FIREFIGHTING

Basic Skills and Techniques

TECHNICAL COLLEGE OF THE LOWCOUNTRY
LEARNING RESOURCES CENTER
POST OFFICE BOX 1288
BEAUFORT, SOUTH CAROLINA 29901-1288

by
Mike Ertel
and
Gregory C. Berk

Publisher
The Goodheart-Willcox Company, Inc.
Tinley Park, Illinois

Copyright 1998

by

THE GOODHEART-WILLCOX COMPANY, INC.

All rights reserved. No part of this book may be reproduced, stored in a retrieval system, or transmitted in any form or by any means, electronic, mechanical, photocopying, recording, or otherwise, without the prior written permission of The Goodheart-Willcox Company, Inc. Manufactured in the United States of America.

Library of Congress Card Catalog Number 96-48400

International Standard Book Number 1-56637-034-5

1 2 3 4 5 6 7 8 9 0   98   01 00 99 98 97

About the Authors

Mike Ertel has had training and practical experience in both firefighting and technical writing. He served as an auxiliary firefighter prior to WWII service in the U.S. Army Air Corps, and received training in fighting aircraft fires while in the military. Following graduation from college after the war, he worked for many years as an industrial engineer. He later became a firefighting training consultant and actively participated in the establishing of state-recognized apprenticeship programs (for which he wrote much of the course material). He has also produced many public fire safety programs for both print and electronic media. During his career, he has authored hundreds of articles and several books, on a variety of subjects. He has taught at Penn College, a division of Pennsylvania State University.

Gregory C. Berk has more than 30 years active involvement in the Fire Service. He began his career as a volunteer firefighter while working in the insurance industry inspecting Highly Protected Risk properties. For the past 20 years, he has been a full-time firefighter, with 19 of those years spent as the Fire Chief of the Flossmoor, Illinois, Volunteer Fire Department. Chief Berk holds a Bachelor of Arts degree from Northern Illinois University, and a Masters in Public Administration from Governors State University. He has taught extensively at the Community College and University levels.

TECHNICAL COLLEGE OF THE LOWCOUNTRY
LEARNING RESOURCES CENTER
POST OFFICE BOX 1288
BEAUFORT, SOUTH CAROLINA 29901-1288

Library of Congress Cataloging in Publication Data
Ertel, Mike.
Firefighting: basic skills and techniques / by Mike Ertel and Gregory C. Berk

    p. cm.
Includes index.
ISBN 1-56637-034-5
1. Fire extinction. I. Berk, Gregory C. II. Title.

TH9310.5.E78   1997
628.9'25—dc21   96-48400
                                                          CIP

INTRODUCTION

Firefighting — Basic Skills and Techniques is a comprehensive text that reflects the diversity of the firefighter's activities and provides the background needed for effective functioning as a member of the "fire team." It is intended for use in community college Fire Science programs, as well as in departmental training operations. The content of this text is closely matched with the basic skills defined in the National Fire Protection Association's Standard 1001, *Standard on Fire Fighter Professional Qualifications*. The relevant portions of Job Performance Requirements from the Standard are displayed at the beginning of each chapter of this text.

The 23 chapters of **Firefighting — Basic Skills and Techniques** provide clear, easy-to-understand explanations of the topics covered, ranging from the physics of combustion to the specific procedures required in hazardous materials incidents. Since firefighting is a highly hazardous occupation, safe work habits and use of proper equipment is strongly emphasized, with chapters on *safety, personal protective equipment,* and *fire behavior*. Proper procedures for handling hazardous materials (HazMat) situations are provided in two comprehensive chapters. One covers the *Awareness Level*, the other the *Operational Level*. Separate chapters also are devoted to various types of equipment and their uses: *hoses, fire streams, portable fire extinguishers, ladders,* and *ropes*. Procedures and equipment for *forcible entry, salvage, overhaul, communications, rescue,* and *emergency medical services* are thoroughly covered in individual chapters. The firefighter's role in education and fire prevention is covered in chapters on *public fire education* and on *fire prevention, inspection, and planning*. Several Appendices at the end of the book cover specialized topics, such as *ladder testing* and *typical radio procedure*.

As an aid to understanding, each chapter of the book includes learning objectives and a list of important technical terms introduced in that chapter. A summary and review questions at the end of the chapter are useful for review to determine if further study is needed. All chapters are thoroughly illustrated with photographs, charts, and drawings.

In most programs, your training will be divided into theoretical and practical sessions. In *theory sessions,* you will use **Firefighting — Basic Skills and Techniques** to study specific topics such as water supply, ventilation, or ladders. In *practical training sessions,* you will participate in hands-on exercises that will help you practice and improve your skills. Typically, these sessions will include some form of testing. Your testing may come in a formal situation, when you will be given a written or practical test to complete. *The ultimate test of any firefighter, however, is the skill demonstrated on the fireground.* We believe that you will find **Firefighting — Basic Skills and Techniques** a very valuable tool for developing those skills.

Mike Ertel
Gregory C. Berk

ACKNOWLEDGMENTS

Developing a book of this complexity would not be possible without the assistance of many individuals and numerous organizations ranging from government agencies to private companies. The authors gratefully acknowledge the help provided by the individuals and organizations listed below.

Special Thanks

The authors are particularly grateful to Chief Harold Anthony of the Williamsport Bureau of Fire, and Ted Kriner of Lycoming County Civil Defense, for sharing their expertise in the specialized areas of (respectively) Public Fire Education and Hazardous Materials.

Fire Departments

Berea (OH) Fire Department, Bon Air (VA) Volunteer Fire Department, Camden (NJ) Fire Department, Cedar Run (PA) Fire Department, Chebanse Township (IL) Fire Protection District, Cleveland Fire Department, First Ward Fire Department, Flossmoor (IL) Fire Department, Hackensack (NJ) Fire Department, Hazel Crest (IL) Fire Department, Homewood (IL) Fire Department, Jersey Shore (PA) Fire Department, Kankakee (IL) Fire Department, Kankakee Township (IL) Fire Protection District, Lansing (IL) Fire Department, Loyalsock (PA) Volunteer Fire Department, Montvale (NJ) Volunteer Fire Department, Richmond (VA) Bureau of Fire, San Francisco Fire Department, South Williamsport (PA) Fire Department, Tinley Park (IL) Fire Department, Williamsport (PA) Bureau of Fire.

Manufacturers and Businesses

Akron Brass; Alco Ladder Co.; Antenna Specialists Division, Allen Telecom Group; Ansul Fire Protection; Barr's Hardware; Blue Water, Ltd.; Chubb National; W. S. Darley and Co.; Duo Safety Ladder Co.; East Jordan Iron Works, Elkhart Brass Mfg. Co., Inc.; Federal Signal Corp.; Frito-Lay, Inc.; Fyrepel Products; Globe Mfg. Co.; Homelite Div. of Textron, Inc.; Institutional Communications Associates; Lab Safety Supply, Inc.; Mine Safety Appliances (MSA); J. W. Moon, Inc.; National Fire Hose Corp.; National Foam; Nipponose Equipment Co.; Nupla Corp.; Pennsylvania Gas and Water; Pierce Manufacturing, Pigeon Mountain Industries, Inc.; H. K. Porter, Inc.; Ramin Pharmacy; Reflexite Corp.; Repco, Inc.; Sampson Fire Sales, Inc.; Susquehanna Equipment Co.; Task Force Tips; U.S. Maritime Services, Inc., Wormold U.S., Inc.; Ziamatic Corp.

Governmental Organizations

National Fire Academy, United States Army, Lycoming County (PA) Civil Defense, United States Fire Administration, Lycoming County Control, Pennsylvania Dept. of Environmental Resources, Pennsylvania State Fire Academy, United States Army Reserve, United States Department of Transportation, United States Marine Corps, Federal Emergency Management Agency.

Other Organizations

CHEMTREC®; Firefighter Safety Study Act Working Group; Foam Task Group, Fire Equipment Working Team, National Wildfire Coordinating Group; Association of American Railroads, Bureau of Explosives; Illinois Firefighters Association; International Association of Fire Chiefs; International Association of Fire Fighters; Rubber Manufacturers Association; Third District Fire Chiefs Association; Williamsport Hospital, Divine Providence Hospital.

Individuals

Assistant Chief Marvin Austin, Retired; Chief Jack Brooks, Retired; Sgt. Bob Burns; Chief Doug Chappell; Roger Cholin; Jason Clark; Jeff Cole; Chief Peg Corson; Bill Dachter; Kyle Day; Chief Pellegrino DeMarco; Betty Eyeler; Capt. John Flanagan; Max L. Foust; Donald Foye, Chief David Fry; R. M. Haluska; Chief William G. Hayes; Dr. Bernie Heilicser; Chief William Henry; Lt. George Hrudka; Tracey Hurne; Lou Hunsinger; Lt. Jim Karnes; Bill Kepner; Chief Matt Kitko; Asst. Chief Terry Lewis, Russell Lindstrom; Warren Lutton; Chief Mike Mancini; Mike Marchese; John Marshall; Chief Gary Mayers; Capt. John McDermott; Bob Miller; Lt. Scott Peoples; Capt. Jim Ritchey; Jack Ruppert; Chief Ralph Schauer Jr.; Brent Shirk; John W. Simon, Pennsylvania State Fire Commissioner; Jon Smith; Mary Smith; Chief Jack Snyder; Marjorie Thompson, Asst. Chief Ron Young ... and Kate.

TABLE OF CONTENTS

Image© 1996 Photo Disc, Inc.

NFPA 1001 Job Performance Requirements

The material on this page consists of those portions of the NFPA 1001 Job Performance Requirements relevant to the material presented in this chapter. Items preceded by the numeral 3 (3-x.x) are Fire Fighter I requirements; those with the numeral 4 (4-x.x) are Fire Fighter II requirements.

3-1.1 For certification at Level I, the fire fighter shall meet the job performance requirements defined in Sections 3-2 through 3-6 of this standard and the requirements defined in Chapter 2, Competencies for the First Responder at the Awareness Level, of NFPA 472, *Standard for Professional Competence of Responders to Hazardous Materials Incidents.*

3-1.1.1 General Knowledge Requirements. The organization of the fire department; the role of the Fire Fighter I in the organization; the mission of fire service; the fire department's standard operating procedures and rules and regulations as they apply to the Fire Fighter I; the role of other agencies as they relate to the fire department; aspects of the fire department's member assistance program; the critical aspects of NFPA 1500, Standard on Fire Department Occupational Safety and Health Program, as they apply to the Fire Fighter I; knot types and usage; the difference between life safety and utility rope; reasons for placing rope out of service; the types of knots to use for given tools, ropes, or situations; hoisting methods for tools and equipment; and using rope to support response activities.

3-1.1.2 General Skill Requirements. The ability to don personal protective clothing within one minute; doff personal protective clothing and prepare for reuse; hoist tools and equipment using ropes and the correct knot; tie a bowline, clove hitch, figure eight on a bight, half hitch, becket or sheet bend, and safety knots; and locate information in departmental documents and standard or code materials.

4-1.1 For certification at Level II, the Fire Fighter I shall meet the job performance requirements defined in Sections 4-2 through 4-5 of this standard and the requirements defined in Chapter 3, Competencies for the First Responder at the Operational Level, of NFPA 472, *Standard for Professional Competence of Responders to Hazardous Materials Incidents.*

4-1.1.1 General Knowledge Requirements. Responsibilities of the Fire Fighter II in assuming and transferring command within an incident management system, performing assigned duties in conformance with applicable NFPA and other safety regulations and authority having jurisdiction procedures, and the role of a Fire Fighter II within the organization.

4-1.1.2 General Skill Requirements. The ability to determine the need for command, organize and coordinate an incident management system until command is transferred, and function within an assigned role in the incident management system.

Reprinted with permission from NFPA 1001, *Fire Fighter Professional Qualifications,* Copyright ©1997, National Fire Protection Association, Quincy, MA 02269. This reprinted material is not the complete and official position of the National Fire Protection Association on the referenced subject, which is represented only by the standard in its entirety.

Introduction to the Fire Service

OBJECTIVES

When you have completed this chapter, you will be able to:

🔥 Describe the development of modern firefighting organizations from early volunteer fire brigades.

🔥 Identify the major effect of the Great Chicago Fire upon building codes and materials used for urban buildings.

🔥 Summarize the role of the individual state Fire Marshal in the overall fire service picture.

🔥 Distinguish between line and staff functions in a modern fire department.

🔥 Describe the significance of developing and using an incident command system.

IMPORTANT TERMS

Federal Emergency
   Management Agency
   (FEMA)
fire mark
fire prevention
full-time paid fire
   department

"good samaritan" laws
incident command
   system (ICS)
Incident Commander
insurance companies
insurers
line functions

motorization
National Emergency
   Training Center
negligence
organization chart
practical training
   sessions

staff functions
State Fire Marshal
steam fire engine
theory sessions
vigil
volunteer fire brigades

Firefighting can be difficult and taxing, but it can also be rewarding. On any given day, a firefighter's duties may include putting out fires, rescuing trapped victims, providing emergency medical services, conducting fire inspections, giving a talk on fire safety to a class of school children, maintaining equipment, or investigating a suspicious fire. The list is almost endless, **Figure 1-1**.

Whatever duty the firefighter is performing, he or she must almost always work as a member of a team. There are few other vocations in which an individual's proficiency and physical safety are so closely tied to the actions of others. The performance of every firefighter can affect the performance of every other member of the organization. See **Figure 1-2**.

All organizations have some sort of a structure and a set of rules which members are expected to follow. Without structure and rules, there is no organization. This does not mean that rules cannot be improved and changed, of course. During an emergency, though, each member of the organization must do whatever is needed to help bring the emergency to a quick and proper conclusion. When ordered to do something in an emergency, do it to the best of your ability, whether or not you agree with the order. Later, when the situation has been stabilized,

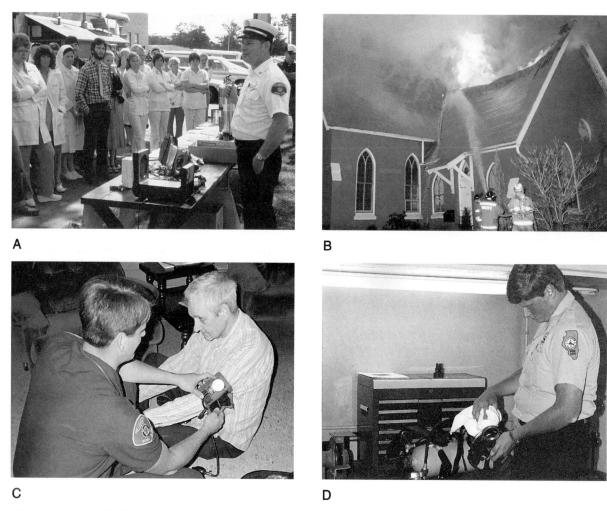

Figure 1-1. The firefighter plays multiple roles. A—Teaching fire safety to hospital personnel.
B—Fighting a fire. (Jon Smith) C—Providing emergency medical services. D—Maintaining equipment.

Figure 1-2. Firefighters depend upon each other. Working together as a team is a must for efficiency and safety. (Warren Lutton)

you can question the order and make suggestions for improving the organization.

To help you better understand the organization of the fire department, this opening chapter will introduce you to the history of the fire service, fire protection responsibilities, and fire department organization.

Fire Service Training

In most programs, your training will be divided into two sections, *theory* and *practice*. Theoretical and practical sessions will be included on almost all topics studied. In **theory** *sessions,* you will study topics such as safety, fire behavior, ventilation, breathing equipment, extinguishers, miscellaneous equipment, fire stream, ladders, and ropes. In *practical training sessions,* you will participate in exercises that will help to improve your skills with hands-on evolutions. See **Figures 1-3** and **1-4.** Typically, these sessions will include some form of testing. Your testing may come in a formal situation, when you will be given a written or practical test to complete. The ultimate test of any firefighter is the skill demonstrated on the fireground. See **Figure 1-5.**

Firefighting efficiency has been enhanced by the continuing quest of fire service personnel for higher levels of education. One objective of this book is to stimulate your interest in learning firefighting techniques by providing a background in the basic areas of fire service training.

Figure 1-3. Training exercises will help you learn and refine the skills you need to become an effective firefighter. (Amoco)

History of the Fire Service

Throughout history, the human race has been concerned about the dangerous aspects of fire. In approximately 24 BC, Augustus Caesar, the emperor of Rome, established a *vigil* to help protect the city from fire. The vigil, a group of watchmen, stood guard at night in order to protect the city from fire. When they detected a fire in a specific district, they alerted the citizens of that area. It was the duty of the Roman citizens to turn out and help fight the fire.

Figure 1-4. These firefighters are taking part in a training evolution at a vacant house that was scheduled for demolition. Note the "Gas Off" sign painted on the house wall—an important safety consideration when such a training activity is being held.

Figure 1-5. The ultimate test of a firefighter's skills and abilities takes place on the fireground itself.

From these early Roman times up to the present, laws have been promulgated to control the use of fire. These laws regulate the manner in which buildings may be constructed and the areas in which fires are allowed. A further advance in fire protection was realized with the establishment of *insurance companies* at about the time of the Great London Fire of 1666. Until that time, it was the responsibility of an owner and his neighbors to rebuild a building that was destroyed by fire. As cities grew and urban areas began to develop, it became harder and harder for neighbors to assist each other. When a fire occurred in a building protected by an insurance company, however, it became the responsibility of the insurance company to replace the building. To protect their interests, the insurance companies began to hire crews of men who acted as fire brigades.

Fire Service in America

In the late 1600s and early 1700s, *volunteer fire brigades* were formed in the major cities of the United States. These fire brigades were hired by individual insurance companies to protect only the properties that the company insured. Therefore the *insurers,* not local government, decided where the brigades would be located and how they would operate.

Obviously, the brigades would be located in areas where the insurance company had the majority of the buildings protected. The fire brigades would be able to know which property owners had purchased insurance by the use of fire marks, **Figure 1-6.** A *fire mark* was the symbol of a specific insurance company, and was placed on the front of the

Figure 1-6. The fire mark identified each house that was covered by an individual insurance company. This is the mark of the Fire Association of Philadelphia, adopted in 1817.

insured building to make it readily visible. When a fire brigade arrived to fight a fire in a building with their company's fire mark, they went to work immediately. However, if a fire brigade arrived and found a rival company's fire mark was on the building, they not only would refuse to fight the fire, but might taunt or even actively hinder the other fire brigade when it arrived. Sometimes, the competition between rival fire companies assumed the proportions of a small riot.

Full-time paid departments

As cities began to develop, it became necessary to provide protection to all building owners. Local government stepped in and took over control of the fire brigades. On April 1, 1853, the nation's first *full-time paid fire department* was established in the city of Cincinnati, Ohio.

At about the same time the first paid fire departments were being established, the *steam fire engine* came into use. This engine permitted more effective firefighting by substituting a more powerful steam-powered pump for a pump operated by human muscle power. See **Figure 1-7.**

Even with the advent of full-time fire departments and better equipment, the towns and cities of the United States were regularly devastated by fire. One of the most celebrated fires in the history of the United States began on October 8, 1871, and eventually destroyed most of the central business and residential areas of Chicago. It eventually became known as the Great Chicago Fire. The cause of the fire has been debated for years, and may never be resolved. However, the important lesson learned from the Great Chicago Fire was that urban areas must be

Figure 1-7. The more powerful pump on a steam fire engine helped make firefighting more efficient. For some fire departments, an old "steamer" like this one is a prized piece of equipment that's carefully maintained and brought out for parades and other public events. (Harold Anthony/Archive Photo)

TECHNICAL COLLEGE OF THE LOWCOUNTRY
LEARNING RESOURCES CENTER
POST OFFICE BOX 1288
BEAUFORT, SOUTH CAROLINA 29901-1288

developed with building materials that were less flammable. As a result of the Great Chicago Fire and other conflagrations that took place at the end of the nineteenth century, far stricter building codes and fire codes were developed.

Motorization of fire apparatus

As the fire service moved into the twentieth century, it began to realize that it must keep up with modern technology. One of the important changes was the *motorization* of fire apparatus, **Figure 1-8.** This not only allowed faster response and a better deployment of equipment, it also meant more powerful pumps with more reliable sources of power. Other advances in technology moved the science of firefighting forward to the point it has reached today. See **Figure 1-9.** It must be remembered, however, that the fire service can never relax. In today's society, new ways of using materials, and new materials of many kinds are constantly being introduced. From a firefighting standpoint, these new materials and new methods often introduce new problems and new challenges. The fire service must work constantly to provide a fire-safe environment for both firefighters and the citizens they protect.

Figure 1-8. Motorized fire apparatus improved response time and gave firefighters more powerful and reliable pumping equipment. (Harold Anthony/Archive Photo)

Fire Protection Responsibilities

To properly understand the organization of the fire service, you must realize that a number of agencies, at several different levels of government, have fire protection responsibilities. The federal government carries out its fire protection responsibilities through the Armed Forces, Forest Service, National Park Service, Consumer Product Safety Commission, and the U.S. Department of Health, Education, and Welfare.

Figure 1-9. The latest fire apparatus takes advantage of advances in technology for greater efficiency and improved safety. This pumper features a raised-roof cab to provide enclosed, protected seating for 8 persons; a large wraparound windshield with high-performance defroster for improved visibility under severe conditions, and retracting fold-down steps for ease of access. (Pierce Manufacturing Co.)

National Emergency Training Center

The one federal agency that has the greatest impact on the local fire service, however, is the *National Emergency Training Center* operated by the *Federal Emergency Management Agency (FEMA)*. The training center, located in Emmitsburg, Maryland, provides a number of valuable services in support of fire departments and related organizations. See **Figure 1-10**. These include the National Fire Academy, the Emergency Management Institute, the Learning Resource Center, the Emergency Management Information Center, the Emergency Education Network, and the publications program of the United States Fire Administration.

National Fire Academy

The Academy offers a wide range of courses to aid in the professional development of fire service personnel and of other persons engaged in fire prevention and control activities. The Academy provides many training programs, both on its own campus and at other sites through its extension service. Among the diverse subjects taught are

Figure 1-10. The campus of the National Emergency Training Center is located in Emmitsburg, Maryland, a suburb of Washington, DC. The NETC is the Federal Emergency Management Agency's focal point for the delivery of emergency management and fire protection training. It coordinates the data of the United States Fire Administration and the resources of the National Fire Academy and the Emergency Management Institute into a single force providing professional training and technical assistance to further national emergency preparedness. As the agency states in one of its publications, "We at NETC are dedicated to working closely with the members of the emergency management community from all over our nation and a growing number of foreign countries to improve preparedness and increase the ability to respond to emergencies of all types. By bringing together people with different backgrounds and expertise, the National Emergency Training Center provides an opportunity to exchange ideas, knowledge and experiences. NETC is more than a training center; it is a resource center and a laboratory where specialized knowledge, technology and training are forged into an effective program. Through this program, NETC graduates are better prepared to meet today's emergency management requirements and the challenges of the future."

volunteer fire service management, firefighter health and safety, hazardous materials incident analysis, and fire/arson detection.

Emergency Management Institute (EMI)

More than 200,000 students per year take part in Emergency Management Institute training programs and EMI-supported emergency management exercises. The Institute offers an Executive Programs Curriculum, a Technical Programs Curriculum, and an Emergency Management Programs Curriculum. Information on both resident and nonresident programs can be obtained from the Institute.

Learning Resource Center (LRC)

With a collection of more than 60,000 books, reports, and other sources, the LRC is an excellent source of information vital to the fire service. Answers to virtually any firefighting question can be obtained by calling the LRC at its toll-free number, (800) 638-1821 (from within the state of Maryland, call (301) 497-1030).

EMIC Program. The Emergency Management Information Center, a part of the Learning Resource Center, makes available for loan a special collection of case studies on accidents and disasters. Case study subjects include weather-related disasters (floods, hurricanes, tornadoes, earthquakes, and blizzards); structure, vehicle, and wildlands fires; explosions and structural collapses, and transportation, HazMat, and nuclear incidents. A given case study may include a variety of media, such as videocassettes, slide/tape presentations, photographic prints, overhead transparencies, books, magazine and journal articles, after-action reports, or government documents.

Emergency Education Network (EENET)

Using satellite broadcast technology, EENET provides nationally available training with a variety of programs and forums on such topics as HazMat, women in the fire service, or sprinkler system technology. The teleconferencing format allows viewers to participate by calling a toll-free number with questions. Information on accessing EENET programs is available from the National Emergency Training Center.

Publications

The U.S. Fire Administration produces many publications of interest to the fire service, both for professional reference and for public fire education purposes. These publications are available without cost to members of the fire service. *Resources on Fire* is a descriptive catalog of the available titles, can be obtained by writing to:

Publications Division
U.S. Fire Administration
16825 S. Seton Avenue
Emmitsburg, MD 21727

State Fire Marshal

In most states, fire protection responsibilities are controlled through the office of the *State Fire Marshal.* See **Figure 1-11.** It must be remembered that the responsibilities of the state in fire matters varies widely from state-to-state. Therefore, a discussion of state involvement in the fire service must be kept in general terms. However, it would appear that in most states, the Fire Marshal is responsible for fire prevention and control, fire data collection, organization of statewide training programs, fire cause and origin investigation, arson investigation, and the protection of state-owned property.

Local Government Responsibilities

Usually, *local* agencies are responsible for delivering fire protection to their citizens. These local delivery systems can be extremely diverse. Obviously, the resources available to a city of a million or more people are different from those available to a city of several thousand people. Large city fire departments are supported by tax dollars and have paid, full-time firefighters. Many smaller communities have fire departments staffed by volunteers

Figure 1-11. Although responsibilities vary from state to state, the State Fire Marshal's office often handles arson investigation and other tasks requiring specialized skills or training. This arson investigator is working with a specially trained dog at the site of a suspicious fire. (Office of the State Fire Marshal of Illinois)

who are paid on a "per call" basis; others are completely unpaid or are a blend of paid (usually drivers) and unpaid personnel. See **Figure 1-12.** These departments may be supported by tax dollars, by private donations, or by a combination of the two. For example, a local volunteer fire department that is basically tax-supported will often raise additional funds necessary for special equipment purchases or other purposes by holding such events as pancake breakfasts, auctions, or dances. Even though smaller departments have fewer resources available than those in large cities, the quality of service they deliver to their citizens is generally equivalent. The level and quality of service delivered to citizens depends more upon the dedication and commitment of the individuals involved than on the size of the department.

Firefighter Responsibilities

Generally, it can be stated that the responsibilities assumed by a firefighter require a conscientious effort to serve the citizens of the community. Despite this dedication to the good of the community, you are not immune from lawsuits. In many states, however, *"good*

Figure 1-12. Many suburban communities, as well as most small towns and rural areas, are protected by firefighting organizations consisting almost entirely of "on-call" personnel. These firefighters may be volunteers or paid on a per-call basis. Smaller departments, such as the two represented by the equipment in this photo, often work together under mutual aid agreements.

samaritan" laws have been passed to protect medical personnel, firefighters, and others in similar roles from frivolous lawsuits.

For a suit to be successfully brought against you, the rule of thumb is that you must have been "willfully and wantonly negligent." Willful and wanton *negligence* would include any act outside the scope of your authority. Consequently, when you perform your firefighting duties in good faith, you are in most cases protected from legal judgments. Since laws vary from state to state, you must take the time to familiarize yourself with the laws that govern your occupation. Time spent understanding the law may help you in the future.

Fire Department Organization

Most fire departments today are organized into staff and line functions. *Staff functions* are those which can be classified as "nonfirefighting" duties. These include administration of the fire department, budget preparation, personnel management, and other aspects of modern organization management. Staff functions can also include the provision of the *fire prevention* services, such as public education of various types and the inspection of commercial, industrial, and public buildings for hazardous conditions. See **Figure 1-13.** Building and fire apparatus

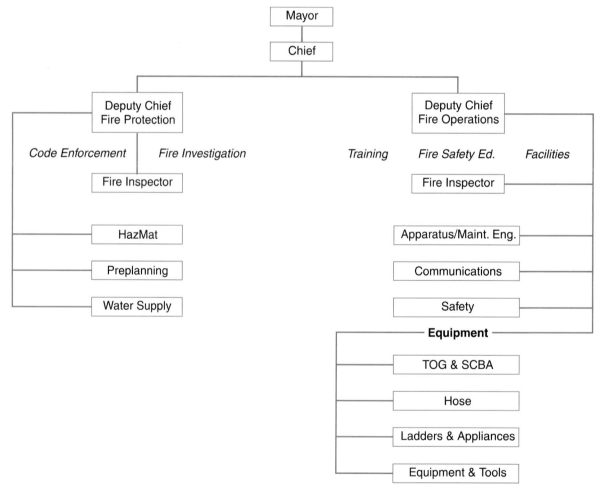

Figure 1-13. Staff functions in a fire department are those not directly related to firefighting, such as budgeting, personnel, and other administrative duties.

maintenance are also considered to be staff functions.

Line functions include those duties that are directly related to the delivery of emergency services to the citizens. Fire suppression, firefighter and paramedic training, and emergency medical services would fall directly under line function heading. See **Figure 1-14.**

Organization Chart

Due to the diversity of the fire service in the United States today, no one *organization chart* will properly represent all departments. To better understand how your own department is organized, it would be helpful for you to draw an organization chart showing all the functions. The sample chart, **Figure 1-15,** demonstrates how the lines of responsibility for both staff and line functions are depicted, and how they relate to your department's ability to serve the citizens. No two organizational charts will look exactly the same, but all such charts are used for the same purpose: they depict the various functions of the department and how they relate to each other in the delivery of service to the citizens of the community.

Incident Command System

An *incident command system (ICS)* is a management tool that a fire department uses to organize any emergency scene. All emergency service providers operating at an incident (whether that incident is large or small), must follow the same rules. An analogy can be drawn with a professional sports team. With such a team, there is one acknowledged leader, the coach. There is a single set of rules that creates the structure for the sport, and a common language that is understood by the coach and all team members. There are also recognized responsibilities that all team members must

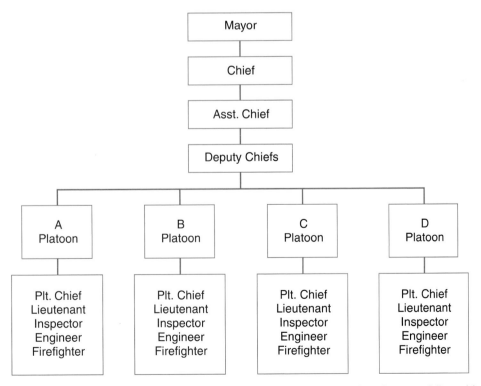

Figure 1-14. The line functions in a fire department are those directly related to providing citizens with firefighting and emergency medical services.

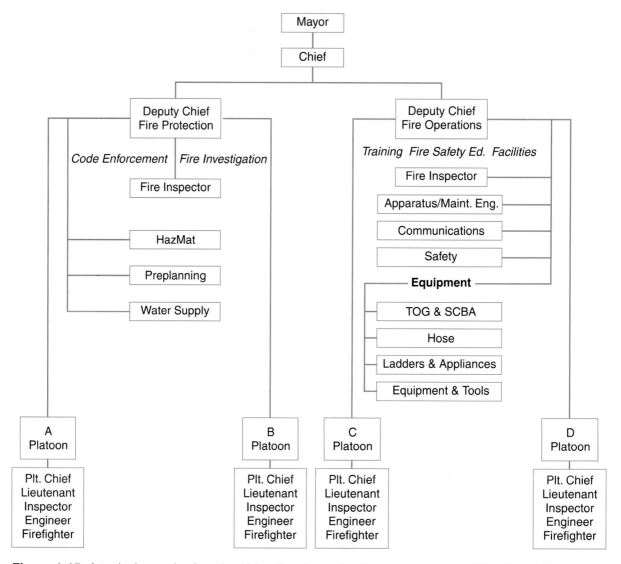

Figure 1-15. A typical organization chart identifies lines of authority and responsibility in the fire department.

accept and carry out on the playing field. The common knowledge and acceptance of specific responsibilities by everyone involved helps to eliminate confusion.

This is as true of an emergency service team as it is of a sports team. The success of any incident command system depends upon the full acceptance by all team members of a unified command structure with a recognized leader, a common language, and agreed-upon responsibilities. All members of the Fire Department must be trained in the requirements of the ICS that is in use.

In addition to the members of your own department being familiar with the structure, leadership, language, and responsibilities of the ICS, all outside companies or agencies responding to an incident must also be willing and able to conform to it. If every responding department or agency operates under its own rules, a large-scale incident could quickly become a large-scale disaster.

Good organizational skills are required in daily Fire Department operations. Under the added stress of an emergency incident, however, those skills can be pushed to the limit.

For this reason, there is great benefit in planning and implementing an emergency response (incident command) system *before* it is needed to cope with a major incident. To be most effectively implemented, the system should be used by all members of the department at *every* emergency incident. Such routine use of the correct procedures will help ensure that the ICS will be fully and effectively used when a large-scale incident occurs.

The ICS Structure

The ICS structure is the set of rules and procedures governing the responsibilities of the personnel and agencies involved. The structure provides for administrative procedures and for such functions as operations, planning, service, and support. While there are currently efforts to develop a standardized ICS for nationwide implementation, there are now many local variations. The important consideration is to *have* an ICS in place, and to *use* that ICS consistently. When an ICS is properly designed and regularly implemented, it becomes as effective a tool for the department as any engine or ambulance or ladder truck.

The basis of an effective ICS is the concept that "there can be only one leader," **Figure 1-16.** That leader is the designated *Incident Commander*, who is ultimately responsible for all decisions. As the scale of an incident increases, assistants (Command Aides) can be added and given specific responsibilities. These aides are answerable to the Incident Commander, and must have free and immediate access to confer on problems. This open line of communication, combined with well-planned reporting procedures, also serves to keep the IC informed about changing conditions on the fire or incident scene.

Operating procedures and lines of authority must be established for each area of responsibility, such as suppression, rescue, communications, medical, and support

services. Provision must be made for additional equipment and supplies, as well as more operating and supervisory personnel in each area as the scale of the incident escalates. *Individual* firefighters and support personnel must have clearly defined roles and must be made aware of their specific responsibilities.

Proper communication is vital to effective functioning of an ICS. Beyond providing sufficient means and proper procedures for physical communication, the ICS must ensure that all persons involved speak a common language. If everyone involved uses the same terminology, the chance for dangerous confusion is greatly reduced.

Figure 1-16. The Incident Commander is the person who is ultimately responsible for decisionmaking on the fireground. Excellent communications capability and a properly developed incident command structure are vital tools for success as the IC. On a very large fire or other incident, other personnel may assume special roles as aides to the Incident Commander, with responsibility for specific tasks or areas.

Summary

Fire departments, like all organizations, must have a structure and a set of rules for its members to follow. The evolution of firefighting organizations into the form we know today can be traced back to Roman times. The immediate ancestors of today's fire departments were the private fire brigades supported by insurance companies. They responded only to fires in premises insured by their owner companies. To provide universal fire protection, communities gradually assumed control and financial responsibility for the fire brigades. In large cities, departments are staffed with full-time paid personnel; smaller communities depend upon volunteers who are often unpaid or paid on a "per call" basis.

Basic responsibility for fire protection rests with local government units. Some support functions are supplied at the state level through the Fire Marshal's office. The federal government provides programs through the Federal Emergency Management Agency. Since 1974, the U.S. Fire Academy has conducted advanced training programs for fire personnel. There are also federal agencies, such as the Forest Service and the armed forces, that maintain their own firefighting operations.

Most departments are organized on a model that includes both staff and line functions. The staff functions are those providing supportive, nonfirefighting services (such as administrative support or fire prevention activities); line functions are directly related to firefighting and emergency medical services.

To meet future challenges, the fire service must be willing to adapt to a changing society. This means that fire service personnel and governmental agencies must understand that the nature of the fire service is constantly changing, and so are the demands placed upon the service by the citizens. Through adopting innovative techniques and procedures, fire departments can continue to deliver the best quality of service to the citizens.

Review Questions

1. Why is it important for firefighters to work together as members of a team?
2. What are the two sections into which firefighter training is usually divided? Give some examples of work done in each section.
3. What is the earliest example of an action aimed at public fire protection?
4. What major change in fire protection took place in the mid-17th Century?
5. How did fire brigades begin? How do they differ from today's fire departments?
6. What major change in fire protection in the United States took place on April 1, 1853?
7. In what way was the steam fire engine an improvement over hand-operated pumpers?
8. What was the important lesson learned from the Great Chicago Fire? What effect did it have on building and fire codes in the United States?
9. Shortly after the turn of the century, a major advance in firefighting equipment took place. What was it?

10. Describe several advantages that resulted from the motorization of fire apparatus?
11. Name at least two U.S. Government agencies that have firefighting responsibilities.
12. Why was the U.S. Fire Academy established? What is its major activity?
13. Which federal agency is currently responsible for operation of the U.S. Fire Academy?
14. List some typical responsibilities of a State Fire Marshal.
15. Aside from size, what is the major way in which large city and small community fire departments differ?

16. What are some typical means that small fire departments use to raise funds for special equipment or other purposes?
17. What is the general term for legislation passed to protect emergency personnel from lawsuits?
18. Usually what must be proven to win a lawsuit against a firefighter or other provider of emergency services?
19. List some typical staff functions of a fire department.
20. What are the primary line functions of a fire department?

Stress vs. Actions

```
                    Firefighter On-Duty
                    Fatalities (1995)
                    96 Deaths
        ┌───────────────────────┴───────────────────────┐
Health/Fitness-Related                        Actions/Operation-Related
Heart Attacks/Strokes/Seizures                Trauma/Asphyxia/Burns/Exposure
48 Deaths                                     48 Deaths
   ┌──────────┴──────────┐                       ┌──────────┴──────────┐
Emergency Ops      Non-emergency Ops         Emergency Ops      Non-emergency Ops
37 Deaths          11 Deaths                 45 Deaths          3 Deaths

 Fireground Ops     Training                  Fireground Ops     Training
 23 Deaths          1 Death                   25 Deaths          2 Deaths

 Rescue/EMS Ops     Other                     Rescue/EMS Ops     Other
 7 Deaths           10 Deaths                 2 Deaths           1 Death

 Responding/Returning                         Responding/Returning
 7 Deaths                                     18 Deaths
```

Firefighting is a dangerous occupation, with an average of more than 100 on-duty deaths each year. Health/fitness-related fatalities typically account for half or more of the total, as shown in this chart based on the United States Fire Administration's 1995 firefighter fatalities survey.

NFPA 1001 Job Performance Requirements

The material on this page consists of those portions of the NFPA 1001 Job Performance Requirements relevant to the material presented in this chapter. Items preceded by the numeral 3 (3-x.x) are Fire Fighter I requirements; those with the numeral 4 (4-x.x) are Fire Fighter II requirements.

3-1.1.1 General Knowledge Requirements. The organization of the fire department; the role of the Fire Fighter I in the organization; the mission of fire service; the fire department's standard operating procedures and rules and regulations as they apply to the Fire Fighter I; the role of other agencies as they relate to the fire department; aspects of the fire department's member assistance program; the critical aspects of NFPA 1500, Standard on Fire Department Occupational Safety and Health Program, as they apply to the Fire Fighter I; knot types and usage; the difference between life safety and utility rope; reasons for placing rope out of service; the types of knots to use for given tools, ropes, or situations; hoisting methods for tools and equipment; and using rope to support response activities.

(3-3.1)

(b) Prerequisite Skills: The ability to control breathing, replace SCBA air cylinders, use SCBA to exit through restricted passages, initiate and complete emergency procedures in the event of SCBA failure or air depletion, and complete donning procedures.

3-3.2 Respond on apparatus to an emergency scene, given personal protective clothing and other necessary personal protective equipment, so that the apparatus is safely mounted and dismounted, seat belts are used while the vehicle is in motion, and other personal protective equipment is correctly used.

(a) Prerequisite Knowledge: Mounting and dismounting procedures for riding fire apparatus; hazards and ways to avoid hazards associated with riding apparatus; prohibited practices; types of department personal protective equipment and the means for usage.

(b) Prerequisite Skills: The ability to use each piece of provided safety equipment.

(3-3.4)

(a) Prerequisite Knowledge: Personnel accountability systems, communication procedures, emergency evacuation methods, what constitutes a safe haven, elements that create or indicate a hazard, and emergency procedures for loss of air supply.

(3-3.9)

(a) Prerequisite Knowledge: Principles of fire streams; types, design, operation, nozzle pressure effects, and flow capabilities of nozzles; precautions to be followed when advancing hose lines to a fire; observable results that a fire stream has been properly applied; dangerous building conditions created by fire; principles of expo-

sure protection; potential long-term consequences of exposure to products of combustion; physical states of matter in which fuels are found; common types of accidents or injuries and their causes; and the application of each size and type of attack line, the role of the backup team in fire attack situations, attack and control techniques for grade level and above and below grade levels, and exposing hidden fires.

3-3.17 Turn off building utilities, given tools and an assignment, so that the assignment is safely completed.

(a) Prerequisite Knowledge: Properties, principles, and safety concerns for electricity, gas, and water systems; utility disconnect methods and associated dangers; and use of required safety equipment.

(b) Prerequisite Skills: The ability to identify utility control devices, operate control valves or switches, and assess for related hazards.

4-1.1.1 General Knowledge Requirements. Responsibilities of the Fire Fighter II in assuming and transferring command within an incident management system, performing assigned duties in conformance with applicable NFPA and other safety regulations and authority having jurisdiction procedures, and the role of a Fire Fighter II within the organization.

(4-4.1)

(b) Prerequisite Knowledge: The ability to operate hand and power tools used for forcible entry and rescue in a safe and efficient manner; use cribbing and shoring material; and choose and apply appropriate techniques for moving or removing vehicle roofs, doors, windshields, windows, steering wheels or columns, and the dashboard.

4-5.2 Maintain power plants, power tools, and lighting equipment, given appropriate tools and manufacturers' instructions, so that equipment is clean and maintained according to manufacturer and departmental guidelines, maintenance is recorded, and equipment is placed in a ready state or reported otherwise.

(a) Prerequisite Knowledge: Types of cleaning methods, correct use of cleaning solvents, manufacturer and departmental guidelines for maintaining equipment and its documentation, and problem-reporting practices.

(b) Prerequisite Skills: The ability to select correct tools; follow guidelines; complete recording and reporting procedures; and operate power plants, power tools, and lighting equipment.

Reprinted with permission from NFPA 1001, *Fire Fighter Professional Qualifications*, Copyright ©1997, National Fire Protection Association, Quincy, MA 02269. This reprinted material is not the complete and official position of the National Fire Protection Association on the referenced subject, which is represented only by the standard in its entirety.

Safety

OBJECTIVES

When you have completed this chapter, you will be able to:

- ⚲ Recognize and describe dangerous building conditions.
- ⚲ Discuss proper procedures to follow when trapped or disoriented.
- ⚲ Demonstrate how to use tools and equipment safely.
- ⚲ List the steps to be taken in dealing with electrical emergencies.
- ⚲ Show how to drive defensively when responding to an alarm.

IMPORTANT TERMS

barcoding
decibels (dB)
decontaminate
defensive driving
duration
firebreaks
fire loading
four-second stopping
   zone
frequency

hydroplaning
intensity
liquefied petroleum gas
   (LPG)
Occupational Health
   and Safety
   Administration
PASS (personal alert
   safety system)

personnel
   accountability
   systems (PAS)
protective equipment
quadrants
radioactive materials
rehabilitation area
scanning
self-contained
   breathing apparatus
   (SCBA)

service drop
space margin
truss construction
twelve-second travel
   path
two-second following
   zone
working equipment

Firefighting is an extremely dangerous occupation, with a rate of death and injury greater than virtually any other field. For this reason, safety information is not confined to this chapter, but is stressed throughout the book. Nearly every chapter points out hazards involved in a particular aspect of firefighting, and describes the safety measures to be taken.

Job Hazards

For generations, firefighters accepted accidents as part of the job of fighting fires; they felt that nothing could be done about them. Something *can* and *is* being done to make firefighting a safer occupation. The job is becoming safer, but there is still a long way to go.

In the routine performance of firefighting duties, a firefighter can suffer:

- Muscle strains from heavy lifting and carrying.
- Puncture wounds of the hands and feet.
- Stress and physical damage from extreme heat and cold.
- Bruises or broken bones from falls on slippery surfaces.
- Respiratory damage from breathing poisonous air.
- Burns from fire and steam.
- Injuries from being hit by falling debris, or from collapse of the floor below or the roof above.
- Electric shock from exposed wires.

Safety is the *business* of the fire service. At the fire scene, your first priority is to save the lives of people who might be trapped in a burning building. At the same time, you must protect your own life.

There is probably no other occupation in which you may be relatively sedentary for weeks, then suddenly be thrust into a situation where you must work at grueling physical labor for 15 or 20 hours straight. During this period of labor, you will be loaded down with 50 pounds or more of protective gear. You will climb steep ladders or several flights of stairs, carrying perhaps another 50 or 100 pounds of equipment. During all of this, of course, you are also subjected to such hazards as extreme heat and cold, an oxygen-deficient atmosphere, toxic gases, falling objects, near-zero visibility, tripping and falling, explosions, high-pressure water streams, swinging axes, slippery surfaces, exposed electrical wiring, chemical fumes, structural collapse, physical strain, and stress (physical, mental, and emotional). See **Figure 2-1.**

And yet during training sessions, you may hear veteran firefighters say, "We do it this way during training sessions; on the fireground, you do it any way you can." *No!* You do it the *safe* way during training

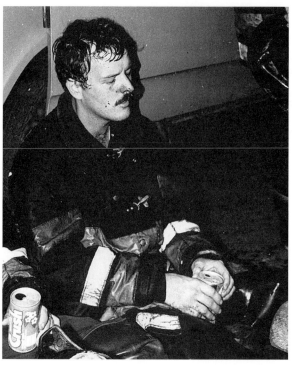

Figure 2-1. Firefighting is exhausting work, often involving heavy physical labor under conditions of extreme heat or cold. Good physical conditioning is a must. (Jon Smith)

sessions, over-and-over again, so that you will do it the safe way *automatically* on the fireground. This business is just *too dangerous* to "do it any way you can."

Firefighter Responsibility for Safety

Safety is something that no one can do for you — it is strictly "do-it-yourself." The standard NFPA 1500, *Fire Department Occupational Safety and Health Program,* places much of the responsibility for firefighter safety squarely where it belongs: on the individual firefighter.

To comply with this standard, you are required to:

- Participate in training activities, both to upgrade your skills and to keep up with technological changes.

- Help to maintain a safe fire station. This goes beyond housekeeping to identifying potentially dangerous conditions or practices and calling them to the attention of the appropriate officer.
- Become knowledgeable about your department's incident management procedures and adhere to them during any emergency incident.
- Follow safe driving procedures when operating an emergency vehicle. When a passenger, ride only in approved safe positions, wearing a safety belt at all times. If needed, wear hearing protection.
- Wear your self-contained breathing apparatus (SCBA) in every situation where the atmosphere *is* hazardous, *could be* hazardous, or *might become* hazardous, **Figure 2-2.** Do not compromise your SCBA with facial hair, buddy breathing, or any other potentially harmful condition or practice.
- Know how to properly care for, and be aware of the limitations of, all items of personal protective equipment.
- Report for duty free of any impairment caused by alcohol or drugs.

Aside from the personal effects of such impairment, you could be endangering other firefighters or civilians. Never permit any member of your department to be on duty while under the influence of drugs or alcohol.

For your own safety, as well as that of your fellow firefighters, take your department's health and safety program seriously. If your department does not have such a program, campaign to get one started.

Causes of Injuries

Each year, the NFPA conducts a national survey of injuries to firefighters. While there are some statistical "ups and downs," the basic pattern remains fairly consistent from year to year. Slightly more than half of all injuries occurred on the fireground. The remaining injuries were incurred, in order of frequency, during nonfire emergencies, in training, and while responding to or returning from a call.

A breakdown of the most common kinds of injuries for each basic activity is shown in chart form in **Figure 2-3.** Note that the major cause of injury, in each category, is *sprains and strains.* The second most common forms of

Figure 2-2. Even when working a structure fire from the outside, wear your SCBA—a shift in wind direction can quickly blanket you with a cloud of choking smoke and hazardous gases.

Figure 2-3. Sprains and strains are the most common forms of injuries to firefighters, making up the largest percentage of reported injuries in each of the categories shown. Columns do not add up to 100 percent due to multiple entries and smaller percentage items that are not shown.

Nature of Injury	Type of Duty				
	Respond/Return	Fire-ground	Nonfire Emergency	Training	Other
Sprain/Strain	55%	36%	46%	49%	52%
Wound, Cut	21%	20%	16%	21%	23%
Burn		10%		9%	
Fracture	4%				
Eye Irritation			3%		4%
Smoke/Gas Inhalation		10%			
Other	20%	24%	35%	21%	21%

injury are bruises and wounds of all type. Taken together, sprains, strains, bruises, and wounds account for *two-thirds* of all firefighter injuries. Wearing proper personal protective gear, combined with learning how to correctly lift and pull heavy objects, will go a long way toward reducing the injury rate.

When looking strictly at *fireground* injuries, causes are divided almost equally between slips and falls (22%), overexertion (22%), and exposure to fire products (20%), as shown in **Figure 2-4.** Injuries resulting from being struck by an object accounted for another 11% of the total; stepping into or otherwise coming into contact with an object (such as a projecting building part) caused another 10% of injuries. The remaining 15% of fireground injuries were from a wide variety of causes. Some injuries continue to be caused by smoke or gas inhalation, which is surprising in light of the quality and availability of modern protective breathing apparatus.

Safety in the Station

During recent years, as many as 25,000 injuries have been reported annually as occurring during training or other nonfireground activities. It is reasonable to assume that most of these injuries occurred in or around the station or other department facilities. You can take a number of precautions to make your station a safer place. These include:
- Practice good housekeeping. Leave nothing lying around where it could

Causes of Fireground Injuries

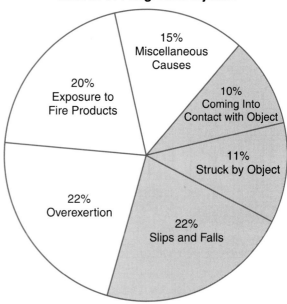

15% Miscellaneous Causes

20% Exposure to Fire Products

10% Coming Into Contact with Object

11% Struck by Object

22% Overexertion

22% Slips and Falls

Figure 2-4. The causes of injuries on the fireground are summarized on this graph. Almost half of the injuries (43%) result from slips and falls, being struck by an object, or coming into contact with a fixed object.

be a tripping or slipping hazard. Pick up tools, ropes, or other items of equipment; promptly wipe up spills of water or other liquids.
- Cover pits. If the facility has a grease pit, park a vehicle over it or fit it with a secure cover.
- Apply nonslip strips. Smooth cement floors can be slippery, especially when wet. Apply strips of nonslip material

to any heavily traveled areas that might be a slipping hazard.

- Pad ladder ends. Prevent possible head injuries by fitting the exposed ends of ladders on apparatus with padded, high-visibility covers.
- Install safety switches. Overhead doors can be equipped with safety switches like those used on elevator doors. If the closing door encounters resistance, it reverses direction.
- Wear safety shoes. Athletic shoes or conventional dress shoes offer little protection from dropped objects, such as a hammer, a coupling, or a nozzle, that could cause broken toes. Wearing steel-toe safety shoes will avoid such problems; safety shoes also provide better footing on slippery surfaces.
- Provide proper ventilation whenever a vehicle engine must be run inside the station. The exhaust gases must be vented to the outside. See **Figure 2-5.**

Communicable Disease Exposure

There is always some danger of exposure to communicable disease when extricating accident victims. Of greatest concern to most firefighters is potential exposure to Hepatitis-B or the HIV virus, which could result from contact with bodily fluids (especially blood) released as a result of the accident.

A highly recommended practice is to wear rubber gloves as a protective layer beneath your turnout gloves. If the turnout gloves become contaminated, they should be removed and disposed of (along with the rubber gloves) in an approved manner. Often, this will involve placing them in a hospital infectious waste container ("burn bag"), such as the one shown in **Figure 2-6.**

Vehicle Fires

Too often, firefighters dismiss fires in automobiles and other vehicles as "nothing to worry about." After all, the fire is out in the

Figure 2-5. To maintain healthy indoor air quality, an exhaust system should be provided for any vehicle that must be run inside the station. This system is designed with a hose that will retract out of the way when the apparatus leaves the station. (Nederman, Inc.)

Figure 2-6. "Burn bags" like the one shown are widely used in hospitals to collect and dispose of infectious medical waste. Turnout gloves or other items that become contaminated with blood or other potentially dangerous body fluids should be placed in such a bag for proper disposal. (Photo courtesy of Lab Safety Supply, Inc., Janesville, WI)

open where you can't become trapped and where nothing is likely to fall on you. How could you get hurt in such a situation?

Quite easily! A motor vehicle fire produces many harmful and toxic gases because of the many plastics and other materials that are burning. Flames can shoot out for a dozen feet in any direction; temperatures can exceed 1500°F (815°C). Parts of the vehicle can explode, throwing out shrapnel; battery acid, gasoline, and other fluids all present some form of hazard. Pound-for-pound, a burning vehicle can be much more hazardous than a structure fire.

Don't dismiss automobile fires as minor; each year, more than 1000 firefighters are injured fighting such fires. For your own protection, treat vehicle fires with respect, and be sure to wear your full turnout gear (including SCBA).

Safe Procedures for Mounting Fire Apparatus

It isn't the recruits who get injured around fire apparatus. Instead, it's usually veteran firefighters who get hurt. Why? Because the situation had become too familiar. At first, we are all intimidated by that big hunk of equipment. Then, as time passes, it becomes as familiar as our own living room or automobile. *That* is when it becomes dangerous, since we take it for granted.

The most important safety hint for working around apparatus is, *Be aware* — know what you are doing at all times. When you board or alight from the equipment, always firmly grasp the rail or other handhold provided. This is particularly important when you are wearing wet boots, because of the danger of slipping. Also, *never* attempt to get on or off the apparatus while it is moving at even a crawl. Treat your apparatus for what it is: a rugged, reliable, but potentially dangerous machine.

Seat belts

Firefighters are frequently surprised to discover that, despite all the fire prevention activities of their department and continuing publicity, many civilians seem unaware of proper fire safety procedures. And yet, despite the years of publicity on the value of vehicle seat belts in saving lives, many of these same firefighters fail to wear the belts in the apparatus (even though, in some states, their use is mandated by law). See **Figure 2-7.** They have a variety of excuses — not valid reasons — for not wearing seat belts:

- *"I'm a good driver, and besides, I'm inside a 15-ton fire apparatus."* True... but what

Figure 2-7. Modern fire apparatus, such as this new Quantum truck, is designed to provide safe enclosed seating for firefighters. Note the heavy-duty seat belts and the provision for comfortable seating while wearing SCBA. (Pierce Manufacturing, Inc.)

if you encounter a terrible driver in a 35-ton tractor-trailer?

- *"I don't want to get trapped by a seat belt."* In a few extremely rare cases, vehicle occupants may have been better off in an accident without a seat belt. Statistically, however, being "thrown clear" of the vehicle is 25 times more likely to result in injury or death, when compared to being restrained by a seat belt.

- *"I can brace my hands against the dash or seat back."* The force of a impact at even the relatively low speed of 30 mph is about the same as falling from a three-story building. Hands and arms wouldn't be much good as shock-absorbers in either case.

- *"I only need seat belts for long trips and high-speed driving."* Statistics show that 75 percent of all vehicle deaths and injuries result from accidents that take place at speeds of less than 40 mph and occur within 25 miles of the driver's home. To improve your chances of avoiding an injury accident, you could always drive at speeds higher than 40 mph and be sure to never get closer to home than 25 miles. (That's been tried — it doesn't work.) When you are driving or riding in any moving vehicle, *always* wear a seat belt.

Hearing protection

Noise pollution, like other forms of pollution, can cause a variety of illnesses in human beings. Exposure to loud noises over a period of time has been shown to cause hearing loss, but also has been considered a contributing factor in other conditions such as high blood pressure, ulcers, nervous tension, fatigue, and even some types of heart disease.

The major characteristics of sound that must be considered are intensity, frequency, and duration. *Intensity* is the volume or "loudness" of the sound: the louder the sound, the more likely it is to cause harm. *Frequency* is the *pitch* of the sound—how "high" or "low" it is. Very high frequency and very low frequency sounds are out of range of human hearing. Loss of hearing in the *middle* frequencies is most serious, since that is the range in which speech occurs. *Duration* is how *long* a sound lasts. The longer the duration of a loud noise, the more potentially damaging it is to hearing.

The loudness of sounds is measured in *decibels (dB)*. When used to measure sounds in the workplace or other environments, decibel measurements are usually given in *dBA*, indicating measurement on a scale covering the range of normal human hearing. There are other scales used with decibel measurements, but they are outside of this discussion.

Prolonged exposure to sounds at an intensity of 90 dBA or higher can cause permanent hearing damage. **Figure 2-8** presents

Common Noise Levels	
Source	*dBA*
Saturn rocket	194
Ram jet	160
Turbo jet	150
Threshold of pain	140
Pipe organ	130
Propeller plane, auto horn	120
Pneumatic drill	110
Siren	105
Passing truck	100
Subway, machine shop	90
Noisy restaurant	80
Inside car with closed windows	70
Office	60
Average home	50
Quiet office	40
Recording studio	30
Whisper	20
Rustling leaves	10
Threshold of hearing	0

Figure 2-8. Examples of some common noises and their decibel ratings. On the weighted dBA scale, an increase of 20 points is a *tenfold* increase. Thus, the restaurant (at 80 dBA) is ten times noisier than the 60 dBA office. Values of 90 dBA or higher can cause permanent hearing damage.

decibel measurements of a number of common sounds. As shown, the sounds of a truck, a siren, and a horn are all above 90 dBA. Many other noises that a firefighter encounters, such as power saws and pneumatic tools, are also above 90dBA.

To protect firefighters from harmful noise levels, sirens and horns should be mounted on apparatus to minimize the amount of sound that is heard inside the cab. Windows of the vehicle should be closed when these devices are being operated. You can help protect yourself from high noise levels by wearing earplugs or earmuffs designed to muffle outside sounds. Earmuffs are the preferred device, but are more expensive and less comfortable than earplugs. They also do not have to be fitted individually.

Occupational Safety and Health Laws

The letters OSHA stand for both the *Occupational Safety and Health Administration* and the act of Congress that created it. OSHA is a federal workplace safety program. The agency is responsible for inspecting for safety and health hazards, investigating workplace accidents, and requiring corrective action. The OSHA legislation applies only to the private sector; thus, a fire brigade in an industrial plant is covered, while a municipal fire department is not.

Some states have adopted similar laws that may, or may not, apply to the public sector. At the municipal level, some governments have adopted the NFPA 1500 standard (Fire Department Occupational Safety and Health Program) for their departments. In still other cases, individual fire departments have fairly thorough procedures for assuring the safety of their personnel.

Federal laws relating to hazardous materials (HazMat) apply nationwide to both the public and private sector. Safety precautions when working with, storing, or transporting such materials must be observed at all times by all persons involved.

Personnel Accountability System

It may not be too great an exaggeration to say that there are almost as many *personnel accountability systems (PAS)* as there are fire departments. Each department develops a system that will meet its own needs, since the requirements of a large city department with thousands of firefighters are obviously different from those of a rural department with 25 firefighters.

The essential element of an accountability system is the ability to identify the location of *each* firefighter at a fire scene or incident. See **Figure 2-9.** Some systems provide a method for logging "time in" and "time out."

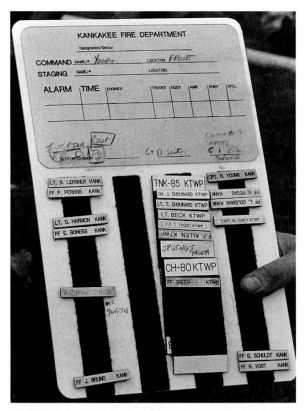

Figure 2-9. This PAS makes use of hook-and-loop fastener tape mounted on a hand-held board. Each firefighter has an individual name tag fastened to his or her helmet with the same material, allowing it to be easily transferred to the PAS board when assigned to a specific area or duty. Tags are also provided to identify placement of apparatus.

This is particularly important when a firefighter is in a hostile environment. If the firefighter remains in that environment beyond the limit set by his or her SCBA air supply, someone needs to know about it and begin an investigation.

A system that works well for smaller departments is a simple board with pegs arranged under the headings,

EXTERIOR INTERIOR
VENTILATION REHAB STAGING

Each firefighter has a name tag on the board. As the firefighter reports for assignment, the incident commander places the name tag on a peg beneath the appropriate heading. The system can quickly be updated as personnel are reassigned; if a firefighter is moved from the interior of the building to an exterior assignment, it is an easy matter to move the name tag from peg to peg. At a glance, the incident commander can assess the way firefighting forces are assigned, and identify the location of each individual. An improvement to this system would be the addition of "time in" and "time out" columns to the INTERIOR heading.

Some systems divide the fireground or incident areas into four sections or *quadrants.* As shown in **Figure 2-10,** the quadrants are labeled with the letters A, B, C, and D. If the fire is in a multistory building, numbers can be added to more accurately identify the location. Thus, if a given firefighter is in the second floor in the B quadrant of the building, his or her location would be identified as "B2."

The systems described are only a *few* of the many possible methods of accounting for personnel. Some departments use a printed log sheet, others use index cards, some use computers. The form of the system is not important, so long as it accurately provides the needed information. To be most effective when it is needed for a major fire or other incident, the PAS should be used consistently at fires and incidents of all sizes. See **Figure 2-11.** That will allow it to become "SOP" (standard operating procedure), firmly fixed in the habit patterns of everyone involved. A further consideration when developing and

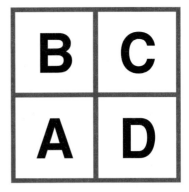

Figure 2-10. Dividing a building or incident area into quadrants (quarters) identified by letters is an aid to locating personnel on the scene. Adding a number for each building floor (C2 would be C quadrant, second floor) allows even more precise location.

Figure 2-11. Consistent use of a personnel accountability system in training and in actual fire situations of all sizes will help ensure that its use will become habitual and expected. For most effective use in major fire operations, where a number of departments are called in to render mutual aid, this system should be adopted by all the fire departments in a given geographic area.

implementing a Personnel Accounting System is cooperation (mutual aid) between departments in a geographical area. Ideally, each of those departments should be using the same system; practically, the systems used by different departments should at least be similar enough to allow everyone to adapt quickly at a major incident.

What of the future? In some respects, it is already here: certain large departments have adopted *barcoding* from industry and business. The bar code on the identification card, bracelet, or tag will contain the firefighter's name, unit, and even such information as blood type, physical limitations, allergies, or other important medical data. Using a scanner and a specially designed computer program, the system can log time-in, time-out information and record the location to which the individual is assigned. The next step may be to adapt satellite tracking and locating technology, which can identify a person's whereabouts, anywhere on Earth, with an accuracy of a few feet in any direction.

Firefighter Rehabilitation

The human body, no matter how good its conditioning, can stand only so much. After a certain amount of emotional, physical, and heat stress, your body's cooling system begins to fail, your judgment becomes impaired, and your ability to work safely is greatly reduced.

For this reason, many departments require that—after a certain amount of time on the fireground—a firefighter be sent to a *rehabilitation area* for rest and evaluation of his or her ability to continue operating effectively. See **Figure 2-12.** The amount of time involved is usually referred to as the "two-air-bottle" rule. This means that after you have worked for two full SCBA air bottles, or 45 minutes elapsed time, you must go to the rehabilitation area. This subject will be discussed in greater detail in Chapter 4, which deals with self-contained breathing apparatus and other personal protective equipment.

Figure 2-12. Firefighters working a large training exercise enjoy a period of rest and "unwinding" on a house porch serving as a rehabilitation area. Proper rest will help minimize fireground injuries due to overexertion or impaired judgment resulting from exhaustion.

Personal Safety

In the main, your safety depends on three things: your physical condition, your equipment, and your knowledge.

Physical Condition

The fire service is unique in the physical demands it makes on people. An athlete always does some form of warm-up exercise before getting into more strenuous activities. This permits the athlete's blood pressure and pulse rate to rise gradually. It also greatly reduces the chance of muscular strain.

Under normal station-house conditions, a firefighter's heart rate is typically about 72 beats per minute. In the 15-20 seconds after an alarm comes in, the rate shoots up to about 120 beats per minute. If you were asleep when the alarm came in, your heart rate would have been about 60, so the increase would be even more dramatic.

For warm-up, you don't have the five or ten minutes that an athlete takes. You don't even have one minute. On the fireground, you are doing a job that would tax the abilities of an athlete in top form, while working under far tougher conditions. The exertion takes a physical toll, but more seriously, it affects your *judgment* :

- You're tired, and the breathing gear is a drag. The air looks pretty clear, so you take off the breathing gear. *Smoke inhalation.*

- You have to move a portable generator. Do it "any way you can" on the fireground. *Strained back.*

- You double-time up three flights of stairs, carrying a 50-foot roll of hose. *Heart attack.*

The best protection you have on the fireground is *good physical conditioning.* Nearly half of all firefighter fatalities are caused by heart attack. It has been estimated that half of these fatal heart attacks could have been prevented by a regular, properly supervised program of exercise, diet, and weight control. See **Figure 2-13.** If you take part in such a program, your chances of surviving a heart attack are doubled. In other words, those who *do not* participate in an exercise/diet/weight control program are four times more likely to suffer a fatal heart attack than those who do.

What percent of fire-related fatalities among firefighters can be attributed, at least in part, to physical condition? There is no way of knowing for sure, but statistics indicate the immediate cause of death as: heart attack, 45%; wounds, blood loss, 22%; smoke inhalation, 15%; dislocation, fracture, 7%; burns, 6%, and other causes, 5%. What percent of these deaths might not have happened if the victim had been in top physical condition? 40%? 50%? 60%?

Equipment

The equipment that a firefighter uses on the job is of two types: *protective equipment* (supplied to protect the firefighter) and *working equipment* (used to perform the job). See **Figure 2-14.** Protective equipment includes helmets, breathing apparatus, turnout coats, boots, lifelines, and so on. Working equipment includes axes, hoses, nozzles, wrenches, and many other items.

You are supplied with very good protective gear. But all the protection in the world

Figure 2-13. Firefighting is a physically demanding job. Those who stay physically fit are far less likely to suffer a fatal heart attack than those who do not exercise and control their weight.

Figure 2-14. On the job, a firefighter uses protective equipment—turnout gear, gloves, and boots—and working equipment, such as hose. Both types of equipment should be carefully maintained to function safely and effectively. (Warren Lutton)

won't do you any good if you don't use it. You may not care about your own safety, but remember that if you *do* go down, four of your comrades are going to have to risk their necks to bring you out. Don't endanger *them* by endangering *yourself*.

In recent years, there have been great gains in firefighter protection. The IAFF, NFPA, NASA, OSHA, the military services, and manufacturers of fire protective equipment, among others, all have had a hand in developing increasingly better equipment. The accident rate among firefighters is generally falling, at least in part because of improved equipment. Personal protective equipment and clothing will be discussed in some detail in Chapter 4.

Care of equipment

Regardless of whether it is "protective" or "working" in nature, any piece of equipment that is abused, neglected, improperly maintained, or used carelessly is a hazard to the user and to everyone nearby.

You can't expect protective breathing apparatus to protect you if you bang it around. Leather helmets (yes, they're still being manufactured) begin to deteriorate at temperatures over 200°F (93°C). Sharp burrs on aluminum ladders can cut and put slivers under the skin. A rounded hammer head might slip off a spike as you pound it and injure your hand. A mushroomed striking surface on a tool can send metal slivers flying in all directions.

Specific instructions for the use, inspection, and maintenance of equipment are given in the appropriate sections of this text. The point to remember is the need for regular and frequent inspection of *everything* you use on the job: ropes, ladders, safety belts, Halligan tools, helmets, face masks, eye protection, all electrical wiring... the list could go on and on. There's no time to inspect and repair equipment on the fireground. It must always be in first-class condition, ready for use.

Knowledge

What are the sounds that tell you a building is about to collapse? What conditions are likely to produce a backdraft explosion? How far out from the side of the building should the butt of the ladder be placed? What does hydrogen cyanide smell like? Does carbon monoxide have an odor? How long will your *self-contained breathing apparatus (SCBA)* give you *complete* protection in dense smoke? What extinguisher do you use on a magnesium fire? Under what conditions do you insert a nozzle in a hole through a roof? How should you break a plate glass window?

If you don't know the answers to the above questions (and many others) or if you are not sure of your answers, or if you have the *wrong* answers—you are a candidate for a serious accident.

Let's take a single, very possible situation and see what can occur:

A tractor-trailer truck carrying a mixed shipment is traveling the southbound lane of a highway through a town. At the point shown on the map, **Figure 2-15,** the trailer is struck from behind by a fast-moving car. The car bursts into flame, setting fire to the load in the trailer. The time is 12:03 p.m. The wind is fairly strong and is blowing from the west.

You are the first on the scene. When you arrive, the tractor is on its side, but the trailer is still upright. The driver of the car was thrown from the vehicle and is obviously dead. There is no sign of life in the tractor, and no indication that the driver has escaped. The trailer is fully involved in flames, and

what appears to be molten metal is flowing out a crack in the bottom. A placard on the side of the trailer, **Figure 2-16,** indicates that *radioactive material* is aboard. There is a large fuel spill from the tractor that is running back toward the burning trailer.

- What is the first thing you should do?
- What are the pros and cons of trying to rescue the truck driver from the overturned tractor?
- What should you do about the fuel spill?
- How do you fight the trailer fire?
- Does this situation call for evacuation of the immediate area? A larger area?
- How can you get information about the trailer contents?
- Should traffic in the northbound lane be stopped?
- What services should you call for?
- How close should you get to the trailer?

Your chances of running into a situation as complicated as this one are remote. In today's highly technological society, however, you are certain to encounter situations with

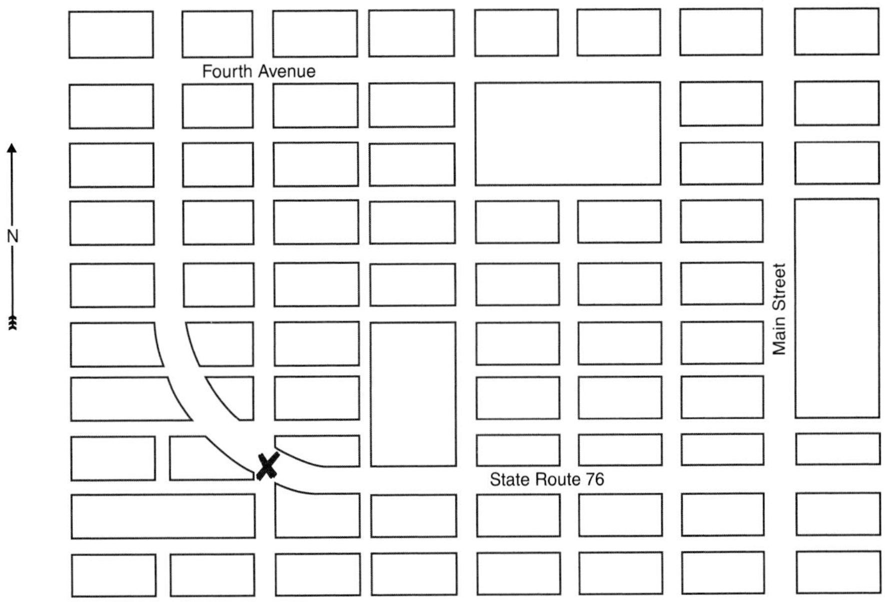

Figure 2-15. Accidents involving cargo transportation, especially trucks and rail cars, can create the double problem of fire and hazardous materials spills. Such situations can occur on streets or rail lines passing through heavily populated areas. "X" indicates the accident site.

Figure 2-16. A prominent warning sign must be displayed on all trucks or other vehicles transporting radioactive materials.

elements that are similar. You are, no doubt, tired of hearing that "no two fires are alike." That statement is nonetheless true. Your safety, the safety of your fellow firefighters, and the safety of the community at large, depend on the knowledge *you* bring to a fire. The fire scene itself is a risky classroom.

Dangerous Building Conditions

The degree and type of danger in any structural fire is determined by these three elements or characteristics:
- Type of construction.
- Materials used in the building's construction.
- Contents of the building.

Type of Construction and Materials

The behavior of fire in a building will vary widely, depending on the type of construction and materials used. For example, large roof expanses supported only at the perimeter,

often found in churches or warehouses, are subject to collapse. See **Figure 2-17.**

Many such buildings employ *truss construction* to support the roof. If the truss is made from wood, the burning of any member may cause the whole thing to fail. If the truss is steel, intense heat will cause it to weaken and twist. In either event, the result is the same: the truss fails, leading to partial or complete roof collapse. If this kind of building requires ventilation, it may be dangerous to go onto the roof to do so. If you must go onto a roof or floor that is suspect, stay on the edges. Walk carefully, probing ahead of you with a pike pole. Buildings that have reinforced concrete beams are far less likely to collapse. Building construction is discussed in detail in Chapter 13, Forcible Entry.

Structural collapse

The collapse of a structure is not a common cause of injury. When a building *does* collapse, however, the injuries are often severe in both number and type. Fortunately, a trained eye and ear will help you spot incipient trouble. If you notice *any* of the following, be especially careful. If two or more signs of trouble are present, don't go into or onto the structure, except when ordered to do so to save lives.
- A rumbling sound inside the structure.

Figure 2-17. Large roofs that are supported only at the perimeter, such as this church roof using laminated wood arches, can collapse suddenly in a fire.

- Sounds of movement of structural members.
- Cracks in the outside walls.
- An abnormal amount of smoke or water leaking through cracks in an outside wall.
- Bulging or distortion of a wall or column.
- A feeling of movement beneath your feet when walking on roof or floors.
- A full water tank on the roof. See **Figure 2-18.**

Older buildings are generally more hazardous than new ones. Building codes were less stringent several generations ago, and in most municipalities, there is no requirement to bring older structures up to modern building code standards. Many older structures do not have fire doors, fire breaks in partitions, or fire walls.

Also, since these buildings frequently do not have any kind of fire detection and warning system, the fire will often be more advanced when you arrive; the smoke and heat will have had a longer time to build up.

Buildings with open stairwells or elevator shafts permit fire or smoke to travel great distances, even skipping one or more floors. You could get caught between two fires—a fire on

the first floor of the building could result in a backdraft explosion on the fourth floor.

Building Contents

Residential fires, especially in older homes, present a number of hazards. Most fireground injuries to firefighters occur at home fires. Junk and stored items may be piled anywhere, blocking your way or just being there to trip over. With houses shut up tight to conserve energy, the buildup of smoke and heat could be intense. Also, many older homes do not have *firebreaks* in the partitions, allowing fire to rise rapidly and weaken overhead structural members.

Beware of basements. They are often the storage place for flammable liquids of all kinds, including paints, paint thinners, and gasoline. The favorite spot to stash this kind of thing is under the cellar steps (thereby cutting off your means of exit).

Fire loading

The greater the *fire loading* (the quantity of combustibles a building contains), the longer and hotter the fire will burn, and the more products of combustion it will produce. A fire loading of 10 pounds of contents per square foot will burn for about an hour. Twenty pounds will burn for two hours, and so on.

For residences, schools, places of assembly, and institutions, you can figure a fire loading of 5 to 10 pounds per square foot, **Figure 2-19.** Business and mercantile establishments have 10 to 20 pounds, while industrial and storage facilities will go 20 to 30 pounds or higher, **Figure 2-20.**

As discussed elsewhere in this chapter, the presence of heat and water with combustibles can produce vast quantities of flammable, explosive, toxic, or irritant gases. The number and quantity of such products of chemical reaction under the conditions you encounter in a fire — even with nothing but "safe" substances around — is truly awesome. Your breathing apparatus and turnout gear are your best (in fact, *only*) protection. In

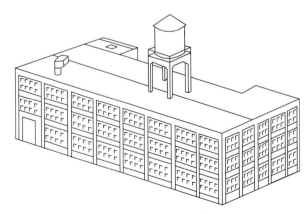

Figure 2-18. When combined with other factors, the weight of a full water tank on the roof of a weakened building could lead to a total or partial structural collapse.

Figure 2-19. Fire loading is the weight of combustibles per square foot that serves as fuel for a fire. Residential structures typically have a loading of between 5 and 10 pounds per square foot, enough to burn for up to an hour. (Bruce)

Figure 2-20. Industrial and storage facilities, such as this warehouse, may have a fire loading of 30 pounds or more per square foot.

spite of the heat and clumsiness of all this equipment, don't be tempted to take it off until told to do so by a responsible officer. Even then, wait until the officer takes off his or her own equipment.

Electrical Shock Hazards

Where you find electrically operated equipment, television sets, electric stoves, computers, large lighted signs, or similar devices, the danger of electrical shock exists, (especially since, with lots of water around, you are well-grounded). The chances for electrical shock also exist when you break into a wall or use a spray nozzle inside a partition. Unless you *know* that the electric power has been shut off, treat this as an electrical fire. Do not touch any electrical equipment or wiring unless you are wearing gloves specifically made for the purpose.

Portable lighting equipment

Portable lighting equipment used in firefighting must project a very great amount of light, which means high-wattage operation. At the same time, this electrically powered equipment must be used in a frequently wet environment. This, of course, makes it doubly dangerous. To guard against electrical shock, manufacturers have used thick insulation on the wiring, provided three-prong grounded plugs, and incorporated ground fault circuit interrupters (GFCIs) to cut off current at the first sign of danger.

Your responsibility is to be sure that the safety features built into the equipment are not compromised. You must regularly check all aspects of the lighting equipment for wear or defects. The integrity of the connectors, insulation, and grounding system must not be compromised in any way. If you discover anything that has been damaged or altered, call it to the attention of the responsible officer.

Electrical emergencies

Most fire departments do not handle electrical emergencies, as such. They do not have the training or the equipment. If you should be confronted with a downed power line, your job is to notify the utility company and keep everybody back. *Period.*

In *any* kind of a structure fire, you must always cut off the electric power at the box before spraying any water around. If you must cut an electric wire, as you might in an electric ballast fire, wear approved insulated gloves and use only an approved electrical wire cutter.

If you are with a department that *does* handle electrical emergencies, you will receive special training. Don't even think of trying to remove a downed charged wire until you have received such training.

Shutting Off Utility Services

Both electricity and gas can pose unnecessary hazards to firefighters in a fire structure. Both utility services must be shut off before firefighters can safely be allowed to enter the structure.

Electric service

Sometimes, you will find a fuse box or circuit breaker box on the outside of a building, usually with an adjacent ON/OFF switch. Moving the switch to the OFF position will disconnect the building's power. If such a box is not outside the building, it will be on the inside. For general location, identify the point where the power lines (called a *service drop*) enter the building. See **Figure 2-21.** Often, the box will be in a basement, but it may be in an attached garage or in a utility room. If you can reach the box safely, cut off the power by using the switch or pulling the main fuses. If you are unable to find or safely approach the box, have your dispatcher notify the electrical utility. Their technicians will disconnect the building at one end of the service drop.

Gas service

The gas meter, often outside and next to a building, will have a shutoff valve located adjacent to it. See **Figure 2-22.** In some cases, the meter and valve may be located some distance from the building, often in a vault near the street. The position of the shutoff valve handle in relation to the supply pipe indicates whether it is ON or OFF. If the handle is parallel to the pipe, gas is flowing though the valve. If the handle is perpendicular to (across) the pipe, the gas valve is closed; no gas is flowing.

In older structures, the gas meter and shutoff may be in the basement. Sometimes, this will mean that the valve is inaccessible or that attempts to reach it would endanger firefighters. As in the case with the electric utility,

Figure 2-21. Sometimes, electrical service to a building can be shut off at an outside fuse or circuit breaker box. If the box is inside the building, its location can often be pinpointed by observing where the conduit from the service drop passes through the wall.

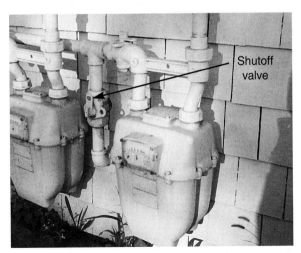

Figure 2-22. Often, gas service to a building can be cut off by locating the gas meter and shutoff valve. Usually, the meter and shutoff will be on an outside wall of the building, but sometimes may be located in a vault near the street. This installation has separate meters for two different tenants in the building, but uses a single shutoff valve on the supply pipe.

ask your dispatcher to notify the gas utility. Their specialist technicians will shut off gas flow to the building.

Homes and businesses in rural areas often depend upon tanks of *liquefied petroleum gas (LP gas, or LPG)* for heating or cooking fuel. The tanks are available in a range of sizes, but all have some form of external shut-off valve. See **Figure 2-23.** At some industrial plants, small LPG tanks are used to power the engines of lift trucks and other material handling devices. As shown in **Figure 2-24,** these tanks are often stored in an outdoor rack.

Radiation Hazards

Since the Three-Mile Island and Chernobyl nuclear power plant accidents, radioactive materials have become an emotional issue. Some people believe that *any* exposure to any sort of radiation constitutes a serious threat to their physical well-being. Much of our fear of radiation is fear of the unknown, the unsensed, the mysterious— you cannot feel, touch, taste, smell, or hear it.

Figure 2-24. Tanks of propane fuel for industrial lift trucks are often stored outside a plant in metal racks.

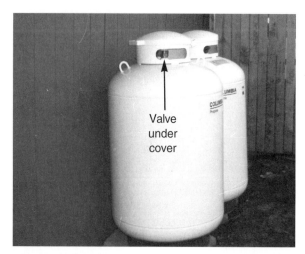

Figure 2-23. Liquefied petroleum gas (most often propane, but other gases and mixed gases are also used) is used for residential heating and cooking, as well as in commercial and industrial applications. The gas is stored in tanks of various sizes outside the buildings. These are residential tanks. Note the protective cover over the shutoff valve atop each tank.

Let's try to put into perspective some of the situations you may encounter:

The truck accident discussed earlier in this chapter would be treated as a life-threatening situation. It could affect your life, as well as the lives of all other people in the area. All you know initially is that there is some kind of radioactive substance aboard the truck. You don't know what kind of material, how much of it, how potent it is, what form it is in, how it is packaged, or anything else of use in determining the degree of danger. You have no choice but to treat it as extremely hazardous, until you *know* otherwise.

Whenever radioactive materials are used, stored, or transported, federal law requires that they must be clearly identified. If a vehicle is carrying radioactive material, it must display a placard like the one shown in **Figure 2-16.**

If the radioactive substance is inside an installation, you are much better off. You are most likely to be in the vicinity of radioactive substances when fighting a fire in an industrial plant or at a hospital. In either case, if you exercise proper caution, there is no great danger. In both kinds of installations, materials are handled according to Nuclear Regulatory Commission regulations. Barring a disaster, trained personnel will probably be on hand to assist.

Industrial application

In a typical industrial situation, the cell housing the nuclear material is a labyrinth design with concrete walls four feet thick. The floor and the ceiling are also concrete. See **Figure 2-25.** The doors are wood, with an eighth-inch-thick lead shield built in. There is little or nothing inside the cell that would support combustion.

The radioactivity source itself is in a container about the size of a cold-medicine capsule. The capsule of radioactive material is fixed to the end of a flexible shaft that feeds in and out through a flexible housing. When not in use, the capsule is kept in a spent-uranium container that absorbs all radiation.

To operate the system, the technician must leave the cell, close the outside doors, and activate exterior controls. When the controls have been activated, a red warning light is activated and the doors cannot be opened.

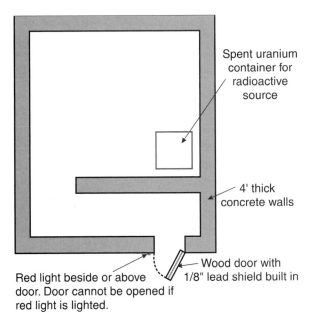

Red light beside or above door. Door cannot be opened if red light is lighted.

Spent uranium container for radioactive source

4' thick concrete walls

Wood door with 1/8" lead shield built in

Figure 2-25. Typical labyrinth construction used for industrial radioactivity sources. The walls, floor, and ceiling are of thick concrete. When the capsule of radioactive material is not in use, it is housed in a container of spent uranium that absorbs all radiation. Whenever the door is opened, the radioactive material is automatically drawn into the protective container.

From a firefighter safety standpoint, everything is relatively simple:

- If the red light is on, do not go in.
- If there is a fire inside the cell and the radioactivity source is in the operating position, let the fire burn. The fire can't do any damage, nor can it spread outside the cell.
- If there is a fire on the outside that burns the wooden door and melts the lead lining, there is no danger from the radioactive material so long as you stay outside the baffle.

Decontamination

If you have reason to believe you have come in contact with any radioactive particles, *decontaminate* immediately. Remove contaminated clothing before entering any vehicle, or leaving the immediate area. Leave your clothing on location to be handled by decontamination personnel. Immediately wash all over with hot water and soap, if available (use cold water and no soap, if that's the best you can do at the time). Get professional medical attention immediately.

Decontamination after skin contact with any hazardous chemicals is done in a similar manner. Strip down and wash thoroughly, using plenty of soap and hot water. Pay special attention to hair. Examine contact area for redness indicating a chemical burn. If the burn is light, treat it as you would an ordinary burn. If the burn is severe or covers a wide area, get medical attention immediately. See Chapters 22 and 23 for more detailed information on hazardous materials.

Taking Proper Action when Trapped or Disoriented

One of humanity's most common fears is the fear of the unknown. Disoriented, alone in the dark, trapped: these are forms of the unknown. Your natural reaction is to kick, scream, run. *Don't!* You are not lost. You are not alone. In a firefighting situation, there are others in there with you. There are also others outside who know you are in there.

Most fires are knocked down in a matter of minutes. Can you survive where you are for a few minutes? Take stock. How is your air supply? If the SCBA bell isn't ringing or the facepiece isn't vibrating, you have at least five minutes. Is the building in danger of immediate collapse? How about the fire itself — is it going to burn *you* in the next few minutes? If there is a closed door between you and the flames, you are probably safe in that respect for at least fifteen minutes. If all the signs say you are safe, for now, *stay where you are! Take stock!*

Personal Alerting Device

You should never enter a burning building, or any other hazardous environment, without wearing a personal alerting device (PAD). Such a device is also referred to frequently as a *PASS (personal alert safety system),* **Figure 2-26.** There are a number of types of such devices on the market, but all have the same purpose: making it easier to locate and rescue you if you become incapacitated. Typically, the alerting device will emit a loud tone if you have not moved within a specified period of time, such as 30 seconds. The device can also be triggered manually in an emergency. The device must be turned on and tested for proper operation before you enter a dangerous environment. See **Figure 2-27.**

Using Your Senses

Make use of your senses. That's why you've got them—to help you survive. Look. Don't assume you can't see anything. *Use* your eyes. Do you see a vague rectangular patch of light? It's a window. That also means an outside wall. Good to know. What else? There's a dim, large lump off to your right. The sofa. It was to your right as you entered the room. At least you know where you are, and you have identified two alternate escape routes. Not bad.

Figure 2-26. A personal alerting device will emit a signal if you do not move in a preset amount of time, helping rescuers to find you more quickly. Such devices represent an important advance in making firefighters' activities safer. (Antenna Specialists Division, Allen Telecom Group)

Figure 2-27. This firefighter is wearing a PASS connected to the harness of his SCBA. The location of the PASS permits easy access for turning it on or off as the firefighter enters and exits a burning building. Failure to do so can be fatal—a recent survey of firefighter fatalities found that 79% of those who died while trapped in a building interior did not have their PASS turned on.

Signaling

Don't move yet. What is between you and that window, or between you and the room door? If you don't know, *stay where you are.* Shout, scream, whistle. Get somebody's attention. Beat on the wall or floor with a piece of wood, your boot, your fist. Use a rhythmic pattern. A single thump doesn't mean anything, but a rhythmic beating is a *signal.*

Moving with a Plan

If you must move, have a *plan.* Usually, you are safer right next to the wall. Be careful how you get there, though. If you know the direction, that's a start. Follow something — a hose or a lifeline — if you can. No such luck? Crouch down. The visibility should be better. Still no luck? Get down on your stomach and crawl (if there is a hole in the floor, at least only *part* of you will fall into it!).

Since you already resemble an insect crawling on the floor, you might as well act like one. Use your arms and hands as antennas. Make wide, sweeping motions. Don't grab, just touch lightly. If you come across a wire, don't grab it—it may be live. Make a fist and extend the center knuckle on your middle finger. *Lightly* brush the wire with that knuckle. See **Figure 2-28.** It might jolt you, but it won't fry you. Do nothing further with the wire unless you have been trained to handle electrical emergencies.

During all this, keep track of where you are and how you got there. You may have to go back. Work slowly and methodically. Don't do anything fast unless you *absolutely must.*

Once you reach the outside wall and the window you identified earlier, you have a choice to make: should you attempt to go out the window, or should you "stay put" at the window, attract attention, and let help come to you? Whenever possible, "staying put" should be your choice — jumping from a building should always be your last resort. If you decide that you *have to* go out through that window, remember that you probably

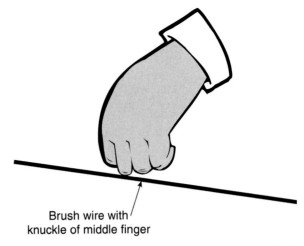

Brush wire with knuckle of middle finger

Figure 2-28. If an exposed wire can't be avoided entirely, the knuckle test can be used to determine whether it is charged. Be sure to brush the wire only lightly to minimize the possible shock.

have more time than you think. Before opening or breaking the window, consider this point: could the rush of oxygen cause a backdraft explosion? You might go out much faster than you had planned. If an explosion isn't likely, you should first throw out mattresses, pillows, blankets, rugs — anything soft to land on. Ease your body out the opening, keeping low, since an explosion is still a possibility. Exit feet first. Ease over onto your stomach and hang by your fingertips. Do whatever you can to shorten the fall. Drop onto a car roof or into a tree or bushes. Make a rope out of a sheet or drapes, or from your own clothing, if you have something substantial like a radiator or heavy bed to tie onto. Let go, and crumple into a heap when you hit.

Operating Emergency Vehicles Safely

Some states give drivers of emergency vehicles privileges that they don't give other drivers. In these states, you may exceed the legal speed limit, go through stop signs and signals without coming to a full stop, even drive the wrong way on a one-way street.

You may do such things *if* you are responding to an emergency, and *if* both your siren and warning lights are operating.

For example, the motor vehicle laws of one state provide that the driver of an emergency vehicle, when responding to an emergency, may:

- "... proceed past a red signal indication or stop sign, but *only after slowing down as may be necessary for safe operation...*"

- "...exceed the maximum speed limits *so long as the driver does not endanger life or property...* "

Note that this law (italics supplied for emphasis) puts the burden for safety on the operator of the emergency vehicle.

In other states, you must obey all traffic laws, regardless of the circumstances. NFPA safety standards also require this. It is doubtful, however, that a police officer would cite you for exceeding the speed limit if you gave proper warning when responding to the emergency, and if you drove in a safe manner.

Driving Responsibly

Drivers of emergency vehicles *do* get arrested for driving in a reckless manner — no law *anywhere* gives a person the right to drive without regard for the safety of others, even when responding to an emergency. In recent years, we have seen an increase in lawsuits against the drivers of emergency vehicles. Other users of the roads who have been injured by fire apparatus or other vehicles that were responding to emergencies have sued, and *won*. If an injured person can show that you were negligent, exhibited disregard for the safety of others, lacked adequate training, or operated the vehicle while under the influence of drugs or alcohol, you could lose everything you own.

However if you were able to show that you were driving within the law, *and* that you had adequate training in the safe operation of your apparatus, you would probably win such a lawsuit.

The material in this section is not intended to be a substitute for training. No book, by itself, can give you such training and the resulting legal protection. If your department cannot provide the hands-on experience you need, check out other sources. Local police departments or sheriff's offices frequently offer such courses, or will know who does. Training in vehicle operation is for your own safety, both physical and financial.

Using warning devices

When attempting to exercise your emergency right-of-way, your first task is to get the attention of the other drivers on the road. Modern technology is on your side: in recent years, vast improvements have been made in warning devices for emergency vehicles. Light bars, **Figure 2-29;** strobe lights, **Figure 2-30,** and portable warning lights, **Figure 2-31,** are all more effective than they were a few years ago. The multiple-function electronic siren, **Figure 2-32,** and powerful loudspeakers, **Figure 2-33,** have added to your ability to get attention.

You cannot rely on your siren and lights alone. Even though your siren sounds very loud to you when you are in the vehicle, the sound doesn't carry as far as you might think. On a noisy city street, even a 200-watt siren

Figure 2-29. Light bars come with various combinations of rotating and strobe lights, in single or contrasting colors, to help catch the attention of other drivers and pedestrians. Some include horns, sirens, or a public address system. (Federal Signal Corporation)

Figure 2-30. Various types of bright strobe light flashers can be mounted on the sides and rear of fire apparatus to alert other drivers on the same and intersecting streets. (Federal Signal Corporation)

Figure 2-31. Firefighters on small town and rural departments often respond to emergencies in their private vehicles. This portable emergency warning light can be mounted on the vehicle's dash or other locations, and is powered by plugging into the cigarette lighter socket. (Federal Signal Corporation)

Figure 2-32. An electronic siren allows you to generate different siren sounds at the click of a switch. Some even emulate the sound of an air horn. This model also includes controls for the vehicle's warning lights. (Federal Signal Corporation)

might not be heard more than about one-half block away (and most emergency vehicle sirens are *100 watts* or less). If you are moving

Figure 2-33. Rugged loudspeakers are used for the sound output of electronic siren units. They are designed to project sound strongly to the front and sides of the apparatus. (Federal Signal Corporation)

fast enough, you can actually "over-drive" the sound of your siren. Your siren isn't likely to be heard for these reasons:

- The background noise of the city.
- The effect of buildings blocking the sound.
- The fact that most cars are well-insulated against cold *and* sound (plus, they have radios and tape players).
- The use of air conditioning that allows many drivers to keep their windows rolled up even in hot weather.

Don't depend on drivers seeing your *lights,* either. Often they just do not pay attention, especially during daytime hours when lights are less effective, anyway.

Your best protection is ***defensive driving.*** Even though your fire apparatus weighs many times more than the average car, you must learn and practice the art of driving defensively.

Checking out the vehicle

Defensive driving starts before you even step inside the vehicle. Check out your apparatus. Check all the fluid levels: brakes, power steering, oil, water. Check tire pressure with a tire gauge for accuracy. Under-inflated and over-inflated tires are dangerous. Adjust all mirrors and clean them, if necessary. Be sure the windshield and all other windows are clean and are clear of any obstructions. Check all lights: warning, driving, and turn signals. Check your siren.

Other precautions

More than 20% of firefighter fatalities result from accidents involving emergency vehicles. The United States Fire Administration recommends the following precautions for emergency vehicle operators, passengers, and officers in charge.

Vehicle Operators

- Make sure you are fully qualified and capable of operating the emergency vehicle you intend to drive.

- Operate the vehicle with due care, exercising the same caution that you would if your passengers and the drivers around you were all members of your family.

- Slower is safer. Do not exceed the posted speed limit. Drive even more slowly when visibility or road conditions warrant a lower speed.

- Always stop at any intersection (such as a railroad crossing) that has a negative right-of-way. Proceed with caution after you are sure other vehicles have stopped and given you the right-of-way.

- Take special precautions at railroad crossings that have no gates or lights, or at any rail crossing where your vision is obscured. Turn off all radios, fans, wipers, sirens, or other sound sources and let the engine idle. Roll down your window and *listen* for any oncoming rail traffic that you might not be able to see.

- Never assume that the operator of another vehicle is aware of the presence of your emergency vehicle. Despite sirens and flashing lights, drivers too often fail to note the approach of a fire vehicle, ambulance, or other emergency equipment.

- Park your vehicle in as safe a place as possible, away from downed power lines, falling debris, and smoke, flame, and toxic gases. When parked on a roadway, use your vehicle's flashing emergency lights (supplemented by flares of portable warning lights, if necessary) to alert other drivers. Always set your parking brake and use wheel chocks, where appropriate, to secure the vehicle.

- Never put your vehicle into motion until all occupants are safely seated and (where available) wearing seat belts. Ideally (and by law in some states), a seat belt would be available for every occupant.

- Never allow anyone to exit your vehicle until you have come to a complete stop.

- When backing the vehicle, always use a competent spotter to guide you.

- Never operate any vehicle (especially an emergency vehicle) while your abilities are impaired by alcohol, drugs, or medications.

Vehicle Passengers

- Always put on your protective clothing before mounting the emergency vehicle.

- Before the vehicle begins to move, make sure that all tools and equipment in the interior are safely secured.

- If the area where you ride is not completely enclosed, always wear your helmet and use eye protection.

- Do not "ride the step" on the back or side of an emergency vehicle; always ride in a seated position inside, wearing a seat belt. See **Figure 2-34.** Do not stand while the vehicle is in motion.

- Before exiting an emergency vehicle, make sure that it has come to a complete stop. Wait for direction before unbuckling your seat belt and standing up.

- Look for oncoming traffic, downed wires, and other hazards before stepping down from an emergency vehicle.

Figure 2-34. Avoid the potential for injury that exists when riding on the outside of a fire vehicle. Always ride in a seated position inside the cab, with seat belt fastened.

- Never try to jump onto or off a moving vehicle.
- When you act as a spotter for an emergency vehicle that is performing a backing maneuver, make sure you are fully aware of its location and direction of movement. Never turn your back on a vehicle that is moving toward you.
- Never board an emergency vehicle while your abilities are impaired by alcohol, drugs, or medications.

Officer in Charge

- Always remember that you are ultimately responsible for the safe and prudent operation of the emergency vehicle, as well as the safety of passengers within it.

Avoiding Vehicle Accidents

A basic law of physics states that two bodies cannot occupy the same space at the same time. This law applies to everything from a game of ping-pong to a vehicle accident. In ping-pong, the ball bounces back toward your opponent because it cannot occupy the same space at the same time as your paddle. Serious damage to a vehicle and injury to occupants often results when that vehicle tries to occupy the same space at the same time as a tree, another vehicle, or a stone wall. Whether or not your state gives you the right to violate traffic laws in an emergency, don't ever try to violate this basic law of physics. The results can be painful, even fatal.

Types of accidents

Accidents don't just "happen." Accidents are *caused*. Those that involve two vehicles occur in one of the patterns shown in **Figure 2-35.** These patterns are:

- Oncoming. Your vehicle collides with one coming toward you.
- Ongoing. Your vehicle collides with one going in the same direction.
- Following. Your vehicle is hit from behind by a car or truck going in the same direction.
- Entering and merging. You are hit at an angle by a car moving into your lane from a merging lane, or one that is pulling out from the curb.
- Intersecting. You are hit broadside by another vehicle at an intersection.

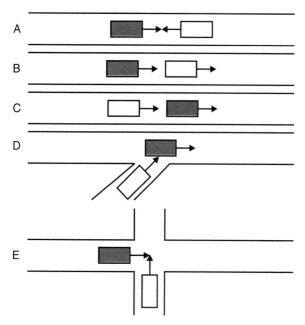

Figure 2-35. Two-vehicle accidents conform to one of these patterns: A, oncoming; B, ongoing; C, following; D, entering and merging, or E, intersecting. Remaining alert and ready to take needed evasive action is the best defense against such accidents.

Contributing highway factors

A number of highway factors can contribute to collisions. These include reduced traction, reduced visibility, and reduced space.

Reduced traction. Skidding can cause a vehicle to change direction or speed, or both. Reduced traction can be caused by loose gravel, holes in the road, bumps, oil, ice, snow, water, and many other road conditions. The more water, the more likely the possibility of *hydroplaning* (skidding on a film of water). The amount of traction lost on wet surfaces will vary. Wet brick offers less traction than wet concrete; a smooth surface less than a slightly rough one. On an icy surface, you have almost no traction with ordinary tires. With snow tires, or even chains, you will have greatly reduced traction.

Reduced visibility. Rain and fog, the time of day, the kind and location of traffic, glare on the highway, high beams from an approaching car—all these can affect your vision and the vision of other drivers. So can highway configurations, such as the brow of a hill, a curve, or a dip. A truck can hide even a large automobile; a small automobile can hide a bicycle or a small child.

Reduced space. Conditions that reduce available space by packing vehicles closer together include heavy traffic, narrow roads and bridges, and road repairs. See **Figure 2-36.** When there is less space available, there is less time to avoid a collision.

When two or more of the preceding factors occur at the same time, the hazards multiply. You could have:

- Poor traction *and* poor visibility.
- Poor traction *and* reduced space.
- Poor visibility *and* reduced space.
- Poor visibility *and* poor traction.
- Poor visibility *and* reduced space *and* poor traction.

Possible maneuvers

If you are moving, you have three choices of things to do to avoid a hazard. You can increase your speed, reduce your speed, or change direction. You also can change direction *together with* an increase or reduction in speed. If you are stopped, you can either pull forward or back up.

So far, this discussion has been mostly about space: the space it will take you to stop

Figure 2-36. When space is reduced by heavy traffic, road repairs, narrow bridges or tunnels, you have less time to react to hazards and less space for evasive action.

or gain control of your vehicle under various conditions of traction, the space where you can (or cannot) see what is going on, the space you have in which to move around. But space, by itself, doesn't mean much. You don't have much space when driving in a filled parking lot, but no one is likely to hit you (if you are the only car moving). It is more practical to think in terms of time. How much *time* do you have to slow down, to speed up, to stop, to move out of the way?

Space and time

When you are driving, you must divide the space along your intended path of travel into three sections: the *following zone*, the *stopping zone*, and the *travel path*. See **Figure 2-37.**

The two-second following zone. You are used to thinking of the distance between your vehicle and the one in front in terms of "car lengths." By themselves, however, car lengths do not mean much. In a traffic jam, two car lengths between vehicles is far more than you need (and the driver behind you will tell you so with his or her horn). At highway speeds, two car lengths could be fatal. The *two-second following zone* is the amount of space you want to keep between

you and the vehicles in front and behind. It refers to the distance your vehicle will travel in two seconds at the current rate of speed. The distance will increase with the speed, so two seconds will give you time to stop, or take evasive action, should the driver in front suddenly stop. The *two-second zone* will give you better visibility, as well. If traction is bad, or you are driving a heavy vehicle such as a pumper, you must increase the "zone" to three or four seconds.

The four-second stopping zone. The *four-second stopping zone* is the minimum distance required to come to a full stop for a fixed object (such as a fallen tree or stalled automobile) or a moving object crossing your path (such as a child running into the street or an intersecting vehicle).

The twelve-second travel path. The distance your vehicle will travel in twelve seconds is the *twelve-second travel path.* This zone gives you time to identify, evaluate, and decide what to do about any potential hazard *before* you reach the four-second stopping zone. On a rural highway, the twelve-second travel path might be as much as one-quarter mile. In an urban area, it will be about one city block.

Figure 2-37. As you drive, mentally mark off zones around your vehicle: the following zone (front and rear), the stopping zone, and the travel zone. As speed increases, the zones will increase in length. You should, however, think of them in terms of seconds, rather than feet or car-lengths.

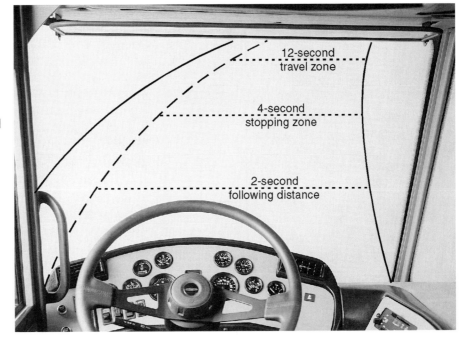

The space margin

Using these time zones as a guide, create a space margin all around your vehicle, **Figure 2-38**. The *space margin* is hazard-free space. It is space in front, in back, and on both sides. This margin gives you time to see, to evaluate, and to react to any hazard, no matter where it comes from. It gives you space in which to maneuver. The size and shape of your space margin will vary with the weather and road, and with traffic conditions. Under normal conditions, the margin should be:

Space ahead. Two seconds following and four seconds stopping. If you are driving a heavy vehicle, increase this to three or four seconds and five or six seconds, respectively. Also increase times if traction is reduced.

Space behind. Two seconds. Again, if you are being followed by a heavy vehicle or if traction is reduced, increase the distance by a second or two. If the vehicle is tailgating you, allow for more space ahead or slow down to the point where the tailgater will pass you, if possible.

Space at the sides. A minimum of one car width on at least one side. It is better to have at least one car width on both sides. If road or traffic conditions do not permit sufficient space at the sides, increase the distance in front.

Time to maneuver

All vehicle maneuvers take time; probably more than you think. When making vehicle maneuvers, you need hazard-free space as indicated in the following list:

- Four seconds when changing lanes, or when merging with high-speed traffic.
- Six seconds when passing through intersections.
- Eight seconds when entering city traffic from a parking space or when making right- or left-hand turns.
- Ten seconds when passing other vehicles.
- Fifteen seconds when entering highway traffic from a stopped position on the shoulder.

Scanning for hazards

The purpose of this time/space margin you build around your vehicle is to give you time to see, register, evaluate, and react to potential hazards. It gives you time to see and adjust to conditions of reduced traction, reduced space, or reduced visibility. All the space in the world won't do you any good if you don't use it wisely. That is the purpose of scanning: to permit you to see and evaluate hazards in a systematic way.

Scanning is the correct and continual use of the eyes. When you scan correctly, your eyes sweep the entire intended path of travel within your twelve-second time zone, **Figure 2-39**. You also make regular checks to the sides and to the rear of your vehicle. Scanning might seem a little awkward at first. After you have made it a habit, however, this practice will reduce the mental strain and

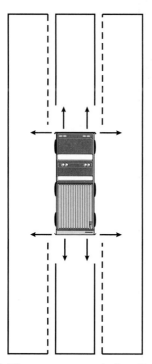

Figure 2-38. The space margin is a hazard-free zone you want to create around your vehicle: ahead, behind, and to both sides. It gives you time to react to hazards and maneuver your vehicle.

fatigue, provide you with more assurance, and leave you with no unpleasant surprises.

Scanning techniques. Use the center of your intended travel path as your point of reference. This will help you stay in your lane. Scan far and near and side-to-side through your twelve-second lead distance. Again, this will be about a block in town and one-quarter mile in rural areas. Using the twelve-second zone, you will be able to better time traffic lights and blend with traffic. You will find that you use your brakes very little.

Keep your eyes moving. Cover the entire space on all sides. Check all mirrors. You should make a complete sweep of the space margin every five seconds in the city and every ten seconds in rural areas. Check your instrument panel every five to ten seconds, as well. Periodically, you will have to make checks of your vehicle's "blind spots." You will have to move your head a bit to see around them.

One of the advantages of scanning is that it prevents you from assuming a fixed stare. A stare becomes fixed if you hold it for more than two seconds. You become oblivious to everything else. Worse yet, a fixed stare rapidly becomes a *blank* stare, in which the mind no longer registers what the eyes see.

What to scan for. Watch for anything, moving or stationary, that can invade your space margin. In commercial areas, this can mean cars pulling out from the side, pedestrians, people pushing handcarts, and many other hazards. In residential areas, it might be children playing, loose pets, piles of wet leaves, or piles of snow. In rural areas, scan for slow-moving vehicles, animals (wild or domestic) crossing the road, fallen rocks or trees, or vehicles entering the highway from farm lanes.

Beware of hazardous road conditions, whether permanent or temporary. Are curves sharp or gradual, flat or banked? Are the lanes wide or narrow, marked or unmarked? Is the road flat or crowned? Are bridge abutments close to the roadway or well out of the way? What about trees, poles, fences, houses, and parking areas? Is the road limited access, or can other vehicles enter at any point without warning?

Keep your eyes moving far-to-near, side-to-side, front-to-back. Watch for *clues*. A ball bouncing into the street is usually followed

Figure 2-39. The practice of scanning will help you quickly identify hazards in time to avoid them. Scan near to far, side to side, front to back, inside to outside. Scanning helps you remain mentally alert, and could save your life.

by a child. Smoke from the tailpipe of a parked car could mean that the car is about to pull out. If the wheels are angled toward the street and the brake lights are glowing, the car will probably pull out *soon.* Make eye contact with the driver to be sure that he or she has seen you. Is the car a sports-type or high-performance model? If so, the driver may be tempted to pull out ahead of you. If the car is badly battered and full of dents and rusty spots, its condition should alert you to a possibly careless driver.

How good is the visibility in your present situation? Can you really see as far and as well as you think you can? Visibility can be poor at twilight, before the other drivers put on their headlights, as well as in patchy ground fog or smoke, in rain or snow, or when you drive directly into the rising or setting sun. If you can't see a problem, you can't prepare for it. What about the other drivers on the road? Can they see you?

Benefits of scanning. As you practice scanning, you will build up a memory bank of conditions and clues. When you encounter similar conditions later, you will remember what you did before and know what to do this time. Don't let your eyes just wander idly

or become fixed. Use them as they were intended to be used. Use them for your own protection and for the protection of others who use the roadways.

When you have developed good visual habits:

- You will be prepared in advance for stops and turns.
- You will notice traffic tie-ups well in advance.
- You will not get trapped behind large trucks or slow-moving vehicles.
- You will not experience unpleasant surprises on the road.
- You will be more aware of vehicles about to pass.
- You will be more aware of your own speed, so that it will be appropriate to conditions and the situation.
- Your signals will flash only when you want them to.
- Your mirrors will always be clean and properly adjusted.
- Your windows will always be clean and not obscured.
- You will not be easily distracted.

SUMMARY

Since the firefighter is exposed to the most severe working conditions of any worker, safety is a *must.* Your safety depends on keeping both your own body and the equipment you use in excellent condition.

Being aware of the dangers of different types of building construction, and of the physical signs that signal imminent structural collapse, are vital to safe firefighting. Know how to master fear of the unknown and how to safely find your way out ofsmoke-filled structures. Also be aware of

proper procedures for handling electrical emergencies. Do not attempt to deal with them unless you have special training.

Make defensive driving an essential part of your vehicle operating time. When driving a piece of fire apparatus, construct a hazard-free "space margin" around you by making use of the two-second following zone, four-second stopping zone, and twelve-second travel path guidelines. Constantly practice scanning for hazards until your reaction to them becomes automatic.

REVIEW QUESTIONS

1. Why is good physical conditioning important for a firefighter?
2. Why shouldn't you wait until you are on the fireground to determine whether all your equipment is in good working condition?
3. At what sound level (measured on the dBA scale) can permanent hearing damage occur?
4. What laws or regulations determine the safety and health standards for your department?
5. How does your knowledge of probable conditions add to your safety?
6. What three characteristics affect the degree of danger in a structure fire?
7. What effect can fire have on a building with wood trusses supporting the roof? Is this effect the same if steel trusses are used?
8. What does the term "fire loading" mean?
9. If you encounter a considerable amount of electrically operated equipment in a fire, what procedure should you follow?
10. Under what conditions should you personally attempt to deal with an electrical emergency?
11. How do you shut off electrical power to a building when the breaker panel is located in an unsafe inside area?
12. What special problems are presented by buildings that include open stairways or elevator shafts?
13. What hazards are you likely to encounter around liquefied petroleum gas?
14. What seven signs warn of possible structural collapse?
15. If you find that radioactive materials are present in a fire, what precautions should you take?
16. What should you do if you become disoriented in a smoke-filled building?
17. Why is a Personnel Accountability System (PAS) important?
18. In what five patterns can a two-vehicle collision occur?
19. Over what distance can you expect your siren to be heard in city traffic?
20. What are the three zones you should establish when driving a vehicle?
21. Define the term "space margin."
22. How much space (expressed in seconds) should you allow when you are changing lanes?
23. How much space (again, expressed in seconds) should you allow when passing another vehicle?
24. Describe in detail the procedure known as "scanning."

NFPA 1001 Job Performance Requirements

The material on this page consists of those portions of the NFPA 1001 Job Performance Requirements relevant to the material presented in this chapter. Items preceded by the numeral 3 (3-x.x) are Fire Fighter I requirements; those with the numeral 4 (4-x.x) are Fire Fighter II requirements.

(3-3.9)

(a) Prerequisite Knowledge: Principles of fire streams; types, design, operation, nozzle pressure effects, and flow capabilities of nozzles; precautions to be followed when advancing hose lines to a fire; observable results that a fire stream has been properly applied; dangerous building conditions created by fire; principles of exposure protection; potential long-term consequences of exposure to products of combustion; physical states of matter in which fuels are found; common types of accidents or injuries and their causes; and the application of each size ond type of attack line, the role of the backup team in fire attack situations, attack and control techniques for grade level and above and below grade levels, and exposing hidden fires.

(3-3.10)

(a) Prerequisite Knowledge: The principles, advantages, limitations, and effects of horizontal, mechanical, and hydraulic ventilation; safety considerations when venting a structure; fire behavior in a structure; the products of combustion found in a structure fire; the signs, causes, effects, and prevention of backdrafts; and the relationship of oxygen concentration to life safety and fire growth.

(3-3.11)

(a) Prerequisite Knowledge: The methods of heat transfer; the principles of thermal layering within a structure on fire; the techniques and safety precautions for venting flat roofs, pitched roofs, and basements; basic indicators of potential collapse or roof failure; the effects of construction types and elapsed time under fire conditions on structural integrity; and the advantages and disadvantages of vertical and trench/strip ventilation.

Reprinted with permission from NFPA 1001, *Fire Fighter Professional Qualifications,* Copyright ©1997, National Fire Protection Association, Quincy, MA 02269. This reprinted material is not the complete and official position of the National Fire Protection Association on the referenced subject, which is represented only by the standard in its entirety.

Fire Behavior

OBJECTIVES

When you have completed this chapter, you will be able to:

- Describe the chemical reactions that take place as a substance burns.
- Discuss how heat moves from place to place, spreading fire.
- Define the term "fire tetrahedron" and discuss its components.
- List and describe the classes of fire (based on the kind of fuel that is burning).
- Identify the phases of burning and the signs of each phase.

IMPORTANT TERMS

backdraft explosion	explosive limits	gas	nonadecane
British Thermal Unit (Btu)	feedback	hydrocarbons	nonane
carbon monoxide	fire	ignition temperature	open-burning phase
chain reaction	fire tetrahedron	incipient phase	products of combustion
combustion	fire triangle	liquid	radiation
compound	flammable limits	methane	solid
conduction	flashover	methane series	smoldering phase
convection	flash point	molecule	
element	fuel		

Fighting fires is hazardous. While some of the risks cannot be avoided, most *can*. And yet, firefighters are constantly being injured and disabled, sometimes permanently, by avoidable hazards. Knowing how fire behaves, and what to expect when things burn, can add greatly to your margin of safety.

This chapter discusses fire behavior as it may be demonstrated in a laboratory, beginning with atoms and molecules. It moves from there to some of the conditions a firefighter might encounter in an actual burning building.

The Chemistry of Fire

Fire is a chemical process that produces heat and light through combining oxygen with another substance, called a *fuel*. To understand fully how this chemical process takes place, it is necessary to understand the physical and chemical changes that can occur in oxygen and in fuels.

Oxygen is an element. An *element* is a simple substance that cannot be broken down into anything simpler by ordinary chemical means. The only way any element can be reduced to smaller particles is by changing its atomic structure, **Figure 3-1.**

Compounds

Oxygen is extremely active: it will combine with many other substances. When one element combines with another element, the result is a new substance called a compound, **Figure 3-2.** Chemically, a *compound* is a distinct substance formed by the union of two or more ingredients in definite proportions. Often, a compound's properties are very different from those of the elements that make it up.

When two atoms of hydrogen combine chemically with one atom of oxygen, the new substance produced is *water*. See **Figure 3-3.** Water, then, is a chemical compound with the formula H_2O. This formula says that each molecule of water is made up of *two* atoms of hydrogen and *one* atom of oxygen.

A *molecule* is the smallest unit of a substance that still retains the characteristics of that substance. A single molecule of water, although it is too small to see, has all the characteristics of a glassful of pure water. But, if that single molecule of water is broken down into components, it once again becomes two atoms of hydrogen and one atom of oxygen, **Figure 3-4.**

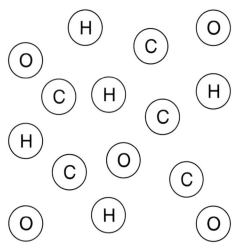

Figure 3-1. Each chemical element has a specific atomic structure. Three of the most common elements are carbon (C), hydrogen (H), and oxygen (O). Atoms of these elements are found in all living matter.

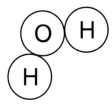

Figure 3-3. Shown is a single molecule of the compound water. It is formed by one oxygen atom and two hydrogen atoms (H_2O).

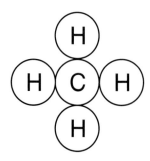

Figure 3-2. When atoms of different elements join together chemically, they form a new substance called a compound. Here, carbon and hydrogen atoms have joined to form the compound methane (CH_4).

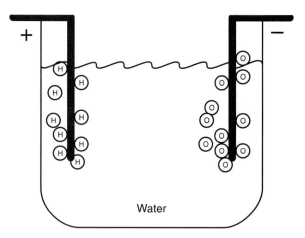

Figure 3-4. The smallest unit of a compound is the molecule; if broken down to individual atoms, it is no longer that compound. The process of electrolysis can be used to break down water into the oxygen and hydrogen atoms that make up its molecules.

Defining a compound as a *distinct substance* means that it is not like the ingredients that make it up. The two elements that make up water, for instance, are both gases. Both are extremely active chemically. This means that they will readily combine with other substances. Water is normally a liquid, and much heavier than the gases that make it up. Water is chemically inactive, which is one of the reasons it is used to put out fires.

States of Matter

In this discussion, the word *normal* refers to the state of matter under these approximate conditions: a temperature of 70°F (21°C), with the barometer at sea level or 14.7 pounds per square inch (101.3 kilopascals). See **Figure 3-5.** Water, under normal conditions, is a liquid. But at 212°F (100°C), the atoms begin to move away from each other and water becomes a gas (steam). Below 32°F (0°C), water becomes a solid. **Solid, liquid,** and *gas* are the three *states* of matter.

Oxygen is normally a gas. But as oxygen (or any gas) cools, the atoms move closer together. At a temperature of –360°F (–218°C), the atoms are so close together that the gas becomes a liquid. At the even colder temperature of –433°F (–258°C), liquid oxygen turns into a pale blue solid, **Figure 3-6.**

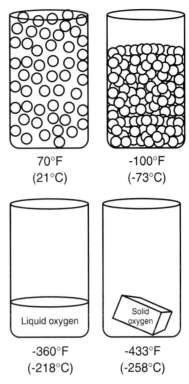

70°F (21°C)   -100°F (-73°C)

Liquid oxygen   Solid oxygen

-360°F (-218°C)   -433°F (-258°C)

Figure 3-6. Under normal conditions, oxygen is a gas. As the temperature decreases, the atoms move closer together until the gas becomes a liquid, and finally a solid.

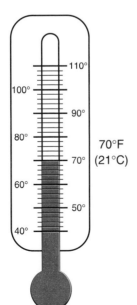

Figure 3-5. When "normal" conditions are referred to, it means that the temperature is 70°F (21°C), and the barometric pressure is 14.7 psi (101.3 kPa).

70°F (21°C)

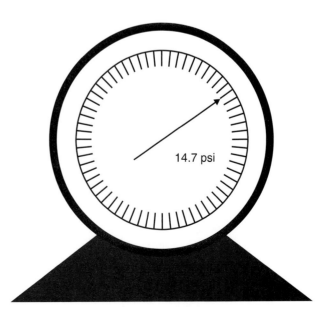

14.7 psi

Changes of pressure can also affect the state of matter. As the pressure on a gas increases, its molecules move closer together. When the pressure is high enough, the gas turns to a liquid. At still higher pressures, the liquid becomes a solid, **Figure 3-7.** Modern manufacturing processes use a combination of high pressure and low temperature to convert gases into liquids and solids.

Since water is made up of oxygen and hydrogen, you might reason that if hydrogen and oxygen were mixed in a container, they would produce water. But this isn't so, until you increase the temperature. This is what happens: the atoms of any gas are usually bound together in pairs. (For example, two atoms of oxygen are bound together to form the molecule O_2. Similarly, hydrogen is usually found in the H_2 form.) But as the temperature increases, the individual atoms in the molecule move apart. When the temperature is high enough, atoms break their bonds. Only then are the individual O atoms free to combine with the H atoms to form water (H_2O). See **Figure 3-8.**

When a fuel (such as hydrogen) combines with oxygen, a new substance is produced. This new substance (in this case, the compound water) is distinct: it doesn't look, act, or feel like the ingredients that make it up. *Heat* is produced when hydrogen unites with oxygen. As shown in **Figure 3-9,** heat is needed to *cause* atoms to combine, but the process also *produces* heat.

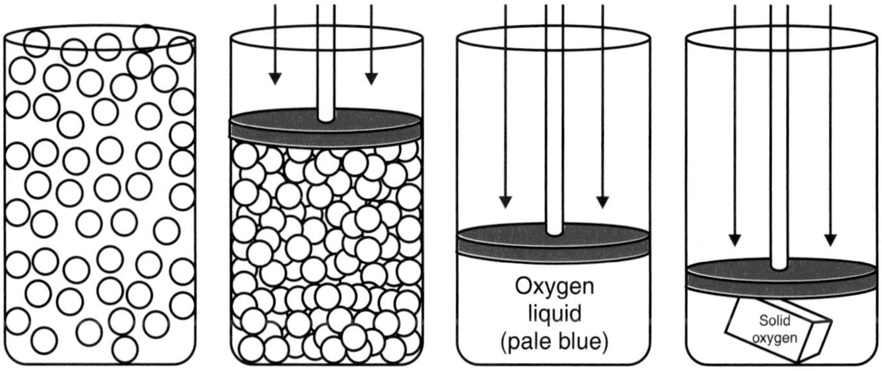

Figure 3-7. Increasing pressure on a gas has the same effect as decreasing temperature. If pressure is sufficiently high, the gas will become a liquid, then a solid.

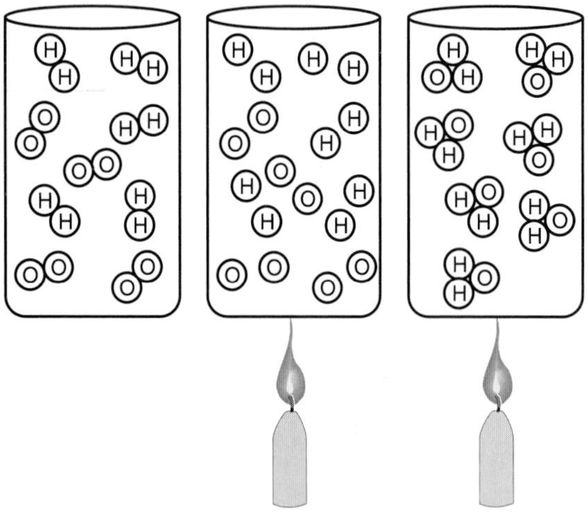

Oxygen liquid (pale blue)

Solid oxygen

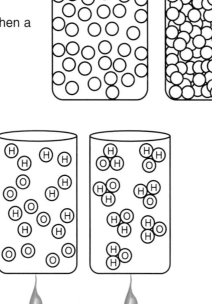

Figure 3-8. As a gas is heated, the atoms move apart. When the temperature is high enough, the atoms will combine into compounds. Here, atoms of hydrogen (H) and oxygen (O) form water.

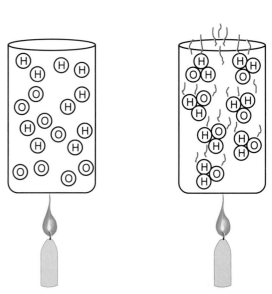

Figure 3-9. Heat is needed for compounds to form, but the process also gives off heat.

How Things Burn

It is not necessary to raise the temperature of the entire container of hydrogen and oxygen to cause *combustion* (the chemical process in which oxygen and a fuel combine). A small spark will have the same result. The spark raises the temperature of a few atoms of hydrogen and oxygen to the point of combustion. The heat produced by the reaction of these few atoms, in turn, heats other nearby atoms to the point of combustion. They then heat others, and so on, until all of the hydrogen or oxygen atoms (or both) are used up. This is known as a *chain reaction,* **Figure 3-10.**

Oxygen and hydrogen, together with the element carbon, are the building blocks of life (and of fire). Plants and animals are composed mostly of these three elements. Compounds of hydrogen and carbon make up a large family of organic chemical compounds known as *hydrocarbons.* The gas that bubbles up in swamps and marshes is a hydrocarbon produced by the decay of plant matter. Chemically, swamp gas is known as *methane.* There is, in fact, a family of related hydrocarbons known as the *methane series* (also called the "paraffin series").

The Methane Series

All of the compounds in the methane series are similar in formula. The general formula for these compounds is $C_nH_{2n}+2$. This means that for every carbon atom there are *two* hydrogen atoms plus *two more* hydrogen atoms. Thus, if there is one carbon atom, there will be two hydrogen atoms plus two more, or a total of four. If there are two carbon atoms, there will be four hydrogen atoms plus two more, or a total of six. See **Figure 3-11.**

The simplest compound in the methane series is methane itself. Methane has one atom of carbon and four atoms of hydrogen (CH_4). Under normal conditions of temperature and pressure, methane is a gas. All the

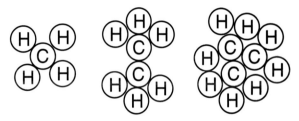

Figure 3-11. In the methane series, there are two hydrogen atoms for each carbon atom. There are two more hydrogen atoms in each molecule, as well.

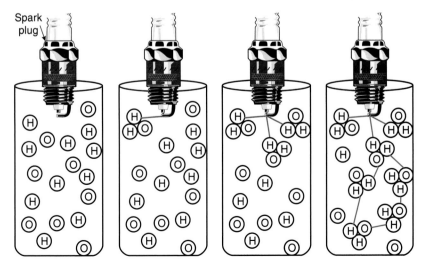

Figure 3-10. A small spark can provide enough heat to raise a few atoms of hydrogen and oxygen to the point of ignition. As they unite chemically, the reaction creates enough heat to raise more atoms to ignition temperature, and so on.

compounds in the methane series that contain one to four carbon atoms are gases. Those with five to fifteen carbon atoms are liquids, and those with more than fifteen atoms of carbon are waxy or fatty solids. See **Figure 3-12.**

Combustion of methane gas

Methane and air (which is about 21% oxygen and 79% nitrogen) in a container will not combine at room temperature. When heat is introduced in the form of a spark, however, methane will burn. A chain reaction occurs, **Figure 3-13,** similar to the one described earlier with hydrogen and oxygen. What happens is this: the heat from the spark causes the carbon and hydrogen atoms making up the methane molecule to move away from each other. The carbon and hydrogen are then more attracted to the oxygen in the air than they are to each other, so some of the carbon will combine with some of the oxygen. Some of the hydrogen will combine with oxygen, as well. If the proportions are exactly right and combustion is complete, what will remain in the container is carbon dioxide (CO_2), water (H_2O), and the nitrogen that was originally in the air. The combustion also releases heat, **Figure 3-14.** The proportions are seldom *exactly* right, however.

In an enclosed fire, such as one in a house, the oxygen soon becomes depleted. During the early stages of the fire, when there is plenty of oxygen, the combustion process produces carbon dioxide (CO_2). As the supply of oxygen decreases, incomplete combustion results. Instead of taking on two atoms of oxygen to form carbon dioxide, the carbon may take on one atom of oxygen. The result is *carbon monoxide* (CO), a highly explosive and poisonous gas. Some of the carbon will not combine at all, but will remain as black particles of soot. See **Figure 3-15.**

Another member of the methane series is *nonane,* one of the components of kerosene. Its formula is C_9H_{20}. Since nonane has more

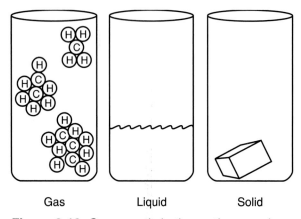

Gas   Liquid   Solid

Figure 3-12. Compounds in the methane series include gases (4 or fewer carbon atoms), liquids (5-15 carbon atoms), and solids (16 or more carbon atoms).

Figure 3-13. Methane will not combine with air at room temperature. However, a heat source (such as a spark) will set off a chain reaction, causing it to burn.

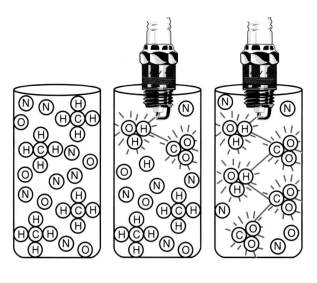

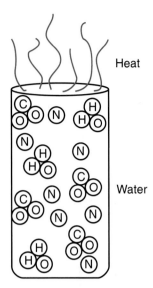

Figure 3-14. When methane burns completely, water, carbon dioxide, and heat are the only products of combustion.

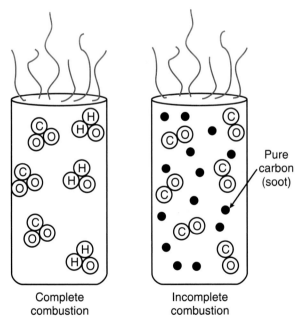

Complete combustion   Incomplete combustion

Figure 3-15. Besides water, heat, and carbon dioxide, *incomplete* combustion produces carbon particles (soot) and carbon monoxide, a toxic and highly flammable gas.

than four carbon atoms and fewer than fifteen, it is normally a liquid. A spark introduced into a container full of nonane would not cause combustion, since liquids do not burn. To burn, a liquid must first be changed into a *gas* (vapor). The gas must then be mixed with the proper amount of air.

Flash point

Heating the container to a temperature of 88°F (31°C) will cause a sufficient number of molecules of nonane to vaporize and mix with the air in the container to form a flammable mixture. The temperature at which this happens is called the flash point. The *flash point* is the lowest temperature at which a substance gives off sufficient vapor to form an ignitable mixture within the vessel used. To cause complete combustion, however (as with the methane), additional heat must be provided. See **Figure 3-16.** The *products of combustion* of nonane vapor in air are water, carbon dioxide, carbon monoxide, soot, and heat.

Paraffin is a solid member of the methane series. Actually, paraffin is made up of a number of waxy methane solids. One of these is *nonadecane* ($C_{19}H_{40}$). As a solid, nonadecane will not burn. Very few solids burn, unless they are first converted to a gas. (One

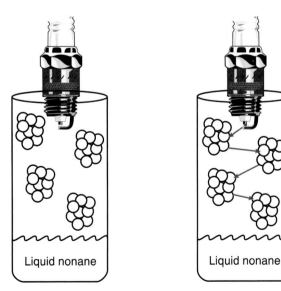

Liquid nonane   Liquid nonane

Figure 3-16. Nonane will not burn at 70°F (21°C), but if the temperature is increased to 88°F (31°C), enough vapor will be produced to sustain a chemical chain reaction. The temperature of 88°F is the *flash point* of nonane.

of the few exceptions is charcoal, which can unite directly with oxygen.) Paraffin melts at about 100°F (38°C), but liquid paraffin will not burn, either. The temperature of the liquid nonadecane must first be raised to its flash point, 390°F (199°C). The products of combustion are the same as those resulting from burning nonane: water, carbon dioxide, carbon monoxide, soot, and heat. See **Figure 3-17.**

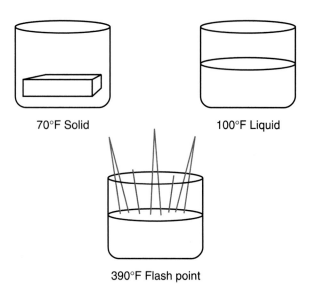

Figure 3-17. Paraffin, a solid in the methane series, melts at about 100°F (38°C). It will not burn as a liquid, however. The temperature must be raised to its flash point, 390°F (199°C) to sustain combustion.

Igniting a mixture of flammable gases in air does not mean that a sustained fire will follow. Every smoker who has used a pocket lighter filled with liquid fuel ("lighter fluid") has had the experience of raising the cap, flicking the spark wheel, and seeing a flash, but no flame. The spark causes the vapor in the cap to burn. This burning does not create enough heat to vaporize and ignite more of the liquid fuel, however. The liquid fuel is not heated to its ignition temperature. See **Figure 3-18.**

Ignition temperature

The *ignition temperature*, which is higher than the flash point, is the temperature that will vaporize the liquid fuel and then ignite the vapor. In other words, there must be a *continuing cycle*. Some of the heat produced by the combustion must vaporize the liquid fuel, so it can ignite. This is known as feedback. In *feedback,* some of the output of a process (in this case, heat) is fed back into the input, **Figure 3-19.**

Not all solid fuels *liquefy* before vaporizing. Wood, for instance, gives off water vapor and carbon dioxide when first heated. With continued heating, it will produce flammable gases. This is why it is nearly impossible to light a block of wood with a spark. A spark will not produce enough heat to drive off the water and CO_2 that prevents combustion. Additional heat must be applied to produce and ignite the flammable gases, **Figure 3-20.**

Figure 3-18. A liquid fuel lighter does not always produce a sustained flame because the initial spark may not result in a flame that will provide heat to vaporize and ignite the liquid fuel.

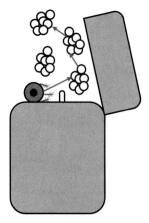
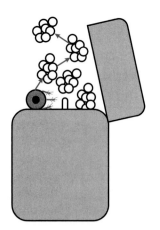
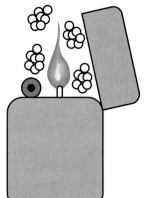

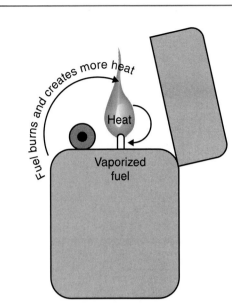

Figure 3-19. Feedback of heat to vaporize additional fuel is important in sustaining flame.

Every automobile driver has had, at some time, the experience of a car that would not start. You find there is a good spark and that the engine is getting gas. The trouble, then, is in the fuel system. Either the engine is getting too much fuel or not enough. The

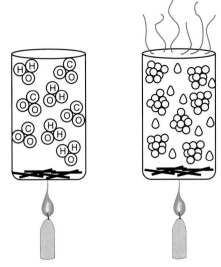

Figure 3-20. A spark does not create enough heat to ignite and sustain a wood fire. Additional heat is needed to drive off water and carbon dioxide and produce flammable gases.

mixture of gasoline vapor and air is either too *rich* (excessive fuel) or too *lean* (excessive air). After a simple adjustment of the fuel system, the car runs fine. See **Figure 3-21.**

Figure 3-21. Fuel and air must mix in the right proportions to permit combustion. Mixtures that are too lean or too rich will not ignite.

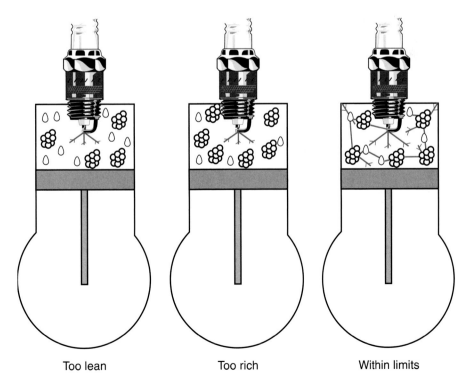

Too lean   Too rich   Within limits

Flammable limits

Too rich or too lean conditions can occur in all mixtures of flammable vapor and air. All gaseous fuels exhibit a *range* of mixtures capable of burning in air. This range is expressed in terms of the percentage of gas vapor to air. It is known as the *flammable limits* or *explosive limits.* With methane gas, for example, these limits are 5.3% and 14%. If the air contains less than 5.3% methane, then mixture is too lean to ignite and burn. If the air contains more than 14% methane, the mixture is too rich. Again, it will not burn. See **Figure 3-22.**

Heat Transfer

The environment always contains two of the three requirements for fire. The air we breathe contains enough oxygen (if it didn't, we wouldn't breathe for long). Even so-called "fireproof" buildings contain fuel. Furniture, curtains, rugs, paints and wallcoverings — all these will burn. The only thing needed for a fire is enough heat to bring these flammables to the flash point, then to the ignition temperature. Heat can be supplied in three ways: convection, conduction, and radiation.

Convection

Convection is the transferring of heat by moving masses of matter. Often, the mass of matter being moved is air. Heated air normally rises. In **Figure 3-23,** heated air is being convected up the flue pipe. The hot flue pipe, in turn, heats the air in the attic. As the attic gets hotter (possibly from overfiring the stove), it drives flammable gases from the accumulated trash. A spark escaping through a crack in the flue pipe (or just more heat) can ignite the gases. Many structure fires begin this way.

Another example of convection starting or spreading fire occurs when plastics are involved. Even supposedly nonflammable plastics can melt, flow, or drip onto something that *is* flammable and set it afire.

Conduction

Conduction is the transferring of heat by *direct contact* from one material to another. In conduction, the direction of flow is always from hot to cool, **Figure 3-24.** A cook, picking up a hot skillet by the handle, may suffer a burned hand. The heat is conducted by direct contact from the pan through the handle to

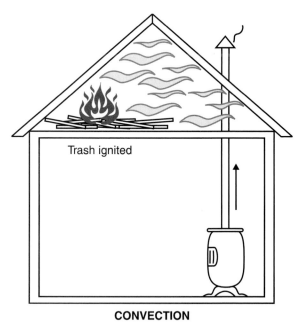

CONVECTION

Figure 3-23. Heat transmitted by convection can ignite material that is far from the original heat source. Heat from the stove, convected up the flue, could cause ignition of trash in the building's attic.

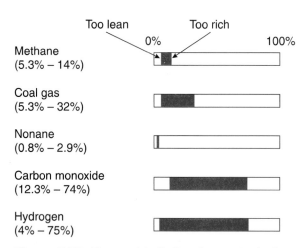

Figure 3-22. Flammable limits of some typical gases. Mixtures below or above the gas's limits will not burn.

Figure 3-24. A cook burning his or her fingers on a hot utensil handle is a good example of direct conduction of heat.

the cook's hand. Iron is a good conductor of heat. Aluminum is even better — it will conduct more heat and will conduct it farther and faster.

A brick is a poor conductor of heat. This is one reason why bricks are used to make chimneys. But if a very hot fire burns long enough on one side of a wall, the bricks can conduct sufficient heat to set fire to a pile of combustible trash on the other side. See **Figure 3-25.** Even though firefighters have the fire out on one side of a brick wall, they must always inspect the other side.

Radiation

The heat felt close to an electric light-bulb is *radiated* heat, or **radiation.** Our planet is warmed by heat radiated from the sun. An important point to remember about radiated heat is that it travels in straight lines, in *all* directions from the source. See **Figure 3-26.** Furthermore, the intensity of radiated heat varies *inversely* with the square of the distance: an object that is two feet from a radiant heat source will get **four** *times hotter than an object four feet away from the source.* In the illustration, the temperature is far higher under the stove than it is at the box of trash in front of the stove. A firefighter working close to a fire can get burned by radiated heat. This is an important reason for always wearing protective clothing.

The Fire Triangle/Tetrahedron

In the fire service, the relationship among fuel, oxygen, and heat is frequently demonstrated by the *fire triangle.* The representation in **Figure 3-27A** shows that to have fire, all three components (fuel, oxygen, heat) must be present.

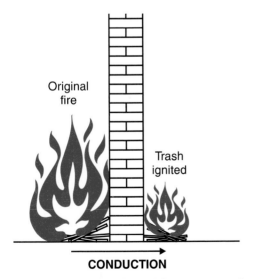

CONDUCTION

Figure 3-25. Even though brick is a poor conductor, a fire that is hot enough (and burning long enough) could cause enough heat to be conducted by the brick to ignite material on the other side.

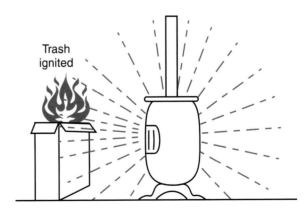

RADIATION

Figure 3-26. A heat source like a light bulb or stove *radiates* heat energy in all directions. The closer an object is to the source, the more heat it will have transmitted to it by radiation. The floor under the stove is receiving more heat than the box of trash.

Figure 3-27. Fire component relationships. A—The traditional *fire triangle*, which has three components: heat, fuel, and oxygen. B—The *fire tetrahedron* adds a fourth component, chemical chain reaction.

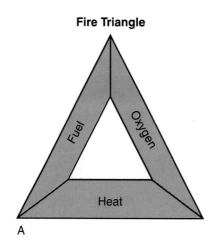

Fire Triangle

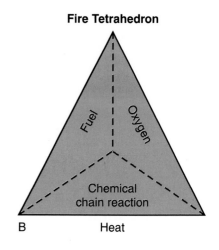

Fire Tetrahedron

However, research done in recent years has added a fourth side to the triangle, making it a *fire tetrahedron,* as shown in **Figure 3-27B.** This fourth side is referred to as the *chemical chain reaction.* Vapors of various gases are given off during the burning process. These vapors contain atoms and molecules that are in the process of change. As oxygen is drawn into the fire, these atoms and molecules combine with it to form new compounds.

Removing Fuel

At first, this method of extinguishing or preventing a fire, **Figure 3-28,** might seem impossible. Simply turning off a burner on a gas stove is an example of removing fuel; so

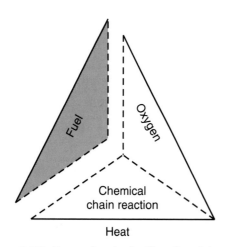

Figure 3-28. Removing fuel will extinguish or prevent a fire.

is carrying a burning mattress out of a home, or cleaning up trash that could catch fire. Sometimes, a burning building cannot be saved. In this case, firefighters may concentrate on applying water to adjacent structures to prevent them from catching fire. The fuel is effectively removed. Oil well fires are frequently extinguished by capping the well to stop the flow of oil, and thus, limit the amount of available fuel.

Removing Oxygen

All combustible materials have flammable limits. Anything that is done to make a mixture *too rich* is, in effect, reducing the oxygen. See **Figure 3-29.** If a person's clothing catches fire, one recommended method is to wrap the victim in a blanket. This excludes oxygen, so the mixture quickly becomes too rich to burn. Simply having the person roll on the ground does the same thing. A covered metal container used to keep oily rags excludes the oxygen needed for combustion.

Removing Heat

When a tank of liquefied flammable gas catches fire, the usual approach of the firefighters is to spray the sides of the tank with cold water. See **Figure 3-30.** This lowers the temperature of the gas below its flash point, and the fire goes out by itself.

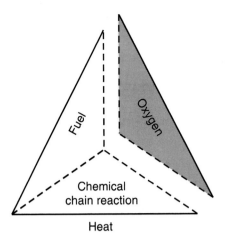

Figure 3-29. Removing oxygen will extinguish or prevent a fire.

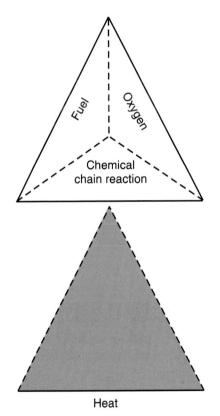

Figure 3-30. Removing heat will extinguish or prevent a fire.

Inhibiting the Chemical Chain Reaction

By stopping the chemical chain reaction, **Figure 3-31,** the fire goes out. This approach

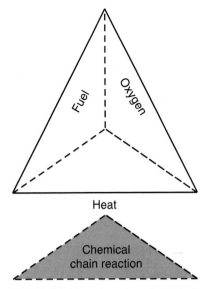

Figure 3-31. Inhibiting the chemical chain reaction will extinguish or prevent a fire.

appears to be a chain-breaking reaction. The agent used will tend to break down the combustion process by replacing some of the necessary elements. Thus, the fire goes out.

Using Water to Control and Extinguish Fire

If you place a cup of water in a small saucepan, it might take several minutes to heat. Put the same amount of water in a frying pan, and it will boil almost immediately, **Figure 3-32.** This occurs because the water in the frying pan has more surface area in contact with the heat. This allows the water to absorb heat much faster.

Figure 3-32. The greater the surface area of water exposed to heat, the quicker the heat will be absorbed.

Solid Stream vs. Fog

For many years, the standard method of fighting fire was to use a solid stream of water. In recent decades, however, the approach has changed. Instead of a solid stream, fire departments have been turning to the application of water in a dispersed form. Nozzles have been developed that break a solid stream of water into coarse drops or even a heavy fog of fine droplets. In this form, water presents many times more surface area to the heat, **Figure 3-33.** Because of this greater surface area, the water absorbs heat faster and turns rapidly to steam. At 212°F (100°C), one cubic foot of water expands to 1700 cubic feet. See **Figure 3-34.** However, fog will not penetrate a deep-seated fire, so a solid stream must be used in such situations.

The Action of Water on Fire

In terms of the fire triangle, water accomplishes the extinguishing of fire in the following manner.

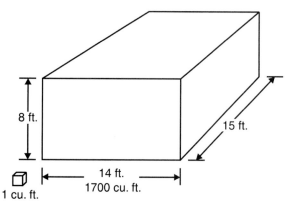

Figure 3-34. A cubic foot of water expands to fill 1700 cubic feet when it is changed to steam. This is equivalent to filling a room that is 8 ft. x 14 ft. x 15 ft.

Removing fuel

Nearly all fuels must be in the form of a gas, or vapor, before they will burn. Since water droplets expand as they turn into steam, the expanding steam removes fuel as it literally forces the flammable gas away from the heat source. In addition, since many gases (such as carbon monoxide) are soluble in water, fuel is removed by going into solution in the water.

A

B

Figure 3-33. A fog stream, (A), presents tremendously increased surface area of water to absorb heat, when compared to the surface area of a solid stream, (B).

Removing oxygen

Just as expanding steam forces the flammable gases away from the heat source, the gases force some of the air away. The steam then mixes with the remaining air. This has the effect of removing the oxygen by diluting the air's oxygen content to the point where it no longer supports combustion.

Removing heat

The measuring unit for heat is the *British Thermal Unit (Btu)*. One Btu is the amount of energy required to raise the temperature one pound of water by one degree Fahrenheit. If water leaves the nozzle at 60°F (16°C), it will absorb 152 Btus to get to the boiling point (212°F or 100°C). Once the water boils, it takes an additional 970 Btus to convert that one pound of boiling water to steam. In going from 60°F to steam, then, one pound of water will absorb 1122 Btus. The heat from the fire, instead of feeding back to raise more fuel to its ignition temperature, is absorbed by the water. With heat removed, the fire can be extinguished.

Classes of Fire

Underwriters' Laboratories (UL) groups fires into three classifications, depending upon the kind of material that is burning. The National Fire Protection Association (NFPA) adds a fourth class. Classes of fire are:

Class A: Ordinary combustibles, such as wood, dry grass, brush, fabrics, paper, or rubber.

Class B: Flammable liquids, including gasoline, kerosene, paints, oils, and many solvents. This class includes liquefied petroleum gas (LPG) and other flammable gases in their liquefied or natural states.

Class C: Live electrical equipment, such as motors, transformers, switches, data processing equipment, and large electric signs. When there is a strong possibility of live electrical equipment being involved, treat any fire as if it is a Class C fire.

Class D: Flammable metals, including sodium, magnesium, titanium, and aluminum. If conditions are right, many other metals will burn, provided they are finely divided enough.

The Phases of Burning

Once combustion takes place, a fire in a combined space will typically progress through several distinct stages. Some authorities list three phases; others recognize four. All agree on the first two phases, called the *incipient phase* and the *open-burning phase* (sometimes called the "free-burning" or "steady burning" phase). The third phase, or *smoldering phase,* is sometimes divided into two separate phases.

First Phase

The first phase is the **incipient phase** or beginning stage. In this stage, the fire is just beginning to burn, **Figure 3-35A**. Oxygen inside the room is at normal level (21% of the air). With this amount of oxygen, the flame burns brightly and combustion is nearly complete. The basic products of combustion during this phase are carbon dioxide, water vapor, and a small amount of carbon monoxide. Depending on the room contents, other gases may be produced. The temperature of the fire's seat may rise to about 1000°F (540°C), but the ceiling temperature will rise only slightly at first. Visibility in the room is fairly good. Ventilation is not a problem, and can usually be accomplished by merely opening a window or door. This fire can be easily extinguished.

Second Phase

The second phase that fire enters, when burning in a confined space, is called the *open-burning phase.* Oxygen in the room is reduced below the normal level, down to a point in the range of 16 to 19 percent. As a result of this lower oxygen content, the flame doesn't burn as brightly, and combustion is less complete.

The room begins to fill with smoke, **Figure 3-35B,** and the carbon monoxide level increases. Ceiling temperatures begin to rise dramatically, and can reach 700°F (371°C). Heat accumulates and begins to bank down from the ceiling to the floor levels. Conditions can become dangerous for firefighters very quickly: *flashover* can occur as the room's contents reach ignition temperature and burst into flame simultaneously. To survive such instantaneous ignition of the whole room, you *must* be wearing breathing apparatus (wear your SCBA *at all times* in a burning building). Extinguishing this fire is possible, with quick action. However, it is reaching the point where major structural involvement can take place. You can produce a vast amount of steam from your application of water to this fire.

Third Phase

The third phase is called the *smoldering phase.* In this phase, oxygen content in the fire area is reduced to approximately 15%. The flames are barely visible, and smoke is dense and becoming darker, **Figure 3-35C.** The increasingly incomplete combustion produces larger amounts of carbon monoxide and other flammable and toxic gases. Temperatures throughout the fire area are very high and dangerous. See **Figure 3-35C.**

Fourth Phase

In the fourth phase, a continuation of the smoldering phase, the oxygen level is 13 % or slightly lower. No flame is possible in this oxygen-depleted atmosphere. Smoke is extremely dense, and the carbon monoxide level continues to rise. The ceiling temperature is up to more than 1200°F (649°C), **Figure 3-35D.** The high temperature drives off flammable gases from the wood, paint, fabrics, chair stuffing, and nearly everything else in the room.

Two sides of the fire triangle are now complete: there is plenty of gaseous fuel, and the material is heated well above ignition temperature. The potential for a *backdraft explosion* is present if the necessary amount of fresh oxygen is improperly introduced to the room. In effect, the room is a time-bomb, **Figure 3-35D.** Refer to the chapter on ventilation for a more complete discussion of this problem.

A

B

C

D

Figure 3-35. The four phases of burning. A—First phase, oxygen content about 21%. The fire burns brightly. B—Second phase, oxygen content about 17%. Flames diminish. C—Third phase, oxygen content about 15%. Flames dimming, smoke becoming dense. D—Fourth phase, oxygen content about 13%. No visible flame, very dense smoke. Backdraft is a serious danger.

SUMMARY

The chemical reaction known as fire requires fuel, oxygen, and heat. Since solid and liquid fuels do not normally burn, heat brings them to the temperature where they will give off a sufficient quantity of flammable gases to ignite. This is known as the flash point. These flammables must be raised to a higher temperature (the ignition temperature) so that they will burn in air. The burning creates enough excess heat to vaporize and ignite more of the fuel, creating a chemical chain reaction. The ratio of flammable vapor to air must be within the flammable (explosive) limits.

Once a fire is burning, it may spread by any or all of the following means of heat transfer: convection, conduction, or radiation. Convection is the transferring of heat by moving masses of matter. Conduction is a flowing condition, as when heat flows through an iron bar. Radiation is heat moving as rays in all directions from a central source. The heat from the sun is radiated heat.

The fire tetrahedron demonstrates that all four factors: fuel, oxygen, heat, and a chemical chain reaction, must be present before there can be a fire. To control or extinguish fire, all that is necessary is to remove any side of the tetrahedron.

Remove the fuel, remove the oxygen, remove the heat, or inhibit the chemical chain reaction, and there can be no fire.

Fire is classed according to the type of fuel that is burning, from Class A (ordinary flammable material) to Class B (flammable liquids), to Class C (electrical equipment), to Class D (combustible metals).

A fire in a closed room, if undetected, will go through four phases of burning. During the first phase, when there is plenty of oxygen, the flames will burn brightly, producing little more than water, carbon dioxide, and heat. The temperature at the seat of the fire may be over 1000°F (540°C). During the second phase, the temperature at the ceiling will rise to 700°F (370°C). As the oxygen content decreases, the flames will be less bright. The fire will start to smoke and produce carbon monoxide. During the third phase, flames will begin to disappear, and smoke will become dense and contain much more carbon monoxide. At the fourth stage of burning, no flames are visible, smoke becomes very dense, carbon monoxide and other flammable and explosive gases will increase dramatically. Temperatures will go up to over 1200°F (650°C). A backdraft explosion is a real threat.

REVIEW QUESTIONS

1. What is the difference between a chemical *element* and a *compound* ?
2. What does the formula for water, H_2O, tell you about the elements that make it up?
3. Describe what happens, step-by-step, in a combustion chain reaction begun by a spark.
4. Why is carbon monoxide considered a dangerous gas?
5. Define the term "flash point." Is it the same as the ignition temperature of a substance?
6. What is the term used to describe the percentages of gas vapor to air above and below which burning cannot take place?

7. Name and describe the three forms of heat transfer.
8. True or false? An object located six feet from a radiant heat source will be only half as hot as an object three feet from the source.
9. What are the three components of the traditional fire triangle?
10. When a fourth component (the chemical chain reaction) is added, the fire triangle becomes the fire _____.
11. Give two examples of extinguishing a fire by removing fuel.
12. Explain why a dispersed form of water (fog) is sometimes more effective in putting out a fire than a solid stream of water.

13. Describe how water removes oxygen from a fire.
14. What do the initials UL and NFPA stand for?
15. How many classes of fire are designated by UL?
16. What kind of material is burning in a Class A fire?
17. What kind of material is burning in a Class B fire?
18. What kind of material is burning in a Class C fire?
19. What kind of material is burning in a Class D fire?
20. In which phase of burning is a backdraft explosion most likely to occur?

The heat-absorbing effect of water is being used here to prevent the spread of fire. The water curtain protects the adjacent structure by absorbing much of the heat radiated by the fire in the burning building.

NFPA 1001 Job Performance Requirements

The material on this page consists of those portions of the NFPA 1001 Job Performance Requirements relevant to the material presented in this chapter. Items preceded by the numeral 3 (3-x.x) are Fire Fighter I requirements; those with the numeral 4 (4-x.x) are Fire Fighter II requirements.

3-1.1.2 General Skill Requirements. The ability to don personal protective clothing within one minute; doff personal protective clothing and prepare for reuse; hoist tools and equipment using ropes and the correct knot; tie a bowline, clove hitch, figure eight on a bight, half hitch, becket or sheet bend, and safety knots; and locate information in departmental documents and standard or code materials.

3-3.1 Use SCBA during emergency operations, given SCBA and other personal protective equipment, so that the SCBA is properly donned and activated within one minute, the SCBA is correctly worn, controlled breathing techniques are used, emergency procedures are enacted if the SCBA fails, all low-air warnings are recognized, respiratory protection is not intentionally compromised, and hazardous areas are exited prior to air depletion.

(a) Prerequisite Knowledge: Conditions that require respiratory protection, uses and limitations of SCBA, components of SCBA, donning procedures, breathing techniques, indications for and emergency procedures used with SCBA, and physical requirements of the SCBA wearer.

(b) Prerequisite Skills: The ability to control breathing, replace SCBA air cylinders, use SCBA to exit through restricted passages, initiate and complete emergency procedures in the event of SCBA failure or air depletion, and complete donning procedures.

(3-3.4)

(b) Prerequisite Skills: The ability to operate as a team member in vision-obscured conditions, locate and follow a guideline, conserve air supply, and evaluate areas for hazards and identify a safe haven.

(3-3.8)

(b) Prerequisite Skills: The ability to use SCBA to exit through restricted passages, set up and use different types of ladders for various types of rescue operations, rescue a fire fighter with functioning respiratory protection, rescue a fire fighter whose respiratory protection is not functioning, rescue a person who has no respiratory protection, and assess areas to determine tenability.

3-5.3 Clean and check ladders, ventilation equipment, self-contained breathing apparatus (SCBA), ropes, salvage equipment, and hand tools, given cleaning tools, cleaning supplies, and an assignment, so that equipment is clean and maintained according to manufacturer's or departmental guidelines, maintenance is recorded, and equipment is placed in a ready state or reported otherwise.

(a) Prerequisite Knowledge: Types of cleaning methods for various tools and equipment, correct use of cleaning solvents, and manufacturer's or departmental guidelines for cleaning equipment and tools.

(b) Prerequisite Skills: The ability to select correct tools for various parts and pieces of equipment, follow guidelines, and complete recording and reporting procedures.

Reprinted with permission from NFPA 1001, *Fire Fighter Professional Qualifications,* Copyright ©1997, National Fire Protection Association, Quincy, MA 02269. This reprinted material is not the complete and official position of the National Fire Protection Association on the referenced subject, which is represented only by the standard in its entirety.

Personal Protective Equipment

OBJECTIVES

When you have completed this chapter, you will be able to:

🔥 Discuss the advantages of the various components that make up the Structural Firefighting Protective Garment.

🔥 Describe the various items of Personal Protective Equipment and the hazards they protect against.

🔥 Identify dangers posed by certain types of fabrics when worn under turnout gear.

🔥 Discuss the reasons for designing turnout gear that will provide less encumbrance.

🔥 Identify the respiratory hazards encountered in firefighting.

🔥 Demonstrate various types of breathing apparatus and identify their safety features.

🔥 Demonstrate proper methods of donning breathing apparatus while wearing full protective clothing.

🔥 Discuss the procedures for periodic inspection and maintenance of breathing apparatus, including procedures for cleaning and sanitizing it.

IMPORTANT TERMS

ammonia	encumbrance	oxygen rebreathing	positive-pressure-type
asphyxia	hemoglobin	apparatus	breathing equipment
carbon dioxide	hydrogen cyanide	oxygen-generating	respiratory process
carbon monoxide	hydrogen sulfide	equipment	Structural Fire Fighting
chlorine	hyperventilation	personal alert safety	Protective Garment
demand-type breathing	oxygen depletion	system (PASS)	sulfur dioxide
equipment		positive pressure	trachea

Until the middle of this century, there were those in the fire service who prided themselves on their ability to enter a burning building and work unprotected from the respiratory hazards of smoke and gases. These individuals, who referred to themselves as "Smoke Eaters," thought they were immune to the effects of the contaminated atmospheres in a fire building.

Today, "Smoke Eaters" are, quite literally, a dying breed — those who thought that they were demonstrating their strength were actually doing serious, irreversible damage to their respiratory systems.

Since the 1960s, firefighters have had available sophisticated breathing apparatus to protect their respiratory systems from smoke and gases. See **Figure 4-1**. The last several

Figure 4-1. Respiratory damage to firefighters has decreased dramatically in recent decades because of the widespread availability and use of self-contained breathing apparatus.

decades have also seen increasing improvements in turnout gear to better protect firefighters from hotter fires and a wider variety of hazards. You have a responsibility to yourself and to your fellow firefighters to be sure that you are wearing all your protective equipment, including self-contained breathing apparatus. It is the responsibility of every fire department to be certain that this equipment is available to firefighters. It is the responsibility of the individual firefighter to *wear* it.

Turnout Gear

From the earliest days of the firefighting service until relatively recently, the protective clothing used by firefighters was made from canvas, rubber, leather, and other natural materials. See **Figure 4-2**. By the 1950s and 1960s, it was becoming increasingly apparent that the old materials were not up to the job any longer. Because of the increasing number of human-made structural materials, fabrics, and other potential fuels, the very nature of fires was changing. Fires were becoming hotter, and their byproducts were becoming more toxic and dangerous.

Fires involving aircraft, as well as shipboard blazes, **Figure 4-3**, made the military services pioneers in the development of new and more effective personal protective gear. New fabrics and new clothing construction methods were tried to improve the thermal and mechanical properties of turnout gear.

As a result, the old canvas "bunker coat" is a thing of the past. Instead, protective clothing is made of modern fibers such as Kevlar®, Nomex®, and PBI (polybenzimidazole). Often, these fibers are used in blends (Kevlar/PBI, etc.) to obtain the best possible combination of qualities, such as resistance to

Figure 4-2. The "bunker gear" of the past, as worn by these firefighters taking part in a training session in the 1960s, consisted of such natural materials as leather, canvas fabric, and rubber. It couldn't stand up to the hotter fires and more dangerous substances found today. Newer materials and fabrics are lighter, tougher, and more resistant to heat and chemicals.

Figure 4-3. The military led the way to a major redesign of firefighters' clothing in response to the need to fight shipboard and aircraft fires. (United States Coast Guard)

direct contact with flame, low heat transmission, resistance to charring, puncture and tear resistance, and the ability to withstand some types of chemical contact.

To allow you to do your job effectively, turnout gear must meet these criteria:

- It must provide thermal protection at the heat levels you are likely to encounter in a fire.

- It must minimize the heat stress that can result from the physical work of fighting the fire. Heat stress can take the form of heat cramps, heat exhaustion, or heatstroke. The last of these is most serious, and can actually be life-threatening.

- It must reduce "protective clothing encumbrance," which is the difficulty of working and moving around that can be attributed to the clothing.

Project FIRES

The early 1970s brought the most important action to date for the improvement of firefighters' protective clothing: a landmark study commonly referred to as Project FIRES (**F**irefighters **I**ntegrated **R**esponse **E**quipment Study). The study, which lasted more than a decade, was conducted by the International Association of Fire Fighters (IAFF). Project FIRES was cosponsored by a number of professional associations and government agencies, and involved fire departments of all sizes, as well as numerous corporations, organizations, and individuals.

The results, after many years and many experiments, included the development of new fibers, new methods of weaving and blending fibers into fabrics, and improved methods of layering and design intended to improve flexibility and ease of movement for the firefighter.

Experimental turnout gear was fabricated using the new fabrics and designs. The clothing was sent to fire departments across the country — large and small, urban and rural — to try out under actual fire conditions. The firefighters who wore the experimental turnout gear provided critical evaluations (you can be sure that if firefighters didn't like something about the equipment, they said so in no uncertain terms).

The modern turnout gear resulting from the study is lighter in weight than its predecessors, while providing superior protection against heat, punctures, cuts, liquid and steam contact, and many other hazards. See **Figure 4-4.**

Even more than fire itself, the IAFF was concerned with the well-being of the *firefighter*. Statistically, few firefighters die of burns; more often, they succumb to stress that shows up as heatstroke or heart attack. This is the area that involved some heavy decision-making, trying to strike the proper balance between protection against heat and flames, and equipment weight that caused physical stress on the firefighter.

The difficulty in moving around and working that is a result of weight and bulk in protective clothing is described as ***encumbrance***. Generally, making clothing thicker and heavier will provide better protection against heat. But with boots, gloves, and helmet, today's turnout clothing can weigh as much as

Figure 4-4. New materials used in turnout gear make it more durable and do a better job of protecting the wearer than traditional natural materials. It will not protect you, however, unless it is used and cared for as if your life depends upon it — which it *does!* (Globe Manufacturing Co.)

50 pounds. Making it thicker and heavier would increase the encumbrance (and thus, physical stress). The tradeoff, therefore, is a little less protection to provide less encumbrance.

To meet current specifications, your turnout clothing must protect you from temperatures as high as 500°F (260°C) for five minutes. At temperatures above 500°F, you are getting into a flashover or backdraft situation. Under such conditions, your clothing must protect you for the approximately 10 seconds required for you and your partner to escape.

How Protective Clothing Works

Although referred to commonly as "turnout" or "bunker" gear, the protective clothing developed in recent years has a formal name. Technically, it is a *Structural Fire Fighting Protective Garment*, **Figure 4-5.** It is composed of three parts: an outer shell, a vapor barrier, and a thermal liner.

- *Outer shell.* This is the first line of protection against the fire or other type of dangerous environment. The shell must resist heat and flame, without charring or burning. It must repel water, and provide good resistance to punctures, cuts, tears, and abrasion. Some shells are pure Nomex fabric; others may be Nomex/Kevlar, PBI/Kevlar, or other blends.

- *Vapor barrier.* This layer is intended to prevent hot or corrosive materials in vapor form from penetrating the garment and reaching the firefighter's body. Materials used for vapor barriers include Nomex, cotton (usually coated with neoprene), or Gore-tex®.

- *Thermal liner.* This layer provides the major protection against heat. It may be a batt of an aramid fiber such as Kevlar, a spun pile of Nomex bonded to a Nomex face fabric, or one of a number of other possible combinations designed to control the transmission of heat.

Figure 4-5. The Structural Fire Fighting Protective Garment uses a variety of "space-age" materials for improved performance with lighter weight. Similar layered construction is used in the pants that are worn with this coat. (International Association of Fire Fighters)

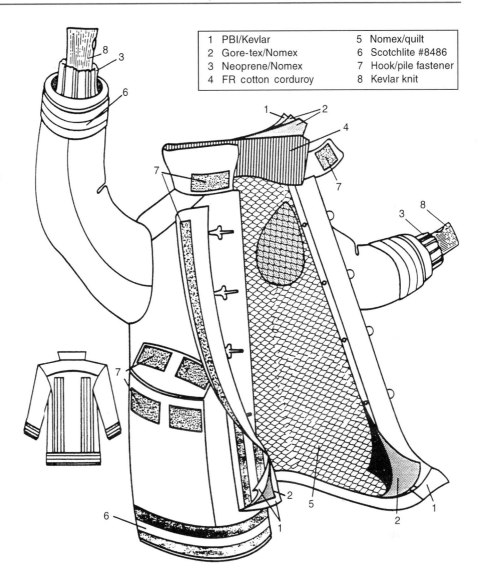

1 PBI/Kevlar	5 Nomex/quilt
2 Gore-tex/Nomex	6 Scotchlite #8486
3 Neoprene/Nomex	7 Hook/pile fastener
4 FR cotton corduroy	8 Kevlar knit

Requirements for turnout gear are listed in NFPA Standard 1971, *Protective Ensemble for Structural Fire Fighting*. Clothing that meets the requirements of NFPA 1971 will state this fact on the label, **Figure 4-6.** If the label does not indicate that the coat or trousers meets NFPA 1971 requirements, it may not provide the protection you need in a structural fire.

Before it was revised in 1991, the NFPA standard required that the thermal liner be sewn into the garment so that it could not be removed. This was a problem, however, since the garment took a very long time to dry after being washed. The revised standard allowed the liner to be removed *only* for washing and drying. Often, the thermal liner and the vapor barrier are a single unit that can be removed or replaced using snaps or similar fasteners.

If you remove the liner for washing and drying, *replace* it as soon as it dries. Never remove the liner in hot weather in an attempt to stay cooler. Doing so will remove most of your protection from the heat generated by a fire. Since the vapor barrier is usually joined to the thermal barrier, you will lose its protection, as well.

In a cold climate, your coat and trousers may also have a *winter liner* for additional

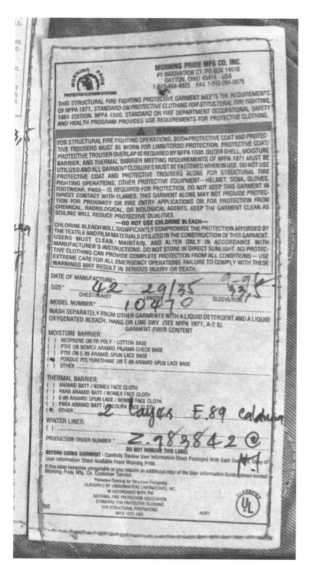

Figure 4-6. Structural Fire Fighting Protective Garments must meet the requirements of NFPA Standard 1971. A label like this one inside the garment identifies it as conforming to the standard. Another label certifies that the garment also meets the requirements of NFPA Standard 1999 on Protective Clothing for Emergency Medical Operations.

Another NFPA standard (1975) describes suitable fabrics for work uniforms ("station clothing") that would be worn beneath the protective outer garments. While such requirements are practical and valuable to persons whose full-time occupation is firefighting, the majority of the nation's firefighting personnel do not wear "station clothing." As part-time or "on-call" members of fire departments, they respond to an alarm wearing the normal clothing of their occupations as pharmacists, teachers, auto mechanics, college students, factory workers, farmers, or homemakers. If you are in this category of firefighter, you may want to use NFPA 1975 for guidance in selecting everyday clothing materials that do not pose a hazard if you must wear them beneath your protective clothing on the fireground.

Even the best protective clothing has its limitations — no garment can protect you from *every* hazard that you can encounter in a fire situation. For example, special protective clothing is needed for dealing with hazardous chemicals (liquids or vapors) or with radioactive substances. See **Figure 4-7.** Even in an "ordinary" structure fire, your protective clothing will not give you much protection against the extreme temperatures involved in a flashover. Temperatures can build to the danger level very rapidly. Watch for these danger signs:

- The air from your SCBA begins to get warm.

- Upholstery and carpet fabrics appear to be steaming.

These are signs that a flashover is imminent. If you detect either of them, alert your partner and get out *immediately*.

Maintaining Protective Clothing

Like all the other equipment used in firefighting, your protective clothing will do its job properly only if it is taken care of. After each use, carefully inspect each piece of equipment for wear or damage. Look for charring. If an item shows charring, it should be discarded

warmth. This removable liner is usually used only when temperatures are very low. The winter liner should meet the same requirements as the thermal liner. Some materials (such as the polyester batting used to line civilian winter jackets) are unsuitable because they cannot withstand the intense heat of a fire.

A

B

Figure 4-7. Special-purpose protective clothing. A—The proximity suit allows a firefighter to work in a radiant heat situation with temperatures as high as 1500°F (816°C) for a limited period. (Fyrepel Products, Inc.) B—A chemical suit protects the wearer from a dangerous environment by sealing him or her inside a chemical-resistant, airtight suit with either self-contained breathing apparatus or an external air line. Such suits are designed primarily for hazardous materials spills and similar situations, rather than firefighting. (MSA)

or (if feasible) returned to the manufacturer for repairs. If material is ripped, it should be repaired by sewing with thread made of Nomex or other approved heat-resistant material. Do not use ordinary sewing thread, since it will be unable to withstand the heat of a fire. Repair or replace any loose fasteners, frayed straps, or other defects you find upon inspection. If reflective trim is no longer bright, it is not able to do its job. Replace it.

An important part of maintaining protective clothing is keeping it clean. In a fire environment, clothing can become loaded with an amazing accumulation of airborne and waterborne products of combustion. Many of

these products are poisonous; some cause cancer. They can be a hazard to you, to your fellow firefighters, to your family and friends.

Once, a number of years ago, a river in the Midwest actually *caught fire*. Of course, the water itself didn't burn — what caught fire was a layer of oil, wood, and other combustible floating debris. In the same way, a layer of soot on your protective clothing can burn if exposed to high temperatures. Even if it does not catch fire, a sooty deposit lessens the effectiveness of your protective clothing. Since it is black, it will *absorb* the radiant energy of the fire, rather than reflecting it (as the fabric is designed to do). This means that your first line of defense against the fire's heat has lost some of its value.

Since there are many different types of protective clothing, with varying combinations of materials, it is impossible to give general cleaning instructions. Follow the recommendations of the manufacturer, which your department should have on file.

Other Protective Equipment

In addition to a coat and trousers, your personal protective equipment will include a helmet, gloves, and boots. Each plays a part in preventing injury and permitting you to function under adverse conditions.

Helmet

The traditional firefighter's helmet of thick leather is basically a museum piece today (although they are still being manufactured). The modern helmet, like its leather predecessor, is a means of protecting you against the impact of falling objects. It also must be resistant to penetration by sharp objects, and provide some degree of protection against heat and chemical attack.

Helmets must conform to NFPA Standard 1972, *Helmets for Structural Fire Fighting.*

The modern fire helmet, **Figure 4-8,** is a highly engineered system consisting of a number of components:

- *Outer shell.* A hard protective layer made from one or a combination of materials such as fiberglass, polycarbonate, Kevlar, or PBI.

- *Impact liner.* An energy-absorbing layer of Styrofoam® or polyurethane foam. In addition to providing impact resistance and penetration resistance, it has heat-insulating properties.

- *Inner shell.* Made from PBI, polycarbonate, or styrene, this layer helps to distribute the force of any impact, as well as providing some heat-insulating value.

- *Crown straps.* These form an inner suspension to help further cushion against impact, and also provide space for air circulation for greater comfort.

Other components of the helmet include a headband, chin strap, face shield, and ear-and-neck protector. During fireground operations,

Figure 4-8. A modern fire helmet is engineered to provide excellent protection against impact, penetration, and heat. This helmet includes an impact-absorbing liner (2) and suspension (8), tough outer shell (1) and heat-resistant inner shell (3), a ratchet-adjustable headband (7), a Nomex strap with quick-release buckle (6), a protective face shield (4), and an ear-neck protector (5). (E.D. Bullard Co.)

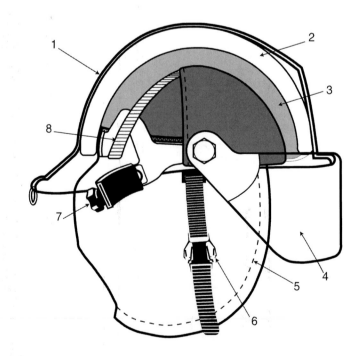

Figure 4-9. A hood made from fire-resistant fabric, such as the ones worn by these firefighters, covers areas between the helmet and turnout coat that would otherwise be exposed. Hoods protect the ears, neck, and scalp — areas where firefighters frequently suffer burns from steam or from flashover or backdraft explosions.

all must be in place to make full use of the helmet's protective features.

Protective hood

To guard against heat and steam burns to the head, ears, neck, and chest, a protective hood made of Nomex or PBI fiber may be worn. See **Figure 4-9.** Such a hood also absorbs perspiration and provides additional warmth in cold weather.

Goggles

In some operations where you are not required to wear an SCBA, such as extrication of an auto accident victim, you should wear impact-resistant goggles for eye protection. This is especially important in situations where you are using tools that can send slivers of metal, wood, or glass flying.

Gloves

Your hands are highly susceptible to injury during firefighting and most other fireground or incident scene activities. For protection, you should wear gloves that conform to NFPA Standard 1973 (*Gloves for Structural Fire Fighting*). See **Figure 4-10.** To guard against hazards ranging from broken glass to caustic chemicals, the gloves must be constructed in several layers. The outer layer, or shell, should be a tough leather. A moisture barrier of neoprene, Gore-tex, or other material will keep hands dry and warm. The inner liner should be Kevlar or other approved protective material; so should the cuffs.

Boots

Substantial waterproof boots with nonslip soles and steel reinforcement are considered a necessity by most firefighters. See **Figure 4-11.** Although some consider leather more comfortable, rubber is more generally used because of its greater resistance to a wide variety of hazardous materials. Boots must conform to NFPA Standard 1974, *Protective Footwear for Structural Fire Fighting*. The boots will typically have a rubber exterior; felt, Kevlar, or Nomex lining, and thick nonslip rubber sole. For resistance to impact and penetration by sharp objects, firefighters' boots have a steel shank, steel toe, and steel midsole.

Breathing Equipment

There should be a basic rule in every fire department that no firefighter can enter a

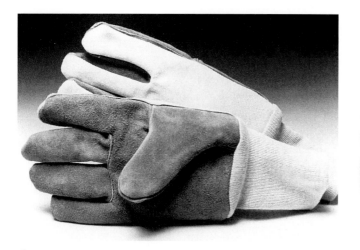

A

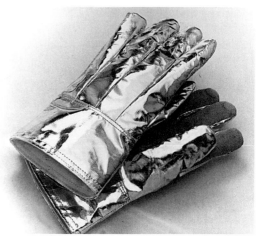

B

Figure 4-10. Protective gloves. A—Very effective insulation allows these flame-resistant gloves to be in limited contact with material as hot as 1000°F (538°C). B—Aluminized backs on these insulated gloves protect against high levels of radiated heat. (Globe Manufacturing Co.)

Figure 4-11. Substantial boots, usually with rubber exterior and thick nonslip soles, are a necessity for firefighting work. (Photo courtesy of Lab Safety Supply, Inc., Janesville, WI)

to wear proper respiratory equipment in a hostile environment can adversely affect your ability to perform necessary tasks on the fireground. To fully realize the importance of wearing proper breathing equipment, you must understand how the human respiratory process works.

Figure 4-12. These firefighters are properly equipped to enter a burning building. In addition to their turnouts, helmets, and SCBAs, note that they have personal alert safety system (PASS) units attached to their waist belts. (Jack Klasey)

building which contains smoke and heated gases without wearing proper respiratory equipment and a *personal alert safety system (PASS)*. See **Figure 4-12.** Failure to wear this equipment can endanger you and those who depend upon you: your partners and persons who might be trapped in the building. Failure

The Respiratory System

The human respiratory system is particularly vulnerable to injury from smoke and heated fire gases. The system, **Figure 4-13,** consists of lungs and associated organs which function to supply oxygen to the bloodstream. The bloodstream then carries this needed oxygen throughout the body.

The *respiratory process* begins each time we inhale air. The air inhaled through your nose or mouth enters your pharynx, passes through the larynx, and enters the trachea. The *trachea* is a relatively large tube which extends from your mouth down into your chest cavity. The flap-like epiglottis guards against foreign matter, such as food or liquid, entering the trachea. Within the chest cavity are the *bronchi*, or bronchial tubes, that branch into smaller tubes (bronchioles) inside your

lungs. Once the air enters the sac-like *alveoli* from the bronchioles, the actual transfer of oxygen into the blood system takes place. It is estimated that there are approximately 300 million alveoli in the human lung. Each tiny air sac, or alveolus, is highly susceptible to damage from smoke or heated gases.

The Importance of Oxygen

The respiratory system is constantly resupplying needed oxygen to the human body through the breathing process. The normal atmosphere, or air that you breathe, contains approximately 21% oxygen. About 78% of the remaining air is nitrogen; the other 1% is made up of miscellaneous gases.

Every fire produces smoke and heated gases that contaminate our breathing air. As a fire continues to burn in a confined space, it

Figure 4-13. The human respiratory system can be seriously affected by the gases and suspended particles in smoke.

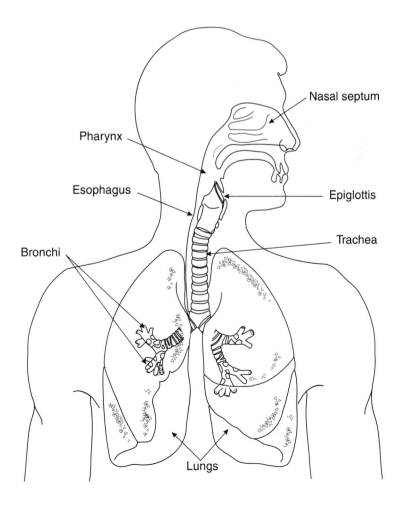

displaces the oxygen in that space with its byproducts. With concentrations of between 15% to 21% oxygen by volume, a human being can continue to function, but with diminished abilities. Whenever the oxygen content drops to approximately 16% or less, however, you can lose consciousness. From 10% to 15% oxygen by volume, judgment is impaired and loss of consciousness is likely to occur. Below 10%, an individual will be unconscious and incapable of caring for himself or herself. When the oxygen content of the air drops below 6%, death will occur in four to six minutes.

It should be obvious that, in terms of *oxygen depletion* alone, you will not be able to carry out your duties within the fire building without proper respiratory protection. In addition to depleting the air's oxygen content, however, fire releases a devil's brew of dangerous gases that can impair your ability to function or can even cause death.

Dangerous Gases

When smoke is encountered inside a burning building, it will ordinarily be a mixture of nitrogen, oxygen, carbon dioxide, and carbon monoxide. Suspended in the smoke will be fine particles of soot and carbon. Depending upon the type of material that is burning, other gases will also be present in varying quantities. It is impossible to give a comprehensive list of all gases that could potentially be found in a fire. Some of the more common dangerous gases, and their potential effects on you as a firefighter, are described below.

Carbon dioxide

Carbon dioxide(CO_2) is a colorless, odorless gas. When concentrations above the normal limits are encountered, you will begin to breathe faster and more deeply, and could experience a reaction called hyperventilation. Hyperventilation will be discussed later in this chapter. Elevated concentrations of carbon dioxide in the bloodstream can cause headaches and a feeling of weakness. If the

carbon dioxide level in the blood reaches approximately 10%, you will lose consciousness; death will occur as a result of an oxygen deficiency.

Carbon monoxide

Carbon monoxide(CO) is a colorless, odorless, tasteless gas that is poisonous in almost any concentration. Also, at the proper concentrations, carbon monoxide can be flammable and explosive. Carbon monoxide is created by the incomplete combustion of burning materials.

Carbon monoxide is highly dangerous because of the way it is attracted to hemoglobin in human blood. **Hemoglobin** is the blood component that combines with oxygen molecules in the lungs and carries the oxygen to other body organs. Hemoglobin, however, has a two-to-three times greater affinity for carbon monoxide than for oxygen. When sufficient amounts of carbon monoxide are present, the hemoglobin attaches to the carbon monoxide and begins to exclude oxygen from the blood. If approximately 60% of the hemoglobin capacity is taken up with carbon monoxide, not enough oxygen can be carried to the vital organs and oxygen deficiency reaches a serious stage.

Common symptoms of carbon monoxide poisoning include headache and extreme physical discomfort. The victim might complain of a racing heart, appear confused or intoxicated, or demonstrate signs of nausea and vomiting. Obviously, if exposure continues beyond this point, unconsciousness and death will result. Carbon monoxide is lethal when it reaches a concentration in air of only 0.5%.

Hydrogen sulfide

Hydrogen sulfide (H_2S) is a gas produced by the burning of rubber, certain plastics, wool, silk, and some synthetic materials. When hydrogen sulfide is present, there is usually a smell of rotten eggs. Hydrogen sulfide attacks the central nervous system and can stop respiratory activity. When inhaled, hydrogen sulfide can cause rapid death, and thus, must be considered a very deadly poison.

Hydrogen cyanide

Hydrogen cyanide (HCN) is an extremely poisonous gas formed in a fire when rubber, plastics, wool, silk, or rayon are being burned. When it is present, there is the odor of bitter almonds. Inhalation in even the most minute amount is likely to be fatal; exposure to a concentration of only 0.003% in air can be lethal within six to eight minutes. Death is caused by *asphyxia*— hydrogen cyanide acts to block the oxygen transfer from the blood to tissue. HCN is predominantly used to fumigate houses, exterminate insects, and to execute criminals on death row.

Ammonia

Ammonia (NH_3) is a colorless gas with an overpowering odor. It is used predominantly as a refrigerant in large commercial cooling units. Ammonia gas in high concentrations can attack the skin and the mucous membranes in the nose, throat, and lungs. A typical physical reaction to the presence of ammonia gas is watering eyes and difficulty in breathing. Suffocation can occur in high concentrations of ammonia gas. When dealing with ammonia leaks of any size, respiratory equipment must be worn, since ammonia attacks the mucous membranes. High concentrations of ammonia gas should only be approached when wearing proper hazardous material suits.

Sulfur dioxide

Sulfur dioxide (SO_2) is a colorless gas with an irritating odor and is considered to be very poisonous. Sulfur dioxide is used as a bleach, in fumigation work, and as a refrigerant in mechanical equipment. Since it is very irritating to the eyes and throat, it usually can be detected very quickly. Sulfur dioxide can be created by the combustion of fuels containing sulfur, such as rubber.

Chlorine

Chlorine (Cl) is a greenish-yellow gas with a very noxious odor, and is widely used in water purification plants and swimming pools. Chlorine has a very irritating effect on the throat and lungs; a concentration of only about four parts per million is considered to be dangerous. Chlorine is heavier than air and will seek lower levels. Firefighters must exercise caution and wear respiratory equipment when working in areas of chlorine spills.

Principles of Breathing Equipment Operation

The basic purpose of breathing equipment is to provide the firefighter with a clean source of air to prevent respiratory system damage from smoke and toxic gases. This may be accomplished in different ways, providing varying amounts of working time in the smoke-filled atmosphere.

Demand-type equipment

"*Demand-type*" breathing equipment derives its name from the fact that airflow only takes place upon inhalation. Use of this type of breathing equipment has been declining steadily, as it is replaced by *positive-pressure* equipment (covered in the next section). As the firefighter breathes in, negative pressure is created on the regulator. It opens and allows air to pass through to the firefighter. If the demand for air is *small*, then the amount of air passing through the regulator is small. If the firefighter gulps air (increases demand), then the amount of air passing through the regulator is much greater.

Under normal operation of a demand-type regulator, the bypass valve is closed. The mainline valve on this type of equipment is kept in the fully open position. Breathing air or oxygen is stored in a cylinder under pressure. With the mainline valve open, the air or oxygen from the tank is allowed to enter the regulator under pressure. Upon demand (inhalation) by the firefighter, the regulator allows a reduced amount of air to pass. This reduced air pressure is more suitable for the firefighter's use. After the firefighter has inhaled an appropriate amount of air, and the "demand" has ceased, the bypass valve closes. When the firefighter exhales, the discharged air is released through an exhaust port.

Breathing apparatus of this type is equipped with an audible alarm that automatically sounds when pressure in the cylinder drops to a certain point. Depending upon the model, this may be from 15 to 60 minutes after use begins. The manufacturer's manual should be consulted to identify the exact point at which the audible alarm will operate. Firefighters should always work in teams of two or more people. Therefore, whenever one firefighter's equipment alarm sounds, all members of the team should evacuate the area. *Never leave your partner alone in the fire building.*

Positive-pressure equipment

Positive-pressure-type breathing equipment is the most-commonly used type today. It is similar in operation to the demand-type, with one exception. With the positive pressure system, a small amount of air is allowed to "leak past" the regulator at all times, **Figure 4-14**. Inside the firefighter's mask, this creates an area of *positive pressure* (air at a pressure slightly higher than the atmosphere outside the mask). The positive pressure within the mask keeps contaminants from leaking into the mask. With demand-type equipment, a *negative* pressure is created inside the mask as the firefighter inhales. If the mask's seal is faulty, the possibility exists that the firefighter could draw contaminants into the mask while inhaling. Like demand-type equipment, positive-pressure units will have a working period of from 15 to 60 minutes, depending upon the storage and pressure capacities of the air cylinder.

Oxygen rebreathing equipment

Closed-circuit *oxygen rebreathing apparatus* includes a small cylinder of pure oxygen. As the firefighter breathes, exhaled air passes through a filter which removes the carbon dioxide. A small amount of pure oxygen is then added to the cleaned air. Thus, the air that the firefighter breathes is a mixture of previously exhaled air and oxygen. The advantage of the rebreathing system is that it

Figure 4-14. In a positive-pressure system, the air pressure inside the face mask is slightly higher than the outside air pressure. This keeps smoke and gases from leaking in.

can provide breathing air for longer periods of time (two to four hours).

Oxygen-generating equipment

Oxygen-generating equipment is similar to the apparatus used for oxygen rebreathing. In addition to removing carbon dioxide from the exhaled air, however, the equipment chemically generates oxygen (rather than supplying it from a cylinder). Working time available with this type of apparatus is normally 30 to 60 minutes.

One limitation of this type of equipment is the warning device that is used. The warning device is a timer that merely indicates how much time has passed since donning the equipment. This timing device doesn't indicate the condition of the chemical in the canister. When the chemical has been depleted, the canister cannot be reused. It must be disposed of in accordance with the manufacturer's directions.

As discussed in an earlier chapter, no firefighter should *ever* enter a hazardous environment without wearing a personal alert device (PAD). Such a device is often referred to as a PASS, or personal alert safety system. The PASS should be attached to your SCBA or coat. It is intended to help fellow firefighters quickly locate you if you should become incapacitated. The device will emit a very loud alarm tone if you do not move in a specific period of time (typically 30 seconds). The PASS can also be activated manually, if necessary.

Equipment Inspections

To be sure that breathing apparatus is in top condition and ready to be used in the next emergency, you must make periodic inspections of that apparatus. Inspections should be made after each use, and at weekly and monthly intervals.

After each use

After each use, carefully inspect the breathing equipment to ensure that it is ready for use in the next emergency. The cylinder should be cleaned and checked for proper pressure. If necessary, it should be refilled. The facepiece and breathing tube should be cleaned and sanitized for the next person to use it. See **Figure 4-15.** If inspection reveals any parts of this equipment are damaged, they should be replaced. The straps should be cleaned and straightened for the next use. It is important to make a simple check of the apparatus to be sure that it has been placed back in service properly. If there is any damage obvious during this visual inspection, pull the equipment out of service until trained maintenance personnel can repair it.

Weekly

Weekly inspections are recommended to be sure that nothing unforeseen has happened to the equipment. Visually inspect the

Figure 4-15. Breathing apparatus should be carefully cleaned and checked after each use. (Warren Lutton)

equipment for cleanliness and general appearance (indicating that it is in good shape). Check the cylinder pressure valve to be sure that the pressure is up to manufacturer's specifications, **Figure 4-16.** If pressure is *not* up to specifications, replace the cylinder.

Figure 4-16. The weekly equipment inspection should include a pressure check on all breathing equipment air tanks. (Warren Lutton)

Monthly

The same procedures followed for weekly and "after use" inspection should be employed for monthly inspections. However, the monthly inspection should also include a check of hose connections from the cylinder to the regulator to be sure that they are properly tightened. See **Figure 4-17.** Check gauges and hoses for air leaks by applying soapy water to these connections. Bubbles will immediately form if a leak is present. Also, be sure to check the mainline and bypass valves to be certain that they are in the proper position.

Be certain to keep proper records of the date and time that each piece of equipment was inspected. These records should also indicate pressure in the cylinder, any problems noted, and the name of the person who conducted the inspection. A file should be kept on each piece of breathing apparatus to make sure that inspections are being carried

out regularly, according to the manufacturer's specifications.

Donning Breathing Apparatus

Figures 4-18 through **4-27** show the typical steps involved in putting on and adjusting self-contained breathing equipment. It is important to your safety to make sure that the equipment is in good condition and functioning properly.

Carefully check all gauges and valves on the apparatus each time you put it on. Listen for the sounding of any low-pressure alarms when you turn the valves on, and listen for hissing sounds that might indicate a leak in the system. When donning the facepiece, be sure to check for proper seal against your skin. If the facepiece does not achieve a proper seal, tighten the head straps.

Also check the exhalation valve to make sure that it functions properly and is not stuck in the closed position. Check the gauges on your regulator to be certain of the amount of air you have available to you. Test the regulator's operation to be sure that it will function properly. Before entering any fire building, make sure that your partner has

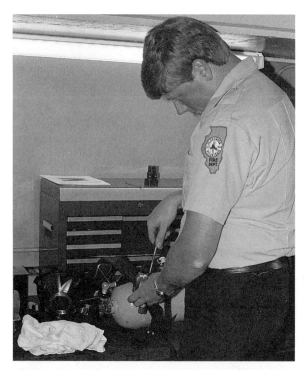

Figure 4-17. Once each month, all breathing apparatus should be thoroughly checked. Hose connections and gauges should be checked for leaks and connections tightened as necessary. (Warren Lutton)

Figure 4-18. Depending upon type of equipment, self-contained breathing equipment may be stored in individual cases or in racks inside a compartment of the truck. (Warren Lutton)

Figure 4-19. To begin donning the equipment, pass the cylinder over your head.

Figure 4-21. Fasten the main buckle across your chest.

Figure 4-20. Slide the cylinder onto your back, so that the harness settles down on your shoulders.

Figure 4-22. Tighten the straps.

Figure 4-23. Fasten the bottom straps at waist level.

Figure 4-25. Slip the facepiece over your head.

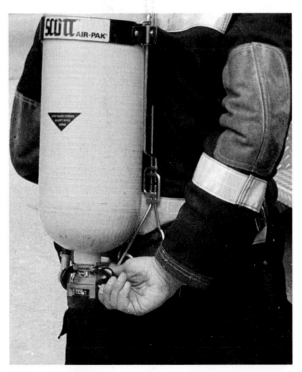

Figure 4-24. Reach behind you and turn on the cylinder valve.

Figure 4-26. Tighten the head straps to obtain a good seal.

Figure 4-27. Connect the facepiece hose to the regulator and check for proper operation of valve.

carried out the appropriate equipment checks and is also prepared to enter.

Working Safely with Breathing Equipment

The fundamental rule to be followed in a fire building while wearing self-contained breathing apparatus is to *always work in pairs*. See **Figure 4-28.** Be sure to stay together — don't allow your partner to wander off to another part of the building.

Because of the smoke, heat, and confusion of the fire, it is possible to lose your sense of direction. Use a safety line or a hose line to be certain of your means of egress. Stay low; crawl on your hands and knees. Use one hand to feel the floor in front of you before you move forward. This can save you from falls through stairways or openings in the floor. Take a handlight with you. Although its use will be somewhat limited at times, it will be helpful.

Whenever you enter a fire building, be sure to locate an alternate means of leaving the structure. Locate and memorize the positions of windows and doors. If your original means of entry becomes unusable, you and your partner can avoid becoming trapped by using an alternate exit.

Figure 4-28. Always work with a partner when wearing self-contained breathing apparatus. Listen for a low-pressure alarm on his or her SCBA, as well as your own.

If a low pressure alarm sounds on either your unit or your partner's, or if any other equipment malfunction occurs, both you and your partner should immediately leave the building.

While you and your partner are inside the fire building, have someone at the exterior keep track of the time that you have been inside, and your general location. If your time in the building approaches or exceeds the air capacity of your equipment, the outside person can send help.

Be aware of your equipment's limitations. For example, self-contained breathing apparatus does not protect you from toxic chemicals that attack exposed skin. This is one of a number of reasons why it is important to know something about the contents of the building you are entering. It is not unusual for a hardware store, for instance, to carry insecticides, solvents, and other chemicals that can produce toxic or dangerous fumes.

Be certain to work at a reasonable pace. Avoid overexertion. When wearing self-contained breathing apparatus, overexertion can easily lead to hyperventilation.

Effects of hyperventilation

Hyperventilation is a respiratory problem caused by overexertion and heavy breathing. When you breathe greater-than-normal amounts of air, the level of oxygen in your bloodstream rises. With the increase of oxygen in the bloodstream, the level of carbon dioxide (CO_2) in the blood drops.

Typical symptoms of hyperventilation include dizziness, impaired vision, anxiety (fear), and numbness or tingling in the extremities. If allowed to continue to an advanced stage, hyperventilation can lead to unconsciousness. Through practice and training in the use of self-contained breathing apparatus, you can reduce the potential for hyperventilating.

SUMMARY

A fundamental rule of firefighting is that no one should be permitted to enter a fire building unless equipped with proper self-contained breathing apparatus. The days of the "Smoke Eater" are gone. Firefighters who do not wear such equipment may find themselves becoming victims of the fire.

Self-contained breathing apparatus supplies the firefighter with air or oxygen to prevent respiratory damage caused by smoke and dangerous gases. Different types of equipment provide varying lengths of working time inside the fire building. The firefighter should know the limitations of the equipment and be thoroughly familiar with the manufacturer's directions and specifications.

Firefighters should always work in pairs or groups for safety and mutual support.

REVIEW QUESTIONS

1. What was the purpose of Project FIRES?
2. What are the three major components of a bunker coat or pants? Describe the functions of each component.
3. What is meant by the term "encumbrance?"
4. What is the purpose of periodically washing turnout clothing?
5. List some of the major hazards a fire helmet is designed to withstand.
6. On the fireground, why are rubber boots preferable to boots made of leather?
7. Why is polyester a poor choice for "station" clothing?
8. What makes carbon monoxide so dangerous? Describe the symptoms of carbon monoxide poisoning.
9. At what percentage of oxygen in air does unconsciousness become likely? How long could you survive in air that contained only 5% oxygen?
10. What concentration of chlorine gas in air is considered dangerous?
11. What feature of positive-pressure-type breathing equipment makes it more desirable than demand-type equipment?
12. What range of working times is possible with either demand-type or positive-pressure-type breathing equipment?
13. In oxygen rebreathing equipment, what happens to exhaled air?
14. What is the most important limitation of oxygen generating equipment?
15. Describe the inspection that should be made after each use of breathing equipment.
16. At a monthly check of breathing equipment, what checks should be made in addition to those conducted after use?
17. When donning breathing equipment, what should be done if a better seal of the facepiece is needed?
18. What would a hissing sound from your breathing equipment indicate?
19. True or false? Wearing self-contained breathing apparatus makes it unnecessary to work in pairs.
20. Describe the effects of hyperventilation.

NFPA 1001 Job Performance Requirements

The material on this page consists of those portions of the NFPA 1001 Job Performance Requirements relevant to the material presented in this chapter. Items preceded by the numeral 3 (3-x.x) are Fire Fighter I requirements; those with the numeral 4 (4-x.x) are Fire Fighter II requirements.

3-3.15 Extinguish incipient Class A, Class B, and Class C fires, given a selection of portable fire extinguishers, so that the correct extinguisher is chosen, the fire is completely extinguished, and proper extinguisher-handling techniques are followed.

(a) Prerequisite Knowledge: The classifications of fire; the types of, rating systems for, and risks associated with each class of fire; and the operating methods of, and limitations of portable extinguishers.

(b) Prerequisite Skills: The ability to operate portable fire extinguishers, approach fire with portable fire extinguishers, select an appropriate extinguisher based on the size and type of fire, and safely carry portable fire extinguishers.

Reprinted with permission from NFPA 1001, *Fire Fighter Professional Qualifications,* Copyright ©1997, National Fire Protection Association, Quincy, MA 02269. This reprinted material is not the complete and official position of the National Fire Protection Association on the referenced subject, which is represented only by the standard in its entirety.

Portable Fire Extinguishers

OBJECTIVES

When you have completed this chapter, you will be able to:

🔥 Explain the principles involved in the chemistry of fire.

🔥 List the methods used to extinguish a fire.

🔥 Explain the classifications of fire.

🔥 Identify the symbols used on portable fire extinguishers and relate them to the fire classifications.

🔥 Explain the appropriate choice of portable fire extinguisher for the various classes of fires.

IMPORTANT TERMS

Btu	extinguishing agents	halogenated	oxygen
carbon dioxide	fire tetrahedron	extinguishing agents	specific heat
chemical chain reaction	firefighting foam agents	heat	test fire
dry chemical	fuel	ignition temperature	vaporize
dry powder			wet water

To understand the proper use of portable fire extinguishers, it is important to have a clear understanding of the limitations of these devices. The following analogy will aid in your understanding:

While working at the scene of a fire, you sustain a small cut to the back of your hand. You wash out the cut and place a small adhesive bandage over it, then go back to work.

If you had cut your hand more severely, though, you might have needed first aid from an EMT or other medical personnel at the scene. They might have applied some butterfly closures and a protective bandage.

What about an even more serious injury, such as a severe gash to your forearm while trying to extricate the victim of an auto accident? A laceration of that size would require advanced medical attention, including possible stitches.

The seriousness of the three injuries can be compared to different sizes of fires, and what level of response is appropriate. In the instance of a very small fire, a portable fire extinguisher would probably extinguish it easily. A larger portable fire extinguisher would be appropriate for a somewhat bigger fire. For a fire equivalent to the severe gash, though, a portable fire extinguisher would probably not be sufficient — a larger response, such as a hose line, would be needed.

It is important to understand that fire extinguishers are excellent when used to control the size of the fire for which they are designed. However, when a fire extinguisher is too small for the fire that you are attempting to control, it simply will not do the job. You must decide, upon your arrival at a fire, whether or not portable fire extinguishers can be used effectively on *this* fire. To make an appropriate decision based upon the size and the type of the fire you have, you must understand the classification and rating system for fire extinguishers. It is also important to be aware of the chemistry of fire, so that you can understand the principles upon which fire extinguishers operate.

The Chemistry of Fire

To help you to understand the chemistry of fire, it would be useful to review the *fire tetrahedron* introduced in chapter 3. The fire tetrahedron is a geometric figure with four triangular faces or sides, **Figure 5-1**. Each of those four sides stands for one of the components necessary for a fire to burn.

The first side of the fire tetrahedron, **Figure 5-2**, is *oxygen*. Oxygen is a gas that makes up approximately 21% of the volume of our atmosphere, or normal breathing air. To sustain a free-burning fire, air must contain 15% to 16% oxygen. When the oxygen content drops below 15%, the ability of the fire to burn is reduced. Once oxygen drops below 8%, a fire can no longer burn; it "suffocates" or

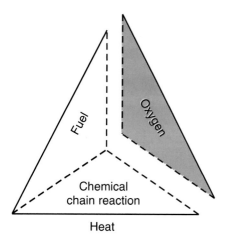

Figure 5-2. Oxygen is vital to burning, but must be present in a concentration above 8% of the total atmosphere for a fire to continue to burn.

"smothers" for lack of oxygen. Oxygen is a vital element of the combustion process. Some fuels contain oxygen that is released as they burn. In such a situation, combustion would continue, even if you were to remove the oxygen from the surrounding atmosphere.

The second side of the fire tetrahedron, **Figure 5-3**, is *fuel*. Fuel is any substance that can burn, and can exist in any one of three physical states: solid, liquid, or gas. The physical state of the fuel particles influences the ability of that fuel to ignite, and the rate at which it can burn.

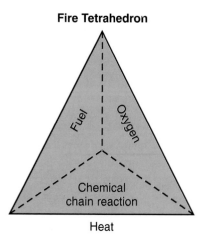

Figure 5-1. The fire tetrahedron serves as a visual reference to the four components that are required for a fire to burn: heat, oxygen, fuel, and a sustained chemical reaction.

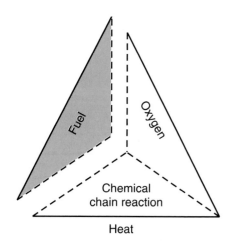

Figure 5-3. Fuel — something to burn — can be a solid, liquid, or gas. To actually ignite, however, the surface of a solid or a liquid must vaporize (change state to a gas).

The third side of the fire tetrahedron, **Figure 5-4**, is *heat*, a form of energy. Intensity of this energy is measured in degrees of temperature. There must be some form of ignition source that provides enough heat to bring the fuel to its ignition temperature. The *ignition temperature* is the level of heat intensity that causes fuel to begin to *vaporize* (change state from solid or liquid to a gas). Fuel must be in the form of a vapor before it will ignite. Ignition temperatures will vary with each individual type of fuel.

The fourth side of the fire tetrahedron, **Figure 5-5**, is the *chemical chain reaction*. During the burning process, a chemical chain reaction takes place in which new products form. These new products may or may not burn. It has been found that the formation or the consumption of certain molecules during

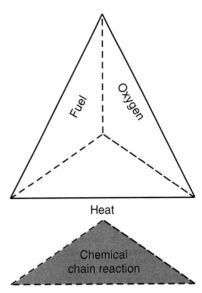

Figure 5-5. The chemical chain reaction that takes place in the burning process is essential to continued burning of the fire. Some extinguishing agents disrupt this reaction and halt the burning process.

the burning process is the key to the reaction that produces fire.

Methods of Extinguishment

By removing any one of the four sides of the fire tetrahedron, you can extinguish a fire. Some methods used to extinguish fires attack only one side of the tetrahedron; others affect two or even three sides to some extent. Methods used to extinguish fire include:

- Removing or displacing the available oxygen.
- Lowering the temperature of the fuel below its ignition temperature.
- Removing the source of fuel or separating the fuel from the heat source.
- Inhibiting the chemical reaction.

Extinguishing Agents

Materials that are used to attack one or more sides of the fire tetrahedron and put out a fire are called *extinguishing agents*. These

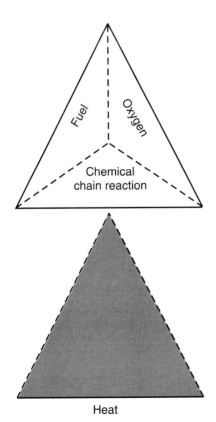

Figure 5-4. When the level of heat intensity (temperature) applied to a fuel is high enough, it will begin to burn. This is called the ignition temperature of the specific fuel.

range from water, the oldest and most common, to "wet water," which is water treated with a chemical wetting agent to make it more effective. Carbon dioxide, dry chemicals, dry powders, and halogenated hydrocarbons are other forms of extinguishing agents. They are described in the following sections.

Water

For many years, *water* has been the most commonly used extinguishing agent, due to its ability to cool and smother the fire. Water is also used because it is usually plentiful and inexpensive. Water extinguishes a fire primarily through cooling the fuel to below its ignition temperature. If the surface of any burning material is cooled to below its ignition temperature, the fire will be extinguished. Water also has a smothering effect: as the water absorbs heat from the fire, it changes from a liquid to a gas (steam, or water vapor). The steam displaces air, depriving the fire of oxygen.

To understand how water can act as an extinguishing agent, you must be familiar with the physical properties of water. Water can act as an effective extinguishing agent due to the following physical characteristics:

- At ordinary temperatures, water is a relatively heavy, yet stable, liquid.
- One *Btu* (British thermal unit) of heat is needed to raise the temperature of one pound of water one degree Fahrenheit, **Figure 5-6**. This is called the *specific heat* of water. Consequently, it would require 112 Btus to raise one pound of water from 100°F to 212°F (38°C to 100°C). It requires 970.3 Btus to convert one pound of water to steam.
- When converting water from a liquid to steam, the volume increases 1,700 times. In a confined space, this large volume of steam displaces an equal volume of air. No other material as readily available as water has the same positive extinguishing effects.

As you keep these physical characteristics in mind, you can begin to understand the

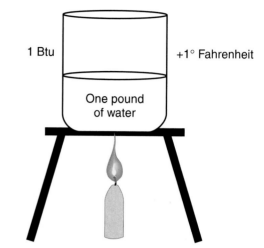

Figure 5-6. The specific heat of water is 1 Btu. This is the amount of heat needed to increase the temperature of one pound of a substance by 1°F.

extinguishing ability of water. When you introduce water into a confined fire, the water is converted to steam by the heat of the fire. The steam envelops the confined area and begins to extinguish the fire. When you apply water to an open fire, the direct application of the water to the material that is burning both cools and smothers the fire. The amount of water required to extinguish a fire will depend upon the amount of heat that must be absorbed. Your ability to extinguish a fire depends upon your ability to apply the water to the fire, **Figure 5-7**. The rate of at which water is applied to the fire must exceed the rate at which heat is generated by the fire.

In addition to its availability and its ability to absorb large amounts of heat, another advantage of water is its ability to be combined with other specialized extinguishing agents. For example, water can be combined with foam-generating solutions to provide a more effective extinguishing agent in certain situations.

Although water is a readily available and inexpensive extinguishing agent, it does have its disadvantages.

For your safety, and the safety of your fellow firefighters, you must always remember that water used for firefighting is typically an excellent conductor of electricity. (Chemically pure water is not a good conduc-

Figure 5-7. Water both cools and smothers a fire by absorbing heat and turning to steam. To successfully extinguish a fire, your hose stream must be sufficient to apply water to the fire at a rate greater than the rate at which the fire generates heat.

tor, but chemically pure water is not often found on the fireground.) The conductivity of water creates a safety hazard for firefighters. In structure fires, care must be taken to be sure that the electrical service is disconnected — solid water streams must never be used on energized electrical equipment. The output of a "fog-only" nozzle can be used safely in such situations, however. Since water freezes at 32°F (0°C), ice can present a hazard to firefighters and equipment in colder climates. It must also be remembered that water can cause a negative reaction if mixed with certain chemicals, such as sodium or potassium. Using water on molten metals or chemicals can cause the explosive production of steam.

Carbon dioxide

Carbon dioxide has been effectively used for many years to extinguish flammable liquid and energized electrical equipment fires. Under normal atmospheric conditions, carbon dioxide is a gas. However, when carbon dioxide is compressed and cooled, it can be stored in a liquid state, **Figure 5-8**. *Carbon dioxide* acts as an extinguishing agent by removing or displacing oxygen from the fire area. The density of carbon dioxide, com-

Figure 5-8. Carbon dioxide gas can be compressed and cooled to a liquid form for use in portable fire extinguishers like this one.

pared to dry air, is 1.529. This means that carbon dioxide is approximately 1 1/2 times heavier than air. This permits it to replace or exclude air from the surface of the burning material, smothering the fire.

Carbon dioxide has a high expansion rate. As shown in **Figure 5-9**, approximately one pound of liquid converts to approximately eight cubic feet of gas. Therefore, a relatively small amount of stored liquid can

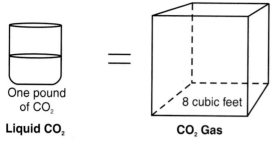

Figure 5-9. Each pound of liquid carbon dioxide will expand to approximately eight cubic feet when it changes state to a gas by being released from a fire extinguisher.

Figure 5-10. Dry chemical extinguishers may be rated only for one type of fire (such as energized electrical equipment), but many are considered *multipurpose* extinguishers. This means they may be used against various kinds of fires. (Photo courtesy of Lab Safety Supply, Inc., Janesville, WI)

convert into a large amount of extinguishing gas. Another major advantage of carbon dioxide as an extinguishing agent is that it does not conduct electricity.

Like water, carbon dioxide also has its disadvantages. Carbon dioxide can be hazardous at approximately 9% concentration. Higher concentration can render a human unconscious in a relatively short period of time and cause death by suffocation. Carbon dioxide is also relatively ineffective on fires involving ordinary combustible materials. Since the gas affords very little cooling effect, the fire may reignite unless hot embers and surfaces are cooled below ignition temperature. Carbon dioxide is also not an effective extinguishing agent for fires involving chemicals containing their own oxygen supply. For example, it cannot smother a fire involving cellulose nitrate, since the combustion of that material creates its own oxygen supply.

Dry chemical extinguishing agents

The term *dry chemical* refers to a mixture of chemical powders that can be used effectively on various types of fires. Commercially available dry chemical extinguishers, **Figure 5-10**, may use one or more of the following as the base chemical for a mixture of powders: sodium bicarbonate, potassium bicarbonate, potassium chloride, or monammonium phosphate. Dry chemicals are finely ground powders that require some form of expulsion force (usually, a compressed gas) to discharge them from a portable fire extinguisher.

Some of the base chemicals used in dry chemical extinguishing agents are more effective than others on specific types of fires. For instance, ordinary dry chemicals, such as sodium bicarbonate, are effective on fires involving flammable liquids but less effective on ordinary combustibles. Multipurpose dry chemicals, such as monammonium phosphate, are effective for use on both ordinary combustibles and flammable liquids.

One of the primary advantages of the dry chemicals is that (again, depending upon the base chemical used) they usually are excellent extinguishers for several types of fires: ordinary combustibles, flammable liquids, and energized electrical equipment. Most dry chemicals do not conduct electricity, but you should make sure, before use, that the extinguisher is rated for electrical equipment fires.

There are several possible adverse effects to the use of dry chemicals as extinguishing agents. When stored for a long period of time, dry chemicals may tend to pack or "cake" inside their container. This does not allow for them to be properly expelled when needed to extinguish a fire. Also, when discharged into confined areas, quantities of dry chemical powder can cause problems with visibility and breathing. Always wear your self-contained breathing apparatus (SCBA) when discharging this type of extinguisher.

Dry chemicals do not provide any cooling effect. Care must be taken that hot embers and hot surfaces do not cause materials to reignite after the extinguishing agent has been applied. Since they are a fine powder, these chemicals leave a messy residue. Also, the chemical reaction of the extinguishing agent in the fire may have corrosive effects.

Dry powder extinguishing agents

The terms "dry chemical" and "dry powder" are used interchangeably. However, there is a difference between them. *Dry powder* extinguishers are specifically intended for use on fires involving combustible metals, such as magnesium or sodium. Like dry chemicals, these extinguishing agents are made up of fine powdered chemicals that have particularly good extinguishing capabilities. However, dry powders may not be used interchangeably with dry chemical extinguishing agents. Dry chemical extinguishers are not effective in fighting combustible metal fires; dry powders are not effective on ordinary combustibles, burning liquids, or electrical fires.

Halogenated agents

Halogenated extinguishing agents are chemical compounds created by the use of the elements bromine, chlorine, fluorine, or iodine. The exact process by which halogenated agents function as extinguishing agents is not completely understood. However, it is believed that they function by inhibiting the chemical chain reaction process in fire. These types of extinguishing agents are most suited for fires involving specific hazards or equipment, such as large computer installations. Where a fixed enclosure is available, total flooding systems are usually designed to allow for adequate concentrations of the extinguishing agent.

One of the primary limitations of the use of halogenated extinguishing agents is that, in high concentrations, they can be toxic. Under normal circumstances, with concentrations of 7% or lower, halogenated extinguishing agents have little or no effect on humans. In concentrations of between 7% and 14%, there can be increasing disorientation. Concentrations above 14% can cause loss of consciousness. For this reason, you must always wear your self-contained breathing apparatus (SCBA) in a situation where this type of extinguishing agent might be discharged.

Because they have been identified as gases that damage the ozone layer, halogenated extinguishing agents are no longer manufactured. Although recently developed agents that are less harmful to the environment are being used in new systems, many existing systems will continue to use the halogenated agents. Once existing supplies of halogenated agents are gone, recycling will make it possible to extend their use for some time. Eventually, however, system replacement and retrofitting of existing systems will eliminate the use of halogenated extinguishing agents.

Foam agents

Firefighting foam agents are used primarily to combat flammable liquid fires, but under special circumstances, foam may be used on fires involving ordinary combustible materials. In most cases, foam is lighter than the burning material to which it is applied. This allows the foam to float on the surface of a flammable liquid and exclude the oxygen from the fire.

Firefighting foams act as an extinguishing agent by creating a blanket to exclude the oxygen from the fire, **Figure 5-11**. This smothering effect is created by the mass of gas-filled bubbles that make up the foam material. Foams may be generated *chemically* through the reaction of two materials in water, or *mechanically* by vigorously mixing a small amount of foaming agent with water.

Figure 5-11. Foams are thick masses of gas bubbles and water that blanket and smother the fire. They are highly effective against flammable liquid fires, and thus are a basic tool for firefighting at airports and in tanker-truck accidents, such as this one. (National Foam)

Protein-forming foams, aqueous film-forming foams, and high-expansion foams are all created by the use of various chemicals. Each has specific applications, based upon the characteristics of its chemical compound. Since foams are water-based, they will conduct electricity and cannot be used on electrical fires.

Firefighting foams are covered in detail in Chapter 8.

Wetting agents (wet water)

Wet water is a term used to describe water to which a wetting agent as been added to improve its extinguishing ability. Wetting agents, **Figure 5-12**, are used to decrease the surface tension of water. This helps water to penetrate below the surface of burning materials and decreases its tendency to run off the surface. By improving the ability of water to cling to the surface material of the fuel in the fire, wetting agents permit you to gain maximum cooling effect from the water. The use of wetting agents also cuts down the amount of water needed and reduces the amount of overhaul necessary, due to its ability to adhere to the surfaces better. Drawbacks include the corrosive effect of wetting agents when in contact with certain types of materials, as well as the problems common to water as an extinguishing agent: freezing and the inability to be used on fires involving energized electrical equipment.

Fire Extinguisher Classification System

The classification system for fire extinguishers is based upon standards established by one of three testing agencies: Underwriters'

Figure 5-12. A wetting agent, such as Class A liquid foam concentrate, can be added to water to diminish surface tension that keeps water from penetrating masses of burning material. The resulting solution of water and wetting agent is referred to as "wet water." Class A foams also are increasingly being used to fight fires involving ordinary combustibles, especially where water is in short supply or where water damage must be kept to a minimum. (National Foam)

Laboratory (UL), Factory Mutual Engineering Company (FM), and the United States Coast Guard (USCG). Portable fire extinguishers are classified by these testing agencies according to their intended use. These classifications carry the letter designations A, B, C, and D. Each letter (reinforced by a symbol of a specific shape and color) denotes the type of material upon which the extinguisher can appropriately be used:

- Class A: (identified by a green triangle) ordinary combustible materials such as paper, cloth, wood, and plastic.
- Class B: (identified by a red square) flammable liquids of all types.

- Class C: (identified by a blue circle) electrical wiring and equipment.
- Class D: (identified by a yellow star) flammable metals.

Extinguishers often will carry more than one letter designation. These multipurpose extinguishers may be used on any of the types of fires designated on their label. Dry chemical extinguishers, for example, are frequently labeled A, B, and C. This means they may be used against fires involving ordinary combustibles, flammable liquids, or electrical equipment.

There also may be a numerical value preceding the letter. Just as the letter denotes the *type* of material that the extinguisher is rated for, the numerical value indicates the relative *size* of fire on which that extinguisher may be used effectively.

Class A (Green Triangle)

Portable fire extinguishers used on Class A fires, **Figure 5-13**, may be expected to adequately extinguish fires involving ordinary combustible materials, such as wood, paper, or cloth. Any extinguisher carrying the capital letter **A** on its label has been certified by one of the testing agencies for fires involving

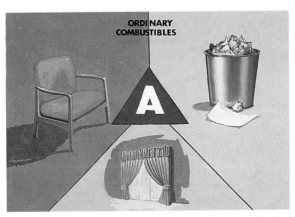

Figure 5-13. Class A extinguishers are marked with a green triangle. This indicates that they can be used for fires involving paper, wood, cloth, plastics, and other ordinary combustibles. (Institutional Communications Associates)

this type of material. A numerical indication usually precedes the letter. The number is relative to the size of a standard *test fire* established by the testing agencies. The number 1 preceding the **A** indicates that this extinguisher could be expected to extinguish a normal test fire. The number 4 in front of the letter indicates that the extinguisher is capable of extinguishing a fire that is four times the size of the standard test fire. By combining the number and the letter, we can determine that a **6A** fire extinguisher, for instance, will be capable of extinguishing a fire three times larger than a **2A** fire extinguisher, or six times larger than a **1A** fire extinguisher.

Class B (Red Square)

Fire extinguishers rated for Class **B** use, **Figure 5-14**, are appropriate for flammable liquid fires. A fire extinguisher carrying a numerical value indicates the relative size of the fire that can be extinguished by this particular extinguisher. However, in the case of Class **B** fire extinguishers, the number may also indicate the square foot area of a flammable liquid fire on which this extinguisher can be successfully used. For instance, a **20B** fire extinguisher should normally be able to extinguish approximately 20 square feet of

flammable liquids fire when used by a person without specific training in fire extinguisher use. A trained operator should be able to extinguish a fire somewhat more than twice that size with the same extinguisher.

Class C (Blue Circle)

Fire extinguishers carrying the Class **C** designation on their labels, **Figure 5-16**, indicate that they may be used safely on fires involving energized electrical equipment. Unlike Class **A** and Class *B*, no number is associated with a Class **C** rating. The Class **C** rating simply means that this extinguishing agent and extinguisher will not conduct electricity when used properly. You must be aware, however, that in order to successfully extinguish any fire involving electrically energized materials, the electrical energy to the equipment must be cut off.

Class D (Yellow Star)

The Class **D** label on an extinguisher indicates that it should be used on fires involving combustible metals. As in the case of Class **C**, no numerical value is usually attached to the Class **D** rating.

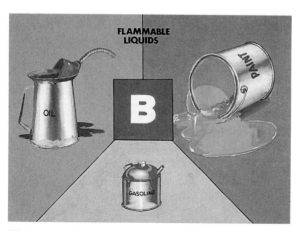

Figure 5-14. The red square indicates an extinguisher suitable for use on Class B fires. These are fires involving flammable liquids. (Institutional Communications Associates)

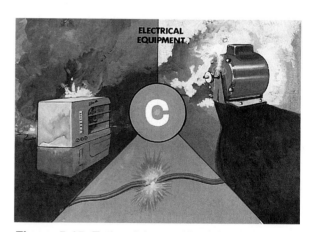

Figure 5-15. Extinguishers with a blue circle are suited for use on Class C fires — those that involve energized electrical equipment. Extinguishing agents for Class C fires must be nonconductive. (Institutional Communications Associates)

SUMMARY

The portable fire extinguisher, when used properly, can be an extremely effective firefighting tool. A trained firefighter can put out what would appear to be a relatively large fire with a portable fire extinguisher. It must be remembered, however, that fire extinguishers have their limitations. If an extinguisher is used improperly, a fire may be allowed to gain an unusual amount of headway because of the time lost in unsuccessfully attempting to extinguish it. When you deal with the public, always be sure to stress that any time they have to use a portable fire extinguisher, they should always call the fire department to be sure that the fire has been properly extinguished.

REVIEW QUESTIONS

1. What is the basic consideration when deciding whether or not to use a portable fire extinguisher?
2. Name the four sides of the fire tetrahedron.
3. What is the general term for materials that are used to attack and put out fires?
4. Describe how water provides both a cooling effect and a smothering effect on a fire.
5. By what amount does volume increase when water is converted from a liquid to steam?
6. How many Btus are needed to convert one pound of water completely to steam?
7. What is the major safety hazard to keep in mind when water is used as an extinguishing agent?
8. Carbon dioxide is heavier than air. How does this help it to be an effective extinguishing agent?
9. What are the disadvantages of carbon dioxide as an extinguishing agent?
10. Distinguish between dry chemical and dry powder extinguishers. Can they be used interchangeably?
11. What type of extinguishing agent would work best for a fire in a large computer room?
12. How do foam agents extinguish a fire? What is their primary use?
13. What are the two methods of generating foams for firefighting?
14. What does the term "wet water" mean?
15. Standards for fire extinguishers are established by testing agencies identified by the abbreviations UL, FM, and USCG. What do those initials stand for?
16. What are the "ordinary combustible materials" for which a Class A extinguisher is suitable?
17. On an extinguisher suitable for flammable liquid fires, what does the number preceding the type letter (for example, 10B) stand for?
18. Can an extinguisher rated for use on an electrical fire successfully extinguish the fire if electrical power is not cut off?
19. If a dry chemical extinguisher is rated for use on ordinary combustibles, flammable liquids, and electrical equipment, what are the shapes and colors of the symbols shown on its label?
20. On what type of fire would you use an extinguisher labeled with a yellow star?

NFPA 1001 Job Performance Requirements

The material on this page consists of those portions of the NFPA 1001 Job Performance Requirements relevant to the material presented in this chapter. Items preceded by the numeral 3 (3-x.x) are Fire Fighter I requirements; those with the numeral 4 (4-x.x) are Fire Fighter II requirements.

3-3.14 Connect a fire department pumper to a water supply as a member of a team, given supply or intake hose, hose tools, and a fire hydrant or static water source, so that connections are tight and water flow is unobstructed.

(a) Prerequisite Knowledge: Loading and off-loading procedures for mobile water supply apparatus; fire hydrant operation; and suitable static water supply sources, procedures, and protocol for connecting to various water sources.

(b) Prerequisite Skills: The ability to hand lay a supply hose, connect and place hard suction hose for drafting operations, deploy portable water tanks as well as the equipment necessary to transfer water between and draft from them, make hydrant-to-pumper hose connections for forward and reverse lays, connect supply hose to a hydrant, and fully open and close the hydrant.

4-5.4 Test the operability of and flow from a fire hydrant, given a Pitot tube, pressure gauge, and other necessary tools, so that the readiness of the hydrant is assured and the flow of water from the hydrant can be calculated and recorded.

(a) Prerequisite Knowledge: How water flow is reduced by hydrant obstructions; direction of hydrant outlets to suitability of use; the effect of mechanical damage, rust, corrosion, failure to open the hydrant fully, and susceptibility to freezing; and the meaning of the terms static, residual, and flow pressure.

(b) Prerequisite Skills: The ability to operate a pressurized hydrant, use a Pitot tube and pressure gauges, detect damage, and record results of test.

Reprinted with permission from NFPA 1001, *Fire Fighter Professional Qualifications,* Copyright ©1997, National Fire Protection Association, Quincy, MA 02269. This reprinted material is not the complete and official position of the National Fire Protection Association on the referenced subject, which is represented only by the standard in its entirety.

Water Supply

OBJECTIVES

When you have completed this chapter, you will be able to:

🔥 Identify the sources of water.

🔥 Describe the physical properties of water.

🔥 List the basic components of a water distribution system.

🔥 Describe the basic components of a fire hydrant.

🔥 Discuss the importance of fire flow tests.

IMPORTANT TERMS

arterial water mains
branch water mains
butts
condensation
distribution system
dry-barrel fire hydrants
evaporation

flow pressure
flow testing
gravity flow
hydrologic cycle
hydrology
normal operating
   pressure

permeability
pitot tube
precipitation
pressure gauge
psi (pounds per square
   inch)
pumping stations

residual pressure
runoff
static pressure
supply water mains
water table
water vapor
wet-barrel fire hydrants

Our station duties were just about completed for the day, when the house bells rang and the speaker indicated a house fire. My partner and I climbed into our seats on the engine and slipped into our SCBAs. As the engine cleared the station drive, the Captain indicated we were headed for the unincorporated area, beyond the city water mains.

When we arrived at the house, we grabbed the preconnected 1 1/2 in. line and headed for the front door. As we paused to put on our masks, the Captain shouted that all the occupants were safely out of the house. As we moved into the hallway, the smoke became heavy. We slowly opened each door

and checked each room, trying to locate the seat of the fire.

About halfway down the hall, we found the fire, located in a family room. My partner opened the nozzle and we pushed our way into the room. To cool and extinguish the fire, we worked the nozzle back and forth and up and down. In a few short moments, the heat began to decrease and the smoke thinned and lifted. Then, we felt the line begin to go limp; my partner grabbed my shoulder and shouted, "We're out of water!" The heat quickly began to grow again, as smoke once more banked down towards the floor. We turned and followed the handline back to the front door.

As we cleared the front door and removed our SCBA masks, the Captain told us that the tanker had not yet arrived; we had run out of water. The frustration in my partner's face was obvious. Just a few minutes more, and we would have had the fire knocked out.

Although water covers approximately 75% of the earth's surface and is the most commonly found compound in our world, firefighters seldom think about it unless it runs out. The primary concern of the fire service regarding water is the availability and the reliability of the water supply. See **Figure 6-1**. This chapter will discuss the terminology, properties, and components of water sources used for firefighting, so that you will be able

Figure 6-1. Tankers are a vital means of water supply for firefighting in rural areas or other locations beyond municipal water mains. Depending upon the size of the fire and the distance to a source of water, two or more tankers may have to be used to ensure an adequate supply of water on the fireground. (Jack Klasey)

to achieve a broader understanding of water supplies and how they function in our total fire suppression system.

The Hydrologic Cycle

The natural water cycle is often referred to as the *hydrologic cycle*. It is important to understand this cycle, which describes the continuous movement of water between the earth and the atmosphere, **Figure 6-2**. *Hydrology* is the science concerned with the distribution of water on earth. It explains the physical and chemical reactions that occur between water and other natural substances and the correlations of those reactions to life on earth. Of the various items that influence the hydrologic cycle, *heat* is the most important. Heat evaporates water from both land and water surfaces. The resulting *water vapor* circulates through the atmosphere and is precipitated back to earth in the form of rain or snow. Once it reaches the earth's surface, water can either soak into the ground or become surface runoff. The path that water follows is decided by the intensity of the rain, combined with the existing moisture content and *permeability* (ability to absorb moisture) of the soil.

Some of the soil moisture usually will evaporate and return to the hydrologic cycle. Another portion of the water may remain in the top layer of the soil to provide moisture for plants. The rest of the water that has soaked into the soil will permeate downward and eventually become a portion of the groundwater. As a part of the natural water cycle, the *water table* (depth at which water is found) will rise or fall as a result of the abundance of, or lack of, water. These groundwater sources can be tapped by wells to provide water for human use. Some water will rise naturally to the surface through springs.

As noted earlier, when the amount of water returning to the earth exceeds the ability of the ground to absorb it, the excess is called *runoff*. It will find its way into streams

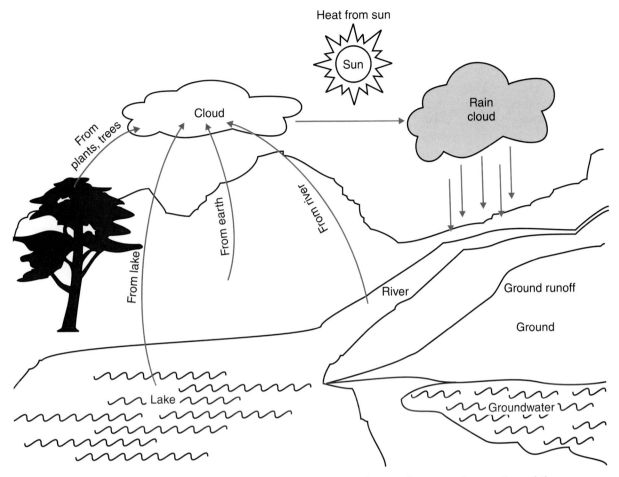

Figure 6-2. The hydrologic cycle is the constant movement of water between the earth and the atmosphere.

and rivers, and eventually into lakes or oceans. The evaporation from the surface of these bodies of water fuels the natural water cycle.

Cycle Components

The components of the hydrologic (natural water) cycle include *evaporation, condensation*, and *precipitation*, **Figure 6-3**. The water on the surface of the earth is constantly being *evaporated* (changed to a gaseous form) by the heat of the sun. This gas, called *water vapor*, is lighter than air and rises until it eventually *condenses* into a cloud formation. The cloud is formed by cooling of the gas so that it returns (condenses) to liquid form. When enough liquid is present in the cloud formation, it becomes heavier than air and

returns to the earth's surface as *precipitation* (rain or snow). The precipitation completes the hydrologic cycle, which begins all over again with evaporation. Actually, this natural water cycle is constantly taking place, so long as there is moisture available.

Physical Characteristics of Water

In its pure state, water is an odorless, tasteless liquid. Under normal atmospheric pressures, the freezing point of water is 32°F (0°C), and its boiling point is 212°F (100°C). Water is made up of the elements hydrogen and oxygen. There are two hydrogen molecules for

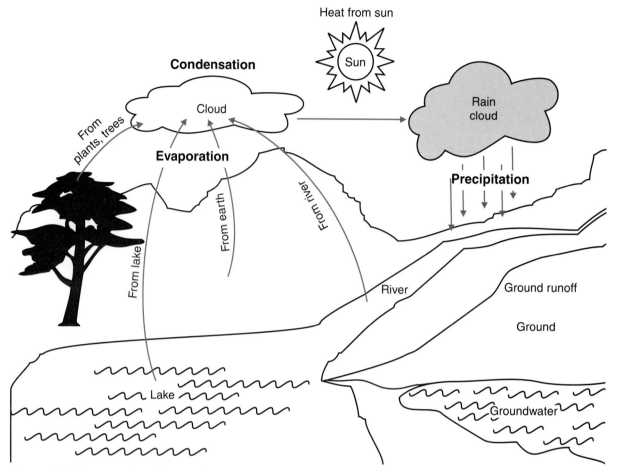

Figure 6-3. Evaporation of water from the earth's surface, condensation in the atmosphere, and a return to earth in the form of precipitation are the three components of the hydrologic cycle.

each oxygen molecule, as shown by water's chemical symbol, H_2O.

Heat always flows from a substance of higher temperature to a substance of lower temperature. One British Thermal Unit (Btu) is the amount of heat required to raise the temperature of one pound of water one degree Fahrenheit. This is also called the specific heat of water. A chart that outlines the basic properties of water is shown as **Figure 6-4**.

Water As an Extinguishing Agent

Because water is relatively abundant and reasonably inexpensive, it has been used for hundreds of years by firefighters to extinguish fire. However, through our knowledge

Basic Physical Properties of Water
◊ Water freezes at 32°F (0°C).
◊ Water boils at 212°F (100°C).
◊ One gallon of water weighs 8.33 lbs. (3.78kg).
◊ One cubic foot of water = 7.48 gallons (28.3 liters).
◊ One cubic foot of water weighs 62.5 lbs. (28.3kg).
◊ Water is incompressible.
◊ One Btu is required to raise the temperature of one pound of water one degree Fahrenheit.
◊ When water converts from liquid to steam, its volume increases about 1700 times at atmospheric pressure.

Figure 6-4. Some of the basic physical properties of water.

of the properties of water, we can better understand why it is effective against fire, because of its ability to absorb large amounts of heat (Btus). The size of the fire (and thus, the amount of the heat that must be absorbed) will determine the amount of water that is required. In a particular fire, the *rate of application* is important; you must be able to apply the water to the fire faster than the heat is generated, **Figure 6-5**.

It should be remembered, however, there are certain limitations to the use of water as an extinguishing agent. Water is capable of conducting electricity, so you must be cautious not to use a solid stream of water as an extinguishing agent around electrically energized equipment. A fine *fog* of water droplets, however, will not conduct electricity, and thus can be used safely around energized equipment. Water may also cause a violent reaction when it comes in contact with certain chemicals, such as phosphorus or sodium. If these chemicals are identified as being present, choose an alternative extinguishing agent. The fact that water freezes at 32°F (0°C) can cause difficulties under normal winter conditions in cold climates.

Water Supply Systems

As you read at the beginning of this chapter, water is not always readily available at the

Figure 6-5. Water can absorb large amounts of heat, making it an effective means of extinguishing fire — if heat can be absorbed faster than it is generated, the temperature of the burning material will fall below the point needed to sustain combustion.

point where it is needed to fight a fire. Often, it must be moved from its source to the point where it is needed. There are basically three methods that can be used to do this: gravity flow, direct pumping, and a combination of the two. A fourth method must be used when the fireground is not within reach of city water mains or a natural water source—such as a creek or farm pond—to draft (pump) from. This method involves using tanker truck relays to bring water from the nearest source to portable canvas reservoirs erected on the fireground.

Gravity Flow Systems

When the water supply is located in an elevation higher than the place which it is going to be used, *gravity flow* is the most practical and economical way of moving it. The use of gravity requires that water be collected and stored in sufficient quantities to ensure a reliable supply at a usable *pressure*. For each foot of elevation above the point of delivery, water exerts approximately 0.434 *psi (pounds per square inch)* pressure. Thus, if the reservoir is located a hundred feet above the point at which the water will be used, 43.4 pounds per square inch of pressure would be available. An early example of the use of the gravity method for moving water was the aqueduct system of ancient Rome. The aqueducts were built to convey water from its source in the mountains to the city of Rome. The same principle is demonstrated by the elevated tanks used in municipal and private water systems, **Figure 6-6**. Such tanks are engineered to contain a specific volume of water at a certain elevation. The limitation of the use of the gravity method of moving water is that the reservoir must be quite large to contain an adequate amount of water.

Pumping Systems

When sufficient elevation is not available to provide a reliable pressure within the system, pumps are added. *Pumping stations*, **Figure 6-7**, are often placed at the source of

A   B

Figure 6-6. Elevated water tanks provide a reliable municipal water supply at a usable pressure through gravity flow. A—A large steel tank of a type used for both municipal and industrial supplies. B—This very large concrete tank supplies the needs of a suburban community outside Chicago.

Figure 6-7. In a pumping station like this, large pumps draw water from a well or other source of supply and channel it under pressure into the distribution system. (Warren Lutton)

supply, where they draw the water from a lake, river, or well. The pumps then increase the pressure and discharge the water into the distribution system. The pumps are engineered to provide an adequate and reliable flow of water through the distribution system.

In some cases, the quality of water requires that it be treated before being discharged into the distribution system. In such cases, the pumps will discharge water from the source of supply into a treatment facility. Usually, the water discharged from the treatment facility is sent to a reservoir or other means of storage. See **Figure 6-8**. A second set of pumps draws clean water from the reservoir and discharges it into the distribution system.

To provide for reliability of the water supply system, duplicate pumps are often

Figure 6-8. A covered in-ground reservoir like this one is used in some communities to store water after it has been treated to remove contaminants. The reservoir discharges into the distribution system. (Warren Lutton)

provided. This set of "backup" pumps often uses a secondary source of power to prevent interruption of water flow. If the primary pumps are powered by electricity from utility lines, the backup pumps are usually powered by an engine that uses fossil fuel, **Figure 6-9**. In this way, the system can continue to pro-

vide water even when the electrical power has been interrupted.

Combination Systems

Many communities combine elevated storage tanks and pumps to provide an adequate and reliable water supply system by providing both. Such a combination allows the community to provide a more even pressure throughout the system. The pumps discharge into the system and are also used to fill the elevated tanks. The elevated tanks then "ride" on the system, providing for a more even water pressure.

Tanker Relay Method

In rural areas and smaller communities without a water main distribution system, the water must sometimes be brought to the fire from a point a mile or more away. To maintain a steady supply of water, two or more tanker trucks will relay water from a water source to the fireground, **Figure 6-10.** In some areas, the water source might be a hydrant at the end of the nearest municipal distribution system; in

Figure 6-9. This diesel engine provides backup pumping power for a water supply system. The batteries in the foreground are used to start the engine if power from utility lines is interrupted. (Warren Lutton)

Figure 6-10. In many areas, water must be brought to the fire-ground in tanker trucks like these. To provide a constant water supply, a relay involving two or more trucks is often set up.

others, it might be a river, lake, retention pond, or other body of water.

Portable canvas tanks are erected on the fireground, **Figure 6-11,** to be used as reservoirs. A pumper then drafts the water from the tank to supply hoselines. Often, a special low-profile strainer is used on the hard suction to permit continued pumping when only a few inches of water remain in the reservoir. See **Figure 6-12**.

The Water Distribution System

To provide water to homes, businesses, and industrial plants, a network of water mains called a *distribution system* is installed throughout the service area. See **Figure 6-13**. For efficient and adequate distribution of water, the system usually includes three types of water mains.

A

B

Figure 6-11. Canvas tanks are used as reservoirs on the fireground. A—The collapsible tank is often carried on a department's tanker, so that it can be quickly erected and filled. B—In a matter of minutes, several firefighters can unfold and set up the tank. Note the hard suction connected to the pumper, ready to be dropped into the tank once it contains water.

Figure 6-12. The low-profile strainer allows maximum efficiency in use of water from a canvas tank. It permits continued drafting with only a few inches of water depth, an advantage when water must be brought from a distant source.

Types of Mains

Arterial water mains, sometimes called primary water mains, are pipes of large diameter (at least 10 inches, but usually even larger). Arterial water mains move large quantities of water to various parts of the community for further distribution. These mains are spaced relatively far apart.

Secondary or *branch water mains* are smaller in size than the arterial water mains and make up the next level of the distribution grid. These mains form the link between the large arterial mains and the smaller supply mains to which fire hydrants and individual customers (homes, businesses, and so on) are connected.

The distribution grid itself consists of a series of smaller *supply water mains*. These mains are arranged to serve the needs of individual customers, and also provide the water supply for all fire hydrants. These mains must be easily accessible for maintenance and repair.

Valves and Pipes

It is important that the distribution system have an adequate number of valves for ease of maintenance. See **Figure 6-14**. These valves should be positioned so that shutting down a section of the system for maintenance

Figure 6-13. A community's water distribution system consists of large arterial water mains, smaller branch mains, and still smaller supply mains to provide thorough coverage. The system supplies the fire hydrant system as well as residences, businesses, and industries.

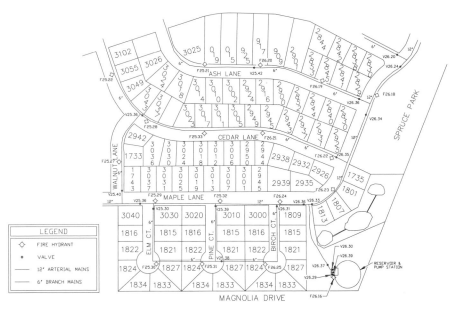

LEGEND
◇ FIRE HYDRANT
• VALVE
— 12' ARTERIAL MAINS
— 6' BRANCH MAINS

Figure 6-14. Valves, installed at the same time as water mains, allow sections to be shut down for maintenance and repair. If an adequate number of valves is installed, smaller sections of the system can be isolated, interrupting service for fewer customers.

Figure 6-15. The auxiliary valve installed in the pipe leading to the hydrant will allow water shut-off for maintenance or repair without affecting adjacent hydrants or water system users. A standpipe and cover will be installed over the valve to permit access after the hole is back-filled. (Warren Lutton)

disrupts as few customers as possible. An auxiliary valve should be installed on the pipe stub that connects the water main to the fire hydrant, **Figure 6-15**. This auxiliary valve will make it possible to shut down a fire hydrant for maintenance without interrupting the flow of water through the main.

Depending upon size, water mains are constructed of different materials. Arterial mains, especially those of larger diameter for use in major cities, are often cast iron, steel, or asbestos cement. The same materials are typically used for branch water mains. Supply mains may be cast iron or steel, but in recent years, plastic has been used extensively. See **Figure 6-16**.

Regardless of the type of pipe that is used, it must be installed properly. The pipe should be carefully supported and backfilled correctly to minimize the possibility of future breaks, **Figure 6-17**. Before being placed in service, the water main must be disinfected and pressure-tested for leaks.

Fire Hydrants

There are basically two types of fire hydrants; wet-barrel and dry-barrel. The *wet-barrel fire hydrant* has water in the barrel at

all times. Consequently, this type of hydrant is not recommended for areas that are subject to freezing temperatures. Under winter conditions, the water in the barrel will freeze, making the hydrant inoperative.

The *dry-barrel fire hydrant* does not have water in the barrel under normal circumstances. The valve used to control water flow is located near the base of the hydrant. When the operating nut is engaged, a shaft extending down the barrel of the hydrant opens the valve, allowing water to enter the barrel of the hydrant. When this type of hydrant is turned off, the valve closes and interrupts the water supply. As the valve closes, drain holes at the

Figure 6-16. Polyvinyl chloride (PVC) plastic pipe has taken a share of the water main market from cast iron and steel pipe. It provides the advantages of lower weight and corrosion resistance.

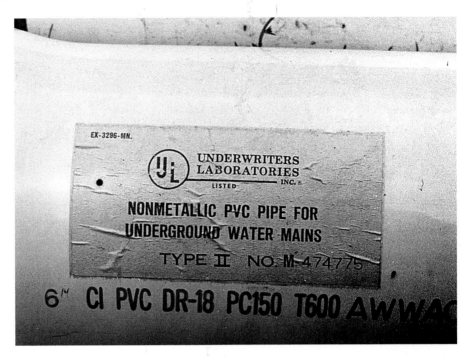

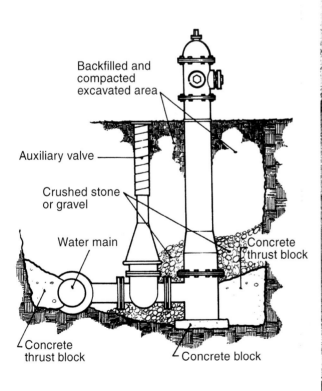

A   B

Figure 6-17. Hydrant installation. A—The pipe and the hydrant must be firmly and properly supported to prevent movement during backfilling that could open joints. B—Careful backfilling of the excavation and compacting of the fill material will result in a troublefree installation.

base of the hydrant open. These holes allow any water remaining in the hydrant barrel to drain out into the surrounding ground. Dry-barrel hydrants are recommended for climates with severe winters. After shutting off a hydrant of this type, make sure that the water is draining from the barrel. If the water is not draining, report the problem immediately to the local agency responsible for hydrant maintenance. If you fail to report an improperly draining hydrant, the hydrant could freeze and become inoperative.

Hydrant Spacing

The exact placement of fire hydrants must take into consideration the nature of the area being protected. In industrial and commercial areas, for example, hydrant spacing should not exceed 300 feet. The American Waterworks Association has a standard on the placement and the installation of hydrants. Local authorities have the right to review and approve the exact placement of hydrants within their community.

Parts of a Fire Hydrant

Hydrants vary in construction, based upon individual manufacturer's specifications. Most modern hydrants, however, have six-inch barrels and a six-inch connection to the city water main. The basic components of the fire hydrant include the barrel, several discharge ports (*butts*), an operating nut, a valve stem, and a valve, **Figure 6-18**. Most fire hydrants will use National Standard Threads (NST) for their hose connections. Most newer hydrants are shipped with an auxiliary valve to isolate the hydrant from the water main when repairs are needed. Whenever a hydrant is in use, the operating valve should be opened completely to assure full waterflow.

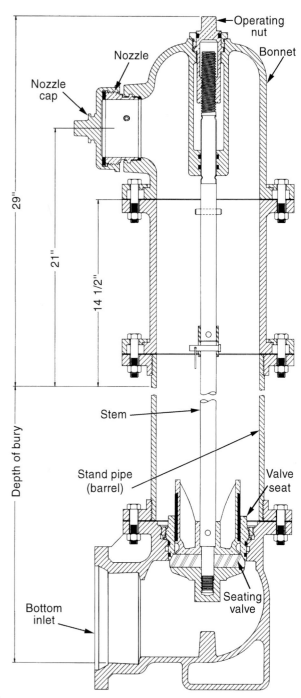

Figure 6-18. The basic components of a fire hydrant. There will be some differences in detail from manufacturer to manufacturer. (East Jordan Iron Works)

Fire Flow Tests

Fire departments should have an established program for annual *flow testing* of hydrants. The results of all flow tests should be recorded and maintained. Over a period of years, these flow test results will establish the normal operating conditions of the various areas of the water distribution system within a community. The tests may make it possible to detect previously unsuspected problems within the water system.

Besides identifying obvious hydrant problems, flow testing makes it possible to identify closed or partly closed valves within the system. For example, when conducting a flow test this year, you find that a hydrant is flowing very poorly. With a history of test results, you establish that this particular area flowed quite well in previous years. Moving to a hydrant on either side of the affected hydrant, you find that the flows are again good. By continuing movement away from the affected hydrant, you can identify the specific area which is causing the problem. Valves within that area can then be checked to see if they are completely open.

Types of Pressures

Conducting flow tests on fire hydrants is a simple procedure. However, in order to understand that procedure, we must first be familiar with four types of pressure: static pressure, residual pressure, normal operating pressure, and flow pressure.

The term *static* implies that there is no motion (something is at rest). **Static pressure** may be generated by gravity, by an elevated water supply, or by a pump. For the purposes of flow testing, static pressure can be defined as *stored potential energy that is available to force water through pipe, hose, fittings, or adaptors*.

Residual describes something that is left over. Consequently, **residual pressure** refers to the pressure remaining in the distribution system when one or more fire hydrants is flowing. Residual pressure is defined as *that part of the pressure that is not used to overcome friction loss while forcing water through hose, pipe, fittings, or adaptors*.

In order to truly understand the relationship between static pressure and residual pressure, you must understand what normal operating pressure is. **Normal operating pres-** *sure* is defined as *the pressure found on the distribution system while normal consumption demands are being met*. Water is constantly being drawn from the system. Each time a homeowner opens a water faucet, he or she is causing a demand on the system. This demand will fluctuate according to the hour of the day, day of the week, or week of the year. Water consumption demand increases in the daytime and decreases at night. Besides the user demands on the system, leakage from the water mains must also be taken into consideration. Therefore, the normal operating pressure must be high enough to overcome the demand upon the system.

The fourth type of pressure, **flow pressure**, is defined as *the forward velocity or force at a discharge opening*. During fire flow tests, you will measure this forward flow pressure by use of a **pitot tube** and a **pressure gauge**. The blade of the pitot tube is inserted into the stream of water and the pressure shown on the gauge is recorded.

Fire Flow Test Procedure

To conduct a flow test, you must choose two hydrants immediately adjacent to each other. Hydrant 1 will be the "static hydrant" and hydrant 2 will be the "flow hydrant."

Static pressure reading

Begin by installing a cap that has been drilled and tapped to accept a pressure gauge on one of the butts of hydrant 1, **Figure 6-19**. Open this hydrant fully, and check for any leaks. If you find no leaks, look at the pressure gauge. Wait a minute or so to be certain that there is no fluctuation of pressure, then record the pressure showing on the gauge. This is the static pressure.

Flow pressure reading

Your partner should be at hydrant 2, and should have removed the cap from one of the butts of that hydrant. After you have recorded your static pressure, signal your partner to fully open hydrant 2. After waiting a

Figure 6-19. Hydrant set up with pressure gauge installed in specially drilled and tapped cap. This gauge is used to determine the static pressure and residual pressure in the water system. (Warren Lutton)

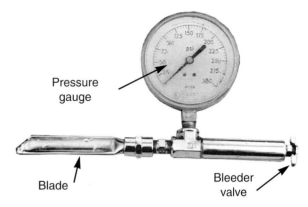

Figure 6-20. A traditional pitot tube. The blade is held in the stream of water and the pressure is read (in psi) from the gauge. The bleeder valve is used to drain trapped air from the pitot tube.

Figure 6-21. This water flow test kit attaches to a hydrant for greater convenience and accuracy when making pitot tube readings of flow pressure. The pitot tube and pressure gauge are mounted on top of the extension that attaches to a hydrant butt. (Western Fire Equipment Co.)

minute or so to allow air in the hydrant barrel to fully discharge, your partner can make a measurement. This can be done using a traditional pitot tube, **Figure 6-20,** or a flow test kit like the one shown in **Figure 6-21**. He or she should insert the small orifice of the pitot tube into the solid stream of water. The pitot tube should be held in the center of the opening and at a distance from the butt that is about half the diameter of the stream. This will help to reduce any turbulence caused by the water flowing out of the butt. While holding the pitot tube in the stream of water, he or she should slowly close the bleeder valve on the tube. This eliminates the air from inside the pitot tube. After the bleeder valve is closed, there will be a solid column of water inside the pitot tube. At this point, the pressure shown on the gauge of the pitot tube can be read.

By watching the gauge for a minute or so, the person making the reading should see slight variations in pressure. He or she should determine the *average* reading on the gauge and record this as the flow pressure.

Residual pressure reading

While your partner has been conducting the flow test, you are still standing at the static hydrant. As soon as hydrant 2 opened, you saw a drop in the pressure shown on your gauge at the static hydrant. This new pressure reading is the residual pressure. As long as hydrant 2 is flowing, you should maintain a relatively constant residual pressure. When your partner closes hydrant 2, your pressure gauge will rise to again show the static pressure.

You have now recorded three useful pieces of information; the static pressure and the residual pressure from hydrant 1, and the flow pressure from hydrant 2. Both hydrants, when shut down, should be checked to be certain that they are properly draining (if they are dry-barrel hydrants). Next, you must now inspect the butt that was used for the flow test on hydrant 2. This inspection is done to determine the *coefficient* that must be used to calculate the flow from this hydrant. **Figure 6-22** identifies the different flow coefficients, based upon the construction of the hydrants. Return the hydrants to service by threading the caps back on the butts. The

field portion of your fire flow test is now complete and you can return to quarters.

As you and your partner sit down to begin the calculations for this flow test, you realize that you have accumulated a number of pieces of information. You know the location of the flow test. You know the date and the time of the flow test. You know the static, residual, and the flow pressures that you recorded during the test. You know, from having examined the butt of the hydrant, the coefficient of flow for that hydrant. As you write down these pieces of information, you realize that one item is still missing: you don't know how much water, in gallons per minute (gpm) was flowing from the hydrant. The final step is to compute the gpm of flow for this test.

Calculating the flow in gpm

In order to compute the gallons per minute for the flow test, you must use this formula:

$$\text{gpm} = 29.83 \times C \times d^2 \times \sqrt{P}.$$

The number 29.83 is a constant derived from physics. "C" is the coefficient of discharge from the hydrant, and "d" is the

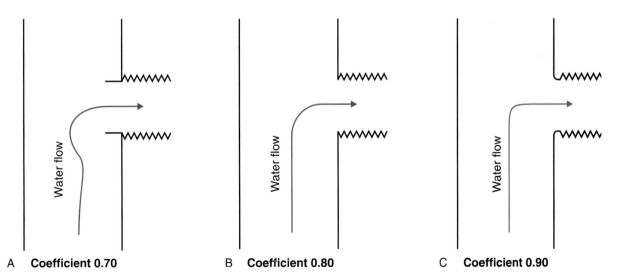

A   **Coefficient 0.70**   B   **Coefficient 0.80**   C   **Coefficient 0.90**

Figure 6-22. The way that the hydrant barrel and butt are joined affects the amount of turbulence in the water flow, and thus the coefficient that must be assigned when computing flow in gallons per minute. A—The butt extends into the barrel, causing considerable turbulence and an assigned coefficient of 0.70. B—Butt is flush with the barrel, resulting in small amount of turbulence and an assigned coefficient of 0.80. C—The butt-to-barrel joint is smoothed and rounded, creating little or no turbulence. The assigned coefficient is 0.90.

diameter of the hydrant butt in inches. "P" is the flow pressure in pounds per square inch that you recorded with your pitot tube.

Let's try a sample flow test, using this information:

Static pressure = 42 psi.
Residual pressure = 30 psi.
Flow pressure = 20 psi.

The coefficient of discharge for the hydrant = .90.

Applying the formula, we would have

$$gpm = 29.83 \times .90 \times 2.5^2 \times \sqrt{20}$$
$$29.83 \times .90 \times 6.25 \times 4.47 = 750.04 \ (750) \ gpm$$

A simpler method of calculating the result of a water flow test is to use one of the readily available charts that shows the gpm flow based upon the diameter of the opening and the flow pressure. There are also several computer programs available that will calculate the flow test results in a relatively short period of time. Possibly the simplest method is the use of a direct-reading flowmeter that provides a read-out of flow in gallons per minute, **Figure 6-23**.

Figure 6-23. This battery-powered portable electronic flowmeter uses a sensor placed in the stream of water and provides a direct digital readout of the water flow in gallons per minute.

SUMMARY

Water is the most commonly found compound on earth, covering about 75% of the earth's surface. Although water is usually abundant, an important concern in firefighting is to be sure that it is readily available at the scene of a fire.

The natural water cycle (hydrologic cycle) includes evaporation, condensation, and precipitation. Water is constantly being evaporated from the surface of the earth by the heat of the sun. The resulting lighter than air gas (water vapor) rises until it cools (condenses) back into a liquid form. The liquid then returns to the earth in the form of rain or snow (precipitation).

Water is an odorless and tasteless liquid. Under normal atmospheric pressure, it freezes at 32°F (0°C) and boils at 212°F (100°C). Water acts as a cooling agent, since it is able to absorb a reasonable amount of heat for the mass involved. The basic consideration in firefighting is that water must be applied at a sufficient rate to exceed the amount of heat generated by the fire. When the rate of application exceeds the heat generated, the fire can be extinguished. Some of the drawbacks of the use of water as an extinguishing agent are that it conducts electricity and is subject to freezing in colder temperatures. Also, water can react violently when in the presence of some chemicals.

Water can be moved by gravity, pumping, or a combination of the two. Modern water systems consist of pumping stations and elevated storage tanks to provide normal operating pressures for the distribution (water main) system. The placement of water mains and fire hydrants is designed to provide the fire service and the consumer with a reliable and adequate supply of water.

Fire hydrants are one of two types: dry-barrel or wet-barrel. Wet-barrel hydrants are constantly filled with water. Dry-barrel hydrants normally contain no water in the barrel. The basic components of a fire hydrant are the barrel, discharge openings (butts), an operating nut, an operating stem, and a valve. Most modern fire hydrants are also equipped with an auxiliary valve that can be shut off to perform maintenance on the hydrant without interrupting water service.

Fire departments should run fire flow tests on a regular basis. The results of these tests, over a period of time, form a history of the operating pressures and the flows for the community's water system.When reviewed regularly, test results can help point out problems that might occur with the water system.

Blockages, major leaks, and possibly closed or partially closed valves can be found through proper flow testing. Since water is the most commonly used extinguishing agent, firefighters need to feel confident that the water system available to them is both adequate and reliable.

REVIEW QUESTIONS

1. Describe the "hydrologic cycle." Why is it important to firefighters?
2. What are the three components of the hydrologic cycle?
3. Water can absorb large amounts of heat. How does this make water an effective tool for extinguishing fire?
4. Identify some situations in which you would *not* use water as an agent for firefighting.
5. Name the three methods used for moving water from the source of supply to a point where it is needed.
6. If water is stored in a tank that is 50 feet above the point of use, what pressure will be available at the point of use?
7. Describe what happens between the source and point of use in a water system that relies solely on pumps for pressure.
8. What tasks do the pumps perform in a combination system?
9. Why do backup pumps normally use a different power source than a system's primary pumps?
10. A community's water distribution system usually includes three different types of mains. Name them and describe how each is used.
11. Why should a water system have valves located at key points?
12. Most fire hydrants today include an auxiliary valve that is located between the hydrant and the supply main. What is the advantage of such a valve placement?
13. What are the two types of fire hydrants?
14. Describe what happens when a dry-barrel fire hydrant is turned on and when it is turned off.
15. What is the recommended spacing for fire hydrants in industrial and commercial districts?
16. What is the name used to identify a discharge port on a fire hydrant?
17. Explain the advantage of maintaining records of the flow tests performed on fire hydrants.
18. Name the three types of pressure that are measured when conducting a fire hydrant flow test.
19. In hydrant testing, what is a pitot tube used to measure?
20. How is the coefficient of flow determined?

NFPA 1001 Job Performance Requirements

The material on this page consists of those portions of the NFPA 1001 Job Performance Requirements relevant to the material presented in this chapter. Items preceded by the numeral 3 (3-x.x) are Fire Fighter I requirements; those with the numeral 4 (4-x.x) are Fire Fighter II requirements.

3-3.6 Attack a passenger vehicle fire operating as a member of a team, given personal protective equipment, attack line, and hand tools, so that hazards are avoided, leaking flammable liquids are identified and controlled, protection from flash fires is maintained, all vehicle compartments are overhauled, and the fire is extinguished.

(a) Prerequisite Knowledge: Principles of fire streams as they relate to fighting automobile fires; precautions to be followed when advancing hose lines toward an automobile; observable results that a fire stream has been properly applied; identifying alternative fuels and the hazards associated with them; dangerous conditions created during an automobile fire; common types of accidents or injuries related to fighting automobile fires and how to avoid them; how to access locked passenger, trunk, and engine compartments; and methods for overhauling an automobile.

(b) Prerequisite Skills: The ability to identify automobile fuel type; assess and control fuel leaks; open, close, and adjust the flow and pattern on nozzles; apply water for maximum effectiveness while maintaining flash fire protection; advance $1^1/2$ in. (38 mm) or larger diameter attack lines; and expose hidden fires by opening all automobile compartments.

3-3.7 Extinguish fires in exterior Class A materials, given fires in stacked or piled and small unattached structures or storage containers that can be fought from the exterior, attack lines, hand tools and master stream devices, and an assignment, so that exposures are protected, the spread of fire is stopped, collapse hazards are avoided, water application is effective, the fire is extinguished, and signs of the origin area(s) and arson are preserved.

(a) Prerequisite Knowledge: Types of attack lines and water streams appropriate for attacking stacked, piled materials and outdoor fires; dangers—such as collapse—associated with stacked and piled materials; various extinguishing agents and their effect on different material configurations; tools and methods to use in breaking up various types of materials; the difficulties related to complete extinguishment of stacked and piled materials; water application methods for exposure protection and fire extinguishment; dangers such as exposure to toxic or hazardous materials associated with storage building and container fires; obvious signs of origin and cause; and techniques for the preservation of fire cause evidence.

(b) Prerequisite Skills: The ability to recognize inherent hazards related to the material's configuration, operate hand lines or master streams, break up material using hand tools and water streams, evaluate for complete extinguishment, operate hose lines and other water application devices, evaluate and modify water application for maximum penetration, search for and expose hidden fires, assess patterns for origin determination, and evaluate for complete extinguishment.

3-3.9 Attack an interior structure fire operating as a member of a team, given an attack line, ladders when needed, personal protective equipment, tools, and an assignment, so that team integrity is maintained, the attack line is properly deployed for advancement, ladders are correctly placed when used, access is gained into the fire area, effective water application practices are used, the fire is approached safely, attack techniques facilitate suppression given the level of the fire, hidden fires are located and controlled, the correct body posture is maintained, hazards are avoided or managed, and the fire is brought under control.

(a) Prerequisite Knowledge: Principles of fire streams; types, design, operation, nozzle pressure effects, and flow capabilities of nozzles; precautions to be followed when advancing hose lines to a fire; observable results that a fire stream has been properly applied; dangerous building conditions created by fire; principles of exposure protection; potential long-term consequences of exposure to products of combustion; physical states of matter in which fuels are found; common types of accidents or injuries and their causes; and the application of each size and type of attack line, the role of the backup team in fire attack situations, attack and control techniques for grade level and above and below grade levels, and exposing hidden fires.

(b) Prerequisite Skills: The ability to prevent water hammers when shutting down nozzles; open, close, and adjust nozzle flow and patterns; apply water using direct, indirect, and combination attacks; advance charged and uncharged $1^1/2$ in. (38 mm) diameter or larger hose lines up ladders and up and down interior and exterior stairways; extend hose lines; replace burst hose sections; operate charged hose lines of $1^1/2$ in. (38 mm) diameter or larger while secured to a ground ladder; couple and uncouple various hand line connections; carry hose; attack fires at grade level and above and below grade levels; and locate and suppress interior wall and subfloor fires.

(Continued on page 150)

Reprinted with permission from NFPA 1001, *Fire Fighter Professional Qualifications,* Copyright ©1997, National Fire Protection Association, Quincy, MA 02269. This reprinted material is not the complete and official position of the National Fire Protection Association on the referenced subject, which is represented only by the standard in its entirety.

Fire Streams

7

OBJECTIVES

When you have completed this chapter, you will be able to:

- Define the term "fire stream" and discuss the different types of streams.
- Describe how to attack Class A and Class B fires with water.
- Demonstrate how to properly open and close a nozzle.
- Define water hammer and tell how to prevent it.
- Briefly trace the development of methods used to get water to a fire.
- Calculate pressure loss in a hose line due to friction or elevation losses.
- Describe the types and uses of foam and other water additives.

IMPORTANT TERMS

burst strength	elevation loss	hydraulics	monitors
constant pressure/	fire pump	impeller pump	nozzle reaction
variable gallonage	fire stream	kickback	solid stream
nozzle	fog stream	kinetic energy	water curtain
deflected stream	friction	master stream	water hammer
deluge set	head loss	momentum	

The advantages of water as a medium for extinguishing fires were discussed in Chapter 3, Fire Behavior. The three ways that water fights fire are *cooling, fuel removal,* and *oxygen removal.* Water cools efficiently because it absorbs a lot of heat when it is converted into steam. The rapid expansion of steam removes fuel by forcing flammable gases away from the fire. The steam further reduces the oxygen content below the level necessary for combustion.

To accomplish these ends, there obviously must be enough water, delivered to the right place, in the right form. The amount and form of water delivered to the fire — the fire stream — will be determined by what kind of fuel is burning, how much fuel there is, where the fire is located, and how close firefighters can get to the fire.

Elementary Firefighting Hydraulics

Hydraulics is the branch of science that deals with the effects of liquids in motion. As applied to firefighting, hydraulics can be described in its most elementary terms: *getting enough water, in the right form, to the fire.* Let's look at the elements of that description, one at a time.

Enough water: You could put out a small fire in a wastebasket with perhaps one cup of water. But for a fire in a warehouse, you might need thousands (even hundreds of thousands) of gallons of water.

In the right form: A fire in a confined area, where everything seems to be burning, will respond best to fog. But a deep-seated fire in an area containing bales of cardboard or other material would require a solid stream.

To the fire: All the water in the world in the perfect form won't do you a bit of good if you don't get it to the fire. Yet, there will often be difficulties: because of intense heat, you can't get in close, or the structure is not safe to enter, or the source of the water is far from the fire.

At one time, firefighters used a simple and direct means of getting the water to the fire: the *bucket brigade.* One person would dip a bucket into a pond or river, fill it with water, and hand it to another firefighter. This person would hand the filled bucket to the next one in line, and so on, until it reached the fire-fighter nearest the fire. That firefighter would throw the water on the fire, then pass the empty bucket back. Meanwhile more filled buckets were moving along the line from the water source to the fire. This system worked fairly well so long as there were plenty of fire-fighters and plenty of buckets.

Next, somebody got the idea of putting water under pressure and running it through pipes to distribute it throughout the city. The easiest way to do this was to dam a small stream on a hill above the city and use it as the source of supply. With this method, fire-fighters could obtain a pressure of about five pounds per square inch (5 psi) for each twelve feet of elevation above the city. Thus, with a hill 60 feet high, they could get about 25 psi coming out of a pipe down in the valley. This was enough to fight most fires. Unfortunately, some parts of town got considerably less than 25 psi and other places didn't get any water at all. The system was pretty uncertain. See **Figure 7-1.**

An obvious solution would be to build the dam on a higher hill, so there could be enough pressure for everybody. But there were some problems with this idea: a higher hill might not be available ... or it might not have a source of water. A better solution was needed.

It came in the form of a machine that would pick up the water and force it through a flexible pipe, or *hose.* This machine, called a

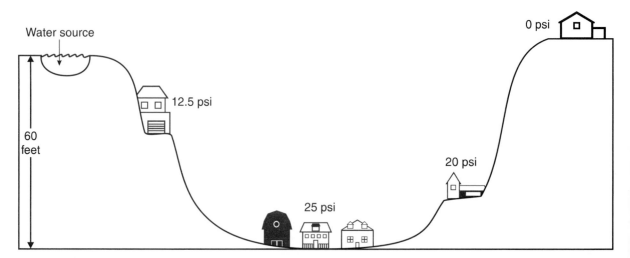

Figure 7-1. A gravity water supply system provides good pressure in some areas, but little or no water in others.

pump, allowed firefighters to use more reliable sources of water such as wells, rivers, and lakes. See **Figure 7-2**. By controlling the operation of the pump they could produce a *fire stream* that delivered as much or as little water as they wanted to the point where it was needed. Thus was born the fire pump, the fire hose, and the modern science of fire hydraulics. Not so simple and direct, perhaps, but more certain. And everybody was pretty happy with it (except, of course, the people who made buckets).

The Fire Stream

The term *fire stream* refers to the size, shape, and compactness that water takes as it leaves the nozzle and reaches its objective. The stream may be a narrow column of water that hits the target with a considerable force, or it may take the form of coarse drops, or a fine mist that will fill a room in a matter of seconds. The engineer and nozzle operator determine the form and force of the stream, the nozzle setting, and water pressure.

The principal reason for using water in fire suppression is its ability to absorb vast amounts of heat. See **Figure 7-3**. But water also has the capacity to destroy, so you must use water in such a way as to absorb the greatest amount of heat while causing the smallest amount of damage. You don't gain much if you use so much water that the building collapses from its weight or the entire contents are so waterlogged that they must be discarded.

Figure 7-3. Water can absorb huge quantities of heat, lowering the temperature of fuel below the point of combustion. In some forms, water also deprives the fire of the oxygen it needs to burn.

Whether caused by fire or by water, the destruction will be about the same.

Big fires require a lot of water to absorb a lot of heat. Small fires require much less water. Therefore, your first suppression priority, upon arrival on the fire scene, is to keep the fire from spreading. Your second, of course, is to extinguish the fire.

In general, you should apply water (especially fog or a broken stream) to the hottest part of the room. This is where the water will absorb the greatest amount of heat. Keep your nozzle moving. Water will put out whatever fire it hits in a very short time. There is no sense throwing more water on a fire once it's out.

Figure 7-2. The development of the hand-operated pump made possible a reliable source of water, at a usable pressure, for firefighting.

Types of Fire Streams

The firefighter has three kinds of fire streams available when using a hand-held nozzle: the solid stream, the deflected (broken) stream, or the fog (spray) stream. Each has its own uses, advantages, and disadvantages.

Solid stream

The *solid stream* is a solid column of water as it leaves the nozzle, **Figure 7-4**. The biggest advantage of the solid stream is that it will travel a long distance. This makes it very useful when the heat is so intense that you cannot get close to the fire. Further, a solid stream will penetrate deep into whatever it hits. This makes it useful for fighting fire in large piles of debris, in bales of cotton or rags, and in material that is stacked on shelves or pallets in stockrooms or warehouses. The disadvantages of the solid stream are that it will not absorb much heat in relation to the amount of water delivered, nor is it effective in dispersing smoke and gases.

A solid stream cannot be used to fight Class B (electrical) fires, since it will conduct electricity back to the nozzle operator.

Deflected stream

A *deflected stream* (sometimes called a "broken stream") is a solid stream that is bounced off a wall, ceiling, or other solid surface. See **Figure 7-5**. This breaks up the solid column of water into drops or a coarse spray, which is useful when the effects of a fog or spray are desired at a distance greater than a fog or spray pattern will travel. It is also useful in fighting fires you can't get at directly because of obstructions. While the deflected stream is not nearly as effective at heat absorption or smoke and gas dispersal as a fog pattern, it is the best alternative when you can't get close enough to the fire to use fog.

Fog or spray stream

In the *fog stream,* the water is broken up into drops as it leaves the nozzle, **Figure 7-6**. The drops may be coarse or fine, depending on nozzle type and setting. This stream provides the maximum heat absorption and the

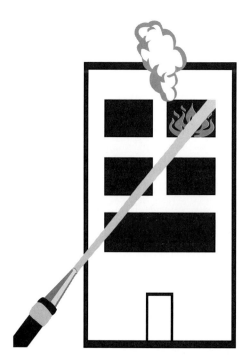

Figure 7-4. The solid stream has good carrying power and enough force to penetrate deep into the burning building. It is less effective than fog at absorbing heat, however.

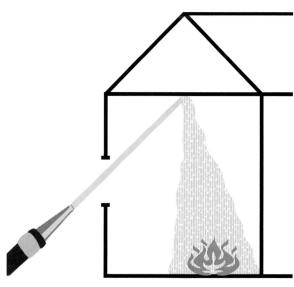

Figure 7-5. The deflected stream is a solid stream that is broken up into coarse drops by aiming it at a solid surface, such as a wall or ceiling. It provides some of the benefits of both solid stream and fog.

Figure 7-6. The fine drops of a fog stream quickly absorb heat and turn to steam, providing both cooling and a smothering action to fight the fire.

maximum gas and smoke dispersal. However, its range is limited — it just will not carry over any great distance.

The spray or fog pattern is the most effective stream to use in such situations as flammable liquid fires, interior fires with heavy smoke, chimney fires, fires in air-conditioning ducts, and widespread fires of low intensity (such as grass or underbrush). Since a fine spray is a poor conductor of electricity, you can also use this pattern to fight electrical fires.

Typical Nozzle Sizes and Pressures

For most inside fires, you will use nozzle sizes ranging from 1 in. to 1 1/4 in. and nozzle pressures of about 30 psi. When using 1 in. to 1 1/4 in. nozzles outside, nozzle pressure should be about 50 psi. With tips on outside lines greater than 1 1/4 in., you will need higher pressure, usually 60 to 80 psi. Most fog applications work best at 80 to 100 psi, although some fog guns operate in the range of 650 to 1000 psi. These latter are for use with high-pressure booster hose.

Fire Pumps

Getting "enough water, in the right form, to the fire" is made easier and more effective through use of a fire pump. Very basically, what a *fire pump* does is increase the distance that water can be moved from the source to the fire. Depending upon a number of circumstances, that distance may range from several hundred feet to more than a mile. The pump makes it possible to regulate the volume and pressure of the water available for firefighting.

Nearly all pumps used in the fire service are of the centrifugal (impeller) type, **Figure 7-7.** An *impeller pump* operates on the principles that

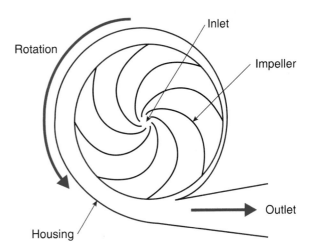

Figure 7-7. Operation of the centrifugal, or impeller, pump is fairly simple. Water enters at the center of the impeller and is forced outward along the rotating impeller blades. It exits from the outlet with the desired flow rate and pressure.

water does not compress and that water always takes the path of least resistance. As the impeller rotates inside the housing, it picks up water at the inlet and *impels* (throws) it toward the outlet. The faster the impeller goes around, the more water is moved toward the outlet.

Pump operation is not nearly as simple as just described, of course. For one thing, every pump seems to have its own little peculiarities. For another, pump efficiency can be affected by variables on the inlet side.

A pump is rated according to the number of gallons per minute (gpm) that it will discharge at a given pressure, measured at the pump outlet. In the United States, that pressure is usually stated in *pounds per square inch* (abbreviated psi); countries using the SI Metric system measure pressure in kilopascals (kPa). Most pump ratings are given at 150 psi. Thus, a pump with a rated capacity of 500 gpm means that it will pump 500 gallons per minute at a pressure of 150 psi. The most common ratings are 500, 750, 1000, 1250, and 1500 gpm (all, of course, at 150 psi).

Lightweight portable pumps, **Figure 7-8**, have many uses. A portable pump can be hand-carried into areas where a fire truck

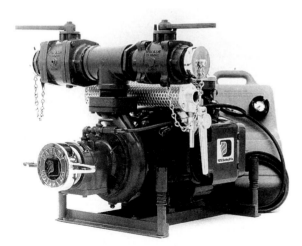

Figure 7-8. This high-volume portable pump weighs approximately 200 pounds, making it easy to move to any point where it is needed. The pump output is 460 gpm at a pressure of 25 psi. (W. S. Darley & Co.)

cannot go. It can be used to fill tankers. It can be used to pump out flooded basements. A portable pump can be left behind at a fire scene in case of a flare-up. A portable pump can do many of the jobs that would normally tie up an engine company's equipment. It can convert any pickup truck or four-wheel-drive vehicle into a highly mobile pumper.

Most fire pumps are equipped with a pressure relief valve to dissipate any large surge in pressure (as might occur if a hose line was shut down suddenly). The pressure relief valve operates to prevent damage to the pump and the hose lines still in operation.

The advantage of using a pump, even where you have good pressure from a hydrant, is *flexibility*. Water flow from a gravity system is pretty much fixed. With a pump system, you can get the amount of pressure and flow that is best suited for the job at hand, **Figure 7-9**.

Pressure Loss

In the discussion of pumps, it was noted that pumps are rated according to their output in gallons per minute at 150 psi. Once the water leaves the pump and starts flowing through a hose, however, it begins to lose pressure. There are two major types of pressure loss, *friction loss* and *elevation loss*. Other, smaller sources of loss can also affect pressure at the nozzle.

Friction loss

Ordinarily, you don't think of water as something that could create friction. In fact, if you have ever skidded on a wet road in an automobile, you would think just the opposite. But *friction* occurs anytime that two material surfaces rub against each other and kinetic energy is converted to heat energy. Even air causes friction — the brilliant streak of a "shooting star" is a falling meteorite heated to a white-hot temperature as it rubs against air molecules in the earth's atmosphere.

Similarly, when water moves through a hose, friction converts some of its *kinetic energy* (energy of motion) to heat energy. The

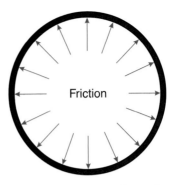

Figure 7-10. As water moves through a hose, it rubs against the inside surfaces of the hose and gives up some of its kinetic energy. The kinetic energy is converted to heat. This process results in lower pressure at the nozzle, and is called "friction loss."

Figure 7-9. Placing a pump between the water source and the nozzle allows you to get the needed amount of pressure and flow to accomplish a specific firefighting task. An engineer usually operates the pump controls on the fireground.

heat is quickly absorbed by the water. The energy conversion caused by friction results in a decrease in the energy that is available to push the water through the hose. This energy is measured in terms of pressure, with the decrease described as "friction loss." Friction loss is primarily due to the rubbing of water against the walls of the hose, **Figure 7-10**. Thus, the farther the water has to travel through a hose line, the greater the loss will be. There will be more loss through 600 feet of hose than through 400 feet.

In the same way, the more water that flows through a line in a given time, the greater the loss will be. There will be more pressure lost due to friction from a flow of 300 gpm than from a flow of 200 gpm. A third factor affecting friction loss is hose diameter. The smaller the inside diameter, the greater the percentage of total water flow that will

rub against the sides of the hose, and the greater the friction loss. See **Figure 7-11**.

Calculating friction loss

An inexpensive pocket calculator can help you find, in seconds, what pump pressure is needed to deliver a desired pressure at the nozzle. Many departments keep such useful items in the cab of each engine.

If a calculator isn't available or practical to use in a given situation, you can make a rough, rule-of-thumb calculation. This is done by first determining the pressure loss *per length of hose*. (For convenience, the calculations that follow are all based on 50-foot lengths of $2\frac{1}{2}$ in. hose.)

The loss is calculated by dividing the pump pressure by a number that consists of the number of lengths of hose used, plus a *friction loss fraction*. That fraction is obtained from the following table, which is based on nozzle size (the larger the nozzle size, the greater the water flow, and thus, the friction loss).

Nozzle Size	Friction Loss Fraction
1 in.	1/10
1 1/8 in.	1/6
1 1/4 in.	1/4
1 1/2 in.	1/2

Figure 7-11. Factors affecting friction loss. A—Length of hose. B—Water flow rate. C—Hose diameter. Note: Discharge patterns shown are illustrative, not actual.

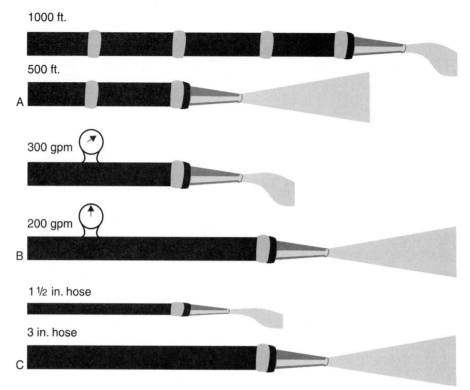

The formula used to determine pressure loss per length of hose:

FL per length = $\dfrac{\text{Pump pressure}}{\substack{\text{Lengths of hose} = \\ \text{denominator of friction loss fraction}}}$

This is easier to understand in the form of a problem. What is the friction loss in six lengths of $2\frac{1}{2}$ in. hose if the pump pressure is 200 psi and you are using a 1 in. tip?
PP (Pump pressure) = 200 psi
LH (Lengths of hose) = 6
FLF (Denominator of friction loss fraction) = 10
   Referring to the chart, the friction loss for a 1 in. tip is $\frac{1}{10}$. The denominator, or bottom part of the fraction, is 10.

$$FL = \frac{PP}{LH + FLF}$$
$$= \frac{200}{6 + 10}$$
$$= \frac{200}{16}$$
$$= 12.5 \text{ (FL per length of hose)}$$

To find the total friction loss, in psi, the result of the calculation is multiplied by the total number of hose lengths:
   Total friction loss: $12.5 \times 6 = 75$ psi

Elevation loss

Another cause of pressure loss is *elevation*, or the vertical distance the water must travel. Water has weight, and each foot in a column of water (such as a hose) presses downward with a pressure of .434 psi. So, for every foot that the nozzle is above the pump, you lose almost one-half psi of pressure. This downward pressure exerted by a fluid is called "head," and the resulting pressure loss is referred to as **head loss** or **elevation loss**.

If you assume 12 feet of vertical distance per story of a building, you can expect to lose 5 psi for each story that your hose is extended. Thus, if your nozzle is on the fifth floor (four stories above ground level), the pressure loss due to elevation will be 20 psi. See **Figure 7-12**.

To determine actual nozzle pressure, you must add together your friction loss and elevation (head) loss, then subtract that total from pump pressure.

Nozzle pressure = Pump pressure − (Friction loss + Head loss)

$$NP = PP - (FL + HL)$$

An example: PP = 200 psi
FL = 75 psi
HL = 20 psi
NP = 200 − (75 + 20)
   = 200 − 95
   = 105

Thus, the nozzle pressure is 105 psi.

Assume that you have a fog nozzle which works best at 95 psi, so the 105 psi in the preceding example is a little too much. Under the same conditions, what pump pressure will you need to get a nozzle pressure of 95 psi? This is not difficult to determine, since nozzle pressure is always *proportional* to pump pressure. No matter how many lengths of hose, no matter what the elevation, pump pressure and nozzle pressure are always proportional. If you raise pump pressure 15 % you will raise nozzle pressure 15 %, and vice versa.

The desired nozzle pressure of 95 psi is 10 psi lower than the 105 psi in the example. The difference amounts to approximately 10 %. Since nozzle pressure and pump pressure are proportional, you must decrease pump pressure by the same percentage. The pump pressure of 200 psi, lowered by 10 % (20 psi), will be 180 psi.

Other pressure losses

In addition to friction and elevation, several other factors can contribute to pressure loss. These factors are bends in the hose, internal roughness, and reduced diameter caused by fittings. See **Figure 7-13**.

Bends in the hose cause a pressure loss as the stream of water is forced to change direction. The sharper the bends, and the more numerous they are, the greater the pressure loss.

Roughness in the rubber lining of the hose will cause turbulent flow and decreased pressure. (Such rough spots can result from allowing vehicles to drive over uncharged hoses.)

Appliances or fittings that effectively *reduce the diameter of the line* will reduce pressure, as well.

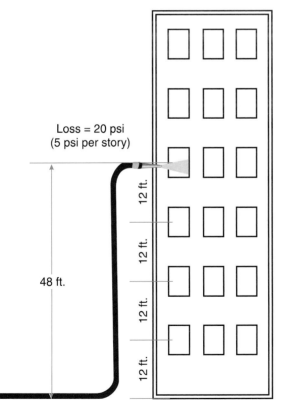

Loss = 20 psi
(5 psi per story)

48 ft.

12 ft.
12 ft.
12 ft.
12 ft.

Figure 7-12. Elevation loss is 5 psi for each building story (12 feet) that the nozzle is above the pump. Thus a hose stretched four floors (48 feet vertically) would lose 20 psi at the nozzle due to elevation alone.

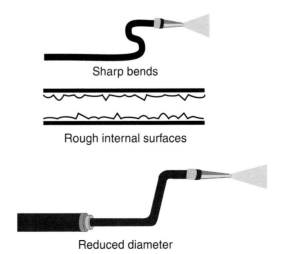

Sharp bends

Rough internal surfaces

Reduced diameter

Figure 7-13. Other causes of pressure loss include sharp bends in the hose, rough internal hose surfaces, and reduced hose diameter.

Losses from these factors are random and highly variable. They cannot be calculated.

Pressure problems in long lays

Getting sufficient nozzle pressure can be a serious problem when hose lays are long, especially when elevations are also involved. The obvious answer is to increase pump pressure as necessary. To a certain extent, this will work. But there is a limit: the *burst strength* of the hose.

Most fire hose is rated for use at either 400 psi or 600 psi. Since there is a fifty percent safety factor, this means that these hose are designed to withstand internal pressures of 600 psi and 900 psi, respectively. But these ratings are assigned when the hose is *new*. After being in use for a time and subjected to the abuse of actual fire service, hose can lose much of its burst strength. After long periods of use, hose rated at 400 psi should not be subjected to pressures of more than 250-300 psi. Remember, it takes only one weak spot to burst and put an entire long lay out of service.

When you must have greater pressure at the nozzle but cannot increase pump pressure because of hose burst strength, you have two alternatives. You can use a siamese to bring together two supply lines, or you can use a larger-diameter supply hose. Either will greatly reduce friction loss and improve pressure at the nozzle.

For example, when you connect two 2¹/₂ in. supply lines through a siamese, the friction loss will be only one-fourth that of a single 2¹/₂ in. line. In this situation, 120 psi will be reduced to 30 psi. See **Figure 7-14**. With *three* siamesed lines, the loss will be one-ninth of the loss encountered with a single line.

The second alternative is to increase the size of the line to reduce friction loss. Going from a 2¹/₂ in. to a 3 in. supply line will reduce friction loss by more than half.

Long lays of 2¹/₂ in. or 3 in. hose are heavy and hard to work with, especially when charged to higher pressures. Smaller, easier-to-use hose can be substituted, but at a high price

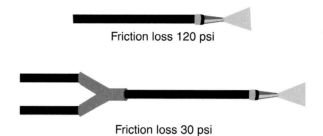

Friction loss 120 psi

Friction loss 30 psi

Figure 7-14. An example of reducing friction loss. A single 2¹/₂ in. line in a given situation might have a friction loss of 120 psi. By using a siamese to split the supply between two 2¹/₂ in. lines, the friction loss decreases dramatically, as shown.

in friction loss. Friction loss in a lay made with 1¹/₂ in. hose will be *13 times greater* than the same lay with 2¹/₂ in. hose, dramatically decreasing pressure available at the nozzle. A workable solution that is often used is to make most of the lay with 2¹/₂ in. hose, then use a reducing coupling and a smaller-diameter hose for the last two or three lengths. This will allow needed flexibility without excessive friction loss. See **Figure 7-15**.

Automatic nozzle

The whole matter of fire hydraulics has been greatly simplified by development of the so-called "automatic" nozzle. The nozzle, formally called a *constant pressure/variable gallonage nozzle*, is built to maintain a constant pressure of about 100 psi. The operator uses a throttle valve to achieve the flow (gallonage) desired, **Figure 7-16**.

With an automatic nozzle, the pump operator is limited only by the pump's maximum intake flow, the discharge pressure that the hose can safely handle, or the engine's maximum safe operating speed. Once any

100 ft. of 2 ¹/₂ in. hose   30 ft. of 1 ¹/₂ in. hose

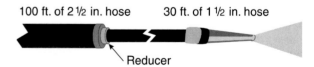

Reducer

Figure 7-15. Using large-diameter hose for most of a long lay, and smaller-diameter hose for the last two or three lengths will provide flexibility without friction loss becoming excessive.

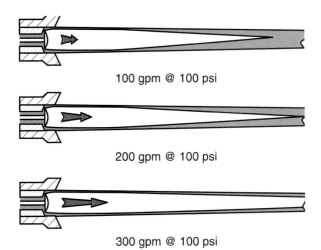

100 gpm @ 100 psi

200 gpm @ 100 psi

300 gpm @ 100 psi

Figure 7-16. An automatic nozzle will maintain a constant pressure as the operator increases or decreases the flow rate to meet changing conditions. (Task Force Tips, Inc.)

one of these pump limits is reached, the nozzle operator is in control. See **Figure 7-17**. There is no need to compensate at the pump for length of hose lay, elevation of the nozzle, or other pressure factors. The automatic nozzle compensates for all the variables between the pump and the nozzle.

Air aspirating nozzle

A recently introduced type of nozzle is the air aspirating nozzle, which mixes approximately nine gallons of air with each gallon of water, resulting in what its developers call a "micro bubble foam water stream." See **Figure 7-18**. The nozzle's patented design, according to its manufacturer, provides the heat-absorbing benefits of a wide angle fog while retaining the penetrating power and range of a straight stream. The nozzle also allows higher water flow rates at lower nozzle pressures with a 1 3/4 in. hose line, reducing the reaction pressure and allowing greater mobility.

Water Hammer

Water flowing through a line under pressure is a body in motion. It has *momentum*, or *kinetic energy*. To understand this, think of an

Figure 7-17. The operator controls flow from an automatic nozzle by pulling the throttle handle backward for full flow or pushing it forward to the "off" position. The flow can be smoothly adjusted to the desired level by moving the handle forward or backward an appropriate distance. (Akron Brass Co.)

automobile traveling down a road and suddenly coming to a stop as the driver jams on the brakes. The car will stop, but objects in the car, moving at the same speed as the car, will try to keep on going. Unless they are restrained (as passengers are with seat belts), these objects will collide with the inside surfaces of the car.

When the flow of water through a hose is cut off by a sudden closing of nozzle, the water will collide violently with the inside surfaces of the nozzle and hose. The shock of impact may be transmitted back to the pump and even the hydrant. The shock of the collision usually will be audible as a sharp clanking sound like a hammer striking a steel pipe. This is called *water hammer*. Since the violent collision of water with the nozzle, hose, and

Figure 7-18. The air-aspirating nozzle breaks up the stream of water into tiny droplets, much like a fog nozzle, but retains the benefits — range and penetrating power — of a straight stream.

other surfaces can burst a hose or seriously damage a pump, water hammer should be avoided. *Always* operate the nozzle shutoff valve slowly and smoothly to prevent this potentially damaging problem.

Using Fire Streams Effectively

Firefighters use five basic fire streams. Since your job is to extinguish the fire while doing the least amount of water damage, the streams are presented in order of those that use the least water to those that use the most. You should always choose the one that is the most effective in extinguishing fire, while using the least water. The basic streams, in order of increasing gallonage, are:

- Fog stream
- Deflected (broken) stream
- Solid stream
- Water curtain
- Master stream.

Most fire departments today use combination nozzles. These nozzles will produce a wide angle fog pattern which can be narrowed to a smaller angle, and further to a solid stream. This flexibility makes them very

useful for meeting changing conditions. See **Figure 7-19**.

Fog Stream

Many fog nozzles are of the constant gallonage type. This means that, regardless of

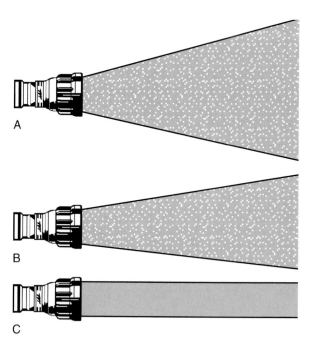

Figure 7-19. Combination nozzles provide varied streams. A—Wide-angle fog. B—Narrow-angle fog. C—Straight stream. (Task Force Tips)

the pattern, the nozzle will always produce the same number of gallons per minute, at any given nozzle pressure. Other nozzles offer variable gallonage, such as 10 to 30 gpm.

As noted earlier, the principal means by which water fights fire is through the absorption of heat. Heat is absorbed through the surface of the water, so the more water surface you can expose to heat, the more heat will be absorbed. Breaking a solid stream into fine drops provides perhaps hundreds of times more surface area than in the original stream. See **Figure 7-20**.

When these fine drops of water absorb sufficient heat, they turn into steam. Under conditions of intense heat, such as you will find in an interior fire, the steam will expand rapidly and try to escape from this confined area. In doing so, it will carry with it a great deal of heat, as well as flammable gases. This is good, since it helps extinguish the fire. But it is also dangerous. For example, if you are positioned in an open doorway, and it is the only escape route for the steam, you can be severely burned. The efficiency of a fog stream in absorbing heat, as noted, makes it both an effective firefighting tool *and* a danger to the firefighter. It must be used with care.

Applying fog

Fog application may be either specific or general. With specific application, you aim the fog nozzle directly at the base of the fire itself or to the place where the heat and smoke are the greatest.

In the latter application, you will most likely aim the nozzle high. If the fire is in a vat of flammable liquid, use a long applicator and direct fog downward to blanket the top of the vat.

You will encounter instances where the fire is too intense, or for other reasons, it is not safe to enter the fire area. If the building has not been ventilated, a *general* fog application might work very well.

This application takes advantage of water's ability to expand tremendously when it turns to steam: one gallon of water (liquid) occupies 0.13 cubic feet of space; as a vapor (steam), it fills a volume of 223 cubic feet. See **Figure 7-21**. When it is turned completely to steam, one gallon of water will absorb about 8100 Btus of heat. Put another way, one gallon of water turned to steam will absorb nearly

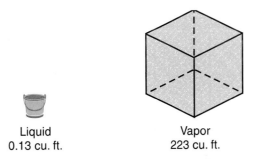

Liquid
0.13 cu. ft.

Vapor
223 cu. ft.

Figure 7-21. Water expands dramatically when it changes state from liquid to gas. One gallon of water, as a liquid, occupies only 0.13 cu. ft. of space. That same gallon, turned to water vapor (steam) has a volume of 223 cu. ft. Drawing is not to scale.

Figure 7-20. Breaking a solid stream into a fog stream of fine drops increases the heat-absorbing surface area by hundreds of times.

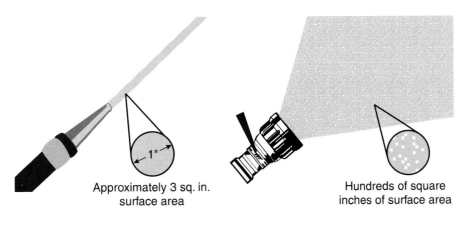

Approximately 3 sq. in. surface area

Hundreds of square inches of surface area

all of the heat produced by burning one pound of wood.

A general fog application is effective only until the building has been ventilated, since it depends upon the cooling and smothering effect of the steam in a confined area. Apply the fog through a small opening, such as a window, aiming toward the ceiling, and keep the nozzle moving in a circular pattern. Stay low, since hot gases will escape through the upper section of the opening. See **Figure 7-22**. Inside the room, steam will form, filling and cooling the airspace and helping to exclude the oxygen that the fire needs to burn. Many fires are extinguished in this way, with little follow-up action needed.

In addition to the types of fires already mentioned, fog is effective in extinguishing widespread, low-intensity fires in grass and

Figure 7-22. When applying fog through a small opening into a confined area, stay low. Hot gases will pour out through the upper portion of the opening.

underbrush, as well as fires in confined spaces such as chimneys, air-conditioning ducts, and chimneys. Fog can also be used as a water curtain to shield a building or object from heat, or to absorb toxic fumes. As fog becomes even more widely used, new applications and techniques will continue to emerge.

The effects of fog

When a fog stream is applied properly, these effects will be immediately apparent:

- A reduction in flame and flame spread.
- A much cooler temperature.
- A clearing of smoke and flammable vapors.

You should see these changes within a short time — 10 to 30 seconds. Remember that the key to extinguishing a fire is to provide enough water, and deliver it to the right place, in the right form. If you do not see dramatic improvement after a 10- to 30-second burst, you might not be getting the water to the *right place* (the source of the fire). Reposition your line and try another burst of fog.

If there is still no improvement, the water may not be in the *right form*. Possibly the fog is not penetrating, and you will have to change to a solid stream. You may need to use an additive, such as "wet water" or foam. In some instances, the best extinguishing agent might not be water — dry chemical might do a better job.

If a 10- to 30-second burst of the chosen stream with the right additive doesn't work, then you may not be getting *enough water* on the fire. Call for additional lines or larger lines.

The old method of just standing around pouring water onto one spot isn't done anymore. The modern approach is the *blitz attack*: hit and move, hit and move, continually changing position and tactics as needed to find the right combination.

Using fog safely

- Be sure the hot steam and gases have an escape route other than the place where you are standing. Usually this means the building must be properly ventilated.

- Wear full protective clothing, including breathing apparatus, **Figure 7-23**. If you are inside a room, the steam and hot gases can be forced around the stream and burn you.

- Keep low, but hold the nozzle high and keep rotating it.

- Start with a wide fog pattern, then narrow it as the smoke and fire diminish. The wide pattern will help protect you from the heat.

- Be sure no one is standing opposite you when you use fog. Standing opposite a fog stream can result in burns as steam is pushed toward the person.

- Fog is not a good conductor of electricity, but a solid stream *is*. To protect yourself from shock, always assume that any electrical equipment is charged. If electricity is likely to be encountered, a "fog only" nozzle is preferred. See **Figure 7-24**. It cannot accidentally be switched to an electrically conductive solid stream. If only a combination nozzle is available, make sure that it is on the fog setting and remains there.

Deflected (Broken) Stream

A fog stream has great heat-absorbing capacity, but will not travel far once it leaves the nozzle. A solid stream carries water long distances, but absorbs heat far less readily. The deflected stream is a compromise: it carries farther than fog and offers better heat absorption than a solid stream.

The deflected stream is a solid stream that is bounced off a wall, ceiling or other surface so that it breaks into drops. No special equipment is needed to produce this stream. All you need is a solid stream and a surface to deflect it.

Figure 7-23. Full protective clothing is a must, especially when using fog in an enclosed area. Encapsulating suits like these can protect you, for a limited time, from temperatures as high as 2000°F (1093°C). They also protect against the effects of many, but not all, dangerous chemicals. (Fyrepel Products, Inc.)

Figure 7-24. A "fog only" nozzle can produce a variety of fog patterns, but not a solid stream. This feature provides some protection against shock in situations where electrical equipment may be "live." (Elkhart Brass Mfg. Co.)

Since deflecting does not produce a spray as fine as that of a fog nozzle, the heat-absorbing properties of this stream are not as great. It will take more water to absorb the same amount of heat, but you can get the water to the source of the fire more effectively.

When you cannot get close enough to the fire to use fog, the deflected stream is often your best attack. Keep your nozzle moving in a pattern that produces the kind of coverage you need. If you are deflecting off a ceiling, a side-to-side, back-and-forth, or circular play might be used effectively. See **Figure 7-25**. Off a wall, an up-and-down play might be best. The situation will dictate which kind of pattern you will use.

Solid Stream

Some kinds of fires cannot be extinguished by either fog or deflected streams. Fires among materials on pallets or in bales, or any type of deep-seated fire, must be fought with a stream that can penetrate deeply. In these situations, the water must be under considerable pressure and delivered in a powerful solid stream. The solid stream has the force and penetrating power that neither the fog nor the deflected stream can provide. See **Figure 7-26**.

When you use a solid stream, however, you need a lot more water to provide a cooling effect equal to the other types of streams. The larger amount of water, however, means the possibility of greater water damage and even building collapse from its accumulated weight.

With any stream, but especially with a solid stream, it is important to keep your nozzle in motion. Otherwise, you will find that you are throwing far more water on one spot than is necessary. What you are after is maximum coverage with the least amount of water.

The force of the solid stream can affect disposition of firefighting personnel: a $1\frac{1}{2}$ in. line with a nozzle pressure of 50 psi is generally the maximum an individual firefighter can safely handle.

Water Curtain

Strictly speaking, a *water curtain* is used to prevent the spread of fire, rather than to actively extinguish it. Typically, a water curtain is set up between two buildings to absorb radiated heat and prevent the spread of fire from one to the other.

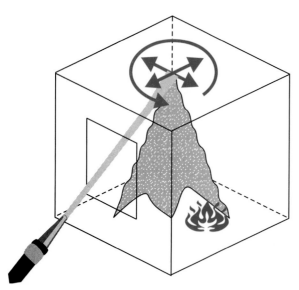

Figure 7-25. When deflecting a stream off a ceiling, one pattern of movement or a combination of patterns can be used. Typical patterns are circular, side-to-side, and back-and-forth.

Figure 7-26. A solid stream provides the force and penetrating power needed for deep-seated fires. (Jon Smith)

In warehouses, permanent water curtains may be installed as part of a sprinkler system. They are located between sections of the building in the same way that fire doors might be used.

A water curtain may be formed in a number of ways. Nozzles made specifically for this purpose produce a fan-shaped stream that may reach a width of 35 feet. See **Figure 7-27**. A coarse fog from a normal fog nozzle acts as a fairly efficient curtain, so does a deflected stream. If large distances are involved, such as in an industrial fire, two solid streams can be used from opposite directions. When they collide in the middle, they will break up against each other, forming a water curtain. The streams may be from hand-held lines or master streams.

Master Stream

A *master stream* is one that is too large to hold and control by hand. As pressure and flow of a hose stream increase, the *kickback* (force exerted in the opposite direction) also increases. Kickback, or *nozzle reaction*, can be calculated by using this formula:

Nozzle Reaction = 1.5 x Nozzle Pressure x Tip Diameter^2

$$NR = 1.5 \times NP \times D^2$$

With a master stream, you will normally use a 1 1/4 in. to 1 3/4 in. tip and a nozzle pressure of about 80 psi (sometimes higher). Using the formula just given and assuming a 1 1/2 in. tip and a nozzle pressure of 80 psi, we can calculate the kickback pressure:

$$NP = 1.5 \times 80 \times (1\ 1/2^2)$$
$$= 1.5 \times 80 \times 2.25$$
$$= 270 \text{ psi}$$

This means that the water leaving the nozzle is exerting a *backward* force of 270 psi. This is obviously too much pressure for one firefighter to hold, much less control for any length of time. Any stream with a waterflow of 350 gpm or higher is considered a master stream, but many master streams have flow rates of 500 to 1000 gpm.

Because of the great forces and flow rates involved, master stream nozzles must be anchored in some way. Frequently, they are permanently mounted on the apparatus body as "deck guns" or *monitors*, **Figure 7-28**. Because it is permanently mounted, a deck

A

B

Figure 7-27. Water curtain nozzle. A—The water curtain may be used to prevent the spread of fire to an adjacent structure by absorbing radiated heat. (Jack Klasey) B—A slot-type orifice on the nozzle produces a fan-shaped spray of water. The end cap can be removed to connect additional hose lengths and water curtain nozzles. (Elkhart Brass Mfg. Co.)

Figure 7-28. A deck gun or monitor, like the one permanently mounted on this apparatus body, can be used to project a master stream with a flow rate as high as 1000 gpm. (W.S. Darley Co.)

Monitor

gun can operate unattended, freeing a firefighter for other duties. However, this can result in pouring more water on a spot than is needed. Also, deck guns are not very maneuverable. Some are equipped with remote controls, greatly increasing their effectiveness.

Some master stream devices are designed for portability. They may be separate units, or deck guns that can be dismounted. Portable master stream devices, **Figure 7-29**, are usually referred to by the term *deluge set*. They are held in place by their own weight and the backward force exerted by the stream. They should never be left unattended unless lashed to something solid. If they get out of control, they can do considerable damage.

On nearly all aerial ladder and aerial platform apparatus, a standpipe leads to a nozzle at the top of the ladder or the platform. Since it is nearly impossible to get good penetration above the fourth floor of a building from lines at ground level, aerial capability is a necessity for most urban fire departments.

A deluge set used on an aerial ladder, **Figure 7-30**, might deliver 750 gpm at 100 psi using a 2 1/2 in. tip. This produces a kickback of almost 950 psi. Because such high pressures and high volumes of water are involved, improper use of deluge equipment can cause damage to the ladder or platform, or to the elevating mechanism. Before attempting to use any piece of equipment of

this type, be sure you understand completely the manufacturer's instructions.

Foam

Many kinds of foam concentrates, foam proportioning systems, and foam delivery

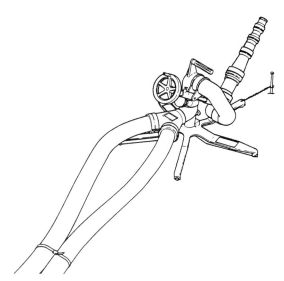

Figure 7-29. A lightweight portable deluge set. This device can be dismounted from the apparatus and placed on the base shown for forward positioning. The deluge set should be anchored before it is charged, to prevent unexpected backward movement. Note the *stacked tips*, ranging from smaller to larger diameter. They can be removed to allow achieving the desired nozzle opening quickly and easily.

Figure 7-30. A ladder pipe can direct a master stream down into the fire from above, with water-flows as high as 750 gpm.

systems are available. The subject of foam and its uses is discussed in detail in Chapter 8.

Other Additives

In addition to foam, there are other agents that can be added to water, although none is as widely used as foam. One prevents water from turning to steam, keeping it a mist of fine liquid particles, for a greater cooling effect. A lubricant can be added to make water "slippery," allowing an increase in pump pressure and reducing friction pressure loss. Another makes water "wetter." Chemically similar to household detergents, this additive breaks down surface tension so that water can penetrate fuel deeper and faster.

SUMMARY

The term "fire stream" refers to the size, shape, and compactness of the stream of water as it leaves the nozzle and reaches the target. With a hand-held nozzle the stream may be solid, broken, or a fog or spray.

Fire hydraulics is the science of getting enough water, in the right form, to the fire. A fire pump increases the distance the water will travel from its source to the nozzle and from the nozzle to the fire. Pumps are rated in terms of gallons per minute discharge at 150 psi. Nozzle pressure is always lower than pump pressure, because some pressure is lost due to friction, elevation, and bends and roughness in the hose. Nozzle pressure is always proportional to pump pressure. To raise or lower nozzle pressure by any given percentage, you must raise or lower pump pressure by the same percentage.

One of the principal advantages of water in fighting fire is by its ability to absorb heat. For this reason, water should be used in a form that will absorb the greatest amount of heat. At the same time, the stream should inflict the least amount of water damage. A fog stream will absorb the greatest amount of heat with the least amount of water damage. A deflected stream breaks a solid stream into small drops that have fairly good heat-absorbing qualities. A solid stream is less heat-absorbing than the first two, but has better carrying and penetrating power. A water curtain is used between buildings to prevent the spread of fire. A master stream is any stream that is too big to hand-hold safely (usually 500 gpm and up).

Additives (other than foam) increase the cooling effect of water, make it slippery, or break down surface tension so that it penetrates better.

REVIEW QUESTIONS

1. Define the term "fire stream."
2. Describe the following streams: solid, deflected, fog, spray.
3. What are the advantages and disadvantages of each of the streams?
4. Which type of fire stream would you most likely use in each of the following situations?
   - a pile of burning mattresses.
   - a fire in a grease duct.
   - a gasoline fire.
   - a grass fire.
   - a room that is fully involved.
   - a hot, smoky fire in a basement.
   - a fire behind a steel partition with only a small access at the top.
5. How can you prevent water hammer?
6. In firefighting terms, what does "hydraulics" mean?
7. What advantages does a fire pump have over a gravity water supply system?
8. What are the most common fire pump ratings? At what pressures are they usually rated?
9. What conditions cause pressure loss in a hose line?
10. What factors affect friction pressure loss?
11. If a pump is producing 225 psi to nine lengths of $2^1/2$ in. hose and you have a $1^1/8$ in. tip, what will your TOTAL friction loss be? What will be the total pressure loss if the nozzle is three floors above the pump?
12. What nozzle pressure do you need when using a standard fog stream inside a residence?
13. Name the five basic fire streams the firefighter can use, depending on the situation.
14. What safety precautions should you observe when using a fog stream indoors?
15. Explain the difference between a specific and a general application of fog.
16. What range of water pressures is usually used to produce an effective fog stream?
17. Describe a deflected stream and how it is used.
18. Under what conditions would you use a solid stream?
19. When using a 1 in. nozzle and a nozzle pressure of 30 psi, what is the amount of kickback?
20. What is the purpose of a water curtain? How is it made?

(Continued from page 130)

(3-3.12)

(b) Prerequisite Skills: The ability to deploy and operate an attack line; remove flooring, ceiling, and wall components to expose void spaces without compromising structural integrity; apply water for maximum effectiveness; expose and extinguish hidden fires in walls, ceilings, and subfloor spaces; recognize and preserve obvious signs of area of origin and arson; and evaluate for complete extinguishment.

3-3.18 Combat a ground cover fire operating as a member of a team, given protective clothing, SCBA if needed, hose lines, extinguishers or hand tools, and an assignment, so that threats to property are reported, threats to personal safety are recognized, retreat is quickly accomplished when warranted, and the assignment is completed.

(a) Prerequisite Knowledge: Types of ground cover fires, parts of ground cover fires, methods to contain or suppress, and safety principles and practices.

(b) Prerequisite Skills: The ability to determine exposure threats based on fire spread potential, protect exposures, construct a fire line or extinguish with hand tools, maintain integrity of established fire lines, and suppress ground cover fires using water.

3-5.4 Clean, inspect, and return fire hose to service, given washing equipment, water, detergent, tools, and replacement gaskets, so that damage is noted and corrected, the hose is clean, and the equipment is placed in a ready state for service.

(a) Prerequisite Knowledge: Departmental procedures for noting a defective hose and removing it from service, cleaning methods, and hose rolls and loads.

(b) Prerequisite Skills: The ability to clean different types of hose; operate hose washing and drying equipment; mark defective hose; and replace coupling gaskets, roll hose, and reload hose.

4-3.1 Extinguish an ignitable liquid fire, operating as a member of a team, given an assignment, an attack line, personal protective equipment, a foam proportioning device, a nozzle, foam concentrates, and a water supply, so that the proper type of foam concentrate is selected for the given fuel and conditions, a properly proportioned foam stream is applied to the surface of the fuel to create and maintain a foam blanket, fire is extinguished, reignition is prevented, team protection is maintained with a foam stream, and the hazard is faced until retreat to safe haven is reached.

(a) Prerequisite Knowledge: Methods by which foam prevents or controls a hazard; principles by which foam is generated; causes for poor foam generation and corrective measures; difference between hydrocarbon and polar solvent fuels and the concentrates that work on each; the characteristics, uses, and limitations of fire-fighting foams; the advantages and disadvantages of using fog nozzles versus foam nozzles for foam application; foam stream application techniques; hazards associated with foam usage; and methods to reduce or avoid hazards.

(b) Prerequisite Skills: The ability to prepare a foam concentrate supply for use, assemble foam stream components, master various foam application techniques, and approach and retreat from spills as part of a coordinated team.

4-3.2 Coordinate an interior attack line team's accomplishment of an assignment in a structure fire, given attack lines, personnel, personal protective equipment, and tools, so that crew integrity is established; attack techniques are selected for the given level of the fire (for example, attic, grade level, upper levels, or basement); attack techniques are communicated to the attack teams; constant team coordination is maintained; fire growth and development is continuously evaluated; search, rescue, and ventilation requirements are communicated or managed; hazards are reported to the attack teams; and incident command is apprised of changing conditions.

(a) Prerequisite Knowledge: Selection of the proper nozzle and hose for fire attack given different fire situations; selection of adapters and appliances to be used for specific fire ground situations; dangerous building conditions created by fire and fire suppression activities; indicators of building collapse; the effects of fire and fire suppres-

sion activities on wood, masonry (brick, block, stone), cast iron, steel, reinforced concrete, gypsum wall board, glass, and plaster on lath; search and rescue and ventilation procedures; indicators of structural instability; suppression approaches and practices for various types of structural fires; and the association between specific tools and special forcible entry needs.

(b) Prerequisite Skills: The ability to assemble a team, choose attack techniques for various levels of a fire (e.g., attic, grade level, upper levels, or basement), evaluate and forecast a fire's growth and development, select proper tools for forcible entry, incorporate search and rescue procedures and ventilation procedures in the completion of the attack team efforts, and determine developing hazardous building or fire conditions.

4-3.3 Control a flammable gas cylinder fire operating as a member of a team, given an assignment, a cylinder outside of a structure, an attack line, personal protective equipment, and tools, so that crew integrity is maintained, contents are identified, safe havens are identified prior to advancing, open valves are closed, flames are not extinguished unless the leaking gas is eliminated, the cylinder is cooled, cylinder integrity is evaluated, hazardous conditions are recognized and acted upon, and the cylinder is faced during approach and retreat.

(a) Prerequisite Knowledge: Characteristics of pressurized flammable gases, elements of a gas cylinder, effects of heat and pressure on closed cylinders, boiling liquid expanding vapor explosion (BLEVE) signs and effects, methods for identifying contents, how to identify safe havens before approaching flammable gas cylinder fires, water stream suage and demands for pressurized cylinder fires, what to do if the fire is prematurely extinguished, valve types and their operation, alternative actions related to various hazards and when to retreat.

(b) Prerequisite Skills: The ability to execute effective advances and retreats, apply various techniques for water application, assess cylinder integrity and changing cylinder conditions, operate control valves, choose effective procedures when conditions change.

4-5.3 Perform an annual service test on fire hose, given a pump, a marking device, pressure gauges, a timer, record sheets, and related equipment, so that procedures are followed, the condition of the hose is evaluated, any damaged hose is removed from service, and the results are recorded.

(a) Prerequisite Knowledge: Procedures for safely conducting hose service testing, indicators that dictate any hose be removed from service, and recording procedures for hose test results.

(b) Prerequisite Skills: The ability to operate hose testing equipment and nozzles and to record results.

NFPA 1001 Job Performance Requirements

The material on this page consists of those portions of the NFPA 1001 Job Performance Requirements relevant to the material presented in this chapter. Items preceded by the numeral 3 (3-x.x) are Fire Fighter I requirements; those with the numeral 4 (4-x.x) are Fire Fighter II requirements.

4-3.1 Extinguish an ignitable liquid fire, operating as a member of a team, given an assignment, an attack line, personal protective equipment, a foam proportioning device, a nozzle, foam concentrates, and a water supply, so that the proper type of foam concentrate is selected for the given fuel and conditions, a properly proportioned foam stream is applied to the surface of the fuel to create and maintain a foam blanket, fire is extinguished, reignition is prevented, team protection is maintained with a foam stream, and the hazard is faced until retreat to safe haven is reached.

(a) Prerequisite Knowledge: Methods by which foam prevents or controls a hazard; principles by which foam is generated; causes for poor foam generation and corrective measures; difference between hydrocarbon and polar solvent fuels and the concentrates that work on each; the characteristics, uses, and limitations of fire-fighting foams; the advantages and disadvantages of using fog nozzles versus foam nozzles for foam application; foam stream application techniques; hazards associated with foam usage; and methods to reduce or avoid hazards.

(b) Prerequisite Skills: The ability to prepare a foam concentrate supply for use, assemble foam stream components, master various foam application techniques, and approach and retreat from spills as part of a coordinated team.

Reprinted with permission from NFPA 1001, *Fire Fighter Professional Qualifications,* Copyright ©1997, National Fire Protection Association, Quincy, MA 02269. This reprinted material is not the complete and official position of the National Fire Protection Association on the referenced subject, which is represented only by the standard in its entirety.

Foam Fire Streams

OBJECTIVES

When you have completed this chapter, you will be able to:

🔥 Describe how foam fire streams control fires and help to prevent or control other hazards.

🔥 Explain how foam is generated and how foam fire streams are formed.

🔥 Explain the difference between hydrocarbons and polar solvents; identify the type of foam to be used on each.

🔥 Describe how foam works and the advantages it provides over plain water as an extinguishing agent.

🔥 Describe the safety precautions and environmental questions that must be taken into account during foam storage, mixing, and application.

🔥 List the causes of poor foam generation and the procedures to be used in correcting problems.

IMPORTANT TERMS

aqueous film	cryogenic	food chain	nonaspirating nozzles
aqueous film-forming foam (AFFF)	density	hazardous vapor	omnivores
	drain time	mitigating foam	polar solvents
aspirating nozzle	dry foam	herbivores	polymer
biodegradable	eductor	high-expansion foams	protein foaming agents
burnback	expansion	hydrocarbons	surfactant
carnivores	expansion ratio	lofted	vapors
Class A foams	fluid foam	low-expansion foams	wet foam
Class B foams	foam solution	medium-expansion foams	wildlands

A favorite children's toy is the bubble kit. It consists of a wire or plastic wand with loop at each end and a bottle of bubble solution. To use the kit, you grasp the wand by the end with the smaller of the two loops, then dip the larger loop into the bubble solution. After removing the wand from the solution, you can form bubbles by blowing into the loop or by waving the wand through the air. See **Figure 8-1.**

The bubble solution consists of water and a foaming concentrate that forms a thin film across the loop of the wand. When you wave the wand through the air or blow into it, the film is forced outward by air pressure. The film encloses a quantity of air and forms a

Figure 8-1. Bubble kits have long been a favorite toy of children. (R.M. Haluska)

bubble. Each bubble formed this way consists of a small amount of water, an even tinier quantity of foaming concentrate, and a comparatively large amount of air. See **Figure 8-2.**

Firefighting foam is produced by using the same principle: a foaming concentrate is mixed with water to form a solution, then air is introduced to create bubbles. The type of foam that results is determined by:

- the type of concentrate used
- the strength of the solution (normally from 0.1% to 6.0% concentrate)
- the amount of air incorporated.

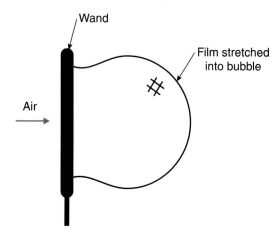

Figure 8-2. The bubble is the basic unit of foam. Whether made by a child with a bubble wand or a firefighter using an aerating nozzle, a bubble consists of small amounts of water and foam concentrate enclosing a volume of air.

Foam concentrates typically consist of three major components:

- a foaming agent that forms the bubbles
- a stabilizer that provides strength to the bubble skin
- a *surfactant* (wetting agent) that reduces the surface tension of the water, causing it to spread more rapidly and penetrate more deeply.

Foam Consistencies

Depending upon your needs, the foam you produce at the fire scene may range from a watery foam solution with practically no bubbles to a thick, dry mass of bubbles that will cling to a vertical surface. Of course, foam is also produced at all stages between these extremes. For convenience, foam is generally considered to be one of four *consistencies:*

Foam solution is a milky-looking fluid with few visible bubbles, **Figure 8-3.** Because of the surfactants it contains, the liquid is able to penetrate deep-seated fires. Since it is almost entirely water, it can be projected as a stream from a distance to reach the burning material.

Wet foam exhibits many more visible bubbles than foam solution, but still consists of far more water than air, **Figure 8-4.** The bubble size ranges widely from tiny to very large, and the foam lacks body. Like foam

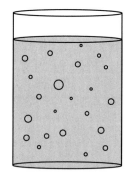

Figure 8-3. A foam solution is nearly all water, and shows few bubbles. Because of the surfactants it contains, however, it is much more effective than plain water.

Figure 8-4. The spherical bubbles of a wet foam trap relatively large quantities of foam solution. It has a fairly fast drain time, which means that it breaks down into water quickly.

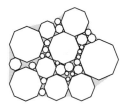

Figure 8-6. Dry foam bubbles are smaller and more tightly packed than those of other types of foam. Dry foam can be applied to inclined or even vertical surfaces. Since little liquid is present, this foam breaks down more slowly than other types.

solution, it has the ability to penetrate deep-seated fires. Wet foam has a fast *drain time,* which is the time required for the foam to break down from bubbles to a water solution.

Fluid foam has more body than wet foam, with a consistency somewhat like watery shaving cream, **Figure 8-5.** The bubble size in the foam ranges from medium to small, so it holds its shape better than wet foam. Fluid foam flows easily, and has a medium to fast drain time.

Dry foam is mostly air. It consists of small to medium bubbles, and resembles whipped cream or beaten egg whites, **Figure 8-6.** Like egg whites, it will hold a peak. Since it holds its shape well and has a slow drain time, dry foam forms a good insulating blanket. Since it will cling to vertical or overhanging surfaces and has a bright white color that reflects heat, it can be used to protect building sides (or even the underside of eaves).

Drain Time

As noted earlier, *drain time* (sometimes referred to as "drainage") is the rate at which

foam releases the solution from the bubbles. Drain time can also be defined as the effective life of the foam. Drain time of a foam affects how it will be used to fight a fire. A fast (short) drain time allows rapid wetting of the fuel by the released solution. A slow drain time means that the foam will remain longer in the form of an insulating and air-excluding blanket. The kind and location of the fire being fought will determine whether a foam with a fast or slow drain time is more suitable.

Expansion

Expansion is the increase in volume of the foam solution that results from the introduction of air. The most important factors affecting the expansion:

- the type of concentrate used
- the ratio of water to concentrate
- the age of the concentrate
- the method used to produce the foam.

Expansion ratio

A little concentrate can go a long way — if you start with a 1% solution at a 10:1 *expansion ratio* (a quite low rate), the foam that is produced would consist of 90% air, 9.9% water, and 0.1% foaming concentrate. With a 10:1 expansion ratio, each gallon of water-concentrate solution would result in 10 gallons of foam. Foam is sometimes described as "low-," "medium-," or "high-expansion," based on its expansion ratio. *Low-expansion foams* have expansion ratios lower than 20:1; *medium-expansion foams* have ratios rang-

Figure 8-5. Fluid foam has more and smaller bubbles than wet foam, so it will hold its shape better. It also breaks down more slowly.

ing from 20:1 to 200:1, and *high-expansion foams* have ratios above 200:1. Ratios as high as 1000:1 are possible.

Foam density

The expansion ratio also affects the density of the foam. *Density* is the weight per unit volume. Low-expansion foam, for example, contains relatively little air, so a given volume (for example, one cubic foot) would weigh more than an equal volume of a medium-expansion foam, which contains proportionally more air. See **Figure 8-7.** A heavier foam offers less wind resistance, and thus will travel better as a fire stream. On the other hand, a less dense foam will not travel as well, but will form a more efficient protective blanket. One of the important advantages of foam as a firefighting agent is the capability of tailoring it to fit the conditions at hand.

How Foam Works

There is nothing magical about foam. The part of the foam that does most of the work is the water. Converting the water to foam essentially improves its firefighting capability. Put simply, it makes the water work better. Here's what it does:

- Foam cools the fuel and the heat source. See **Figure 8-8.** As you've noticed, when a regular water stream is applied to a fire, most of it splashes or runs off almost immediately. Foam does not run off; it holds the water in place so it can absorb heat. As liquid water absorbs heat, it turns to steam. In addition, the wetting agent used in foam causes the water to assume the form of a thin film, which absorbs heat more easily. By absorbing radiant heat, the foam blanket helps to prevent rekindling, or *burnback.*

- Foam blankets the fuel source, excluding the oxygen needed to support combustion. See **Figure 8-9.**

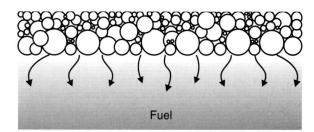

Figure 8-8. Unlike plain water, which quickly runs off, foam holds a blanket of moisture in contact with the fuel. The foam gradually releases liquid as it breaks down.

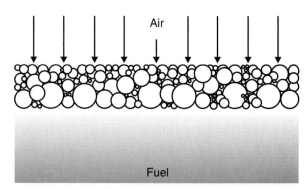

Figure 8-9. The blanket of foam forms a barrier on top of the fuel, "starving" it of the oxygen needed for continued combustion.

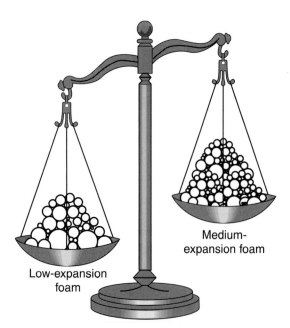

Figure 8-7. Since it contains a higher proportion of water to air, low-expansion foam weighs more than an equal volume of medium-expansion foam.

- The foam blanket suppresses the release of flammable vapors, **Figure 8-10.** This is why foam is often applied to gasoline spills, even though they are not burning. The foam holds back the vapors. It keeps them from reaching a fuel source and igniting.

- Foam separates flames from the fuel surface, cutting off the supply of combustible material.

Types of Foam

Foams are made to fight either Class A fires or Class B fires. As described in an earlier chapter, Class A fires are those involving ordinary solid combustibles, such as wood, paper, rubber, hay, textiles, and similar substances. Since Class A foams have excellent wetting properties, they are very effective on such fires. If there is a significant amount of melted plastic involved, however, a Class A foam would not be fully effective. *Class A foams* are made from hydrocarbon-based surfactants and detergents, and do not have the strong film-forming properties of a Class B foam. Class A foams will be discussed in greater detail later in this chapter.

Class B Foams

Class B foams are formulated to extinguish fires involving flammable liquids and

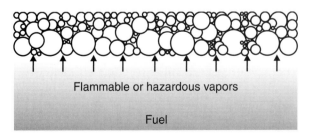

Figure 8-10. Just as it keeps oxygen from reaching the fuel, a blanket of foam forms a barrier to keep toxic or flammable vapors from escaping into the atmosphere.

gases, grease, and melted plastics. The majority of flammable liquids are *hydrocarbons,* compounds of the elements carbon and hydrogen in varying amounts. These organic compounds are not soluble in water. Common hydrocarbons are gasoline, benzene, and naphtha.

Polar solvents are a class of flammable liquids that must be treated separately. Since these substances (alcohols, ketones, esters, and aldehydes) are water-soluble, they will quickly break down most foams. Special foaming concentrates are made to fight fires involving polar solvents.

To cope with the different types of fuels and other factors involved in Class B fires, five types of foam concentrates are in general use. They are aqueous film-forming foams (AFFF), alcohol-resistant AFFF concentrate, protein foaming agents, fluoroprotein foam concentrates, and film-forming fluoroprotein concentrates.

Aqueous film-forming foams

These concentrates are synthetics based on varied combinations of fluorochemical and hydrocarbon surfactants and solvents. *Aqueous film-forming foam (AFFF)* concentrates produce a high quality foam with very little energy input. They produce foams which have low viscosity and are very fast-spreading. Such a foam will blanket the entire surface of a hydrocarbon fire, spreading an *aqueous film* (thin film of water) over the fuel to exclude oxygen and halt vaporization, **Figure 8-11.** Foams expanded from AFFF concentrates can be used on Class B fires and mixed Class A and Class B fires. Aqueous film-forming foams can be adapted to a large number of foam delivery systems, so they are in widespread use.

Alcohol-resistant AFFF concentrates

Since polar solvents cause standard foams to break down rapidly, they must be handled differently from other flammable liquids. Adding a *polymer* (substance with large molecules formed by the repeated linking of

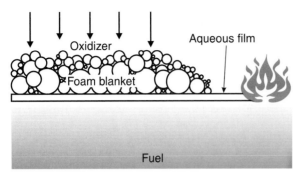

Figure 8-11. Aqueous Film-Forming Foam (AFFF) releases a thin film of water that rapidly spreads over the surface of the fuel. It excludes oxygen and traps fuel vapors. (Ansul Fire Protection)

smaller molecules) to AFFF concentrate provides a solution to the problem. Some polymers are found in nature, but most are synthetics under the general category of plastics. The synthetic polymer added to AFFF concentrate provides a film that will resist breaking down of the foam by the solvents. See **Figure 8-12.** Foams made from alcohol-resistant AFFF concentrates can be used on either hydrocarbon or polar solvent fires.

Protein foaming agents

The concentrates known as *protein foaming agents* are made from natural proteins found in animal byproducts (hooves, horns, feathers). The protein provides strength and elasticity to the bubbles in the foam developed from the concentrate. The

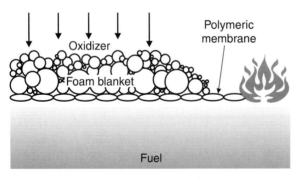

Figure 8-12. Alcohol-resistant foams generate a thin layer of polymeric (plastic) material over the surface of a polar solvent to prevent the solvent from breaking down the foam.
(Ansul Fire Protection)

foam is viscous, dense, stable, and shows good heat resistance. It retains water well and prevents burnback.

Fluoroprotein foam concentrates

These concentrates are similar to the protein foaming agents, but have fluorinated surface agents added to improve their resistance to contamination by fuels. This makes them suitable for fighting fires in situations where the foam must be plunged into the fuel rather than being spread gently on the burning fuel surface. They exhibit excellent vapor blocking and burnback prevention qualities.

Film-forming fluoroprotein concentrates

Similar in composition to the fluoroprotein foam concentrates, this group of foam-producing agents is designed to form an aqueous (water) film on the surface of a flammable liquid. They spread fast and level quickly to completely cover the surface. The main application for these foams is in firefighting at bulk storage and transportation facilities for hydrocarbon fuels.

Hazardous Vapor Mitigating Foam

Hazardous materials incidents do not occur strictly in areas with heavy concentrations of industrial plants — they can occur in the central business district of a city, in a residential neighborhood, in a rural area, even in a desert or on the ocean. Why? Because four out of five (80%) hazardous material spills occur during *transportation*. This means that any area where a truck, train, bus, barge, cargo ship, or airplane can operate is a potential HazMat site.

It has been estimated that approximately 40% of all firefighting foam is actually used for incidents that do not involve fire — most often, for spills of materials posing some hazard to life or property. Some experts contend that spills create more fire department activity than do fires. See **Figure 8-13.**

In many spills, the greatest danger is from the *vapors* (gases resulting from evaporation)

Figure 8-13. An estimated 40 percent of all foam used by fire departments is spread over spills of materials that are not burning, but are considered to be hazardous.

the hazardous materials give off. These vapors may be flammable, toxic, or corrosive (or a combination of these properties). Several methods are typically used to deal with such problems. They include:

- Covering the spill with an absorbent material. Sand is sometimes used, but materials especially manufactured for this purpose are more effective.
- Covering the spill with a sheet of plastic or other nonporous material. This sometimes works, but often is unworkable because the spill is too large. Also, vapors can still escape around the edge of the covering material. In some cases, the spilled material or its vapors will dissolve plastic.
- Covering the spill with foam. Standard firefighting foams are often effective on spills, since they both trap and absorb vapors. Also, since the foams release water, they dilute the material that is giving off the vapors. Foam can reduce hazardous vapor release into the atmosphere by 80% or more. Standard foams cannot be used effectively on all substances, however. As noted earlier, spills of polar solvents call for special foams that will

not break down readily. Other chemicals, especially strong acids or alkalis, require the use of a special *hazardous vapor mitigating foam.* A number of different foams are made for use on specific chemicals or groups of chemicals. A chart showing the effectiveness of firefighting foams in mitigating certain vapors will be found in the Appendix.

Identify the Hazard

Before you can select and apply a foam, you must know what you are dealing with — doing the wrong thing can be worse than doing nothing. For example, if you used a fast-draining foam on a highly water-reactive material such as sulfur trioxide, you would generate a far greater and more hazardous cloud of vapor than if you had done nothing.

Methods for properly identifying the hazardous substance, and where to find information on correctly dealing with it, will be discussed in Chapters 22 and 23 of this book.

Class A Foams

Foams for use in fighting Class A fires have only been in use since the 1980s, when they were introduced for use in burning *wildlands.* Increasingly, Class A foams are being adopted by municipal fire departments, however, because of the advantages they offer:

- They make more effective use of limited water resources than traditional hose streams. This is especially important in rural or undeveloped areas removed from municipal water supplies.
- They minimize structural stress (and thus the danger of collapse), since there is far less weight of water being placed on the structure.
- They lessen the potential for water damage to structure and contents.
- They help prevent some smoke damage by absorbing smoke from the fire.

Often, the damage caused by smoke and water is more extensive (and thus more costly to repair) than the damage caused by the fire.

- They can cling to and protect vertical or slanting surfaces by reflecting heat.

Class A foams are used at higher dilutions than Class B foams. While a Class B foam solution will typically contain 3% to 6% concentrate, Class A solutions usually have 0.1% to 1.0% concentrate. The amount of concentrate used depends upon the kinds of fuel involved, the nature of the fire (smoldering or burning strongly), the method used to generate the foam, and the method of application to be used.

Foam can be especially useful in situations where a structure is inaccessible or too dangerous to enter. By using an aspirating nozzle or a blower fan, **Figure 8-14**, you could produce foam with an expansion as high as 1000:1 and use it to fill an entire three-dimensional space (such as a fully involved cellar). This will have a number of positive effects: cooling the entire area by absorbing large amounts of heat, absorbing flammable vapors, and cutting off the air supply needed for continued combustion of the fuel. At such a high expansion ratio, you also will be putting a comparatively small amount of water into the structure.

Safe use of foam

Any use of foam on the fireground or at an incident entails a certain amount of risk, since a clinging, viscous foam can hide hazards. It can fill or cover a hole in the ground or the floor, hide items that have sharp edges or points, cover tripping hazards, and make some surfaces slippery (concentrate is more slippery than foam itself).

You have to be particularly careful if you enter a space that has been completely filled with foam. The foam reduces visibility to zero — you literally cannot see your hand in front of your face. This means *disorientation* — one or two steps into a foam-filled room will leave you with no sense of direction. You will also find that sound is greatly muffled, so you can't rely on your sense of hearing for direction. For the same reason, the effectiveness of your PASS locator device will be greatly reduced. *Never* enter a foam-filled space without wearing your SCBA and using a lifeline that you can follow back to safety. If you are

Figure 8-14. A blower fan can be used with high-expansion foam to generate sufficient material to fill an entire room or other enclosed space. (Ansul Fire Protection)

searching for someone in a foam-filled area, one way to improve visibility is to use a coarse fog stream. It will cut through the foam and make it easier to see where you are going.

In general, foam concentrates and solutions are no more toxic than shampoos or household detergents; they may, however (like those products), cause skin irritation or an allergic reaction in some people. There also is a possibility of eye or upper respiratory tract irritation from vapors. The solutions should not be ingested, of course. If backpack tanks are used to store and transport the solutions, be sure they are prominently labeled to avoid having them mistaken for containers of drinking water. If foam solution is accidentally ingested, you should seek immediate medical attention.

Foam handling precautions

When handling foam concentrates, you should observe these precautions:

- Before working with the concentrate, read the label, the Material Safety Data Sheet, and any other instructions provided by the manufacturer.

- Wear proper protective clothing: goggles, rubber or plastic gloves, rubber boots. Apply protective cream to exposed skin to help prevent irritation or allergenic reactions.

- Immediately remove any clothing that becomes soaked with concentrate. Clothing should be rinsed or washed thoroughly before it is worn again.

- Avoid breathing vapors from foam concentrate. Outdoors, work with the wind to your back. If working indoors, make sure there is adequate ventilation, or wear your SCBA.

- If concentrate splashes on your skin, wash it off immediately.

- If concentrate splashes into your eyes, flood with water for 15 minutes. Get medical attention promptly.

Foam and the Environment

You've probably seen cartoons of a tiny fish being swallowed by a larger fish, which in turn is being swallowed by a still larger fish, and so on. See **Figure 8-15.** This is sometimes described as an illustration of the *food chain.* Actually, the food chain is quite a bit more complex. At the beginning of the chain are plants (some of them microscopic in size), which convert light from the sun, and the elements carbon, hydrogen, and oxygen from the environment, into organic compounds called carbohydrates. The plants are a food source for animals known as *herbivores* (plant eaters), which are in turn the food sources for *carnivores* (meat eaters). At the very top of the food chain are the *omnivores*, which eat both plants and animals. Human beings are omnivores.

What does all this have to do with firefighting foam?

As noted earlier, foam is considered nontoxic to humans. That's not the case, however, for all creatures. It can have a serious effect on plant life — especially the most basic types of plants, the simple *algae* that grow in ponds, rivers, and other bodies of water. It also can directly harm many of the plant eaters that live in water. Indirectly, of course, it can affect the carnivores and omnivores by reducing the supply of available food.

Firefighting foams also have a negative effect on the bacteria that break down sewage into harmless components. These bacteria,

Figure 8-15. This illustration is sometimes used to portray the food chain, but the actual chain is considerably more complex. Foam must be used carefully to prevent damage to the tiny plants that form the first link of the food chain.

which are extremely sensitive to firefighting foams, are a vital element of municipal sewage treatment and also exist in natural watercourses, such as rivers.

Not all foams are equally harmful to algae and bacteria. Of the two types of foam in general use (protein-based and synthetic detergent-based), the protein-based materials are considered far less damaging. Sewage-plant bacteria that might be killed by a concentration of detergent-based foam as low as one part-per-million (PPM) could survive a concentration of several thousand PPM of protein-based foam.

Avoiding Water Contamination

The potential for environmental damage does not mean that the use of foams should be abandoned — they are too powerful a weapon to eliminate from the arsenal — but it *does* mean we should use them carefully and appropriately.

To prevent contamination of water, keep all mixing and storage areas well away from natural bodies of water. Maintain a 100-foot to 200-foot buffer between foam preparation areas and the high-water line of reservoirs or other water supplies. *Do not* apply foam directly to any body of water, unless it is absolutely necessary.

Handling concentrate spills

If foam concentrate is spilled, it must be cleaned up immediately, since it poses both an environmental hazard and a firefighter injury hazard. The firefighter injury hazard results from its slippery nature, which could cause a fall. The environmental hazard, of course, is possible water contamination.

Obviously, a foam concentrate spill, even a small one, should never be "washed down" into storm drains or watercourses. If possible, cover the spill with an absorbent material, then shovel it into a container for proper disposal. Most foams are *biodegradable,* which means that soil bacteria will break them down into harmless components. The time required

ranges from 14 to 30 days. Larger spills should be dealt with by containing them and notifying the proper authorities (as specified by department operating procedures).

Mixing Foam Solutions

Mixing of foam solutions can be done manually or automatically. Both methods have advantages and disadvantages. All types of proportioning systems, however, must be thoroughly cleaned after use because of the chemical action of the foam concentrate. The concentrate corrodes metal, and also strips lubricants from surfaces exposed to it.

Manual Methods

The major advantage of manual mixing is that it involves far less investment in equipment than automatic mixing. In some cases, you can use equipment that is already on hand. The major disadvantage of manual methods is less-precise proportioning of concentrate to water. As a result, it will usually be more difficult to get exactly the foam quality that you desire.

Getting the correct proportion of foam concentrate to water is important. If there is too little concentrate, the foam will be less than fully effective. If too much concentrate is used, the duration of the foam will be reduced. Overproportioning is also wasteful. There are four basic methods of manual proportioning: batch mix, suction-side regulator, in-line proportioner (eductor), and around-the-pump proportioner.

Batch mix

This method is also known as the "pre-mix" or "dump-in" method, since it involves mixing a specified amount of concentrate with a known amount of water. See **Figure 8-16.** The batch mix method can be used with a tank, a backpack, or an extinguisher. If, for example, you were going to mix a batch of foam in a 500-gallon (1893 liter) tank, you

Figure 8-16. Batch mixing is a common manual preparation method for foam. Mixing 5 gallons of foam concentrate with 500 gallons of water will produce a 1% foam solution. (Ansul Fire Protection)

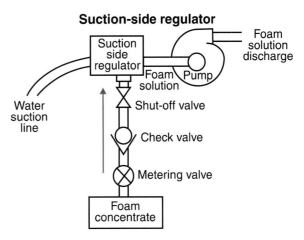

Figure 8-17. The suction-side regulator mixes water and foam concentrate before the water stream enters the pump. The check valve ensures one-way flow. (Foam Task Group, Fire Equipment Working Team, National Wildfire Coordinating Group)

would fill the tank nearly full of water — leaving room for the quantity of concentrate you will add. For a 1% solution, add 5 gallons (19 liters) of concentrate; for a 3% solution, add 15 gallons (57 liters). *Always* add the concentrate to the water, not vice versa, to keep foaming to a minimum. A disadvantage of batch mixing is that you will get foam whether you need it or not.

Suction-side regulator

In this method, the vacuum created by the operation of the pump is used to pull concentrate into the water stream at the inlet side of the pump. See **Figure 8-17.** The major disadvantage of this method is the need to regulate the metering valve every time there is a change in flow.

In-line proportioner (eductor)

The *eductor* uses venturi action to pull the concentrate into the water stream on the pressure side of the pump. See **Figure 8-18.** An important advantage of the eductor is that it eliminates many of the problems associated with exposure of the tank and pump to the concentrate. These problems include corrosion, contamination, lubricant removal, and possible seal breakdown. The most serious drawback to this method is that eductors

work within specified concentration ranges. To change ranges, you must use a different eductor. See **Figure 8-19.** Adjustment of concentrate proportioning is done manually.

Around-the-pump proportioner

As shown in **Figure 8-20,** this method diverts some of the flow from the discharge side of the pump through a venturi, where it mixes with foam concentrate. The solution is then piped back to the inlet side. The around-the-pump proportioner is more flexible than the eductor, but it also must be adjusted manually to account for changes in flow rate.

Automatic Mixing

Although automatic systems require a greater equipment investment than manual methods, they have a number of advantages. These include:

- The ability to accurately maintain the desired proportioning over a wide range of flows and pressures.
- Addition of the concentrate at the discharge side of the pump, minimizing corrosion and other tank and pump problems associated with manual systems.

Figure 8-18. In-line proportioner. A—The eductor, or in-line proportioner, mixes concentrate with water on the outlet side of the pump. Since the foam concentrate does not pass through the pump, corrosion of pump parts is reduced. (Foam Task Group, Fire Equipment Working Team, National Wildfire Coordinating Group) B—Venturi action draws concentrate into the stream of water to provide correct proportioning. (Ansul Fire Protection)

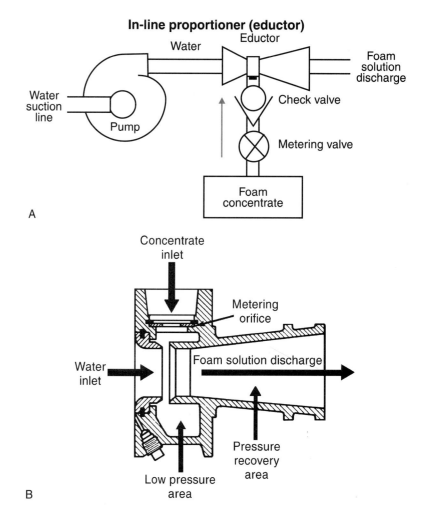

Figure 8-19. Eductors are made in different sizes to provide different concentration ranges. (Ansul Fire Protection)

- The capability of changing concentrate-to-water proportions with relative ease during operation.
- Elimination of any restriction on the length or number of hose lays.

There are three automatic proportioning systems in general use: the balanced-pressure bladder tank, the balanced-pressure pump, and the direct injection proportioner.

Balanced-pressure bladder tank

In this system, **Figure 8-21**, the concentrate is held in a bladder inside a pressure tank. Some of the flow from the pump is used to pressurize the tank, increasing and decreasing as the flow rate changes. The increase or decrease of pressure on the bladder causes the flow rate of the concentrate to change accord-

Around-the-pump proportioner

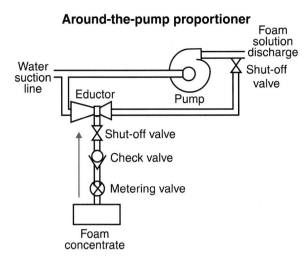

Figure 8-20. The around-the-pump proportioner diverts some of the pump discharge back through a venturi to mix with foam concentrate. The mixture is then blended with water at the inlet side of the pump. (Foam Task Group, Fire Equipment Working Team, National Wildfire Coordinating Group)

ingly. The major disadvantage of this system is the need to periodically refill the bladder with concentrate, interrupting the flow of foam.

Balanced-pressure pump

This system uses a pilot-operated relief valve to sense pressure coming from the water pump. A separate pump delivers concentrate to a venturi, where it enters the

Balanced-pressure bladder tank proportioner

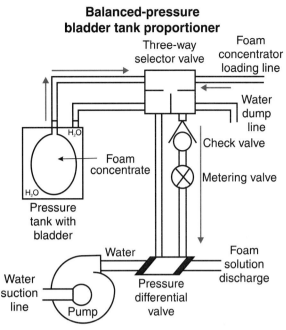

Figure 8-21. Flow from the pump pressurizes the bladder tank, assuring a uniform percentage of concentrate being introduced to the system. Foam flow must be interrupted periodically to refill the bladder. (Foam Task Group, Fire Equipment Working Team, National Wildfire Coordinating Group)

water stream in proportion to the pressure differential across the venturi. See **Figure 8-22.** The concentrate tank can be refilled without interrupting the flow of foam.

Figure 8-22. Foam concentrate is handled by a separate pump in the balanced pressure proportioner. The concentrate tank can be refilled without a break in foam production. (Foam Task Group, Fire Equipment Working Team, National Wildfire Coordinating Group)

Balanced-pressure pump proportioner

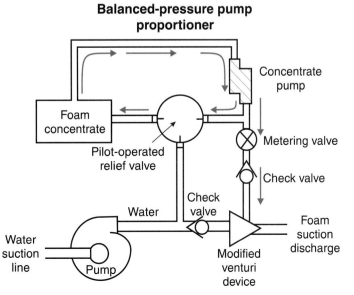

Direct injection proportioner

A sensor located on the discharge side of the water pump determines the water flow rate and transmits this information to a microprocessor. The microprocessor identifies the desired mix ratio as set on the apparatus' control panel, and combines this information with the water flow rate to compute the proper flow rate for concentrate. The processor then directs a separate pump to deliver concentrate at that rate, producing the proper proportion for foam. See **Figure 8-23.** This is a very flexible system, allowing different densities and types of foam to be delivered as needed. It also permits the concentrate supply to be replenished without interrupting the production of foam.

Foam Delivery

Once you have concentrate mixed in the correct proportion with water, you must convert the solution to foam, then deliver the foam to the point where it is needed. A number of options are available; the equipment you have and the nature of the problem will determine which of those options is best.

Conventional nozzles

You can use either a straight bore or a fog nozzle to deliver a foam solution, but neither of these *nonaspirating nozzles* will produce a stable foam. See **Figure 8-24.** At best, the foam delivered by either a straight or fog nozzle will be similar to "wet water." It will have good penetrating ability and will more thoroughly wet the fuel than will ordinary water. However, it will not provide the heat reflection and insulating properties that are offered by a more fully developed foam.

Aspirating nozzles

An expansion chamber in the *aspirating nozzle*, **Figure 8-25**, mixes fine jets of solution with air to create foam. The size of the cham-

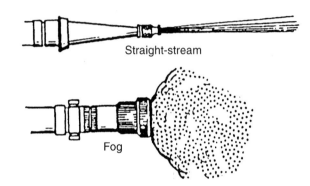

Straight-stream

Fog

Figure 8-24. "Normal" nozzles — either straight-bore or fog — can be used to deliver a stream of foam solution. The foam they produce, however, is not stable. (Foam Task Group, Fire Equipment Working Team, National Wildfire Coordinating Group)

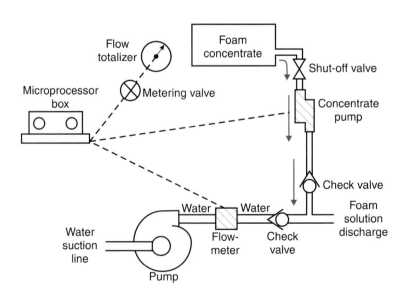

Figure 8-23. The most flexible (and most costly) automatic foam system is the direct injection proportioner. A microprocessor controls its operation. (Foam Task Group, Fire Equipment Working Team, National Wildfire Coordinating Group)

Flow totalizer

Foam concentrate

Shut-off valve

Microprocessor box

Metering valve

Concentrate pump

Check valve

Foam solution discharge

Water   Water

Flow-meter   Check valve

Water suction line

Pump

ber affects the type of foam produced — a smaller chamber will generate a wetter foam that will project further from the nozzle, while a larger chamber creates a drier foam that does not project as well, but will cling better to vertical surfaces.

Low-expansion aspirating nozzles produce foams with expansion rates of up to 20:1; medium-expansion nozzles, up to 200:1.

High-expansion foam generators

This equipment is used to produce huge quantities of foam for blanketing large spills or completely filling enclosed spaces such as cellars. It can produce foam with expansion ratios as high as 1000:1 by spraying a mist of foam solution onto a screen, then forcing air through the screen to form bubbles. See **Figure 8-26.**

Compressed-air foam systems

By injecting compressed air before the foam solution reaches the nozzle, these systems achieve a thoroughly blended, uniform, and very stable foam. See **Figure 8-27.** Because the compressed air adds energy to the stream,

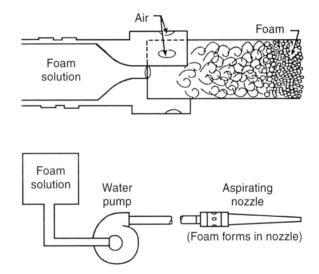

Figure 8-25. Aspirating nozzles produce low-density or medium-density foams by mixing fine jets of foam solution with air to generate the desired product. (Foam Task Group, Fire Equipment Working Team, National Wildfire Coordinating Group)

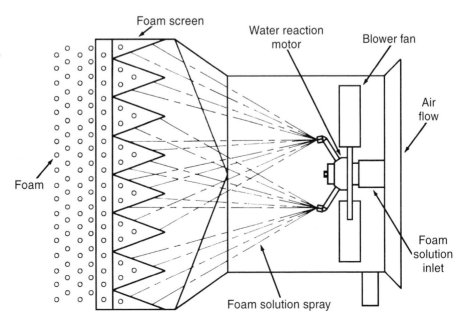

Figure 8-26. Very large quantities of high-expansion foam are produced by equipment of this type. As shown, foam solution is sprayed onto a screen, then turned into dense foam by a high volume of air from a blower fan. (Ansul Fire Protection)

Figure 8-27.
Compressed air systems like this one produce very stable foam that can be projected for long distances. (Foam Task Group, Fire Equipment Working Team, National Wildfire Coordinating Group)

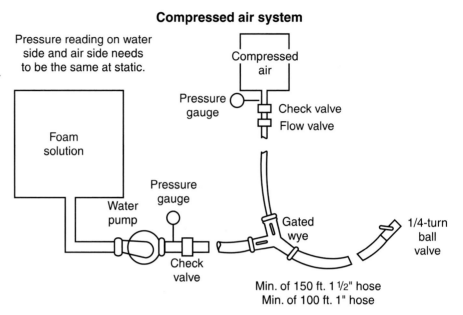

Compressed air system

Pressure reading on water side and air side needs to be the same at static.

Compressed air

Pressure gauge

Check valve

Flow valve

Foam solution

Water pump

Pressure gauge

Check valve

Gated wye

1/4-turn ball valve

Min. of 150 ft. 1 1/2" hose
Min. of 100 ft. 1" hose

the foam can be projected for a greater distance than with other systems. Disadvantages of the compressed-air system are its greater equipment costs and its more complicated operation.

Aspirated vs nonaspirated foam

As is the case with many other aspects of firefighting, the question of whether aspirated or nonaspirated foam is best depends upon the situation. See **Figure 8-28.** Each has its uses. An aspirating nozzle will produce a higher expansion ratio, and the resulting foam will have a longer drain time and provide greater protection against burnback. On the other hand, a straight pipe or narrow fog nozzle will project a nonaspirated foam more effectively, at the same flow rate, for better penetration. A fog pattern also will provide a greater measure of heat shielding for the firefighter behind the nozzle.

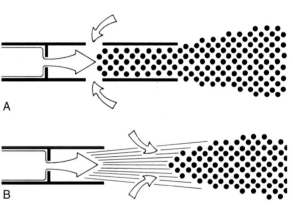

Figure 8-28. Types of nozzles. A—Aspirated nozzle mixes air with foam solution in an expansion chamber, producing a more stable foam with a higher expansion ratio than a nonaspirated nozzle. B—In a nonaspirated nozzle, air and foam solution mix after the solution leaves the nozzle. The material, which has a lower expansion ratio, can be projected a greater distance than a foam from an aspirated nozzle. (Ansul Fire Protection)

Foam Application

Generally, foams are *lofted* (projected into the air) over the fire, so the blanket of material can settle down on top of the burning fuel. See **Figure 8-29.** As noted earlier, foams have both a cooling and a smothering effect — they absorb heat as their water content turns to steam, and they exclude oxygen needed for combustion. Foam is an efficient way to apply water to the fire, since it does not run off as readily and contains wetting agents that allow it to penetrate the mass of burning material.

Figure 8-29. For greatest effect, especially with burning liquids, foams are typically lofted and allowed to settle onto the burning material. This firefighter is practicing foam application at a training facility. (Ansul Fire Protection)

The amount of water that is effectively applied to the fire depends on the water content of the foam itself, the amount of water evaporated, the stability of the foam (how fast it breaks down and drains away), and the type of fuel involved. To be fully effective, a foam must have the ability to break down sufficiently to wet the fire, while remaining stable enough to maintain an unbroken blanket over the burning material.

There are some situations in which foam should not be used, or where a specialized type of foam must be applied. These include:

- Liquefied or *cryogenic* (extremely cold) gases. High-expansion foam is sometimes effective in containing cryogenic spills.
- Liquids flowing from overhead or pressurized tanks.
- Any material that reacts violently with water, such as metallic sodium or potassium.
- Charged electrical equipment (foam *will* conduct electricity).
- Hot oils or other heated liquids that could respond to foam application by violent frothing and boilover.

- Polar solvents, such as alcohol. Foams specially formulated for such situations must be used.

Poor Foam Generation or Performance

While there are a number of possible causes of poor foam generation, and even more for poor performance, most will fall into one of these general categories:

- Wrong foam type. The most obvious example of this is applying a standard aqueous film-forming foam to an alcohol or other polar solvent spill. The solvent will quickly break down the foam. An alcohol-resistant AFFF would provide effective blanketing
- Improper foam application. For example, plunging a standard foam into a burning liquid, rather than lofting it so that it settles as a blanket on top of the fire, will lose much of the foam's effectiveness. If a plunging attack is necessary because of fire conditions, a fluoroprotein foam should be used. These foams are specially formulated

to shed fuels, so that they will float to the surface and form an effective blanket that blocks vapors and prevents burnback.

- Foam generator problems. This could include malfunctioning of the equipment, or (especially with manual methods) improper proportioning of concentrate to water, resulting in a foam that contains too little or too much water for the desired application.

- Unrealistic expectations. Foam is not magic — no single foam will work in every conceivable situation, and there are some situations (as noted earlier) in which no foam will work effectively. Learn the limitations of each foam you use and work within those limitations.

SUMMARY

Firefighting foam is made up of three components: a foaming concentrate, water, and air. The concentrate includes a foaming agent, a wetting agent, and a stabilizer. Depending upon the kind and amount of concentrate used and the methods employed for mixing and delivery, foam may range from a watery solution with few bubbles to a very dense, dry mass of bubbles that will cling to even a vertical surface.

Foams are available with expansion ratios that are rated as low (up to 20:1), medium (up to 200:1) or high (up to 1000:1); they also are classified as fast or slow draining, depending upon the speed at which they break down and release water.

Foam extinguishes fire by cooling the heat source, separating the fuel from oxygen needed for combustion, suppressing flammable vapors, and separating flammable vapors from a heat source that could cause them to ignite. The wetting agent (surfactant) used in foams helps the water to spread out in a thin film and to penetrate into the burning material. In addition to use in extinguishing fires, foam is widely used as a blanketing agent to contain vapors from spills of hazardous materials.

Class A foams are for use on ordinary combustibles, such as wood; Class B foams are used on burning liquids, such as gasoline. Alcohol-resistant foams are used on spills or fires involving polar solvents. These solvents cause standard foams to rapidly break down.

Safety considerations involving foams include the danger of disorientation when entering a space filled with foam; the need to wear eye protection, gloves, and an SCBA when handling concentrates, and avoiding ingestion of water contaminated with concentrate. Environmental concerns must be observed carefully, since firefighting foams can be lethal to organisms in bodies of water, as well as to beneficial bacteria used in sewage treatment.

Both manual and automatic systems are available for mixing concentrate and water in the proper proportions. Automatic systems are highly accurate, but more expensive than manual systems. Manual methods are less precise, but also much less costly. Delivery of foam to the fire or spills can be done with straight nozzles, fog nozzles, or aspirating-type nozzles. The aspirating nozzles deliver more stable and thicker foams than straight or fog nozzles. Special equipment is used to produce foam with expansion ratios as high as 1000:1. In most situations, foam is lofted onto the fire so that it will settle as a blanket. Special fluoroprotein foams are used when it is necessary to plunge foam into a liquid fuel, rather than lofting it.

Foam problems may stem from improper choice of type of foam, improper application, errors in preparation, or equipment malfunctions. Foam has limitations; knowing what they are and working within them is important.

REVIEW QUESTIONS

1. What are the major components of a typical foam concentrate?
2. Foam is described as having four different consistencies. What are they?
3. What is meant by the term "drain time"?
4. Distinguish between hydrocarbons and polar solvents. Give two examples of each.
5. Under what conditions must you use an alcohol-resistant foam?
6. What does the term "aqueous film-forming" mean?
7. When the expansion ratio of a foam is given as 20:1, what is meant? At that ratio, how many gallons of concentrate would be needed to generate 20 gallons of foam?
8. What is the purpose of the wetting agents that are included in most foam concentrates?
9. Describe some reasons why foam would be chosen as the primary firefighting agent in a structure fire.
10. Under what conditions would you use Class A foam? Class B?
11. Although they are considered generally nontoxic, foam concentrate can cause some physical problems for humans. What are they?
12. Why should you exercise care when using firefighting foam near bodies of water?
13. When batch-mixing foam, how many gallons of concentrate must be added to 500 gallons of water to produce a 3% foam solution?
14. In addition to batch mixing, what other manual proportioning methods are used?
15. In the suction-side regulator shown as Figure 8-17, what is the purpose of the *check valve?*
16. The automatic direct injection proportioner includes a microprocessor. What does the microprocessor do?
17. Describe the operation of an aspirating nozzle.
18. What would be the usual maximum expansion ratio possible with a high-expansion foam generator? For what purposes would you use the foam that is produced?
19. How is foam normally applied to a horizontal surface?
20. What are the four general categories of reasons for poor foam generation or performance?

NFPA 1001 Job Performance Requirements

The material on this page consists of those portions of the NFPA 1001 Job Performance Requirements relevant to the material presented in this chapter. Items preceded by the numeral 3 (3-x.x) are Fire Fighter I requirements; those with the numeral 4 (4-x.x) are Fire Fighter II requirements.

(3-3.7)

(a) Prerequisite Knowledge: Types of attack lines and water streams appropriate for attacking stacked, piled materials and outdoor fires; dangers—such as collapse—associated with stacked and piled materials; various extinguishing agents and their effect on different material configurations; tools and methods to use in breaking up various types of materials; the difficulties related to complete extinguishment; dangers such as exposure protection and fire extinguishment; dangers such as exposure to toxic or hazardous materials associated with storage building and container fires; obvious signs or origin and cause; and techniques for the preservation of fire cause evidence.

(3-3.9)

(a) Prerequisite Knowledge: Principles of fire streams; types, design, operation, nozzle pressure effects, and flow capabilities of nozzles; precautions to be followed when advancing hose lines to a fire; observable results that a fire stream has been properly applied; dangerous building conditions created by fire; principles of exposure protection; potential long-term consequences of exposure to products of combustion; physical states of matter in which fuels are found; common types of accidents or injuries and their causes; and the application of each size and type of attack line, the role of the backup team in fire attack situations, attack and control techniques for grade level and above and below grade levels, and exposing hidden fires.

(b) Prerequisite Skills: The ability to prevent water hammers when shutting down nozzles; open, close, and adjust nozzle flow and patterns; apply water using direct, indirect, and combination attacks; advance charged and uncharged $1\frac{1}{2}$ in. (38 mm) diameter or larger hose lines up ladders and up and down interior and exterior stairways; extend hose lines; replace burst hose sections; operate charged hose lines of $1\frac{1}{2}$ in. (38 mm) diameter or larger while secured to a ground ladder; couple and uncouple various hose line connections; carry hose; attack fires at grade level and above and below grade levels; and locate and suppress interior wall and subfloor fires.

(3-3.14)

(b) Prerequisite Skills: The ability to hand lay a supply hose, connect and place hard suction hose for drafting operations, deploy portable water tanks as well as the equipment necessary to transfer water between and draft from them, make hydrant-to-pumper hose connections from forward and reverse lays, connect supply hose to a hydrant, and fully open and close the hydrant.

3-5.4 Clean, inspect, and return fire hose to service, given washing equipment, water, detergent, tools, and replacement gaskets, so that damage is noted and corrected, the hose is clean, and the equipment is placed in a ready state for service.

(a) Prerequisite Knowledge: Departmental procedures for noting a defective hose and removing it from service, cleaning methods, and hose rolls and loads.

(b) Prerequisite Skills: The ability to clean different types of hose; operate hose washing and drying equipment; mark defective hose; and replace coupling gaskets, roll hose, and reload hose.

(4-3.2)

(a) Prerequisite Knowledge: Selection of the proper nozzle and hose for fire attack given different fire situations; selection of adapters and appliances to be used for specific fire ground situations; dangerous building conditions created by fire and fire suppression activities; indicators of building collapse; the effects of fire and fire suppression activities on wood, masonry (brick, block, stone), cast iron, steel, reinforced concrete, gypsum wall board, glass, and plaster on lath; search and rescue and ventilation procedures; indicators of structural instability; suppression approaches and practices for various types of structural fires; and the association between specific tools and special forcible entry needs.

4-5.3 Perform an annual service test on fire hose, given a pump, a marking device, pressure gauges, a timer, record sheets, and related equipment, so that procedures are followed, the condition of the hose is evaluated, any damaged hose is removed from service, and the results are recorded.

(a) Prerequisite Knowledge: Procedures for safely conducting hose service testing, indicators that dictate any hose be removed from service, and recording procedures for hose test results.

(b) Prerequisite Skills: The ability to operate hose testing equipment and nozzles and to record results.

Reprinted with permission from NFPA 1001, *Fire Fighter Professional Qualifications,* Copyright ©1997, National Fire Protection Association, Quincy, MA 02269. This reprinted material is not the complete and official position of the National Fire Protection Association on the referenced subject, which is represented only by the standard in its entirety.

Hoses, Nozzles, Fittings, and Appliances

OBJECTIVES

When you have completed this chapter, you will be able to:

🔥 Identify the sizes, types, amounts, and uses of hose carried on a pumper.

🔥 Identify and describe the uses of the hose and adapters, fittings, and appliances carried on a pumper. This includes the methods used to replace a burst line or extend a line.

🔥 Demonstrate the hose rolls used by a department.

🔥 Demonstrate how to couple hose and attach nozzles.

🔥 Demonstrate the ability to load hose on an apparatus and make the appropriate finishes.

🔥 Demonstrate how to connect hose to a hydrant, and how to fully open and close a hydrant. This includes making hydrant/pumper connections.

🔥 Identify, select, and demonstrate the use of any nozzle carried on a pumper.

🔥 Describe the precautions to take when advancing hose to a fire.

🔥 Use appropriate drags and carries to advance dry lines safely and efficiently. This includes connecting to a standpipe and working a charged line from a ladder.

🔥 Demonstrate how to properly and safely advance charged lines.

🔥 Demonstrate the inspection and maintenance of fire hose, couplings, and nozzles.

IMPORTANT TERMS

abrasion-resistance
accordion load
appliances
booster hose
butts
cellar nozzle
combination load
constant gallonage
  nozzle
cross-fold finish
divided load
donut finish
donut roll
finishes
fitting

flexibility
fog nozzle
fog-only nozzle
gate valve
hard suction hose
high-pressure fog
  nozzles
horseshoe load
hose
hose adapters
hose bridges
hose cap
hose clamp
hose jacket
hose line

hose pipe
hose roller
hose strap
in-line pumping
intake manifold
loads
nozzle
piercing nozzle
reverse lay
shutoff
siamese fittings
single roll
skid finish
straight lay
straight-bore playpipe

straight-to-reverse lay
strainer
suction hose
suppressants
taking a hydrant
tip
variable gallonage
  nozzle
water hammer
water thief
working hose
wye fittings

Most of the time, water — plain water — is the cheapest, most efficient, and best substance for putting out fires. But water's efficiency depends on delivering the right amount, in the right form, at the right time and place. Fighting fires is, at best, hard work. Efficiency, from the point of view of the firefighter, means working *smarter*, not *harder*.

The firefighter must know instantly what size hose to lay, what fittings will be needed, and how many feet of hose will be needed. Getting hooked up and then finding out that an additional fifty feet of hose is required means a lot of extra work. Worse, it means extra time for the fire to grow and spread, making the job still harder.

What are Hoses, Nozzles, Fittings, and Appliances?

Different fire situations require different applications of water and other *suppressants*. You may need a lot of water for a long time, or a lot of water for a very short time. You may need a small amount of water for a short time, or for a long time. You may need a powerful, compact stream to penetrate deep into the base of a fire or a fine mist to cool and clear the air. There are all sorts of variations and combinations. You achieve the various combinations through the proper selection of hoses, nozzles, and appliances.

A *hose* is a flexible pipe, often made from rubber, that is used to convey fluids from a faucet or hydrant to a point some distance away. Some hoses are flexible only by comparison with a cast-iron pipe, but they have *some* flexibility. Others are quite easily folded or bent around corners and obstructions. *Flexibility* is an advantage when you must fold hose so you can get the maximum amount on a truck. The strength and *abrasion-resistance* of such hose comes from its fabric outer cover. Older canvas-covered hoses must be dried after every use, since the cover might be weakened by rot and mildew. Modern hose is manufactured with a jacket of synthetic fabric, usually polyester, that will not rot or mildew. This allows hose to be packed wet or dry.

Flexibility is *not* an advantage when you must draft water from a pond or stream, because the suction pressure will collapse the hose. *Hard suction hose* is made to be quite rigid so that pressure will not collapse it. See **Figure 9-1.** Both *booster hose* and hard

Figure 9-1. The rigid construction of a hard suction hose is apparent in this photo. Firefighters are disconnecting a hard suction from a pumper after using it to draft water from a portable canvas tank at a mutual aid training exercise.

suction hose are rubber-covered, so they don't have to be dried after every use. Hose that is used to pull water from a pressurized source (and thus, is in no danger of collapsing) is referred to as "soft suction" hose.

A *nozzle* is defined as "a short tube with a taper or constriction that is used to direct a flow of fluid." Nowhere have nozzles been developed to the extent that they have in the fire service. You can obtain nozzles to provide any kind of a stream or pattern desired, from a solid compact penetrating stream to a wide-patterned mist. Modern nozzles can provide nearly every kind of stream between these extremes.

In the fire service, a *fitting* is, roughly, anything that attaches to a hose. These include adapters to connect different sizes and styles of threads, those with two male threads or two female threads, devices to combine two or more streams of water into one or to divide one stream into two or more, and shutoffs used between the source and the nozzle.

As the term implies, *appliances* are anything that can be applied to a completed hose line, but that do not become a part of the line itself. These include hose straps, hose jackets, hose clamps, and several other items.

A *hose line* is all of the hose, fittings, and nozzles used to bring the water from the point of origin (hydrant, pond, or stream) to the point of application (the fire). It includes everything mentioned so far, with the exception of appliances, which are external to the line itself.

Hose Identification

The identification of the various kinds of hose is really quite simple. There are really only three basic kinds: suction hose, working hose, and booster hose. *Suction hose* is available in various lengths and has long handles on the *butts* (couplings). Suction hose also comes in hard and soft types, as noted previously. Most *working hose* comes in fifty-foot lengths. Booster hose is on reels. See **Figure 9-2.**

The more common sizes of suction hose used by fire departments are 2¹/2 in., 3 in.,

A

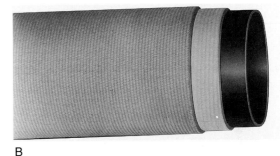

B

C

Figure 9-2. Commonly used types of hoses. A—Single-jacket hose, used primarily by industrial fire brigades. B—Double-jacket hose, the primary attack hose used by fire departments. C—Hard suction hose. The outer jacket has spring-steel wire molded in to help prevent hose collapse under suction. (National Fire Hose Corp.)

4 in., 4¹/2 in., 5 in., and 6 in. The 2¹/2 in. and 3 in. hoses are available as hard suction only, the other sizes in either hard or soft forms. Working hose sizes are 1¹/2 in., 1³/4 in., 2¹/2 in., and 3 in. The 1³/4 in. hose is supplied 1¹/2 in. couplings, so it can be used interchangeably with the smaller-diameter hose. The 3 in. hose can be obtained with either 2¹/2 in. or 3 in. couplings. Booster hose is either ³/4 in. or 1 in. diameter.

Uses of various-size hoses

Booster lines have been traditionally used on minor incidents, such as small debris fires. While they permit immediate response, they are limited to the capacity of the water tank and should never be relied upon for a protective fog pattern. Some departments have a policy that prohibits use of booster lines in a structure fire unless ordered by an officer, and backed up with 1 1/2 in. or larger hose.

Most structure fires and outside fires are put out with a 1 1/2 in. or larger hose line. Such lines are also used in washing-down operations. In many situations, firefighters can get a 1 1/2 in. line to a fire easier and faster than a booster line, and it will supply far more water in terms of gallons per minute.

A 1 3/4 in. hose will deliver, at high pressure, as much water as a 2 1/2 in. line. But such high pressure is harder to handle for one or two firefighters on a nozzle.

The workhorse of the fire service has traditionally been the 2 1/2 in. hose, which can deliver large volumes of water at manageable pressures. The 2 1/2 in. line is also a good supply line from hydrant to pumper, from pumper to pumper, or to a master stream.

The 3 in. hose is not suitable for handlines. It is used mainly in situations where large amounts of water are consumed, such as ladder pipes, standpipes, sprinkler systems, or master streams.

With greater water demands in today's structure fires, the 5 in. line is being more widely used for supply. Formerly, it was used as a supply line only at really big fires where a vast amount of water was needed.

Nozzles

In the not-too-distant past, nozzle selection was a simple job: the firefighter used the old, reliable playpipe. It was usually made of cast brass and weighed about 20 pounds. It had a handle to open and close it, and came in several tip sizes. That was it. The ***straight-bore playpipe*** is still being manufactured, and most pumpers carry at least one. In fact,

the straight stream, which once seemed headed for oblivion, is regaining popularity. Departments that have returned to using the straight stream feel that it knocks down fire more rapidly, while producing less steam to possibly scald firefighters. Playpipes are available in both traditional metal and lightweight plastic.

Today, a bewildering variety of nozzles is available. Rather than brass, the modern nozzle is more likely to be made of aluminum, steel, or lightweight plastic. Instead of producing just one kind of stream, the modern nozzle can often deliver a variety of streams and patterns.

Nozzles are classified by the kind of stream or streams they will produce. The three *basic* streams are solid, fog, and foam, but there are also combinations, such as solid/fog, variable/fog, fog/foam, and solid/fog/foam.

Most nozzles consist of three separate sections, **Figure 9-3.** The part that threads onto the hose (called the *playpipe*) has two

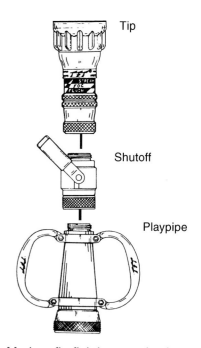

Figure 9-3. Modern firefighting nozzles have three separate sections, which permits the interchanging of tips for different waterflow quantities and patterns. (Task Force Tips)

handles so that two firefighters can control it. This is necessary because of the high discharge rate. The middle section, which includes the handle, is called the *shutoff*. When the shutoff handle is in the forward position, the nozzle is closed. When the handle is lying back against the base, it is open. The outermost section is the *tip*, which determines how much water will flow. Straight tips range in diameter from 1/2 in. to 15/8 in., in increments of 1/8 in. The straight tips can also be replaced with adjustable fog nozzles that will deliver anything from a solid stream to a wide fog pattern.

The simplest nozzle of all, the *hose pipe*, is made to fit either 11/2 in. or 21/2 in. hose. There is no shutoff or control. This nozzle is not much used by fire departments.

The *fog-only nozzle* is intended mostly for fighting electrical fires. A fog stream will not conduct electricity for a distance of more than a few feet. The reason for a "fog-only" nozzle is to prevent accidental switching to straight stream, which could cause electrocution. The fog pattern is adjustable over a moderate range.

As the term is frequently used, *fog nozzle* refers to a wide variety of combination solid stream/fog nozzles. See **Figure 9-4**. These versatile nozzles will produce a solid stream and a range of fog patterns from narrow (about 30°) to extra-wide (about 190°).

Fog nozzles may be classified as constant gallonage or variable gallonage. At any given pressure, a *constant gallonage nozzle* will produce the same flow in gallons per minute (gpm) whether the setting is for a solid stream or one of the fog patterns. A *variable gallonage nozzle* permits the *operator* to determine the amount of flow. Thus, for a small fire, the firefighter can reduce the flow and the water damage, but will still have the capacity of greater flow if that is needed. Typical gallonages of these nozzles are 3 to 18 gpm, 50 to 350 gpm, and 150 to 1000 gpm. Fog nozzle gallonages are usually rated at 100 psi, although high-pressure fog nozzles are rated at 300-1000 psi. As with most other noz-

A

B

C

Figure 9-4. Fog nozzles. A—Pistol-grip type for use on 11/2 in. lines. It is a constant-gallonage type rated for 85 gpm. B—Variable gallonage nozzle, rated from 60-400 gpm, adjustable from solid stream to fog pattern, for use on 21/2 in. hose lines. C—Playpipe-style variable-gallonage adjustable nozzle, with the same rating as B. (Akron Brass Co.)

zles, the forward handle position is closed and the extreme back position is open. The kind of stream (solid or fog pattern) is determined by rotating a collar on the barrel. Gallonage is usually set the same way.

Most *high-pressure fog nozzles* look like guns, and are usually called "guns." Since they operate in a pressure range of 300-1000 psi, they are always attached to high-pressure booster lines. As with other fog nozzles, these are combination nozzles: they produce a range of fog patterns as well as a solid stream. The open/close control on a fog gun is a trigger mechanism. This makes them well-suited to short bursts which further reduces water use and damage.

Foam nozzles are discussed, along with foam-producing equipment, elsewhere in this text.

Special nozzles

Two special nozzles that are extensively used are the cellar nozzle and the piercing nozzle. These can save time, effort, help keep you out of danger, and minimize damage to the building you are trying to save.

The *cellar nozzle*, **Figure 9-5**, has a rotating head that produces a fog which projects up, down, and sideways. Depending on the nozzle size, the sideways fog pattern will be anywhere from 25 to 50 feet in diameter. All the firefighter needs to do is cut a small hole in the floor, lower the nozzle a few feet into the cellar, and turn it on. A nozzle with a 25-foot range can cover a 40-foot basement completely by lowering it into holes cut 12 feet from each end wall. Don't let the name restrict your thinking — a cellar nozzle can also be used to fight an attic fire. Again, simply cut a couple small holes in the roof and insert the nozzle. **Caution:** if you are not certain that the floor or roof is safe, lay down a short ladder and work from that.

The *piercing nozzle* is a fog nozzle that is sometimes referred to as a "partition nozzle." As shown in **Figure 9-6**, it is fairly long (often three to six feet), with an end made of sharpened tool steel, hard stainless steel, or carbide. A piercing nozzle can be pushed or driven into a wall, ceiling, or floor. Because of the small hole it makes and the fog stream, this nozzle causes a minimum amount of cutting and water damage.

Hose Adapters and Fittings

Properly speaking, *hose adapters* are fittings. They are used to connect two threads that normally wouldn't go together, either because of thread size or thread type. Examples would be 2½ in. to 1½ in. hose, 2½ in. female thread to another 2½ in. female thread, and pipe thread to hose thread.

Typical adapters are double male, double female, intake, and reducer. See **Figure 9-7.** Most threads in fire department fittings are National Standard Threads (NST). Some departments and buildings use their own

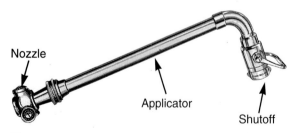

Figure 9-5. The cellar nozzle has a rotating head that produces a fog pattern up to 60 feet in diameter. It can be inserted into a basement or other confined space by cutting a small hole on a floor or wall. This nozzle is shown mounted on a rigid metal applicator, but it can also be threaded directly onto the end of a hose. (Elkhart Brass Mfg. Co.)

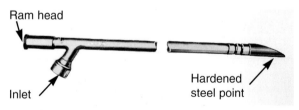

Figure 9-6. The sharpened steel point of a piercing nozzle allows it to be pushed or driven through a building partition into adjoining rooms or confined spaces. This nozzle is often used in aircraft fires, since it can easily penetrate the aluminum skin of the aircraft. (Akron Brass Co.)

Figure 9-7. Commonly used hose adapters. A—Double male. B—Double female. C—Reducer. (Elkhart Brass Mfg. Co.)

threads, however, which are not NST. In such instances, special adapters will be necessary to match the nonstandard threads to NST threads.

Siamese and wye fittings

Both *siamese fittings* and *wye fittings* (connections) are shaped like the letter "Y." It is not really hard to tell them apart, though, because the thread patterns are exactly opposite. The siamese has a male thread at one end and two female threads at the other, while the wye has a female thread on one end and two male threads on the other. The siamese, **Figure 9-8**, is used for *combining* two supply lines into one working line. The wye shown in **Figure 9-9** is just the opposite; it is used to *divide* one supply line into two working lines. Often, there is a clapper valve inside the fitting to keep water from flowing out an unused opening. Each outlet may also have a gate valve, **Figure 9-10.** To keep friction loss to a minimum, a siamese should be inserted as close to the fire as possible, while a wye should be close to the hydrant or pumper.

Water thief

The *water thief* has one gated outlet that is the same size as the inlet and two or more smaller gated outlets, **Figure 9-11.** This provides the option of using one large line or two or more smaller ones. All the outlets from a water thief cannot be used at the same time, because the pressure loss would be too great.

Figure 9-8. Siamese fitting, used to combine two supply lines into a single working line. Both inlets have a female thread, the outlet has a male thread. A clapper valve automatically seals off the second inlet if only one supply line is connected. The device on the left side of the fitting is a drain valve. (Elkhart Brass Mfg. Co.)

The most common water thief sizes are a 5 in. inlet/outlet with four 2 1/2 in. gated outlets, and a 2 1/2 in. inlet/outlet with two 1 1/2 in. gated outlets.

Gate valve

The *gate valve* is used to shut off one line independently of others from the same source. See **Figure 9-12.** An example would

Figure 9-9. A wye fitting divides the output of a single supply line between two working lines. This single inlet has a female thread; the two outlets, male threads. (Elkhart Brass Mfg. Co.)

Figure 9-11. A water thief has three outlets, allowing a choice of charging one large line or two smaller ones. Gate valves provide individual control of outlets. (Elkhart Brass Mfg. Co.)

Figure 9-10. A gated wye. The gate valves on the outlets allow them to be opened and closed independently. This permits a hose connected to the first outlet to go into use immediately while the second hose is being connected. (Elkhart Brass Mfg. Co.)

Figure 9-12. A gate valve can be installed at a hydrant to control a single hose line, or at one outlet of a plain wye fitting to independently control one of the hose lines. (Elkhart Brass Mfg. Co.)

Intake manifold

What is called an ***intake manifold*** is actually a three-way hydrant wye. It is normally attached to a vehicle and used to bring three intake lines into a 6 in. pump intake. The manifold may also be used as a three-way gated wye to allow independent use of three lines. A common intake manifold configuration is a 6 in. inlet with three 2 1/2 in. gated outlets.

Hose cap

The ***hose cap*** is a closed, threaded fitting that can be used to block off a line or as a

be shutting off one of several lines coming from a hydrant without shutting down the entire hydrant. A gate valve is also used in conjunction with a nozzle that does not have its own shutoff, such as a cellar nozzle.

thread protector. The hose cap is available in sizes from 1 1/2 in. to 6 in. See **Figure 9-13.**

Strainer

A *strainer* is attached to the end of a hard suction hose when drafting from a pond or stream to keep rocks and other debris out of the pump. Strainer sizes are 2 1/2 in., 4 in., 4 1/2 in. and 5 in. See **Figure 9-14.**

Hose Appliances

There are three accessory items that are described as "hose appliances": the hose strap, the hose clamp, and the hose jacket.

Hose (ladder) strap

Originally intended for securing a charged line to a ladder, the *hose strap* has many other uses. It can be employed to secure a ladder to a building, to serve as a carrying strap or a safety belt, or formed into a rescue harness, for example. Its uses are limited only by the firefighter's ingenuity and imagination. See **Figure 9-15.**

Hose clamp

The *hose clamp*, **Figure 9-16**, is used any time that an emergency shutoff of a working line is needed (most often, for the replacement of a burst line). It also can be used to insert additional lengths of line. If the need for a shutoff is known in advance, however, it

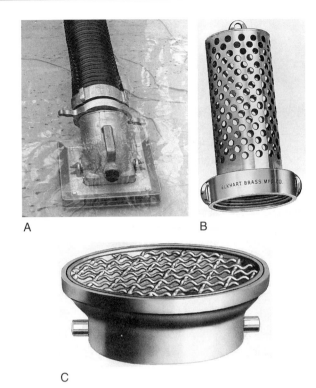

A   B

C

Figure 9-14. Strainers for use on suction hose. A—A low-profile strainer for use in portable water tanks to make maximum use of limited water supplies. B—A barrel strainer with rocker lugs. C—A flat strainer with pin lugs. Most fittings are offered by manufacturers with either type of lug. (Elkhart Brass Mfg. Co.)

Figure 9-15. A hose strap is strong and flexible. It has numerous uses on the fireground.

is better to use a gate valve (if available). A gate valve is less damaging to hose than a clamp. Another use of the hose clamp is shown in **Figure 9-17.** Most clamps will handle any working line up to 3 in. in size (except booster line, which cannot be clamped).

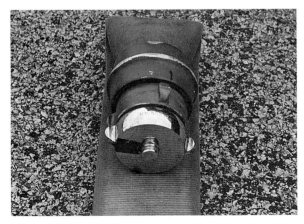

Figure 9-13. The hose cap can be placed on the end of a line to protect threads from damage.

Figure 9-16. A mechanical hose clamp is most often used to shut off a working line in emergency. The long handle provides enough leverage to pinch the charged hose shut. There are many styles of hose clamps available. (Akron Brass Co.)

Figure 9-17. Using a hose clamp as a flow control device. After connecting the line to the pumper, the engineer can bring pump pressure to the required discharge level. When the call for water is received, the clamp is released to charge the line. This clamp uses a small hydraulic cylinder to improve leverage. (Ziamatic Corp.)

Hose jacket

To temporarily seal a burst hose, a device called a *hose jacket* is used. The jacket is used by placing it under the hose, rotating the line so the burst area is horizontal, then snapping the jacket closed. The hose jacket can also be used to join damaged or mismatched couplings, or to join different sizes of hose (provided they are reasonably close in diameter, such as 2½ in. and 3 in.). See **Figure 9-18**.

Working with Hose

Proper procedures for loading hose on apparatus, making connection to hydrants or

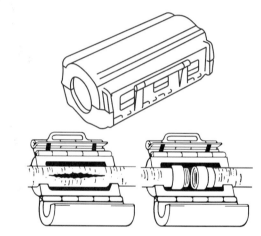

A

B

Figure 9-18. Hose jacket. A—The primary use of the hose jacket is to seal a burst hose. B—It can also be used to temporarily join mismatched couplings or hoses with two different (but reasonably close) diameters.

standpipes, connecting nozzles, and advancing hose lines are vital to effective firefighting. Proper hose care and periodic inspection and testing are also necessary. These topics are discussed in the following sections.

Loading Hose on Fire Apparatus

There are a number of different ways to load the hose on an apparatus. The kind of fireground situation your department is most likely to encounter will determine which possible loading method is best. In a city, for example, buildings will be close together, so you will need a number of lines for containment and extinguishment. The lines will be short, since several hydrants will be available close to the fire. In a rural area, on the other hand, containment is not quite the problem that it is in the city. You will need fewer, but longer, hose lines.

Other factors that will determine which hose load is best for a department are the number of firefighters likely to be available to lay hose, and how many pieces of apparatus will respond to an alarm. Some departments send out at least two pumpers, with each loaded for a different situation.

Departments sometimes load a certain way because "we have always done it like this," but that is not always a good reason, and may not result in the best load.

Types of loads

The most frequently used *loads* are the horseshoe (or "U") load, the accordion load, the divided load, and the combination load. Typical *finishes* are the cross-fold finish, the donut finish, and the skid finish. Each of these loads and finishes has a number of variations. You will probably have to adapt them somewhat to meet local practices.

The *horseshoe load*, **Figure 9-19**, has the advantage of eliminating about half the sharp bends that other loads have. Sharp bends are damaging to hose. This load is especially good where you are likely to have long hose lays. It is not suited for shoulder or underarm hose carries, however.

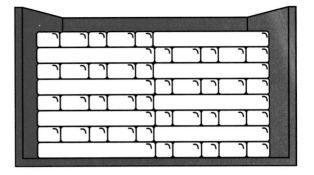

Figure 9-19. The horseshoe load is easier on hose than some other loads, because the folds are less sharp. This load is well-suited to situations where a long hose lay is the norm.

When making this or any other load, do not jam the hose in too tightly, or it will bind when you pull it off the apparatus. At the back of the load (the rear of the apparatus), stagger the folds so that every other one is about six inches shorter than those on either side. This method is less damaging to the hose, since the folds are a little less sharp. Also the hose will pull off the apparatus more easily.

The *accordion load*, **Figure 9-20**, is more versatile than the horseshoe load. It lends itself to shoulder and underarm carries. This is also the basic load used in conjunction with the

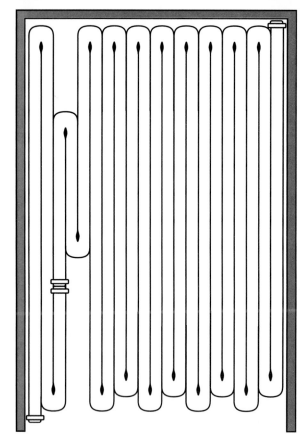

Figure 9-20. The accordion load permits easy use of shoulder and underarm carries. By staggering alternate folds, the chance of binding when paying out is minimized. The reverse bend allows the double coupling to be pulled straight out so that it does not bind.

divided and combination loads. Stagger every other fold, front and back, to prevent possible binding due to too-tight folds. It is not good practice to make a double coupling reverse itself as the hose pays out. Where the hose is packed in tight, this will cause it to bind. If you

are faced with this situation while loading hose, simply put in a reverse bend (a short fold), so the coupling will pull straight out.

A *divided load* is really two accordion loads in one hose bed. As shown in **Figure 9-21**, the two loads are divided by a piece of board, the length and height of the hose bed. This board is called a *baffle board*. The divided load may be used to provide either one long stretch of hose or two shorter ones. In the latter configuration, one section can be used for a straight lay and the other for a reverse lay.

A *combination load* also uses a baffle board. See **Figure 9-22**. On one side of the board is 2¹/₂ in. hose used for a supply line to the pump. On the other side are two 1¹/₂ in.

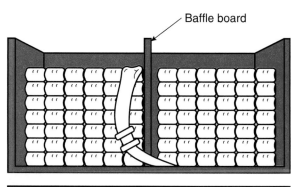

Baffle board

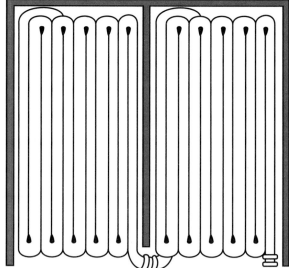

Figure 9-21. The divided load can be set up as a single long stretch of hose, or two shorter hose lines for greater flexibility. The hose bed is divided in half with a baffle board.

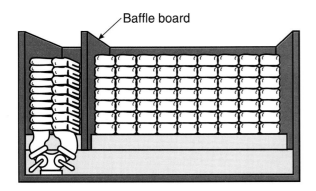

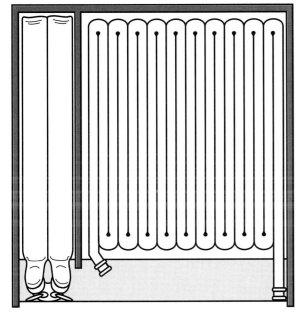

Figure 9-22. Like the divided load, the combination load uses a baffle board. In this load, however, each section of the hose bed holds a different size or type of hose. This permits great flexibility.

preconnected lines for attack use. The 1 1/2 in. lines should be connected to a gated wye to permit separate operation of the lines. This will permit the easy shutdown of one line for repositioning, extending, or replacing a burst section, without shutting down the entire attack system. This type of load can also be used for larger preconnected attack lines, such as 2 1/2 in.

Hose finishes

Hose *finishes* are intended to provide a sufficient amount of immediately available hose to take to a hydrant or to begin advancing a nozzle. Another advantage is that finishes quickly put enough weight on the ground to assist in paying off the regularly loaded hose.

The *cross-fold finish*, **Figure 9-23**, and the *donut finish*, **Figure 9-24**, are both excellent for taking a hydrant. The donut finish is somewhat easier to use. As shown in **Figure 9-25**, you can simply wrap it around the hydrant while the apparatus moves away. The cross-fold finish will provide more hose than the donut.

The *skid finish*, **Figure 9-26**, is best for advancing hose to the fire. It will provide about three lengths of ready hose on the ground. It is adaptable for the shoulder carry,

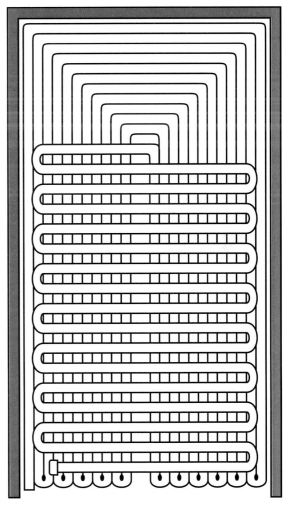

Figure 9-23. The cross-fold finish makes hose easily accessible when connecting to a hydrant. In this example, the cross-fold finish is atop a horseshoe load.

Front of hose bed

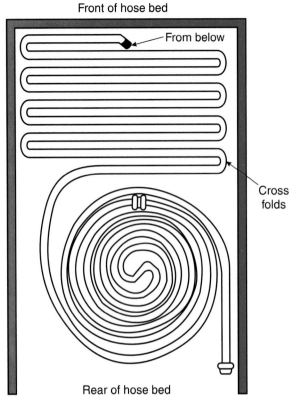

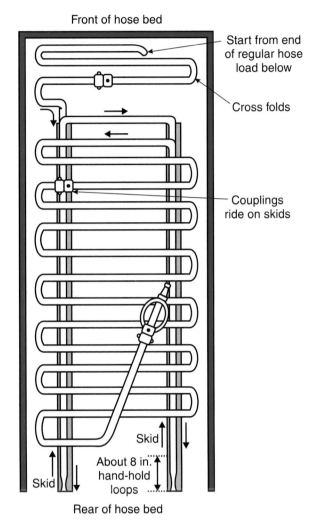

Front of hose bed

Figure 9-24. The donut finish employs a donut roll of hose atop the load for quick access. It is easily pulled off onto the ground when taking a hydrant.

the underarm carry, or any of the other common hose advancement methods. Three lengths in front of the fire structure is usually enough to put the nozzle where you want it.

Figure 9-26. A skid load finish uses two long folds of hose as "skids," so that about three lengths of hose can easily be pulled off the top of the load. It is a good finish for advancing hose to a fire.

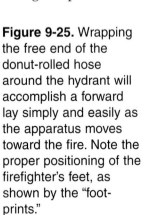

Figure 9-25. Wrapping the free end of the donut-rolled hose around the hydrant will accomplish a forward lay simply and easily as the apparatus moves toward the fire. Note the proper positioning of the firefighter's feet, as shown by the "footprints."

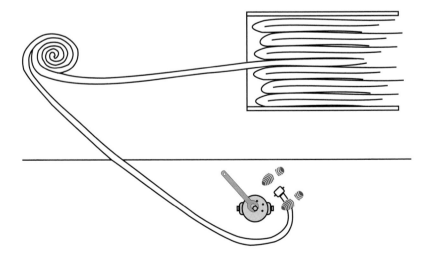

Hose rolls

Normally, for ease of storage and carrying, hose is rolled. The hose may be in single-roll form or in donut (double-roll) form.

The *single roll* is usually made with the male butt inside to protect the thread, **Figure 9-27.** After washing, however, if the hose is to be stored on a rack, it is normally rolled with the male butt *out*. This facilitates placing the hose on an apparatus later. (Local practices will vary.)

To roll hose with the male coupling in, begin by laying the hose out flat. Grasp the hose several inches back of the male coupling and fold it over so the coupling rests on the hose. Now, simply roll up the hose. After some practice, you will be able to do this quickly and smoothly.

The *donut roll* (sometimes called double roll) keeps both butts to the outside for easier access. See **Figure 9-28.** It is done by folding the hose back on itself approximately halfway along its length. The male butt should be on top of the hose, three to four feet behind the female butt. The hose is then rolled from the fold toward the butts. This job goes better if there are two firefighters available to do it. One firefighter rolls the hose, the other keeps the hose flat and aligned.

A

B

C

Figure 9-28. Donut roll hose technique. A—The donut roll is begun by folding the hose back on itself, leaving about 4 ft. between butts. B—Rolling begins from the folded end, usually with one firefighter rolling the hose and a second helping to hold it straight. C—The completed donut roll. (Warren Lutton)

A

B

Figure 9-27. Single hose roll technique. A—A single roll of hose is made by starting with the male butt turned in. B—The hose is then rolled to the end. After washing hose, however, this procedure is usually reversed, with the female half of the coupling at the center of the roll.

Making Hose Lays

Firefighters have a number of different ways to lay hose lines, and use a number of different terms to refer to them. In some places, firefighters call it a "hose lay," while in others, it is called a "hose stretch." The "straight lay" used by one department is a "forward lay" to another. In the same way, a "reverse lay" and a "back stretch" designate the same method. No matter what it is called, the lay that will be used depends on the situation. Each has advantages and disadvantages.

Straight lay

Straight lay hose is laid from the hydrant to the fire, **Figure 9-29.** That is, the truck first stops at the hydrant nearest the fire. A fire-

fighter pulls off sufficient hose to connect to the hydrant. The truck then proceeds to the fire, paying out hose as it goes.

Reverse lay

In some instances, the truck will reach the fire and the nearest practical hydrant will be on the other side of the building. This calls for a *reverse lay*, from the fire to the hydrant. See **Figure 9-30.** In this case, a firefighter will unload sufficient hose to go from that point to the fire *plus* one additional section for each floor up to the fire floor, and two sections for the fire floor itself. That is, if the firefighter is 50 feet from the building and the fire is on the third floor, five 50-foot sections (or 250 feet) of hose will be needed. One section is needed to

Figure 9-29. In a straight lay (forward lay), a firefighter connects hose to the hydrant nearest the fire, while the truck moves ahead, paying out hose.

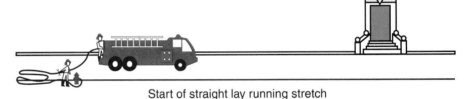

Start of straight lay running stretch

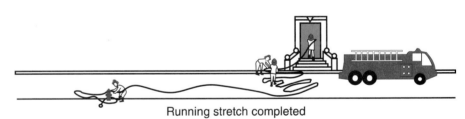

Running stretch completed

Figure 9-30. In a reverse lay, the movement is from the fire to the hydrant. A firefighter is dropped off near the building with the appropriate amount of hose for use. The truck then moves to the hydrant, paying out additional hose as it goes.

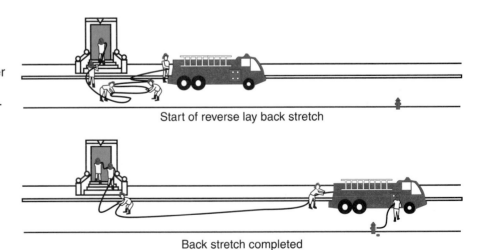

Start of reverse lay back stretch

Back stretch completed

reach from the drop-off point to the building, one section for each of the two floors below the fire floor, and two for the fire floor. After dropping off the firefighter and the necessary hose, the truck proceeds to the hydrant, paying out hose as it goes.

Hose is often loaded on a truck with the female fitting toward the fire. Since the *nozzle* also has a female fitting, a double male coupling is needed to join them. Similarly, the firefighter taking the hydrant will need a double female coupling in this situation.

Straight-to-reverse lay

Occasionally, a *straight-to-reverse lay* (times called a "mixed lay") must be made. This happens when there is some form of obstruction between the hydrant and the fire, so that neither a straight nor a reverse lay is practical. In this situation, one truck will start a straight lay from the hydrant and proceed as close to the fire as possible. Another truck will start a reverse lay from the fire toward the hydrant. Where the lays meet, a double female is used to connect the two lines.

For most situations, *in-line pumping* is used for better control of pressure in the attack lines. This means that water flow from the hydrant to the attack lines is through the truck's pump, **Figure 9-31.** Assuming a straight lay, one firefighter will step off at the hydrant with sufficient hose to connect, then the truck will proceed to the fire. The remaining firefighters will immediately attack the fire using lines preconnected to the tank on the

truck. This gets water on the fire while the person at the hydrant and the engineer are still connecting lines. Since the amount of water in the tank is limited, it is important to quickly begin pumping water from the hydrant.

Connecting to a hydrant

The process of connecting a line to a hydrant is often referred to as *taking a hydrant*. The procedure described in the following paragraphs assumes that you are making a straight lay from the hydrant to the fire, and that the load is finished with a donut roll (this will not always be the case).

When the truck stops near the hydrant, place a spanner wrench and a hydrant wrench in the right-hand pocket of your turnout coat. Take hold of the donut roll and place it on the ground. Do not drop it or throw it down, since this could damage the coupling so that you cannot connect the hose.

As you leave the truck, pick up a two-way gate valve with your right hand. With your left, grasp the end of the hose right behind the coupling and walk to the hydrant. Lay the gate valve beside the hydrant temporarily. Wrap the end of the hose around the hydrant and hold it in place with your foot (again placed right behind the coupling). See **Figure 9-32.**

NOTE: When taking a hydrant, always observe this safety precaution: hold the hose with either the hand or foot that is on the side to which the hose would be pulled if it got snagged on the truck as it moved

Figure 9-31. In-line pumping is used whenever possible, since it permits better control of pressure in the attack lines.

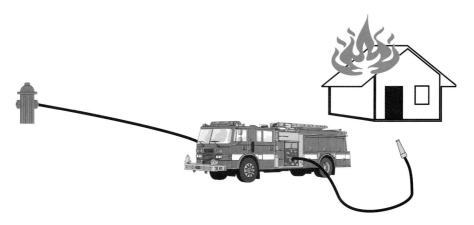

Figure 9-32. Hold the hose in place with your foot as the truck pulls away. Observe the safety precaution noted in the text. After loosening the hydrant cap with your wrench, place it on the valve nut, ready for use.

Figure 9-33. Align the threads of the hose coupling with the valve threads and rotate until it is hand-tight. Use your spanner to snug it into place.

away. That is, if the hose would pull to the left, hold it with your left foot or left hand. If it would pull to the right, use your right foot or hand. That way, a snagged hose will pull *away* from you, not across your body.

Using your hydrant wrench, loosen a hydrant cap. Place the wrench on the operating (valve) nut, ready for use when the engineer calls for water.

Attach the two-way gate valve to the hydrant, making sure it is snugged up tight. Pick up the hose by grasping it just behind coupling with the hand that is on the side away from the hydrant. With other hand, grasp the rotating collar of the coupling. See **Figure 9-33.** (Never handle couplings by placing your fingers inside them. Many firefighters have broken or even lost fingers that way.) Match the coupling to the hydrant fitting, and rotate the collar one-quarter turn counter-clockwise to engage the thread. Next, rotate the collar clockwise until it is finger-tight. Tighten all fittings with your spanner wrench.

Move the gate valve lever on the side with the hose connected to the "ON" position. Make sure the other side is in the "OFF" position. Do not *open* the hydrant until you are signaled to do so by the engineer. When you *do* receive the signal for water, open the hydrant valve fully.

There are some variations in how water is turned on. Some departments open the hydrant but keep the gate valve closed until water is called for. Other departments put hose clamps on the attack lines and pressurize to that point. The clamps are released when the engineer signals for water.

Connecting to a standpipe

Schools, hospitals, factories, hotels, apartment houses, and similar occupancies frequently have standpipe protection. At several places on each floor, there are cabinets containing hose that is preconnected to the standpipe. This hose is an unlined linen material, and not a bad hose for the purpose. Unfortunately, it hangs in the cabinet for years, is never taken off and refolded, and is never tested. For fire department purposes, the hose is useless.

Procedures for connecting to a standpipe at a modern high-rise building follow this general pattern:

1. Take three donut rolls of 1½ in. hose to the floor *just below* the fire floor. This will give you one hose length for the stairway and two for the fire floor.
2. Connect the hose to the standpipe at the nearest cabinet. Connect the other two lengths of hose and install the nozzle.

3. Advance the hose up the stairway. Extend it past the fire floor a short distance and back again.
4. When the line is in position, call for water. Open the nozzle just enough to exhaust the air. Do not enter fire floor until the line is charged.

Coupling hose and nozzles

Hoses can be coupled by either one or two persons. It goes faster with two, but sometimes one firefighter must do it alone.

During hose washing, inspecting, and loading procedures, firefighters should check for the presence and condition of the gasket in the female half of the coupling. The gasket may not be there or it may be so badly damaged that it will not seal. So, before you start to make a connection, make sure the gasket is there and that it will seal properly.

One-person hose couple. Follow these steps to couple hose when working alone:
1. Hold the female half in your right hand and place your left foot on the hose just behind the male half. See **Figure 9-34.**
2. Bring the two parts of the coupling together, then rotate the swivel of female half counterclockwise until you hear or feel the slight click of the threads engaging. Rotate swivel clockwise until tight. If the gasket is in good condition, a hand-tight connection should seal properly.

An alternative one-person method for coupling hose is described below:
1. Spread feet apart about shoulder width for proper balance.
2. Stoop slightly and clamp the female end of the hose under your right arm. Allow the coupling to rest on your left thigh.
3. Using your left hand, bring the male and female portions of the coupling together. Connect the hose by rotating the female coupling half with your right hand.

Two-person hose couple. The *two-person hose couple* has several advantages over the one-person method. To begin with, it's faster just because you have two sets of hands working. Further, it allows coupling two

Figure 9-34. Placing your foot behind the male half of the coupling will tilt it upward for easier joining of the two hose lengths. (Warren Lutton)

lengths of hose (or a hose and a nozzle) while advancing toward the fire.

To make a two-person couple, the firefighters face each other and hold the coupling halves at about waist level, as shown in **Figure 9-35.** The firefighter with the male half holds it firm and level, pointing straight at the other person. The person with the male half doesn't try to align the coupling or even look directly at it. All the aligning and rotation should be done by the person with the female portion of the coupling.

Figure 9-35. Two-person hose couple or nozzle attachment. Each firefighter holds one coupling half at waist level. The halves (or coupling half and nozzle, as shown here) are then brought together, aligned, and tightened. (Warren Lutton)

Attaching a nozzle. Connecting a nozzle to a hose line is similar to making a hose connection, using the same basic one-person or two-person techniques. When working alone, first rotate the nozzle about one-half turn counterclockwise to engage the threads. Then, rotate the nozzle clockwise until tight. See **Figure 9-36.**

A

B

Figure 9-36. One-person nozzle attachment. A—Attaching a nozzle using the same basic technique as the one-person hose couple shown in Figure 9-33. B—Alternate method usable for coupling hose or attaching a nozzle.

Attaching a nozzle — reverse lay

The information on coupling hoses and attaching nozzles assumed that you were making a straight lay (from the hydrant to the fire). On a reverse lay, from the fire toward the hydrant, the procedure for attaching a nozzle is somewhat different. You will have a female coupling half facing the fire instead of a male coupling half. For such situations, pumpers usually have at least one nozzle with a double male coupling already attached. When making a connection under these circumstances, the firefighter with the nozzle holds it level and steady, and the person holding the hose end makes the alignment and tightens the connection.

Advancing Hose Lines

There are many kinds of hose line advances. At a major fire, you may make any of the following advances:

- into a structure
- up an inside stairway to an upper floor
- up an outside stairway to an upper floor
- down an inside stairway to a lower floor
- down an outside stairway to a lower floor
- to an upper floor by hoisting
- up a ladder to an upper floor window.

At a working fire, you will use every ounce of energy you've got and then some, so it is very important to conserve energy wherever and whenever you can. Substitute efficiency for brute force; brainpower for musclepower.

Efficiency requires knowing in advance what to do and who will do it. It is knowing the *right amount* of hose to lay, neither more nor less than is needed. The job can get very rough when you need just *a little* more hose than was laid out. Efficiency is having everything ready *before* you turn the water on. Efficiency means working together smoothly as a team.

How much hose is needed?

If you have five sections of hose laid out and charged, then find out you need ten more feet, you've got a job on your hands. Similarly, if you have a couple hundred feet extra at the foot of the ladder, you've got a problem. You need the *right* amount. If you are advancing up an inside stairway or a fire escape, allow one section (50 feet) for each floor below the fire floor, plus two sections for the fire floor itself. If you are advancing up a ladder, allow *15* feet per floor, plus two sections for the fire floor.

The hose bed on most pumpers is about ten feet long. Therefore, every fold you see at the end of the hose bed represents *20* feet of hose. Every *coupling* you pull off the hose bed represents 50 feet of hose. Thus, if you are parked 50 feet from the front door of a house and the fire is on the second floor, you will need 50 feet to get to the front door, 50 feet for the first floor, and 100 feet for the second floor. Four lengths will give you what you need, but for good measure, pull off to the next coupling. When you take hose off the bed, pull off a couple of folds at a time and keep each group separate from the others. This will help you keep track of how much hose you have removed. Also, it will prevent the hose from getting tangled up like a bowl of spaghetti.

A number of factors will determine what type of hose advancement you will use. Among the more important are:

- *The hose load.* What hose sizes do you have available? How is the hose loaded on the vehicle?
- *The length of stretch.* One firefighter can quickly stretch three or four lengths of 1½ in. hose with little trouble. But stretching ten or fifteen lengths would be a lot more difficult.
- *The number of firefighters.* With enough firefighters you can lay any amount of hose anywhere. But working with restricted numbers, you must learn to work efficiently.
- *The type of structure.* Obviously, a twenty-story high-rise is going to present a different set of problems than will a one-story bungalow. A wide, low structure (such as a warehouse) will be still different.

Carrying vs dragging hose

In general, it is better to *carry* hose rather than drag it. Fifty feet of 1½ in. hose weighs only 18 pounds. Fifty feet of 2½ in. hose weighs about 32 pounds. Either amount of weight is easy to carry. When you try to drag it, however, the task becomes harder, since there will be friction between the hose and the pavement. Also, hose gets hung up going around corners. Carrying hose is far less damaging to it than dragging. At times, there is no alternative to dragging. In such cases, watch out for hose-damaging conditions such as sharp debris or injurious chemicals.

Types of carries

For longer lays, such as going up several flights of stairs, deep into a building, or a long way from the apparatus, you should use either the shoulder carry or the underarm carry. Remember, you need enough hose to get to the building, one length for each floor, and two lengths for the fire floor.

For both the shoulder carry and the underarm carry, someone at the apparatus should load the carriers and keep track of how many lengths of hose are being put into use. You don't want to have to extend the line.

Shoulder carry. The first firefighter places the nozzle over one shoulder and walks forward 25 feet. See **Figure 9-37.** The loader places three loops of hose on the shoulder of second firefighter, who then moves forward 25 feet. The loader places three loops of hose on the shoulder of the next. The loader can increase the number of loops of hose on succeeding firefighters, because they won't have to walk so far. When enough hose has been loaded, all walk toward the fire while maintaining a 25-foot interval. The last firefighter loaded pays off hose first, then the next-to-last, and so forth. As each firefighter is relieved of the load, she or he moves forward to assist those in front.

Figure 9-37. In the shoulder carry, firefighters are spaced about 25 feet apart as they advance hose. Carriers pay off hose in reverse order of loading. (Warren Lutton)

Underarm carry. This is basically the same as the shoulder carry. The only difference is that the firefighters carry hose under their arms rather than on their shoulders. See **Figure 9-38.**

Short lay hose advance

The first firefighter places the nozzle over his or her left shoulder, with the hose crossing the chest to the left. A second firefighter picks up the hose at the first coupling and places the hose over one shoulder with the coupling resting on his or her chest. The third firefighter

Figure 9-38. The underarm carry differs from the shoulder carry only in the way firefighters hold the hose as they advance.

does the same at the next coupling. They walk toward the fire in unison, keeping an interval of about 25 feet between them.

Long advance

One firefighter can stretch several hundred feet of hose by the method shown in **Figure 9-39**:
1. Pull a little over two lengths from the apparatus.
2. Walk back to the first double coupling and pull it so that it is even with the nozzle. This will pull more hose from the apparatus.
3. Pull the next coupling even with the nozzle, then the next coupling, and so on.
4. When you have enough hose off the apparatus, walk forward with the nozzle, paying out hose as you go. At the new position, repeat the whole process, pulling hose even with the nozzle, so that

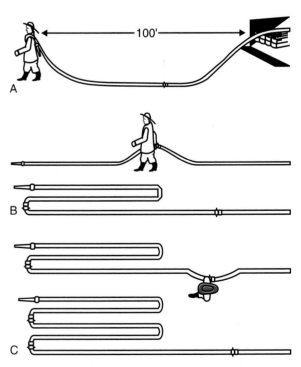

Figure 9-39. One-firefighter hose stretch. A—Pull approximately 100 ft. of hose off the hose bed. B—Pull the first coupling even with the nozzle. C—Pull the next coupling even with the nozzle. Repeat as needed to pull enough hose off the truck. The hose can then be advanced further in the same way.

additional lengths are pulled off the apparatus. Repeat the forward movement until you have the nozzle where you need it.

Advancing hose up a fire escape

Assuming the fire is on the fourth floor, four firefighters would be used in the advancement. See **Figures 9-40** to **9-44.**

1. While hose is being brought to the fire escape and flaked out beside it, the firefighter who will operate the nozzle climbs to the fourth floor, carrying a rope. After fastening one end of the rope to the fire escape, he or she drops the free end to the ground.
2. Two other firefighters position themselves on the fire escape balconies at the second and third floors. See **Figure 9-40.**
3. The firefighter on the ground folds the nozzle back over the hose to form a two-foot loop, then ties a clove hitch around the nozzle. (The firefighter first makes certain to tie the nozzle handle in the "off" position.) A half-hitch is used to secure the hose near the top of the loop. See **Figure 9-41.**
4. Acting in unison, firefighters on the balconies and the ground hoist the hose upward, **Figure 9-42.**
5. The firefighter on the third floor flakes out excess hose, working from the building side of the balcony to the outside. See **Figure 9-43.**
6. Before calling for water, firefighters tie the hose at the second- and third-floor balconies to relieve strain on the couplings. See **Figure 9-44.**

Advancing hose up a ladder; working from a ladder

Since these two topics are very closely related, they will be discussed together.

1. Tie the ladder firmly in place, using any approved method.
2. Near the foot of the ladder, flake out sufficient hose for the necessary advance.
3. The nozzle operator places the nozzle over one shoulder and starts to climb the ladder. See **Figure 9-45.**

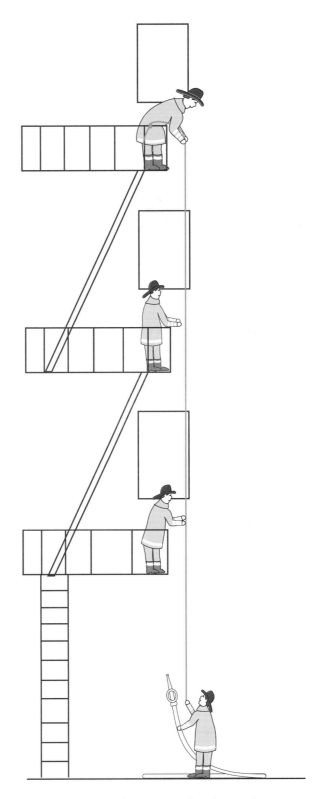

Figure 9-40. Firefighters station themselves on all three balconies. A rope is tied to fourth floor railing and dropped to ground to hoist hose.

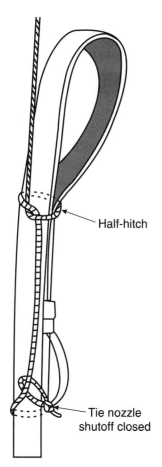

Figure 9-41. The hose is attached to the hoisting rope with a clove hitch and a half-hitch.

4. The next firefighter grasps the hose about halfway between the nozzle and the first double coupling and places it over one shoulder. This firefighter starts climbing the ladder, staying ten feet behind the nozzle operator.

5. The next firefighter grasps the hose at the double coupling. Laying the coupling across his or her chest, the firefighter starts climbing. Again, this firefighter must maintain the ten-foot distance from the person next highest on the ladder.

6. Once the hose is in place, a hose strap is used to tie it securely behind the nozzle. It should also be secured to the bottom of the ladder. If the nozzle is taken inside the building, secure the hose inside as well. Do not call for water until the hose is completely secured.

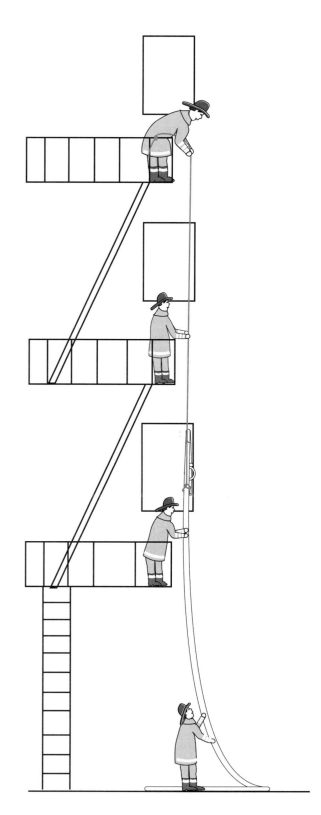

Figure 9-42. Firefighters work together to hoist the hose to the upper levels of the fire escape.

Figure 9-43. As hose is hoisted upward, the firefighter on the third floor balcony flakes out the excess, ready for use.

Figure 9-44. Tying the hose to the fire escape balconies on the second and third floors will take strain off the hose couplings.

A   B

Figure 9-45. Advancing hose up a ladder. A—The first firefighter places the nozzle over one shoulder and starts to climb. B—The next firefighter grasps the hose and starts climbing, staying about ten feet behind the nozzle operator. (Warren Lutton)

Advancing charged lines

There is seldom need to advance a charged line any great distance, if it has been properly placed to begin with. When fire hose is charged, it becomes stiff and unwieldy and does not bend readily. It also becomes heavy: the water in one length of 2½ in. hose weighs 106 lbs.; in a length of 3 in. hose, 150 lbs. As stated earlier, with enough firefighters, you can pick hose up and set it down anywhere. But the modern firefighter uses brainpower, not musclepower, whenever possible.

It just does not make sense to try working a charged 2½ in. line up a stairway or fire escape. It is far quicker and easier, in the long run, to cut off the water and drain the line, then move the hose. If there is a gate valve between the nozzle and the pump, simply shut off the line you have to move. If there is no gate valve, shut off the flow of water temporarily with a hose clamp.

But the *best* way to handle this situation is to avoid it: make sure the line is properly positioned before you call for water.

Extending a Hose Line

Extending a line and replacing a burst section are basically the same procedure. (When you replace a burst section, however, you must remove the burst section completely before adding the new one.) One firefighter can handle such tasks, but two or more firefighters can do them easier and faster. To extend a line:

1. Bring a donut roll of hose to the point that you plan to insert it. Place the roll so the male coupling is toward the female end of the existing joint.
2. Position a hose clamp as close as possible to the joint that will be broken. Insert hose in the clamp. Slowly close and lock the clamp to cut off water flow.
3. Break the line and connect the new hose to the matching butts.
4. Extend line with additional hose, as required.
5. Unlock and slowly release the clamp so water can flow through the line again.

Normally, sealing a burst in a section temporarily with a hose jacket is preferred to taking the line out of service. There are occasions, though, when you will have to replace a section of hose on the fireground (for example, when the burst area is too long to seal).

Replacing a burst section

1. Bring the replacement hose section up and stretch it parallel to the section to be

replaced. Match the butts of the two hose sections: male beside male, female beside female.

2. Use a hose clamp to slowly cut off water-flow.
3. Uncouple the burst section and move it aside.
4. Insert new section of hose and connect the couplings.
5. Unlock and slowly release the clamp.

Protecting Hose on the Fireground

Modern fire hose is usually a double jacket of fabric with a synthetic rubber lining. The rubber is soft and pliable and has very low burst strength. Jackets are usually made of cotton, synthetic fibers, or a combination of the two. The outer jacket is woven to provide abrasion resistance, the inner one to give the hose good handling qualities. Together, the jackets provide the high burst strength needed for hose used in modern firefighting.

It might seem odd to think of fire hose as "protective equipment," but there are times when it is the best protective equipment you have:

- You use it to clear the air of smoke so you can see where you are going.

- You use it to form a protective spray to keep heat and flames away from you.

- You use it to cool a room to prevent a possible flashover.

These are all excellent reasons for taking good care of hose, since one length failing at a crucial time could leave you in a hazardous position.

Most departments pressure-test hose at least once a year, but much can happen to a length of hose in 365 days. (For that matter, a lot can happen in 24 hours after it is tested.) One of your many jobs is to protect your hose so *it* can protect you.

The jacket on a hose is tough, but it is not indestructible. Dragging hose over a sharp surface, such as a window with broken glass still in the frame, will cut through the jacket and

weaken it. A *hose roller*, **Figure 9-46**, will protect a hose against chafing and cutting when it is pulled over a sharp edge. This device will also make it much easier to pull the hose.

If a hose is laid over a sharp edge, such as a curb, vibration of the pump will cause chafing at that point. This can wear through the jacket. Use chafing blocks if the hose must be in this position any length of time. See **Figure 9-47.**

Do not permit vehicles to drive over hose, especially hose that is empty. This can

Figure 9-46. A hose roller protects the hose from chafing and cutting when it is pulled over a sharp or rough edge. It also reduced friction, making hose-pulling easier. (Akron Brass)

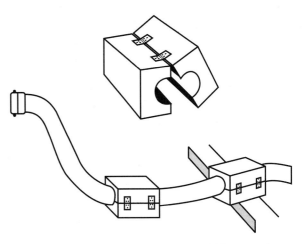

Figure 9-47. Chafing blocks should be used to prevent vibration from causing a hose to wear at the point where it is laid over a curb or similar edge.

cause the rubber lining to separate from the jacket. To prevent this type of damage, use *hose bridges* whenever you must lay hose across a street. See **Figure 9-48.** If possible, choose hydrants and position your pumpers so that you do not have to lay lines across a street. Don't lay hose across a *railroad track*, unless that track can be closed to train traffic.

Always exhaust the air from a line as soon as it is charged, to avoid excessive air pressure buildup. When closing a nozzle, do so slowly. Air in the line or too-rapid closing of a nozzle can cause *water hammer*, a pressure surge that can reach as high as seven times the static pressure. Thus, if the pump pressure is a modest 150 psi (1034 kPa), the surge could reach over a 1000 psi (over 7000 kPa). Such high pressure can cause the hose to burst, or literally tear the lining out of it.

Do not drop hose or throw it around. Rough handling can damage coupling threads or knock a coupling out of round. In either case, the hose length will be useless until it is repaired.

During subfreezing weather, a coating of ice will form on hose, making the jacket fibers stiff. When this happens, handle with care. Any bending will cause the fibers to break. If hose should become frozen to the pavement, don't try to pry it up. This will also cause the fibers to

break. Very carefully chop around the hose with an axe, then without bending the hose, load it (and the attached ice) onto the apparatus,

Heat causes rubber to harden, and when rubber hardens, it cracks and leaks. Usually, you cannot prevent heat damage at a fire. But do not store hose in direct sunlight, near a radiator, or near any other heat source. There is no sense asking for trouble.

Gasoline, oils, and many solvents will attack and dissolve rubber. As much as possible, keep hose away from these substances on the fireground. Don't identify hose by stenciling with oil-based paint or ink. For the same reason, don't lubricate couplings with oil or grease of any kind. A good cleaning will usually free a balky but undamaged coupling. If you must lubricate, use dry graphite powder.

Injurious substances, such as solvents, acids, and alkalis, may be found at almost any fire. Playing water into the building will wash these substances out and into the gutter along the curb. To avoid bringing hose in contact with these damaging materials, do not lay hose directly in the gutter. Lay it parallel to the curb, but up on the sidewalk or a foot or two toward the middle of the street.

Older hoses with jackets made from cotton canvas will mildew and rot if they are not thoroughly dried before being stored.

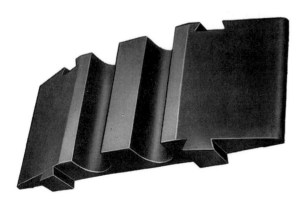

A

B

Figure 9-48. A hose bridge protects hose from damage by vehicles driving over it. A—A typical hose bridge. B—Hose bridges in use.

Manufacturers of hose with synthetic jackets claim that such hose does not have to be dried after use. In a sense, this is true: synthetics won't rot. But the acids, solvents, and other substances that a hose may come into contact with can do considerable damage. More important, however, is the fact that such substances are often hazardous to your health. After every fire, you should wash *all* hose used. Drying may not be necessary with synthetic coverings.

Hose Inspection and Maintenance

The ultimate test of any material or thing is one that shows how it will perform; that it will do its job without falling apart or flying apart. For this reason, most fire departments test hose on a regular schedule, usually once a year.

These periodic tests for hose that has been in use are referred to as "service tests." To service-test hose, set up a line consisting of one to six lengths and a nozzle.

Leak test

Pressurize the line with water at 50 psi (345 kPa), then exhaust the air and close the nozzle. Examine the entire line for leakage.

Burst test

If there is no leakage, increase the pump pressure to 250 psi (1724 kPa) and hold at that pressure for a minimum of five minutes. In addition to the hose being able to withstand this pressure, there must be no indication that a coupling has moved.

Lengths of hose that pass both tests are dried and returned to service. Those showing any sign of failure are either repaired and retested or are removed permanently from fire use.

CAUTION: Hose tests (especially the burst test) can be extremely dangerous. *Do not attempt to test hose until you understand and are able to follow all safety requirements.*

Annual hose testing is not enough, however. Anything can happen to a length of hose at a fire. After each use, every length that was taken off the hose bed should be washed and inspected thoroughly before being placed back into service. Look for any signs of discoloration or deterioration that could be caused by chemicals, high heat, or mildew. Mildew has a strong, musty odor that is unmistakable. Look for cuts or abrasions in the jacket. Look for any signs of jacket fraying, especially where couplings are attached. Look for any indication that a coupling has moved. If a hose has been frozen, it must be leak- and burst-tested.

Feel the rubber through the jacket. It must be soft and pliable, and firmly bonded to the jacket. Check inside the female coupling for a gasket. There must be a soft, pliable gasket present to properly seal the joint. The gasket should have no cuts or splits, and no areas of excessive roughness. Pressure test any questionable lengths of hose before putting them back in service.

Check both couplings for signs of damage or corrosion. Threads should not show nicks or gouges. Male threads are especially subject to damage. Make sure both butts (couplings) are round. Be sure the female thread swivels easily. If it does not, there could be some grit or small stones in it. If the swivel won't free up, it should be replaced. If any butt looks suspicious, thread it all the way into a mating butt.

If a nozzle appears to be damaged, it probably *has* been damaged. Look over every nozzle that has been used for any sign of physical abuse. Tips may be knocked out of round, and they occasionally get burrs inside. Both conditions can adversely affect the stream. Adjustable nozzles sometimes have small stones or other foreign matter trapped somewhere. Sometimes, you can hear a rattle if you shake a nozzle that has foreign matter inside it. Again, if there is any question, call for a functional test. If the nozzle is adjustable, test it on all possible settings. It is better to uncover problems in quarters rather than at the fire scene.

SUMMARY

Hoses may be either hard or soft. Hard hose is used for drafting water from rivers and ponds; soft hose is used for working and supply lines. Soft hose from 1½ in. to 3 in. is working line; anything larger is supply line.

Many kinds of nozzles are available, but the most versatile is the combination solid stream/fog nozzle. This type of nozzle will provide any kind of a stream you need on a handheld line from a penetrating solid stream to a fog pattern.

Adapters are fittings that are used to connect two threads that ordinarily would not match. Other fittings are the siamese, used to join two lines into one, and the wye, used to separate one supply line into two working lines.

The kind of hose load that a department uses depends in large part on the kind of area served. Where supply lines will be long, the horseshoe load has advantages. Where supply lines will be short and multiple attack lines are often needed, an accordion, split, or combination load will probably be best. The two most common hose rolls are the single roll and the donut roll. The donut roll is convenient for extending a line, since it does not have to be unrolled completely to be put into use.

In making a straight lay, the hose is laid from the hydrant to the fire. A lay from the fire to the hydrant is called a reverse lay. Sometimes, hose is laid part way from the hydrant to the fire and part way from the fire to the hydrant. This is called a mixed lay. For most fires, in-line pumping is used, even when there is sufficient water pressure from a hydrant. The reason for using a pump is the ability to get the exact amount of pressure that you need.

The hose load, length of stretch, number of firefighters available, and the severity and nature of the fire determine the method you will use to advance hose lines. Do not call for water until your lines are in place and there is a sufficient amount properly positioned for advancement. Do not open or attempt to enter the fire structure or fire floor until you have a charged line in your hands. With proper positioning you will not have to advance the charged lines very far.

During the course of a fire, hose can be damaged in many ways. A hose that won't hold up during a fire is worse than no hose at all. Protect your hose as you would your breathing apparatus. After every use, hose should be inspected for damage to the jacket, lining, or couplings. Every length of hose should be service-tested at least once a year.

REVIEW QUESTIONS

1. Define the term "hoseline."
2. Distinguish between fittings and appliances.
3. What sizes (diameters) of working hose are used? Give an application for each size.
4. What is the difference between a siamese and a wye?
5. Describe the use of a water thief.
6. Under what circumstances would you use a hose jacket?
7. Describe the procedure for replacing a burst hose section.
8. State the procedure one firefighter would use to attach a nozzle to a hose. Assume you are using a straight hose lay.
9. What are the advantages of a combination hose load?
10. Describe three finishes and state their uses.
11. What is a reverse lay? Why is it made?
12. What is the advantage of in-line pumping?
13. Describe three types of fog nozzles.
14. When is a "fog-only" nozzle used? Why?
15. What is the advantage of a variable gallonage nozzle?
16. Describe the method of using a cellar nozzle.
17. What conditions or substances found at fires are damaging to hose?
18. What procedure would you use to attack a fire on the eighth floor of a high-rise building equipped with exterior fire escapes?
19. State the procedure for advancing hose up a ladder and working with charged line on a ladder.
20. How often should you leak-test and pressure-test fire hose?

NFPA 1001 Job Performance Requirements

The material on this page consists of those portions of the NFPA 1001 Job Performance Requirements relevant to the material presented in this chapter. Items preceded by the numeral 3 (3-x.x) are Fire Fighter I requirements; those with the numeral 4 (4-x.x) are Fire Fighter II requirements.

3-3.10 Perform horizontal ventilation on a structure operating as part of a team, given an assignment, personal protective equipment, ventilation tools, equipment, and ladders, so that the ventilation openings are free of obstructions, tools are safely used, ladders are properly used, ventilation devices are properly placed, and the structure is cleared of smoke.

(a) Prerequisite Knowledge: The principles, advantages, limitations, and effects of horizontal, mechanical, and hydraulic ventilation; safety considerations when venting a structure; fire behavior in a structure; the products of combustion found in a structure fire; the signs, causes, effects, and prevention of backdrafts; and the relationship of oxygen concentration to life safety and fire growth.

(b) Prerequisite Skills: The ability to transport and operate ventilation tools and equipment and ladders and to use safe procedures for breaking window and door glass and removing obstructions.

3-3.11 Perform vertical ventilation on a structure operating as part of a team, given an assignment, personal protective equipment, ground and roof ladders, and tools, so that ladders are properly positioned for ventilation, a sufficient opening is created, all ventilation barriers are removed, structural integrity is not compromised, products of combustion are released from the structure, and the team retreats from the area when ventilation is accomplished.

(a) Prerequisite Knowledge: The methods of heat transfer; the principles of thermal layering within a structure on fire; the techniques and safety precautions for venting flat roofs, pitched roofs, and basements; basic indicators of potential collapse or roof failure; the effects of construction types and elapsed time under fire conditions on structural integrity; and the advantages and disadvantages of vertical and trench/strip ventilation.

(b) Prerequisite Skills: The ability to transport and operate ventilation tools and equipment; hoist ventilation tools to a roof; cut roofing and flooring materials to vent flat roofs, pitched roofs, and basements; sound a roof for integrity; clear an opening with hand tools; select, carry, deploy, and secure ground ladders for ventilation activities; deploy roof ladders on pitched roofs while secured to a ground ladder; carry ventilation-related tools and equipment while ascending and descending ladders.

4-3.2 Coordinate an interior attack line team's accomplishment of an assignment in a structure fire, given attack lines, personnel, personal protective equipment, and tools, so that crew integrity is established; attack techniques are selected for the given level of the fire (for example, attic, grade level, upper levels, or basement); attack techniques are communicated to the attack teams; constant team coordination is maintained; fire growth and development is continuously evaluated; search, rescue, and ventilation requirements are communicated or managed; hazards are reported to the attack teams; and incident command is apprised of changing conditions.

(a) Prerequisite Knowledge: Selection of the proper nozzle and hose for fire attack given different fire situations; selection of adapters and appliances to be used for specific fire ground situations; dangerous building conditions created by fire and fire suppression activities; indicators of building collapse; the effects of fire and fire suppression activities on wood, masonry (brick, block, stone), cast iron, steel, reinforced concrete, gypsum wall board, glass, and plaster on lath; search and rescue and ventilation procedures; indicators of structural instability; suppression approaches and practices for various types of structural fires; and the association between specific tools and special forcible entry needs.

(b) Prerequisite Skills: The ability to assemble a team, choose attack techniques for various levels of a fire (e.g., attic, grade level, upper levels, or basement), evaluate and forecast a fire's growth and development, select proper tools for forcible entry, incorporate search and rescue procedures and ventilation procedures in the completion of the attack team efforts, and determine developing hazardous building or fire conditions.

Reprinted with permission from NFPA 1001, *Fire Fighter Professional Qualifications,* Copyright ©1997, National Fire Protection Association, Quincy, MA 02269. This reprinted material is not the complete and official position of the National Fire Protection Association on the referenced subject, which is represented only by the standard in its entirety.

Ventilation

OBJECTIVES

When you have completed this chapter, you will be able to:

- Discuss the principles, advantages, and effects of ventilation.
- Describe the dangers encountered when performing ventilation.
- Explain how backdraft explosions occur.
- Describe the different types of roof construction and how they affect ventilation.
- List the types of tools used in ventilation and describe how they are used.
- Describe the locations and sizes of openings needed for effective ventilation.

IMPORTANT TERMS

arched roof
backdraft explosion
flashover
flat roof
forced ventilation

HVAC
hydraulic ventilation
natural ventilation
negative pressure
 ventilation

pitched roof
positive pressure
 ventilation
smoke ejector
strip ventilation

trench ventilation
ventilation
venting devices
wear surface

Responding to a structure fire, you hear the dispatcher tell the officer of your engine, "The police officer on the scene reports that you have a working fire and that everyone is out." Your mind races through all the things you will be doing in the next few minutes. You feel a sense of relief that you won't have to worry about a rescue. As your engine rounds the corner, you catch a glimpse of the building charged with smoke, **Figure 10-1.** You pull on your mask as you step off the engine (you *never* enter a burning structure without wearing your SCBA). With your partner, you grab the preconnected hand line. As you reach the front door, your officer forces it open. The smoke and the heat quickly drive you to the floor, **Figure 10-2.** Going is slow! The sweat pours off your face and drips into your mask.

Just about the time you begin to think that you will be unable to advance further, you hear the sound of a power saw being started somewhere overhead. See **Figure 10-3.** As you inch forward, you hear the saw blade make contact with the roof deck. See **Figure 10-4.** After several minutes, the ceiling falls from above. Almost immediately, the smoke rises out the vent hole and you can see in front of you. The temperature drops sharply, and the fire, which you couldn't locate a few short minutes before, appears before you. As

Figure 10-1. The sight of a building heavily charged with smoke often greets firefighters on arrival. (Warren Lutton)

Figure 10-2. Heat and smoke banking down from the ceiling will often drive firefighters to the floor as they advance into the building.

Figure 10-3. A truck company member starts a power saw as he prepares to open the roof and vent smoke. Note the roof ladder being placed to provide firmer footing on the steeply pitched surface. (Jack Klasey)

you and your partner make your attack, the thought crosses your mind, "leave it to the truckees to show up right on time!"

Benefits of Ventilation

This story clearly illustrates the dramatic effect that proper ventilation, along with a

Figure 10-4. A power saw can quickly create an opening in a roof to vent smoke and hot gases.

well-coordinated attack, can have on your ability to safely extinguish a confined fire. *Ventilation* is the planned release of smoke and gases from a confined area. You must remember that the release of these gases can also aid in the rescue of trapped victims. Ventilation creates a safer environment and allows the rescuer to quickly search the area.

The proper release of smoke and gases can also reduce structural damage. It reduces the potential for a backdraft, as well as the effects of mushrooming. Ventilation makes firefighting easier, and helps to confine the spread of the fire itself.

Questions to Ask Before Ventilating

Before an officer orders ventilation of a building, there are three questions that must be asked, based on the fireground situation. The answers to these questions will help to create the plan of attack that the officer uses when ordering you to ventilate.

Is ventilation required at this time?

This question must be based on conditions at the fire scene, **Figure 10-5.** Heat, smoke, and gases that are trapped within the

Figure 10-5. As firefighters prepare to enter an involved building, the officer in charge must decide if ventilation is needed, where ventilation will take place, and whether it will be natural or forced.

structure must be considered. Life hazards to both building occupants and firefighters are also important.

Where must you ventilate?

This answer depends on the type of building construction, the occupants and contents of the building, and the location and extent of the fire. External factors at the fireground, such as exposures to the fire building, wind direction, and access, also must be considered.

What type of ventilation is required?

Based upon the answers to the two previous questions, the officer may order you to use either natural ventilation or forced ventilation. **Natural ventilation** includes the use of all openings found or made in the fire building. This will allow the smoke and gases to be released naturally through these openings. **Forced ventilation** can easily be accomplished with the use of water fog or mechanical forced-air ventilation.

Phases of Fire

To better understand the principles of ventilation, you must review the phases or stages that a fire goes through as it burns in a confined space.

As described in Chapter 3, a fire in a closed room, if undetected, will go through four phases of burning. During the first (*incipient*) phase, when there is plenty of oxygen, the flames will burn brightly. Although the temperature at the seat of the fire may be over 1000°F (540°C), room temperature will not rise significantly at first. In this phase, the fire will produce little more than water, carbon dioxide, and heat.

During the second phase (described as *open-burning* or *free-burning*), the temperature at the ceiling will rise to 700°F (370°C), or even higher. As the oxygen content decreases, the flames will be less bright. The fire will start to smoke and produce carbon monoxide. Two legs of the fire triangle are complete: there is plenty of gaseous fuel, heated to well above ignition temperature. If there is sufficient oxygen present, the entire room may burst into flame, a state of instantaneous combustion known as *flashover*.

During the third (*smoldering*) phase, flames will begin to disappear. Temperatures throughout the confined space will be very

high, and the smoke will become dense and contain much more carbon monoxide. At the fourth stage of burning, no flames are visible, smoke becomes very dense, and carbon monoxide and other flammable and explosive gases will increase dramatically. Temperatures will go up to over 1200°F (650°C). The high temperature drives off flammable gases from the wood, paint, fabrics, chair stuffing, and nearly everything else in the room. If there is *not* sufficient oxygen in the confined space, the fire could eventually "smother itself" and go out.

Backdraft explosion dangers

In the fourth phase, lack of oxygen in the confined space can pose a serious threat to firefighter safety. If oxygen is suddenly introduced to the room (for example, by your action in cutting through a wall or door panel) the room contents can instantly begin burning in a violent **backdraft explosion**. The potential for a backdraft explosion can often be recognized by the presence of a heavy volume of dense black smoke moving under a great deal of pressure. Proper ventilation of the space involved in fire can avoid such a hazardous situation. You should consider attacking this fire indirectly, coordinating your attack with the ventilation effort. Application of a water stream at this phase will produce a very large amount of steam.

Behavior of Gases

It is essential to be familiar with the physical properties of gases, particularly under fire conditions. Your understanding of how these gases react will become an important tool during ventilation procedures.

When fire burns in an enclosed area, the gases in the air expand and rise to the ceiling as they are heated. Cooler air moves into the area to replace the heated air. As the cooler air is heated in turn, it rises toward the ceiling. This causes a continuous motion of the atmosphere within the confined area. See **Figure 10-6.** As the amount of available oxygen within the area diminishes, the fire moves through the four phases of burning into the smoldering phase.

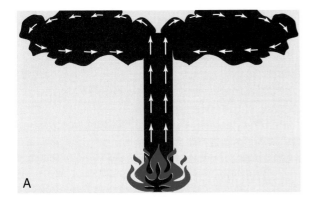

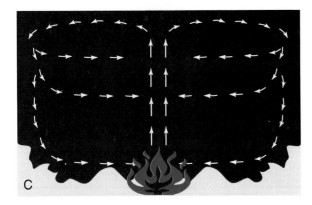

Figure 10-6. The movement of heated gases. A—Heated air rises to the ceiling, then spreads laterally. B—Lateral circulation continues as the heated gases and smoke bank downward from the ceiling. C—Eventually, heated air and smoke fill the entire space.

You can now understand how an entire building may be exposed by the travel of heat and smoke. When the building is several stories high and the fire is burning on a lower floor, heated gases and smoke will rise to the top floor. Unless released by proper ventilation, the heated gases may then mushroom downward, causing further fire spread, **Figure 10-7.**

Preventing Fire Spread Through Duct Systems

One major factor in the travel of heat and smoke within a building is the forced-air *HVAC* (heating, ventilation, and air conditioning) system. The HVAC system is a network of ducts designed to carry heated or cooled air to all parts of a building, so once fire penetrates the ductwork it has a clear path throughout the building. See **Figure 10-8.**

To minimize the spread of heat and smoke through the ductwork, the HVAC system's blower fan should be shut down during any building fire. Many modern buildings that are equipped with automatic fire detection and alarm systems can be wired to immediately shut down the HVAC system in case of fire. Whenever you are dealing with a fire in a building with a forced-air HVAC system, check to determine that the system is *not* operating. If it *is* still operating, shut it down immediately by cutting off power to the blower fan. During overhaul operations, be sure to check the HVAC system to be sure that it is in a safe condition.

Venting Devices

Architects or fire protection engineers often make provision, when designing a large building, for devices that will help to vent the products of combustion in the event of a fire. Some types of *venting devices* are designed for automatic operation; others are manual. Every firefighter and fire officer should be familiar with the operation of such venting devices. Proper pre-fire planning by your Department will identify buildings equipped

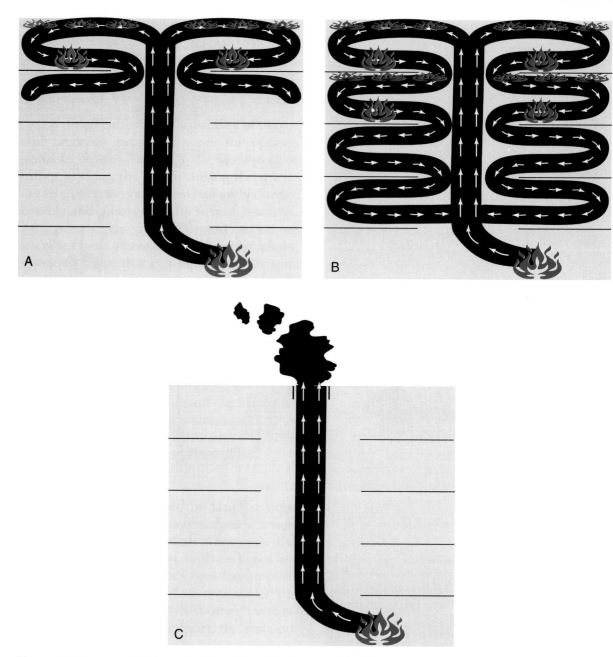

Figure 10-7. In a multi-story structure, there is danger of the fire spreading vertically. A—Smoke and hot gases rise to the top floor, causing combustion there. B—The mushrooming effect can cause the fire to spread downward to intervening floors until the entire structure is involved. C—Proper venting allows the hot gases to escape, preventing the downward spread of the fire.

with such devices, and provide information on their method of operation.

During a fire in a building equipped with automatic devices, one firefighter should be assigned to verify that they have opened. If they have not, the firefighter can operate them manually once he or she receives from the Incident Commander an order to ventilate the building. Buildings with manually operated venting devices are handled in a similar way — a firefighter is assigned to open them upon receipt of the order to ventilate.

Figure 10-8. Many buildings have forced-air systems for heating and air conditioning. The ducts for such a system can quickly spread smoke and heated gases from a fire to other parts of the building.

Roof Construction

To properly ventilate a building, you must understand the various construction components of that building. On the fireground, you often must open roofs. Your ability to properly carry out this procedure requires that you have a basic knowledge of roof construction. The various roof designs, as shown in **Figure 10-9**, include:

- Flat
- Gable
- Shed
- Hip
- Gambrel
- Butterfly
- Mansard
- Lantern.

Figure 10-10 shows typical roof construction, with a deck (also called sheathing) attached to the rafters, then a layer of roofing paper and a *wear surface* or covering. The wear surface is the exposed part of the roof that protects the building from weather. Wear surfaces that you may encounter include wood shingles, composition shingles, composition

Common Roof Designs

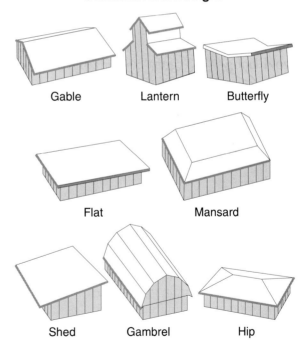

Gable   Lantern   Butterfly

Flat   Mansard

Shed   Gambrel   Hip

Figure 10-9. There are many roof designs used for residential and commercial structures. The ones shown are most common.

roofing paper, rubber membrane, tile, slate, sheet metal, and built-up tar and gravel roofs. The type of roof covering used will vary,

Figure 10-10.
Construction of a typical residential roof. There are many different wear surfaces, or coverings, used (depending upon local building codes and owner tastes).

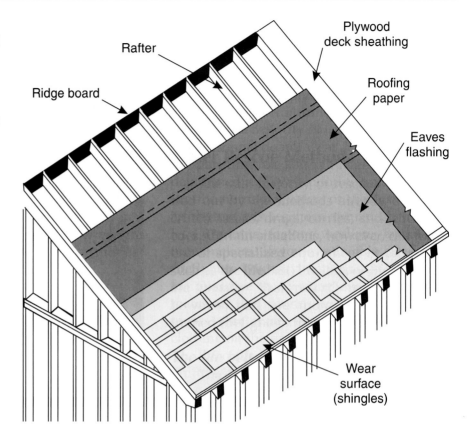

based upon architectural preference and local building codes.

Regardless of the roof design or style, or the type of covering used, there are several general procedures to follow in opening up a roof. Choose the highest point on the roof *above* the seat of the fire. Note the direction of the wind. Stand with your back to the wind as you work, so that the flames, smoke, and hot gases are blown *away* from you as they are released. Make sure that there is a backup hose line for your personal protection. Provide a second way off the roof in case something unexpected happens. Note any heavy or large objects located on the roof, such as air-handling equipment.

Roof Types

Although there are different roof designs or styles, there are basically only three ways that a roof can be constructed. A roof can be pitched, flat, or arched.

Pitched roof

A *pitched roof* is one that is higher in the center than it is at the edges, or higher at one side than the other. The degree of roof incline, or *pitch*, will vary with the style of the building. It can be gradual or very steep.

Safety must be your first concern when attempting to open up any type of roof, but is especially important on a pitched roof. Depending upon the degree of incline, there is the possibility of slipping and falling from a pitched roof. For this reason, you should always use a roof ladder when operating on this type of roof, **Figure 10-11.** It will provide you with a more secure footing and allow you to open the roof with less chance of falling. A safety line may be used for additional security.

To begin the ventilation procedure, first locate the roof supports. Tap the roof structure with an axe or other tool. The area between supports will sound hollow, and your tool will tend to bounce. When you are near or on top of a roof support, the sound will be more solid. This means there will be less tendency for the tool to bounce.

Once you have located the roof support, mark off the area that you intend to open. One large opening, as shown in **Figure 10-12,** will provide better ventilation than several small openings. For this reason, it is recommended that you open a hole at least 4 ft. by 4 ft. (1.2 m by 1.2 m). Next, remove the roof wear surface by cutting the material with your axe. Once the material has been cut, it should be peeled back out of the way. Using the proper tool, cut the roof deck adjacent to the roof supports, **Figure 10-13.** To maintain the integrity of the roof structure, always try to avoid cutting into the roof supports. When using an axe, try to employ short chopping strokes, If you must swing the axe high to provide more force, be sure to check above

Figure 10-11. A roof ladder provides safety when ventilating a steeply pitched roof. Note that the firefighter is sliding the axe along the rail of the ladder as he climbs.

Figure 10-12. Proper location for venting a pitched roof. One large opening is more effective than several smaller ones. The ceiling below the vent should be broken through to allow the escape of heat and smoke.

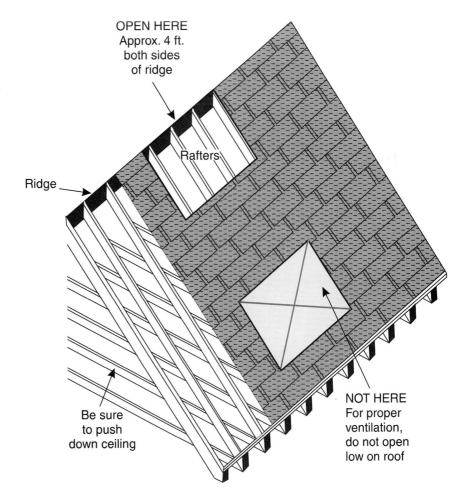

Figure 10-13. A chain saw or other heavy duty saw will make quick work of cutting through a roof deck to ventilate a building. (Warren Lutton)

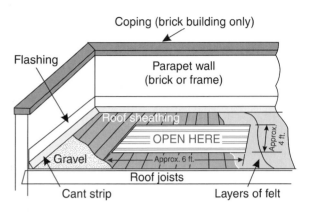

Figure 10-14. Some types of flat-roof construction, such as this built-up layer of felt, tar, and gravel, can be ventilated with hand-held tools. When the roof deck is concrete or metal, however, existing openings often must be used.

you for obstructions such as electrical wires. Also, make sure that you always know where your fellow firefighters are located, to avoid hitting any of them.

Flat roof

Flat roofs are found on larger commercial, industrial, and multiple-dwelling structures. *Flat roof* construction is similar to that of a floor. The structural material may be metal, wood, or concrete, while the roof covering material is similar to that found on pitched roofs. The material used to construct a flat roof will determine your ability to cut through the roof, **Figure 10-14.** Obviously, you would find it extremely difficult to cut through a concrete roof with normal fire department tools. Instead, you should look for large existing openings in the roof and use them for ventilation.

Arched roof

An *arched roof* can be formed with either trusses or short rafter sections that are beveled and bolted together at an angle to form the arch. You will often find that an arched roof built with trusses will have concealed spaces formed by installing a ceiling

on the lower portion of the truss. These concealed spaces can cause serious problems in ventilating such a roof. With this style of construction, you will sometimes have to pull down the ceiling from the inside. The procedure to follow in opening an arched roof is similar to that used for pitched or flat roofs. However, extreme caution must be exercised, because of the tendency of arched roofs to collapse with little or no warning. Always test the structural integrity of an arched roof before walking on it.

Trench (Strip) Ventilation

Some structures are very long, in proportion to their width, because of the type of use. Examples would be boarding or racing stables, rental storage buildings, and some types of warehouses and manufacturing buildings. Such structures present some unique ventilation problems.

One technique that often can be used effectively is called *trench ventilation*, or sometimes, *strip ventilation.* In this method, an opening is made through the roof completely across the building's width. The opening should be approximately four feet in width. See **Figure 10-15.** To be effective in stopping the spread of fire, the trench must

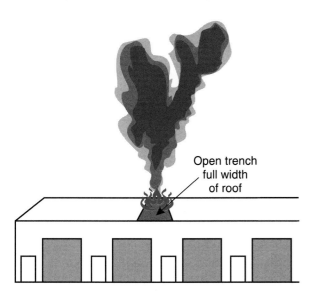

Figure 10-15. To ventilate a very long, narrow structure, the trench ventilation method can often be used effectively.

be cut well ahead of the advancing blaze. As the fire approaches the trench, the smoke and heated air will vent out of the trench, preventing spread of the fire to areas beyond.

Roof Precautions

Regardless of its construction type, any roof that feels spongy or weak is in danger of collapse. The spongy feeling under your feet indicates the presence of structural damage to the roof. Exercise extreme caution when operating on any roof that feels spongy. Preferably, you should abandon roof operations when it becomes apparent that structural damage has occurred.

When operating on any roof, be sure to have a backup line available to protect the roof crew. The number of firefighters allowed to work on any roof should be kept to an absolute minimum, and a second means of escape should always be available. While ventilation procedures are taking place, keep a constant vigil for evidence of structural weakness and possible collapse.

Normally, you should avoid introducing water from a hose line into a vent hole. This would cause the ventilation process to stop.

Such improperly directed lines not only disrupt the natural ventilation process, but will force the heated gases back down into the building. This will adversely affect any crew working inside. Only under the most unusual circumstances should you discharge a hose stream into a ventilation opening.

Types of Ventilation

Ventilation, either natural or forced, may be accomplished either vertically or horizontally. Horizontal ventilation is most often used in single-story dwelling fires. Vertical ventilation is used in multiple-story buildings or (by opening the roof) in larger single-story buildings such as factories or warehouses. Regardless of the type of ventilation involved, the ventilation precautions listed in **Figure 10-16** should be observed.

Vertical Ventilation

Vertical ventilation uses the natural convection process by allowing heated gases to rise and exit the building through natural or created openings. To put vertical ventilation to the best use, you must consider the location of the fire and the direction that you want the smoke and hot gases to travel within the building. Consideration must also be given to the type of building construction. You must also be aware of the direction of the wind and how it will affect your exposures. The extent of the fire within the building, the possibility of severe structural damage, and the amount of contents can all affect your ability to use vertical ventilation.

Choosing the highest accessible location in the building will allow you to put vertical ventilation to the most effective use. Whenever possible, ventilate by using the natural openings found in the building itself. These can include skylights, ventilating shafts, elevator shafts, and built-in ventilation hatches.

VENTILATION PROCEDURES		
Hazards Involved in Ventilation	**Possible Consequences**	**Approved Practice**
Opening below fire	Backdraft explosion No ventilation value	Open above fire
Opening too soon	Lines not laid Fire intensifies Increased loss Additional work time Additional life hazard	Lay and charge lines simultaneously Be prepared to fight fire
Opening wrong place	No ventilation Backdraft explosion Spread fire to uninvolved areas Increased loss Additional work time Additional life hazard Adverse criticism	Have previous knowledge of building Open over vertical shafts Know contents Know hallways and partitions
Opening into blind attic	No ventilation Backdraft explosion Loss of time Additional loss Additional life hazard	Have previous knowledge of building Use pike pole to open ceiling below
Opening insufficient in size	Ineffective ventilation Backdraft explosion Loss of time Additional loss Additional life hazard	Open large enough hole in first place Know size of areas below
Involve exposures	Spread of fire Increased loss Additional work time Additional life hazard	Know surrounding buildings in advance Know horizontal openings Know roof structures Watch wind direction and velocity Have lines covering exposures Know heat and gas behavior
Life hazard to firefighters	Roof collapse Explosions below Bad smoke and gas conditions Escape difficult in emergency Injury from axe	Know building construction in advance (if doubtful, lay ladder flat on roof) Delay lower openings for ventilation above Know contents of building Cut from wind side of opening Paint top 15 in. of ladders white Work from diagonally opposite corners of cut when two firefighters are cutting
Delayed ventilation	Backdraft explosion Roof unsafe Entire building involved Excessive losses Increased life hazard	Prompt decisions Prompt action
Public criticism	Hurts reputation of department Lowers morale of department Lessens public support Promotes political interference Lowers departmental efficiency	Know buildings in advance Know principles and proper methods of ventilation Use judgment Do a workmanlike job Explain department practices to public Explain reasons for ventilation Admit your mistakes Have department trained and disciplined Know smoke and gas behavior

Figure 10-16. This table presents some of the hazards involved in ventilation, along with possible consequences and the approved practices to follow.

Horizontal Ventilation

In its simplest form, horizontal ventilation may involve nothing more than opening windows and doors to create a natural draft through the fire building. Sometimes, due to difficulty of access or the location of the fire, windows must be broken from the outside to provide ventilation. See **Figure 10-17.** Horizontal ventilation is typically used in single-family dwellings where attics are not involved in the fire. Buildings with high windows, attic spaces with louvers, individual floors of multiple-story structures, and buildings with large unsupported open spaces under the roof, are all highly likely candidates for horizontal ventilation.

Ventilating a single room of a residence by opening windows should be done, whenever possible, as shown in **Figure 10-18.** Open the windows two-thirds from the top and one-third from the bottom. When you do this, the lighter hot air rises and quickly escapes out the larger top opening of the window as heavier, cooler air enters through the bottom. The distance between the top of the window and the ceiling or the roof can affect this process. When the distance between the top of the window and the ceiling is large, hot gases will escape at a lower rate.

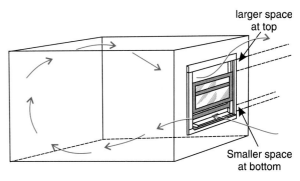

Figure 10-18. The proper method of opening a window for ventilating smoke and heated gases. Lighter heated air will escape more quickly through the larger opening at the top.

Whenever possible, open the lower half of a window on the windward side of the building, and the upper half of a window on the leeward side. Cool heavier air entering on the windward side forces the lighter hot air to escape through the upper half of the window on the leeward side. This is called cross-ventilation, **Figure 10-19.** The construction of the building and the wind conditions can be used to your advantage in expediting ventilation.

Ventilating a basement

The removal of products of combustion from a basement or cellar can be extremely important to achieving a swift and effective attack on the fire. Within the building, there are certain areas that should be looked at as you seek ways to ventilate the basement. The most accessible and effective ventilation points will often be the tops of internal shafts or the tops of stairwells.

Figure 10-17. Horizontal ventilation is sometimes achieved by breaking a window pane from the outside. A pike pole is often used, since its length minimizes the danger of injury from the falling glass.

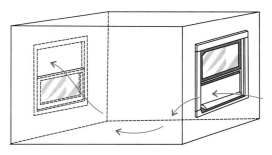

Figure 10-19. Cross-ventilation takes advantage of building construction and wind conditions to more quickly clear smoke and heated air from a room.

The building's exterior also presents some excellent sites to consider for ventilating the basement. Any door leading from the basement to the outside is an easily used ventilation location. Other openings that can be used are street-level windows, trapdoors, light wells, and sidewalk elevators. The decision on the type of ventilation to use (positive-pressure or negative-pressure) must be made by the Incident Commander, based upon the situation and local procedures.

Mechanical Ventilation

Forced air mechanical ventilation can be used to expedite the movement of the smoke or heated gases from any area. This method is often used when natural ventilation is unsuitable, or when the fire is in an area with no outside ventilation. When the fire is in an interior room of a larger building, you must move the smoke and heated gases through interior corridors to the outside. In doing so, you are subjecting other parts of the building to the adverse effects of the heated gases and smoke. During this operation, make sure that all door and window openings to other rooms in the building are closed to keep out heated gases and smoke. You can then use power fans to move the smoke and hot gases to the outside. The ventilation activity can make use of either negative or positive pressure.

Negative pressure ventilation

In *negative pressure ventilation*, **Figure 10-20**, a fan called a *smoke ejector* is positioned in a doorway or window opening. The air stream is directed outward, causing a lowering of air pressure inside the building. Fresh air is drawn in through other openings as the smoke is "pulled" out of the structure by the fan.

An alternative method to moving the smoke and gases through the hallways is to use a plastic tube. When you attach this tube to the smoke ejector, you can control movement of the smoke and hot gases to the outside.

Figure 10-20. Power fans can be used for mechanical ventilation. The method shown is called "negative pressure ventilation," and uses the fan as a smoke ejector when natural ventilation is inadequate or when the fire is located in an area with no outside ventilation. Inset shows one method for hanging fan in a doorway or window opening, using a spring-loaded bar. For most effective venting of smoke, the areas above and below the fan should be closed using salvage covers or other materials. (Warren Lutton)

Positive pressure ventilation

In *positive pressure ventilation*, a fan is placed outside the building in a position that permits it to blow a stream of air directly into a door or window opening. See **Figure 10-21.** This arrangement introduces fresh air, while creating a *positive* pressure inside the structure. By creating a pressure inside the building that is higher than the outside atmospheric pressure, smoke and heated gases will be forced out of the structure. Movement of fresh air and of heated gases within the fire building can be controlled by systematically opening or closing doors and windows.

Figure 10-21. Locating a fan outside the structure to blow a stream of air into an opening is known as the "positive pressure" method of ventilation. Increasing the air pressure inside the structure will drive smoke and heated gases to the outside.

Proper placement of the fan outside the building is vital to effectively using the positive pressure method. The fan must be set up so that the stream or "cone" of air it projects completely covers the selected opening. See **Figure 10-22.** Typically, placing the fan 4-6 feet from the opening will accomplish this, but the distance will vary with opening and fan size. The air-moving capacity of the fan may be a factor, as well — a powerful fan can be placed nearer the opening than one which moves a lesser volume of air. If you expect to use the positive pressure method under fire conditions, experiment *in advance* with your ventilation equipment to establish the proper working distance for each fan.

Hydraulic (fog stream) ventilation

Another method of removing smoke from the area in which you are operating is to use the water fog from your hose line. This method, called *hydraulic ventilation*, is accomplished by placing the nozzle on full fog and pointing it out an open window. The venturi effect of the fog stream exiting the window will draw hot gases and smoke from the room. Be careful to watch for the seat of the fire and for possible flare-ups. This method is sometimes

used by the hose crew until proper vertical ventilation can be accomplished. It allows the crew to create a more tenable environment in

Figure 10-22. When setting up for positive pressure ventilation, care must be taken to place the fan so that its stream of moving air covers the entire opening. If it does not, effectiveness of the technique will be greatly diminished.

which to work, as well as a draft that makes it easier to locate the seat of the fire.

Ventilation Equipment

Some of the hand and power tools most commonly used for ventilation are shown in Figure 10-23. The decision to use any specific tool should be based upon the standard procedures of the local department and the personal preferences of the firefighter. When the fireground officer requests a specific job, he or she will often specify an appropriate tool for the job that needs to be done.

A   B

Figure 10-23. Ventilation tools. A—This fan, approximately 24 in. in diameter, is powered by a small gasoline engine. It provides sufficient airflow for effective positive pressure ventilation. B—A selection of hand and power tools used for ventilation tasks.

VENTILATION: WHEN, WHERE, AND HOW

When to Vent

- When charged lines are in position and ready to advance.
- When points of spread are protected.
- When higher and adjacent exposures are protected.
- *Immediately*, if life is endangered and rescue must be effected.

When *Not* to Vent

- When ventilation would create drafts or explosions that would spread the fire or intensify its condition.
- When it is likely to create severe exposure to other buildings or floors.
- When venting might liberate volumes of heat, smoke, or gases into other parts of the structure that are occupied by the public, resulting in panic.

Where to Vent

At the roof (quick ventilation):
- Remove skylights or scuttles; break skylight glass, if necessary. Remove or break ceiling skylights below roof skylights.
- Open bulkhead doors and windows to relieve shafts and floors.

At the roof (cutting openings):
- Directly over fire or other hot spots at the highest level possible.
- Area adjoining scuttles to augment preliminary venting and provide adequate area.
- Over blind drafts.
- Immediately adjacent to chimneys, flues, or stacks.
- Breach ceilings below cut roof openings, as required.

Floor above fire:
- Open windows, top and bottom. Open doors.
- If a severe condition exists, cut openings in floor adjacent to windows and doors.

Cellars and basements:
- At top of shaft leading from cellar or basement.
- Sidewalk trapdoors, sidewalk elevators, deadlights.
- Exterior doors leading from exits.
- Light and vent windows at street level.
- If a severe condition exists, cut openings in floor adjacent to windows and doors.

If vapors or gases that are heavier than air are present:
- Ventilate each end of area at floor level to produce maximum circulation.
- Use exhaust fans, blowers, air-movers.
- In addition to normal venting, use suction for exhaust, as necessary, especially in excessively low areas.

Exposures:
- Vent away from exposures unless unavoidable. Provide protective water curtain.

Where Not to Vent

- Through the proscenium wall of a theater.
- Through fire doors.
- Into an exit or passageway that could prevent egress or deter firefighting operations.
- Through doors or windows facing a fire escape. This could jeopardize safety of occupants or of fire companies working at upper levels.

How to Vent

- Make proper use of tools and equipment.
- Work from the windward side, if possible.
- Make openings at proper locations and of adequate size.
- Make one large opening in preference to many small openings.
- Use existing openings (skylights, scuttles, doors, windows) to best advantage.
- Make full use of smoke ejectors, fans, and blowers, when needed.
- Make effective use of ladders to reach otherwise inaccessible areas.

Continued

Door and Window Precautions

- Before resorting to physical damage to obtain ventilation, check to see if doors or windows are unlocked.
- Always work from the side when opening doors or windows or when breaking glass for ventilation. Avoid a position directly in front of the opening.
- When breaking glass, start at the highest area, then work downward. Clean sash of remaining jagged pieces of glass.
- Use the flat side of the axe to break glass. Work from the side to avoid injuries caused by the broken glass "following" the tool handle. Wear eye protection and gloves at all times.
- Use extreme caution when glass is hot to the touch. This indicates conditions capable of causing a backdraft explosion.
- Beware of flying glass at all times. Do not break glass indiscriminately. To avoid injury to those working below, warn them before breaking the glass.

SUMMARY

Ventilation can be defined as the planned release of fire, heat, smoke, or gases to follow a predetermined course under the direction and control of the firefighting forces. Ventilation is used to improve rescue operations by directing fire, heat, smoke, and gases away from trapped occupants; prevent the further spread of fire, vertically or horizontally; help the firefighting forces to reach the seat of the fire quickly, and reduce property damage from fire and smoke.

Several quick decisions must be made at the fireground scene by the fire officer. Those decisions include whether or not ventilation is required, where ventilation is needed, and what type of ventilation should be performed.

Safe and effective ventilation requires knowledge of such areas as the phases through which a fire progresses, and the behavior of heated gases. Knowing the different types of roof construction and how to properly vent them is very important.

REVIEW QUESTIONS

1. Define the term "ventilation" as used in the fire service.
2. What are some advantages of ventilating a burning structure?
3. What three questions must an officer on the scene ask when deciding whether or not to ventilate?
4. Name and describe the two types of ventilation.
5. What temperature could be measured at the ceisling of a room in the fourth stage of burning? Can flames be seen?
6. A state of instantaneous combustion is known as _____.
7. Describe the movement of air in a confined space where a fire is burning.
8. Describe the conditions that make a backdraft explosion possible. What event can cause such an explosion?
9. List some kinds of materials that may be used at roof coverings or wear surfaces.
10. What are the three basic types of roof construction?
11. When ventilating a pitched roof, what safety precautions should you take?
12. Why shouldn't you cut through roof supports when you are opening a roof for ventilation?
13. On what types of buildings are you most likely to find a flat roof?
14. What method must usually be used to ventilate a building with a concrete roof deck?
15. Describe the reasons why it may be difficult or dangerous to ventilate a structure with an arched roof.
16. What does a spongy feeling underfoot tell you about a roof?
17. Why should you avoid, if at all possible, introducing water from a hose line into a vent hole? Describe the results of such an action.
18. Define both vertical and horizontal ventilation.
19. In natural vertical ventilation, where should the vent opening be located?
20. When using mechanical ventilation to move heated gases and smoke through interior corridors, what precautions should you take?

NFPA 1001 Job Performance Requirements

The material on this page consists of those portions of the NFPA 1001 Job Performance Requirements relevant to the material presented in this chapter. Items preceded by the numeral 3 (3-x.x) are Fire Fighter I requirements; those with the numeral 4 (4-x.x) are Fire Fighter II requirements.

3-3.5 Set up ground ladders, given single and extension ladders, an assignment, and team members as appropriate, so that hazards are assessed, the ladder is stable, the angle is proper for climbing, extension ladders are extended to the proper height with the fly locked, the top is placed against a reliable structural component, and the assignment is accomplished.

(a) Prerequisite Knowledge: Parts of a ladder, hazards associated with setting up ladders, what constitutes a stable foundation for ladder placement, different angles for various tasks, safety limits to the degree of angulation, and what constitutes a reliable structural component for top placement.

(b) Prerequisite Skills: The ability to carry ladders, raise ladders, extend ladders and lock flies, determine that a wall and roof will support the ladder, judge extension ladder height requirements, and place the ladder to avoid obvious hazards.

(3-3.8)

(b) Prerequisite Skills: The ability to use SCBA to exit through restricted passages, set up and use different types of ladders for various types of rescue operations, rescue a fire fighter with functioning respiratory protection, rescue a fire fighter whose respiratory protection is not functioning, rescue a person who has no respiratory protection, and assess areas to determine tenability.

(3-3.9)

(b) Prerequisite Skills: The ability to prevent water hammers when shutting down nozzles; open, close, and adjust nozzle flow and patterns; apply water using direct, indirect, and combination attacks; advance charged and uncharged 1 1/2 in. (38 mm) diameter or larger hose lines up ladders and up and down interior and exterior stairways; extend hose lines; replace burst hose sections; operate charged hose lines of 1 1/2 in. (38 mm) diameter or larger while secured to a ground ladder; couple and uncouple various hand line connections; carry hose; attack fires at grade level and above and below grade levels; and locate and suppress interior wall and subfloor fires.

(3-3.11)

(b) Prerequisite Skills: The ability to transport and operate ventilation tools and equipment; hoist ventilation tools to a roof; cut roofing and flooring materials to vent flat roofs, pitched roofs, and basements; sound a roof for integrity; clear an opening with hand tools; select, carry, deploy, and secure ground ladders for ventilation activities; deploy roof ladders on pitched roofs while secured to a ground ladder; carry ventilation-related tools and equipment while ascending and descending ladders.

3-5.3 Clean and check ladders, ventilation equipment, self-contained breathing apparatus (SCBA), ropes, salvage equipment, and hand tools, given cleaning tools, cleaning supplies, and an assignment, so that equipment is clean and maintained according to manufacturer's or departmental guidelines, maintenance is recorded, and equipment is placed in a ready state or reported otherwise.

(a) Prerequisite Knowledge: Types of cleaning methods for various tools and equipment, correct use of cleaning solvents, and manufacturer's or departmental guidelines for cleaning equipment and tools.

(b) Prerequisite Skills: The ability to select correct tools for various parts and pieces of equipment, follow guidelines, and complete recording and reporting procedures.

Reprinted with permission from NFPA 1001, *Fire Fighter Professional Qualifications,* Copyright ©1997, National Fire Protection Association, Quincy, MA 02269. This reprinted material is not the complete and official position of the National Fire Protection Association on the referenced subject, which is represented only by the standard in its entirety.

Ladders

OBJECTIVES

When you have completed this chapter, you will be able to:

- Identify various types and sizes of ladders.
- Select the proper ladder for a given application.
- Discuss materials and other elements of ladder construction.
- Describe the load safety features of ladders.
- Explain how to inspect and maintain ladders.
- Describe various types of ladder carries and the proper techniques for different ladder raises.
- Discuss and demonstrate safe ladder climbing practice, including ascent and descent while carrying tools and equipment.

IMPORTANT TERMS

"A" ladder	char	fly	rungs
Bangor ladders	"D" distance	folding ladder	teasers
beam carry	effective length	heat indicators	tie rods
beam raise	flat carry	permanent set	tormenters
beams	flat raise	pompier ladder	trusses

Fire department emblems almost always include a representation of a ladder. And well they should — the ladder is essential to firefighting operations. Ladders are used not only for climbing, but also as bridges, light-duty battering rams, stretchers, water chutes, and many other purposes that human ingenuity has conceived.

When properly maintained, handled, and used, modern ladders are safe; if maintenance, handling, and use are improper, they become traps. With a constant emphasis on safety, this chapter discusses ladder types and construction, proper inspection and maintenance, and proven techniques for carrying, raising, and climbing ladders.

Selecting the Proper Ladder

On the fireground, *time* is your one great enemy. The *longer* the fire burns, the worse it gets. The longer the fire burns, the more people are in danger. The longer the fire burns, the tougher the job of extinguishing it becomes.

If you had plenty of time at your disposal, you could take all the ladders off the apparatus, measure and weigh them, look up their specifications, then decide which of them to use. But time is what you *don't* have on the fireground; time is your *enemy*.

You must be able to instantly answer such questions as, "What ladders are available?" "Which one will do the job best?" "How many firefighters will be needed to carry and raise the ladder?" "What special fire conditions make this kind or style of ladder preferable to another?" "What safety considerations are involved?"

Fire apparatus carry many different lengths and styles of ladders. The reason for all the ladders is that, in any given situation, there is always one that is *best*. Your job is to know which one that is.

Ladder Types and Sizes

The types of ladders most commonly used in the fire service are the wall ladder, extension ladder, roof ladder, attic ladder, extension ladder with poles, and the aerial ladder.

Wall (straight) ladder

This is a single-section ladder that typically ranges in size from 10 to 35 feet, but is sometimes longer. See **Figure 11-1.** Some departments no longer use wall ladders. They have replaced them with roof ladders which will do anything a wall ladder will do, and more.

Extension ladder

As the name indicates, an extension ladder is made up of two or more ladders, nested together, that can be extended to almost their combined lengths. See **Figure 11-2.** For example, a three-section extension ladder with a closed length of 16 feet can be extended to any length up to about 40 feet.

Roof ladder

This ladder resembles a wall ladder, but has swivel hooks at the top, **Figure 11-3.** You

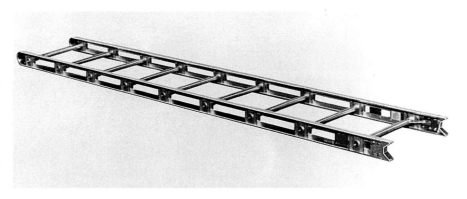

Figure 11-1. A typical wall ladder of the aluminum truss-beam type. Some are 35 feet or more in length. Although fire ladders seem simple in construction, they are precision tools and should be treated as such. (Aluminum Ladder Company)

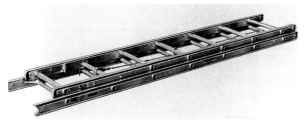

A

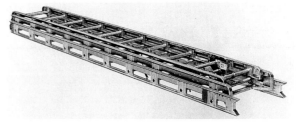

B

Figure 11-2. Extension ladders are two or more ladders, nested together, that can be extended to nearly their combined length. A—Two-section solid-beam extension ladder. B—Three-section truss-beam extension ladder. (Aluminum Ladder Company)

Figure 11-3. The roof ladder has hooks at one end. They can be folded flat or swiveled out to anchor the ladder over the ridge of a roof. Because they are more versatile, roof ladders are replacing wall ladders in many cases. (Aluminum Ladder Company)

can use it in any place where you would use a wall ladder; while the hooks increase its usefulness. To provide greater stability, you can hook them over roof gables, cornices, window sills, and similar edges.

Attic ladder

This is a narrow extension ladder used for entry through attic trapdoors and other tight places. Attic ladders are just a shade over a foot wide. When fully extended, they range from 10 to 15 feet in length.

Extension ladder with poles

This is basically an ordinary extension ladder that has poles (also called *tormenters*

or *teasers*) attached to its sides to aid in raising and steadying it. Most ladders of this type are 40 feet or more in length.

Aerial ladders

These are truck-mounted extension ladders, and are hydraulically operated on most modern equipment. See **Figure 11-4.** Most aerial ladders are between 75 and 100 feet in length; some are longer. An aerial ladder may have fixed piping for water.

Other aerial devices

In addition to the aerial ladder, there are several similar truck-mounted extension devices in use. Some fire departments may

A

B

Figure 11-4. Aerial ladder. A—This early version of the truck-mounted aerial ladder was hand-cranked and could extend approximately 50 feet. (Harold Anthony/Archive Photo) B—Today's aerial ladders, operated with hydraulic cylinders, are often 100 feet or more in length. These devices are typically built to a department's specification. A unique feature of this apparatus is independently steerable rear wheels, providing a shorter turning radius and greater maneuverability for positioning. (Pierce Manufacturing, Inc.)

have all of these, in addition to aerial ladders; others may not even have an aerial ladder. Other aerial devices include:

Tower. This is an aerial ladder with a platform (called a "bucket") at its tip. It will have fixed piping for water and a master stream nozzle. See **Figure 11-5.**

Telesquirt. This is an articulated boom that includes piping for water and a master stream nozzle. It is positioned and operated with ground-level controls on the truck. See **Figure 11-6.**

Snorkel. First developed by the Chicago Fire Department, the snorkel is now widely used by fire departments worldwide. It is an articulated boom with a bucket attached. The movement of the articulated boom can be controlled from the bucket or from the truck-mounted controls, making it a highly versatile tool for both rescue work and firefighting. See **Figure 11-7.**

The major advantage of the aerial ladder and other aerial devices, other than length, is that the free end need not be supported. This permits them to be used in situations where a regular ladder would be destroyed by fire or where conditions would otherwise be too hazardous for a firefighter to work. For example, a firefighter working from the bucket of a snorkel can ventilate a roof that would be too dangerous to stand on. The bucket can be used as an elevator to more rapidly and safely raise and lower firefighting personnel or rescued persons. See **Figure 11-8.** If civilians must be removed from upper floors of a structure, the snorkel bucket is safer than a ladder (as well as less harrowing) for those being rescued.

Aerial devices must be exceptionally strong because of the uses to which they are subjected. The NFPA standard requires that any aerial device be capable of supporting a

A   B

Figure 11-5. Tower unit. A—A tower permits attack from above the fire, directing a stream into areas that could not easily be reached from ground level. (Jon Smith) B—The construction of a tower unit (an aerial ladder with a bucket attached to the end) is clearly visible in this photo. Note the two monitors mounted on the front of the platform. (Pierce Manufacturing, Inc.)

Figure 11-6. Controls on the truck are used to maneuver and position the master stream nozzle at the end of the articulated telesquirt boom. The boom may reach up to 75 feet. (Pierce Manufacturing, Inc.)

Figure 11-7. The snorkel is a hybrid aerial device that combines the telesquirt's articulated arm with the platform or "basket" of the tower. Equipped with a master stream nozzle, the snorkel is an extremely versatile piece of apparatus. (Jon Smith)

Figure 11-8. The snorkel basket can be used to quickly and safely hoist firefighters and equipment to a building roof. These firefighters are preparing to ventilate the roof of a burning commercial building.

weight of 250 lbs. (113 kg) at its tip when the device is fully extended in a *horizontal* position.

Special-purpose Ladders

In addition to the six basic ladder types just discussed, there are a number of special-purpose ladders available.

The *"A" ladder*, **Figure 11-9**, is collapsible, resembling a tall stepladder in appearance. It may be used as either a straight ladder or free-standing (stepladder-type) ladder.

The very narrow *folding ladder* folds in half vertically (beam-to-beam), **Figure 11-10**. In some departments, these are referred to as

Figure 11-9. The jointed, collapsible "A" ladder resembles a stepladder. The joint can be locked to allow its use as a single ladder. (Aluminum Ladder Company)

Figure 11-10. The folding ladder collapses into a long, thin bundle that can be worked into very tight quarters. (Aluminum Ladder Company)

"attic ladders," and are used in the same way. This ladder can be worked into some very tight places.

A *pompier ladder*, **Figure 11-11**, looks different from other ladders, with its top hook and rungs passing through the single center beam. Pompier ladders can be used in a lot of tight places, and they are very light (a 20-foot pompier ladder weighs only about 25 pounds). This versatile ladder is probably not used by the fire service to anywhere near the extent that it could be.

Ladder Construction

Fire ladders are usually made from wood, aluminum, a combination of wood and aluminum, or fiberglass. Ladders are sometimes, but rarely, made of steel or magnesium. There are two basic styles of ladder construction, solid-beam and truss-beam. The terms used to describe ladder components are shown in **Figure 11-12.**

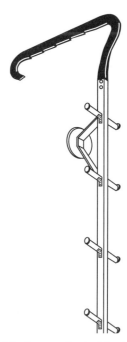

Figure 11-11. A pompier ladder is a very light ladder with a large hook at the top that makes it very versatile. "Pompier" is the French word for fireman.

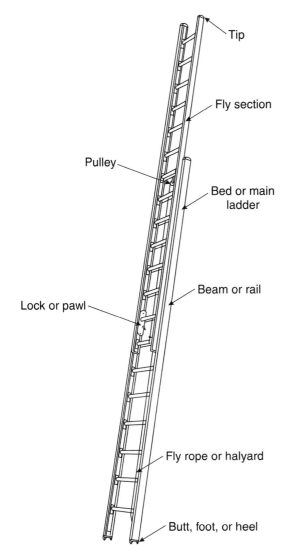

Figure 11-12. Names of the major parts of an extension ladder. Many of the names apply to the corresponding parts of other types of ladders, as well. Note that the tip ends of the ladder rails are rounded, while the butt ends have safety shoes or points to prevent slipping. A ladder should never be raised with the rounded ends down, since climbing it would be very dangerous. (Duo-Safety Ladder Co.)

Labels on figure: Tip; Fly section; Pulley; Bed or main ladder; Lock or pawl; Beam or rail; Fly rope or halyard; Butt, foot, or heel

Solid Beam Wood Ladders

This is the traditional fire department ladder, although few are being manufactured currently. The **beams** (also called *rails*) are made of a light wood such as Douglas fir or spruce. The beams on longer ladders are wider and thicker, allowing them to support greater weight. *Rungs* are made from a tough hardwood, such as hickory, ash, or oak. Rungs may be glued or bolted (or both) to the beams. Some ladders also have **tie rods** for greater strength. These are long bolts that go through every fourth rung, from beam to beam. Wood ladders have a protective coating of varnish.

Truss Beam Wood Ladders

Wood truss ladders are somewhat lighter than solid beam ladders of the same weight-carrying capacity. The beam of a truss ladder is actually two rails of smaller cross-section, held together by *trusses* that also serve as rung support blocks. The hickory, ash, or oak rungs are typically glued and bolted to the trusses. Tie rods are usually used about every four rungs.

Aluminum Ladders

Ladders constructed from aluminum may be of either the solid beam or truss construction. Actually the term "solid beam" isn't truly accurate, since the beams are made from hollow aluminum tubing. They look solid, however, and are quite strong and rigid. The aluminum used is age-hardened at 350°F to 400°F (177°C to 204°C) for ten hours. The rungs may be welded or expanded (or both) into the beams, **Figure 11-13.** Aluminum truss and wood truss models are similar in construction, but metal ladders are fastened with rivets, rather than glue and bolts. The aluminum truss construction provides great strength without excessive weight.

Wood and Aluminum Truss Ladders

These are conventional-style truss ladders with wood beams and aluminum trusses and rungs. Bolted construction is used, **Figure 11-14.**

Fiberglass Ladders

Fiberglass, consists of a resin (plastic) reinforced with glass fabric. It is consistent in its density and strength, will not rot or corrode,

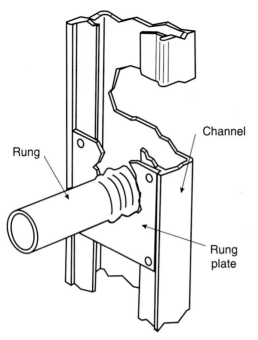

Figure 11-13. Construction of a solid beam aluminum wall ladder. The rung is welded to the channel, and is also expanded on both sides of the rung plate. (Duo-Safety Ladder Co.)

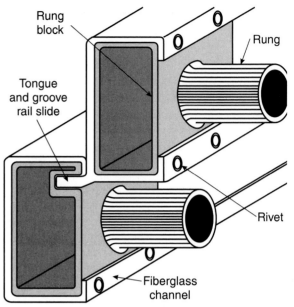

Figure 11-15. Fiberglass ladders are nonconductive. They have continuous rails of fiberglass with no connecting metal pieces between the individual rung assemblies. The ladder sections have full-length tongue and groove slides for rigidity. Rungs are expanded on both sides of the rung block and welded to the block. Rung blocks are riveted to the fiberglass rails. (Duo-Safety Ladder Co.)

and does not conduct electricity when dry. Nearly all fiberglass ladders use solid beam construction. Rungs are either fiberglass or aluminum. See **Figure 11-15**. If rungs are fiberglass, they are usually riveted. If rungs are aluminum, they are welded to aluminum blocks

and the blocks are riveted to the beams. Aluminum rungs are sometimes assembled directly to the beams with expansion plugs.

Figure 11-14. Combination wood and aluminum truss-type ladders use wooden beams in combination with aluminum truss blocks and rungs. This extension ladder example shows the bolted construction used. (Duo-Safety Ladder Co.)

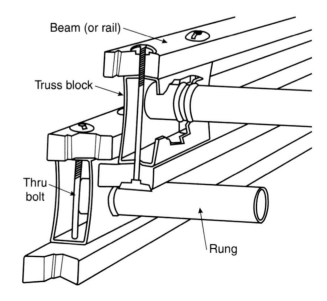

Ladder Materials

Each of the major ladder construction materials (wood, aluminum, fiberglass) has advantages and disadvantages.

Wood

Advantages: Wood is a nonconductor of electricity when dry. It is also an excellent insulator against heat. If wood gets too hot, it will burn, but the burn is on the surface. The inside will remain strong. If wood is exposed to excessive heat, it will burn more deeply, or *char*. This is easily detected.

Disadvantages: Wood dries out, splits, and splinters, so it requires frequent inspection and maintenance. Wood ladders should be periodically scraped and a coat of spar varnish applied. With proper care and maintenance, a wood ladder has a ten-year life span, at best. Wood ladders are heavier than aluminum. They are also more expensive. Few wooden ladders are being manufactured at present.

Aluminum

Advantages: The greatest advantage aluminum has over other ladder materials is its combination of lightweight and great strength. Aluminum requires no attention to its surface. In a short time, aluminum loses its shiny appearance as the surface oxidizes. The dull gray coating that forms, aluminum oxide, serves as a protective finish.

Disadvantages: Aluminum is a good conductor of electricity, making it a serious shock hazard around charged electric wires. It will also conduct heat rapidly, so even a brief exposure to high temperature may permanently weaken a ladder. With sufficient heat, the ladder may even collapse under its own weight. A ladder that has been weakened may show no visible effects. The only way to tell whether a ladder has been weakened by heat is to test the metal for hardness. Since strength and hardness are directly related, significantly lower hardness indicates a weakened ladder. **Heat indicators** like those in **Figure 11-16** change color when exposed to a temperature that could cause weakening. A dot that has changed color is a warning that the ladder should be tested. Manufacturers are providing ladders with indicators already in place. They also can be purchased and affixed to existing ladders. Obviously, indicators should be applied only to ladders that are known to be structurally sound.

Wood and Aluminum

Advantages: The beams are nonconductors of electricity when dry, and the wooden portions will not conduct heat or be seriously weakened by heat exposure. These ladders are lighter than solid wood ladders, but not as light as aluminum.

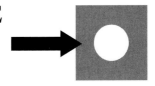

REMOVE LADDER FROM SERVICE AND TEST IF ANY HEAT SENSOR TURNS DARK

Figure 11-16. Heat indicators (sensors) change color when exposed to a temperature higher than that for which they are rated. This allows them to be used as a means of warning that an aluminum ladder may have been dangerously weakened by heat exposure. The white dot on the label will darken after being exposed to a temperature of 300°F (149°C). (Duo-Safety Ladder Co.)

Disadvantages: The aluminum parts are affected by heat. The wood parts require frequent inspection and maintenance.

Fiberglass

Advantages: Fiberglass doesn't dry out or split, and is a nonconductor of electricity when dry. It is highly resistant to chemical attack. It is a slow conductor of heat and will withstand brief exposure to high temperatures without permanently losing strength. Fiberglass will burn only when exposed to direct flame. Burned areas will be obvious, indicating a weakened condition. Fiberglass requires little maintenance.

Disadvantages: Fiberglass is heavier than wood, so fiberglass ladders longer than 24 feet are not practical. If overloaded, fiberglass will not take a permanent bend (but it *will* be weakened by the overload). A weakened fiberglass ladder may suddenly fail without warning.

Weight of Materials

One major consideration in choosing ladder material is *weight* — firefighters will have to carry and raise the ladder. Since many departments must work today with reduced numbers of firefighters, weight is an important (but not the only) factor to consider when choosing ladders.

There can be a considerable variation in the weight of ladders of different types and materials. All ladders in the following list are 20 feet long and 18 inches wide.

Ladder Type	Weight (pounds)
Wall, aluminum, solid beam	40
Wall, wood and aluminum	55
Wall, wood, solid beam	59
Roof, aluminum, solid beam	52
Roof, aluminum, truss	62
Roof, wood, truss	66
Extension, aluminum, solid beam	51
Extension, fiberglass	73

Ladder Carries

While there is no one correct way to carry a ladder or to raise a ladder, it is important to settle upon and use uniform methods. Standardized carries not only eliminate confusion within a department, they also allow members of different departments to work together efficiently and safely.

Sprains and strains are among the commonest injuries to firefighters. Improper lifting and handling of heavy objects such as extension ladders is one of the major causes of strains and sprains. A three-section extension ladder, for instance, may weigh 250 pounds or more. Helping to carry, raise, and position such a heavy ladder can cause you to use your arms, and particularly your back, in unaccustomed ways. When lifting, always move slowly and steadily. Don't *jerk* heavy objects; use your legs, not your back, to do the work. See **Figure 11-17.**

Figure 11-17. When lifting a ladder or any other heavy object, use your legs, not your back. Lift slowly and steadily, rather than jerking the load upward.

In addition to protecting *you* from injury, using proper ladder-carrying techniques will protect the *ladder* from damage. Ladders seldom get damaged while you are climbing them. They are damaged in handling, by being dropped and banged around. Carrying a ladder smoothly, so that you can raise it efficiently, marks you as a "pro."

Carrying Techniques

A ladder may be carried with the rungs perpendicular to the ground, or parallel to the ground. The first method is called a *beam carry*; the second, a *flat carry*. See **Figure 11-18.**

Unless you are told otherwise, carry wall and extension ladders with the butt facing in the direction you are moving. This avoids the need to reverse the ladder end-for-end before raising it. A roof ladder is pointed in just the opposite direction, with the hooks facing forward. See **Figure 11-19.** Again, this avoids the need to reverse it before use.

When carrying a ladder, and especially when turning, be aware of the location of fellow firefighters and spectators. Being bowled

Figure 11-19. A roof ladder is carried with the hook end forward. Do not open the hooks before reaching the structure.

Figure 11-18. When performing either a beam carry or a flat carry, the butt end of the ladder is usually pointed in the direction of travel. A—Beam carry. B—Flat carry.

A

B

over by a ladder may seem funny on the Saturday morning TV cartoons, but it's not at all humorous in real life.

Types of Carries

Standardized carries involving from one to six firefighters have been developed over the years. They are described in step-by-step fashion on the following pages.

One-person carry

This carry is suitable for short ladders. Begin by standing facing the butt end of the ladder to be carried. Position yourself so that the shoulder next to the ladder is slightly ahead of the ladder's middle. This will raise the front end of the ladder slightly when it is carried, making it easier to control. Lift the ladder and place the underside of the top beam on your shoulder. Extend the arm that is passing through the ladder to grasp the second rung ahead of you. Extend your free arm forward, parallel to the ladder, to help control it. See **Figure 11-20.**

Two-person carry

This is a good carry for medium-length ladders. The two firefighters begin by standing next to the apparatus, facing in the direction of travel. The person in front stands between the second and third rungs, the one in back between the last two rungs. Moving together, the two remove ladder from the apparatus and place the top beam on their shoulders. They each pass an arm through the ladder and grasp a rung in front of them, **Figure 11-21.** As they move toward the building, the person at the butt end controls positioning of the ladder.

Alternate two-person carry

This resembles the standard two-person carry, except that the two firefighters tuck the ladder under their arms and grasp a rung, rather than resting the beam on their shoulders. The firefighter at the front should extend his or her free arm to help control the ladder. See **Figure 11-22**

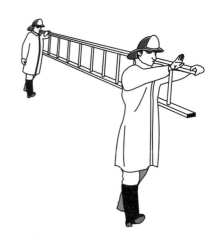

Figure 11-21. In the standard two-person carry, firefighters rest the top beam on their shoulders and grasp a rung with one hand. The free arm of the lead firefighter is extended to help control the ladder.

Figure 11-20. A one-person carry is suitable for short ladders. The free arm should be extended forward for better balance and control.

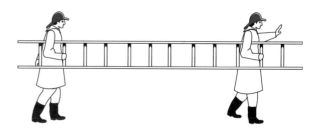

Figure 11-22. An alternate two-person carry, in which the ladder is tucked under the firefighters' arms, instead of being carried on the shoulders.

Three- or four-person carry

To carry and raise a 30-foot truss ladder or a 35-foot extension ladder, at least three firefighters will be needed. In a three-person carry, one firefighter is at each end of the ladder, while the third supports the middle. The four-person carry, with two at each end, is more common, however. It is described in the following paragraphs.

When the ladder is *mounted on the apparatus*, two firefighters position themselves at each end of the ladder, with their backs to the direction of travel. Those on the outside reach across and grasp the underside of the top beam with both hands. Those on the inside do the same, grasping the underside of the bottom beam. On a signal, all four firefighters lift the ladder from the apparatus and swing it onto their shoulders. As they do so, they pivot to face the direction of travel, **Figure 11-23.** To relieve some of the weight being carried on their shoulders, the firefighters each support the ladder with the palm of one hand. The two persons at the butt end of the ladder determine its positioning.

When the ladder is *lying flat on the ground*, the same sequence of actions is followed, except that firefighters must follow safe lifting techniques to prevent back injury. The proper method of lifting is to bend your knees as you grasp a rung with the hand nearest the ladder. At the signal to lift, rise straight up, using the *leg* (not back) muscles, then pivot and rest the ladder on your shoulder.

Five- or six-person carry

These carries are used for an extension ladder that is equipped with poles (tormentors).

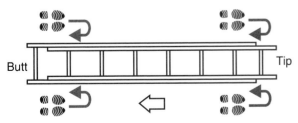

Figure 11-23. In the four-person carry, the firefighters grasp the ends of the ladder, then pivot to face forward as they swing it onto their shoulders.

They are identical in execution, except that the five-person carry uses one (rather than two) firefighters at the butt end of the ladder.

The firefighters form two lines at the rear of the apparatus. The two nearest the equipment begin to slide the ladder out. The next pair of firefighters grasp the end and help to pull it further out. When the ladder is fully off the apparatus, the firefighters place it on their shoulders, as described for the four-person carry. The one or two persons (depending upon whether five or six fighters are performing the carry) at the butt end control the ladder's positioning.

Returning ladders

Returning ladders to their original positions on the apparatus is essentially the same as removing them, except that all actions are reversed.

Ladder Raises

Perhaps nowhere in firefighting is teamwork more essential than in the raising of ladders. The longer and heavier the ladder, the more necessary it becomes to "work by the numbers." Everybody *must* do what he or she is supposed to do, at the right time, or the ladder could topple. The result would likely be a damaged ladder and some damaged firefighters.

It takes the same number of firefighters to raise a ladder as to carry it. At the start of the raise, all assume the same positions they occupied while carrying the ladder. The ladder butt carriers position and control the butt. The tip carriers start the raise near the tip.

During training, especially, it helps to have an extra, experienced firefighter available to observe and to give the commands. The firefighters carrying the ladder position it, then lower it to the ground. On the command "one," they assume positions to carry out the raise. As described later, they work "by the numbers" to raise the ladder into place.

Ladder Placement

With the exception of such short units as roof and attic ladders, fire ladders are carried butt forward for ease of control and positioning. Placement of the butt is important, since it will determine the angle of the ladder once it is in place. If the angle is too steep, the ladder will be unstable. If it is too shallow, the ladder will be weakened and might collapse. The proper angle is 75.5°.

The distance of the butt from the building (the *"D" distance*) is determined by the *effective length* of the ladder. If a 40-foot ladder is resting with its tip against the building, its effective length is 40 feet. If it is resting against an eave with 4 feet of ladder projecting above the eave, the effective length is 36 feet. See **Figure 11-24.**

The most common method of determining the D distance, and the one recommended by manufacturers, is to simply divide the effective length by 4. This will produce the proper 75.5° angle. See **Figure 11-25.** To help achieve the correct angle, some ladders are now supplied with a positioning label attached to the side rail.

For a ladder with an effective length of 40 feet, the D distance is thus 10 feet; for a 36-foot effective length, the D distance is 9 feet. Some departments use a different formula to provide a slightly lower angle. They divide by either 4 or 5, then add 2 feet to the result. The lower angle, with more weight on the tip, is believed to make the ladder more stable: there is less tendency for it to topple backward or tip to the side. At a lower (less than 75.5°) angle, however, the ladder's load-carrying capacity is reduced.

If the ladder will rest against an overhang, the depth of the overhang must be added to the D distance. For example, if you calculate a D distance of 9 feet and the beams of the ladder rest against an overhang that projects 2 feet, you should position the ladder butt *11 feet* from the wall of the building (9 feet + 2 feet = 11 feet.). See **Figure 11-26.**

Another factor to consider in placing a ladder is its relationship to a window or other opening. If you are going to enter the window or play a hose into it, you will not want to position the ladder in the center of the opening. If you do, the ladder will get in your way. Since most people are right-handed, placement to the left of the window is most common.

When an extension ladder is in position on the building, should the *fly* (section of ladder that is extended) be on the upper or the lower side? This is something of a controversy. Some departments do it one way, some the other; ladder manufacturers state emphatically that the fly should always be on the upper side. They say that their product is designed to work best and most safely with the fly on the side away from the building. If your firefighters have been doing it the other way for years and years, it will probably be pretty hard to get them to change.

Types of Raises

A ladder may be raised by either a flat raise or a beam raise. These terms refer to the position of the ladder with respect to the ground. If the ladder is lying with its rungs parallel to the ground, it is in position for a *flat raise*. If the rungs are perpendicular to the ground, it will be a **beam raise**.

Raises may also be thought of as parallel or perpendicular. *Parallel* means that the ladder is lying alongside (or parallel to) the building wall. *Perpendicular* means that the ladder is at a right angle to the building, with the ladder tip pointing away. The perpendicular raise is the easiest and most direct when there are no obstacles overhead or on the ground. The parallel raise is slightly less convenient, but works well when there isn't enough room to use a perpendicular raise. A parallel raise is also preferable to the raise commonly used under an overhead obstruction.

Caution: For all its rugged appearance and strength, a fire ladder is a precision implement. Do not throw it on the ground. Lay it down. Do not slam the tip against the building. Place it there gently. To mistreat a ladder is to shorten its useful

Figure 11-24. Effective length of a ladder is the distance from the ground to the point where it contacts the building. At left, where the tip rests against the building, the effective length of a 40-foot ladder is 40 feet. At right, the ladder projects four feet above the eave of the building, so the effective length is only 36 feet. The distance ("D") of the butt from the building wall is found by dividing the effective length by 4.

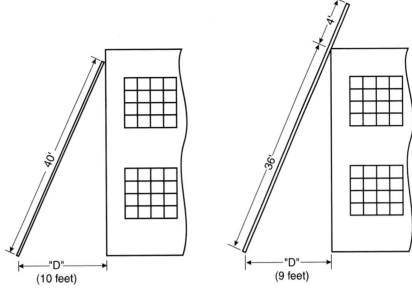

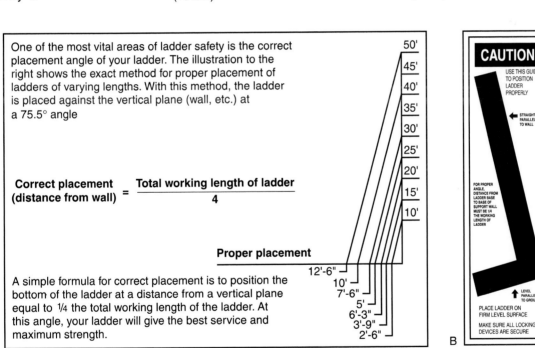

Figure 11-25. Ladder placement angle. A—The correct 75.5° angle is easily found by using the formula shown. (Duo-Safety Ladder Co.) B—This label is provided on new ladders from one manufacturer to indicate when the ladder is positioned at the correct angle. The company has labels available to be placed on older ladders. (Aluminum Ladder Company)

life, destroy its smooth operation, and possibly weaken it to the point where it is hazardous to the person who has to climb it (that person might well be *you*). To protect your hands, always wear gloves when handling or raising ladders.

One-person flat raise

This is the best raise for one firefighter. You can use it to raise a 16- to 20-foot ladder. Begin by placing the butt of the ladder against the building. Move to the tip and face the building. Keeping your back straight,

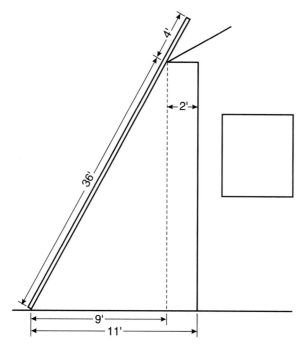

Figure 11-26. When a ladder rests against an overhang, the overhang depth must be added to the "D" distance. In this example, a 36-foot effective length means that the "D" distance is 9 feet (36 divided by 4). The overhang projects two feet, so this must be added to the "D" distance. Thus the distance from the building wall to the butt of the ladder will be 11 feet.

bend your knees and pick up the rung closest to you with one hand. Lift with your legs (not your back). Grasp the second rung and proceed forward, working hand-over-hand until ladder is vertical against the building. See **Figure 11-27.**

With both hands, grasp a lower rung and lift the ladder (again, use your *legs*). Move the butt away from the wall to the calculated D distance.

Two-person perpendicular raise (wall ladder)

This is the easiest raise for two firefighters, provided there are no obstructions overhead or on the ground. It is intended for 20-foot to 28-foot ladders.

The first firefighter begins by placing the ladder in the flat position, with the butt the D distance from the building. He or she then

Figure 11-27. In the one-person flat raise, the wall of the building is used as a "backstop" to hold the butt end of the ladder steady while it is tilted upright.

stands at the butt of the ladder, facing the tip. Placing both feet on bottom rung, the firefighter then grasps the second, third, or fourth rung with both hands, and shifts her or his body backward to act as a counterweight. See **Figure 11-28.**

The second firefighter stands next to the ladder, near the tip, facing away from the building. That firefighter assumes a lifting stance with back straight and knees bent. Grasping a rung with the hand nearest the ladder (palm down and knuckles toward tip), the

Figure 11-28. For a two-person perpendicular raise, the firefighter at the butt end of the ladder serves as a counterweight. He or she places both feet on the bottom rung, and grasps the next rung upward.

firefighter lifts up and pivots under the ladder in one smooth motion. He or she is now facing the butt, with the tip of the ladder raised overhead. Placing hands on alternate rungs and moving toward the butt, the firefighter can "walk the ladder up," **Figure 11-29.**

As the ladder approaches an upright position, the first firefighter can step off the bottom rung and grasp the beams to assist in raising. When the ladder is vertical, the sec-

Figure 11-29. With one person serving as a counterweight on the butt end, the second person can "walk" the ladder up to a vertical position.

ond firefighter should place one foot on bottom rung and grasp a rung with both hands at shoulder height, **Figure 11-30.** Working together, the two firefighters lower the ladder gently against the building.

Two-person perpendicular raise (extension ladder)

Begin by positioning the ladder flat, with the fly down. Follow the steps described for raising the wall ladder, until the ladder is vertical. The first firefighter (the one facing away from the building) steadies the ladder. The second firefighter places one foot on bottom rung, then unties the halyard and extends the fly to the desired height. Once the halyard is retied, the two firefighters gently lower the ladder against the building.

Two-person parallel beam raise (wall ladder)

The first firefighter positions the ladder on one beam, parallel to the building, and the desired D distance from it. Placing his or her forward foot at the end of the bottom beam, the firefighter shifts the other foot as far back as possible. He or she then grasps the third or fourth rung with one hand, and the top beam near the butt with the other hand. See **Figure 11-31.**

At the same time, the second firefighter stands about one-third the ladder length from the tip, facing in that direction. This firefighter grasps a rung with the hand nearest the ladder, palm backward.

At a signal, the first firefighter (at the butt) shifts his or her weight backward and pulls up on the ladder beam, while the first firefighter (near the tip) lifts the ladder and swings under it. While swinging under the ladder, this firefighter pivots to face the butt, **Figure 11-32.** Placing his or her free hand beneath the lower beam, this firefighter now walks toward the butt, raising the ladder. As the ladder reaches vertical, the first firefighter helps lower the second beam to rest on the ground, moves to the side nearest the building, and grasps both beams at shoulder

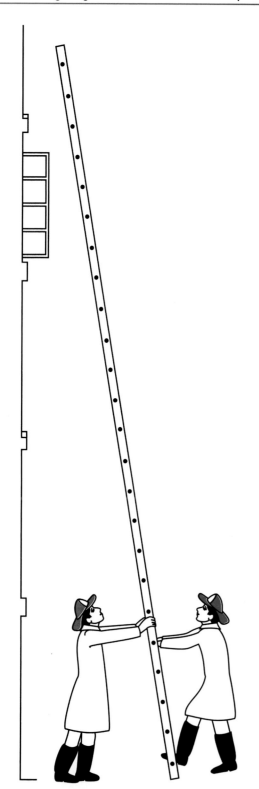

Figure 11-30. Once the ladder is vertical, the two firefighters will be facing each other with the ladder between them. They work together to gently lay the ladder tip against the building.

Figure 11-31. For a two-person parallel beam raise, the ladder is rested on one beam, with the butt the desired distance from the wall. The person at the butt end places a foot at the end of the rail to serve as a stop.

Figure 11-32. The firefighter at the tip end lifts the ladder, swings under it, then pivots to face the butt end. He or she can then "walk" the ladder into a vertical position while the second firefighter anchors and steadies it.

height. The second firefighter braces the ladder from the opposite side, and the two work together to gently lower it against the building.

Two-person parallel beam raise (extension ladder)

Begin by positioning the ladder with the fly facing away from the building. Follow the steps described for raising the wall ladder, until the ladder is vertical. The first firefighter (the one facing away from the building) steadies the ladder. The second firefighter places one foot on bottom rung, then unties

Figure 11-33. The two-person beam raise with an extension ladder uses the same steps as a wall ladder, until it is vertical. One firefighter then steadies it from behind, while the second braces a foot on the bottom rung and uses the halyard to raise the fly to the desired height.

the halyard and extends the fly to the desired height, **Figure 11-33.** Once the halyard is retied, the two firefighters gently lower the ladder against the building.

Two-person parallel flat raise (wall ladder)

Begin by placing the ladder flat on the ground, with the inside beam resting the D distance from the building.

Follow the procedure as described for the two-person perpendicular raise until the ladder is vertical. The firefighter that started at the butt end moves to the beam side nearest the building. The second firefighter moves to the opposite side, so they are facing each other. Each firefighter grasps the ladder beam nearest him or her with one hand waist high and the other shoulder high. Tilt the ladder toward the building slightly, then rotate it one-quarter turn so rungs are parallel to the building. Lower the ladder gently against the building.

Two-person parallel flat raise (extension ladder)

Begin by placing the ladder flat on the ground, with the fly down and the inside beam resting the D distance from the building. Follow the procedure described for the parallel flat raise until the ladder has been turned.

The first firefighter (the one facing away from the building) steadies the ladder. The second firefighter places one foot on bottom rung, then unties the halyard and extends the fly to the desired height. Once the halyard is retied, the two firefighters gently lower the ladder against the building.

Two-person roof ladder raise (one-story building)

Begin by raising a wall or extension ladder in the normal manner, with the tips extending above the eaves of the building. Stand the roof ladder next to the wall ladder and leaning against it, **Figure 11-34A.** The roof ladder should be positioned so that when the hooks are opened, they will point away from the wall ladder.

One firefighter steadies the wall ladder at the ground level, while the second climbs high enough to be able to reach the roof ladder hooks. He or she then opens the hooks, locking them in the open position. The firefighter on the ladder locks one leg over a rung, then grasps both beams of the roof ladder near the hooks. The firefighter on the ground grasps both beams of the roof ladder near the butt. Together, they lift and swing the roof ladder so that it lies with its lower beam resting on one beam of the wall ladder, **Figure 11-34B.**

The two firefighters next push the roof ladder upward until part of its length is above the eaves, **Figure 11-34C.** The ladder is then turned flat to lie on the roof, with the hooks downward. The firefighter on the ladder continues to push it upward until the hooks drop over the roof peak, **Figure 11-34D.** He or she then pulls backward on the roof ladder to make sure that the hooks are engaged.

Two-person roof ladder raise (two-story building)

When the ladder must be moved to the roof of a two-story building, the initial procedure is the same: The roof ladder, with hooks extended, is placed on edge, resting on one beam of the wall ladder, **Figure 11-35A.** Then, however, the two firefighters must physically lift it to the roof, rather than sliding it into place. The firefighter on the ladder slips his or her arm through the roof ladder, behind the second or third rung from the tip. The firefighter on the ground does the same with the second or third rung from the butt of the roof ladder. Resting the roof ladder beam on their shoulders, the two firefighters climb in unison to move the ladder to the roof, **Figure 11-35B.** Positioning is done in the same way described for the one-story raise, **Figure 11-35C.**

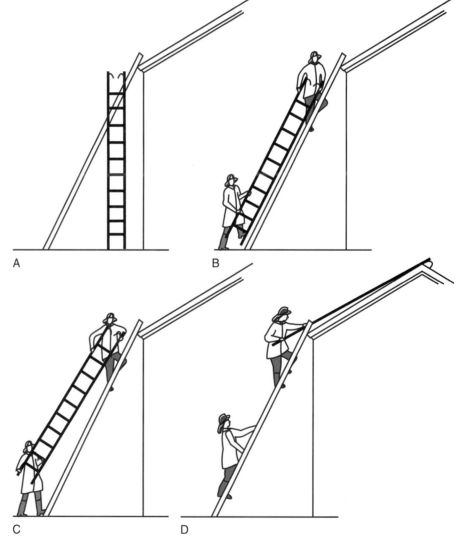

Figure 11-34. Two-person roof ladder raise. A— Stand roof ladder against beam of wall ladder. B—Firefighter on ladder grasps top of roof ladder and opens hooks. Roof ladder is swung up to rest on one beam of wall ladder. C—Firefighters push roof ladder upward until it extends above the eaves. D—Ladder is laid flat on roof, hooks down, and pushed upward until hooks drop over peak.

A

B

C

D

Figure 11-35. Roof ladder raise for two-story building. A—Firefighters rest roof ladder on beam of wall ladder. B—With arms hooked through rings of roof ladder, the firefighters climb in unison. C— At the eave, ladder is slid onto roof and positioned so hooks lock over peak.

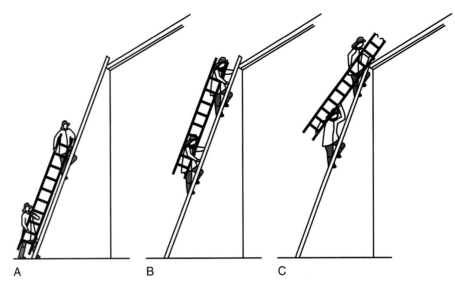

A   B   C

Three- or four-person perpendicular flat raise (extension ladder)

The only difference between the three-person and four-person raises is the number of firefighters at the butt of the ladder: one or two, depending upon availability of personnel. The following description assumes that four persons are working together.

To begin the raise, position ladder flat on the ground with the butt the necessary D distance from the building. The fly should be down. The firefighters at the butt end place their feet on the bottom rung and lean backward to serve as counterweights, as described for two-person raises. See **Figure 11-36A.** The two persons at the tip end stand on opposite sides of the ladder, facing the tip and out one-third the ladder's length back from it. Each grasps a beam, using the hand nearest the ladder. With a smooth swinging motion, the two lift the ladder tip and swing beneath it. A turning movement while they swing the ladder upward leaves these two firefighters facing the butt of the ladder. They then "walk" the ladder to an upright position, **Figure 11-36B.**

The two firefighters at the butt end now remove one foot apiece from the bottom rung, and the two who began at the tip end now place one foot each on the bottom rung. If all four look upward toward the tip, they can easily keep the ladder balanced. One of

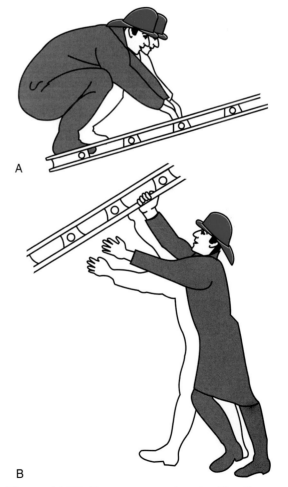

A

B

Figure 11-36. Four-person raise. A—Two firefighters position themselves at butt end to serve as counterweights. B—Two firefighters "walk" ladder up to vertical.

the firefighters then unties the halyard and raises the fly to the desired height. After the halyard is retied, the ladder is gently lowered against the building.

Three- or four-person parallel flat raise (extension ladder)

The initial procedure is the same as the raise just described, except that the ladder is placed parallel to the building. Once the ladder is raised to an upright position, it must be rotated one-quarter turn to properly orient it to the building.

To turn the ladder, the two firefighters farthest from the building move to the ladder beams. At a command, the four firefighters first tilt the ladder slightly so its weight is on one beam end, then rotate one-quarter turn. When the quarter-turn is completed, the fly should be away from the building. The firefighter nearest the halyard should untie it, and raise the ladder to the desired height. After the halyard has been retied, the ladder can be lowered gently against the building.

Five- or six-person perpendicular raise

This raise is used for longer ladders equipped with staypoles ("tormentors"). These ladders are usually referred to as *Bangor ladders*, and are often more than 40 feet in length when fully extended. Raises are best performed with six persons, but can be done with five by assigning only one person to the butt end. The description that follows assumes six firefighters are available.

This raise begins with the ladder perpendicular to the building and flat on the ground, with the fly facing down. The butt should be the D distance from the building. The firefighters are positioned as follows:

- Two at the butt end, facing the tip.
- Two at the tip end, facing the tip.
- Two spread out to the sides, about one-third the ladder's length from the tip. These are the pole holders. See **Figure 11-37A**.

The firefighters at the butt end step on the bottom rung and lean backward to serve

as counterweights. The firefighters near the tip lift the ladder and swing under, turning to face the butt end. As the ladder tip begins to rise, the pole holders start to push upward as well, **Figure 11-37B**. The poles are also used to correct any tendency of the ladder to swing to one side or to rise unevenly.

Once the ladder is in a vertical position, the pole holders move to a *steadying* position. One moves so that the pole is parallel to the building; the other so that his or her pole is perpendicular. Thus the two poles form a right angle, with the ladder at the intersection, as shown in **Figure 11-38A**. The two firefighters originally at the tip now move to the beams of the ladder, facing each other. Each grasps the beam with one hand at shoulder height and the other at waist height, then braces one foot against the beam at the point where it meets the ground. The firefighters who began at the butt end now step off the bottom rung. Each braces one foot against the beam end where it rests on the ground. One of these firefighters operates the halyard to raise the extension, then re-ties it after the desired height is achieved. The firefighters gently lower the ladder against the building, **Figure 11-38B**. The poles are placed against the ground under the ladder for additional support.

Five- or six-person parallel raise

This raise is accomplished in the same way as the perpendicular raise, except that the ladder is rotated one-quarter turn after it is vertical. The pole holders assist in steadying the ladder as it is rotated perpendicular to the building.

Other Raises

There are three other raises (overhead obstruction, church, hotel) that are difficult to perform well and are more hazardous than those already described. For these reasons, they should be used only as a last resort.

Overhead obstruction raise

If a parallel raise is possible, it should be used in preference to this one, especially if the

Figure 11-37. Six-person ladder raise. A—Positioning of firefighters at start of raise. B—Use of tormentor poles to help raise ladder to vertical.

obstruction is an electrical wire. Touching a charged power line with a metal or wet wooden ladder can result in a severe (possibly *fatal*) electrical shock.

Unlike other raises in which the butt is positioned first, the *tip* is placed as close as possible to the building for this raise. The ladder is perpendicular to the building. The raise is accomplished most easily if four firefighters are available.

Two of the firefighters stand on either side of the tip, with their backs to the building. The other two stand at the butt, facing the building. All four should be alert to any obstacle that could interfere with the raise or cause injury.

The two persons at the tip lift it upward and inward toward the building. The two

persons at the butt end hold it low and keep "feeding" the ladder to the firefighters at the tip end as they raise it. When the obstacle has been cleared and the ladder is nearly vertical, the butt can be positioned at the D distance and the tip rested against the wall.

Church (dome) raise

This raise is used in places where there are no walls, posts, or other surfaces against which to rest the tip of the ladder. This raise requires, at minimum, six firefighters. Also needed are two lengths of rope that are more than twice the distance from the ground to the tip of the ladder when it is fully extended. Thus, if the ladder tip will be 40 feet above the ground when fully raised, you will need two 100-foot lengths of rope.

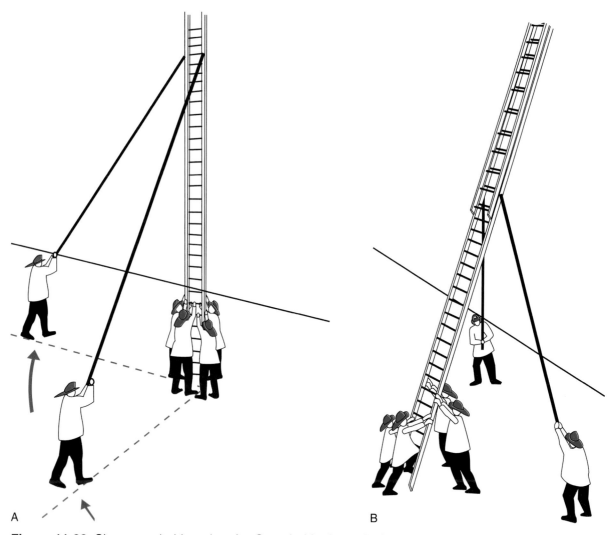

Figure 11-38. Six-person ladder raise. A—Once ladder is vertical, tormentors should be positioned as shown while fly section of ladder is raised. B—Tormentors are repositioned as shown to steady ladder as it is lowered against building.

Begin by extending the fly several feet and making sure the locks are engaged. Make a loop in the middle of one of the ropes. Form a half-hitch under the top rung and around one beam of the ladder, then place the loop over the beam end. Snug the knot tight for security. Repeat with the second rope. See **Figure 11-39.**

Use one of the standard raises to place the ladder in a vertical position. Two of the firefighters should face each other with the ladder between them, holding the beams at shoulder height. The other four firefighters each take a rope end and wrap it around

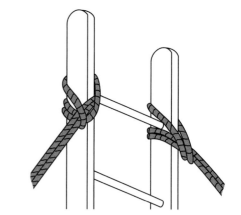

Figure 11-39. Method of securing steadying ropes to extension ladder tip for a church raise.

themselves for control. The rope should pass between one arm and the firefighter's body, wrap below the buttocks, and be held by the free hand. The four firefighters walk diagonally outward from the ladder, feeding rope as they go, to form a square, **Figure 11-40.** The firefighters should keep their eyes on the tip of the ladder as they walk outward.

One of the firefighters holding the ladder will untie the halyard and raise the fly to the desired height. As the fly is raised, the four rope holders can pay out additional rope as needed. The ropes should be kept snug. The ladder is now ready for use.

Hotel (factory) raise

This raise is used when people must be rescued from windows on two or more floors simultaneously, or when firefighters must enter or leave windows on several floors at

Figure 11-40. Four firefighters with ropes act as "outriggers" to steady vertical ladder in a church raise. This raise is used in situations where the ladder tip cannot be rested against a support.

the same time. The total raise should always be made with a Bangor ladder. This raise requires two ropes that are slightly longer than the ladder will be when raised. Like the church raise, a minimum of six persons must be involved.

The ladder should be positioned for either a parallel or perpendicular raise, so that the butt will be 4 feet from the building when the raise has been completed. Extend the fly so that three or four rungs are protruding. Be certain that all locks are engaged. Tie one end of each rope around a beam and the third or fourth rung of the fly. Use clove hitches to secure the rope to the ladder.

After raising the ladder to the desired height, the two firefighters on the butt end should stand at either side, grasping the beams at waist and shoulder heights. The two rope holders move about 10 feet directly behind the firefighters at the sides of the ladder, while the pole holders move out to positions at a 45° angle to the beams. This permits the ladder to be held in a nearly vertical position, so it will be within reach of firefighters on several floors at the same time. See **Figure 11-41.**

Figure 11-41.
Positioning of six firefighters to steady extension ladder in nearly vertical position. This is called the hotel or factory raise.

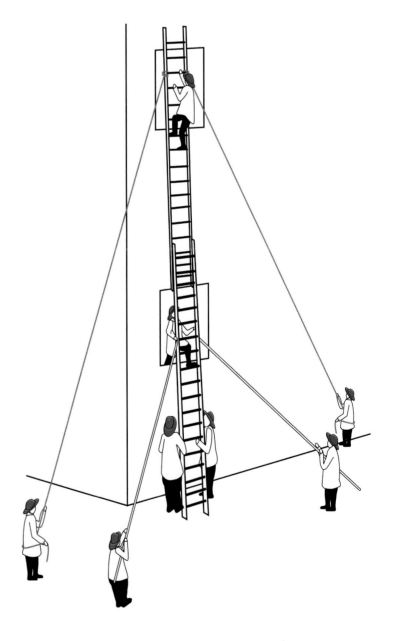

Climbing Ladders

Climbing ladders isn't the safest sport in the world, but going up the ladder doesn't have to be particularly dangerous, either. This is true if the ladder is structurally sound and properly placed, and the climber knows what she or he is doing.

Structural Soundness

Ladders for fire department use are made to exacting standards. They will remain safe and effective tools for many years, if they are not abused. Most damage to ladders results from sloppy handling. Occasionally, unavoidable abuse will occur at a fire. If you know that a particular ladder has been damaged, discuss it with your officer or the safety officer. The last thing either of these officers wants is to have firefighters injured because of faulty equipment.

Proper Placement

Before you climb, check the ladder for proper placement. It should rest evenly on safety shoes or spurs. Both beams should be solidly against the building. The butt should be the D distance from the building.

Climbing

Most important, don't try to set any speed records: you're more likely to end up in the hospital than in the record book. Make a conscious effort to move more slowly and deliberately than you know you can.

Before you start to climb, stand at the foot of the ladder, with your toes in line with the butt. Extend your arms and fingers straight out from the shoulder. A rung should be in line with the middle of your hand. This tells you whether or not the angle of the ladder is correct. It also gives you the proper erect position for climbing. Climb with your body perpendicular to the ground. In other words, don't hug the ladder. In the erect position, you will have

better control of your balance, and your knees won't bang into the rungs as you climb.

Other climbing tips

- Climb in the way that is most natural to you. You can climb using the movement pattern right arm/right leg, left arm/left leg, or you could alternate limbs: right arm/left leg, left arm/right leg.

- Climb steadily and smoothly. Work for form, rather than speed. Speed will come with practice.

- Step on every rung, and climb with your legs, not your arms. Push yourself up, don't pull yourself up. Grasp every rung or every other rung, but don't reach up — grasp the rung directly in front of your shoulder. See **Figure 11-42.**

- Step on the balls of your feet, not the underside of the arch. An arch is not intended to bear weight on its underside.

- Step in the center of each rung. This will reduce ladder wobble.

- Unless you are carrying tools, place your hands on the rungs, not the beams. This will allow you to test the soundness of the rungs before placing your full body weight on them.

- There should be no more than one firefighter per 10 feet of ladder working length, **Figure 11-43.** There should never be more than four persons on a ladder at a given time, no matter what its length (this doesn't apply to aerial ladders).

- When climbing, look up and ahead. Don't look down; you already know where you started. It's where you are going that counts.

- Take good care of yourself. When working from a ladder, always secure yourself with either a leg lock or a safety belt. If you use a leg lock, the leg that is *opposite* the side of the ladder where you are working is the one to lock in place. See **Figure 11-44.**

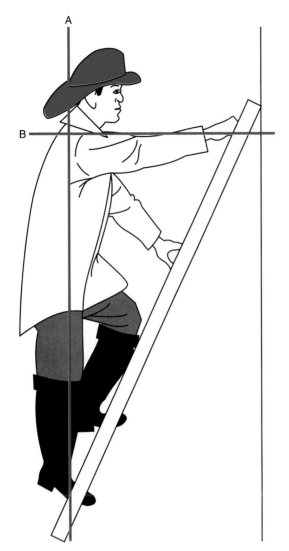

Figure 11-42. When climbing a ladder, your body should be kept in a vertical position (A). Reach out to grasp the rung in front of you, at shoulder height (B). Place the ball of your foot, not the instep, on the rungs.

- Wear gloves for hand protection whenever you carry, raise, or climb a ladder.
- Secure the ladder at the top with a ladder strap or rope hose tool.

Carrying Tools and Equipment

The best and safest way to get equipment up to a roof or upper floor of a building is to pull it up with a rope. That isn't always practical, or even possible. There are times when

Figure 11-43. For each 10-foot working length of ladder, only one firefighter should be climbing. Note that the ladder is at a safe angle, with sufficient projection above the eaves. The firefighter is grasping the rung at shoulder level as he climbs, and is placing the ball of his foot (not the arch) on the rung.

you have no choice but to climb a ladder carrying an axe, a roof ladder, an extinguisher, or some other piece of equipment.

When you carry a heavy object up a ladder, it is very important that you climb in an erect position, so that you keep your balance.

If the object you are carrying is light enough and of the proper configuration, slide it along one beam, **Figure 11-45.** You can do this with an axe, a pike pole, a claw bar, or similar objects. Other things, like a roof ladder or a load of hose, can be carried on your shoulder. Nozzles and extinguishers, however, must be carried in one hand. Regardless of the load you are carrying, be sure to balance yourself by sliding your free hand along under the beam on that side.

Figure 11-44. A leg lock around a rung and the ladder beam will allow you to safely work with both hands while on a ladder. (Warren Lutton)

Figure 11-45. Many lighter objects, such as an axe or pike pole, can be most easily carried up a ladder by sliding along one beam.

Ladder Rescue

The method of ladder rescue that is described is most suitable for victims who are conscious and somewhat able to help themselves. With some modification, it can be used for an unconscious person, as well.

Training is done with a mannequin or another firefighter acting as the "victim." In a real situation, however, you may be assisting a person who is not accustomed to heights. The victim may become terrified and either freeze or pass out. The victim that passes out is the more dangerous one for the rescuer, since he or she could slip off the ladder unless you react quickly. You are suddenly faced with dealing with an unconscious person on the ladder, while protecting yourself from a fall.

As you bring a conscious victim down the ladder, it is important to keep talking to him or her. By maintaining a constant commentary ("we're about halfway there," "you're doing great," "just a little way to go"), you'll reassure the victim and cope with his or her fears. Tell the victim what you are doing, every step of the way, and give the victim firm, clear directions on what you expect of him or her. Use a calm, matter-of-fact tone to convey the idea that what you are doing is routine and that you are in full control of the situation.

Preventing panic reactions keeps both you and the victim safe.

As you move down the ladder, your feet should be one rung below those of the victim. Keep your body close to the victim, which will not only provide reassurance, but will help you maintain control if he or she loses consciousness. Your arms should encircle the victim, grasping the rungs at your shoulder level (chest level on the victim). See **Figure 11-46**. Keep in step with the victim, letting him or her set the pace. Keep your knees close together.

If the victim loses consciousness, allow him or her to slide slowly downward until their crotch rests on your knee. Control speed of the slide with your body pressure. By repeating this procedure, one rung at a time,

Figure 11-46. When helping a conscious victim down a ladder, encircle his or her waist with your arms as you grasp the rungs. This will help reassure the victim, as well as giving you full control. Note the use of a safety rope. (Donald Foye)

you can gradually lower the victim to the ground. In this situation, you should slide your hands along the beams, rather than grasping the rungs, to maintain constant contact with the ladder.

Using a safety rope

Using a safety rope with a ladder rescue makes the process less hazardous for both rescuer and victim. In addition, the greater sense of security provided by the safety rope makes the experience far less terrifying for the person being rescued. In a real rescue, use a safety rope whenever possible.

To use a safety rope, tie a bowline with a loop large enough to fit loosely over a person's shoulders. Place the loop over the victim's shoulders and beneath his or her arms. Bring the free end of the rope over a rung above the level of the victim's head and drop it to the ground. Firefighters on the ground will now be able to support the weight and control the descent rate of the victim as you move him or her down the ladder.

Working from Ladders

When you first think of it, working from a ladder doesn't seem to be very different from working with the same equipment on the ground. In one sense, it is very much the same: when working with an axe, for example, you must use the same precautions that you would use on the ground. But, there are some major differences that you must take into account, as well. If you drop that axe while you are on the ground, you probably won't do too much damage. But if you drop it from a ladder, it could seriously injure or kill someone.

When working on a ladder, you have no place to run. If a hose runs wild, if a wind shift sends a lot of poisonous smoke your way, if flames break out a window next to your ladder, you are pretty well *stuck* where you are. To get out of the way, you can't move forward, back, or sideways — you can move only up or down. Moving up or down can't be done very fast, either. This means that you must remain extra alert to everything that goes on around you.

Whenever possible, wear a life belt when working from a ladder. But sometimes this is neither possible nor practical. The leg lock, which has already been discussed, will hold you securely. By locking the leg opposite the side to which you are working, you will exert a counterbalancing force that will help keep you stable. Should anything go wrong, however, you can unlock a safety belt faster than you can get out of a leg lock.

When working with hose lines on a ladder, the hose should be tied to the ladder with a ladder strap or rope hose tool before the water is turned on. This precaution will prevent a kickback that could knock you off the ladder.

Care of Ladders

Ladders do fail. It doesn't happen often, but it does happen. When a ladder fails, firefighters get hurt. There is no absolute guarantee that any given ladder is safe. But you can make the odds heavily in your favor by frequent inspection and good maintenance practices.

Aluminum ladders are affected adversely by both acids and alkalis. These substances that often found in smoke. When mixed with water, they can concentrate into strong enough solutions in crevices (such as the point where a rung joins a beam) to dangerously weaken the member. To prevent this, they must be washed thoroughly after each use at a fire or other exposure to chemicals. Washing should be done with a solution of biodegradable detergent and water, applied with a soft brush, with special attention to joints and crevices. The ladder should then be rinsed thoroughly with lukewarm water and wiped dry.

Wooden ladders can be damaged by too little moisture or too much moisture. If kept in an excessively damp atmosphere, they can warp and rot. If they are kept in too-dry a situation (stored near heat ducts, for example, or left in direct sunlight), they can dry out and split. Wooden ladders will also dry out if

their protective coating of varnish is removed. Many of the substances present at a fire will soften and destroy varnish.

After every use (especially use at a fire), a wooden ladder should be rinsed down with clear water that is warm (not hot). Again, pay close attention to crevices and joints. After washing, wipe the ladder dry with a clean, soft cloth.

Visual Inspection and Testing

Like all other tools of the firefighting trade, ladders must be inspected after every use — whether that use was at a fire or not. If a ladder has been struck or badly jolted while on the apparatus, it must also be inspected.

This inspection should be *tactile* as well as visual: if something appears to be suspicious check it further with your fingertips or fingernails. This will help you identify dents, cracks, or surface irregularities that might indicate an attack by heat or chemicals.

Your visual inspection should cover all parts of the ladder and identify any signs of strain or physical damage. Look for fractured rails or rungs. Twist, push, and pull rungs to detect any signs of looseness. Identify any splinters that could cause hand injuries. Look for damaged pawls, improperly adjusted wires, damaged or missing fasteners, worn or missing halyards. Examine any heat indicator labels for a color change showing the ladder had been exposed to excessive heat.

Any ladder that does not pass your visual and tactile tests with flying colors must be taken out of active use. Such ladders must not be placed back on apparatus until they have been service tested and meet the requirements of NFPA Standard 1932.

Testing

When should a ladder be tested? The general rule is that a ladder must be tested at least once each year. In addition, a ladder must be service-tested:

- Before being placed in service for the first time.

- After it has been subjected to loads exceeding the NFPA recommended level.
- After it has been used in any unusual manner (such as forcing open a door).
- After it has been repaired.
- At any time there is a question about its safety (for example, following possible exposure to excessive heat).

The NFPA specifies several types of tests for ladders. The primary ladder test, however, is the Horizontal Bending Test (also called the Center Load Test). An abbreviated version of the test follows:

Prepare for testing by placing the ladder so that it is supported under each end rung, as shown in **Figure 11-47.** There must be sufficient space between the ladder and floor to allow for deflection of the ladder under load.

If the ladder being tested is an extension type, it must be fully extended to its normal working height, as indicated on the base of the ladder. Pawls must be engaged and prevented from disengaging by fastening a strap tightly around corresponding rungs on the fly and base sections. Three-section ladders, of course, must be strapped in two locations to prevent disengagement of the pawls.

Measure the distance between the two points where the ladder is supported, then divide that distance by two to find the precise midpoint. Measure and mark the location. This is where the test load will be applied (the load should extend no more than 16 inches to either side of the midpoint).

To conduct the test:

1. Apply a 350 lb. (158.8 kg) load at the midpoint of the ladder. Wait one minute, then remove the load.
2. Measure the distance from the midpoint of the ladder to a point on the floor or ground directly below. Record the distance (this is your *base measurement*).
3. Apply a 500 lb. (226.8 kg) load to the midpoint of the ladder. Wait five minutes, then remove the load.
4. Wait five minutes more, then measure the distance from the midpoint of the ladder to the floor or ground.
5. If the ladder breaks or is obviously damaged by the load, it has failed the test.
6. If the ladder sustains a *permanent set* (difference between the two measurements) that is greater than allowable, it has failed the test. The allowable permanent set for various ladder lengths is:

Ladder length	Allowable set
25 ft. or less	1/2 in. (12.7 mm)
Over 25 ft., but under 35 ft.	1 in. (25.4 mm)
35 ft. or more	1.5 in. (38.1 mm)

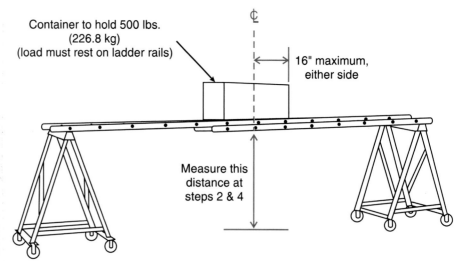

Figure 11-47. This is the general setup for testing a ladder, using the Horizontal Bending Test. Since the ladder can fail suddenly, be sure to keep all body parts from under the ladder while it is loaded. (Duo-Safety Ladder Co.)

Container to hold 500 lbs. (226.8 kg) (load must rest on ladder rails)

16" maximum, either side

Measure this distance at steps 2 & 4

If the difference between the base measurement and the second (load) measurement is greater than shown, the ladder must be removed from service and either repaired or destroyed.

This abbreviated version is intended to make you familiar with the basic load test procedure. Before conducting such a test, consult NFPA Standard 1932 for the complete procedure. The Standard also describes additional ladder tests in detail.

Ladder maintenance

Wipe wood ladders dry after they have been wet. Oil all pawls and pulleys with a good quality lubricating oil. Use softened candle wax or a high-quality grease to lubricate guides, grooves, and other bearing surfaces (both wood and aluminum ladders). If varnish is damaged or worn off a wood ladder, sand lightly and apply a new coat of spar varnish. Sharpen dull spurs. Remove any splinters (burrs on aluminum) and make sure the surface is smooth. *Never* paint a ladder, since the paint will hide defects that could be dangerous. If any part is worn or suspect, replace it — remember, you are depending on this ladder to hold you safely when you are 30 or 40 feet in the air.

Determining Safe Ladder Loads

The amount of weight that a ladder can safely carry is determined by the side rails — they are engineered to support a particular load over a specific span (distance). The specified loading is valid only if the ladder is set at the proper 75.5° angle, and has passed the NFPA Horizontal Bending Test.

The general guidelines for maximum safe ladder loads are:

- folding and pompier ladders: 300 lbs. (136 kg).
- single (wall) and roof ladders: 750 lbs. (340 kg), distributed.
- extension ladders: 750 lbs. (340 kg), distributed.

The maximum concentrated load for any type of ladder is 500 lbs. (226.8 kg).

NOTE: The weights listed include tools, equipment, personal protective gear, charged hoselines, and weight of the firefighter(s). If the ladder is set to an angle other than 75.5°, the maximum allowable weight is 250 lbs. (113.4 kg).

SUMMARY

The ladders in most common use by fire departments are the wall (or straight) ladder, extension ladder, roof ladder, attic ladder, and aerial ladder. In addition, most departments use one or more special purpose ladders.

Most ladders used in the fire service are wood, aluminum, wood and aluminum, or fiberglass. Each material has its advantages and disadvantages. Ladders may be of either solid or truss construction. The beams on solid ladders are made of one piece of wood or aluminum. Truss construction consists of two rails held together by bolts, rivets, or welds at the rung blocks. The advantage of truss construction is greater strength with less weight than solid beam ladders.

Standardized ladder carries and raises were developed to prevent injury to the firefighter and damage to the ladder. The ladder carry and raise should be one smooth operation. Only practice will make it so. Nearly all raises are performed by one to six firefighters. The number will be determined by the length and weight of the ladder, and by the type of raise. Raises are done perpendicular to the building or parallel with it, and may begin with the ladder lying flat (raise) or standing on one edge (beam raise). Whatever the raise, it is essential that the firefighters doing it work together. Each must know what is done by the person in each position. They must be able to work "by the numbers" to lift in unison.

For maximum strength and stability, the ladder butt must be the correct distance from the building. Various formulas exist, but the most common is to use a distance equal to one-fourth the effective length of the ladder. Most departments place the fly of an extension ladder away from the building when raising it; others place it toward the building. Local practices prevail in most ladder work.

Before you climb a ladder, make sure it is at the proper angle. Climb with your body perpendicular to the ground, and climb on the balls of your feet. Place your feet in the center of the rungs. When working on a ladder, there is no place to escape, so you must always be aware of what is going on around you. Wear a life belt or use a leg lock. It is safer to hoist tools and equipment than to carry them while climbing. Hoses should be tied in place before being charged to prevent kickback.

Ladder rescues can be hazardous to the rescuer and the rescued, since the victim may be terrified. Stay as close as possible to the person being rescued and whenever possible, use a safety rope. Talk reassuringly, explaining what you are doing.

Ladders sometimes fail, causing injuries. Most failures can be prevented by proper treatment, maintenance, and inspection. Wash aluminum ladders with a mild detergent solution, wood ladders with plain water. Dry them thoroughly. While washing and drying, inspect carefully for conditions that could indicate weakening.

REVIEW QUESTIONS

1. Name the six ladders most often used in the fire service. State their identifying characteristics.
2. Why do many fire departments prefer to use roof ladders, rather than wall ladders?
3. What is the difference between a solid beam and a truss ladder?
4. What materials are most commonly used in ladder construction? What are the advantages and disadvantages of each?
5. What is the proper way to lift heavy objects?
6. What is the difference between a flat carry and a beam carry?
7. When carrying a ladder, which end is usually in front?
8. How many firefighters are usually needed to raise an extension ladder?
9. Describe the difference between a perpendicular flat raise and a horizontal beam raise.
10. If a 45-foot ladder is projecting five feet above an eave, how far from the building should the ladder butt be?
11. What is the distribution of firefighters in a three-person flat raise? In a four-person flat raise?
12. How is a church (dome) raise different from other types of ladder raises? How many firefighters must take part in a church raise?
13. State three of the precautions you should take when climbing a ladder.
14. Why should you place your weight on the ball of your foot, rather than the arch, while climbing a ladder?
15. Describe the procedure for climbing a ladder while carrying an axe.
16. What procedure should you follow when assisting a conscious person during a ladder rescue?
17. Describe the defects to watch for when inspecting an aluminum ladder.
18. What is the proper procedure for cleaning and preserving a wooden ladder?
19. What is the maximum weight load permitted on a wall ladder?
20. What is the maximum allowable permanent set for a 20-foot roof ladder, as measured using the NFPA Horizontal Bending Test?

NFPA 1001 Job Performance Requirements

The material on this page consists of those portions of the NFPA 1001 Job Performance Requirements relevant to the material presented in this chapter. Items preceded by the numeral 3 (3-x.x) are Fire Fighter I requirements; those with the numeral 4 (4-x.x) are Fire Fighter II requirements.

3-1.1.1 General Knowledge Requirements. The organization of the fire department; the role of the Fire Fighter I in the organization; the mission of fire service; the fire department's standard operating procedures and rules and regulations as they apply to the Fire Fighter I; the role of other agencies as they relate to the fire department; aspects of the fire department's member assistance program; the critical aspects of NFPA 1500, Standard on Fire Department Occupational Safety and Health Program, as they apply to the Fire Fighter I; knot types and usage; the difference between life safety and utility rope; reasons for placing rope out of service; the types of knots to use for given tools, ropes, or situations; hoisting methods for tools and equipment; and using rope to support response activities.

3-1.1.2 General Skill Requirements. The ability to don personal protective clothing within one minute; doff personal protective clothing and prepare for reuse; hoist tools and equipment using ropes and the correct knot; tie a bowline, clove hitch, figure eight on a bight, half hitch, becket or sheet bend, and safety knots; and locate information in departmental documents and standard or code materials.

3-5.3 Clean and check ladders, ventilation equipment, self-contained breathing apparatus (SCBA), ropes, salvage equipment, and hand tools, given cleaning tools, cleaning supplies, and an assignment, so that equipment is clean and maintained according to manufacturer's or departmental guidelines, maintenance is recorded, and equipment is placed in a ready state or reported otherwise.

(a) Prerequisite Knowledge: Types of cleaning methods for various tools and equipment, correct use of cleaning solvents, and manufacturer's or departmental guidelines for cleaning equipment and tools.

(b) Prerequisite Skills: The ability to select correct tools for various parts and pieces of equipment, follow guidelines, and complete recording and reporting procedures.

Reprinted with permission from NFPA 1001, *Fire Fighter Professional Qualifications,* Copyright ©1997, National Fire Protection Association, Quincy, MA 02269. This reprinted material is not the complete and official position of the National Fire Protection Association on the referenced subject, which is represented only by the standard in its entirety.

Ropes

OBJECTIVES

When you have completed this chapter, you will be able to:

🔥 Identify various rope materials and describe the advantages and disadvantages of each.

🔥 Describe the "rope basics": the bight, loop, round turn, and half-hitch.

🔥 Recognize and describe the uses for each type of knot.

🔥 Give instructions for tying the more commonly used knots.

🔥 List procedures for the inspection, cleaning, maintenance, and storing of rope.

🔥 Discuss the recommended sizes of rope for various firefighting and rescue tasks.

🔥 Demonstrate tying knots to support a firefighter.

🔥 Discuss the uses of rope to secure ladders, hoses, and other equipment.

IMPORTANT TERMS

bight	half-hitch	running bowline	standing part
bowline on a bight	kernmantle	safety ropes	tensile strength
chimney hitch	loop	sheepshank	utility ropes
clove hitch	rescue knot	sheet bend	working end
elasticity	rope hose tool	slippery hitch	working strength
elongation	round turn	square knot	

WORKING WITH ROPES

Potentially, every rope is a lifeline. Each time you handle a piece of rope, you should remember this — you would never be casual about a rope if you thought it might be used one day to save your own life.

Rope has come under close scrutiny in recent years, partly because of some tragic accidents, and partly because of increased interest in activities such as mountain climbing. As a result, ropes and their use are undergoing improvement.

As with all other firefighting equipment, the safe and efficient use of rope depends on its care and handling. An improperly tied knot may come loose just when it is needed most. A rope subjected to abrasion or deterioration may support only a fraction of its rated load.

In addition to rescue, ropes are used in the fire service for hoisting equipment, raising ladders, tying down hose nozzles, pulling heavy objects, lashing, splinting, and many more tasks. See **Figure 12-1**. You must know instantly what size rope and type of knot to use in a given situation. Such knowledge comes only with repeated practice.

Ropes that are used for rescue or other activities upon which human life might depend are called *safety ropes.* Those used for hauling equipment, securing ladders, or any of the other assorted tying and pulling activities on the fireground or in the station are referred to as *utility ropes.* Don't confuse the two — never use a utility rope for a safety rope task, or vice versa.

Rope Materials

Until the recent past, ropes used in the fire service were made of natural fibers: manila, hemp, and sisal. Manila, made of fibers from the banana plant, became the preferred material because of its properties of flexibility, strength, and reliability. See **Figure 12-2**. Modern technology has developed artificial fibers that are replacing natural fibers in the manufacture of ropes. Today, most ropes being purchased by fire departments for safety lines, rescue work, and hoisting are made of nylon. This fiber is lighter, stronger, more resistant to abrasion than manila, hemp, or sisal. Other artificial fibers are also used for ropes.

Nearly all nylon ropes for fire and rescue applications are of the type of construction known as *kernmantle.* The kern (or core) is composed of braided or twisted nylon strands. The mantle (sheath) is braided nylon. See **Figure 12-3**. Because the fibers are uni-

Figure 12-1. Rope has many uses on the fireground. This firefighter is using a rope hose tool as a safety line while practicing ventilation techniques on a steeply pitched roof during a training exercise. (Warren Lutton)

Figure 12-2. Manila has been the favored rope material in the fire service for many years, because it is strong, flexible, and reliable. In recent years, however, it has been replaced by nylon and other artificial materials.

Figure 12-3. Most ropes of nylon and other artificial fibers are of kernmantle construction. The strong, continuous-fiber core is called the "kern." The "mantle," or cover, is braided from material of a contrasting color. This allows abrasion and other damage to show up quickly, providing improved safety.

form and the braids and twists can be varied, manufacturers have control over the amount of stretch and spin that is characteristic of this type of rope.

One advantage nylon-fiber ropes have over ropes made of natural fibers is greater flexibility. This greater flexibility makes knots easier to tie and untie. The material is non-slip, so the knots hold better, as well.

One of the advantages of kernmantle nylon ropes is the sharp color contrast between the sheath and the core. Typical color combinations are an orange sheath over a black core, white over orange, and red over white. If the sheath has been cut or worn away at any point (indicating weakening of that section), you can see it easily. In some cases, you can cut out the worn part and have two shorter ropes. In others, you might have to retire the rope from life support use. Don't take unnecessary chances.

The rope recommended for water rescue is made from polypropylene rather than nylon. Polypropylene is lighter than nylon and will float. These rescue ropes have a yellow sheath that makes them highly visible on water.

All ropes, especially those used in rescue work, must have some *elasticity*. That is, they must stretch under load and then return to their original length. The elasticity ensures that, in case of a fall, the rope will absorb much of the shock that would otherwise be transmitted to the firefighter's body and cause injury. By absorbing this impact, the rope acts much like the shock absorber in an automobile. One objection to nylon ropes has been that they stretch and lose their original elasticity (and thus, their ability to absorb impact). However, this happens only if the rope has previously been overloaded or abused in some way.

Rope Strength Ratings

All ropes are rated on tensile strength. *Tensile strength* is the breaking point of the rope when one end is anchored and a pull is exerted on the other end. Tensile strength is often expressed as the number of pounds of pull it takes to break a sample. Thus, as shown in **Figure 12-4**, the amount of pull it takes to break a length of 7/16 in. nylon rope is 7000 pounds.

Elasticity and elongation

Other characteristics determined when rope is tested are its elasticity and elongation. *Elasticity* refers to the amount (usually expressed as a percentage) that a sample of rope can be stretched and still return to its original length. *Elongation* is the amount of *permanent* stretch a rope reaches at its breaking point. To express it somewhat differently, so long as a rope is stretched within its elastic limits, it will always return to its original length. Once a rope has been elongated, some of its original elasticity is lost. The rope will no longer absorb as great a shock load. If the rope reaches its elongation limit, it will snap.

Most ropes, manila or nylon, will retain their elasticity, or ability to absorb shock, if they are not loaded beyond 15 percent of their tensile strength. The *working strength* is always within the elastic limits of the rope. You cannot exceed the working strength by very much without doing permanent damage; that is, weakening the rope.

The tensile and working strengths of representative manila and nylon ropes, as shown in Figure 10-3, apply only to *new* ropes used for descent, rescue, and safety purposes. Once ropes have been exposed to dirt, corrosives, sharp bends, or excessive heat, their safe load-carrying capacity is reduced significantly. For example, once you have used a rescue rope to jerk a pumper out of the mud, you had better not use it again for anything more critical than tying Christmas packages. Never use life support ropes for anything *but* life support.

Safety demands that you use the proper strength rope for the job. While you can always use a rope stronger than recommended for a given application, it can be very dangerous to use one that is weaker. The minimum recommended rope sizes for hoisting tools and equipment are 1/2 in. to 5/8 in. manila or 3/8 in. to 1/2 in. nylon; for heavy loads and rescue work, 3/4 in. to 1 in. manila or 7/16 in. to 5/8 in. nylon.

Working strength

The only strength rating that concerns the firefighter is the *working* strength. Forget about tensile strength. That just tells you at what load the rope will break. Your job isn't breaking ropes. Your job is rescuing people and hauling firefighting equipment. You must select a rope that will bear a static load which does not exceed its working strength. For example, you have to raise a 450-pound load using nylon rope. Referring to **Figure 12-4**, should you use a 9/32 in. rope or a 3/8 in. rope? You must use the size *next larger* than your expected load (in this case, 3/8 in.). For your own safety, memorize the working strength of every size and type rope you will use.

What if the load should drop? Won't this put additional strain on the rope? Yes, it will.

Figure 12-4. Tensile and working strengths, in pounds, of manila and nylon ropes. Working strength is generally considered to be 15 percent of the tensile strength.

TENSILE STRENGTH (NEW)						
	9/32"	3/8"	7/16"	1/2"	5/8"	3/4"
Manila		1350		2650	4400	5400
Nylon	2400	3700	7000	7600	11,500	

WORKING STRENGTH (NEW)						
	9/32"	3/8"	7/16"	1/2"	5/8"	3/4"
Manila		202		397	660	810
Nylon	360	555	1050	1140	1725	

But, because of its elasticity and elongation capabilities, a rope will absorb a shock load greater than its working strength. As long as the static load does not exceed the working strength, and the rope is in good condition, it will do the job.

How long should the rope be? To put it most simply, "a little longer than you actually need." If you have to descend a 100-foot cliff using a 75-foot rope, the last 25 feet might be a bit rough. If somebody 50 feet up is going to hoist an axe, he or she will need 50 feet of rope plus a foot or two left over to tie around the axe. If you have a pulley 60 feet up and you will pull something up from the ground, you will need 120 feet, plus enough additional to securely tie the equipment for hoisting. When working with rope, "too much" is always preferable to "too little."

An easy method of making a rough measurement of rope is shown in **Figure 12-5**. Although the distance will vary from person to person, the distance from hand to hand with arms outstretched is approximately six feet. From the center of the chest to the end of an outstretched arm is approximately three feet. For greater accuracy, measure the actual distances on your own body.

KNOTS

Whenever you tie a knot or loop a rope around an object, you actually weaken the rope. This occurs because the outside fibers take most of the strain at the bend. The sharper the bend, the more damage you inflict, so a bend around a one-inch pipe will do more harm than a bend around a telephone pole. Obviously, going around sharp corners is even worse. Despite the weakening they cause, knots are a vital part of using rope for practical firefighting and rescue tasks.

All knots are made from combinations of three basic elements: the *bight*, the *loop*, and the *round turn*. There are also two phrases that describe sections of the rope in terms of their function, the *standing part* and the *running part*. These terms will be used in the descriptions of the various knots that follow, so you should have them clear in your mind.

The *bight* is simply a bend or reversing of direction of the rope. The sides of the bight are parallel. A *loop* is formed when one of the sides of the bight is crossed over the other. The *round turn* is a continuation of the loop, in which the pieces of the rope are again parallel. It could also be described as a bight with a loop in it. See **Figure 12-6**. The section of rope that will be used for work, such as pulling or hoisting, is the *standing part*. The portion of the rope used to make bights, loops, and round turns as a knot is formed is the *working end* (also called the "running part" or "loose end"). See **Figure 12-7**.

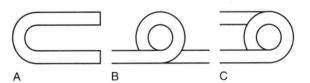

Figure 12-6. Basic elements of a knot. A—The bight. B—The loop. C—The round turn.

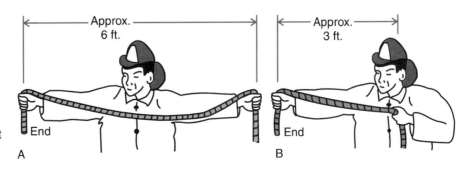

Figure 12-5. An easy method of estimating the length of rope. A—Use outstretched arms to measure six-foot increments. B—For three-foot increments, measure from mid-chest to end of one outstretched arm.

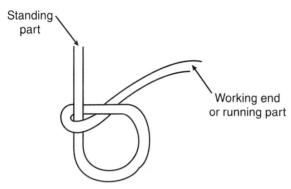

Figure 12-7. The working end (running part) of a rope is used to tie a knot. The standing part is used to do the work of hoisting or pulling.

Types of Knots

Although there are many different types of knots used for a variety of special applications, fewer than a dozen of them are used routinely in firefighting and rescue work.

Half-hitch

The *half-hitch*, **Figure 12-8**, is the simplest and most versatile knot used in the fire service. It is used in hoisting, in conjunction with other knots as a safety factor, and for many other purposes. It consists of a simple loop that may be formed on an object or formed in the hands and then applied.

Clove hitch

The *clove hitch* is really two half-hitches, with one the reverse of the other. Like the half-hitch, it may be formed on an object, as shown in **Figure 12-9**. A clove hitch can also be formed in the hand, **Figure 12-10**, then slipped over the end of an object. One shortcoming of this knot is that its loops can loosen when strain is alternately applied and released. To prevent this, use one or more properly spaced half-hitches (safety knots) in conjunction with the clove hitch.

Figure 12-8. The half-hitch is a knot that consists of a simple loop. It is easily formed on an object, or in the hand.

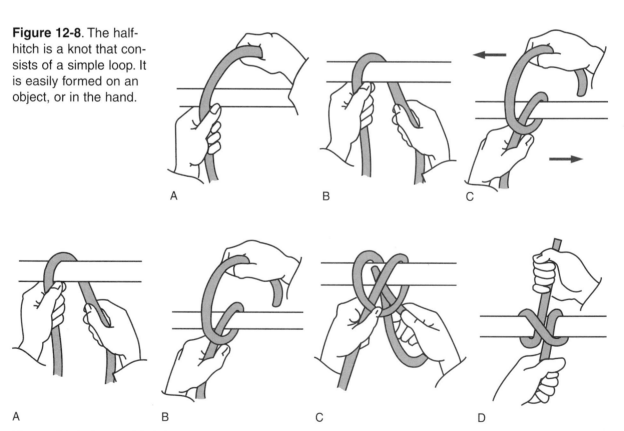

Figure 12-9. A clove hitch is an easy knot to tie. It consists of two half-hitches, with the direction of the working end reversed for the second one.

Figure 12-10. The clove hitch can also be formed in the hand and slipped over the end of an object.

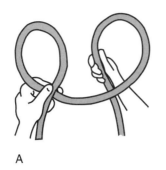
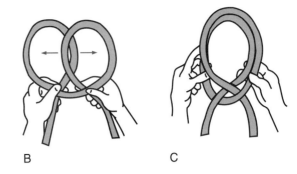

A   B   C

Square knot

The *square knot*, **Figure 12-11,** has only one use on the fireground: tying together two ropes of the same diameter. Generally, the square knot should be avoided because it can become untied if the free end is jerked. Furthermore, it's extremely difficult to untie if it gets wet. Follow these steps to tie the square knot:

A. Bring the two ropes together and wrap one completely around the other, making one full turn.
B. Bring the working ends up and wrap one complete turn.
C. Pull on the free ends to tighten. Note that both parts of each rope enter and leave the bight on the same side.

Sheet bend

The *sheet bend*, sometimes called a *becket bend*, is used principally to tie together two ropes of different diameters. See **Figure 12-12.** Since it is not likely to slip once it has been set, the sheet bend is useful on the fireground. Follow these steps to tie the sheet bend:

A. Form a bight from the working end of the larger rope. Pass working end of the smaller rope through bight diagonally from bottom to top.
B. Pass the small rope end behind the bight.

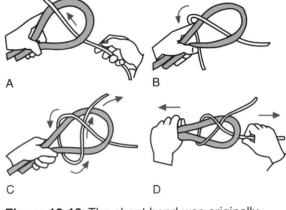

A   B

C   D

Figure 12-12. The sheet bend was originally used on ships to tie together ropes, called "sheets," that were used to hoist the sails. On the fireground, it is used primarily to join two ropes of different diameters.

C. Bring the small rope over the near side of bight, under itself, then over the far side of the bight.
D. To tighten, pull on the standing part of the small rope.

Bowline

When properly tied, the bowline will neither slip nor tighten. These desirable properties make it very useful on the fireground for hoisting and rescue work. It may be formed in the hand, as shown in **Figure 12-13,** or

Figure 12-11. The square knot is used to tie together ropes of the same diameter. It can be hard to untie when ropes are wet.

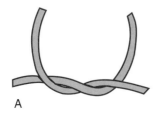

A   B   C

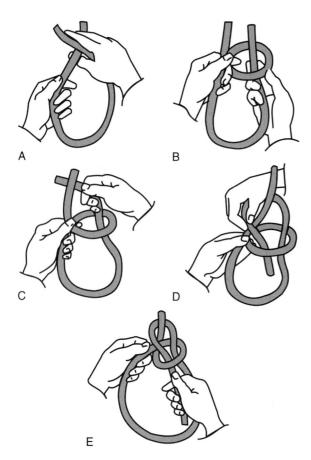

A

B

C

D

E

Figure 12-13. The bowline is one of the most useful knots for hoisting or rescue work.

around an object. Follow these steps to tie the bowline:

A. Cross the working end over the standing part.
B. With your left hand, form a loop of the standing part over working end. Hold this loop in position with your left hand until the knot is formed.
C. Bring the working end behind the standing part.
D. Pass the working end down through the loop.
E. Pull the free end against the working end to tighten the knot.

Running bowline

The *running bowline* is a bowline with the standing part passed through it to form a loop that is easily tightened or loosened. This knot is used in pulling charged and uncharged hose lines up the side of a building. The ability to loosen and tighten the knot easily makes it ideal for this purpose.

Rescue knot

The *rescue knot* is really a combination of two knots: the bowline on a bight and the slippery hitch. The formation of these two knots will be shown separately for ease of understanding, although they are frequently used together. As the name implies, the rescue knot is used when a person must be raised or lowered a vertical distance. It may be used in the rescue of an injured person provided that person is properly packaged for movement.

Bowline on a bight. The *bowline on a bight*, **Figure 12-14**, is formed in the same way as a conventional bowline, but is made with a double strand of rope. The bight formed by doubling the rope is used as the working end. Follow these steps to tie the bowline on a bight:

A. Measure 1-1/2 arm lengths (8-9 feet) of rope. Form a bight so that the working end overlaps the standing part by a little over four feet. Grasp the doubled rope with your left hand about four (4) feet from the bight. Lay the bight over the standing part just above your left hand.
B. With your left hand, loop the standing part of rope over the bight, as if you were making a regular bowline.
C. Pull the bight down through the loop about eight inches.
D. Pass the bight behind the loop and standing part.
E. Pull the bight up behind the loop.
F. Pull down on the double rope, just below the loop, to tighten the bowline.

Slippery hitch. To complete the rescue knot by tying a slippery hitch, first slip the two loops formed by the bowline on a bight over the victim's legs. The standing part of the rope should run up the victim's chest, with the working part hanging free. Follow these steps to tie the *slippery hitch*, **Figure 12-15**:

Figure 12-14. The bowline on a bight is made with a doubled rope, but tied in the same way as a bowline.

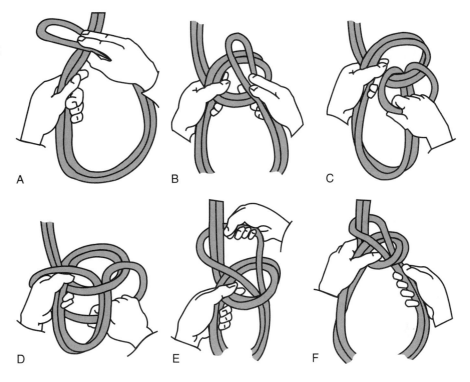

Figure 12-15. The slippery hitch is typically used in combination with a bowline on a bight to hoist or lower a victim in an upright position.

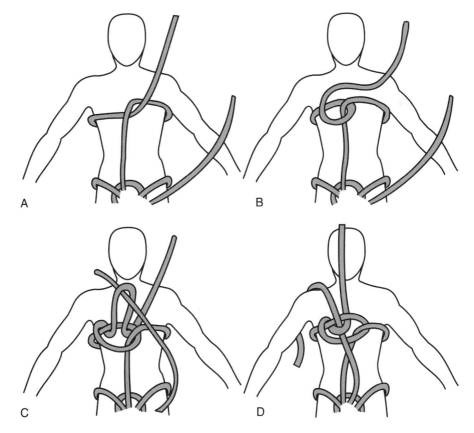

A. Form a half-hitch, using standing part of rope, around the victim's chest just below armpits.
B. Form a loop beneath the half-hitch.
C. As shown, form a bight from the standing part above the loop. Tuck the bight behind the hitch and bring it up through the loop. Bring the free end (working part) of the rope up and pass it through the bight.
D. Pull upward on the standing part to tighten the knot. The rescue knot, when properly made, will hold a person in an upright position while he or she is being raised or lowered. See **Figures 12-16** and **12-17.**

Figure 12-17. A victim can be lowered in an upright position by using the rescue knot. Note that one rescuer is steadying the victim with a guy line, while the second rescuer is controlling the speed of descent with a rope passed under a ladder rung then wrapped around his waist. (Donald Foye)

Figure 12-16. The completed rescue knot. Note that the bowline on a bight passes below the victim's buttocks to serve as a sling "seat." (Donald Foye)

Sheepshank

The *sheepshank*, **Figure 12-18**, is used to shorten or tighten a rope that is tied between two objects. An example would be a rope tied between trees for use in crowd control. Follow these steps to tie this simple knot:
A. Form a double bight at the point where you want to shorten the rope.
B. Tie a half-hitch around each bight and pull tight.

Chimney hitch

The *chimney hitch*, **Figure 12-19**, is a slip knot that slips only when you want it to slip. The chimney hitch is used in situations where you must loosen and retighten a line frequently, tie around very large objects, or descend a steep roof (where you have a good strong chimney to tie onto).
A. Pass free end of rope around chimney or other object that will serve as an anchor.

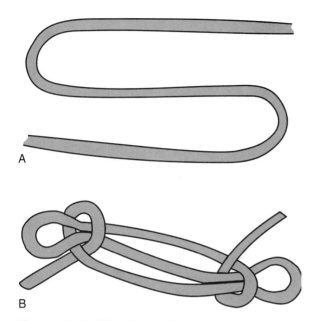

A

B

Figure 12-18. The sheepshank is used to shorten a rope that is tied between two points.

B. Cross the working end behind the standing part to form an "X" shape.
C. Pass the working end through the loop at the top of the "X."
D. Cross the working end behind the standing part again, and then pass it through the loop once more.
E. Tie a half-hitch around standing part of the rope below the loop. Snug up the knot. This knot will not slip under tension, but can be easily slid up or down the standing part when tension is released.

Rope Hose Tool

Probably the best way to secure such items as ladders and hoses is the rope hose tool, **Figure 12-20**. Very simply, the *rope hose tool* is a length of rope about six feet long, with its ends joined to form a circle. A strong metal hook is attached.

The rope hose tool is called "the tool with a hundred uses," but it has many more than that. You can use it as a safety belt or a rescue harness, a means of carrying a line up a ladder, a way to secure a nozzle or hose to a ladder, or to fasten a ladder to a building. If less length is needed, you can make the tool shorter by simply twisting the rope. **Figure 12-18** shows a few of the many uses of the rope hose tool.

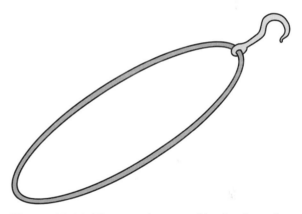

Figure 12-20. The rope hose tool is simply a circle of rope with a strong hook attached. It has numerous uses on the fireground.

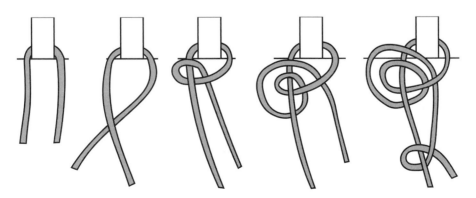

Figure 12-19. Steps involved in tying the chimney hitch. The knot can be easily slid along the standing part when tension is released, but "locks up" when tension is applied.

Figure 12-21. Some of the many ways a rope hose tool can be used on the fireground.

If a rope tool is not available, or if it does not have sufficient length for the job at hand, you will have to secure objects with a rope. A *clove hitch* will suffice for most securing applications. This hitch is quick and easy to tie and untie. A *bowline*, because it will not slip, is even better for many securing operations.

When entering an upper floor from a ladder, it is important to secure the ladder as a means of egress. Very often ladders are moved from one spot to another. A firefighter who needs a ladder will grab the first and most convenient one available. You could be in serious trouble if you had to get out in a hurry and found your ladder was gone. Securing a ladder at the top will help prevent its being moved.

When you tie a rope to something, make sure that the object you choose as an anchor will not move. Tie to a radiator, a heavy chest of drawers, a steam pipe, a heavy bed, a solid-looking doorknob — the leg of a small wooden chair just won't do.

Sometimes, you will have to improvise an anchor. For example, you could drive the pick of your axe hard into a roof and tie to that. The axe would probably be a safer anchor than a crumbling chimney.

Crossing on a Rope

It looks easy enough, and you've seen it hundreds of times on TV: your favorite actor, Joe Macho, ties the rope zip-zip, swings onto it and moves swiftly across, hand over hand, 89 stories above ground. If Joe Macho can do it, you can do it, right?

Wrong! If the rope really *is* 89 stories above the ground, some stuntman is out there. Joe is back in his dressing room, probably trying to work up the courage to stand on a chair to straighten a picture. If you really are seeing Joe on the rope, he's in front of a backdrop and his feet aren't even off the floor.

Far too many people are injured trying to do descents, rappelling, or sliding a line without really knowing what they are doing. Whole books are written on the subject. Experts give courses in this kind of thing. Don't try any high-up rope stuff without proper training.

While it is unlikely, you might someday find yourself in a situation where you must cross on a rope. For this reason, you should practice it. A bowline is a good knot to use, since it will neither slip nor tighten. For this activity, your minimum rope size should be either a 3/4 in. manila or 7/16 in. kernmantle nylon in good condition. Tie the rope high enough so that your feet will be just barely off the ground. Wear a safety belt with a safety line over the traverse rope. Stand on something high enough so you can test your knots by putting most of your weight on the rope. Once you are certain of the knots, start across. Once you become confident of your ability, raise the rope so your feet will be five or six feet off the ground. But don't go any higher than that without adequate equipment and proper training.

CARING FOR ROPE

Ropes are one of the firefighters' most important tools, and deserve proper care to provide long, safe, and useful service. Observe the following "do's" and "don'ts" of rope care:

- *Do* hang a new manila rope, after uncoiling it, in the hose tower. Fasten a weight to the bottom to stretch the rope. This will give a permanent set to the strands and cause the fibers to lie flat. The rope will be softer and more pliable.

- *Don't* tar or oil a rope. The fibers of a manila rope have already been impregnated with a lubricant. Nylon ropes don't need lubrication.

- *Don't* allow rope to come into contact with oils, acids, alkalis, or chemicals. Even fumes from such chemicals can harm rope fibers. If you suspect that a nylon rope has been contaminated, wash it in warm (not hot) water with a mild detergent. Rinse with cold water and a fabric softener. Dry it in a location that is out of direct sunlight. Wash a manila rope with plain warm water.

- *Don't* drag a rope across the ground, where its fibers can be damaged by sand and other grit. Dragging a rope, especially at a fire scene, also can cause it to come into contact with injurious chemicals, such as acids.

- *Don't* put sharp bends into a rope or saw it back and forth across sharp corners, broken glass, or metal edges. This breaks the outer fibers. Use an edge roller (similar to a hose roller) if you must pull or lower a rope over a sharp edge. See **Figure 12-22**.

- *Don't* overload a rope beyond its rated capacity. Avoid sudden jerks with a heavy load (for example, when trying to pull a stalled vehicle).

- *Do* use life support ropes for life support purposes only.

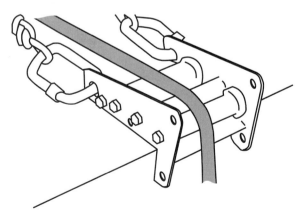

Figure 12-22. A special roller is used to keep ropes from being damaged when they pass over a sharp edge, such as a building parapet. (Pigeon Mountain)

- *Don't* expose ropes unnecessarily to intense sunlight. This discolors the rope and weakens the fibers.

- *Don't* expose rope to high temperatures on the fireground, if they can be avoided. Excessive heat drives out the lubricant in manila ropes, making them brittle. It also weakens nylon ropes.

- *Don't* wait until a fire or other emergency to find out that you have a defective rope. *Do* inspect ropes after every use.

- *Do* allow wet ropes to dry thoroughly out of direct sunlight before storing them or putting them back into service.

- *Do* keep a record of ropes just as you would on any other life support equipment.

Inspecting Rope

After necessary rinsing and drying of rope, carefully inspect it by passing the entire length through your hands. Turn the rope frequently so you can examine all surfaces. Look carefully for discoloration that could result from exposure to acids or other chemicals. Look for cuts and abrasions.

Untwist manila rope so that the strands separate. Sniff for mildew. Observe for sand or grit caught within the strands. Look for a powdery condition, indicating that rope has been attacked by acids. Replace any rope that shows signs of damage that could cause it to fail.

SUMMARY

Ropes have many uses in the fire service. To perform well and safely, they must be treated with respect. Every firefighter must treat a rope as if it will be used to save his or her own life.

For many years, manila ropes were preferred for fire and rescue work. Recently, however, nylon ropes have gained wide acceptance because they are lighter, stronger, and more resistant to abrasion. No rope, however, should be loaded beyond its working strength (15 percent of the tensile strength). Overloading a rope causes it to lose its ability to absorb shock loads. Life support ropes should never be used for any other purpose.

All knots are formed from the three basic elements: the bight, the loop, and the round turn. You must learn to make all of the knots used by your department.

The rope hose tool is extremely useful. Many firefighters would not think of climbing a ladder or entering a burning building without one. It can be used to carry or secure many items. You should always secure a ladder at the top to prevent it from tipping over or from being moved by another firefighter. When you secure to anything, be sure that it will provide enough support.

Crossing on a rope, rappelling, and similar activities require knowledge, skill, the proper equipment, and the proper training. Practice these skills at low levels. But do not attempt any intricate high rope work without special training.

After every use, rope should be washed, dried, and inspected carefully before being placed back on the apparatus. Any rope which is suspect should be replaced.

REVIEW QUESTIONS

1. Define the term "kernmantle."
2. List three ways in which nylon ropes are better than manila for fire and rescue purposes.
3. Why should a rope have some elasticity?
4. What is the difference between tensile strength and working strength?
5. Describe the basic elements of the knot: the bight, the loop, and the round turn. Distinguish between the standing part and the running part of a rope.
6. What diameter rope (manila and nylon) should be used for rescue work? For hoisting tools and equipment?
7. What color and material are used for water rescue ropes? Why?
8. Why is the square knot not recommended for general use on the fireground?
9. State one fireground use for each of the following knots:
   A. Bowline.
   B. Running bowline.
   C. Sheepshank.
   D. Sheet bend (becket bend).
   E. Chimney hitch.
   F. Half-hitch.
   G. Clove hitch.
   H. Square knot.
10. Give five uses for a rope hose tool.
11. State two reasons for securing a ladder at the top.

An important use of the rope hose tool is to secure the top end of a ladder in place. The rope should be attached to a solid structure on the roof or parapet to prevent shifting of the ladder.

NFPA 1001 Job Performance Requirements

The material on this page consists of those portions of the NFPA 1001 Job Performance Requirements relevant to the material presented in this chapter. Items preceded by the numeral 3 (3-x.x) are Fire Fighter I requirements; those with the numeral 4 (4-x.x) are Fire Fighter II requirements.

3-3.3 Force entry into a structure, given personal protective equipment, tools, and an assignment, so that the tools are used properly, the barrier is removed, and the opening is in a safe condition and ready for entry.

(a) Prerequisite Knowledge: Basic construction of typical doors, windows, and walls within the department's community or service area; operation of doors, windows, and locks; and the dangers associated with forcing entry through doors, windows, and walls.

(b) Prerequisite Skills: The ability to transport and operate hand and power tools and to force entry through doors, windows, and walls using assorted methods and tools.

3-5.3 Clean and check ladders, ventilation equipment, self-contained breathing apparatus (SCBA), ropes, salvage equipment, and hand tools, given cleaning tools, cleaning supplies, and an assignment, so that equipment is clean and maintained according to manufacturer's or departmental guidelines, maintenance is recorded, and equipment is placed in a ready state or reported otherwise.

(a) Prerequisite Knowledge: Types of cleaning methods for various tools and equipment, correct use of cleaning solvents, and manufacturer's or departmental guidelines for cleaning equipment and tools.

(b) Prerequisite Skills: The ability to select correct tools for various parts and pieces of equipment, follow guidelines, and complete recording and reporting procedures.

(4-3.2)

(a) Prerequisite Knowledge: Selection of the proper nozzle and hose for fire attack given different fire situations; selection of adapters and appliances to be used for specific fire ground situations; dangerous building conditions created by fire and fire suppression activities; indicators of building collapse; the effects of fire and fire suppression activities on wood, masonry (brick, block, stone), cast iron, steel, reinforced concrete, gypsum wall board, glass, and plaster on lath; search and rescue and ventilation procedures; indicators of structural instability; suppression approaches and practices for various types of structural fires; and the association between specific tools and special forcible entry needs.

Reprinted with permission from NFPA 1001, *Fire Fighter Professional Qualifications,* Copyright ©1997, National Fire Protection Association, Quincy, MA 02269. This reprinted material is not the complete and official position of the National Fire Protection Association on the referenced subject, which is represented only by the standard in its entirety.

Forcible Entry

OBJECTIVES

When you have completed this chapter, you will be able to:

- Identify the most commonly used forcible entry tools.
- Describe typical uses of forcible entry tools.
- Demonstrate the safe hoisting of forcible entry tools.
- Describe the basic construction features of buildings.
- Demonstrate forcible entry procedures.
- Clean, maintain, and inspect forcible entry tools.

IMPORTANT TERMS

anchor bolts	duck bill lock breaker	hydraulic shearing and	screw jack
axe	electric-powered	prying rescue kit	sill
bale hook	circular saw	insulated wire cutter	sledge hammer
balloon framing	fire stop	Kelly tool	sole plate
bar and cable cutter	floor joists	leverage	subflooring
battering ram	forcible entry	oxyacetylene cutting	tin snips
bearing wall	foundation wall	outfit	universal spanner
brick veneer	framing anchors	pike pole	wrench
bridging	gasoline-powered	platform construction	utility bar
chain saw	circular saw	pneumatic chisel	voids
claw bar	girder	portable electric	wall studs
closet hook	hacksaw	generator	wood-frame structure
crowbar	Halligan tool	reciprocating saw	

The Need for Forcible Entry

Too often, in the public mind, firefighters are seen as gleefully smashing windows, chopping holes in ceilings and floors, and generally having a good time. Of course, every firefighter knows that ventilating a roof or pulling a ceiling is hardly *fun;* instead, it's plain hot, hard work. It is important to get across to the public, however, that firefighters don't do this sort of thing unnecessarily, much less for enjoyment!

Forcible entry is, by its very nature, destructive. Its tools are the tools of destruction, not construction — nobody uses an axe to lay a carpet or a Halligan tool to hang a picture.

Compounding the entry problem is the growing security consciousness of many people, especially in urban areas. There was a time when practically nobody locked a house door; today nearly everybody does. Homes often have chain locks, bars, deadbolts, window bars, and are beginning to take on the appearance of bank vaults or prisons. This means that, increasingly, firefighters are running into situations where they must use force to get into a building.

If there is no other way to get in, by all means use force, but don't break in unless it is absolutely necessary. And then, do the minimum possible amount of damage. Don't chop the door down if it can be pried open. Don't pry it open until you have tried to open it the conventional way (it *might* be unlocked).

In addition to the public relations value of using a minimum amount of force to gain entry, there are other good reasons:

- Smashing things creates jagged edges that can cause injury to firefighters and others on the scene.

- Breaking in a window or door might cause an unfavorable ventilation situation that will be hard to remedy quickly.

- The firefighter's job is to save property, not destroy it.

Choosing Forcible Entry Tools

Have you have ever watched a skilled mechanic or carpenter work? You knew, from the minute the person picked up a tool, that he or she was indeed highly skilled. Just the way that he or she handled a piece of equipment told you that this was a person who was confident and "in command" of the situation. Much of that confidence, of course, came from years of doing the job and doing it well.

A firefighter is every bit as much a skilled craftsperson as, say, a patternmaker. See **Figure 13-1.** A vital difference is the time

Figure 13-1. The firefighter is called upon to select the right tool for the job without hesitation, then use it in the most effective manner. A well-trained firefighter displays a high level of skill in the use of tools and equipment.

available to make a decision; the patternmaker can take time, even a lot of time, to figure out what to do next. The firefighter must decide almost instantly which tool will do the job most efficiently, safely, and with the least amount of damage. Handling your equipment with command tells anyone watching that you are a skilled worker. Command comes with repetitive use, repetitive practice.

Sometimes, a fire scene covers an area as large as a city block, or even several blocks. Fortunately, this doesn't happen very often. Most fires are confined to one or two small rooms. Sometimes, there may be a dozen firefighters or more working in this confined area. This means that you must carry and use equipment in such a way that you will not injure a fellow firefighter. For instance, when using an axe, you can't swing it freely, as if you were in a forest. Instead, you have to learn to raise the axe to no more than shoulder height when cutting. The same principle applies to all other potentially dangerous equipment.

Working Safely

All forcible entry tools are to a greater or lesser extent dangerous. If they were not, they couldn't do their job. Your responsibility is to use them in such a way that you will not endanger yourself or those around you. This means watching how you carry a pike pole or chain saw. It means looking in all directions before you swing an axe or a Halligan tool. It also means avoiding the use of anything that might cause a flame or spark in an atmosphere that is heavily charged with fumes or dust.

The condition of the tool has a great deal to do with how safe it is to use. If the tool has a wooden handle, you had better make sure that the handle isn't cracked. Just as important, make certain that whatever is attached to the handle is on *tight.* On metal tools, watch out for slivers or chips of metal that could fly off and hit someone. Beware of the *dull* axe! A dull axe is more dangerous than a sharp one — it will bounce off hard wood and embed itself into something a little softer, such as your leg.

Be particularly careful around electricity. Don't use an axe to cut electrical wiring (the wood handle is a good insulator, but not when it's wet). Don't jab a pinch bar, pike pole, or similar implement into a wall close to an electric outlet, unless you are *absolutely sure* the electricity has been shut off. Guesses don't count, because a wrong one can kill you.

Tools for Forcible Entry

You will recognize some forcible entry tools as implements you have seen all your life. The hacksaw, axe, and tin snips are common items. Some others, such as the duck bill lock breaker, are special purpose tools peculiar to the emergency services. Their use might not be immediately apparent. Some are multipurpose tools with a wide range of applications that you will have to learn.

Not much uniformity exists in what specific tools are called. Some of the names are trade names, given by the manufacturer. Other names are local or regional. Many tools have two or more names (for example, the Halligan tool is called a "hooligan tool" in some places). If they call a tool a "fidget wid-

get" in your department, you will have to call it a fidget widget, too, if you hope to communicate effectively.

The lengths and weights given in the following tool descriptions are approximate and for identification purposes only. Some tools come in many different sizes. Since tools must often be hoisted with a rope for use by firefighters working one or more stories above the ground, the descriptions include hoisting directions, where appropriate.

Axes

The *axe* is a tool that is made in a number of different types, or *patterns,* for various uses. Two basic patterns, pick point and flathead, are widely used in firefighting, **Figure 13-2.** The crash axe is a specialized pattern developed for rescue work.

Pick point. A basic tool with a steel head and wood handle. Length is usually 30 in. and weight, 6 lbs. Typical uses include chopping through walls or wood roofs, forcing doors and windows, cutting wire and cable (in an emergency), scraping broken glass from window frames, and pulling cylinder locks. The pick end of the axe is used to go through hard plaster or cinder block, to break lock hasps, to break tempered glass, to pry up decking, and by being driven into a pitched roof, to provide foot support for a firefighter.

Flathead. A tool similar in length, weight, and materials to the pick point axe. The axe blade is used for the same purposes as the pick point axe, while the flat head is

Figure 13-2. The two basic axe patterns used in the fire service are the pick point axe, at top, and the flathead axe, at bottom. Each has a number of uses beyond chopping work. (Nupla Corp.)

used for such hammering tasks as driving a chisel or Kelly tool, pounding stakes, or breaking masonry. The flat side of the axe is used when breaking ordinary window glass.

Crash. This all-steel axe is shorter (15 in.) and lighter (2 1/2 lbs.) than the pick point or flathead axe. The crash axe has a pick point, a serrated blade, and a handle that is insulated for 200,000 volts. The crash axe can be used to cut metal, break out automobile windshields, or cut out locks.

Follow these suggestions for using axes safely and effectively on the fireground:

- To hoist an axe, tie clove hitches and half-hitches, as needed, around the head and handle. **Figure 13-3** shows a typical arrangement used to hoist an axe or similar tool. Note that the axe is hoisted handle-first.

- Always carry an axe with the blade pointed away from the body. If it has a pick, the pick should be shielded, **Figure 13-4.** Never carry an axe over your shoulder.

- If chopping flooring or roofing, do so close to the supporting members. The axe will bounce less. Stand firmly with feet spread about a shoulder-width apart. If you are right-handed, keep your left foot well out of the way.

- Chop so that only the toe of the axe enters the wood. It should enter at an angle to the direction of the grain, **Figure 13-5.**

Figure 13-3. An axe and a pike pole ready for hoisting. Most tools are secured for hoisting with a combination of clove hitches and half-hitches. The two tools shown are hoisted in opposite directions: the axe is pulled up handle first, while the pike pole is hoisted hook first.

Figure 13-4. Point the axe blade away from your body when you carry it, as shown here. If the axe you are carrying is a pick point pattern, shield the pick with your hand.

Figure 13-5. When using an axe to chop, enter the wood at an angle to the grain for most effective cutting. Use care to keep your feet well away from the area being cut.

- To force a lightweight door, insert the axe blade just above or below the bolt, as shown in **Figure 13-6.** Push or pull the handle in the direction opposite the hinges.

- Use the flat side of the axe to break ordinary window glass. See **Figure 13-7.** Keep your hands above the point of impact, and stand well to the side, out of the way of flying glass. *Make sure nobody is directly in line on the other side of the window.*

- If you *must* go through a tempered glass door (an expensive choice), stand to one side with your back to the door. Hit the glass sharply with the point of your pick, and be ready for a shower of glass fragments.

- When you use an axe to force a window, place the blade right in the center of the sash. This will prevent jamming the window.

Bale hook

Sometimes called a "cargo hook" or "longshoreman's hook," the steel *bale hook* has a wooden cross-handle. The tool is about

Figure 13-6. Many ordinary entry doors can be forced by inserting the axe blade just above or below the lock. When leverage is applied to the axe handle, the casing will often be spread far enough to allow the bolt to slip out of the strike plate or keeper.

Figure 13-7. Break ordinary glass with a blow from the flat side of the axe. Always wear a face shield to protect against flying glass, and make sure other firefighters are well out of the way.

11 in. long and weighs approximately 1 lb. It is used for a variety of purposes, especially removal of boxes, bales, burned mattresses, and other debris. It is also useful for opening stuffed furniture during overhaul. The hook also can be used to remove an automobile windshield, **Figure 13-8.**

Bar and cable cutter

Also called a bolt cutter, the *bar and cable cutter* can typically cut bolts and cable up to 1/2 in. diameter, as well as padlock hasps and some door chains. *Safety note:* Do not use on charged electrical wiring. Depending upon model and manufacturer, the cutter may be 36 in. to 42 in. long and weigh between 12 and 18 lbs. See **Figure 13-9.** To hoist a bar and cable cutter, tie a clove hitch around it.

Battering ram

This steel tool is typically 4 ft. in length and weighs about 50 lbs. See **Figure 13-10.** The *battering ram* has a notched end, used to break through brick or stone walls and partitions, and a rounded end for softer material, such as plaster or cinder block. The rounded

end can also be used to knock down light steel doors.

Safety note: When you break through a brick wall, the hole you make must be diamond-shaped to keep the wall from collapsing. See **Figure 13-11.**

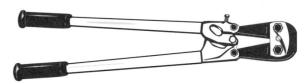

Figure 13-9. The long handles of the bar and cable cutter provide the leverage needed to cut steel bolts or similar stock up to 1/2 in. in diameter.

Figure 13-10. The battering ram is sometimes the only tool that can do the job of forcing entry. The notched end is used to break through harder material, such as brick or stone. For plaster and other relatively softer materials, the rounded end is used.

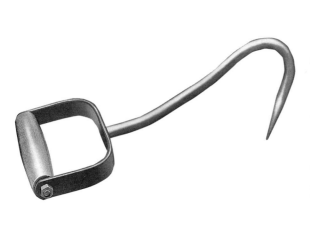

A

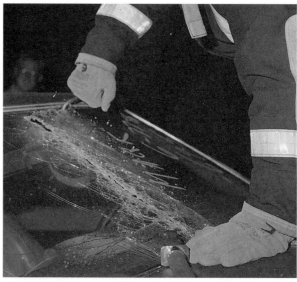

B

Figure 13-8. The bale hook. A—The steel hook has a wooden "D" handle to provide a firm grip. (Elkhart Brass Co.) B—One common use for the bale hook is ripping open a section of an automobile windshield.

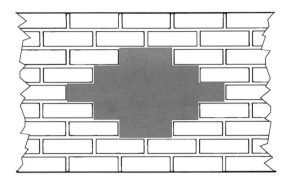

Figure 13-11. The safest pattern for breaching a brick or block wall is the diamond, since it has the least effect upon the wall's structural strength. The upper section of the diamond acts somewhat like an arch, supporting the masonry above it.

Claw bar

Typically three ft. long and approximately 8 lbs. in weight, the steel *claw bar* is also known as a "New York State Lock Breaker," or a "New York bar." See **Figure 13-12.** The

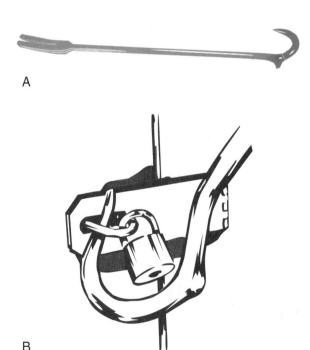

Figure 13-12. The claw bar. A—With a hook at one end and a claw at the other, this tool has many prying uses. B—The hook can be inserted in the staple of a hasp, them twisted to quickly force entry.

hooked end is inserted through the shackle of a padlock or the staple of a hasp, then leverage is applied to break it open. The claw bar is used for heavy prying, such as doors, gates, shutters, and automobile trunks or hoods. It can also be used as a ceiling hook in close quarters.

To hoist a claw bar, tie two half-hitches and safety above the claw, and another half-hitch around the bar below the heel.

Closet hook

The *closet hook* is a pike pole head with a short shaft and "D" handle, **Figure 13-13.** It is used as a pike pole in confined spaces such as halls, closets, and crawl spaces. It can be used to rip open upholstery, as well. The tool is approximately 32 in. long and weighs 5 1/2 lbs.

Crowbar

Longer (4 1/2 ft.) and heavier (13 lbs.) than a claw bar, the *crowbar* is used to force doors, lift and move heavy objects, or break through plaster.

To hoist this tool, tie two half-hitches and a safety around the thin portion of bar, and another half-hitch on the thick portion of bar, about one-third from the top. See **Figure 13-14.**

Duck bill lock breaker

Two ft. in length and weighing about 10 lbs., the *duck bill lock breaker* has a bronze head and rubber-covered steel handle. It is inserted into a padlock shackle, then struck with flathead axe to break the shackle.

Halligan tool

An extremely versatile device, the *Halligan tool* (**Figure 13-15**) can be used as a crowbar, pick, or sledge hammer. Typical uses are forcing entry doors (opening either "in" or "out"), prying or twisting hasp locks,

Figure 13-13. A shortened version of the pike pole, the closet hook is ideal for work in confined spaces. (Ziamatic Corp.)

Figure 13-14. When hoisting a crow bar, use the combination of knots shown in this illustration. The bar is hoisted with its thicker end upward, to keep it from slipping out of the knots.

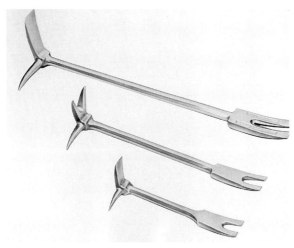

Figure 13-15. The Halligan is the firefighter's "all-purpose" tool. It can be used for almost any prying or pounding tasks. It also can be used, by driving the pick into a pitched roof, as an anchor for a firefighter. It is available in sizes ranging from 18 in. to approximately 36 in., as shown here. (Ziamatic)

opening windows, removing hinge pins, removing manhole covers, shutting off gas cocks, breaking glass, and anchoring a firefighter on a pitched roof. Known in some areas as a "Hooligan Tool," it varies in length and weight, depending upon manufacturer. Typically, length is between 30 in. and 36 in. and weight, 30 lbs. to 36 lbs.

When hoisting a Halligan tool, tie two half-hitches and a safety around the lower part of the bar, just above the claw. At the top, place a half-hitch around bar under the adze.

The Halligan tool is kind of a cross between a Kelly tool (see description) and a claw tool. In fact, the Halligan tool is so useful that some departments require each firefighter to provide his or her own. Some specific techniques for use include:

- To force a door that opens "in," insert the adze blade of the tool near the lock, then pull the handle toward the center of the door.

- To force a door that opens "out," insert the adze blade near the lock, then pull the handle *away* from the center of the door.

- To break the staple holding a padlock, insert the pick through the staple and pull downward to provide a lever effect.

- To breach a brick wall, use the hammer end of the tool to loosen a brick. Pull that brick out with the pick. Use the claw end to pry out additional bricks, creating a diamond-shaped opening to avoid collapse of the wall. See **Figure 13-16.**

- To remove flooring, drive the pick into a joint and pry upward. Pull up additional sections as needed with the pick, using the flat side of the tool against a joist as a fulcrum, **Figure 13-17.**

- To remove baseboard, insert the claw behind it and pry it away from the wall.

- To remove door or window framing or molding, use the adze blade or pick and pry outward.

Hydraulic shearing and prying rescue kit

The *hydraulic shearing and prying rescue kit,* **Figure 13-18,** is a powerful tool that may be either gasoline-operated or powered by a vehicle's 12-volt electrical system. Typical uses are to pry open steel doors, cut auto centerposts, jack up a vehicle, or pull steering wheels or other vehicle parts to extricate vic-

Figure 13-16. Using a Halligan tool to breach a brick wall. A—Loosen a brick by pounding with the hammer end. B—Use the pick to lever out the loose brick. C—Pry out more bricks with the claw end, working to keep the opening a diamond shape for safety.

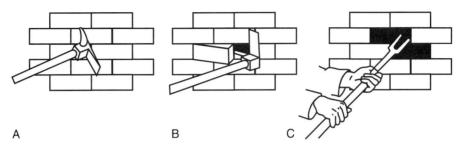

A   B   C

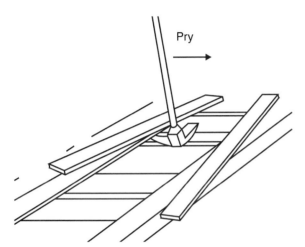

Figure 13-17. The flat side of the Halligan tool can be rested on a joist and used as a fulcrum for prying up floor boards with the pick point of the tool.

Figure 13-18. Hydraulic force provides the "muscle" to cut through metal or provide heavy duty prying effort in rescue and forcible entry situations. (H.K. Porter Co.)

tims of auto accidents. This equipment should not be used in an explosive atmosphere, but a pumper should be on standby in case of unforeseen combustion. This kit is normally not hoisted, partly due to its weight (125-200 lbs., depending on manufacturer).

Insulated wire cutter

This steel cutter, with insulated handles, is usually 24 in. to 28 in. long and weighs 6-7 lbs. It can be used to cut all charged electrical wires 110 volt or above. Typically rated for a maximum of 20,000 volts, the *insulated wire cutter* must be used with an approved insulated glove. To hoist this cutter, use a clove hitch.

Kelly tool

The strong, lightweight, highly versatile *Kelly tool* has many uses: prying windows

and doors, forcing auto trunk lids, breaking glass, prying decking, driving stakes, and removing hinge pins. The short (2 ft.) length of this tool makes it easy to handle in restricted quarters. See **Figure 13-19.** To hoist the Kelly tool, tie a clove hitch just below the head, and a half-hitch one-third the distance from the opposite end.

Oxyacetylene cutting outfit

An *oxyacetylene cutting outfit* is a portable unit consisting of tanks, hoses, and torch, used to cut steel bars or to cut through steel doors on autos or buildings. It can also be used in an emergency, *with extreme caution,* to thaw frozen hydrants and couplings. Typically, the kit weighs 30 lbs. and is 24 in. long. To hoist, tie a clove hitch around the handle.

Figure 13-19. Similar to the Halligan tool, but without the pick point, the Kelly tool is widely used for prying and pounding tasks.

Safety note: Do not use cutting outfit in an explosive atmosphere. Before using, make sure tanks are full to rated capacity. Always wear eye protection against intense light.

Pike pole

A widely-used tool, the *pike pole* consists of a steel head with spike and hook, mounted on a wood or fiberglass handle that may be from 6 ft. to 16 ft. in length. See **Figure 13-20.** Depending on size, a pike pole weighs from 4 lbs. to 16 lbs.

The pike pole is an implement designed for pulling, not prying. It has an almost endless number of uses, such as:

- Pulling down lath and plaster from ceilings or walls, **Figure 13-21.** (When pulling ceilings, the best length is about two feet less than the floor-to-ceiling distance.)

- Pulling down overhead obstructions. *Safety note:* Do not pull down charged electrical wires.

- Opening high windows, such as those used in factories and warehouses, **Figure 13-22.**

Figure 13-20. The pike pole is a pulling tool, and should never be used for prying, since the handle will break in such a situation. Pike poles have handles of fiberglass (top) or wood (bottom) and are available in various lengths. (Ziamatic)

Figure 13-21. Pulling down plaster and lath to open a ceiling is one of the most common uses of the pike pole. A face shield should be worn to protect against dust and debris.

Figure 13-22. The length and hooked end of a pike pole make it useful for opening high windows in industrial buildings.

- Advancing lines up a fire escape or open stairway.
- Quickly raising a fire extinguisher (or any other object you can hook onto) one or two stories.
- Being used with a salvage cover to make a water chute.
- Being used to improvise a stretcher out of coats or blankets.

Pneumatic chisel

The *pneumatic chisel,* **Figure 13-23,** is used for both rescue and forcible entry tasks. It can be used to cut through auto roofs and centerposts, remove auto locks, cut bolts, cut steel casement window frames, break cinder blocks, or make a starting hole for a battering ram. *Safety note:* Wear full body and eye protection when using the pneumatic chisel. To hoist chisel kit, tie a clove hitch around the handle.

Portable electric generator

The gasoline-driven *portable electric generator* supplies power for lights, smoke ejectors, saws, and other tools when no other source is available. The typical generator, **Figure 13-24,** weighs 115 lbs. to 250 lbs., and supplies 3000 to 5000 watts of 110 volt AC power.

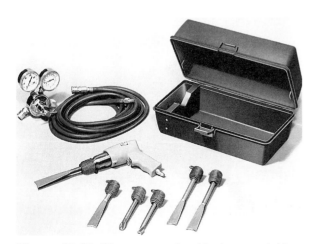

Figure 13-23. The pneumatic chisel can quickly and easily cut through steel or masonry for forcible entry and rescue tasks. (Ziamatic Corp.)

Figure 13-24. A gasoline-powered generator is often necessary to provide power for lighting or operating tools on the fireground. Various sizes are available.

Saws

Most departments have available a variety of hand and power saws suited to the various cutting requirements presented by forcible entry, ventilation, rescue, and overhaul applications. See **Figure 13-25.** The most commonly found types of saws are described in the following paragraphs.

Chain. Usually powered by gasoline, the *chain saw* can quickly open a roof or the side of a building. It is also used extensively to clear fallen trees and similar storm debris. Chain saws are available in many sizes, but a length of 3 ft. and a weight in the 20 lb. range is typical. *Safety note:* Do not use in explosive atmosphere. To hoist a chain saw, tie a clove hitch through the handle.

Circular (electric-powered). Sometimes referred to as a rescue saw, the *electric-powered circular saw* is typically used to open walls or floors. Depending upon size and model, circular saws weigh from 35 lbs. to 80 lbs. *Safety note:* Do not use in an explosive atmosphere. To hoist a circular saw, tie a clove hitch through the handle.

Circular (gasoline-powered). Although similar in size and operation to the electric version, the *gasoline-powered circular saw* is more powerful and more portable. It can cut wood, steel, and concrete, and is used to open the roof, walls, or floors. It also can be used to

Figure 13-25. Typical saws used for forcible entry or rescue work. Clockwise, from left, are the hacksaw, reciprocating saw, gasoline-powered circular (rescue) saw, and an electric chain saw. In addition to tools using gasoline or electric power, pneumatically powered tools are available (but are much less common). (Warren Lutton)

cut out a victim trapped in a vehicle. Depending upon size and model, circular saws weigh from 35 lbs. to 80 lbs. *Safety note:* Do not use in an explosive atmosphere. To hoist a circular saw, tie a clove hitch through the handle.

Hacksaw. The small (length, 18 in.; weight, 1 lb.), manually operated *hacksaw* is designed for cutting bolts, bars, lock hasps, and other metal objects. To hoist this saw, tie a half-hitch through the frame.

Reciprocating. The *reciprocating saw,* sometimes called a saber saw, is ideal for cutting wood or steel in small, tight areas. Typical uses are cutting around a chimney, cutting out a lock, or cutting small openings in walls, roofs, floors, or flashing. Reciprocating saws are considerably lighter than circular saws, typically weighing 25 lbs. or less. *Safety note:* Do not use in an explosive atmosphere. To hoist a reciprocating saw, tie a clove hitch through the handle.

Screw jack

The *screw jack* is a powerful manual jack that can be used to raise a vehicle or force an overhead door. A typical screw jack is 30 in. long and weighs about 8 lbs. To hoist a screw jack, tie a clove hitch around it.

Sledge hammer

Typical uses for the long-handled 10 lb. to 16 lb. *sledge hammer* are breaking out wall tile or concrete, freeing iron bars set in masonry, and driving out a lock with a chisel. To hoist a sledge hammer, tie a clove hitch around the head, with a safety around the handle below the head, and a half-hitch around the handle one-third the distance from the other end.

Tin snips

Heavy-duty *tin snips* are used to open sheet metal roofing, cut flashing, or cut steel window casements. To hoist, tie a clove hitch through the handles.

Universal spanner wrench

Made from either steel or aluminum, the *universal spanner wrench* is used for connecting hose, shutting off a gas cock, and as a prying tool. See **Figure 13-26.** To hoist a spanner wrench, tie a clove hitch through the hook end.

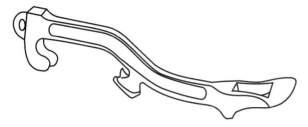

Figure 13-26. The universal spanner wrench is used for many tightening and prying tasks. It is usually about 10 in. long.

Utility bar

The *utility bar* is a multipurpose steel bar, usually 28 in. to 35 in. long and weighing approximately 10 lbs. As shown in **Figure 13-27**, it has a hammer head at one end and a claw at the other, and can be used as a wrecking bar, crow bar, hatchet, hammer, or sheet metal ripper.

To hoist a utility bar, tie a clove hitch around the head, and a half-hitch near the claw end.

Using Forcible Entry Tools

The tools of forcible entry are also the tools of ventilation and overhaul. We tend to think of ventilation and overhaul as operations that save property. Forcible entry is no less so, since its ultimate aim is to minimize the damage caused by fire. We seem to put the emphasis on "forcible," when we should probably be thinking in terms of "skillful" entry. The higher the level of skill displayed by the firefighter, the less damage to the property and the fewer accidents. If you chop down a door, there's no doubt about it: it's

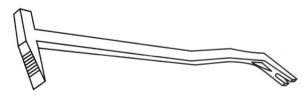

Figure 13-27. The utility bar is useful for ripping sheet metal, prying open doors or windows, and other activities requiring pounding or the application of leverage.

down. If you pry it open skillfully, however, there is hardly a mark to show what you have done. If you smash through a roof, it may look as if it were hit by a bomb. If you cut a neat hole, though, it will show you for what you are, a skilled and careful worker.

The activities of forcible entry — cutting, prying, pushing, pulling — are also the activities of ventilation and overhaul. To perform these activities, you have available the wide range of tools described earlier in this chapter. Some of these tools are single-purpose; others have a wide range of uses. But even the multiple-use tools have their limitations. Selecting the *best* tools for the particular activity is another way in which you demonstrate your skill.

For instance, a fire axe can be used to pry open windows and light doors. However, its wooden handle simply will not take the strain involved in forcing a locked, heavy steel door. A utility bar, claw bar, or Kelly tool is much better adapted to this kind of heavy prying. The pike pole is intended for pulling. Innumerable pike pole handles are broken every year, however, by firefighters who try to use pike poles as if they were crow bars. The skilled worker shows skill as much in the selection of tools as he or she does in using them.

Forcing doors

Don't automatically assume that a door is locked — try to open it in the normal way before attempting to force it. (For the same reason, don't chop through a door until you have tried unsuccessfully to force it.)

When you *do* force a door, the normal procedure is to insert the forcing tool near the lock. Then, move the tool in the direction that the door is intended to open. See **Figure 13-28.** The *leverage* (multiplied force) you are applying may spread the jamb far enough to allow the locking bolt to clear the strike plate or keeper. The door will swing open with barely a mark to show how it was done.

Some steel doors, especially those that are electrically operated, are opened with a gear mechanism. Any attempt to force such a

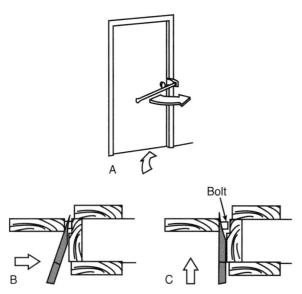

Figure 13-28. Forcing a door. A—Inserting the blade of the forcing tool above the lock, then moving the handle away from the hinges will often open the door. B—View from above, showing how the blade is inserted between door and jamb. C—Moving tool handle away from hinge side of the door forces jamb and door apart, allowing the bolt to slip out of keeper.

door will cause it to seize tighter than ever. Try to find an alternative means of entry. If none exists, you will probably have to use a battering ram on the door. But entry might be easier, and the damage less costly to repair, if you go through a wall. Steel garage doors may have glass panels that can be broken out to allow you to reach the unlocking mechanism, **Figure 13-29.**

Forcing windows

Basically, follow the rule of "try before you pry, and pry before you break." This is a good guide, but only a guide. Sometimes, breaking a single pane and unlocking a window or door is the quickest and least destructive way to gain entry. If you must pry open a sash-type window, pry at the center and in the direction that the window would normally open, **Figure 13-30.** Prying at the center is less likely to break the glass.

Windows in many factory buildings have steel frames and are glazed with wire glass. These are almost impossible to pry open without doing excessive damage. The best way to open such a window, provided you don't find one that is unlocked, is to cut out one pane of the glass. Using an axe or other sharp tool, cut the wire glass alongside the sash. Once a pane is out, you should be able to reach in and unlock the window. When cut-

Figure 13-29. Breaking a window in a steel garage door often will allow you to release the locking mechanism with the least damage to the door.

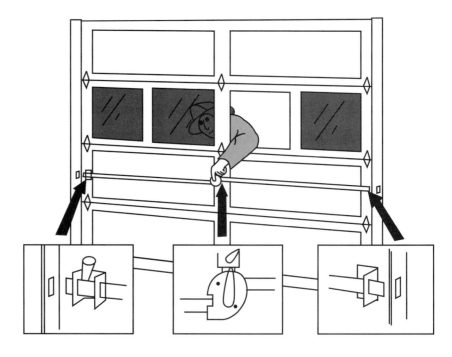

removing some siding from an exterior wall, use an axe or a power saw to cut the underlying sheathing. Cut close to the studs, but not into them. The lines of nail heads will tell you where the studs are located. If you must breach a solid *brick* or *cinder block* wall, remember to make the hole in the shape of a diamond, as described earlier in this chapter. Such a diamond pattern will not weaken the wall to nearly the extent that it would be weakened by a square hole with the same area.

When opening roofs for entry, use the same basic procedures that you would to open a roof for ventilation. There is one important exception, however: when opening a roof for entry, do not make your opening directly over the fire or anywhere near the fire.

Structural Hazards

It has been said that many (and perhaps most) of the buildings constructed in this country are built to burn, and to collapse. This is especially true of older buildings. They appear to have been constructed without regard to preventing the spread of fire, without thought for the safety of the inhabitants, and without concern for the safety of firefighters.

When an airplane crashes, large amounts of money are spent to investigate the cause of the crash and make engineering changes to prevent the same kind of accident from happening again. When a building burns, however, we simply build another one just like it or turn the site into a parking lot. We then forget about the whole thing.

But buildings, especially one- and two-family residences, are not designed as carefully as airplanes. In fact, for most part, they were never *designed* at all, not in the true sense of the word. Most of our construction practices just developed through long years of trial and error.

The best thing a firefighter can do is to become familiar with the various kinds of

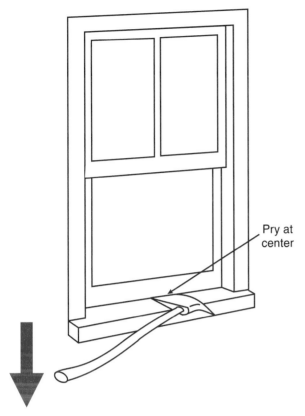

Figure 13-30. Glass breakage is less likely if a window is forced by placing the forcing tool in the center of the sash.

ting or breaking glass, always wear protective clothing, including a face shield. Stand to one side to avoid the shower of broken glass.

Breaching walls

For safety, assume that every wall is a *bearing wall* (one that supports part of the weight of the building). If the structure has been weakened by fire, such walls can lose some of their strength. If a considerable amount of water has already been thrown into the building, the load on the already weakened structure will have increased greatly. The building could be on the point of collapse.

If the building is a *wood-frame structure*, nearly all its weight is supported by the wall studs. Removing siding, sheathing, or other coverings from a small area will not do very much to weaken the structure if you do not cut through, or remove one or more studs. After

construction used in the area and the types of hazards associated with each. If a housing development is being built, observe how the units are put together, **Figure 13-31.**

Imagine one of the houses or apartment units on fire. What problems would the fire present in the attic? In the cellar? In a bedroom? In a kitchen? What hazards would the firefighter face? Whenever you are in a building, make it a habit to examine that building structurally and determine what you would do in any kind of fire. Do this whenever you

are in a public building, a store, an office building, or the home of a friend. (One day, your friend might have reason to thank you for it.)

Construction Techniques and Problems

A building may be constructed on a concrete slab or on a *foundation wall* that allows for a cellar or a crawl space beneath the first floor. If the building is on a slab, firefighter safety is somewhat enhanced — the first floor, at least, cannot collapse into a lower level.

Platform construction

When a foundation is poured, *anchor bolts* are embedded in its top surface about every four feet. These bolts are used to fasten the *sill* (the first piece of wood) to the foundation. The builders then nail a joist header to the sill. If the distance across the basement (the *span*) is relatively short, *floor joists* can bridge the entire distance. They rest on the sill and are nailed to the header, **Figure 13-32.**

Figure 13-31. Observe different types of buildings as they are being constructed. This will help you become familiar with potential fire problems in such structures and plan how you would respond to them. (Howard Bud Smith)

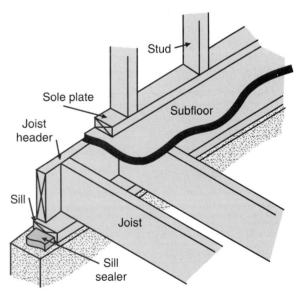

Figure 13-32. Floor joists are nailed to the joist header and rest on the sill. For longer spans, a girder is installed along the centerline of the space to serve as a support for the opposite ends of the joists. The subfloor is laid on the joists, and the sole plate of the wall section is nailed into place.

If the span is longer, a *girder* will be installed down the centerline of the basement or crawl space. The joists are placed perpendicular to the girder, with one end resting on it and the other end on the sill. The girder greatly reduces the chance of collapse of the first floor. *Subflooring* is then laid on top of the joists and nailed in place. Next, the *sole plate* is installed by nailing through the subfloor to the joists. *Wall studs* are nailed to the sole plate. This type of framing is called *platform construction*, since a deck or platform is built at each floor level.

If there is to be a second floor, a double plate is placed on top of the wall studs. Joist headers, floor joists, and subflooring are installed, just as they were for the first floor. On longer spans, a bearing wall is typically installed parallel to, and directly over the girder. Like the exterior walls, the bearing wall has a double plate on top of the studs, **Figure 13-33.** Besides serving as support for the second floor joists, the double plate on the outside and bearing walls acts as a *fire stop.* It prevents the space between the studs from acting as a chimney that would conduct heat and smoke up to the floors above. Similarly, the fire stopping above the double plate prevents the horizontal spread of fire between the first floor ceiling and the subflooring for the second floor.

Balloon framing

Balloon framing is seldom used today, but many older homes are of this type of construction. The main difference between platform framing and balloon framing is the length of the wall studs. In platform framing, as described, the wall studs are only one story high. In balloon framing, however, the studs in both exterior walls and bearing walls extend the entire height of the building, from the foundation to the rafters. See **Figure 13-34.** Most often, fire stopping was not put between the studs when the building was framed. Therefore, a fire starting in the basement can go directly up a wall to the attic.

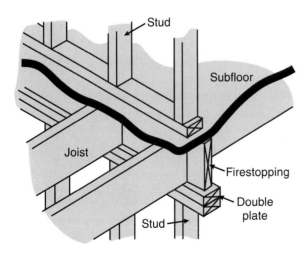

Figure 13-33. An interior bearing wall is topped with a double plate. In a single-story building, the bottom chord of the roof truss would rest on the double plate. In a two-story structure, shown here, floor joists and a continuous fire stop are attached to the plate. The subfloor and wall sections are the same as those on the first floor.

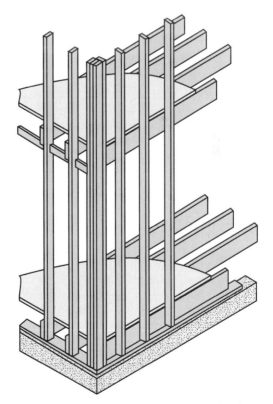

Figure 13-34. Balloon framing is found today only in older structures. Continuous spaces between wall studs running the full height of the wall form a flue for smoke and hot gases.

Such a building can become fully involved in fire in a very short time.

Framing anchors

Framing anchors are sheet metal angle plates that are nailed to a girder or joist header, **Figure 13-35.** The joists are then placed against the anchor and nailed in place. From the point of view of the firefighter, this construction method can be extremely hazardous. In a fire, the anchor will rapidly absorb heat and conduct it to the nails, causing them to loosen. The anchor can then twist, allowing the joist to fall. Many local codes require the use of framing anchors. If your community does so, be aware of this potential hazard in new or remodeled buildings.

The problem is compounded by the fact that the use of bridging between joists is being discontinued. *Bridging* is the term applied to cross pieces that go from the bottom on one joist to the top of the joist beside it. These are installed in pairs forming an "X," **Figure 13-36.** Bridging may be of wood or metal. The purpose is to keep the joists vertical and to spread the load from joist to joist.

If subflooring is strongly nailed to the joists, the floor framing will be more rigid. Sometimes, the subfloor is both nailed and

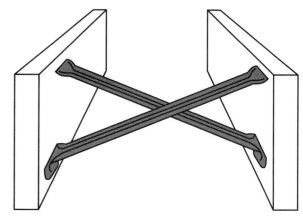

Figure 13-36. Bridging helps spread the load between joists and helps to keep the joists vertical. Either metal bridging, shown here, or wood bridging may be used.

glued for greater strength and rigidity. Under certain circumstances, however, the use of glue can actually *increase* the hazard to firefighters. When they use glue, some builders feel that they don't have to use as many nails. But adhesives tend to lose their strength as the temperature increases. At the temperatures found in full involvement, adhesives have no strength at all. Thus, the structure becomes less strong and rigid than if the normal number of nails, alone, had been used to fasten the subflooring.

Trusses

A truss, shown in **Figure 13-37,** is often used in construction to carry the roof load between the supporting walls. From a firefighting standpoint, the truss is an "all-or-nothing" proposition; it all holds together or none of it does. In other words, if any member of a truss fails, the entire truss fails. The two most likely points for failure are the center of the bottom chord and the peak. The peak is particularly vulnerable, since it is the highest point of the structure, where heat will accumulate.

Structural voids

Older buildings frequently present difficult problems for the firefighter. Often these structures have stairways, or even elevator

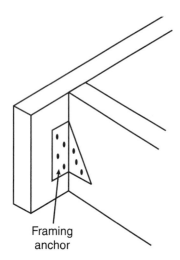

Framing anchor

Figure 13-35. Framing anchors, joist hangers, and other metal plates used to fasten and reinforce structural joints can actually weaken the structure under fire conditions.

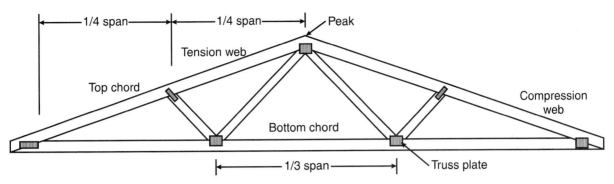

Figure 13-37. A truss of the type typically used in residential construction. In a fire, a truss can fail quickly and without warning, usually at the peak or in the center of the bottom chord.

shafts, that have been bricked or boarded up. Ceilings have been lowered, and false ceilings of sheet metal or other materials installed. Partitions have been added or removed. All of these changes create vertical and horizontal *voids* (openings) in the structure. In such voids, fire can move rapidly, unobstructed and unobserved. Sometimes, the "improvements" made through the building's history weaken the structure. At other times, they may block access of firefighters to fire areas.

Fire stopping

Sometimes fire stopping is made of a non-combustible material. Usually, however, it is made of the same wood that is used for studs, joists, and rafters. Thus, if a house is framed with 2 x 4s, the fire stopping will be 2 x 4 lumber nailed between the studs and other places. It is important that fire stopping be the same size as the structural members to which it is attached. A barrier must close up the entire area to prevent the spread of fire. Fire stopping should be applied at any spot where there is a lengthy void. Proper placement of fire stopping will greatly reduce the spread of fire and the danger of building collapse.

Brick veneer

Many building codes require that buildings in urban areas must have a noncombustible exterior. Often, this is accomplished by covering the walls with a single layer of brick, which is known as **brick veneer.** See **Figure 13-38.** Even where its use is not

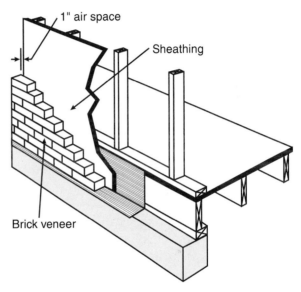

Figure 13-38. Brick veneer construction is the application of a single course of brick to a wood-framed building, primarily for appearance. The brick is connected to the structure by stainless steel ties.

required, brick veneer is often applied to give the building the appearance of solid brick construction. As a method of preventing the *spread* of fire (from the inside out or the outside in), brick veneer is of little value. It might protect a house from being touched off by a grass fire, but otherwise affords little protection.

Brick veneer is usually applied by nailing stainless steel tabs to the building's exterior. The tabs are bent out and embedded in the mortar between courses of the brick. These tabs are the only thing securing the brick to the building. In a fire, a buildup of hot gases can cause the walls to bulge. The underlying wood siding or sheathing might burn away, or the intense heat might cause the nails holding the tabs to loosen. A whole section of brick wall could come tumbling down, injuring any firefighter who might be underneath when it happens.

A building collapse is not always directly caused by fire damage to the structure. It is most likely to occur in buildings where stored materials absorb water being used to extinguish the fire. Such materials as bales of paper, cloth, cotton, mattresses, overstuffed furniture, or carpeting can soak up vast quantities of water. The weight of the water might be enough to cause a collapse, even though the building is still structurally sound.

Building Collapse Warning Signs

The signs of structural collapse were described earlier in the chapter on safety. If you notice any one of the signs or conditions listed below, be especially watchful. If you notice two or more, do not go into or onto the building, unless ordered to do so to save lives. If you are inside, get out, unless you are there to save lives. Even then, use your judgment. If you cannot effect a rescue in a very short time, you will have to abandon the effort. Should this become necessary, you may feel some guilt about abandoning your effort. But you will certainly prevent even greater danger to those who would have to try rescuing you. Sometimes, there are no easy answers.

As previously stated, the signs of imminent structural collapse are:
- A rumbling sound coming from inside the building.
- Sounds of movement of structural members.
- Any cracks in the outside walls.
- An abnormal amount of smoke or water leaking through cracks in an outside wall.

- Any bulging or distortion of walls or columns.
- A feeling of movement beneath you when walking on floors or roof.

Tool Cleaning, Maintenance, and Inspection

Cleaning and properly maintaining forcible entry tools not only allows them to properly perform the work they were designed to do; it also makes injury-causing accidents less likely to occur. **Figures 13-39** to **13-41** illustrate key areas to be inspected and maintained on widely used hand tools.

Hand Tools

In general, sharp edges should be kept sharp. They cut better, and are less likely to slip and hit something you didn't intend to cut. Surfaces used for pounding must be flat, not rounded. A flat surface is less likely to slip off the intended target and hit something else.

Tool handles must be sound and smooth, and heads must be firmly attached to them. Splinters on wood handles and burrs on steel or aluminum handles must be removed before they embed themselves deeply in a

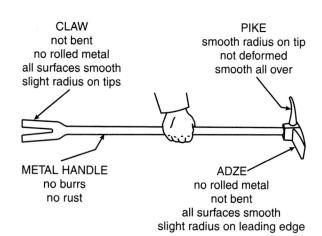

Figure 13-39. Areas to inspect and maintain on a Halligan tool.

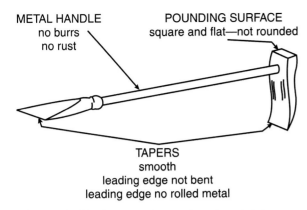

Figure 13-40. Areas to inspect and maintain on a Kelly tool and similar devices.

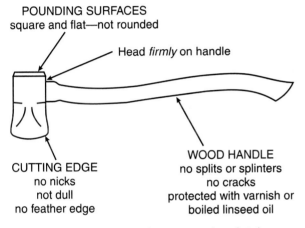

Figure 13-41. Areas to inspect and maintain on an axe and similar tools with wooden handles.

user's hand. A cracked wooden handle can pinch your hand or it can break in two while you are using it. Loose tool heads must be tightened with wedges so they do not fly off and possibly injure someone nearby.

When an axe handle is wet, it is hard enough to hold onto. When it is wet and greasy, it is practically impossible to control. The same applies to all the other muck that can get on your equipment during a fire. In addition, many of the byproducts of fire are acidic. These substances can corrode metal or weaken leather and fabric in a very short time. All tools and equipment must be cleaned after every use, for their protection and your own safety. Wash metal and wood surfaces with detergent and warm water, then dry them thoroughly with a clean cloth. Unpainted metal surfaces, especially those used for cutting or prying, should be protected with a light coat of rust preventative.

Pay special attention to the following:

Claw (on hammer, claw tool, Halligan tool, or similar tools): Must not be bent or have any rolled metal. If bent, use a ball peen hammer and an anvil to straighten. File to remove rolled metal. Put a slight radius on the leading edge of claw.

Cutting edge (on axe, hatchet, bolt cutter, or similar tools): Inspect for nicks, rolled metal, and dullness. Grind to sharpen, being careful to avoid overheating the metal, which would remove its temper. Remove feather edge with fine abrasive stone.

Prying edge (on Kelly bar, Halligan tool, crowbar, or similar tool): Inspect for rolled metal and bent corners. Use a ball peen hammer and anvil to straighten bent edges and corners. File or grind to remove rolled metal. A prying edge should not be sharp, like the cutting edge of an axe. File it to a slight radius.

Metal handle (Halligan tool, spanner wrench, cable cutters, or similar tools): If bent, straighten with a ball peen hammer and anvil. Check for burrs and rust. Use a file to remove any burrs, and sand lightly to remove rust. Apply a light coat of rust preventative.

Wood handle (on axe, hatchet, pike pole, or similar tools): Look for splinters, splits, and cracks. Check to see if handle is firmly in head. Sand or file handle to eliminate splinters. If the handle is split or cracked, repair is seldom effective. Replace it. Tighten a loose head with wedges or pin, or soak it in water to swell the wood.

Insulation (20,000-volt-rated wire cutter): Inspect for damage, splitting, tearing, excessive wear, or any other condition that could expose a user to electrical shock. Report the condition to your officer. Insulation must be tested for electrical leakage annually.

Pike, pick, or hook (on axe, Halligan tool, claw bar, or similar tool): Check for smooth radius on tip; rest of surface must also be smooth. Use a file or abrasive stone to correct any defects.

Pivots (on cable cutter, tin snips, or similar tools): Check for smooth, free movement. If necessary, apply a dry film lubricant.

Taper (on axe, Kelly bar, Halligan tool, or similar tool): Inspect for smoothness. Use a file or abrasive stone to remove all roughness. Straighten bent edges and corners. Apply rust preventative to all exposed metal surfaces, especially cutting edges.

Power Tools

Equipment that is electrically or gasoline-powered should be wiped down with a nonconducting solvent (such as Stoddard solvent), then dried with a dry cloth.

Inspecting electrically driven equipment

- Check electrical cord plug, and all electrical connections to be sure they are sound.
- Check insulation for cracks, tears, or other damage.
- Inspect moving parts for damage and proper adjustment.
- Check all fasteners for proper tightness.
- Test weekly for proper functioning.

Inspecting gasoline-driven equipment

- Check spark plug to be sure it is not fouled.
- Check wiring for damage.
- Check to see that gas tank is full.
- Inspect moving parts for damage and proper adjustment.
- Check all fasteners for proper tightness.
- Test weekly for proper functioning.

SUMMARY

Forcible entry tools can be dangerous. Carry and use them with concern for your own safety and the safety of those working with you. Always remember that a firefighter is a skilled worker who has developed those skills only after repeated practice in using the tools of the trade.

Know the names of all the tools you use, the names of the parts of each tool, and where it is on the apparatus. When you have finished using a tool, always return it to its designated place on the apparatus.

Very often, tools are raised from the ground to a higher point on the building. You must know how to tie each tool in such a way that it will not slip out of the knot and fall (possibly injuring somebody). And you must be able to do this even when you can't see very well. This takes practice.

Forcible entry tools are basically the same tools that are used for ventilation and overhaul. As in ventilation and overhaul, they must be used in a manner that will save property and not destroy it. Always "try before you pry and pry before you chop."

Certain walls, outside and inside, bear a portion of the weight of the structure. The building might already have been weakened by the fire, heat, and the additional weight of the water used in extinguishment. You will have to learn enough about building design and construction to know where it is safest to cut into the structure and how much to cut. Observe buildings during their construction to plan what should be done in a fire. Make it a habit, when in any kind of a building, to look around and learn in advance what problems you might encounter.

Most wood-frame buildings are of platform or balloon construction. In balloon frame, the studs go from the foundation to the rafters. If there are not fire stops between the studs, a fire can go from the cellar to the attic as readily as it can go up a chimney. Platform construction is a little safer, because the cavities between studs are closed at each floor level. Older buildings are extremely unpredictable, since they may contain many voids where fire can spread undetected.

Collapse might also be brought on by the added weight of water that has been absorbed by the building contents. The building can collapse even though it has not been greatly weakened by the fire itself.

Dull cutting edges and various types of damage or excessive wear can reduce the efficiency of your tools. Worse, these conditions can make the tools hazardous to use. After every use, you must wash, dry, inspect, and if needed, repair your tools to make sure they are ready for the next time they are needed.

REVIEW QUESTIONS

1. What is the safe way to carry an axe?
2. Why is a dull axe more dangerous than a sharp one?
3. When breaching a brick wall, what shape should the hole be? Why?
4. What is the difference between a closet hook and a pike pole?
5. What is the maximum diameter steel bar you can cut with a bar and cable cutter?
6. Under what condition should you not use a gasoline-powered rescue saw?
7. State five uses for a Halligan tool.
8. How do you determine the best length of pike pole for pulling ceiling lath and plaster?
9. How do you tie a sledge hammer for hoisting?
10. What should you do before attempting to force a door or window?
11. When forcing a window, where should you place your axe blade?
12. Why is an axe not suitable for prying steel doors?
13. After use, what should you look for in inspecting a Halligan tool? A portable generator? A pike pole?
14. Distinguish between platform framing and balloon framing.
15. What hazard do framing anchors present?
16. How can the use of glue in flooring increase the possibility of danger to firefighters?
17. Why are fires in old buildings unpredictable?
18. What is fire stopping?
19. Why is brick veneer hazardous?
20. What are the seven signs of potential building collapse?

NFPA 1001 Job Performance Requirements

The material on this page consists of those portions of the NFPA 1001 Job Performance Requirements relevant to the material presented in this chapter. Items preceded by the numeral 3 (3-x.x) are Fire Fighter I requirements; those with the numeral 4 (4-x.x) are Fire Fighter II requirements.

3-3.8 Conduct a search and rescue in a structure operating as a member of a team, given an assignment, obscured vision conditions, personal protective equipment, a flashlight, forcible entry tools, hose lines, and ladders when necessary, so that ladders are correctly placed when used, all assigned areas are searched, all victims are located and removed, team integrity is maintained, and team members' safety—including respiratory protection—is not compromised.

(a) Prerequisite Knowledge: Use of forcible entry tools during rescue operation, ladder operations for rescue, psychological effects of operating in obscured conditions and ways to manage them, methods to determine if an area is tenable, primary and secondary search techniques, team members' roles and goals, methods to use and indicators of finding victims, victim removal methods (including various carries), and considerations related to respiratory protection.

(b) Prerequisite Skills: The ability to use SCBA to exit through restricted passages, set up and use different types of ladders for various types of rescue operations, rescue a fire fighter with functioning respiratory protection, rescue a fire fighter whose respiratory protection is not functioning, rescue a person who has no respiratory protection, and assess areas to determine tenability.

(3-3.9)

(b) Prerequisite Skills: The ability to prevent water hammers when shutting down nozzles; open, close, and adjust nozzle flow and patterns; apply water using direct, indirect, and combination attacks; advance charged and uncharged $1^1/2$ in. (38 mm) diameter or larger hose lines up ladders and up and down interior and exterior stairways; extend hose lines; replace burst hose sections; operate charged hose lines of $1^1/2$ in. (38 mm) diameter or larger while secured to a ground ladder; couple and uncouple various hand line connections; carry hose; attack fires at grade level and above and below grade levels; and locate and suppress interior wall and subfloor fires.

4-4.1 Extricate a victim entrapped in a motor vehicle as part of a team, given stabilization and extrication tools, so that the vehicle is stabilized, the victim can be disentangled without undue further injury, and hazards are managed.

(a) Prerequisite Knowledge: The fire department's role at a vehicle accident, points of strength and weakness in auto body construction, dangers associated with vehicle components and systems, the uses and limitations of hand and power extrication equipment, and safety procedures when using various types of extrication equipment.

(b) Prerequisite Skills: The ability to operate hand and power tools used for forcible entry and rescue in a safe and efficient manner; use cribbing and shoring material; and choose and apply appropriate techniques for moving or removing vehicle roofs, doors, windshields, windows, steering wheels or columns, and the dashboard.

4-4.2 Assist rescue operation teams, given standard operating procedures, necessary rescue equipment, and an assignment, so that procedures are followed, rescue items are quickly recognized and retrieved, and the assignment is completed.

(a) Prerequisite Knowledge: The fire fighter's role at a special rescue operation, the hazards associated with special rescue operations, types and uses for rescue tools, and rescue practices and goals.

(b) Prerequisite Skills: The ability to identify and retrieve various types of rescue tools, establish public barriers, and assist rescue teams as a member of the team when assigned.

Reprinted with permission from NFPA 1001, *Fire Fighter Professional Qualifications*, Copyright ©1997, National Fire Protection Association, Quincy, MA 02269. This reprinted material is not the complete and official position of the National Fire Protection Association on the referenced subject, which is represented only by the standard in its entirety.

Rescue

OBJECTIVES

When you have completed this chapter, you will be able to:

- Describe the procedure for searching out victims in burning, smoke-filled buildings and other hostile environments.
- Discuss how to remove injured persons from the immediate hazard, using whatever material and manpower are available on the spot.
- Describe proper use of a life net.
- Explain the procedure for removing debris, rubble, and other material found at cave-ins.
- Discuss methods used for extracting a victim from a vehicle accident.

IMPORTANT TERMS

aggravating	fireman's carry	life belt	rubble
ambulatory	fireman's drag	life safety harness	safety line
carries	fore-and-aft carry	life net	seat carry
cave-in	horizontal packstrap	one-person crutch	secure
cervical collar	carry	assist	two-person crutch assist
chair litter carry	horizontal position	packaging	vertical packstrap carry
collapsed building	improvise	paramedics	vertical position
drags	incline drag	pneumatic lifting bag	

Firefighter Responsibilities for Rescue

In a typical ambulance emergency, at least two ambulance personnel (who often are trained *paramedics*) are usually present. They are fully equipped with heart monitors, blood pressure equipment, stretchers, splints, and other equipment, and they are in direct radio contact with a doctor at a nearby hospital. Usually, they also have one more vital thing going for them: time. They have five minutes, ten minutes, maybe half an hour or more before they must move the victim.

The *firefighter* in a rescue situation, however, often has little or nothing to work with except what is in the immediate area. When removing a victim from a burning building, there is precious little of that vital element, time. Whatever must be done, must be done *immediately*. To further complicate matters, if the victim is injured, the rescue must be carried out without *aggravating* (making worse) those injuries.

Of course, there are situations in which you will have a relatively large amount of time to do surveys, apply backboards, splints, cervical collars, or whatever is needed. You will be able to follow the proper methods of packaging and moving injured persons, which presuppose that the greatest threat to the victim is his or her own injuries.

But more often, you will encounter situations in which you have a seriously injured victim who is also threatened with immediate building collapse, fire, or a poisonous or oxygen-depleted atmosphere. You do not have the time nor will you always have the equipment you have been taught to use for the safe movement of injured persons. In these situations, the firefighter must *improvise* and solve the problem with whatever is available, **Figure 14-1.**

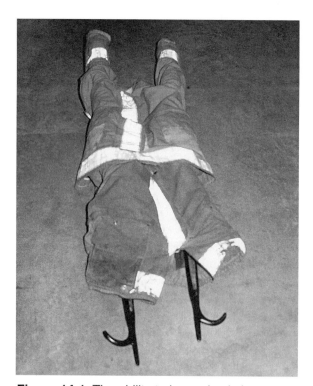

Figure 14-1. The ability to improvise is important in search and rescue situations. This stretcher was quickly improvised from two pike poles and two coats. (Warren Lutton)

It's not as difficult as it sounds: you improvise all the time. For example, you need to drive a stake but you don't have a hammer. So, you improvise: you use a rock. Another example: you arrive at your favorite trout stream, then discover all your fishing flies are back home on your workbench. Again, you improvise. You cut a bit of lining out of your jacket, pull a few hairs from your head, and tie the whole works onto a hook. Naturally, your improvised fly makes it possible to land the biggest brown trout you've ever caught (or was that just a "fish story?").

Improvising on the Fireground

You are inside a burning building, where the ceiling has fallen and a beam has hit a fellow firefighter. He has possible neck and back injuries. The whole works is likely to come down at any minute, but you want to avoid aggravating his injuries if at all possible. It's time to improvise. What can you use to substitute for a *cervical collar* to immobilize his neck? *The foam rubber padding from a chair.* Tie it into place around his neck with a lamp cord. What can you use as a stretcher? Pry a closet door off the hinges, then slide him onto that and drag him out. What if the crunching, grinding, bumping sounds from the building tell you that you don't even have time for the collar and stretcher substitutes? *Improvise* again — protect his neck with a rolled-up curtain and drag him out by the heels!

Moving the Victim

There are a number of traditional *carries* or *drags* that can be used by one or several rescuers to remove an injured person from an area of immediate hazard. Which of them you use will depend on these factors:

- The extent and location of injuries.
- The immediacy of the hazard (how much time you have).
- The materials at hand.
- The number of firefighters available to effect rescue.

Extent and location of victim's injuries

Don't overlook the possibility that the victim may be in good enough shape to walk. If he or she is *ambulatory*, you will both get out of danger a lot quicker, **Figure 14-2.** If the injured person cannot walk, it is generally better to keep him or her in a horizontal position, or as near as possible to horizontal. This is especially true if victim is unconscious or if time and visibility do not permit a complete survey of injuries.

To remove the victim from danger, use a door or other substitute for a stretcher. If a door is not available, use a long coffee table, a length of carpet, a blanket, drapery, or whatever else is at hand. If no stretcher substitute is readily available, drag the victim out by arms or heels, whichever seems best. If you can't drag the victim by arms or heels, use the *fireman's drag*: tie the victim's hands together loosely and place them over your head and around your neck.

Figure 14-2. If an injured person can walk with your assistance, you can move him or her to safety much more rapidly than if you had to perform a carry or drag. (Donald Foye)

Immediacy of the hazard

Let's face it, rescuing an injured person from a burning building is a panic situation. But *don't* panic. If you do, you won't help either yourself or the victim. Stop and ask yourself this question: "Do I really have to get that person out of the building right now, by myself?" If the answer is not an unqualified "yes," get help. The ambulance crew with their equipment is best. Anyone who can work with you is next-best. A single-handed rescue, although it is sometimes necessary, is definitely the *last* resort.

Materials at hand

As mentioned earlier, a door makes a satisfactory stretcher or litter; so does threading two pike poles through the sleeves of a couple of jackets. Rugs, drapes, or blankets also work well. In an extreme situation, you can tie the victim's hands or feet together and drag him or her out of danger with your belt. If need be, you can even drag the victim by the hair — if you use a steady, gentle pull, it won't even hurt. Don't spend too much time looking for the "right" thing to do the job, however. If you have that kind of time, you have time to get the ambulance crew in. Otherwise, use whatever is at hand.

Number of firefighters to effect rescue

The technique you use to carry out a rescue depends upon the number of people available to take part. If you must work alone, you are limited to dragging or carrying the victim. Which drag or carry you use will depend on victim's condition, how much time you have, and what materials are available. These techniques are explained in detail later in this chapter.

With two or more rescuers, you have more and better options open to you. Obviously, the more people you have, the more support you can give, and the less you will aggravate the victim's injuries.

Again, the nature and extent of the victim's injuries and the immediacy of the external hazard will determine which technique you will use.

Removal of Victim by One Rescuer

Moving a victim to safety in a *vertical position* (either walking or being carried) is often faster, but movement in a *horizontal position* is usually safer for both the rescuer and the rescued. For the nonambulatory victim, your choice is between a drag and a carry, with the drag considered to be safer and more effective in most cases. Choice of the actual technique to be used is affected by condition of the victim, strength and skills of the rescuer, and the circumstances under which the rescue must be performed.

One-person crutch assist

If victim is conscious and not severely injured, the *one-person crutch assist* is usually the quickest way out. To achieve the best support, the victim should place one arm around the rescuer's neck. The rescuer then grasps the wrist of that arm with his or her outside hand. Next, the rescuer wraps his or her inside arm firmly but gently around victim's lower chest to provide support. Rescuer and victim then simply walk out.

Fireman's drag

Place the victim on his or her back. Form a loop of curtain or whatever is available, then slip the loop around victim under the armpits. Drop to your hands and knees over the victim, and put the other end of loop around your neck. Crawl to safety on your hands and knees, dragging the victim with you. A variation of this drag is simply to tie victim's wrists together and place them around your neck, **Figure 14-3.**

Note: If you believe that the victim has neck injuries, make an extra loop to place behind victim's head and around your neck. This will keep victim's head fairly level as you drag him or her to safety.

Incline drag

The *incline drag* is used for easing a victim down a stairway, **Figure 14-4.** If the victim is unconscious, tie his or her wrists together to prevent injury to arms. With the victim lying on his or her back, position your-

Figure 14-3. A variation of the fireman's drag, in which the victim's hands are tied together and looped around the rescuer's neck. The fireman's drag keeps you and the victim close to the floor, where the air is better. It also can be used by a firefighter wearing self-contained breathing apparatus. (Donald Foye)

Figure 14-4. The incline drag is useful for easing a victim down one or more flights of stairs. As shown, it allows the rescuer to protect the victim's head from injury. (Donald Foye)

self behind the person's head, and grasp him or her under the armpits. Support the victim's head in the crook of one arm for protection. Use your knees for support as much as possible as you back down the stairway.

Vertical packstrap carry

This carry is useful for moving an unconscious victim. It *cannot* be used, however, if you are wearing self-contained breathing apparatus.

To perform the *vertical packstrap carry*, raise the victim to a sitting position on a stool, the edge of a table, or something of similar height. Loop a tablecloth, curtain, or similar length of cloth under the victim's arms and over your own shoulders. Bring the ends under your arms and tie them together behind your back. Bend over slightly to raise victim off his or her feet, **Figure 14-5.** With practice, the loop may be formed before placing it around victim (the loop must be snug, however). A slightly quicker version of this carry can be accomplished by simply tying the victim's wrists together and looping them over your head. This method should not be used if the victim has arm injuries, of course. An important advantage of the packstrap carry is that it leaves the rescuer's hands free.

Horizontal packstrap carry

The *horizontal packstrap carry* is similar to the vertical packstrap carry, except that it is performed on hands and knees, **Figure 14-6**, rather than walking upright. Like the vertical carry, it cannot be used when wearing self-contained breathing apparatus.

Begin with the victim lying on his or her stomach. Form a loop and pass it under victim's shoulders. Lie down atop the victim, back-to-back, and put your arms through the

Figure 14-6. If the victim is unconscious, a horizontal packstrap carry can be used. After placing the loop, the rescuer simply rolls over, raises up on hands and knees, and crawls to safety with the victim.

loop. Roll over onto your stomach, bringing victim onto your back. Raise up on your hands and knees, and crawl to safety.

The fireman's carry

This carry should be used as a last resort, since it will aggravate any injuries a victim might have. But if you have to get someone out of danger immediately, this is probably the quickest rescue method. *Note:* It is theoretically possible to make this carry while wearing self-contained breathing apparatus, but quite difficult to accomplish in practical terms.

Begin the *fireman's carry* by turning the victim face down. Standing at the victim's head, place your hands under the armpits and lift him or her to a kneeling position, facing you. Slide your hands down to a point just above the waist and raise victim to an almost-standing position. Slip your left knee between victim's legs for additional support. Grasp the victim's left wrist with your right hand and lift that arm over your head and onto your left shoulder. Holding the victim close to you, ease

A   B

Figure 14-5. The vertical packstrap carry. A—Using a loop of cloth to secure the victim. B—Variation with the victim's arms tied and looped over rescuer's head. (Donald Foye)

your left hand between his or her legs and lift. The victim should now be draped over your left shoulder, ready to be carried.

Removal of Victim by Two Rescuers

As noted earlier, the availability of two or more rescuers greatly increases the options available. It also decreases the likelihood of further injuring the victim during the rescue process, since the victim can be handled more securely and more gently by several rescuers. Only a few of the more common carries are described here. There are a number of others, especially those that can be done with *more than* two rescuers.

Two-person crutch assist

The *two-person crutch assist* is similar to the one-person version, except that one rescuer is on each side of the victim. It is a familiar sight during football season, when it is used to help injured players off the field. The two-person crutch assist is a simple and effective means of moving a victim whose injuries do not dictate horizontal transportation.

Seat carry

The *seat carry* should be familiar from your childhood. Two rescuers kneel beside the victim, facing each other. They raise the victim to a sitting position, with each placing one arm behind the victim's back for support. Both rescuers slide their free arm under the victim's thighs and grasp each other's wrists. For better control and support, the rescuers grasp each other's forearms behind the victim's back. If victim is conscious or semiconscious, she or he can place arms around rescuers' shoulders for additional support. Rescuers then rise together slowly, and carry the victim to a safe place. See **Figure 14-7**.

Fore-and-aft carry

This carry is relatively easy to perform, and can be effectively used with a victim who is unconscious. See **Figure 14-8**. It should *not* be used, however, if the victim has leg or back injuries.

Figure 14-7. The seat carry is a secure and easy to perform carry when two persons are available to evacuate a victim. (Donald Foye)

Figure 14-8. An unconscious person can easily be evacuated by two firefighters with the fore-and-aft carry. It should not be used if the victim has suffered chest, leg, or back injuries. (Donald Foye)

To make the *fore-and-aft carry*, one rescuer stands at victim's feet, facing away; the other, at the victim's head facing toward the victim. The rescuer at the head kneels and raises the victim into a semi-sitting position.

The rescuer then slips his or her arms under victim's armpits and grasps one wrist with the other hand. The second rescuer slightly spreads victim's legs, then backs up until he or she is between the victim's knees. Passing one arm under each knee, the rescuer grasps one wrist with the other hand. Both rescuers rise slowly, in unison, and move forward in step.

Chair litter carry

If a chair is available, the *chair litter carry* is an excellent carry to use, **Figure 14-9.** It is fast, easy, and less likely than other carries to cause further harm to an already injured victim. All that is necessary is to be sure the victim is firmly seated (if you have time, tie the person to the chair). The rescuer at the front squats and reaches behind his or her back to grasp the chair legs. The rescuer behind the chair grips the side of the chair back. At a signal, the rescuer behind the chair tilts it backward and lifts, while the rescuer in front rises and lifts. Once the chair and victim have been raised, they can be easily transported to safety.

Improvised stretcher

When two or more rescuers are available, any kind of a stretcher is usually preferred to the carries just described. The use of a stretcher helps avoid aggravating any injuries the victim has suffered. You can almost always improvise a stretcher out of something: a door, a wide board, a table, a blanket, two jackets and two poles, a padded short ladder. See **Figure 14-10.**

Ladder Rescues

Most people are afraid of heights. Firefighters, who scramble up and down ladders as a part of their everyday life, might forget that. For this reason, even if the person you are rescuing is completely uninjured, you still may have a problem: fear could cause the person either to freeze or to let go. If the person lets go, you might get knocked off the ladder and go down, too.

In a ladder rescue, you must provide both physical and moral support. Staying close enough to let the victim feel your presence, and keeping up a constant line of reassuring talk will help: "OK, bring your left foot down to the next rung. That's good. Now

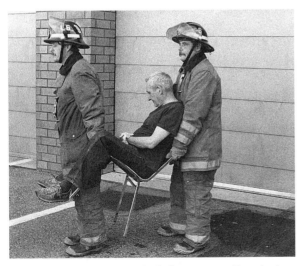

Figure 14-9. Use the chair litter carry, if a chair is available, to move a victim whose injuries might be aggravated by other types of carries or drags. (Donald Foye)

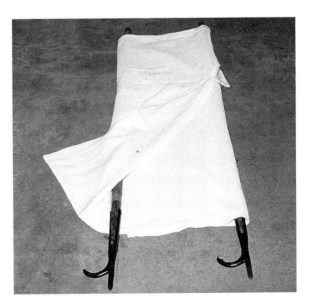

Figure 14-10. One of the many methods for improvising a stretcher is to fold a blanket around two pike poles or other wood supports. The stretcher can be prepared quickly, and will safely support most victims during evacuation.

the right one. You're doing fine, we're halfway down. Now, again the left. And the right. Good ..." Working with a frightened victim in that way will help make sure that you'll both get down.

When helping a victim down a ladder, your best position is one rung below with your hands on the rung in front of you. See **Figure 14-11.** You should keep your knees close together. If the victim should let go or pass out, you can maintain control of the situation. Ease the victim to the ground, one rung at a time, supporting his or her weight on your knees as shown in the illustration.

Using a safety line

A safer method for everybody involves the use of a *safety line*. Tie a rope around victim's chest just under the armpits, using a bowline or other knot that will not slip and constrict the victim's chest. Loop the rope over an upper rung of the ladder. One or two firefighters on the ground should hold the rope and pay it out (keeping it snug, however) as you descend. They should be prepared for

A   B

Figure 14-11. Ladder rescue. A—To safely bring a victim down a ladder, position yourself one rung lower and grasp the rung in front of the victim. B—If the victim passes out, you can maintain control by supporting his or her weight with your knees and descending rung-by-rung. (Donald Foye)

a sudden strain on the rope if the victim lets go, slips, or passes out.

If the victim is not conscious, you may have to tie him or her in a rescue knot to be lowered to the ground, using the ladder as a derrick.

Other Rescue Methods

The vast majority of rescues will be carried out by the methods already described: crutch assists, drags, carries, and ladder rescues. Certain situations, however, call for the use of specialized equipment or techniques, such as the life belt, life line, or life net. These are usually "last resort" rescue methods, however, and are more suited to use by trained firefighters than by civilians.

The life belt

The *life belt* or *life safety harness* is a rescue device that you don't use unless you absolutely have to. Since it requires thorough training to use safely, you are unlikely to ever use this device in the rescue of a civilian (ladder rescues are safer).

When working from an aerial ladder or a snorkel, you *must* wear a life belt or harness, however, and you must be trained in its use. Imagine a situation in which you are up on an aerial ladder and high heat from the fire makes collapse of the ladder imminent. Or, imagine you are in a snorkel basket and a sudden high wind makes it too risky to remain. In either case, you must evacuate *immediately* and *straight down*. It doesn't happen often, but it *does* happen, and that is when there is no substitute for it.

Inspecting a life safety harness. If the harness or belt has sustained an impact in arresting a fall, it *must* be removed from service and discarded, *regardless of its appearance*. Follow this procedure for inspecting a life safety belt or harness before it is used:

- Grasp a strap with your hands about eight inches apart, with the side that will be against your body facing toward you. Bend the strap away from you and inspect it carefully for any indication of fraying, broken fibers, cuts, pulled stitches, or discoloration that might indicate attack by chemicals or heat. Repeat the inspection on all surfaces or all straps.

- Next, check all buckles and D-rings for damage, distortion, or wear. Make sure they are firmly anchored. Inspect all riveted connections for cracks, looseness or discoloration; look for broken, missing, or distorted grommets. Inspect the tongue for excessive looseness in any direction.

- Finally, hold the harness out in front of you at arm's length and examine it carefully for overall condition and appearance. Remember, you might find yourself trusting your life to this piece of equipment!

The life net

Few firefighters, even veterans, have ever seen an actual life net rescue. And with luck, they never will. A *life net* rescue is dangerous for both the rescued and the rescuers. Why, then, do we practice it? For the same reason that you carry fire insurance on your home: "just in case." With luck you'll never need it, but you still buy it. The fact is that situations *do* develop where the life net, dangerous as it is, the best and only means of rescue. Your chances of avoiding injury, whether you are a rescuer or the rescued, are far better if you have had regular practice.

Use of the life net. The following sections provide general instructions for deploying and holding a life net, as well as instructions for safely jumping into such a net.

- Do not open the net in view of the rescue victim. He or she may very well jump before the net or rescuers are ready.

- As you unfold net, check to make sure the hinge locks have snapped into place. They can jam on a piece of grit and not engage fully, making the net unsafe to use.

- When the net is moved into position to receive a jumper, it must be held by no fewer than eight firefighters who are evenly spaced around its rim.

- Hold the net by gripping the frame with palms up and thumbs underneath rail. Hold the net at shoulder height, with elbows well out to the sides of your body. This allows your arms to "give" as shock absorbers when the jumper strikes the net.

- Watch the jumper at all times and be prepared for unexpected moves. Stand with your left foot forward, and be ready to move in any direction, so that you will catch the jumper in the center of the net.

- If more than one person is to be rescued, you must ready the net for the next jumper as soon as each person has landed. When the first person lands, quickly drop side of net farthest from building and raise other side, so he or she will roll off. Reposition the net quickly to get ready for next person to be rescued.

Since the safety net is more frequently used to rescue fire personnel than civilians, every firefighter must practice landing in a net. Remember, when you are jumping from a distance of only thirty feet, you hit bottom at a speed of thirty miles per hour. This is fast enough to do considerable damage to even the hardiest of people. You have to do it right. Here's how:

1. Never jump until told to do so by your instructor!
2. Don't actually *jump*, since jumping makes your landing point less predictable. Instead, *step* from the building "at attention" with your eyes straight ahead.
3. Remain "at attention" as you fall. It is easier to control your body position this way.
4. Just before you hit, raise your arms and pull up your legs so that you land in a sitting position. Landing on your feet can cause severe injuries.

When you practice jumping, start at a height no greater than ten feet. Once you have mastered this height, gradually increase the distance. For safety, *do not* exceed thirty feet in practice jumps.

Searching for Fire Victims

In search operations, you must set priorities and be methodical. Your search priorities will focus on building areas where people are most likely to be, and on areas where there will most likely be survivors. The search method you follow must ensure that you will cover all of the areas in the structure with the least amount of danger to the occupants, to yourself, and the other searchers.

Setting search priorities

Before you enter a fire building to make a search, get as much information as you can about the possible location of the victim. Try to have witnesses draw or describe the layout of the building. Even a mental image of the interior of the building will make your job easier during the search. Also, attempt to *verify* the information given to you about the victim — many searches have been conducted for victims that were not in the building at the time of the fire. There is no sense endangering yourself and your partner looking for someone who is not there.

The time of day that a fire occurs is often your best guide to where people will be in a structure. Since most fatal fires in residences occur at night, the victims will usually be found in the bedrooms or in adjacent hallways. During the daytime and early evening hours, victims are most likely to be in the living room, kitchen, or recreation areas of the home.

Your search should begin in the area where survivors will probably be found. Once this area has been searched, extend your activities to other, less probable parts of the structure. Do not expect persons involved in a fire to behave rationally. They are often panicky and disoriented. Frequently, their one thought is to get away from the smoke and flames, no matter how much more deeply this may get them into trouble.

Don't take anything for granted: check *everything* and *everywhere*. Victims (especially children) will find the most obscure places to hide, since they are frightened and are trying to hide from their fears. Always look under and behind furniture and inside closets and cabinets. If you have been able to obtain the name of the person you are searching for, *use it*. Continually call out the name and listen for any response (however faint) that could lead you to the victim's hiding place.

Search principles

The basic principles of search apply whether you are looking for potential survivors in a smoke-filled building, a demolished building, a crash, cave-in, or whatever. Each presents its unique hazards, but the same precautions apply. Regardless of the nature of the disaster: don't go in alone; look for alternate ways out, and search systematically, following all applicable precautions and procedures. General precautions and procedures are described in the following sections.

Before you go in. For your own safety and the safety of your fellow firefighters (who may be called upon to rescue *you*), take a number of precautions before entering a building to search.

- Get as much information as possible from people who have already escaped from the building. Do not trust information provided by casual bystanders.
- Have your breathing apparatus in place.
- Do not go in alone.
- Be sure you have more than one way out of the building.
- Carry along a spare rope to use as a guideline so that you can find your way out.
- Whenever possible, enter a smoke-filled building from the leeward side.

Once inside. Following a specific set of search procedures will make your search more efficient, improve the possibility of locating survivors, and minimize risk to yourself and fellow firefighters.

- Start out along an outside wall, ventilating as you go. Caution: Do not ventilate the *windward* side until the *leeward* side has been ventilated.

- Work in pairs, and keep in close touch with your partner.

- Stay low, where the visibility is better.

- Visibility will be poor, at best. Rely on your sense of touch, making wide sweeping motions with your arms.

- Search systematically, so that your work will not have to be duplicated or some areas left unsearched.

- Search one room completely before going on to another room.

- Move up and down stairs on your hands and knees. You will be much less likely to fall through a hole.

- Look for flame spread and report it to the officer in command.

- Be alert. Listen for groans, heavy breathing, pounding noises, or the whimpering of a child.

- Children and some adults may try to hide from fire. Search under beds, behind doors and drapes, under tables and desks, in closets. Search anything big enough to hold a small child.

- People, especially children, may be in their beds, so pull covers off gently.

- If you can open a door only part-way, a body may be blocking it. You might have to take the door off its hinges.

- If you find a door that is bolted from the inside or held with a chain lock, take it as an almost-sure sign that someone is inside.

- If you make contact with a victim, talk and keep talking. This will calm the victim, who may help out by crawling toward you. If movement is too dangerous, tell victim to remain where he or she is.

- Whenever possible, crawl with or drag the victim, so that you can both stay low, where the best air is.

- Once outside, place the person you have rescued into the custody of a responsible party, so he or she can't attempt to reenter the building to save a pet or recover a prized possession.

A typical search

You are first on the scene at a fire in a house with the floor plan illustrated in **Figure 14-12.** As you arrive, no flames are showing, but heavy smoke is erupting from attic and second floor. As shown in the illustration, you and your partner enter by ladder through a second story window. As you enter, check behind the drapes on both sides of the window. Keep low, since visibility is better near the floor. Proceed along the broken line to *Point 1*. Probe under the bed, using a gentle, sweeping motion with an arm, leg, or axe *handle* (anything that will reach more than halfway under the bed). Pull the covers off to make sure nobody is on the bed.

Proceed to *Point 2*, and probe under the bed as you did before. If you do not find a victim, turn the mattress 90 degrees to indicate that the bed has been searched. Continue along the broken line to *Point 3* and probe under the desk. Turn the chair upside down on top of the desk to show it has been searched.

Proceed to *Points 4* and *5*, and probe under the second bed. As before, rotate the mattress to show that it has been done. Now, move to *Point 6*. Probe under the chest of drawers.

Follow the wall of the room, past the hallway door to *Point 7*, the closet. Probe inside the closet, paying special attention to corners and the spaces behind hanging clothing (terrified people sometimes try to hide from fire). Proceed along the wall to the end of room, then back through the center of the room to the hallway door, *Point 8*.

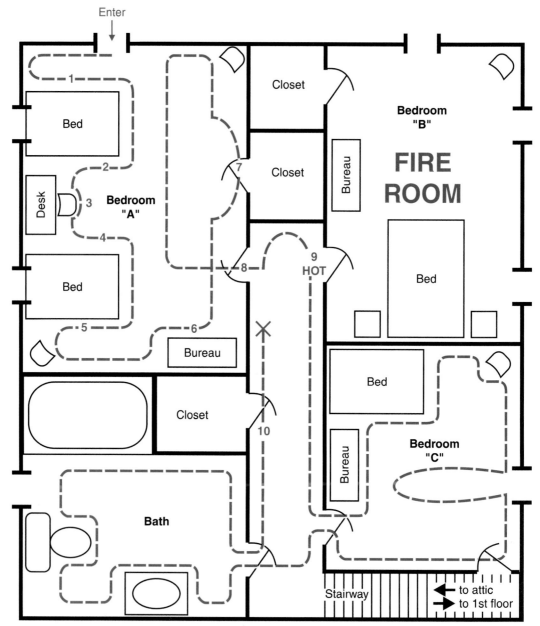

Figure 14-12. This floor plan shows a typical search pattern for the second floor of a residence. A thorough, systematic search for possible victims is essential.

Feel the door to the hallway. If it is hot, *do not open* unless you have a charged line in your hands. If it is cool, open very carefully. If the door opens toward you, place your toe a few inches away from the door so the pressure of fire gases won't blow it in on you. If door opens away from you, grasp the knob with both hands and push gently. If door doesn't open easily, it may be held back by debris, pressure

from gases outside the room, or an unconscious body. Proceed with caution.

If you can open the door without a problem, exit the room. Close the door and tie a curtain, pillowcase, or some other "flag" to the doorknob to show that the room has been searched.

Cross the hall to *Point 9*, the door to Bedroom "B." Feel the door; if it is *hot*, do not attempt to open it. If anyone is inside, there is little chance that they are still alive. Bypass this room for now.

Move to Bedroom "C," as indicated by the dashed line. Again, feel the door. If it is cool, enter cautiously, using the same door-opening precautions as you did when leaving Bedroom "A." Search the room as you did before. When finished, close the door and tie some sort of "flag" to the knob.

Cross the hall to the bathroom. Check to see if the door is hot or cool. If the door is locked, it probably means someone is in that room. Pry the door open with blade of axe. Search the room. If you find a victim, follow the rescue procedures described earlier. If no one is found, close the door and tie a "flag" to the knob.

Move to *Point 10*, the hall closet. Check this space as you did the other closets. When finished, close and "flag" the door.

If the attic door was open when you checked Bedroom "C," you should check the attic as soon as possible. Do not search the attic until you have completed your search of the more likely areas.

Proceed to *Point X*, outside Bedroom "B." By now, a charged line should be available, allowing you to move into that room from the hallway. If a charged line has not been advanced, exit by the same window you used to enter. Move the ladder and enter the hot room through its window with a charged line.

Other Search and Rescue Situations

In time of natural disaster (such as earthquakes, tornadoes, hurricanes, or floods), firefighters often bear the brunt of search and rescue work in collapsed or badly damaged structures. A collapsed excavation (*cave-in*) is also frequently the scene of search activities. Firefighters are also called in to assist when industrial accidents occur, or to remove persons trapped between floors in elevator cars due to power failures or other malfunctions.

Collapsed buildings

A *collapsed building* is one that has had to bear a load too heavy for its construction (the collapse is actually an attempt at achieving structural stability). Anything you do in a collapsed structure can potentially cause a further collapse. Even so, if there is a possibility of survivors inside, you have to try a rescue. People have been brought out alive several days, even a week or more, after a collapse. The following precautions are aimed at avoiding the biggest hazard of rescue in a collapsed structure: more of the building falling in and trapping you.

- Walk along the outside edges of the floor, close to structural members.

- Search the accessible areas before going into areas where the *rubble* (debris) is more dense. Usually this means moving along the exterior walls where there might be a lean-to effect. See **Figure 14-13.**

- Do not move even the smallest piece of rubble unless you have to, and then only with extreme caution.

- Proceed slowly. If you must tunnel into the debris, shore up as you go.

- If victim is fairly safe for now and not in immediate danger from injuries, do not attempt a single-handed rescue. Call for help and proper rescue equipment. Stay with victim as much as possible, reassuring him or her.

Search techniques. As stated earlier in this chapter, a pile of rubble is unstable, at best. The material has reached a temporary state of equilibrium. The least thing you do may cause it to collapse even more. For this reason, you should never climb around on a collapsed structure, since a further collapse could injure you, or cause additional injury to anyone trapped in the rubble.

At the beginning, removal of debris might be a pick-and-shovel operation. But it is safer to work with your hands, wearing thick gloves. First, remove the easy pieces - the material that shows no resistance. This

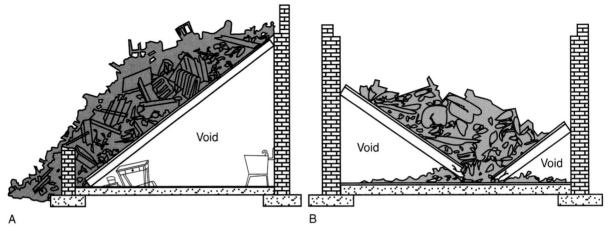

A   B

Figure 14-13. In a building collapse, voids are often created by floor sections leaning against walls at one side. A—A typical lean-to effect that creates a large void along one wall. B—A V-type collapse that creates smaller voids along parallel walls.

probably means that it isn't supporting anything. As you remove pieces, shift them well to the side or well behind you. Don't pile up debris close to your path of travel. It might come tumbling down on you. Don't be hasty. Work slowly and carefully.

When you have most of the loose pieces out of the way, you can see the situation more clearly. What you have left is like a house of cards: move the wrong one and the whole works falls down. Try to move a piece just a little. See what everything else does. If nothing else moves, you might be able to pull it out carefully. Repeat the process as often as necessary.

You'll find that you can't move some pieces that are supporting a pile of other material. You will have to go around or over or under them. Here is where you might have to start making trenches and tunnels, supporting and shoring up as you go. See **Figure 14-14.**

You might, however, be able to jack up a section, using hydraulic or mechanical jacks. An alternative method is to use a *pneumatic lifting bag* (often referred to simply as an "air bag") that is capable of lifting several tons. These bags, when deflated, can be slipped into spaces only an inch or two high, then inflated from an air cylinder. Depending upon the model and type, an air bag will raise objects anywhere from a few inches to more than a yard. Since they have a large area of ground contact to spread the pressure, these devices can be used on soft or uneven surfaces. If you raise a section, shore it up and

Figure 14-14. To reach survivors in the small voids left by a pancake-type collapse, you will usually have to trench or tunnel very carefully through the rubble. Extreme care is needed to avoid further collapse of the unstable debris.

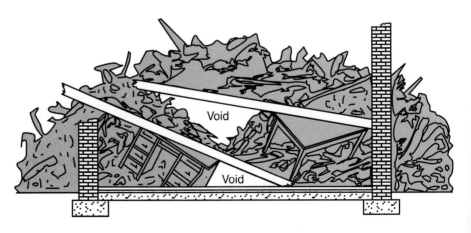

move the jack or air bag elsewhere. As you remove debris, you will have to support what is left to prevent further collapse.

As you get close to where survivors are likely to be, debris removal becomes a very careful hand operation. It is extremely difficult to recognize an unconscious human body when it is covered with dirt and debris. You will have to work slowly, shoring as you move forward. The farther into the collapsed structure you go, the greater the possibility of further collapse becomes. Listen for any movement, indicating that what's left of the structure is moving on its own. If you are ordered out, get out *without delay*.

Cave-ins

A ground cave-in is very much like a building collapse, since it is an unstable situation, at best. Do not walk close to the edge of a collapsed excavation. If you *must* approach the edge, stretch out flat on the ground. Keep your body perpendicular to the edge and have someone hang on to your ankles. If victim of the cave-in is not seriously injured, and if further collapse is not imminent, don't try a single-handed rescue. Wait for help and the proper equipment.

Industrial accidents

Many industrial plants have their own trained rescue teams. The members of such teams have received special instruction on the hazards likely to be encountered, and have planned for and practiced required techniques for rescue. If your fire company is called in on an accident at such a plant, you will most likely be present on a "standby" basis, to assist if needed. If fire department personnel take part in the actual rescue effort, they will often be under the direction of a person from the plant rescue team who has the required special knowledge.

Special hazards. Almost every community has locations that present firefighters with hazards peculiar to that area: abandoned commercial and industrial buildings; quarries and mines, bulk storage terminals

for grain and other commodities, and such natural hazards as steep cliffs or swamps. In the same way that the department does pre-fire planning for various locations, plans should be made for dealing with accidents and potential rescue operations at sites presenting special hazards.

Elevator rescues

Although elevators may be one of the safest methods of travel (they don't run into things, and things don't run into them), they do sometimes malfunction. Since safety interlocks make it virtually impossible for an elevator to drop more than a few feet, most elevator incidents involve becoming "stuck" between floors. This happens, in most cases, due to a power failure; in rare instances, the cause is a malfunction of the elevator mechanism itself.

The passengers in the car are seldom in actual danger - the greatest hazard is panic resulting from being confined in such a small space. For the safety of both firefighters and the persons being rescued, power to the elevator motor must be *shut off* to prevent unexpected movement of the car.

Most often, you will approach the car from above, since an emergency exit hatch is built into its roof. To do so, you must first open the doors to the elevator shaft on the floor immediately above the point where the car is stopped. A special key is needed to open the doors, and usually must be obtained from the manager or maintenance person for the building (in some communities, keys for elevator doors are carried on equipment of companies with elevator-equipped buildings in their response area).

After opening the doors, lower a short ladder to the roof of the car. The emergency hatch can then be opened, and a second ladder lowered to provide a means of egress from the car. Some people are frightened by the need to climb a ladder, so you may have to help them climb up to the open door. Injured or disabled persons may have to be packaged and hoisted from the car.

Vehicle Rescue

Many times, you have seen the wreckage of an automobile and wondered if anyone got out alive ... then later learned that the occupants escaped with only minor injuries. Never assume that, just because a twisted pile of metal is barely recognizable as an automobile, there are no survivors.

Since automobiles, planes, trains, and buses are made of metal, there isn't much chance of further collapse once the thing has stopped moving. The major dangers in this kind of search and rescue are fuel spills and possible ignition, hazardous material in cargoes, electrocution (if the vehicle has crashed into a power line), and possible panic among survivors. If there has been a fuel spill, you may have to take up the fuel with an absorbent before attempting rescue; hazardous material may require removal by specially trained personnel before rescue can be carried out. If charged power lines are lying across vehicle (treat *all* power lines as charged lines until you are sure they are not charged), have them removed by qualified personnel before you attempt to enter.

The general principles of search apply: look for survivors where survival is most likely. Start your search there.

When you locate survivors, your first impulse will be to "get them out of there." Any feeling human being would react in the same way. But your first impulse may be the *worst* impulse. There may be other, more urgent tasks that must be done first. In many cases, you will have to secure the vehicle, gain entry for life support and packaging, and open roof or side of the vehicle before you can begin to remove any victims.

Securing the Vehicle

If the vehicle is standing on its wheels on a relatively flat surface, you probably do not need to *secure* it (other than blocking wheels with a brick or board). But when the vehicle is resting precariously on its side, or is on an incline, or is about to roll off the edge of an embankment, you can't do anything until it is stabilized. An unsecured vehicle could roll over or slide or roll down a slope, causing further (possibly fatal) injuries to those inside, including rescue personnel.

Use whatever is at hand — boards, jacks, a block and tackle, a winch — to support the vehicle so that it cannot move in any direction. See **Figure 14-15**. Once you think it is safe, try to rock it gently. If it moves the slightest bit, prop it up some more. Do not attempt any further action until you are certain that the vehicle will not roll over or slide.

Gaining Entry

The victim cannot be moved until you know the nature and extent of injuries, have begun life support procedures, and have completed *packaging* (preparation for safe movement). To do this, first try the doors. One of them might open. Most often, though, you will have to open a hole in the vehicle just large enough for rescue people to wiggle through to the inside.

If the car has rolled over, the windows have probably been broken. In this case, all

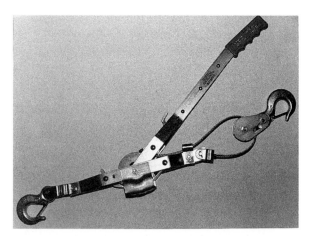

Figure 14-15. To secure a vehicle and prevent it from rolling over, a small portable winch or "come-along" like this one is a useful tool. This type of winch has other rescue applications, as well.

you will have to do is remove any glass still in the frame. If the windows are intact, the quickest way in will probably be through removing the windshield or rear window. First, remove the trim. Next, use a sharp knife with a curved blade, such as a linoleum knife, to cut away the rubber molding from the sides and top. This often can be done in one smooth action, starting at the bottom on one side and ending at the bottom on the other side. Finally, work the blade behind the glass and pop the glass out.

Using a sharp-edged forcible entry tool, such as a crash axe, you can cut away half a windshield or rear window, **Figure 14-16.** Cut down the middle and around the edges, then pry the glass out.

Unless you can see from the outside that the victim is bleeding badly, take your time and work cautiously. It can take an hour or even much longer to extricate an injured person from a vehicle.

Once inside, turn off the vehicle ignition, just in case. Do a survey of life-threatening injuries, as described in the chapter on Emergency Medical Care in this text. Once you are certain that there are no unattended life-threatening conditions, begin the package for removal. Again, use the packaging techniques described in this text or your training program. Unless the car is on fire or about to explode, do not attempt to move injured

Figure 14-16. A crash axe or similar forcible entry tool can be used to cut away half the windshield or rear window to gain access to victims inside a vehicle. (Warren Lutton)

people until they are carefully packaged. If the driver has been impaled on the steering wheel column, do not attempt to pull out the column. Cut it loose from the vehicle and leave it in place when you remove the driver.

Opening a Vehicle for Removal

While some rescue personnel are attending to the injured inside the vehicle, others should be preparing an opening for removing the victims. Obviously, the small hole that the rescue people wiggled through won't be sufficient. You will probably need a large opening.

Where and how this opening should be made will depend on the exact nature of the victim's injuries, the condition of the vehicle, the equipment at hand, and other factors. Those working inside will know how best to move the victim to prevent further injuries.

You might have to cut away door posts and doors or even cut off most of the top of the vehicle. When choosing the method for opening, bear in mind that the condition of the injured person or persons must be the first consideration.

A gasoline-powered rescue saw is fast. It can cut the entire top off a car in a few minutes, but is extremely noisy. If an injured person is near shock, the noise would be bad for him or her. An oxyacetylene torch will cut through thick posts. But if any flammables are near, or people are close to the area being cut, it cannot be used.

Various types of hydraulic cutters and spreaders are on the market today. Some are gasoline-operated, some operate off the rescue vehicle's electrical system, some are hand-pumped. They are all relatively quiet. Depending on the make, they can exert a cutting or spreading force of anywhere from four to twenty tons.

Many hand rescue tools are also available. The crash axe, the fire axe, and all kinds of pry bars will cut, spread, and move metal. One implement that looks like a large can opener will take the top off a car in a matter of minutes.

SUMMARY

In emergency rescues, the firefighter often must improvise. The method used to remove a victim from a hazardous situation is determined by the location and extent of the victim's injuries, how much time is available, the materials at hand, the number of firefighters available to help.

Usually, in moving an injured person, a horizontal method is best, but may not be the quickest. Circumstances will dictate whether safety or speed should be given the most importance. Ladder rescues are particularly hazardous since the victim is probably not used to heights and may either freeze or let go. A safety line will provide an extra measure of physical security and assurance. Life belts, life lines, and life nets represent "last resort" rescue methods, and are more often used for trained firefighters than for civilians.

In fire search and rescue operations you must set priorities and be methodical. First search where the people are most likely to be at the time of day the fire occurs. Search one room thoroughly before proceeding to the next. Leave signs indicating that you have searched the complete room, including under beds and in closets. Remember that children and elderly people may try to hide from the fire in unexpected places.

Before going into the building, get all the reliable information you can gather. Don't go in alone. Carry a spare rope for a guideline and be sure you have more than one way out.

Search in pairs and use a systematic approach. Use all your senses, especially touch and hearing. If you locate a survivor, talk to him or her and keep talking as you move them to safety. Once out, put survivor in the custody of a reliable person so he or she can't go back in.

The real danger in collapsed buildings is that anything you do may cause further collapse. Move slowly and shore up as you go, searching for voids in the rubble where survivors will most likely be found. Cave-ins also present the danger of further collapse. Approach the edge horizontally with someone holding onto your feet. If you go in, wear breathing apparatus, in case you should become buried.

In the case of vehicle crashes, there is a danger of electrocution, fuel explosion, or hazardous material spills. You may have to wait until specially trained personnel complete their tasks before going in.

People have been removed uninjured from motor vehicles that look like a pile of twisted metal. Don't let the condition of the vehicle mislead you as to the condition of those inside. You may have to make sure the car won't tip over or roll down an embankment before you can begin rescue. While paramedics are working inside, rescue workers on the outside should begin preparing an opening to remove injured persons. The method used to open up the vehicle will depend on the vehicle's position and contents, the kinds of injuries sustained by its occupants, and the equipment at hand.

REVIEW QUESTIONS

1. When making emergency rescues, you often have to improvise. Describe at least three improvised substitutes for each of the following:
   A leg splint
   A tourniquet
   A cervical collar

2. List the four factors that determine which drag or carry you would use when removing a victim from a hazardous situation.

3. Describe how to perform each of the following carries and drags:
   The vertical packstrap carry
   The incline drag
   The seat carry
   The fireman's drag
   The two-person crutch assist
   Ladder rescue with safety line

4. Describe the procedure for inspecting a life safety harness.

5. What is the proper procedure for jumping into a life net?

6. Where you would begin the search for victims in a house fire at 8 p.m.? At 6 a.m.?

7. Describe your reasons for selecting the two "first search" areas you selected in the preceding question.

8. What should you do before going into a burning house on a search and rescue operation?

9. What extra equipment should you carry in a situation where you are attempting a single-handed rescue in a burning house?

10. Describe the procedure for searching the second floor of a house during a fire that occurs after midnight.

11. What is the biggest danger in searching a collapsed building? What should you do about it?

12. When you remove rubble and debris in a search for a victim, where should you place it?

13. In an area where trapped persons might be found, why shouldn't you use a pick and shovel?

14. How should you approach the edge of an excavation that has caved in?

15. What steps should you take before attempting to remove injured persons from a wrecked vehicle?

16. Why might you sometimes have to shore up a wrecked vehicle?

17. Describe some common methods used to create an opening in a vehicle so that paramedics can enter and assist injured occupants.

18. Why should paramedics or ambulance personnel enter a vehicle before occupant removal operations are begun?

19. What methods could you use to open a vehicle for the removal of injured persons?

20. What factors should you consider when determining the best method of opening a vehicle to remove injured occupants?

NFPA 1001 Job Performance Requirements

The material on this page consists of those portions of the NFPA 1001 Job Performance Requirements relevant to the material presented in this chapter. The following is drawn from the Entrance Requirements section of NFPA 1001.

2-3 Emergency medical care performance capabilities for entry-level personnel shall be developed and validated by the authority having jurisdiction. At a minimum, the performance requirements shall include infection control, CPR, bleeding control, and shock management.

Reprinted with permission from NFPA 1001, *Fire Fighter Professional Qualifications,* Copyright ©1997, National Fire Protection Association, Quincy, MA 02269. This reprinted material is not the complete and official position of the National Fire Protection Association on the referenced subject, which is represented only by the standard in its entirety.

Emergency Medical Services

OBJECTIVES

When you have completed this chapter, you will be able to:

- Demonstrate primary and secondary surveys for life-threatening injuries.
- Describe the signs and symptoms of cardiac arrest.
- List the procedures involved in cardiopulmonary resuscitation.
- Identify and describe at least three types of external bleeding.
- Discuss the techniques necessary for controlling external bleeding.
- Describe the types of burns and the appropriate emergency medical care for each.
- List the types of fractures and describe the necessary emergency medical care for each type.
- Identify the signs and symptoms of shock and describe the appropriate emergency medical care.

IMPORTANT TERMS

anaphylactic shock	compound fracture	minor burns	septic shock
arterial bleeding	critical burn	moderate burns	shock
artery	degree	neurogenic shock	simple fracture
assessment	dermis	neutral position	spiral fracture
burn	epidermis	oblique fracture	third-degree burns
capillaries	first-degree burns	primary survey	tourniquet
capillary bleeding	greenstick fracture	psychogenic shock	unresponsive
cardiogenic shock	hemorrhagic shock	respiratory shock	vein
cardiopulmonary	impacted fracture	rule of nines	venous bleeding
resuscitation	medical history	secondary survey	vital signs
comminuted fracture	metabolic shock	second-degree burns	

Although emergency medical services are available from both public-sector and private-sector providers, this chapter will deal specifically with the services provided by fire departments. Fire service personnel frequently find themselves faced with the need to provide emergency medical services to either fellow firefighters or to citizens.

The firefighter has a responsibility to provide the best possible medical services that he or she can during an emergency. This chapter is not intended to provide you with a detailed medical services course, but rather to make you familiar with the basic elements needed to provide care to the sick and injured.

During the late 1960s, it became apparent that a better system of pre-hospital care had to be developed to improve survival rates for the sick and injured while being transported to a medical facility. The fire department became a logical choice as service provider, because many departments already operated local ambulances. Throughout the 1970s, intensive training programs of emergency medical technicians (EMTs) and EMT/paramedics flourished, **Figure 15-1.** State by state, the emergency medical services system grew into a nationwide network capable of providing pre-hospital emergency medical services. Today, in almost all urban areas and most rural areas, care can be provided to the sick and injured by trained emergency medical technicians. As the system grew, the demand by citizens increased. Today, many local governments require all public safety personnel to be trained as either EMTs or paramedics, **Figure 15-2.**

Figure 15-1. In addition to firefighters and police officers with emergency medical technician (EMT) training, many employees of private ambulance services are certified as EMTs or EMT/paramedics.

Medical History

Your assessment of the patient will begin when you first receive the call for help. Regardless of how the request is received, *some* basic information will be given to you. Most often, the information will be as simple as, "possible heart attack," or "automobile accident." Based upon that information, you have begun the process of taking a *medical history*. As you respond to the scene of the incident, you and your partner may discuss what you expect to face upon your arrival. Once you arrive, you may be able to determine whether or not the environment had any effect on the patient's illness or injury. For example, in a single-vehicle accident, you may want to ask, "How did the accident happen?" "What were the weather conditions?" "The road conditions?" "Did the driver lose consciousness?" "Does the driver remember

Figure 15-2. Both police and fire personnel in this community are trained as paramedics and staff this mobile intensive care unit.

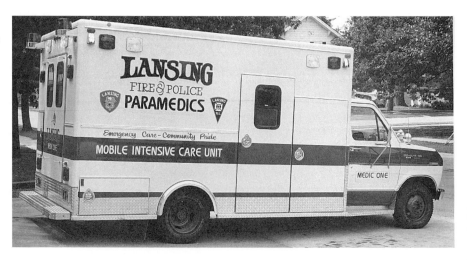

the accident?" "What is the last thing the driver remembers?"

By asking questions such as these, you may find a mechanical problem or faulty driving technique was the reason for the accident: the driver sharply applied brakes on an icy road, lost control, and skidded into a tree. You might, however, find that the driver lost consciousness prior to the accident and does not remember anything about it. In such a case, you have the responsibility for asking *additional* questions. Those should include pertinent inquiries about the patient's medical history. "Is the patient a diabetic?" "Has the patient ever lost consciousness like this before?" "Is the patient an epileptic?" "Does the patient have a heart condition?" All of these questions are aimed at attempting to identify the *cause* of the loss of consciousness.

Be observant. By becoming aware of the environmental conditions around the patient, you can reduce potential injuries to yourself and your partners. For example, in the case of a possible electrocution, be sure to determine the cause of the electric shock *before* touching the patient. In cases involving hazardous materials, concern for your own safety should dictate determining the type of hazardous material before rushing into the area. Your observations and caution will lead to better patient care.

Through the entire process of taking history and assessing the patient, it is important that you remain calm and in control. In many difficult situations, your ability to maintain your composure will provide a calming effect for everyone concerned. By being able to gain control of the situation in this manner, you are demonstrating your ability as a professional.

Patient Assessment

Proper treatment of any patient depends upon an *accurate* assessment of the patient's illness or injury. The **assessment** of the illness or injury that you make in the field can be compared to the foundation of a house. See **Figure 15-3.** When the foundation is strong and solid, the builders can continue the construction of the house without interruption. If the foundation develops cracks or problems, however, the builder must stop work on the house and repair the foundation before continuing. When your assessment of the patients' illness or injury in the field is accurate, the doctors and nurses in the hospital can continue patient care without delay. If your assessment is inaccurate or incomplete, however, they must interrupt treatment to correct the problems with your assessment. You must remember that, in the delivery of pre-hospital care, you are the eyes, ears, and hands of the physician.

Primary Survey

Begin the *primary survey* with an assessment of "the ABCs." As shown in **Figure 15-4,** "A" stands for airway, "B" for breathing, and "C" for circulation.

To complete a primary survey of a patient, you must establish whether or not the patient is conscious. This can be done by using the

Figure 15-3. Like the strong foundation needed for uninterrupted house construction, your accurate assessment of a patient's illness or injury allows hospital personnel to continue treatment without a break when you bring the patient into the facility.

Primary Survey

A = Airway

B = Breathing

C = Circulation

Figure 15-4. In the primary survey, check the patient for an unobstructed airway, proper breathing, and adequate circulation.

"shake and shout" method, **Figure 15-5**, when no evidence of *spinal trauma* exists. This method involves placing your hands on the patient's shoulders and gently shaking him or her while calling the patient's name. This will help you determine whether or not the patient is conscious.

Airway

The first step is to establish whether or not the patient has an adequate airway. In assessing the airway, you should determine whether or not the airway is open and can exchange air freely. If the airway is not open, you must immediately take the necessary steps to secure an open airway for the patient. If an obstructed airway is not immediately corrected, the patient will die.

If the mechanism of injury or the presence of pain indicates cervical spine injury, you should place a cervical collar on the patient as soon as you establish whether the patient has an adequate airway. In most cases, it is appropriate to assume (with the mechanism of injury present), that an unconscious patient has a cervical spine injury. Placing a cervical collar on the patient during the primary survey will help avoid further spinal injury.

Breathing

If you determine that the airway is not obstructed, then your next step is to establish whether or not breathing is taking place. You can check for breathing by listening for the exchange of air, **Figure 15-6**, looking for the rise and fall of the patient's chest, or by holding your hand near the patient's mouth or nose to feel for the exchange of air.

Circulation

The final part of the primary survey is to determine whether or not there is adequate circulation in order to sustain life. The simplest method of checking for the presence or absence of circulation is to feel for a pulse in the carotid artery. Do this by placing the fingers of your hand along the side of the patient's throat,

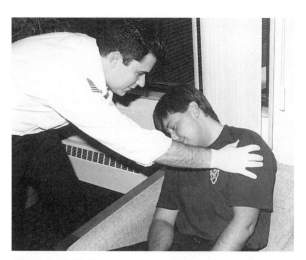

Figure 15-5. Determining whether the patient is conscious can be done by using the "shake and shout" method. Place your hands on the patient's shoulders and gently shake while calling his or her name. (Warren Lutton)

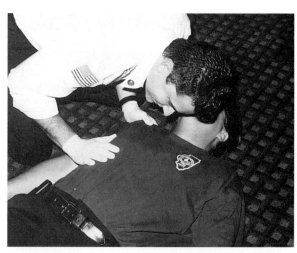

Figure 15-6. To determine whether a patient is breathing, listen for the exchange of air. (Warren Lutton)

Figure 15-7. If you determine that your patient has an adequate airway, but is not breathing, or does not have adequate circulation, you must *immediately* begin cardiopulmonary resuscitation (CPR). Cardiopulmonary resuscitation will be discussed later in this chapter. Any *other* ABC-related problem that you discover during your survey should be treated immediately — do not wait until you have completed the survey.

Secondary Survey

The *secondary survey* involves conducting a physical examination of a patient. You should do everything possible to respect the privacy of the patient, consistent with your responsibility to avoid further injury. For example, instead of conducting a thorough physical examination in a crowded restaurant, it may be more appropriate (when the conditions permit) to move the patient to your ambulance to conduct a complete examination. However, the patient should be moved *only* if you are certain that movement of the patient will not cause additional injury.

As you conduct this secondary survey, it is important for you to make full use of your senses. Use your sense of *sight* to observe the normal landmarks of the patient's anatomy. You will look for the symmetry of the

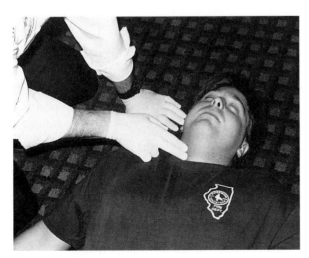

Figure 15-7. Adequate circulation can be established by feeling for a pulse in the carotid artery on the side of the patient's neck. (Warren Lutton)

patient's body. You will look for swelling, skin discoloration, and bleeding. You should also be aware of any discharges from the body, such as cerebral fluid, urine, feces, or vomitus. You will use the sense of *touch* as you feel the different parts of the patient's body for the presence of swelling, tenderness, pulses, instability of structures, and the presence of subcutaneous air. You will use your sense of *hearing* as you listen for significant sounds from the patient. The patient will typically indicate the presence of pain by moaning, complaining, or crying out. You can sometimes identify the presence of a broken bone by hearing when you touch it. You will use your sense of *smell* to detect odors that might help with your history of the patient. For instances, you might smell alcohol on a patient's breath, or you might detect an odor in an industrial situation that indicates the possibility of a hazardous material problem. By using your senses, you will be able to carry out a complete secondary survey of the patient.

Protecting yourself

Any time that you are likely to be in physical contact with a patient, you must take proper precautions to avoid exposure to communicable diseases. The simplest and most basic form of protection is to wear latex examination gloves, **Figure 15-8.** This precaution can protect you from exposure that could result from contact with disease organisms on the skin or in body fluids. If the patient is *known* to have a serious communicable disease, additional protective equipment should be worn to avoid exposure. See **Figure 15-9.**

Checking vital signs

Your secondary survey of the patient should begin with a set of *vital signs*. To indicate the present physical status of the patient, you should include a pulse count, a respiratory count, and a blood pressure reading.

If your patient is conscious, one of the first things you should establish is the nature of the patient's primary or chief complaint,

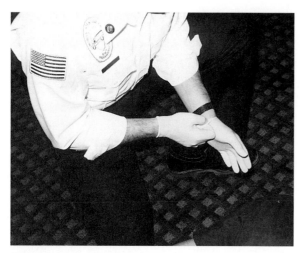

Figure 15-8. Whenever you come into physical contact with a patient, you should wear surgical gloves to avoid possible exposure to disease. (Warren Lutton)

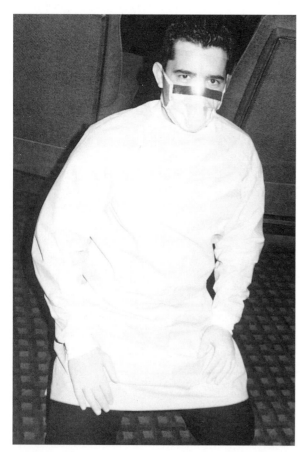

Figure 15-9. If a patient is known to have a communicable disease, you must take further precautions, such as wearing a mask and gown. (Warren Lutton)

Figure 15-10. Once this has been identified, you will be able to zero in on the area most affecting the patient. However, do not be misled. There are times when patients or family members or bystanders will mislead you, either intentionally or unintentionally. Always attempt to verify and confirm any information that you receive. With a conscious patient, you will be able to use the patient himself or herself to help you confirm the injury or illness that is causing the problem.

If the patient is unconscious, however, you must rely on family members or bystanders to provide you with the primary or chief complaint. See **Figure 15-11.** Often, the information you receive will not add a great deal to your knowledge: "He just clutched his chest and collapsed." At other times, though, the information will be more helpful. "The student was doing a gymnastics maneuver on the balance beam when her foot slipped. As she fell, her head struck the beam. She has not been conscious since we called you."

The purpose of the primary and secondary survey is to either confirm or rule out the existence of a life-threatening situation. The actual physical survey should be done

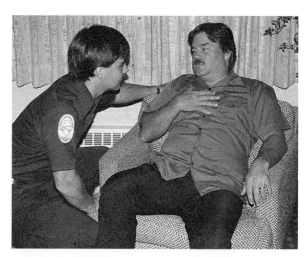

Figure 15-10. Try to establish the chief complaint, or major problem, of the patient. If the patient is conscious, you can ask him or her; if not, you may have to talk to relatives or bystanders. (Warren Lutton)

Figure 15-11. Verifying the chief complaint often involves gathering information from someone other than the patient. In this disaster drill, the unconscious person at right cannot communicate, so information is being sought from another firefighter-victim. (Warren Lutton)

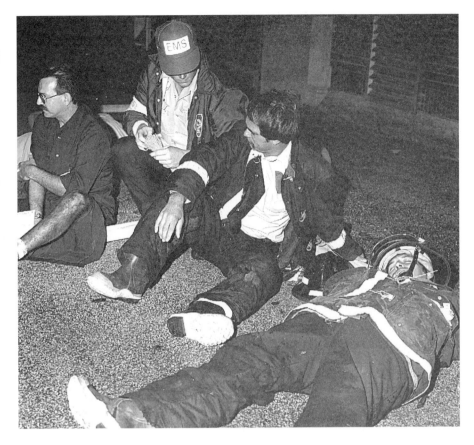

quickly and systematically to identify life-threatening injuries without delay. A systematic secondary survey should begin at the patient's head, then move downward.

Head

You should first visually inspect for any obvious signs of head injury. If injuries are found, they should be examined thoroughly to see if they are potentially life-threatening. If no obvious injuries are found, then a hands-on inspection of the patient's head should be conducted to check for structural integrity of the skull, facial bones, and jaw. See **Figure 15-12.** You should closely check the scalp for lacerations, bruising, or blunt trauma. Next, examine the ears, nose, and mouth for the presence of fluids and for any damage that may have occurred. During this inspection, try not to move your patient anymore than is absolutely necessary.

Next, conduct a neurological exam by verifying the level of consciousness of the patient.

Does the patient respond to a verbal stimulus? Does the patient respond to pain? What are the motor and sensory responses of the patient? Can the patient move his or her arms and legs?

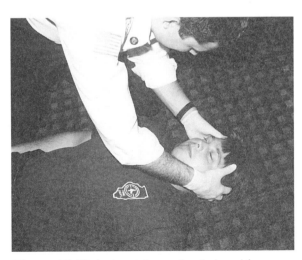

Figure 15-12. Inspect the patient's head for structural integrity of the skull and related structures. (Warren Lutton)

Does the patient feel your hands placed upon him or her? When you are called upon to describe the neurological state of the patient, do so as completely and specifically as possible. For example, "the patient responds to pain, but not to a verbal stimulus. The patient was unable to squeeze my hands when requested to do so." Do not simply say that the patient is "lethargic," or "unconscious," or "nonresponsive." These are not adequate descriptions of the patient's condition.

If you find a life-threatening injury at any time during the secondary survey, *immediately* take the necessary steps to stabilize that injury before continuing with the secondary survey.

Neck

The next part of the patient's anatomy to inspect is the neck, **Figure 15-13**. Look to see if the structure of the neck is intact. Is the Adam's apple midline and where you would expect it to be? Is there a deformity to the neck? Use your fingertips to feel for any deformity to the patient's cervical spine. (If you chose to place a cervical collar on the patient during the primary survey, you would have conducted this inspection at that time.) While inspecting the neck, you should

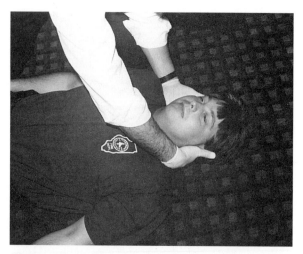

Figure 15-13. Examine the patient's neck for injury. Check for medallions or other jewelry bearing medical condition information. (Warren Lutton)

look to see if the patient is wearing a medallion or other jewelry warning of a medical condition. The presence or absence of any warning device should be noted.

Chest

After inspecting the patient's neck, move to the chest area and conduct a thorough inspection for injuries. Look at the chest to determine if there is any bruising, for instance, from a steering wheel. A crushed chest is considered life-threatening and should be dealt with immediately. You should also look carefully for penetrating injuries, such as gunshot wounds or stab wounds. These also will usually be considered life-threatening and would require immediate response. When you palpate the chest, you also should be looking for the possibility of any broken ribs or the lack of structural integrity of any of the normal structures of the chest.

When you inspect the patient's chest, you must loosen or remove any restrictive clothing. Keep in mind the patient's right to privacy; if at all possible, conduct the examination in either your ambulance or a secured area. To more easily inspect the chest, divide the large area into four smaller areas that are more manageable. As shown in **Figure 15-14**, the easiest way to make this division is to draw an imaginary vertical line down the center of the chest and an imaginary horizontal line across the nipple line. You should develop your own method of inspecting these areas, so you do not omit any of them. A suggestion would be to start in the upper right-hand quadrant, proceed to the lower right-hand quadrant, then to the lower left-hand quadrant, and finally, to the upper left-hand quadrant. It is important to devise a method that you are comfortable with and to use this method every time you do a survey of a patient.

Back and spine

Although you will often find it difficult to do a thorough examination of an uncon-

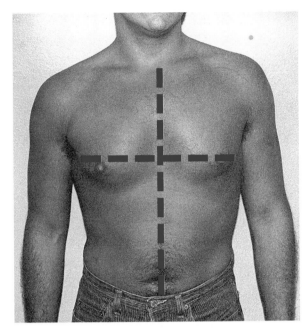

Figure 15-14. Use imaginary lines, as shown, to divide the patient's chest into four smaller areas for thorough inspection. The same type of division is done for inspection of the abdomen, with the horizontal line passing through the navel.

scious patient's back and spine, you must not omit this exam. Because of the possibility of further damage if there is spinal injury, you must move the patient as little as possible. By sliding your hand beneath the patient, **Figure 15-15**, you should be able to feel the patient's back and spine, while causing very little movement. Be sure to remind the patient that he or she should immediately make you aware of any pain your touch causes. As with the other parts of the anatomy, you are checking the back and spine for symmetry and structural integrity.

Abdomen

Examine the abdomen with care to be certain that you detect even injuries that are not immediately visible. During the palpation of the abdomen, the patient should be asked to indicate whether any action you take causes pain. Since the abdomen is a relatively large area, it should be broken down into four areas, just as you did the chest. Divide it vertically along the midline of the body and

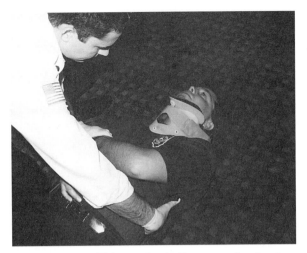

Figure 15-15. This method allows you to check the patient's spine with the least possible movement to prevent possible further injury. (Warren Lutton)

horizontally by drawing an imaginary line through the navel.

In a trauma situation, it is advisable to take a girth measurement of the abdomen after you complete the abdominal examination, **Figure 15-16**. Record the time of the measurement, so it can be used as a reference: an increase in girth over time indicates the possibility of internal bleeding. The key indicator of

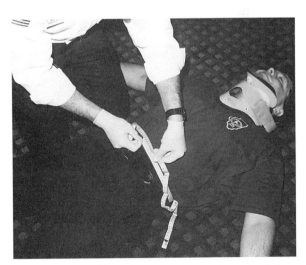

Figure 15-16. Use a tape measure to establish a benchmark for later measurements that would indicate internal bleeding was taking place. (Warren Lutton)

possible internal bleeding would be the fact that the abdomen was soft upon initial inspection but became rigid as time progressed.

Pelvic region

After checking the abdomen, inspect the pelvic region of the body for possible fractures. This can be done by placing your hands on the outside of the hips and making three movements: pushing inward, pushing up and down, and rocking the hips back and forth. See **Figure 15-17.** This three-way inspection of the hips will reveal any possible fracture in the pelvic region.

Extremities

Both legs and both arms should be inspected carefully for injury. When conscious, the patient should be asked to place his or her feet against the EMT or paramedic's hands, then push and pull as illustrated in **Figure 15-18.** The patient should also be requested to squeeze the EMT's hands with his or her hands to demonstrate that equal force can be exerted. See **Figure 15-19.**

At all times when doing a patient assessment, the EMT or paramedic should check for pulses and talk continuously to the patient. This will help to reassure the patient

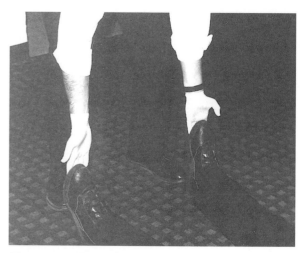

Figure 15-18. Check for foot and leg injuries by asking the patient to push against your hands, as shown. (Warren Lutton)

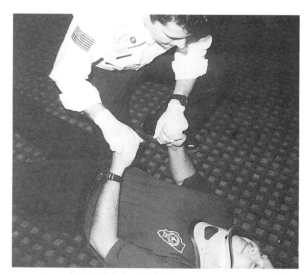

Figure 15-19. If the patient cannot squeeze your hands with equal force, the weakness is likely due to injury. (Warren Lutton)

and to gain as much information from the patient as possible.

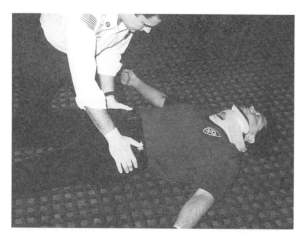

Figure 15-17. Possible fractures in the pelvic region can be detected by attempting movement of the patient's hips in various directions. (Warren Lutton)

Cardiopulmonary Resuscitation

Any time that a life-threatening injury is discovered, action must be taken immediately. When the primary survey indicates that there is no breathing and circulation has stopped, time is of the essence. Action must be taken within four to six minutes of the patient's heart stopping, or irreversible brain damage will result. To be prepared to handle such situations, all fire service personnel should be trained in *cardiopulmonary resuscitation* (CPR) techniques, as prescribed by the American Heart Association. When the heart has stopped, proper external chest massage and artificial respiration can give a patient the chance for full recovery.

When you first encounter an unconscious patient, you should establish whether or not the patient is *unresponsive*. This can be done by gently shaking the patient physically and shouting at him or her to see if there is a response. This "shake and shout" method should *not* be used if you suspect that the patient has head or neck injuries. If the patient proves to be unresponsive, your first priority will be to open that patient's airway. See **Figure 15-20.** Second, check to see if the patient is breathing. Third, check to see if the patient has a pulse and is therefore circulating blood.

If you determine that cardiopulmonary resuscitation is required, the only possible way that you can effectively help the patient

is to have been properly trained in CPR procedures. Since these procedures are quite detailed, attendance at a CPR class is highly recommended. Contact the nearest American Heart Association office or your local hospital for the location of CPR classes.

External Bleeding

You may, during your secondary survey of the patient, note the presence of external bleeding. If you do, you should realize that there are three possible sources, or *types*, of bleeding. In decreasing order of severity, they are: arterial bleeding, venous bleeding, and capillary bleeding.

Arterial bleeding is caused when one of the arteries in the patient's body is cut. An *artery* is one of the major vessels that carries blood from the heart to other parts of the body. Arterial bleeding is usually indicated by appearance: the blood is bright red and usually "spurts" from the wound due to the pumping action of the heart. Direct pressure should be applied to the wound to slow or stop the loss of blood.

The second type of bleeding that you may encounter is *venous bleeding*, which is caused when one of the veins in the patient's body has been cut. A *vein* is one of the blood vessels that carries blood from the system back to the patient's heart. Venous bleeding can be recognized because the blood is usually a darker red color than arterial blood. The darker color is the result of the oxygen having been taken from the blood by the body. The darker blood is being returned to the heart and lungs to be reoxygenated and sent back to the patient's system. The second means of recognizing venous bleeding is that venous bleeding typically does not spurt from the wound, as in the case of arterial bleeding. This is because the blood is returning to the heart and is not as strongly affected by the heart's pumping action.

The third type of bleeding that you may encounter is *capillary bleeding*. This bleeding

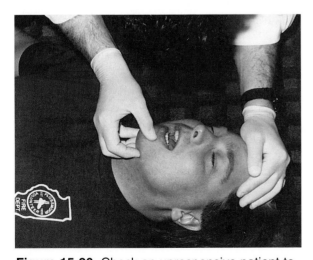

Figure 15-20. Check an unresponsive patient to be sure that he or she has a clear airway. If you have been trained to do so, begin administering CPR as necessary. (Warren Lutton)

results from tiny blood vessels near the surface of the skin (*capillaries*) being cut. It is in the capillaries that the nourishment and oxygen in the blood is transferred to the body. Capillaries are much smaller than either arteries or veins, so loss of blood from capillary bleeding is usually much less than from arterial or venous bleeding. Typical capillary bleeding results from scrapes and abrasions.

Controlling External Bleeding

The easiest and one of the most effective ways of controlling bleeding is to apply direct pressure to the wound, **Figure 15-21**. Bleeding can almost always be stopped by applying pressure directly over the wound. When applying pressure, a sterile dressing is preferred. However, if no sterile dressing is available, pressure can be applied with your hand. If bleeding continues after you have applied pressure directly to the wound, it may be necessary to locate a pressure point and apply pressure to that point in addition to the direct pressure.

Pressure points in the body are those where an artery crosses over a bony structure, **Figure 15-22**. By applying pressure to this

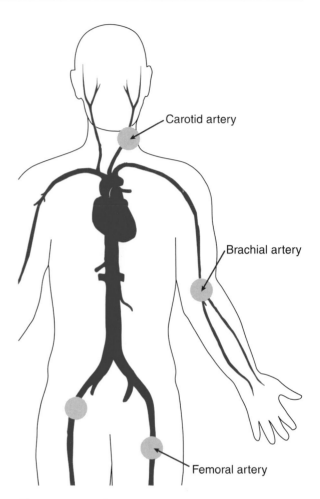

Figure 15-22. Pressure points are located where an artery crosses a bony structure. In addition to those shown here, there are pressure points in the armpits and in the knee area.

area, the artery is compressed against the bone to slow or stop the flow of blood through it. The effect is similar to stepping on a garden hose where it crosses a concrete sidewalk. The most readily accessible pressure points are located in the armpits, the interior of the elbow, the groin, and in the knee area. By applying pressure at these points, you will stop the flow of blood "downstream" (below the point where you are pressing). The combination of direct pressure over the wound and the use of the pressure points, should either stop or control most bleeding sufficiently to allow transporting the patient to a medical facility.

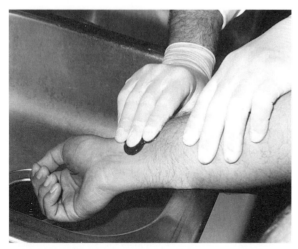

Figure 15-21. Bleeding is most easily controlled by direct pressure to the wound as shown. Sometimes, direct pressure is supplemented by use of a pressure point, such as the interior of the elbow. (Warren Lutton)

You should consider the use of a *tourniquet* in only the most extreme cases. Tourniquets are not recommended because pressure from the tightly wrapped material can cause damage to nerves and blood vessels. A tight tourniquet can cause complete stoppage of circulation in the limb; if maintained for too long a period, the lack of circulation could result in the loss of the arm or leg. A tourniquet should be considered a last resort, never the standard method of controlling bleeding.

Burns

Your skin is the largest organ in your body. It provides a covering that, along with the skeletal system, protects all of the vital organs of your body from potential injury. Your skin automatically acts to help protect you from the environment and allows your body the necessary time to adapt to that environment.

The skin has two major layers. The outermost layer is called the *epidermis*, **Figure 15-23.** The epidermis is sometimes referred to as the "wear layer" of the skin. It is the part of the skin that is constantly rubbing off and being replaced from below by other cells. The epidermis is watertight and is usually resistant to germs.

The second major layer of skin is called the dermis. The *dermis* is a deeper layer of skin located below the epidermis. It is within the dermis that sweat glands, oil glands, hair follicles, nerve endings, and blood vessels are located.

A *burn* is a type of injury that can permanently damage the skin. If severe enough, the burn can damage both the epidermis and dermis. There are four ways in which the skin can be damaged by a burn:

- heat burns.
- chemical burns.
- electrical burns.
- radiation burns.

The most common type of burn is the heat burn. The relative seriousness of any burn depends upon the *degree* of the burn (how deeply skin is damaged) and the amount of the body surface that has been affected. The larger the loss of protective skin

Figure 15-23. Structure of the human skin. The seriousness or "degree" of a burn is determined by how deeply the skin is damaged.

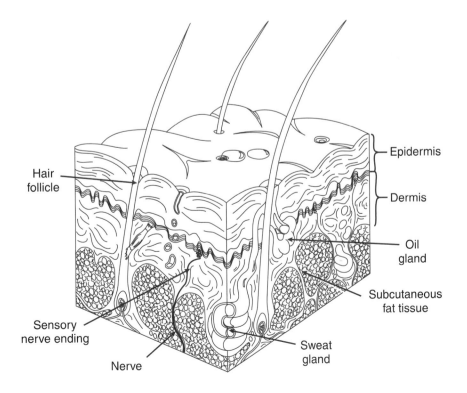

Hair follicle

Epidermis

Dermis

Oil gland

Subcutaneous fat tissue

Sensory nerve ending

Nerve

Sweat gland

covering, the greater the injury that will result from the burn. Severe burns can result in large fluid loss and extreme pain, which can cause the patient to go into shock. The severity of the burn is indicated by referring to it (in increasing order of severity) as first-degree, second-degree, or third-degree.

First-Degree Burns

First-degree burns affect only the outermost areas of the epidermis. They are characterized by a reddening of the skin area, and often by swelling. First-degree burns result from minor exposure to relatively low temperatures. Typical first-degree burns are those that result from sunburn, momentarily touching a hot pan, or touching the tip of a match immediately after it has been blown out.

Second-Degree Burns

Second-degree burns involve deeper damage to the skin than first-degree burns. In a second-degree burn, damage to the dermis layer is beginning to take place. Second-degree burns are usually characterized by a considerable amount of pain, a deep reddening and the presence of blisters. The skin area may also swell. Because of the deeper damage to the skin, second-degree burns are more serious than first-degree burns.

Third-Degree Burns

Third-degree burns, usually referred to as "full thickness burns," are the most serious degree of burns. With a third-degree burn, the entire skin has been damaged: both the dermis and epidermis have been burned. Skin that has suffered a third-degree burn often will appear to be dry, white, or pale; however, it may also be brown or even heavily charred. Third-degree burns are characterized by the loss of pain sensations, since nerve endings in the dermis have been burned away.

Extent of Burns

The depth of the burn will determine whether it is first-degree, second-degree, or third-degree. However, in order to properly determine severity, you should also estimate the amount of the body surface that has been burned. A general reference guide to determining the amount of body surface that has been burned is often referred to as the "rule of nines." See **Figure 15-24**. The *rule of nines* divides the body into areas, with a percentage of the body surface area assigned to each. By using the rule of nines, you can determine the extent of burns in terms of body surface area.

To properly determine burn severity, you must factor in the degree (first, second, third) of the burn, location and extent of the burns, and the age of the patient. You will then be able to classify the burn as minor, moderate, or critical. These classifications of burn injuries are important in determining the proper treatment to use.

Minor burns

Minor burns are usually considered to be first-degree burns that cover less than 20 percent of the body surface. Second-degree burns that cover less than 15 percent of the body surface also may be considered as minor burns. In some cases, even a third-degree burn (if it covers less than 2 percent of the body area) can be considered a minor burn. NOTE: Burns to the hands, feet, or face (even first-degree burns) should *not* be considered minor burns.

Moderate burns

Moderate burns require prompt medical attention. When first-degree burns cover more than 50 percent of the body surface, they should be classified as moderate burns. Any second-degree burn that covers 15 percent or more of the body surface should also be considered a moderate burn. Third-degree burns covering between 3 and 10 percent of the body surface should be considered moderate burns. If the third-degree burns are to

Figure 15-24. The "rule of nines" can be used to determine the percentage of body surface affected by a burn. The numbers represent percentages of the entire body surface. For example, on an adult, the torso represents approximately 36 percent, or one-third, of the total body area. Note that proportions are different for infants and small children.

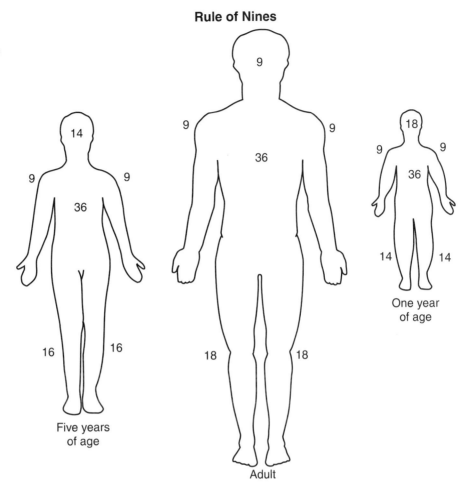

Rule of Nines

Five years of age

Adult

One year of age

the face, hands, genitals, or feet, they should be considered critical.

Critical burns

A *critical burn* is any second-degree burn that involves more than 30 percent of the body area, or any third-degree burn that covers more than 10 percent of the body area. Remember that third-degree burns involving the face, hands, feet, or genitals — regardless of extent — should be classified as critical. Third-degree burns involving the hands and feet are classified as critical due to the potential for loss of function because of damage to tendons and ligaments. Third-degree burns to the face are considered to be critical due to the potential damage to the respiratory tract.

Any burn involving the respiratory tract should *always* be considered critical.

Treatment of Burns

The treatment of heat (thermal) burns will depend upon the severity of the burn and the percentage of the body surface that has been involved. You should be aware that burns can be deceptive — they may appear at first to be less serious than they actually are. First-degree burns and most second-degree burns should be treated by the continuous application of cold water for at least five minutes. The application of grease, butter, or petroleum jelly is not recommended for burn treatment. Cover the burn with a sterile, moist dressing and continue cold applications for the relief of pain. Transport the patient to a medical facility as soon as possible for continued evaluation and treatment.

Treatment for extensive first- and second-degree burns and for any third-degree burns should begin with providing support for the respiratory system. Assuming that the respiratory system is properly cared for, cover the burns with sterile dressings and apply cold water for the reduction or relief of pain. Monitor the patient constantly for signs and symptoms of shock. If symptoms of shock develop, immediately begin treatment. These patients should be transported immediately to a proper medical facility for continued care.

CAUTION: If the burn covers a large surface area, the application of cold water may cause shivering and hypothermia.

Chemical burns

When you are faced with a chemical burn, your first priority should be to identify the agent that caused the burn. Once the agent has been identified as one that will not react with water, immediately begin to flush the burn area with large amounts of water. Remove the patient's clothing from the affected area, being careful to avoid direct contact with any chemical that may have been absorbed by the fabric. Continue flushing the burned area with water and transport the patient to a medical facility as soon as possible for continued treatment. NOTE: A burn caused by *lime* requires special precautions: since water can aggravate lime burns, it should not be used unless *large quantities* are available for flushing the affected area. If a large amount of water is not available with a lime burn, attempt to brush as much of the lime off the patient as is possible without exposing yourself. Remove any clothing covering the affected area, cover lightly with a sterile dressing, and transport the patient to a medical facility.

Electrical burns

Before you can begin to treat a patient with an electrical burn, you must first locate and remove the source of the burn. Whenever you treat a patient who has been burned by electrical energy, first check to be certain that he or she is breathing and has a good pulse (an electric shock can stop the heart). In most cases, electricity will cause both an entrance burn and an exit burn. Attempt to locate both these burns. Treat them as you would thermal burns. Immediately transport the patient to a proper medical facility.

Radiation burns

As with electrical burns, your first priority in dealing with burns caused by nuclear radiation is to locate the source and take necessary measures to protect yourself from exposure to the radiation. Transport the patient to an appropriate medical facility as quickly as possible.

Injuries to the Skeletal System

The human skeleton consists of more than 200 bones, **Figure 15-25.** These bones give the body form and provide protection for vital organs of the body. Injuries involving broken bones (called *fractures*) are commonly encountered by emergency service personnel.

Classification of Fractures

When a bone is fractured and skin has *not* been broken, the injury is referred to as a closed or **simple fracture**. When a bone is fractured and protrudes through the skin, the injury is called an open or **compound fracture**. Compound fractures are more serious than simple fractures due to the risk of infection from the open wound. In addition to being either simple or compound in nature, a fracture is classified by the *way* that the bone is broken. See **Figure 15-26.**

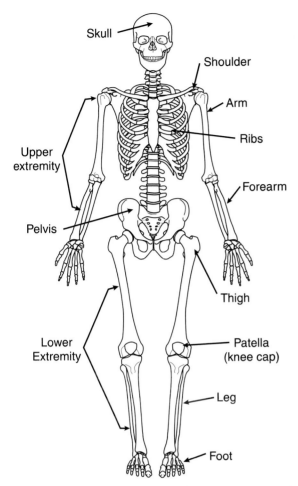

Figure 15-25. The human skeleton supports and gives form to the body. It is comprised of more than 200 bones.

Greenstick fracture

The *greenstick fracture* is characterized by an incomplete breaking of the bone. This type of fracture is most often encountered in children, whose bones have not yet become brittle.

Spiral fracture

The *spiral fracture* is characterized by a twisting type of break line. This type of fracture can occur when one part of the bone is held stationary, while the other portion of the bone is subjected to a twisting force.

Impacted fracture

An *impacted fracture* is characterized by many fine incomplete fracture lines at the point of injury. The bone is greatly weakened. This type of break results from the ends of the bones being forced together.

Oblique fracture

The *oblique fracture* is characterized by a break line angling through the bone. It differs from the spiral break since the break line is diagonally across the bone, rather than spiraling around it.

Comminuted fracture

The *comminuted fracture* is characterized by the bone being broken in more than

Types of Fractures

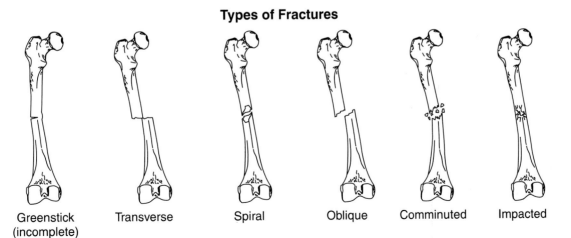

Greenstick (incomplete)   Transverse   Spiral   Oblique   Comminuted   Impacted

Figure 15-26. Bones can fracture in a number of different ways. The types of fractures shown are the common ones.

two pieces. As shown in **Figure 15-26**, the bone can have many small breaks.

In examining a patient with a fracture, you may note several common signs and symptoms that indicate the possibility of a broken bone. In some cases, the patient will tell you that he or she "felt it snap." There may be swelling and bruising present at the fracture site. Deformity, angulation, or shortening of the limb may be present. During your secondary survey, the patient may complain of tenderness and pain in the area of the fracture. Often, you will hear a grating sound when you gently palpate or manipulate the bone. As a result of pain, the patient often will "guard" the area in an attempt to keep you from moving it. Finally, in the case of a compound (open) fracture, you may be able to see the portions of the bone extending through the skin.

CAUTION: Always be sure to check for distal pulses.

Splinting

The main reason for splinting a possible fracture is to prevent further injury while the patient is transported to a medical facility. See **Figure 15-27**. Also, splinting will help prevent a closed fracture from becoming an open fracture by not allowing the ends of the bone to move around and cut through the skin. If not immobilized with a splint, the broken ends of a bone may cause damage to muscles, blood vessels, or nerves, and can even restrict the flow of blood by pinching off a blood vessel. Immobilizing the affected area will prevent further damage. Additionally, it should be remembered that through proper immobilization of the affected area, you can greatly reduce the amount of pain that the patient will feel during transportation to the medical facility.

General splinting considerations

Whenever you have a patient with a possible fracture, make every effort to apply a

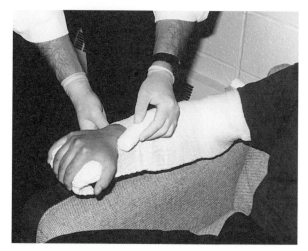

Figure 15-27. A splint is used to reduce mobility of an injured extremity. The arms are referred to as "upper extremities," and the legs as "lower extremities." By preventing movement, the splint reduces the chance of further injury while the patient is being transported to a medical facility. (Warren Lutton)

splint before moving him or her. Proper splinting and immobilization before transporting the patient to the hospital will reduce both the amount of pain and potential for further injury. In most cases, fractures that have severely deformed an arm or leg should immediately be splinted. You should immobilize the limb in the exact position that you found it. The patient often will have, prior to your arrival, found a "neutral position" for the injured area. This *neutral position* is the one that causes the patient the least pain, and thus can best be tolerated. Try to immobilize fractures in the neutral position chosen by the patient. After applying a splint be sure to check distal pulses to make certain you have not interrupted circulation.

Shock

In many accident or fire situations, victims will "go into shock" as a result of their injuries. *Shock* is a general term for a condition in which the body's cardiovascular system breaks down and fails to provide sufficient blood circulation to the body. The cardiovascular system is that portion of the body which delivers adequate blood supply to all parts of the body in order to provide them with oxygen and food. To sustain life, vital organs such as the brain, heart, and kidneys must be nourished by a constant supply of blood. These vital organs simply cannot survive without this continuous flow of blood to them. When a person suffers from shock, the vital functions of the body will begin to slow down. In situations where the underlying cause for the shock is severe, death can result.

Types of Shock

To better understand how shock affects the patient's body, you must be familiar with the various types of shock. These types of shock include:

Hemorrhagic shock

The loss of blood, whether inside or outside the body, causes *hemorrhagic shock*. As the amount of blood in the system decreases, the ability of the heart to provide an adequate supply of blood to the vital organs at an acceptable pressure is reduced. If blood loss is extensive, the severity of the hemorrhagic shock will increase.

Respiratory shock

The inability of the patient to breathe adequate amounts of oxygen results in *respiratory shock*, usually referred to as "respiratory failure." In many cases, this can be caused by injuries or obstructions to the respiratory system. As the amount of oxygen available to the vital organs decreases, the severity of the respiratory shock will increase.

Cardiogenic shock

Cardiogenic shock results from the inability of the heart itself to pump adequate blood to vital organs of the body. Cardiogenic shock can be caused by trauma to the heart muscle itself or by damage to the heart muscle as a result of cardiac problems. Regardless of the cause, the result is the same. The heart as a pump can no longer effectively function.

Anaphylactic shock

The inability of the human body to tolerate a particular substance causes *anaphylactic shock*. Substances that "trigger" anaphylactic shock may be encountered by ingesting foods or medicines, through injections, or through insect stings. If the allergic reaction of the body is severe, anaphylactic shock will increase. In some cases, it becomes fatal.

Neurogenic shock

Neurogenic shock is caused by inability of the central nervous system to convey messages to various parts of the body. The most common cause of neurogenic shock is an injury to the spine. In neurogenic shock, the blood vessels will dilate and more blood than usual is required to fill the cardiovascular system. If the dilation process is severe enough, there simply will not be enough blood within the system to provide adequate blood flow to the organs.

Psychogenic shock

Often referred to as fainting, *psychogenic shock* is the immediate reaction of the nervous system to a temporary reduction of the blood supply to the vital organs. The reduced blood supply is caused by sudden dilation of the blood vessels within the brain. This interrupts the blood flow to the brain, resulting in loss of consciousness.

Septic shock

The existence of extreme amount of poisons or bacteria within the cardiovascular system causes *septic shock*. Development of septic shock is much less sudden than the other types of shock described in this section. It typically results during the course of a long period of hospitalization for serious injuries or surgery.

Metabolic shock

Metabolic shock results from prolonged periods of fluid loss due to vomiting, diarrhea, or urination. These continued fluid losses, when untreated, will cause a metabolic imbalance within the system.

Treatment of Shock

The primary concern in the treatment of shock, no matter which type of shock is involved, is identifying the underlying cause of the problem. For example, the underlying cause in hemorrhagic shock is loss of blood; the underlying cause in anaphylactic shock is an allergic reaction. By identifying the underlying cause, you will be able to determine the proper treatment to reduce the effects of shock. The basic procedure for treating shock is to place the patient in a supine position and elevate his or her legs to help increase the blood flow to the vital organs. See **Figure 15-28.** Every effort should be made to maintain the patient's body heat, as well. Take the time to calm and reassure the patient, and transport him or her to a proper medical facility as soon as possible.

In areas where advanced life support procedures are available, intravenous therapy should be initiated by paramedics as soon as possible. Through the administration of intravenous solutions, additional fluids will be infused into the cardiovascular system and help to provide more volume within the system. Different types of intravenous solutions will be used, determined by the type of shock that is involved. The decision of the type of solution to be used should be made by your project medical director.

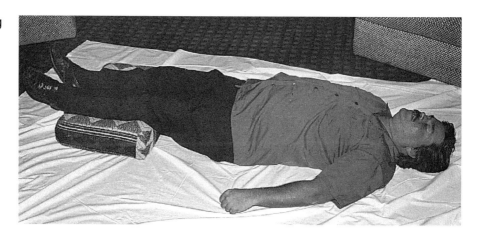

Figure 15-28. Elevating the patient's legs to maintain blood flow to vital organs is a basic step in treating shock. (Warren Lutton)

SUMMARY

Firefighting personnel, whether or not they are trained as emergency medical technicians or paramedics, will frequently encounter emergency situations. Many of these emergency situations will involve illness or injury to citizens or other firefighters. To be prepared to deal with these emergencies, you should make the effort to train yourself in the proper handling of such situations. All fire service personnel should be trained in CPR procedures and in basic first aid for such problems as bleeding, fractures, burns, and shock. The key to proper handling of emergency medical situations is to recognize the severity of the situation, understand your limitations, and (based upon your abilities), provide treatment, and transport the patient to the nearest medical facility for continued care.

REVIEW QUESTIONS

1. As emergency medical services were developed in the 1960s and 1970s, why did fire departments become the logical choice as service provider?

2. In an emergency medical service situation involving an accident, why is it important to be aware of the environmental factors involved?

3. Why can your assessment of the patient in the field be compared to the foundation of a house?

4. What are the three conditions you must establish in your primary survey of the patient?

5. What factors would lead you to place a cervical collar on the patient during your primary survey?

6. Describe how you would use your senses in conducting a secondary survey of a patient.

7. What are the measurements usually referred to as the "vital signs?"

8. Describe the method recommended for thoroughly examining the chest and abdomen of a patient.

9. In a trauma situation, why is it advisable to make a girth measurement of the abdomen and record it along with the time it was made?

10. When a patient's heartbeat or breathing have stopped, how quickly must CPR be administered to avoid irreversible brain damage?

11. What are the signs that distinguish venous bleeding from arterial bleeding?

12. If direct pressure is not sufficient to stop bleeding, what can you do? Why should a tourniquet be avoided whenever possible?

13. What is the name of the skin layer that is sometimes referred to as the "wear layer?"

14. Name the four ways in which the skin can be damaged by a burn.

15. Which is more serious, a first-degree burn or a third-degree burn? Why?

16. Why are burns to the hands, face, genitals, or feet never considered to be "minor" burns?

17. What must you do before beginning treatment of a patient with chemical, electrical, or radiation burns?

18. Describe the difference between a simple fracture and a compound fracture.

19. What is the purpose of applying a splint when a patient has suffered a fracture?

20. Describe the basic procedure for treating shock.

NFPA 1001 Job Performance Requirements

The material on this page consists of those portions of the NFPA 1001 Job Performance Requirements relevant to the material presented in this chapter. Items preceded by the numeral 3 (3-x.x) are Fire Fighter I requirements; those with the numeral 4 (4-x.x) are Fire Fighter II requirements.

(3-3.10)

(b) Prerequisite Skills: The ability to transport and operate ventilation tools and equipment and ladders and to use safe procedures for breaking window and door glass and removing obstructions.

3-3.13 Conserve property as a member of a team, given salvage tools and equipment and an assignment, so that the building and its contents are protected from further damage.

(a) Prerequisite Knowledge: The purpose of property conservation and its value to the public, methods used to protect property, types of and uses for salvage covers, operation at properties protected with automatic sprinklers, how to stop the flow of water from an automatic sprinkler head, identification of the main control valve on an automatic sprinkler system, and forcible entry issues related to salvage.

(b) Prerequisite Skills: The ability to cluster furniture; deploy covering materials; roll and fold salvage covers for reuse; construct water chutes and catch-alls; remove water; cover building openings, including doors, windows, floor openings, and roof openings; separate, remove, and relocate charred material to a safe location while protecting the area of origin for cause determination; stop the flow of water from a sprinkler with sprinkler wedges or stoppers; and operate a main control valve on an automatic sprinkler system.

3-5.3 Clean and check ladders, ventilation equipment, self-contained breathing apparatus (SCBA), ropes, salvage equipment, and hand tools, given cleaning tools, cleaning supplies, and an assignment, so that equipment is clean and maintained according to manufacturer's or departmental guidelines, maintenance is recorded, and equipment is placed in a ready state or reported otherwise.

(a) Prerequisite Knowledge: Types of cleaning methods for various tools and equipment, correct use of cleaning solvents, and manufacturer's or departmental guidelines for cleaning equipment and tools.

(b) Prerequisite Skills: The ability to select correct tools for various parts and pieces of equipment, follow guidelines, and complete recording and reporting procedures.

Reprinted with permission from NFPA 1001, *Fire Fighter Professional Qualifications,* Copyright ©1997, National Fire Protection Association, Quincy, MA 02269. This reprinted material is not the complete and official position of the National Fire Protection Association on the referenced subject, which is represented only by the standard in its entirety.

Salvage

OBJECTIVES

When you have completed this chapter, you will be able to:

- Discuss the purpose of salvage and its value to the public and the fire department.
- Identify and describe the uses of the common items of salvage equipment.
- Describe salvage cover folds and rolls.
- Demonstrate salvage cover throws and spreads.
- Describe the construction of water chutes and catchalls for the removal of water and debris.
- Discuss methods of closing openings made during firefighting operations.

IMPORTANT TERMS

accordion fold	chute	one-person roll	salvage cover
balloon throw	grommets	one-person throw	soil pipe
blocking	grouping	public relations value	two-person fold
building paper	kits	routing	two-person throw
catchall	one-person fold	salvage	

It was a nasty, hot fire. The partitions had no fire stops, so the flames went straight to the attic from the origin point in the cellar. All four floors were damaged extensively. It happened early on a Christmas morning, and the last of the firefighters didn't leave until the middle of the afternoon.

Later, when the homeowner was permitted in, he was amazed at what the firefighters had done. They had protected the turkey by putting it in the oven (it was the coolest place in the house, they said). The Christmas presents had been removed to the protection of one of the fire trucks. Everything movable had been taken to the front of the house, which was not involved in the fire. Large quantities of plaster and lath pulled down to get at the fire inside the walls had been shoveled into the back yard. To prevent further damage by the elements, building paper had been nailed across the roof and down the rear wall.

The homeowner, himself a former firefighter, was lavish in his praise of the fire department. When interviewed by the local newspaper, he expressed amazement that there was so little water or smoke damage to the *contents* of the house: nearly all the damage was caused by the fire itself. In an editorial, the newspaper praised the fire department.

About two months later, when the family was once again in its home, one of the firefighters paid a visit. He just wanted to thank them, he said, for the nice things they said about the department. He had spent most of Christmas saving their home and he was thanking *them!*

This true story demonstrates the **public relations value** of good salvage practices. All fire departments, whether volunteer or paid, need the support of their communities. They get that support by earning it, as did the fire department mentioned in this story. (The homeowner, by the way, is one of the authors of this book. The firefighters who did such a superb salvage job were members of the Montvale, NJ, Volunteer Fire Department.)

The Importance of Salvage

Have you ever heard anyone complain that "the firemen did more damage than the fire"? Of course you have. Is the statement ever justified? Think about it.

The firefighter has a lot of jobs. And he or she has to do them all well. But the three most important of these, ranked in order of importance, are:

1. Saving lives.
2. Extinguishing or containing fires.
3. Protecting and salvaging property.

Common sense tells you that these priorities are in the right order. But while you *must* concentrate most of your efforts on the first two, you cannot ignore **salvage** (protecting building and contents from unnecessary damage). Once the fire is out, this is one of the things that the public notices. The building owner or occupant is a member of that public. He or she will be very vocal about the job you did.

In addition to saving valuable property for its own sake, you must consider salvage as public relations. During a time of increasing costs and decreasing tax revenues in many cities, good public relations become an important tool for the fire department.

The salvage aspect of the firefighter's job has become increasingly important. As you are carrying out fire extinguishment and search and rescue activities, you must be considering salvage possibilities, as well. At times, the circumstances may dictate that the fireground commander shift the concentration of effort from firefighting to the salvage of valuables.

Causes of Damage

Damage to the contents of a building can come from at least five sources: fire, heat, smoke, water, building collapse.

- *Fire:* The charred remains of furniture and bits and pieces of other building contents that remain after a room has been involved in fire are familiar to every firefighter. See **Figure 16-1.**

- *Heat:* Blisters paint and varnish, and melts glass, plastics, and even metal. Heat damage may occur some distance from the fire itself.

- *Smoke:* Sometimes it seems that smoke can penetrate and discolor anything: clothing, draperies, even pottery. The discoloration and smell can be difficult, if not impossible, to get rid of. Like heat damage, smoke damage is often remote from the fire.

- *Water:* The damage that water can do ranges from staining floors, loosening paint and plaster and discoloring fabrics, to collapsing a floor because of its weight. The judicious use and removal of water in fighting fires can be a kind of salvage operation in itself.

- *Building collapse:* This may be brought about by the weight of the water applied in firefighting, as noted above, or by the weakening of structural members by the fire itself. Collapse of a building can result in the total destruction of the building and its contents.

Salvage begins with the extinguishment of the fire and the proper ventilation to remove

Figure 16-1. Actual fire damage such as this is only part of the damage done when a building burns. Heat, smoke, and water can also cause extensive damage; building collapse may result in a total loss. (Williamsport Bureau of Fire)

or reduce heat and smoke. It can also involve the application of water fog (as opposed to a solid stream) to reduce the amount and weight of water needed to cool the burning material and force the smoke from the area.

Salvage may involve simply moving the contents to a safe part of the room, away from the fire and areas to which it might spread. Also, contents must be protected from damage by water. Keep valuables away from stairways and ceiling light fixtures, since water being applied to an upper floor tends to pour down both enroute to a lower level. If fire is burning underneath a room, the contents (especially heavy pieces) should be moved away from the immediate area to prevent smoke and heat damage. Another reason for moving heavy pieces is that their weight might cause a weakened floor to collapse.

Salvage Equipment

In some departments, salvage equipment is assembled into *kits* for specific applications. A roof repair kit, for example, might contain a roofer's hatchet, a linoleum knife,

nails, building paper, and other necessary items. See **Figure 16-2.**

The use of kits has both advantages and disadvantages. On the one hand, if you have to close up a hole in a roof, it's nice to have everything you need in one place. On the other hand, if someone needs a hatchet, and the only one he can think of is in the roof repair kit, guess what happens?

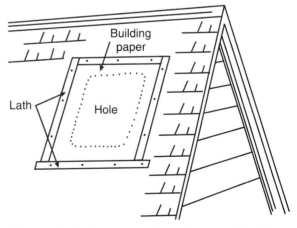

Figure 16-2. Some departments assemble kits of tools and materials for specific applications, such as this temporary roof repair intended to prevent further damage from rain or snow.

Some of the more common items of salvage equipment and their uses include:

- Basket: carry small, loose articles and debris.
- Broom: sweeping plaster, ashes, and water.
- *Building paper* (also called tar paper): temporary patching of openings in walls or roofs.
- Electric cable on reel: providing power for smoke ejectors, lights, pumps, and other electrical devices.
- Hammer: driving nails to put building paper over holes in walls and roofs, securing doors and windows, constructing water chutes, braces, and other needed items.
- Hard sleeve: pumping water out of basements.
- Hatchet: trimming during roof repair.
- Nails: fastening building paper in place to cover openings.
- Pike pole: making water chutes, serving as a prop.
- Plastic sheeting: covering openings in walls or roofs (same uses as building paper).
- Portable light: supplying light for search and rescue, salvage, or any operation where a battery-powered light is needed.
- Portable pump: removing water from cellars.
- *Salvage cover:* covering household contents or merchandise in a store to protect against smoke and water damage. Also, serving as a water chute, catchall, carrier, or temporary means of closing roofs and walls. The salvage cover, **Figure 16-3**, is the basic salvage tool.
- Shovel: removing dirt, debris, and sometimes, water.
- Smoke ejector: removing smoke to reduce chance of backdraft explosion, prevent smoke damage, and clear the air for visibility.

Figure 16-3. The basic salvage tool is the salvage cover made from either natural (cotton canvas) or synthetic (vinyl or nylon) materials. To be available and effective when needed, covers must be carefully cleaned after use and repaired as necessary. (Globe)

- Squeegee: removing small amounts of water from floors, walls, or other large flat surfaces.
- Staple gun: tacking down plastic sheeting or building paper.
- Wet vac: removing small amounts of water from floors.

Salvage Cover Rolls and Folds

A salvage cover can be rolled or folded in a number of different ways to permit easy use by one or two firefighters. For consistency and ease of use, the same roll of fold should always be employed. Four of the more common rolls and folds are described in the following paragraphs.

One-person roll

"One-person" in the name *one-person roll* refers to the number of firefighters it takes to put the salvage cover into use. It takes *two* firefighters to roll it, following the steps shown in the diagram, **Figure 16-4**:

1. Two firefighters stand, facing each other, at the points marked "A" and "B." They spread the salvage cover smoothly on the floor, making sure all folds and ripples are out of it. See **Figure 16-5**. Each

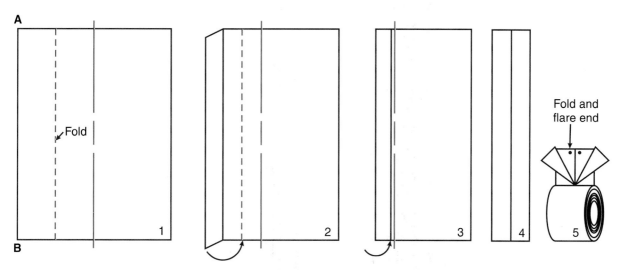

Figure 16-4. Steps needed to perform the one-person roll for a salvage cover.

Figure 16-5. Spreading the salvage cover prior to folding and rolling. (Warren Lutton)

Figure 16-6. Folding the cover to the center, then folding again. (Warren Lutton)

person takes hold of the cover with one hand halfway between the outside edge and the centerline. (Represented by the dotted line marked "fold" on the diagram). With the other hand, each person takes hold of the corner.

2. Working together, they bring the outside edge in to the middle. They pull it tight and smooth, eliminating wrinkles and air pockets, **Figure 16-6.**

3. With one hand, each person takes hold of the double thickness at the center and at the folded edge. Again, they fold to the center.

4. They then repeat steps 1, 2, and 3 with left-hand side of the cover, **Figure 16-7.** They smooth out the cover, making sure all edges are straight and square, as shown in **Figure 16-8.** Then, both firefighters move to one end of the cover, one on each side of the center, **Figure 16-9.** They begin to roll it up like a jelly roll, keeping the roll tight.

Figure 16-7. Repeating the folding steps with the other half of the salvage cover. (Warren Lutton)

Figure 16-9. Both firefighters move to the same end of the folded cover and begin to roll it tightly. (Warren Lutton)

Figure 16-8. The cover is smoothed and squared prior to rolling. (Warren Lutton)

Figure 16-10. The ends of the cover are flared out so they can be tucked in to hold the roll together. (Warren Lutton)

5. After rolling to about two feet from the end, they fold that end down toward the roll, making a flap about a foot long. As shown in **Figure 16-10**, they flare out the ends of the flap, then tuck the roll into the flap like a newspaper carrier folds a newspaper for delivery. If a cover is not used, it should be removed from the truck at least once a month, unrolled, inspected, and rerolled.

One-person fold

The *one-person fold* is not as easy to use as the one-person roll, but it is preferred by some departments.

1. Spread the cover on floor with seam side down, as shown in **Figure 16-11**. Two firefighters face each other, as in the one-person roll.
2. Place your inside hand one-fourth the distance from the outside edge to the center. Hold the cover down with this hand. With outside hand grasp a corner of cover and fold it over until the edge is halfway to the center.
3. Fold again, bringing the folded edge the same distance as in step 2.
4. Repeat step 3, bringing the folded edge to within three or four inches of the center.

Figure 16-11. Steps used to perform the one-person fold for a salvage cover.

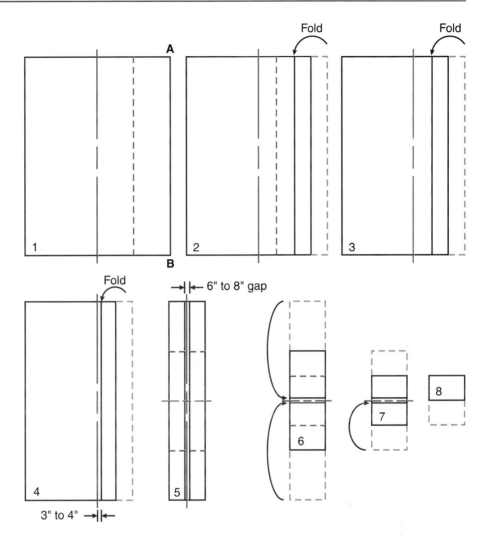

5. Move to the other side of cover and make the same two folds. There should be a gap of six to eight inches in the center.
6. Fold the top half of the cover to within three or four inches of center, then move to the opposite end and fold it the same way. There should be a gap of six to eight inches in the center.
7. Fold each half again, as above. Be sure to maintain gap of six to eight inches.
8. Fold cover again.

Accordion fold

The *accordion fold* allows use of ballooning or of the one-person or two-person throws. A cover folded this way is easy to carry.
1. Spread the cover flat on the floor, seam side down. Two firefighters kneel at posi-

tions "A" and "B." Fold the corners in about 10 in., as shown in **Figure 16-12.**
2. Place your outside hand, palm down, half the distance from the outside edge to the center. Hold the cover down with this hand. With your inside hand grasp the corner of cover and fold it over until the edge is two-to-three inches from the center.
3. Repeat step 2.
4. Move, with your partner, to the other end of the cover. Repeat steps 2 and 3. Leave a gap of four to six inches at the center.
5. Reposition yourself opposite your partner, as shown by "A" and "B" in the illustration. Place outside hand about one foot from the end of the cover. With your inside hand, grasp the folded cover about one foot closer to the center. Pull

Figure 16-12. Steps involved in accordion-folding a salvage cover.

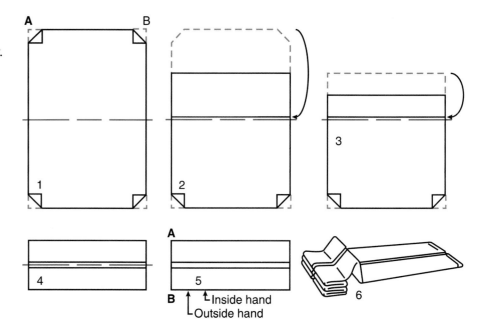

cover up with inside hand and fold it over the outside hand, aligning the fold with the end of the cover.

6. Repeat step 5 as many times as needed to completely fold cover.

Two-person fold

The *two-person fold* should be used only if two firefighters will be available to spread the cover.

1. Firefighters "A" and "B" position themselves along the long edge, as shown in **Figure 16-13.** Each picks up a corner and

moves to the opposite side, lining up the edges exactly.

2. Repeat step 1. The cover is now one-quarter its full width.

3. Firefighter "B" moves to a corner, beside Firefighter "A," as shown. Each takes a corner, folding the cover in half from top to bottom.

4. Fold again from bottom to top.

5. Make a final fold from top to bottom.

If the two-person fold is properly done, all four corners of the salvage cover will be together, close to the middle of the folded

Figure 16-13. Steps needed to perform the two-person fold for a salvage cover.

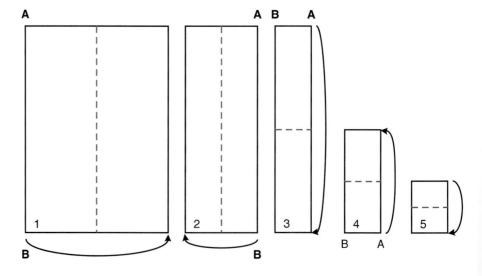

cover. If they are not, the cover will be difficult to spread.

Spreading the Salvage Cover

In a residential fire, one salvage cover can typically be used to protect the contents of an entire room. The key to this efficient salvage practice is proper *grouping* of the room contents.

Grouping room contents

Provided the building is structurally sound, you should move the contents toward the center of the room away from open stairways. Do not group contents under a ceiling light fixture, however, since water often drains from upper floors through such fixtures. First, position the largest pieces, such as beds, sofas, or large tables. Next, group chests of drawers, small bookcases, stereos, and similar items at the foot of the bed or sofa. Place small chairs and items like lamps or framed pictures on top of the sofa or bed. As you move each piece, slip the rug from underneath it. When all items are in place, roll up the rug and place it on top of the pile to serve as a ridge pole, **Figure 16-14.** The salvage cover will be spread over the pile, using one of the throws described in the succeeding sections.

The one-person throw

With a properly folded or rolled salvage cover, one firefighter can easily and efficiently cover a pile of furniture in a residence or grouped stock in a store. To perform the *one-person throw:*

1. Stand at one end of the pile to be covered and unroll enough of the cover to touch the floor. Then, unroll approximately another foot to tuck under the material being covered.
2. Place the roll on top of the pile and walk along the pile to the other end, unrolling as you go.
3. When the cover is completely unrolled, open it sufficiently to grasp one outside edge with each hand. Snap both hands up and out to spread the cover over entire pile of contents, **Figure 16-15.** Repeat for other end.

The balloon throw

The *balloon throw* requires two firefighters, but is the quickest method for quickly covering a lot of material. The trick is to get enough air under the salvage cover to float it over the material that you are covering. To perform the balloon throw:

1. Unroll the salvage cover. Two firefighters stand facing each other at opposite ends of material to be covered. Hold cover by the corners and stretch tight between you and your partner.
2. Drop the edge of cover that is closest to pile. Make several accordion folds in the salvage cover, as shown in **Figure 16-16.**

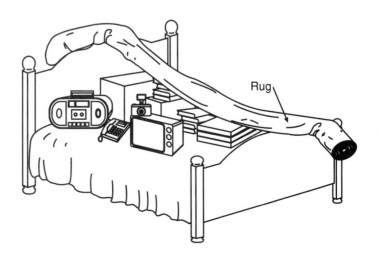

Figure 16-14. Careful grouping of room contents will usually make it possible to cover an entire roomful of furnishings with a single salvage cover. Note use of rolled rug to serve as a "ridge pole" under the salvage cover. This will cause water to run off, rather than puddling and soaking through the cover.

Rug

Figure 16-15. In the one-person throw, the cover is unrolled atop the pile of material to be protected, then "snapped" open from each end in turn.

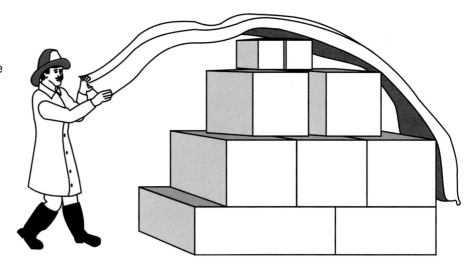

Figure 16-16. Two fire-fighters loosely accordion-fold the salvage cover in preparation for making a balloon throw.

3. Stretching cover tight between you, move the edge furthest from the pile down, away, then *up*. Make a smooth arc with the cover, trapping as much air as possible,
4. Continuing the arc motion and reaching as high as you can, float the cover over the material to be protected, **Figure 16-17.**
5. Straighten the cover and tuck it in around the material.

The two-person throw

The *two-person throw* is similar in some respects to the balloon throw, except that the salvage cover is only partially unfolded before being spread. To perform the two-person throw:

1. Open the folded cover to reveal the four corners. The person carrying the cover takes the two bottom corners. The other firefighter takes hold of the top two corners.
2. Back away from each other until the cover is stretched alongside the material to be covered. Proceed as in the balloon throw.

Care of Salvage Equipment

There is no time or place on the fire-ground to repair equipment. It must be ready

Figure 16-17. The firefighters arc the leading edge of the cover high over the pile, trapping air beneath the cover. This allows them to "float" the cover into place.

for use when you arrive on the fireground. In other words, it has to be ready *all the time.*

After each use, every piece of salvage equipment must be cleaned and inspected for damage. Wooden handles must be examined for cracks and splits, batteries checked for charge, and edges that are supposed to be sharp must be inspected for sharpness. Don't put anything back on the vehicle until you are sure it is in first-class condition.

Maintaining salvage covers

Since salvage covers are used for so many purposes, and because one cover may be used to protect several thousand dollars worth of household furnishings or merchandise, you should pay special attention to their condition.

Older salvage covers are made from natural fibers, usually a cotton canvas. The newer covers are made of vinyl, nylon, and other synthetic materials, **Figure 16-18.** These newer covers will not mildew. After a fire, however, they may be covered with ashes, dirt, acids, and other byproducts of fire. They will sometimes get holes punched in them. All salvage covers, regardless of the material used, must be washed, dried, inspected, and repaired as necessary for future use.

To clean a cover, spread it out on a clean concrete floor and wash it down using clear

Figure 16-18. Newer salvage covers are made of synthetic materials that will not rot or mildew. They still must be cleaned after use and carefully inspected for damage. Holes and tears should be repaired promptly and securely to prolong the useful life of the cover. (Ziamatic)

water and a broom. If the cover has become stained, it may be necessary to add detergent or soap powder to the wash water. If you do use soap or detergent, hang the cover by the *grommets* (metal-reinforced holes) and rinse it thoroughly to remove all traces. If left in the cloth of a cover made of natural material, soaps and detergents will destroy the cover's waterproof characteristics.

After washing, hang the cover indoors to dry, suspending it by the grommets. Do not fold the cover until it is thoroughly dry. Folding a damp cover made of natural materials will cause it to mildew.

After the cover has dried thoroughly, spread it out on a clean, dry floor for inspection. Three or four firefighters then line up, side-by-side, and raise the cover above their heads. They slowly pass the cover backward over their heads, looking for a ray of light that would indicate a hole. When a firefighter spots a hole, he or she calls out and presses the palm of one hand against the hole. A firefighter on the outside draws a circle around the hole with a chalk. After inspection is complete, patch all holes on both sides. Depending upon the material, the holes can be repaired with rubber cement and tire patches, or with a patching kit suggested by the manufacturer.

Minimizing Water Damage

Water can damage a building and its contents in a number of ways.

It will soak INTO and discolor some items. It encourages mildew and rotting. It will cause wooden floors to warp. It loosens the glue bonds in furniture, floor tiles, or wallpaper. In extreme cases, because of its weight, water can cause a building to weaken and collapse. For these reasons, you *must* control and eventually remove all water used in extinguishing a fire.

You control water, and minimize the damage it causes, in three ways:
- *Limiting water use.* Where applicable, use short bursts from a fog nozzle instead of a continuous flow from a solid stream nozzle. Use water only as needed to clear and cool the air, prevent the spread of fire, and extinguish fire. Any additional use causes unnecessary damage and creates more work for you.
- *Blocking and routing water.* By **blocking**, you prevent water from flowing

where it will cause unnecessary damage and present removal difficulties. See **Figure 16-19.** *Routing* directs the flow of water to where it will do the least damage and be easy to dispose of. Whenever large amounts of water must be used in containing and extinguishing a fire, you *must* block and route water to minimize damage.
- *Catching water.* Small amounts of water are less of a problem, and can be caught in a container. Often, you can catch the water that drips to a lower floor in a garbage can, a large plastic trash bag, a wash tub, or even a child's play pool. Salvage containers are manufactured for this purpose, but something you find in the fire structure might do just as well.

Handling Water on the Fire Scene

The floor plan of a typical second-floor one bedroom apartment is shown in **Figure 16-20.** The first-floor apartment, directly below it, has an identical layout. When you arrive on the scene, you find that the kitchen of the second floor apartment is fully involved but the fire hasn't spread. The apartment is expensively furnished, as are those beside and below it. Obviously, the potential

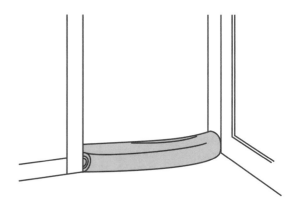

Figure 16-19. Salvage covers and other materials can be used to block the flow of water to minimize damage. Here, a rolled cover is being used to block a doorway.

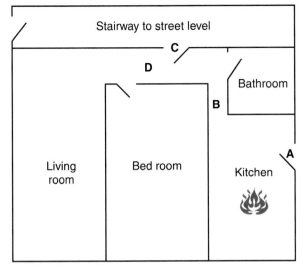

Figure 16-20. Floor plan for a typical one-bedroom apartment. This apartment is located on the second floor, and has a fire in the kitchen.

for water damage is as great as (and possibly even greater than) that of damage from fire or smoke.

If there is an outside door (as shown at A on the plan), the obvious thing to do is to block the flow of water at B. Once the fire is out, or at least well under control, you can simply open the outside door and let the accumulated water flow down the side of the building.

Even if there is no outside door, you still have several good choices. Block the flow of water at C (the apartment's front door) and D (the hallway). At C, all you must do is close the door and block the crack at the floor with a towel. With the hallway blocked as well, water can be routed into the bathroom for disposal. This can be accomplished by unbolting the toilet fixture from the floor and letting the water flow down the *soil pipe* (large drain). Place a strainer over the pipe to prevent debris from blocking it.

An equally effective way of minimizing water damage is to block the hallway at D, and also block the water from entering the bathroom. Open the apartment door and construct a *chute* to channel water down the stairway. This can be done simply by opening a salvage cover part-way and rolling up the sides to form the chute, **Figure 16-21.** You can run the chute down the stairway and out the street door. A refinement is to use a ladder or two pike poles, starting at the middle of the stairway, to make the chute more rigid and continue it out the door. This will improve

Figure 16-21. A salvage cover can easily be spread down a stairway to form a chute that will guide water to a cellar or outdoors.

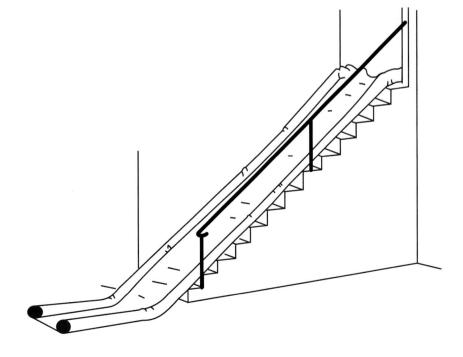

drainage and help prevent water from entering apartments on the first floor.

If none of the foregoing methods is practical, you may have to use one of the more destructive means of disposing of water. Essentially, they involve routing the water from the second floor to the first floor and then to the cellar. If a significant amount of water has already fallen to the first floor, adding more might cause the floor to collapse. In such a case, the first step is to cut a hole in the *first* floor, directly beneath the point where you plan to cut through the second floor. See **Figure 16-22.** Next, cut a hole in the first floor *ceiling,* directly above the hole in the floor. This is to prevent water from moving laterally across the ceiling, doing unnecessary damage. Finally, cut a hole through the flooring on the second floor, in line with those you cut below. *Caution:* Deciding on the hole location calls for some planning. You want to locate holes in a place where the water will accumulate (a low spot),

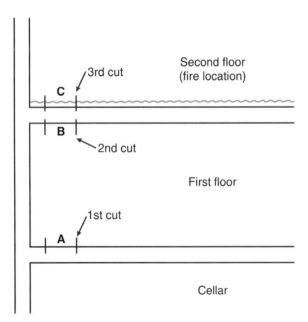

Figure 16-22. To drain water from the second floor to the cellar, cut drain holes in three steps. Cut the first-floor hole (A) first, then the hole through the ceiling of the first floor (B). Finally, cut through the flooring on the second floor (C).

but not where firefighters are likely to step in them and become injured.

When routing water from floor to floor, be sure that any valuables are moved out of the way or covered with a salvage cover.

Another way to remove large quantities of water is to cut a small hole in the outside wall at floor level and let the water drain down the side of the building. This method should not be used if one of the less destructive methods will work.

You might have to guide the water to make it go where you want it to go. A wide pushbroom, a squeegee, even a regular kitchen broom or a snow shovel will do the job. Where available, the squeegee is best because it will leave the floor quite dry. This means there will be a minimum amount of damage to linoleum, floor tiles, or wooden floors.

When water is routed down a bathroom soil pipe or a cellar drain, be sure to cover the pipe or drain with a strainer to keep it from becoming blocked by debris. A strainer designed for use with a suction hose will work well for this purpose.

An alternative to routing water into the cellar is to construct a water chute in the room under the fire floor and route the water out a window or a door. See **Figure 16-23.**

You can use a salvage cover to construct a *catchall* for removing water and debris. Simply roll up the four sides of the cover to form a shallow pool. If one end is left open, water and debris may be swept in, and then the end is rolled up for disposal. See **Figure 16-24.** When the catchall is full, at least four firefighters will be needed to carry it out and dispose of the contents.

Closing Up a Fire Structure

After the fire is extinguished, it will usually be necessary to close up all openings to protect against any additional damage to the structure from rain, snow, or wind. This applies to existing openings, such as doors or windows that have been broken or forced

Figure 16-23. Using a salvage cover to convey water from an upstairs room to a window on the lower floor. This avoids the need to cut through one floor (and to later pump water out of the cellar). Use a wall ladder to support the chute from the top of the stepladder to the window.

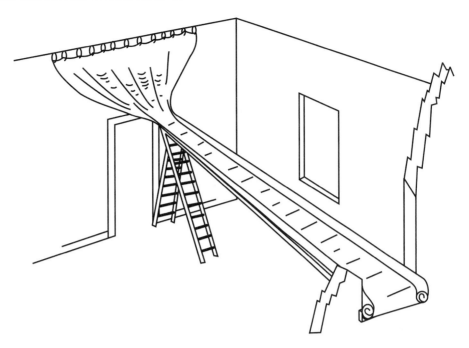

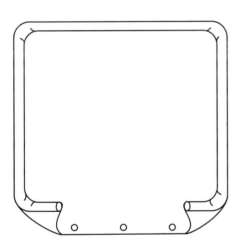

Figure 16-24. A catchall is formed by rolling up the sides of a salvage cover to hold water and debris. One side can be left open, as shown here, to sweep water, dirt, and debris onto the salvage cover. The cover can then be carried outside and emptied.

open, and to openings that have been made by the fire itself, or by efforts to gain access to the burning areas, or to ventilate the structure. Building paper or plastic sheeting can be fastened in place with a staple gun or hammer and nails. You can also close a large area with a salvage cover nailed through the grommets. On a roof (especially a flat roof),

you should place boards or bricks around the hole and fasten the plastic or tar paper over them to form a curb that will prevent water from puddling and leaking inside. See **Figure 16-25.** If you are covering a large hole with tar paper, you may have to overlap several sheets. An alternative is to use a salvage cover for a one-piece covering.

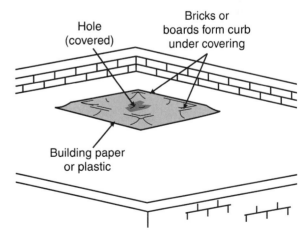

Figure 16-25. On a roof that is flat or has only a slight slope, construct a curb of bricks or scrap wood around a hole before covering it with building paper or plastic. This will help prevent rainwater or melted snow from entering the hole to cause further damage.

SUMMARY

The public relations aspect of salvage is important to the firefighter and to the department. A good salvage job is good public relations.

Salvage means protecting the contents of the building from fire, heat, smoke, water damage, and building collapse. This often involves moving contents to a safe place or covering them to protect against water and smoke damage.

The salvage cover is the basic piece of salvage equipment. Its uses are limited only by the imagination of the users. It can be folded or rolled in a number of ways, depending on whether one or more firefighters are to spread it. For ease of use, the same fold or roll, should always be used.

A single salvage cover is often used to cover a great quantity of building contents that have been grouped in a compact arrangement. Care must be taken to provide a tent-like configuration so that water will run off and not be trapped in pockets so that it can leak or soak through. Salvage covers should be carefully cleaned and repaired after each use.

Water damage can be held to a minimum by limiting the amount of water used, by blocking the flow to unaffected areas, by routing the water to where it can do little or no damage, or by catching small amounts of water. It can be routed down a toilet soil pipe, a drain, out a door or to the outdoors by use of a water chute.

When routing water by means of holes in the floor, be sure you first protect any valuables on the lower floors. Do not cut holes where firefighters are likely to step into them.

REVIEW QUESTIONS

1. In order of importance, what are the three job priorities of the firefighter?
2. Why is salvage important to the homeowner? To the fire department?
3. In protecting property through good salvage practices, what hazards are you protecting the property from?
4. List at least three ways of protecting property from damage or loss in a fire.
5. Name ten common tools or other items used in salvage operations.
6. State some advantages and disadvantages to using salvage kits.
7. Name three salvage cover rolls or folds. How many persons are required to spread each of them?
8. Describe the technique used in performing the balloon throw.
9. Why must a salvage cover be rinsed thoroughly after being washed with soap or a detergent?
10. Why must a salvage cover made from natural materials be dried thoroughly before it is folded?
11. What are the purposes for which water is used in a fire situation?
12. Describe the kinds of damage water can cause to a structure and its contents.
13. List the three basic means used to minimize water damage at a fire.
14. What is the advantage of blocking the flow of water?
15. State five methods used to route water.
16. List two ways to use a water chute.
17. What procedure should be used when routing water from floor to floor?
18. When routing water down a soil pipe or drain, what precaution should you take to avoid blocking the pipe or drain?
19. List as many ways as you can to remove water and debris from a structure without using fire department equipment.
20. Describe the materials and methods used to close outside holes in a structure.

Before the widespread adoption of dry-barrel models, firefighters in northern climates often had to thaw out frozen hydrants. This well-dressed trio of firefighters in Williamsport, Pennsylvania, is demonstrating the thawing technique, which involved igniting kerosene in the hydrant barrel to melt the ice. (Harold Anthony/Archive Photo)

NFPA 1001 Job Performance Requirements

The material on this page consists of those portions of the NFPA 1001 Job Performance Requirements relevant to the material presented in this chapter. Items preceded by the numeral 3 (3-x.x) are Fire Fighter I requirements; those with the numeral 4 (4-x.x) are Fire Fighter II requirements.

3-3.12 Overhaul a fire scene, given personal protective equipment, attack line, hand tools, a flashlight, and an assignment, so that structural integrity is not compromised, all hidden fires are discovered, fire cause evidence is preserved, and the fire is extinguished.

(a) Prerequisite Knowledge: Types of fire attack lines and water application devices most effective for overhaul, water application methods for extinguishment that limit water damage, types of tools and methods used to expose hidden fire, dangers associated with overhaul, obvious signs of area of origin or signs of arson, and reasons for protection of fire scene.

(b) Prerequisite Skills: The ability to deploy and operate an attack line; remove flooring, ceiling, and wall components to expose void spaces without compromising structural integrity; apply water for maximum effectiveness; expose and extinguish hidden fires in walls, ceilings, and subfloor spaces; recognize and preserve obvious signs of area of origin and arson; and evaluate for complete extinguishment.

3-3.13 Conserve property as a member of a team, given salvage tools and equipment and an assignment, so that the building and its contents are protected from further damage.

(a) Prerequisite Knowledge: The purpose of property conservation and its value to the public, methods used to protect property, types of and uses for salvage covers, operations at properties protected with automatic sprinklers, how to stop the flow of water from an automatic sprinkler head, identification of the main control valve on an automatic sprinkler system, and forcible entry issues related to salvage.

(b) Prerequisite Skills: The ability to cluster furniture; deploy covering materials; roll and fold salvage covers

for reuse; construct water chutes and catch-alls; remove water; cover building openings, including doors, windows, floor openings, and roof openings; separate, remove, and relocate charred material to a safe location while protecting the area of origin for cause determination; stop the flow of water from a sprinkler with sprinkler wedges or stoppers; and operate a main control valve on an automatic sprinkler system.

(4-3.2)

(a) Prerequisite Knowledge: Selection of the proper nozzle and hose for fire attack given different fire situations; selection of adapters and appliances to be used for specific fire ground situations; dangerous building conditions created by fire and fire suppression activities; indicators of building collapse; the effects of fire and fire suppression activities on wood, masonry (brick, block, stone), cast iron, steel, reinforced concrete, gypsum wall board, glass, and plaster on lath; search and rescue and ventilation procedures; indicators of structural instability; suppression approaches and practices for various types of structural fires; and the association between specific tools and special forcible entry needs.

4-3.4 Protect evidence of fire cause and origin, given a flashlight and overhaul tools, so that the evidence is properly noted and protected from further disturbance until investigators can arrive on the scene.

(a) Prerequisite Knowledge: Methods to assess origin and cause; types of evidence; means to protect various types of evidence; the role and relationship of Fire Fighter IIs, criminal investigators, and insurance investigators in fire investigations; and the effects and problems associated with removing property or evidence from the scene.

(b) Prerequisite Skills: The ability to locate the fire's origin area, recognize possible causes, and protect the evidence.

Reprinted with permission from NFPA 1001, *Fire Fighter Professional Qualifications,* Copyright ©1997, National Fire Protection Association, Quincy, MA 02269. This reprinted material is not the complete and official position of the National Fire Protection Association on the referenced subject, which is represented only by the standard in its entirety.

Overhaul

OBJECTIVES

When you have completed this chapter, you will be able to:

- Identify the elements involved in planning for overhaul operations.
- Discuss dangers and safety precautions to be observed during overhaul.
- Describe procedures used in overhauling structures, contents, and storage areas.
- List procedures used in exterior overhaul.
- Discuss indications that point to possible arson.
- Describe techniques used in overhauling vehicle fires.
- Discuss the public relations aspects of overhaul.

IMPORTANT TERMS

arson	decontaminating	heat detector	re-ignition
baled materials	flammable	LPG (liquefied	salvageable
char	foreign bodies	petroleum gas)	smolder
creosote	habitable	overhaul	social services

Never *assume* that a fire is out. Some years ago, as an experiment, the New York City Fire Department ignited a bale of cotton, then lowered it into the East River. A week later, they pulled the bale out of the water and broke it open. The cotton was still smoldering!

Fire can remain hidden for very long periods in areas above ceilings and in walls. It can *smolder,* or burn without visible flame, in mattresses and in piles of debris. Fire can mushroom from its point of origin to a distant part of the same building, or even to an adjacent building.

Searching for Hidden Fire

Overhaul is the process of conducting a thorough search for and then extinguishing any hidden fire, smoldering material, or even sparks. This process applies not only to the structure itself, but to any the contents of that structure that could have been exposed to fire. Further, overhaul means leaving the building in as safe, secure, and serviceable condition as possible.

Sometimes the fire is extinguished by the occupants of the building, by an automatic sprinkler system, or by another fire company acting under a mutual aid agreement. The fire department having jurisdiction usually is responsible for overhaul, however.

Planning for Overhaul

The first thing to determine is whether or not it is safe to work in the building. A number of factors must be taken into consideration:

- How extensive was the main body of fire?
- How hot was it?
- Was it located in a spot where it could weaken structural members of the building?
- How much water was used?
- Could the contents of the building have absorbed a dangerous weight of water?

Obviously, a widespread fire is likely to cause a general weakening of the building's structure, with more severe weakening in particular areas. See **Figure 17-1.**

A localized but intense fire often will cause serious damage and weakening in a limited or specific area. For example, it could weaken the area where the joist or beam ends rest on a bearing wall. The ends might have burned away, or they may have pulled away from bearing surfaces because the walls have bulged. The beams or joists could be sagging and near collapse because of the added weight of water used in extinguishing the fire.

The amount of water used will have a great deal to do with the safety of the building. One inch of water on a 20 ft. x 40 ft. floor (the size of a large living room) will add 4000 lbs. (2 tons!) to the weight on that floor, **Figure 17-2.** Such contents as mattresses, heavy carpeting, bales of cloth, or stacks of paper will absorb and hold many pounds of water. This added weight can cause beams to sag and pull away from their supporting members, or even to snap in the middle.

A thorough inspection by an experienced officer to determine the safety of the structure

Figure 17-1. A widespread fire, like this one, will usually cause a general weakening of the building's structure. The degree of weakening must be taken into account when planning overhaul.

should be done before heavy overhaul operations begin. Once the structural safety of the building is established, the officer in charge should determine the starting and finishing points for overhaul. This officer should assign the areas that each firefighter should work in, both for safety and to prevent duplication of effort.

Overhaul Preparations

The officer should designate a specific place (or places) for tools. Bring in all of the tools needed need right at the beginning — few activities are more fatiguing and demoralizing than making countless trips to the apparatus for "just one more tool."

Figure 17-2. A one-inch layer of water on the floor of this room will add two tons of weight to be supported by the structure.

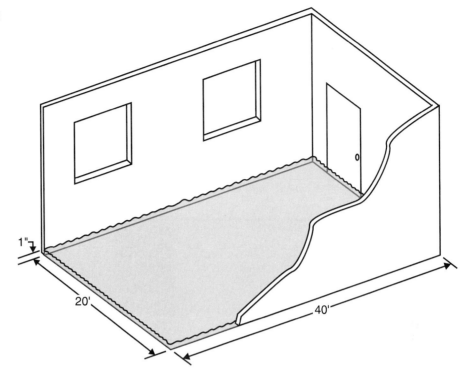

1"

20'

40'

Depending on the nature of the fire, the tools most frequently used in overhaul are:

Attic ladder	Axe
Ceiling tool	Charged line
Halligan or claw tool	Hand water pump
Heat detector	Pitchfork
Portable gas detector	Portable light
Power saw	Salvage cover
Scoop shovel	Six-foot pike pole
Smoke ejector	Squeegee

Adequate lighting is essential to a thorough and safe overhaul job. A portable generator can supply electricity for general lighting. Powerful, battery-operated lights are used for looking into crevices, holes, and other dark areas.

Before overhaul begins, electricity to the building (or at least to the fire area) should be shut off at the breaker panel, if not already shut off. This is to prevent the hazard of electric shock to firefighters who must probe around wires, appliances, and other electrically charged contents.

Since gas pipes can be broken during a fire, service should be cut off. Piped-in fuel gas should be shut off at the street valve, while bottled gas (*LPG*, or *liquefied petroleum gas*) is turned off at the tank. See **Figure 17-3.**

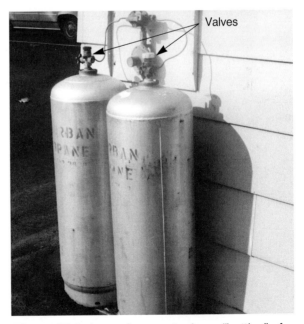

Valves

Figure 17-3. In rural areas, tanks or "bottles" of liquefied petroleum gas provide the household supply for cooking and heating. Before overhaul begins, the tank valve should be closed to cut off the supply to house lines.

Sometimes, older buildings have gas lines with soldered connections. The solder can melt in the heat of a fire, allowing highly flammable, asphyxiating gases to leak into a large area.

Fire can flare up suddenly and intensely during overhaul. Close or cover doors and windows to slow down the spread of fire. Always have at least a 1 1/2 in. charged line ready in each area of overhaul. This charged line will be used to protect you as well as to extinguish the fire.

Dangers during Overhaul

Overhaul is, perhaps, the most dangerous time in firefighting. "The worst is over," you think, so you can relax and let down your guard a little. *Don't relax* — this is where the injuries can really mount up.

The most common kinds of injuries that occur during overhaul result from:

- *Falls.* Tripping over debris, slipping on wet or icy floors, or stepping into holes can cause cuts, bruises, even broken bones.

- *Cuts.* Broken glass, splintered wood, protruding nails, or sharp edges from hanging tin ceilings can gash your skin.

- *Strains.* Lifting heavy debris or building contents can strain and tear muscles. Be particularly careful of unexpectedly heavy objects — a soaked mattress weighs much more than a dry one.

- *Eye injuries.* **Foreign bodies** in the eyes, such as plaster dust, wood fibers, or bits of charcoal can be painful and can cause corneal damage .

- *Bruises and cuts.* Being hit by objects pulled or thrown from above, or by a tool wielded by another firefighter, can cause injuries ranging from slight to severe.

Eye injuries from airborne material and cuts and bruises from being hit by tools or falling objects usually result from firefighters working too close together. During overhaul, you have to watch out in all directions: back and front, up and down, and both sides. Officers should not participate in the actual labor of overhaul. Their job is to look out for the safety of firefighters.

Chemical hazards

Drugstores, body shops, factories, laboratories, and even private homes (especially in cellars and garages), are repositories of vast amounts and numbers of chemicals. See **Figure 17-4.** So long as these chemicals are sealed in their original containers, these are relatively safe to be around. When released, however, many are hazardous. Nearly every place you go, you will encounter such materials; some are flammable, some release strong acids or caustics, and others release poisonous vapors.

Under normal conditions, containers of chemicals should be approached with caution. Under fire conditions, be far *more* cautious. Many containers have plastic tops that will melt in the heat of a fire. Metal containers often have soldered side, bottom, and top seams as well as soldered handle attaching points. Solder will soften or melt completely when exposed to intense heat, allowing

Figure 17-4. Many residential and business buildings have shelves full of chemicals like these. Fire can weaken or damage packaging, causing potentially hazardous situations. Notice than most of the containers are labeled, but actual contents may not always match the label.

container seams to open. Handle all containers carefully, especially if they appear to have been exposed to high heat. Don't pick them up by the handles, which may no longer be firmly attached. Lift them carefully from the bottom, and do not allow them to tip, since the top may be melted or missing entirely.

Nearly all authorities recommend that firefighters wear protective breathing apparatus throughout the overhaul procedure. Even the best of these devices, **Figure 17-5**, is cumbersome and severely restricts your vision. For this reason, you may be tempted, when the smoke clears a little, to remove the facepiece (or even the whole thing). *Don't take the chance* — you can't see most of the vapors that can harm or kill you. If you drop a container of poison, you won't have time to get your apparatus and put it on. Also, there is always the danger of a flare-up, or even a flashover, during overhaul. Wear your protective breathing apparatus until overhaul is over.

Figure 17-5. Breathing apparatus is uncomfortable to wear during overhaul, but could be a lifesaver if poisonous fumes are present or a sudden flare-up occurs.

Always wear gloves during overhaul. They will help protect you from falling embers, sharp objects, and corrosive and poisonous materials.

Dust hazards

Dust is often *flammable,* and in the proper proportion with air, *explosive.* Dusts that can catch fire or explode are found in places where large amounts of cloth is present, such as clothing manufacturing and dry cleaning establishments, and in flour mills and grain storage areas. Under the right conditions, even fine sawdust or the dust raised during overhaul may be capable of burning or exploding. Don't take chances. If you find that you are raising a lot of dust during overhaul, dampen it with a fog nozzle or evacuate it with a smoke ejector.

Work purposefully and efficiently, but do not rush. The worst of the fire is under control, at least for now. Take your time to think about what you are doing and why you are doing it. *Take the time to be safe.*

Overhaul Procedures

As noted earlier, the real job of overhaul begins when the main body of fire has been knocked down. Since there is less need for haste, firefighters can plan a systematic job. In the long run, this will save time and effort, prevent injuries, avoid duplication, and get better results.

The overhaul plan for any given building will be based on a number of factors:

- *Location of the fire.* If the fire was in a wall, it might have spread upward to the attic or even across the attic and into an adjoining building. On the other band, a mattress fire may require only a thorough overhaul of the mattress, the bed, and the immediate surrounding area.

- *Intensity and extent of the fire.* A trash fire in a wastebasket will generate relatively little heat. If it is obvious that the fire did not spread beyond the confines of the wastebasket, there is little need for further overhaul. The opposite is true of a chimney fire, especially where a heavy layer of *creosote* has built up. Such a fire can be extremely hot. If the chimney is not in particularly good condition, you may have to open parts of the wall around it to make sure it has not spread.

- *Type of construction.* If the building is constructed of fire-resistant material such as concrete block, there is obviously little overhaul needed for the building itself. You won't have to tear out any walls. But wooden floors, roofs, pipe recesses, and any vertical openings through which heat can convect should be checked thoroughly.

- *Kind, amount, and distribution of contents.* This will be considered in a later section of this chapter.

- *Amount of water used.* As noted earlier, an inch of water on the floor of a 20 ft. x 40 ft. room will add 2 tons to the weight on that floor. If there is a large amount of water on the floors of the building, the first step may be to start removing water. Start with the bottom floor and work up, so that water from above will not add weight (and thus, the danger of collapse) to the lower floors.

While the fire is being brought under control, an officer or an experienced firefighter should examine the areas surrounding the fire to determine if the fire is spreading, and if so, in what direction. This preliminary survey should include all vertical paths such as stairways, elevator shafts, pipe and wire raceways, or heating ducts. Knowledge gained here will help greatly in carrying out a complete overhaul later.

Using your senses

When you overhaul, start at the main fire area and work away in all directions. Work upward, sideways, and downward. Use your senses. *Listen* for a crackling or a roaring sound in walls and floors. *Look* for fresh smoke coming from cracks in the floor, around baseboards, or in outside walls. Look for cobwebs in a wall or ceiling you have opened up — if they are present, there isn't much chance of fire in that area. *Touch* the walls with your bare hand, **Figure 17-6.** If you can hold your bare hand against a plaster wall long enough to say "It's OK here, Chief," it probably *is* OK.

Heat detectors have been greatly improved. A hand-held *heat detector* looks like a conventional flashlight. It will find heat sources behind walls, in dense smoke, and in other hiding places. It will detect a lighted cigarette at 18 feet. An alarm will sound when the detector is pointed directly at a heat source. The pitch of the alarm changes, depending upon the temperature of the heat source.

Checking the structure

In a frame building, you will have to open all possible channels of fire spread. Look for concealed fire in partitions, floors, ceilings, and walls, **Figure 17-7.** If you find charring, keep working in a direction away from the fire until the wood shows clear. The same applies to the area around pipes and

Figure 17-6. Holding your bare hand against a wall will help you determine if fire is still burning inside the wall.

Figure 17-7. In a frame structure, you must look for concealed fire in floors, ceilings, and walls. Begin at the origin of the fire (indicated by an X in the photo), and work outward until you find no more charring.

around heating and air conditioning ducts. Wet down anything that appears suspicious. If you have to pull down plaster from a ceiling or wall, move all items of value out of the way and use salvage covers to protect them from plaster dust.

The least damaging way to overhaul a wall is to carefully remove the baseboard. Punch holes in the plaster or gypsum board in the area of the wall normally covered by the baseboard. When you are satisfied there is no fire inside that wall, lay the baseboard on the floor next to that wall. The owner can then repair the wall with a minimum of work and expense.

Window and door frames are common places for fire to remain hidden. Often, on an older double-hung window, the pulley rope will burn through and the sash weight will drop off. The rope remains smoldering, like a fuse. Carefully remove trim from around windows and doors and check these areas thoroughly.

If you must remove floorboards, the safest and least damaging way is to cut them alongside a joist. Using an axe head, sound for a joist by tapping the floor. You will hear a higher sound at a joist than between joists. If you have reason to suspect that the joist ends have burned or pulled away, or are sagging, saw rather than chop the floorboards. The vibration from chopping might cause part of the floor to collapse under you. Prying floorboards, if you can, is safer than chopping them.

If the fire is very hot or extensive, it is wise to leave a few firefighters with charged lines at the scene when the rest return to the station. No matter how thorough an overhaul operation might be, it can never be perfect. If you do not take this precaution, you might find yourself returning in a little while to fight a fire as big or bigger than the original one.

Overhauling building contents

As you are fighting the main body of fire, move as many flammable materials as you can away from the fire. The more you can get out of harm's way, the less overhauling you will have to do later.

Once the fire is knocked down and overhaul begins, give yourself some working room. If you are in a bedroom, take the bed apart. Next, clear a space at each end of the room.

Starting from the fire location, work from top to bottom. Remove drapes and pictures before you move chairs and rugs. Work systematically away from the fire. Put burned material at one end of the room, unburned and *salvageable* materials at the other end. Handle unburned valuables carefully to avoid damaging them (and remember, what looks like junk to you, may be valuable to the owner). Place heavy objects close to walls, where the floor is strongest.

Water can do a lot of damage. For this reason, dip suspicious items in water, whenever possible, rather than hosing them down. Fill the bathtub half-full of water for dipping such items. If a bath tub isn't handy, make a tank by draping a salvage cover over some furniture. Put water in that and use it for dipping. Whenever you can, overhaul with tools, rather than water. It is less damaging.

Remember the bale of cotton that was still burning after a week underwater in New York? In the same way, fire can penetrate deep inside a mattress or overstuffed chair. Since these things can burst into flame when air reaches the smoldering material, it is best to remove them to a yard or sidewalk before ripping them open. Generally, such items are not salvageable.

Items that you find on top of dressers, chests of drawers, or desks should be placed inside the drawers. Purses, wallets, jewelry, and other valuables must be turned over to the officer in charge.

Overhauling stores and warehouses

Most of what was said about overhauling the contents of a home apply as well to the contents of a retail store or a warehouse. As much as possible, do your overhauling with tools, rather than water. Segregate burned items from those that are unburned. Use extra care with items of value.

As you would do in a residential fire, begin in the immediate vicinity of the fire and systematically work away. Overhaul only those items that have come in contact with the fire. Don't even move merchandise which is distant from the fire and shows only slight discoloration from smoke. If possible, segregate burned items for a later inventory of loss.

In stockrooms or storage areas, move materials from one shelf to another. Remember that you can encounter hazardous materials anywhere. Pick up containers by the bottom and not by the handle. Be careful

not to break bottles, which might contain flammable or poisonous substances.

Again, it is better to dip burned items in water, instead of soaking them with a hose. Since you might be dipping items of considerable size, you will probably need a large tank made from a salvage cover. Do not construct such a tank in the middle of a floor or where the joists or beams have been weakened. The total weight of the water and what you are dipping might be too great for the floor to support. For example, a ten-foot-square tank filled five feet deep with water weighs well over 30,000 pounds. Build a tank only where there is strong support underneath.

Baled materials. In storage areas where *baled materials* (such as cotton, cloth, paper, or hay) are kept, you will encounter special problems. See **Figure 17-8.** Frequently such places are densely packed with bales from floor to ceiling. When soaked, the bales become extremely heavy and tend to expand.

In this situation, your first priority in overhaul will be to remove weight from the floor so that it doesn't collapse. Fortunately, you will usually find a forklift truck available

Figure 17-8. Baled or stacked items, such as these pallets of cardboard cartons, can absorb huge amounts of water and become very heavy. Soaked materials of this type should be moved from the building during overhaul.

in such places to move the bales. Select a convenient window and cut it down to the level of the floor, **Figure 17-9.** Starting at the middle of the floor (the weakest point), move the bales to the window. *Make sure that no people or equipment are under that window,* then simply push bales out for overhaul or later disposition. If you must make such openings at windows on several floors, be sure the windows are not in line *vertically.* If they are, the wall could be weakened enough to make it collapse.

When overhauling bales that may still be smoldering, you will need a solid stream. A fog simply will not penetrate deep enough. So-called "wet water" will help, but is not a guaranteed solution. You will have to break open baled material until you can see no more evidence of burning.

In lumber yards, coal piles, or rubbish heaps, segregate burned from unburned material. In other words, remove the fuel supply. Such places usually have forklifts, bulldozers, or bucket loaders that make the job a little easier.

Burning hay. A special hazard is presented by piles of hay, sawdust, straw, and similar materials. The fire can eat out pockets,

Figure 17-10. The pile looks sound and solid enough from the outside, but if you step onto the thin layer of material over such a pocket, it will give way. You could fall into an inferno. If you must go onto any pile of combustible material, use a ladder or a plank to spread your weight and provide support.

Earlier in this chapter, the flammable and explosive hazard presented by airborne dust was described. Dust can also be a possible source of *re-ignition,* causing the fire to unexpectedly flare up again. A layer of dust on any flat surface can smolder with very little smoke showing, and can act as a fuse. In flour mills, sawmills, woodworking shops, or any place where quantities of dust are produced, carefully examine all flat surfaces. Check belts, beams, pulleys, ledges, or any other dust-catching surface that may have been exposed to fire. Also inspect any place a burning ember may have landed.

Business records. Any business records you find while overhauling, even if they are partly burned, should be set aside and preserved. They might look useless to you, but will help a trained accountant establish fire loss.

Before returning to quarters, replace any sprinkler heads that have opened with serviceable heads of the same temperature rating.

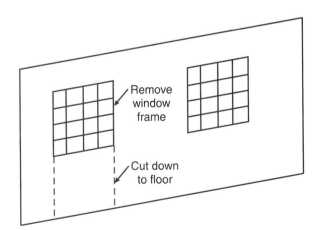

Figure 17-9. Cutting a window down to floor level will allow you to move water-soaked baled material out of the building. Altering an individual window in this way does not seriously weaken a structure. If done on several floors, however, the altered windows should not be aligned one above the other.

Figure 17-10. Fire can burn inside a pile of hay, sawdust, or similar material and form a pocket. A firefighter walking over such a burning pocket could break through the surface and be seriously burned. Always used a plank or ladder for support in this situation.

After all heads are in place, turn the system's water supply on again. In spite of all your overhaul efforts, the fire still could re-ignite.

If the business where the fire occurred uses large refrigeration or freezer units (a supermarket, butcher shop, or dairy, for example), see to it that electrical power is restored to units in working condition. This will prevent unnecessary further loss.

If the fire was very hot or widespread, it is wise to leave a few firefighters with charged lines at the scene. This is especially true if arson is suspected. It will prevent the arsonist from re-igniting the fire. Also it will permit fire department investigators to enter the premises at will. This precaution will also prevent the destruction of evidence that remains on the scene.

If poisonous or other hazardous materials are present at the fire scene, thoroughly wash down all tools and equipment used before returning it to the apparatus. Otherwise, you might have a major job *decontaminating* the entire apparatus and the firehouse.

Exterior overhaul

Normally, overhaul is accomplished more easily and safely, and with fewer costly repairs, from the inside. But sometimes, you *must* pull off siding or open a roof to get at hot spots.

When working on a roof, always assume it has been weakened by fire. Otherwise, why are you there? Lay a ladder flat on the roof surface and work from that to avoid the possibility of falling through. If the roof is pitched, use a roof ladder and make sure the hooks are set firmly, **Figure 17-11.**

Always open the roof directly over the fire. If you first open the roof anywhere else, flames will be drawn toward that opening, spreading the fire.

A shovel will remove loose shingles as fast as any other tool. To open a metal roof, cut it and then peel it back. Around a skylight or chimney, cut diagonally and peel back. Work with your back to the wind, so that if flames shoot up they will not come toward you.

Figure 17-11. A roof ladder provides secure footing when opening a pitched roof to ventilate during the fire, or to get at hot spots during exterior overhaul.

Vehicular fire overhaul

Whether the cause of the vehicle fire was electrical or not, disconnect the battery. The fire may have burned the insulation from some wires, which could short-circuit and cause re-ignition. Remove all seats. Look in, under, and around them. Look under floor mats, as well. If the seats show signs of burning, cut them open to make sure that there is no smoldering material inside. Check the contents of the car's trunk, removing anything that could be smoldering. Look carefully under the hood. Scrape all burned wires to remove any smoldering insulation. Check the engine compartment and the underside of the vehicle for burning grease or insulation.

Suspected Arson

According to one nationwide study, about three of every one hundred fires is *arson* (deliberately set or *incendiary* in nature) The frequency of arson fires may well be higher than that, since evidence of the crime is often destroyed by the fire itself or by firefighters in the process of extinguishing it. As a result of this lack of evidence, arsonists are seldom apprehended and even more rarely, convicted.

Valuable evidence is often destroyed during this cleanup operation we call overhaul. If you find any indication that the fire might have been arson, bring it to the attention of an officer or to another firefighter. Don't wait until later — call attention to evidence when you find it. This will allow it to be preserved for possible use in court.

Causes for suspicion

What might be considered an indication that a fire is arson? A "yes" answer to any of the following should be cause for suspicion:

- Was anybody running away from the fire building as you arrived on the scene?
- Are there one or more "regulars" who seem to show up at every fire?
- Has a door been forced? A window broken out? A fire door blocked open?
- Are there empty fuel cans in or near the building? (It's amazing how often an arsonist will leave an empty can at the scene.)
- Is something where it shouldn't be? Excelsior or crumpled papers strewn about? An electric iron plugged in and lying in a wastebasket full of paper?
- Is there any sign of a burglary, such as rooms or desks that have been ransacked? Arson fires are often set to cover a burglary or other crime.

If you find anything that "just doesn't look right," report it. Also, call it to someone else's attention, so that person can back up your story. If at all possible, avoid moving any evidence that points to arson. If you *must* move some evidence to get at the fire, note exactly where it was, how it was lying, and any other pertinent information. Again, make sure you have a witness who can corroborate your testimony if you have to go to court.

When it is necessary to move a piece of evidence, handle it carefully and in a manner that will not obscure any fingerprints. With modern techniques, experts can now restore and record fingerprints, even on a badly charred can. Put any evidence you find in a safe place and notify an officer of that location.

Do not discuss the possibility of arson with anyone outside the chain of command, unless directed to do so. An arsonist who feels that he or she has not been detected may get careless.

Overhaul and Public Relations

Just for a moment, look at the overhaul process through the eyes of the occupant or owner of the house you just saved. This person probably knows nothing about firefighting. He or she looks up and sees that you have opened the ceiling. The person will wonder, and possibly even ask, "Why did you make a hole in my ceiling? There wasn't any fire up there, was there?" Point out the line of *char* going up the wall and across the ceiling toward the light fixture, and explain how it could have set fire to the lath.

The homeowner may wonder why you had to cut into his (or her) favorite overstuffed chair. Explain the problem: fire could smolder in there for hours, then suddenly break out.

Answering such questions is an important public relations responsibility for a fire department. Once the fire is out and the overhaul process is finished, a senior member of the department should explain to the owner or occupant what firefighters did and why they did it. If the department did a job that they could be proud of, the explanation will be easy. This fire will be a major topic of conversation of the people involved for days to come. They will tell their friends and their friends will tell their friends. And fire departments need all the friends they can get.

Before returning to quarters, clean up as much as possible. If you had to make any holes in the roof or outside walls, close them up temporarily with heavy plastic sheeting to prevent weather damage. Remove broken glass and sharp metal from the sidewalk and surrounding area. If there is no water dripping, uncover furniture, to show that it has not been damaged. Show everything you did to protect the inhabitants and their property. Return jewelry, money, and other valuables, or show the owner where they were placed for safekeeping.

Tell the occupants about the **social services** available to people who have had fires. Better yet, contact the social service agencies yourself, with the owner's permission. Also, tell the owner what must be done to return the structure to a safe, *habitable* condition. But do not make any recommendations about who should do the work. Leave that up to the property owner.

People who have experienced a serious house fire are often shocked, confused, and bewildered. They don't know where to turn or what to do next. To help people in this situation, the United States Fire Administration, in cooperation with the Hollywood, Florida, Fire Department, has produced a 14-page booklet filled with helpful suggestions. Entitled *After the Fire: Returning to Normal*, this book should do exactly that: help people get back to normal living. It describes procedures for taking inventory of the loss, replacing important documents, cleaning clothing and books, contacting social service agencies for help, even replacing burned cash!

This excellent publication provides most of the information that fire victims need to get their lives back in order. Copies are available free to fire departments for distribution to persons who have suffered fire losses. To obtain a supply of *After the Fire: Returning to Normal* for use by your department, write to:

The U.S. Fire Administration
Federal Emergency Management Agency
Washington, DC 20472

SUMMARY

After the main body of fire has been extinguished, small pockets of burning material can remain, unseen and unsuspected, for long periods of time. The purpose of overhaul is to find and extinguish all potential sources of re-ignition. A secondary purpose is to return the fire building to as nearly serviceable condition as possible.

Successful overhaul requires careful planning. The overhaul plan should include starting and finishing points, a determination of the tools needed, and who should do what. It also should include shutting off gas and electricity, and provision for adequate lighting. You must have charged line or lines readily available.

During this operation, firefighters must be constantly on guard against injuries, the danger posed by hazardous materials, and the potential for dust explosions. Breathing apparatus, gloves, and other protective equipment should be worn at all times.

Having a good plan for overhaul of both the structure and its contents will make the job more efficient and safer. Start at the fire location and work away from it. Work from top to bottom. Handle unburned articles carefully, and protect any valuable items you find. Segregate burned from unburned. Overhaul with tools rather than water. As much as possible, dip items in water rather than spraying them with a hose. Bulky overstuffed furniture and mattresses should be overhauled outside of the fire structure.

In stores and storage areas use the same general kind of a plan that you would use elsewhere. Overhaul only items that have come into contact with fire. Segregate for loss inventory. Protect any records you find, no matter how badly burned. If you must construct a large tank for dipping, be sure there is strong support underneath. Water-soaked baled materials must be removed from the building for overhaul because of their weight and the danger of their bursting into flame when opened. Be careful when working on piles of hay or other such combustibles. The fire may have eaten out a pocket that will not support your weight. Work on such piles from a ladder or a plank.

Before leaving the fire scene, replace open sprinkler heads, reactivate refrigeration and freezer units, and wash down any tools that have been in contact with hazardous materials. If exterior overhaul was necessary, close up any holes to avoid further damage by rain or snow.

Be alert for signs that a fire might be arson. If arson is suspected, preserve any evidence you find, and report your suspicions. Whenever possible, ask another firefighter to act as a witness to your actions.

Remember the public relations aspect of overhaul. Anything you do will reflect, favorably or unfavorably, on the entire department. Make sure it is favorable. Handle valuable and salvageable items carefully. Protect records. Clean up and move any dangerous or sharp objects to a safe place. Cover outside openings to prevent weather damage. Explain to the owner or occupant everything that the department did to extinguish the fire and protect against further damage. Tell the owner what is needed to make the structure safe and habitable again.

REVIEW QUESTIONS

1. Define what is meant by "overhaul." Why must it be done?
2. What factors must you consider in determining whether or not it is safe to overhaul a structure?
3. What tools and equipment are needed for a complete overhaul?
4. Give two reasons why you should always have a charged line handy during overhaul.
5. What are the most common accidents that occur during overhaul?
6. How should you handle metal containers containing chemicals after those containers have been exposed to fire?
7. Why shouldn't you remove your protective breathing apparatus during overhaul?
8. What is the correct procedure for handling valuables discovered during overhaul?
9. In what ways can dust be hazardous?
10. What factors determine the plan for structural overhaul?
11. How can your senses tell you where there may be hidden fire?
12. Why is dipping items preferable to soaking them with a hose?
13. What precaution must be observed when using a salvage cover to make a dipping tank?
14. State the general plan for starting and finishing overhaul.
15. What special hazard does a pile of hay or similar material present?
16. If it is necessary to walk on a pile of hay that may be burning internally, what precaution should be taken?
17. Under what circumstances should the department leave behind several firefighters with charged lines after returning to quarters?
18. If you find evidence of arson, what should you do with it?
19. What is the first step in overhauling a vehicle that has burned?
20. Why should a senior member of your department thoroughly explain your overhaul practices to the owner or occupant of a building after a fire?

NFPA 1001 Job Performance Requirements

The material on this page consists of those portions of the NFPA 1001 Job Performance Requirements relevant to the material presented in this chapter. Items preceded by the numeral 3 (3-x.x) are Fire Fighter I requirements; those with the numeral 4 (4-x.x) are Fire Fighter II requirements.

3-5.1 Perform a fire safety survey in a private dwelling, given survey forms and procedures, so that fire and life-safety hazards are identified, recommendations for their correction are made to the occupant, and unresolved issues are referred to the proper authority.

(a) Prerequisite Knowledge: Organizational policy and procedures, common causes of fire and their prevention, the importance of a fire safety survey and public fire education programs to fire department public relations and the community, and referral procedures.

(b) Prerequisite Skills: The ability to complete forms, recognize hazards, match findings to preapproved recommendations, and effectively communicate findings to occupants or referrals.

3-5.2 Present fire safety information to station visitors or small groups, given prepared materials, so that all information is presented, the information is accurate, and questions are answered or referred.

(a) Prerequisite Knowledge: Parts of informational materials and how to use them, basic presentation skills, and departmental standard operating procedures for giving fire station tours.

(b) Prerequisite Skills: The ability to document presentations and to use prepared materials.

4-5.1 Prepare a preincident survey, given forms, necessary tools, and an assignment, so that all required occupancy information is recorded, items of concern are noted, and accurate sketches or diagrams are prepared.

(a) Prerequisite Knowledge: The sources of water supply for fire protection; the fundamentals of fire suppression and detection systems; common symbols used in diagramming construction features, utilities, hazards, and fire protection systems; departmental requirements for a preincident survey and form completion; and the importance of accurate diagrams.

(b) Prerequisite Skills: The ability to identify the components of fire suppression and detection systems; sketch the site, buildings, and special features; detect hazards and special considerations to include in the preincident sketch; and complete all related departmental forms.

Reprinted with permission from NFPA 1001, *Fire Fighter Professional Qualifications,* Copyright ©1997, National Fire Protection Association, Quincy, MA 02269. This reprinted material is not the complete and official position of the National Fire Protection Association on the referenced subject, which is represented only by the standard in its entirety.

Public Fire Education

OBJECTIVES

When you have completed this chapter, you will be able to:

- Teach basic fire prevention techniques.
- Instruct homeowners in the importance of smoke detectors and an escape plan for fire survival.
- Teach adults and children how to report a fire.
- Conduct fire station tours.
- Make use of the media for fire prevention and education activities.
- Conduct school fire drills.
- Identify sources of free or low-cost fire safety materials.

IMPORTANT TERMS

911 system
escape plan
fire prevention through
   education

Fire Prevention Week
fire safety
public service
   announcements (PSAs)

right-hand and left-
   hand search
smoke detector
Stop, Drop, and Roll

United States Fire
   Administration

On a warm June evening in a small East Coast city, firefighters at Station One are in the training room going over pumping evolutions when suddenly, the alarm sounds:

"Station One...structure fire, 101 Main Street. Flames showing."

When they arrive on the scene, they find the structure is well-involved. See **Figure 18-1.** After the fire is extinguished, an investigation determines that the cause was grease igniting on the stove. Apparently, the fire department didn't do its job properly.

What does that mean? The firefighters did what they were supposed to do — they put out the fire, didn't they?

Of course, they did. But the fire service is changing: we can no longer think that "putting the wet stuff on the red stuff" is our only job. You might say that a good fire department is one that never has a fire. In other words, one that does an outstanding job of educating the public on how to eliminate fire hazards. That's why we could say that the department with the grease fire "didn't do its job properly." What happened in that fire was a failure to educate the homeowner on how to prevent kitchen fires. *Fire prevention through education* must become an important part of every fire department's program if we are to reduce the number of

Figure 18-1. People usually think of their home as a place of safety, but most fires, fire injuries, and fire deaths occur in residential buildings. (Harold Anthony/Archive Photo)

fires (and resulting injuries and fatalities) in our communities.

Responsibility for Fire Safety Education

Most fire departments have certain members assigned to fire prevention and education duties. Often these members also perform inspections and other duties, and are designated as "fire inspectors" (in some departments, they are called "fire marshals," but have similar responsibilities). It should be understood, however, that *every* firefighter is responsible for fire prevention through education. As a visible representative of the department, your words and actions can be very effective in helping to educate the public. This is especially true of children — just by your position, they look up to you and naturally learn from you. What they learn could save them from the ravages of fire.

In this country, most fires and fire-related deaths and injuries occur in residential settings. Thus, the main goal of fire safety education should be to educate adults and children in making the home fire-safe and what to do if a fire *does* occur.

A well-rounded program for all age, social, and ethnic groups should be a must. Each group has a specific need and should be dealt with accordingly. For example, preschool children often play with matches and lighters, causing many fires. Elderly persons may forget they have something on the stove until a fire starts or the house is filled with smoke. Other community members may have physical or mental disabilities. You may have to overcome language barriers to reach some groups. Uncovering and dealing with such problems is a part of developing an effective program.

Educating the Children

While the department should provide a comprehensive and pro-active fire prevention program to all segments of the community, it should specifically target the children. If children are properly educated in fire safety at an early age, they will continue to carry these good habits with them for the rest of their lives.

School Programs

Make every effort to institute a *fire safety* program in your community's school system. Approach the responsible school administrator with your program. See **Figure 18-2.** Present a well-balanced, organized program to the school official. If possible, have all your information in a brochure to present at the time of the meeting.

Make sure that your program stresses fire safety all year long, not just during *Fire Prevention Week.* Assure school personnel that your department can make the teaching hours flexible, and that each part of the program will be designed for the appropriate age group. See **Figure 18-3.** An important help in developing good fire safety education programs is the wealth of school-oriented fire safety information available from most insurance companies. The materials available run the gamut from videos to coloring books and are available free or at a nominal cost. See the "Information Source" heading at the end of this chapter.

Following are some items to teach in your fire prevention program.

Figure 18-2. Meet with the responsible school administrator to discuss making fire safety presentations in the schools. Be well-prepared for the meeting, with an organized presentation that will help you "sell" the idea.

Stop, Drop, and Roll

This exercise in burn prevention is both an educational and fun activity. To be effective in teaching *Stop, Drop, and Roll* and other techniques to students, the firefighter must become totally involved — you have to actually *do* the exercise with the students. Teach your students that they should never run if their clothing catches fire. Instead, they

Figure 18-3. A classroom fire safety presentation should be appropriate to the age level of the students in the classroom. These students are dressed to go outdoors for the next part of this firefighter's program.

should **stop, drop** to the floor or ground, protect eyes and breathing passages by placing their hands palms down across their face, then **roll** back and forth to extinguish the fire. These steps are illustrated in **Figure 18-4.**

Crawl Low in Smoke

As every firefighter should know, *smoke kills!* One of the first lifesaving techniques you should teach is to how to properly crawl low in smoke. The place where the air in a smoke-filled room is most bearable and least toxic is about 18″ above the floor. For this reason, you should show students how to keep their heads at the proper level while crawling, rather than "plowing the floor with their noses." See **Figure 18-5.**

Calling the Fire Department

Notifying the fire department can be done in different ways, depending on the established notification process for the given community. Some communities use a designated seven-digit telephone number, but more and more areas are adopting the 911 emergency system. The three-digit number is

Figure 18-5. Teach students to crawl properly. Emphasize that the area about 18 inches above the floor of a smoke-filled room will provide the best breathing conditions when they are crawling to safety.

easier to remember and is more quickly dialed in an emergency situation. See **Figure 18-6.** The *911 system* uses special computer equipment and programs that help dispatchers identify the location from which the call is being made. This is a real advantage when the

A

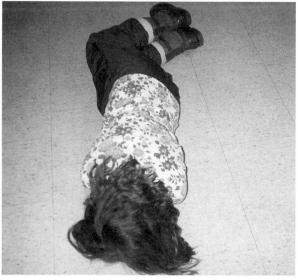

B

Figure 18-4. Each year, many children are seriously burned when their clothing catches fire. Teaching them the effective "Stop, Drop, and Roll" technique will help them react properly and could save their lives. A—After stopping, the child should drop to the floor or ground and use his or her hands to cover the face. B—The child should then roll over and over to extinguish the flames.

Figure 18-6. Dialing 911. An actual telephone or a realistic play telephone can be used to teach children how to dial the emergency number and report a fire or other incident.

caller is a young child, or is confused or otherwise impaired.

When you teach students how to use the phone to notify the fire department, role-playing is probably the easiest way to achieve success. The firefighter should play the dispatch center operator and the child plays the person reporting the fire. If possible, use a play telephone or actual instrument that will allow the child to practice actually dialing the emergency number.

Guide the student through responses to the following questions:

What is the problem? (Is it a fire? A person who is injured? Some other type of emergency?)

Where is it located? (Street address and cross street, if known.)

Who is calling to report the problem? (Name and telephone number.)

What kind of fire (or other incident) is it? (Kind of structure, location within the building, whether the occupants have evacuated premises.)

Be sure that you stress how important it is to *immediately* get out of any structure that is on fire and place the call to the fire department from a telephone in a safe location: a neighbor's home or a pay phone. Remind students that it is important to learn their address and phone number, so that they will be able to use this information if they ever have to report a fire. While maintaining a friendly and warm approach, make sure that the students understand that reporting an emergency is serious business, not a game. Avoid frightening the children, but make them aware that calling in a false alarm is a crime and they could get in trouble for doing it.

School Exit Drills

Most (perhaps all) communities in this country have mandatory school exit drill procedures. Often, these fire drills are conducted on a regular basis by school personnel. In such a situation, periodic visits by a fire department representative will help to ensure that proper procedures are being followed. Fire drills may be made a part of a regular fire safety education program in the school.

Fire Station Tours

One of the greatest tools for the firefighter is public education; there is no better way to use this tool than offering fire station tours, **Figure 18-7.** All tours should be structured for the age group that is touring. The person or persons conducting the tour should be able to relate well to that age group (when doing a

Figure 18-7. On fire station tours, show your apparatus and explain its functions. For safety, however, do not allow children to climb on it.

tour, your personality means everything). When taking children on a station tour, set up tour guidelines immediately to prevent accidents and possible injuries. Basic tour safety guidelines (your experience will probably provide some additional ones) include:

- Do not climb on apparatus.

- Stay together as a group.

- If an alarm sounds, move to a safe area designated by the guide.

Start your tour at the front door of the station. Show the alarm room, offices, bunkroom, kitchen, dayroom, and any other areas of interest. In each area, explain what you are showing in laymen's terms, not firefighter jargon. Take the time to answer any questions raised by members of the group.

One of the most important aspects of the station tour is the opportunity to show the public (especially children) how you look in turnout gear, **Figure 18-8.** When in the bunkroom, demonstrate the use of the bunker pants. Dress and undress in front of the audience, explaining each piece of equipment you put on (including your SCBA). This will help children overcome their fear. Explain to them that, if they are ever in a fire,

Figure 18-8. By letting children observe you as you put on your turnout gear (including the SCBA), they will learn that there is a friendly, helpful, real person under the somewhat frightening exterior. (Donald Foye)

they should not hide under the bed, in the closet or under the covers, but to call out to firefighters. When conducting a tour for an adult audience, you should also explain the costs of the various equipment you are demonstrating, including the trucks. This will help members of the public become more aware of the money that is needed to operate a fire department. Finish your tours by asking if there are any questions, and thanking the members of the tour group for their interest and support of their fire department.

Programs for Adults

In addition to fire station tours, there are a number of possible fire education activities that can be provided to the adult residents of your community. Some of these may be carried out as a speaker before specific groups; others may be part of public events where large numbers of people can be exposed to your message (such as community festivals or events in malls or other shopping areas. Local media (newspapers, radio, cable television) also offer opportunities to reach a wide audience.

Smoke Detector Awareness

Without a doubt, one of the most important lifesaving inventions of the twentieth century has been the *smoke detector.* Since being introduced only a few short years ago, the detector has been proven to significantly reduce life loss and damage in fires in this country and the world. Every firefighter should make this a topic of paramount importance at every possible opportunity. In teaching any of your fire prevention classes, always demonstrate a smoke detector to drive home the point that "Smoke Detectors Save Lives."

Make your audience aware that a single smoke detector is not sufficient for the average-sized home. Smoke detectors should be installed in each sleeping area of the home, and on each level of a building that is not all on one floor. Detectors should be tested at least monthly, and a new battery installed once each year (a low battery beep will signal intermittently when the battery needs replacing). See **Figure 18-9.** A campaign that has been successfully used in many communities is to promote the idea of changing smoke detector batteries each Fall, on the day when the homeowner changes clocks from Daylight Saving Time to Standard Time.

Alerting others in a fire

Another important consideration you should explain to your audience is the need to alert other occupants of the structure when a fire occurs. If a central fire alarm station is available, it should be activated. If not, shouting, knocking on doors or blowing a whistle are some ways to notify other occupants.

Persons who are hearing-impaired will not be alerted by such audible signals, however. Special detectors are now being manufactured to alert people with hearing disabilities. These include detectors with built-in strobe lights, **Figure 18-10,** and detec-

Figure 18-10. This smoke detector, designed for households where one or more residents is hearing-impaired, uses a bright flashing strobe light as well as an audible signal. (First Alert)

Figure 18-9. The widespread use of smoke detectors has caused a dramatic decrease in the number of deaths and injuries from residential fires. Never miss an opportunity to let people know that "Smoke Detectors Save Lives," but that regular testing and annual battery replacement are vital to keep them operating properly.

tors that make a bed vibrate. Still others are in the design phase.

Home fire drills

Smoke detectors reach their maximum value only when they are combined with home fire drills. Since most fires and fire deaths occur in the home, it is essential to have an *escape plan* and make sure that all members of the household are familiar with it through practice. This involves planning at least two ways out of each room and out of the house or apartment in the event of a fire, **Figure 18-11.** If the household includes one or more handicapped persons, special escape procedures and even some structural alterations may be necessary.

Figure 18-11. Every household should have a plan for evacuation in case of fire, and two means of exiting each room and the building itself. One possible method of providing a second means of egress from second-story rooms is an escape ladder like this one. (First Alert)

Make your audience aware of the danger of returning to the fire area. Once a person has exited the building they should not reenter until the fire department gives the all clear.

Survival Procedures

As all firefighters know, the most dangerous time for a fire is when people are sleeping. How an occupant of the building responds to the smoke detector alarm can mean the difference between life or death. It is crucial that the firefighter demonstrates the proper survival techniques.

The first thing that should be taught when the alarm sounds is the importance of avoiding disorientation. Upon hearing the alarm, the occupant should roll out of bed onto the floor, while maintaining hand contact with the bed. The occupant should then crawl and do a right-hand or left-hand search to locate the door of the bedroom. Explain that, for someone in a smoke-filled structure, a *right-hand and left-hand search* is using the sense of touch to find a way out. Then, demonstrate the technique of rolling out of bed, keeping one hand in contact with it. Show how the hand that is not on the bed is used to feel for the wall. Then, demonstrate following the wall to a means of egress. Remind your audience that they should never stand up into the smoke that is in the room.

Tell your audience that the bedroom door should be kept closed when sleeping. Explain that a common ordinary wood door will keep out smoke and fire for 15 minutes or more. Show how, upon reaching the door, it should be checked for heat by feeling it with the backs of the hands, starting at bottom and moving toward the top. There are two reasons for using the back of the hand: the back is more sensitive to heat, and if the back of the hand is burned, the person can still crawl and hold onto objects. Warn your audience that if the door is found to be hot, it should not be opened — the occupant should use a second means of egress. Tell them that if the door is cold, it should be opened slowly and carefully. If no smoke or heat is encountered, egress should be made using this route.

Kitchen Fire Safety

Kitchen fire safety should be an important part of your fire safety program. A large majority of the residential fires that occur daily in this country start in the kitchen. Grease igniting on the stove is one of the main fire causes. Time should be taken to show the value of always cooking with the pot handles turned inward. Also stress the importance of keeping a lid accessible to cover a pan and having a fire extinguisher nearby. Advocate wearing tight-fitting (not loose) clothing when cooking, and suggest keeping small appliances unplugged when not in use. See **Figure 18-12.** Always use examples of kitchen utensils when doing demonstrations. This can be done by using a tabletop as the "stove," if an actual stove is not available. For part of your demonstration, wear a bathrobe to demonstrate the danger of catching the sleeves on the handles of pots containing boiling material. Explain that resulting spill can cause severe burns to you or a young child. Also note that a drooping sleeve can touch a burner and catch fire. Display small appliances that have been involved in actual fires as examples of what can happen. Your department is sure to have a number of such items as toasters, curling irons, and hot plates.

Programs for Business

The best way to get business people involved in fire safety and fire prevention programs is to visit them directly. Don't call, don't write— they will be "too busy right now, later, perhaps." And that "later, perhaps" will be a

Figure 18-12. When demonstrating the safe use of appliances, always unplug an item after use. Explain why you are doing so.

long time coming. Visit in person, and in uniform. When you visit a business, present only one item and be prepared to present that subject briefly and clearly. If you can tie your presentation in with some recent incident — for example, a local fire that got out of control because the employees didn't know how to use fire extinguishers — use that as an introduction. Before you leave, make sure you have a definite time and date commitment from the business owner or manager to make presentation to his employees.

Using the Media in Fire Safety Education

A good working relationship with the newspapers, radio stations, and television operations (both broadcast and cable) in your area is very important to success in your fire department's public relations and education efforts. Keep your department pro-active with the media. Do press releases on fires as soon as investigations are started and completed. You call them, do not wait for them to call you. Remember, the media could do you more harm than good if they wanted to; keep them on your side. Do seasonal public safety announcements.

Radio, television, and newspapers are all more than willing to help you get your fire safety messages out to the public. For example, you could try to establish a public safety column in your local newspaper, working in conjunction with your police department. Over-the-air electronic media—radio and television—are required by law to provide *public service announcements (PSAs).* Most cable television operations also will provide free air time for fire safety tips.

Your public service announcements and other fire safety efforts in the media should not be just a "Fire Prevention Week" drive but a year-round effort. Plan your messages around the kinds of hazards that are presented seasonally. Christmas tree safety, leaf burning, kitchen safety, Halloween safety, outdoor cooking, fireplaces, heating systems, etc. Write and record your own public service announcements. Don't worry about them not looking or sounding as smooth as those done by professional broadcasters. The messages will have more impact if they are obviously done by a professional firefighter, not someone that is trying to look like one. Home audio and video equipment is often good enough to produce PSAs, but contact your radio or television station — they might allow you to use their equipment. See **Figure 18-13.** They usually will be glad to help you any way they can. **Figures 18-14** and **18-15** are two sample PSAs you can adapt for use by your department and record for broadcast. Radio stations will usually want PSAs to be either 30 or 60 seconds in length, but some use shorter lengths, such as 10 seconds.

Contact your local stations to determine the lengths they prefer before recording your messages.

To give your fire safety programs a better chance of reaching a broad audience, it may be in your best interest to seek help from other members of the community and form a committee on fire prevention. This committee should include members of the news media, service organizations, and senior citizen groups, as well as persons with special skills or needs, such as educators, engineers, handicapped persons, and public housing residents. The group should be of a manageable size, and should meet on a regular basis, such as monthly or quarterly. Among the activities of the group could be evaluating current fire safety education efforts, identifying community needs, and helping to plan and develop new programs.

Figure 18-13. Video can be a powerful tool for fire safety education and department public relations. The material this camera operator is videotaping at a training exercise can later be used for PSAs and other purposes. (Jack Klasey)

Figure 18-14. A sample script for a 30-second public service announcement (PSA) on automotive fire safety. Insert your name and your department's name at the appropriate points.

```
THIS IS _____ OF THE WILLIAMSPORT BUREAU OF FIRE
WITH SOME FIRE SAFETY TIPS CONCERNING YOUR
AUTOMOBILE.

NEVER STORE GASOLINE IN YOUR TRUNK, THE VAPORS
COULD IGNITE AND CAUSE AN EXPLOSION. ALSO, A
MINOR REAREND COLLISION COULD RESULT IN A MAJOR
TRAGEDY.

DON'T DRIVE OR PARK IN AREAS OF DRY GRASS OR
LEAVES. THE INTENSE HEAT FROM THE CATALYTIC
CONVERTER COULD START A FIRE.

USE YOUR ASHTRAY. . . . NEVER THROW SMOKING
MATERIAL OUT THE WINDOW.

CARRY AND MAINTAIN AN APPROVED FIRE EXTINGUISHER.
KNOW HOW TO USE IT.
```

Figure 18-15. Another sample PSA script, this one aimed at senior citizens. Most radio and television stations use either 30 second or 60 second "spots."

```
THIS IS _____ WITH SOME FIRE SAFETY TIPS FOR
SENIOR CITIZENS.

BE CAREFUL WHEN PREPARING YOUR MEALS.

USE THE FRONT BURNERS AS MUCH AS POSSIBLE, BUT
TURN HANDLES IN.

USE A LARGE FRYING PAN ON A SMALL BURNER. THERE
WILL BE LESS CHANCE OF OIL OR GREASE SPLASHING
ON THE HOT ELEMENTS.

BE CAREFUL WHEN WEARING A BATHROBE WITH LOOSE
SLEEVES AS THEY IGNITE EASILY AND YOU MAY NOT
BE AWARE OF THIS BECAUSE OF THE AIR SPACE
BETWEEN YOUR BODY AND THE GARMENT.

FOR MORE INFORMATION CONTACT THE WILLIAMSPORT
BUREAU OF FIRE AT 555-7537.

USE SMOKE DETECTORS. THEY SAVE LIVES.
```

Information Source

A vast amount of material is available to assist in the delivery of a good fire prevention and education program. Much of it is free or obtainable at a very low cost. The *United States Fire Administration* publishes the *Public Fire Education Resource Directory*. This directory, **Figure 18-16**, is a "compendium of available print, audiovisual and exhibit materials from a variety of sources. Materials are organized into thirteen categories of fire problems, with each entry listing the publication's title, description, cost (if any), suggestions for most appropriate audiences and source listings to contact for more information." This publication is free and can be obtained by writing to :

Federal Emergency Management
Agency
United States Fire Administration
P.O. Box 70274
Washington, DC 20024

The Fire Administration publishes other excellent public fire education materials which are also free to the fire service. Write to the above address for a copy of their publications catalog.

Figure 18-16. This directory lists hundreds of public fire education materials. Many are available free or at a nominal charge.

SUMMARY

One reason fires occur is because fire departments have not done a good enough job of teaching public fire education, protection, and safety. We have to do a better job. School programs and programs for various youth and adult groups are one method of carrying out this responsibility. Fire station tours are also important, and can be very effective when conducted properly. As a public service, newspapers and radio and television stations are more than willing to help you get fire prevention messages out to the public. Such messages can include burn prevention, smoke detectors, reporting a fire, and other fire safety topics.

REVIEW QUESTIONS

1. Every fire that you successfully fight is also a failure for your department. Why is this so?
2. In what type of structure do most fires occur?
3. Who has the responsibility to provide fire prevention to the community?
4. Why is it most important to teach fire prevention to children?
5. In any fire department, which firefighters are responsible for fire prevention?
6. In delivering a program, what should you instruct your audience to do if their clothes catch fire?
7. When instructing people in how to escape from a smoke-filled environment, what should you tell them to do?
8. When encountering a closed door in a fire structure, how should a resident determine if it is safe to open that door?
9. Often fire and other emergencies are reported by young children. What information must all children know to be able to report an emergency?
10. Why is a fire station tour of extreme importance in your fire safety program?
11. Why are newspapers, radio, and television usually more than willing to help fire departments with their fire prevention programs?

Building citizen awareness of the fire service has always been important to departments' public fire education efforts. This turn-of-the-century photo shows firefighters ready to join a local Independence Day parade. In many communities, fire equipment is a popular component of every civic celebration. (Harold Anthony/Archive Photo)

NFPA 1001 Job Performance Requirements

The material on this page consists of those portions of the NFPA 1001 Job Performance Requirements relevant to the material presented in this chapter. Items preceded by the numeral 3 (3-x.x) are Fire Fighter I requirements; those with the numeral 4 (4-x.x) are Fire Fighter II requirements.

3-5.1 Perform a fire safety survey in a private dwelling, given survey forms and procedures, so that fire and life-safety hazards are identified, recommendations for their correction are made to the occupant, and unresolved issues are referred to the proper authority.

(a) Prerequisite Knowledge: Organizational policy and procedures, common causes of fire and their prevention, the importance of a fire safety survey and public fire education programs to fire department public relations and the community, and referral procedures.

(b) Prerequisite Skills: The ability to complete forms, recognize hazards, match findings to preapproved recommendations, and effectively communicate findings to occupants or referrals.

4-2.1 Complete a basic incident report, given the report forms, guidelines, and information, so that all pertinent information is recorded, the information is accurate, and the report is complete.

(a) Prerequisite Knowledge: Content requirements for basic incident reports, the purpose and usefulness of accurate reports, consequences of inaccurate reports,

how to obtain necessary information, and required coding procedures.

(b) Prerequisite Skills: The ability to determine necessary codes, proof reports, and operate fire department computers or other equipment necessary to complete reports.

4-5.1 Prepare a preincident survey, given forms, necessary tools, and an assignment, so that all required occupancy information is recorded, items of concern are noted, and accurate sketches or diagrams are prepared.

(a) Prerequisite Knowledge: The sources of water supply for fire protection; the fundamentals of fire suppression and detection systems; common symbols used in diagramming construction features, utilities, hazards, and fire protection systems; departmental requirements for a preincident survey and form completion; and the importance of accurate diagrams.

(b) Prerequisite Skills: The ability to identify the components of fire suppression and detection systems; sketch the site, buildings, and special features; detect hazards and special considerations to include in the preincident sketch; and complete all related departmental forms.

Reprinted with permission from NFPA 1001, *Fire Fighter Professional Qualifications,* Copyright ©1997, National Fire Protection Association, Quincy, MA 02269. This reprinted material is not the complete and official position of the National Fire Protection Association on the referenced subject,a which is represented only by the standard in its entirety.

Fire Prevention, Inspection, and Planning

OBJECTIVES

When you have completed this chapter, you will be able to:

- List the common causes of fire and how to prevent them.
- Describe basic fire inspection procedures.
- Describe the importance, during prefire planning, of developing building diagrams that record the locations of specific hazards.
- Identify the information needed to prepare a building inspection report.

IMPORTANT TERMS

codes
combination
  construction
common hazards
conflagration hazards
construction
enforcement
exposure hazards
exposures

fireground commander
fire hazard
fire prevention
fire-resistive
  construction
fuel hazard
heat hazard
heavy timber
  construction

inspections
noncombustible
  construction
occupancy
ordinary joist
  construction
oxygen hazard
personal hazards

prefire plan
protection
radiation hazards
special hazards
statutory requirements
target hazards
transportation hazards

Although they are less glamorous than fire suppression activities and gain less public attention, fire *prevention* activities are certainly no less important. When we joined the fire department, we were taught — from our first day on the job — the basic evolutions and skills necessary to fight fire. When fire prevention was discussed, however, what first came to your mind? Probably something along the lines of "The fire inspectors take care of that." In fact, after a fire has been extinguished, an engine company will sometimes call a fire inspector to the scene to explain to the owner of the building how the fire started.

But wait a minute! As firefighters, isn't our major responsibility saving lives and protecting property? The best way to accomplish those requirements is to keep fires from occurring: a fire that doesn't take place can't damage property or take human life. In other words, the best tool we have available to us is *fire prevention*, **Figure 19-1.**

Instead of being strictly a task for inspectors, fire prevention is every firefighter's *duty*. The main objective for each of us should be to prevent fires before they start. Inspections should not be accomplished in order to complete a list or meet a quota; each inspection

Figure 19-1. Residential fire inspections provide an excellent opportunity for "one-on-one" fire safety education with homeowners or occupants. By taking a positive approach in dealing with inspections, you will be helping to build support for the fire department, as well as working to prevent fires. (Warren Lutton)

Figure 19-2. An effective fire prevention program must include three elements: education, enforcement, and engineering. Paying proper attention to all three elements will help save lives and prevent property losses.

should be done with quality, rather than quantity, in mind. Fire prevention should be made a part of our daily schedules, not be put off because other things might be more important. Through a high-quality fire prevention program, we can accomplish our objective of saving lives and protecting property.

The Three "Es" of Fire Prevention

Three "E" words are at the heart of a department's fire prevention efforts. Those three words are *education, enforcement*, and *engineering*, **Figure 19-2**. It is the goal of every fire prevention program to increase public awareness of fire and life safety problems and to attempt to eliminate those problems when identified. This can be done through education of the public, enforcement activities such as fire inspections, and work with engineering personnel to develop fire-safe buildings.

Education

One responsibility of firefighters is to educate building owners and occupants to be fire-safe at home, in the workplace, and at play. Fire safety should relate to all aspects of our lives. Effective public education programs, as described in Chapter 18, can work to make citizens aware of the fire problem in America today. Citizens need to be taught the importance of summoning the fire department without delay. They should be made fully familiar with evacuation from their home and/or workplace. They must be taught the importance of using travel smoke detectors when on vacation, and how to evacuate safely from a hotel or motel. Fire prevention is a 24-hour-a-day job; you must teach people to be fire-safe around the clock.

Enforcement

Enforcement usually refers to the process of inspecting structures for fire code violations and any followup necessary (including legal action) to ensure that any violations have been corrected. Enforcement also includes the review of plans for new structures, or alterations to existing ones, to assure compliance with fire codes, **Figure 19-3.**

Inspections of existing properties are done to assure that proper exits have been provided, that flammable material is stored properly (particularly in business and industrial structures), that smoking and other fire safety rules are being observed, and that occupancy loads in places of public assembly (such as restaurants) have not been exceeded. Another fire department enforcement activity is controlling the sale of hazardous materials, such as gasoline, chemicals, or fireworks.

Enforcement of the fire prevention *codes* (municipal laws) can be done through voluntary cooperation. By using the opportunity to educate the public about fire hazards, a fire inspector should be able to gain some degree of voluntary compliance at each inspection. Time should be taken to explain why something is a hazard and what should be done to correct it. If the owner or occupant indicates that correcting the problem would create a hardship for their business or occupancy, work with them to achieve code compliance through finding an alternate solution.

More difficult problems may require allowing the property owner or occupant a period of time to comply. Your requests for compliance with the code provisions should be reasonable. If the property owner or the occupant simply refuses to comply within a reasonable length of time, then the matter should be turned over to a higher authority. Such a refusal by the owner or occupant may require legal action to gain compliance, **Figure 19-4.** In such a case, your ability to document previous attempts to gain compliance will be extremely important.

Engineering

It is important that fire service personnel, especially those in fire prevention, have a basic understanding of engineering principles. They should work hand-in-hand with fire protection engineers and architects to help design a fire-safe structure. As firefighters, they have a vested interest in this objective. Once the building is occupied, the engineer and architect's jobs are done ... but the firefighter's job is just starting. Since we must protect these buildings for many years to come, we should work closely with the people who are building them. Organizations such as the Society of Fire Protection Engineers are constantly striving to develop ways to provide safer buildings.

Figure 19-3. Reviewing plans for new or altered structures to make sure they meet fire code provisions is an important fire prevention activity. The person responsible for reviewing plans should have a good working knowledge of construction practices, as well as a thorough familiarity with the code. (Warren Lutton)

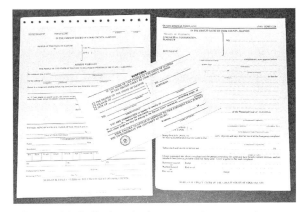

Figure 19-4. Refusal of a property owner to remedy violations of the fire code may call for legal action to enforce compliance. Forms such as these are used to initiate legal action.

Fire inspection programs can accomplish two goals for the fire department. The first goal is to identify fire hazards in a structure and to eliminate those hazards through enforcement of the appropriate codes. The second goal is to familiarize the fire department with the properties within its jurisdiction. We often refer to this familiarization process as prefire planning. It will be discussed in greater detail later in this chapter.

Fire Hazards

A *fire hazard* is a condition that could encourage a fire to start or could increase the severity of the fire once it has begun. To be able to identify fire hazards, you must have a thorough knowledge of the *fire tetrahedron*. The fire tetrahedron was described in detail in Chapter 3.

To understand how a situation can become hazardous and lead to a fire, you must think in terms of *three* hazards: the *fuel hazard*, the *heat hazard*, and the *oxygen hazard*. If any one of these can be eliminated, a fire cannot occur. Fire service personnel must to be able to identify situations in which these hazards exist and take the necessary steps to eliminate them.

Fuel hazards can take on many forms, since fuel to burn is readily available. Fuel includes ordinary combustible materials, such as wood, cloth, or paper, **Figure 19-5.** Flammable liquids such as gasoline, oil, and alcohol are also fuels. In special processes, fuels may be combustible gases or specific chemicals. In agricultural and grain processing, grain dust can be a fuel hazard. In woodworking facilities, sawdust is a fuel hazard; in manufacturing plants, fuel hazards include combustible metals and plastics.

In your search for fire hazards, the source of heat and methods of heat movement must be taken into consideration. As described in Chapter 3, heat travels by one of the three methods; *conduction*, *radiation*, or *convection*. If a fuel is located close to a heat

Figure 19-5. Many homes have storage areas filled with ordinary combustibles, such as this stack of boxes, paper sacks, and other materials. An accumulation of such material can represent a fuel hazard.

source, there is a potential heat hazard, **Figure 19-6.** One of your responsibilities as a fire inspector is to try to physically separate fuels from heat sources.

The term *common hazards* refers to the *frequency* with which particular hazards occur, not to their severity. A common hazard may be found as a condition in almost any type of occupancy. Typical common hazards are poor housekeeping practices, faulty electrical systems, faulty heating systems, and unsafe materials storage. See **Figure 19-7.**

Personal hazards are particularly dangerous because they arise from an individual's disregard of common-sense fire safety rules. A typical personal hazard would be an individual smoking in an area that is clearly designated as a nonsmoking area. The indifference of a supervisor to maintaining a fire-safe workplace is another example of a personal hazard. Although these hazards are hard to define, they are present anywhere that human beings are present.

Special hazards are those particular to an occupancy or process. Some examples of special hazards include spray painting, storage of flammable liquids, welding, grain dusts, and the use of processing chemicals. See **Figure 19-8.** Since special hazards are particular to an

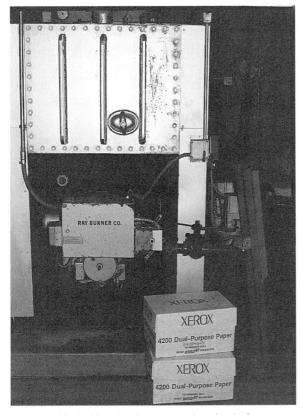

Figure 19-6. Physically separating fuels from a heat source is an important fire prevention responsibility. In this case, the boxes of paper should not be stored in close proximity to the heating system burner. The situation represents a potential heat hazard.

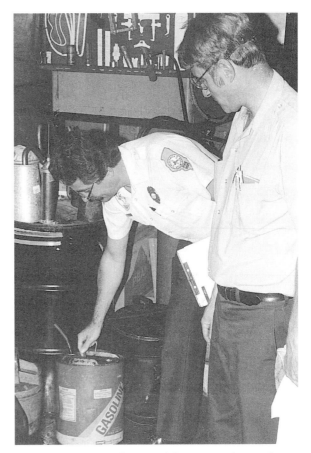

Figure 19-7. Unsafe materials storage is one form of common hazard. This inspector is making a business owner aware of proper procedures for storing flammable liquids. (Warren Lutton)

Figure 19-8. One special hazard that is often encountered is welding. Because of the use of flammable gases and the flying sparks produced by welding and cutting processes, the inspector should make sure that all code provisions are properly met. (Liquid Carbonic)

operation or process, take care during an inspection to identify such hazards.

Any hazards that could potentially lead to large life loss or large property loss from fire are considered to be *target hazards*. Examples of target hazards include nursing homes, hospitals, lumber yards, and chemical plants.

Another group of hazards consists of those related to the movement of materials. These hazards can be classified as *transportation hazards*, **Figure 19-9.** Hazards created by the location or proximity of one structure to another are called *exposure hazards*. An extreme example of an exposure hazard might be the location of a large liquefied petroleum gas storage facility adjacent to a hospital.

Although not seen to the same extent today as they were in the past, *conflagration hazards* still must be considered. This is a condition in which a large number of buildings may be lost due to their proximity to other buildings and the type of material used in their construction. Such situations were once common in cities filled with closely packed wooden buildings.

Radiation hazards can create problems that are potentially very serious, **Figure 19-10.**

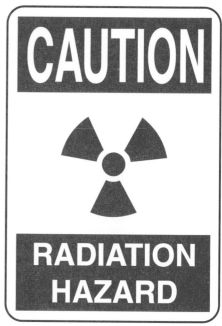

Figure 19-10. Building areas or containers that present radiation hazards are required to display prominent markings. Wording on signs may vary, but the symbol in the center is standardized.

Figure 19-9. Movement of materials by road, rail, water, or air creates transportation hazards. This truck, piled high with baled straw, could have a hard-to-extinguish fire in its cargo.

Any incident involving radioactive materials must be handled with the most extreme caution.

Inspection Procedures

The frequency with which inspections are conducted will vary greatly from community to community, and often, within a community itself. Variation within a community usually results from state statutes or local ordinances that require certain types of occupancies or structures to be inspected more frequently than others. To be certain of complying with such *statutory requirements*, you should become very familiar with both local and state laws governing fire inspections. Fire service personnel have a responsibility to bring all hazardous conditions to the attention of the appropriate people, and to follow up to be certain that there has been compliance with codes.

Using the "C.O.P.E." Method

When you conduct a fire inspection, you will be looking for four items that can be represented by the acronym *C.O.P.E.* These four letters stand for *construction, occupancy, protection,* and *exposures*. By carefully checking each of these four items, you will carry out a thorough and systematic inspection of the building.

Construction

Construction refers to the method and materials used to build a building. Type of construction is important because it determines the ability of a fire to burn or spread within a structure. Common types of construction may include:

Fire-resistive. The term *fire-resistive construction* is used to describe a building which is built completely of noncombustible material. It does *not* mean "fireproof," since a building is normally filled with combustible *contents*, **Figure 19-11.** Under normal conditions,

Figure 19-11. Although this building is being constructed of fire-resistive materials, it will eventually be filled with contents that can burn. Combustible contents mean that no building is truly "fireproof."

buildings of fire-resistive construction will burn at a slower rate than buildings of other construction types. The fire will likely involve a smaller area of the building, as well.

Noncombustible. This type of construction has walls, partitions, and structural members that are noncombustible, but that do not qualify as fire-resistive. Typical *noncombustible construction* will have bearing walls with a minimum fire resistance rating of two hours. This means that the material from which the wall is constructed has been tested under conditions of standard heat intensity, and that it will withstand that heat—without burning or failing structurally—for a minimum of two hours. The roof and floor construction and their support structures must have a minimum one-hour fire resistance rating to be classified as noncombustible. Openings in floors, including the stairwells, must be within an enclosure with a one-hour fire resistance rating.

Heavy timber. This type of construction is often referred to as "mill construction," since it was used for many of the large textile mills built in New England towns in the nineteenth century. In *heavy timber construction,* the columns, beams, and girders are large wood timbers. For a building to be classified as "heavy timber" construction, wood columns must be at least eight inches in any dimension. Wood beams and girders must not be less than six inches in the least dimension, nor less than 10 inches in depth.

Ordinary joist. This type of construction is also typically referred to as *ordinary* or *wood-frame* construction. In this type of construction, the roofs, floor and interior framing are wholly or partially constructed of wood (of lesser dimensions than in heavy timber construction). *Ordinary joist construction* has bearing walls with a minimum fire resistance rating of two hours and nonbearing walls of noncombustible construction.

Combination. Different types of construction may have been used in any particular building, especially as a result of building additions made after the original construction. When you encounter a building that involved *combination construction*, be sure you first identify the primary type of construction. Next, make sure to note any areas of different construction type that could be a hazard to you and other firefighters. For example, be sure to identify the existence of any *exterior attachments* when you are checking the construction of a building. It is quite possible, for example, that you might encounter a totally fire-resistive building with a combustible exterior attachment, such as a covered wooden outside stairway.

Occupancy

For the purpose of fire inspection, *occupancy* classifications are made according to the type of hazard that they present. The nine occupancy classifications that follow are typical.

Assembly. This classification includes all places of assembly where people gather in large numbers. For the purposes of this discussion, we might consider applying this classification to places where 20 or more people are gathered.

Office. These occupancies are traditionally used for the transaction of day-to-day business. Also, the premises occupied by professionals, such as doctors and lawyers, can be classified as office occupancy.

Educational. These occupancies are structures in which classroom teaching is conducted. Primarily, this means schools.

Industrial. These occupancies include all facilities used to manufacture goods or process a material.

Institutional. These occupancies include hospitals, nursing homes, prisons, and other buildings or complexes housing persons who are ill, incarcerated, or unable to live independently.

Mercantile. Occupancies in which the retail sale of goods and services is conducted.

Residential. These occupancies are single- or multiple-family living units that provide food preparation areas, sleeping accommodations, storage, and other amenities.

Storage. These occupancies are extensive in floor area, and are used for the warehousing of materials.

Mixed. In these occupancies, two or more of the above classes of occupancies are in evidence.

Protection

Protection may be broken down into two classifications; public and private. When reviewing the public protection available to a building, you should look first at the fire protection capabilities of the community. This will include the capabilities of the fire department, and the approximate travel time from the nearest fire station to the occupancy at different times of the day. Another vital protection item is the public water system that is available to fight a fire occurring in this building. Conduct flow tests to ensure current knowledge of water system capabilities.

When you review private protection capabilities, note such items as automatic fire detection systems and automatic sprinkler systems. Identify the locations of standpipes, both wet and dry, and the location of their connection for the fire department. Establish the presence of fire doors. During inspection, check these doors for proper operation. Note also the availability and location of portable fire extinguishers.

Exposures

When reviewing *exposures*, look at four things: the construction of the adjacent exposures, the occupancy of those exposures, the protection afforded within those exposures, and the distance between the exposure and the building being inspected. All these items of information can be important during a fire.

To complete the inspection, you should make a sketch of the building, noting all the information you have gathered on construction, occupancy, protection, and exposures. You should also obtain such general information as the names of the property owner and occupants, the address of the owners (if different from the building being inspected), and emergency telephone numbers at which the owners or occupants may be reached.

Residential Inspections

Because most fatal fires occur in private dwellings, *residential* inspections deserve some attention of their own. Unfortunately, very few fire prevention codes allow fire departments the authority to inspect private dwellings. This is a carryover from the old English common law concept ("a man's home is his castle") that government officials cannot enter a private home without the owner's permission. Thus, any residential inspection program must rely heavily upon educating the homeowner to gain his or her cooperation.

The hazards that you would inspect for in a residential dwelling would not vary greatly from those previously discussed, so no attempt will be made to review them. Instead, this section will focus on the residential inspection program as an effective public education tool. Because you are dealing one-on-one with the property owner, you have the ability to educate him or her regarding

fire safety, **Figure 19-12.** You are also talking to and dealing with the individual who can make immediate corrections when any hazards are found.

If someone comes into your home to sell you a product and immediately begins to demand that you buy this or that item, that salesperson will probably meet with little success. You would resent the person's attitude and resist buying his or her product. The same holds true for you as a fire inspector. First of all, you must remember that (in most cases)

Figure 19-12. When you conduct a residential inspection, you have a very good opportunity for individualized fire safety education. You cannot only identify a problem, but are able to make the homeowner (and family members) aware of the cause and possible consequences. You can also make specific recommendations for correction. (Warren Lutton)

you are an *invited guest*. As a guest in someone's home, you are more likely to meet with success by suggesting or recommending courses of action, rather than issuing orders or making demands. Before you begin the inspection, establish a favorable atmosphere: thank the homeowner for the opportunity to enter the home and spending the time needed to create a fire-safe dwelling. Then, take a few moments to explain the inspection process.

Everyone remembers instructions better and are more likely to act on them if they know *why*. As you conduct the inspection, tell the homeowner about each problem as you discover it, and explain why it *is* a problem. After you are certain that the homeowner understands the problem, explain the alternatives available that will lead to the necessary correction.

For example, rather than flatly stating "that chimney needs cleaning," make sure that the homeowner knows why it is a danger and should be cleaned. You might say something like:

"There's a buildup of creosote in your chimney that could catch fire. The creosote is a byproduct of burning soft wood. It builds up on the walls of the chimney and, when heated sufficiently, will catch fire. Creosote burns very hot, so the heat created by it burning inside the chimney could cause a fire in the attic or walls. A periodic cleaning of the chimney will prevent a dangerous buildup of creosote. You can find someone to do the work by looking under 'chimney cleaning' in your telephone directory."

Remember that, when you are performing a residential inspection in uniform, *you* are "the fire department." After you have gone, the homeowner doesn't tell a neighbor that "Josh Shanks was here today." Instead, the homeowner is going to refer to the fact that "the Fire Department was here today." In a very real sense, the way you look and everything you say and do reflects upon the entire fire department. For this reason, you should always dress neatly and be courteous and professional in manner. The impression that you leave with the homeowner can be a

very valuable means of public education, as well as a good public relations tool for the department.

As noted earlier, you should explain to the homeowner everything that you will be doing and that it will be a learning process for both of you. Maintain a positive attitude, and be complimentary whenever you can. Be constructive in your comments. If you write anything down, be sure to leave a copy with the homeowner. As you leave the premises, be certain to again thank the owner for the opportunity to have made the inspection, **Figure 19-13.** Your contact with this homeowner during the inspection can be the most

Figure 19-13. Thank the owner for the opportunity to have made the inspection as you leave the premises, and be sure to leave a copy of any written reports or recommendations. (Warren Lutton)

positive step you can take to provide him or her with a fire-safe dwelling.

Prefire Planning

Effective prefire planning is a vital resource for the fireground commander. During a fire, the *fireground commander* must manage an extremely large amount of information. In most cases, the time cannot be taken during the fire to obtain needed information. For example, if the fireground commander does not know the capacity of the fire hydrants adjacent to a fire building, he or she could make the wrong decision concerning placement of engine companies at that fire. Or, if the commander does not know the location of the sprinkler system's fire department connection, valuable time could be lost sending an engine company to the wrong side of the building.

Surveying the Response Area

Prefire planning is somewhat like hospitalization insurance—you hope you will never need it, but if you do, you're glad you've got it. Statistics have proven that, with complete prefire planning, extinguishment is quicker, less property is lost, and fewer firefighters get injured. Complete prefire planning includes an on-site survey of all major structures within the first-alarm response area, of the best routes to reach a specific structure, and of the water sources available for each structure.

Major structures

Are the structures built of wood or of fire resistant materials? What are the occupancies and hazards? Are they apartment buildings, single-family houses, warehouses, commercial buildings, factories, schools, hospitals? What about the contents? Are they slow-burning, fast-burning, explosive? Do they contain hazardous materials? Are the buildings equipped with fire doors, sprinklers, standpipes? Will other buildings close by need protection? Are there any special entry problems, such as security areas?

Routes

How large is your first response area? In a city it may be only a few square blocks. In a rural area, it might be many square miles. Some departments have prescribed routes, others do not. You will be concerned not only with the shortest route, but also the most reliable. For example, the shortest route won't be at all reliable if it includes a heavily traveled railroad grade crossing. What about rush hour traffic? A longer route using secondary streets actually might be faster than a shorter route that uses traffic-clogged main streets. What about temporary conditions? Road construction or flooding could cause serious delays. You will need up-to-the-minute information on these conditions, and must know what alternatives are available to work around them.

Water supply

Where is the water? What is the source, and how reliable is that source? Will you have to draft from a stream or pond, or can you hook up to a hydrant? If so, does the hydrant have enough flow or pressure for your needs? Can you connect to a given hydrant without taking the water that supplies a sprinkler system?

Computers in Prefire Planning

Prefire planning requires the gathering and filing of large amounts of information. Fortunately, much of this information can be put on computers. In some places, it already is on computers. When an alarm comes in, so does the information on structures, floor plans, descriptions of contents (including hazardous materials), route maps, and locations of water supplies. Response apparatus in some communities are already equipped with computers to access to this information. In the future, probably all emergency vehicles will be so equipped. But that is in the future. For now, most firefighters have to carry that information in their heads, or perhaps in a notebook on the apparatus.

Fireground Advantages

Upon arrival at the scene, a properly prepared *prefire plan* will give the commander the information necessary to make sound fireground decisions. Without such a prefire plan, the commander's approach to a given fire situation would be haphazard, at best. The prefire plan is developed by assembling information regarding the building's construction, occupancy, exposures, and the available public and private protection. This information is primarily gathered during fire prevention inspections. The prefire plan presents the needed information in a usable form that will help the fireground commander make quicker and more accurate decisions.

The duties of firefighting can be more easily accomplished when an effective prefire plan has been developed for a building. Knowledge of the building, its occupants, and other vital information can save time and energy, and potentially, lives and property.

SUMMARY

Fire prevention is best effected by eliminating conditions that cause fires and by educating the public to the practices that cause fires. An effective fire inspection program will uncover hazardous conditions. Only through education of the public will you effectively eliminate those hazardous conditions.

Fire inspections of dwellings coupled with a good public education program will go a long way toward preventing fires. When conducting home fire inspections, be polite and well-mannered. Explain what you are doing, and explain why a condition or practice is hazardous. Be as complimentary and positive as possible.

Prefire planning gives the fireground commander the tools necessary to make appropriate and competent decisions. When used properly, a good prefire plan can help the commander be more efficient and effective on the fireground.

As awareness of the services available to the public grows, fire prevention and public education will take an increasing amount of fire department time. As a firefighter, you must be prepared to deal with the demand from citizens for increased service.

REVIEW QUESTIONS

1. As firefighters, what is our greatest responsibility?

2. Should individual firefighters have any responsibility for fire prevention? Why?

3. What are the "three Es" of fire prevention?

4. List at least three things that citizens should be taught as part of fire prevention education.

5. Why do fire inspectors review plans for new buildings or alterations to existing structures?

6. List several reasons why buildings are inspected by fire department personnel.

7. What can be done if a property owner refuses to bring a building into compliance with the fire code?

8. What two goals do inspection programs achieve for a fire department?

9. Define the term, "fire hazard."

10. In addition to ordinary combustibles, what kinds of fuel hazards might be found in a manufacturing plant? In a grain elevator? In a cabinetmaking shop?

11. What is a "target hazard?" Provide several examples.

12. Why are conflagration hazards less likely today than they were a number of years ago?

13. What do the letters in the acronym C.O.P.E. represent?

14. Describe the difference between fire-resistive and noncombustible construction.

15. Which classes of occupancy have the greatest potential for injury and death in case of fire?

16. List some typical private protection components that could be found in a commercial or industrial building.

17. Why is the cooperation of the property owner important when conducting a residential fire inspection?

18. What is the advantage of explaining hazards and violations to the homeowner as you discover them?

19. Why is prefire planning important to efficiently and effectively fighting a fire?

20. Using a street map of your own community, pick two widely separated spots and determine the shortest route to get from your fire station to each of these points. Is the shortest route, in each case, always the best or fastest route? If not, state why, and determine the best alternate.

NFPA 1001 Job Performance Requirements

The material on this page consists of those portions of the NFPA 1001 Job Performance Requirements relevant to the material presented in this chapter. Items preceded by the numeral 3 (3-x.x) are Fire Fighter I requirements; those with the numeral 4 (4-x.x) are Fire Fighter II requirements.

3-2.1 Initiate the response to a reported emergency, given the report of an emergency, fire department standard operating procedures, and communications equipment, so that all necessary information is obtained, communications equipment is operated properly, and the information is promptly and accurately relayed to the dispatch center.

(a) Prerequisite Knowledge: Procedures for reporting an emergency, departmental standard operating procedures for taking and receiving alarms, radio codes or procedures, and information needs of dispatch center.
(b) Prerequisite Skills: The ability to operate fire department communications equipment, relay information, and record information.

3-2.2 Receive a business or personal telephone call, given a fire department business phone, so that proper procedures for answering the phone are used and the caller's information is relayed.

(a) Prerequisite Knowledge: Fire department procedures for answering nonemergency telephone calls.
(b) Prerequisite Skills: The ability to operate fire station telephone and intercom equipment.

3-2.3 Transmit and receive messages via the fire department radio, given a fire department radio and operating procedures, so that the information is promptly relayed and is accurate, complete, and clear.

(a) Prerequisite Knowledge: Departmental radio procedures and etiquette for routine traffic, emergency traffic, and emergency evacuation signals.
(b) Prerequisite Skills: The ability to operate radio equipment and discriminate between routine and emergency traffic.

4-2.2 Communicate the need for team assistance, given fire department communications equipment, standard operating procedures (SOPs), and a team, so that the supervisor is consistently informed of team needs, departmental SOPs are followed, and the assignment is accomplished safely.

(a) Prerequisite Knowledge: Standard operating procedures for alarm assignments and fire department radio communication procedures.
(b) Prerequisite Skills: The ability to operate fire department communications equipment.

(4-5.1)

(a) Prerequisite Knowledge: The sources of water supply for fire protection; the fundamentals of fire suppression and detection systems; common symbols used in diagramming construction features, utilities, hazards, and fire protection systems; departmental requirements for a preincident survey and form completion; and the importance of accurate diagrams.

Reprinted with permission from NFPA 1001, *Fire Fighter Professional Qualifications,* Copyright ©1997, National Fire Protection Association, Quincy, MA 02269. This reprinted material is not the complete and official position of the National Fire Protection Association on the referenced subject, which is represented only by the standard in its entirety.

Communications

OBJECTIVES

When you have completed this chapter, you will be able to:

- Describe how to instruct a citizen to report a fire or other emergency.
- Explain how to receive a report of an emergency and initiate action.
- Discuss the purpose and function of alarm-receiving equipment.
- Describe proper methods for handling of personal and business phone calls.
- Explain the requirements of a fire department radio procedure.
- Describe how to respond to multiple alarms and calls for special assistance.
- Demonstrate proper techniques for producing written reports.

IMPORTANT TERMS

911
abstract
central dispatching
    agencies
communication

concrete
decode
Dispatch
DOA
encode

inference
noise
OD
sensitive information
summary

telecommunications
    systems
telecommunicator
transmit

Many fire department emblems include a representation of a megaphone, the "walkie-talkie" of the 19th and early 20th centuries. If the user had a powerful voice, the megaphone would help it carry to a range of several hundred feet. Firefighters of that time could not have even dreamed of the sophisticated communications equipment available today. Using an instrument that weighs only a few ounces and fits comfortably in the palm of one hand, a person can converse easily and clearly with someone just down the street — or halfway around the world.

But communication involves more than just conversation. It goes beyond just saying words. For true *communication* to take place, someone must also hear and understand those words. Since a firefighter constantly deals in emergency situations (a time when people often fail to communicate clearly), he or she must make doubly sure that he or she *understands* and is *understood*. In these situations, the firefighter's responsibility is to convey clear information and to be sure that the information that is received is accurate.

The Communication Process

The process of human communication can be represented by a diagram, as shown in **Figure 20-1.** At **A,** you form a mental image of something (the "idea"). You want to tell someone about this idea. To do this, you must encode it. This is because the idea is a mental image and that is all. Few (if any) of us can transmit an idea directly from one mind to another. So we must *encode* the idea, or put it in a form that can be transmitted from one person to another. At **B,** the encoding step, you can do a number of things to encode the message, depending upon its complexity. You can simply point with one finger and another person will possibly get the idea. If the idea is more complex, you probably will have to put the idea into words, either spoken or written.

You now *transmit* the message (move it through time and/or space), **C.** Someone a short distance away can see you point your finger or hear your words. If you write the message in a letter, it may be read a thousand miles away and three days later.

However you transmit it, the receiver eventually will see or hear your message. He or she must then *decode* it (translate the words back into a mental image), **D.** If this mental image, **E,** is very similar to the one you originally encoded, then both the sender and the receiver have done a good job of communicating.

Let's apply this to a real-life situation, **Figure 20-2.** Harold Jones is walking down the street and sees smoke coming from one of the windows of a house. As luck would have it, there is a police patrol car passing by. Jones may simply have to wave at the police officer to get his or her attention, then point to the house. The officer might nod to Jones to acknowledge the message, then pick up the car's radio microphone and relay the information to headquarters. Help will be on the way in moments.

Figure 20-3 shows a different situation: There's no handy patrol car on the street, so Jones goes to a neighboring home and asks to use the telephone. He dials the emergency number and tells the dispatcher, "There is smoke coming from the house at 512 Maple Street." Again, help will be on the way quickly.

These two messages were encoded and received without difficulty. At times, however, something can happen to prevent your message from getting through as you intended. This is known as "noise." In communications science, *noise* is anything that interferes with the purity of the message. Noise can occur at any stage of the communication process.

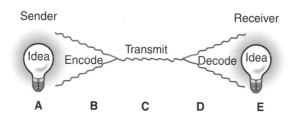

Figure 20-1. Communication begins with forming an idea (A). The sender encodes it (B), and then transmits it (C) to the receiver. The receiver decodes it (D), and forms a mental image (E). If that mental image is very close to the one formed by the sender, communication has taken place.

Figure 20-2. An idea can be communicated without a single word being spoken: Jones gets the police officer's attention and points to the burning house. The officer nods to acknowledge the information, then turns in the alarm.

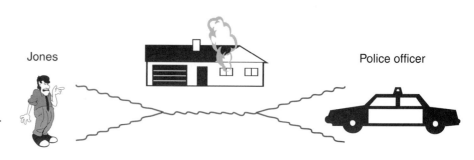

Figure 20-3. The message that smoke is coming from a house at a specific address was transmitted simply and clearly to Dispatch in this example.

Noise

What if Jones is deep in thought when he walks past the house with the smoke coming from the window? As shown in **Figure 20-4**, he may see the smoke, but doesn't register the idea of fire. If there's no idea to be encoded, there's nothing to transmit or receive.

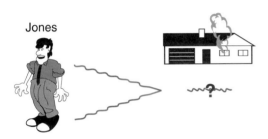

Figure 20-4. If there's no mental image (idea), there is no encoding and no message transmitted. Jones didn't notice the smoke coming from the house, so he couldn't attempt to communicate information about it.

Noise in the encoding stage, **Figure 20-5A**, can also interfere with transmission of the message. As shown, Jones finds a telephone and promptly calls the fire department. But, like many people, he doesn't communicate well under stress. The call might go like this after it's answered by dispatcher Terry Smith:

Smith: *"Fire Department, Smith speaking."*
Jones: *"Oh, this is terrible."*
Smith: *"What's the problem?"*
Jones: *"This is awful. There are children in there."*
Smith: *"Where?"*
Jones: *"In the fire. Send help right away."*

And he hangs up. Jones has not encoded the message in a way that can be used by the fire department. (In some areas with sophisticated 911 systems, the dispatcher will be able to identify the telephone number and address from which the call was made. In many others, however, there would be no way to recover this vital information.)

Figure 20-5. Noise in the transmission disrupts communication. A—Noise in the encoding stage prevents communication of the idea. B—Communication can also be made more difficult by noise at the receiving end.

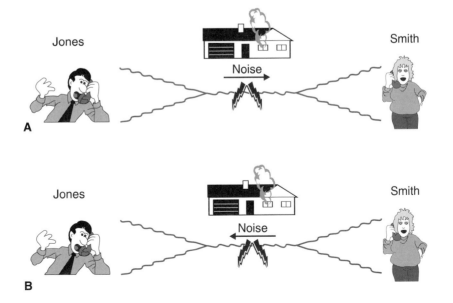

The person receiving the call may complicate the problem, **Figure 20-5B**. A person calling to report a fire often is excited and nervous. If the dispatcher is impatient or responds in an intimidating manner, the caller may become even more nervous. Such a call might be like this example:

Smith: *"FIREDEPARTMENTSMITHS-PEAKIN."*

Jones: *"This is awful. There's smoke..."*

Smith: *"SPEAKUP, WILLYA?"*

Jones: *"There's smoke..."*

Smith: *"TALK LOUDER, I CAN'T HEAR..."*

Jones: (Hangs up)

Smith has only made the caller so nervous that he can't encode the message at all.

There might *literally* be noise in the transmission, **Figure 20-6**. It might be a loud motorcycle passing by, at just the wrong time:

Jones: *"There is smoke coming from the house at ... VRRRROOOOMMMMM-MMMMM."*

It might be a bad telephone connection, or another alarm coming in at exactly the same time. Noise in transmission can be caused by any number of things, and can originate at either end of the call.

As depicted in **Figure 20-7**, there may also be noise in the decoding process: Jones may send the message correctly, but Smith might "hear" a different message.

Jones: *"There is smoke coming from the house at 512 Maple Street."*

However, Maple Street is a short street in an out-of-the-way part of town. Maple *Avenue* is a major thoroughfare. So Smith might "hear" "Maple Avenue", rather than "Maple Street."

Helping Callers Communicate

As you can see, getting a clear message from anybody who is upset or excited is extremely difficult. But it is your job, as a firefighter, to make sure that the information you get is complete and accurate. That means, as shown in **Figure 20-8**, that you must actively help in the communication process by being supportive and by asking questions to clarify any possible misunderstandings. A call that is an effective communication might go like this:

Smith: *"Fire Department. Smith speaking. May I help you?"*

Jones: *"Oh, this is awful..."*

Smith: *"Do you want to report a fire?"*

Jones: *"Yes. Please hurry, there are children in there."*

Smith: *"Would you please give me the address of the building that's on fire?"*

Figure 20-6. Literal noise can interfere with communication, as in the case of this passing motorcycle that "wiped out" the address Jones was giving to Smith.

Figure 20-7. Noise at the receiving end is illustrated here: Jones said Maple *Street*, and Smith mentally substituted Maple *Avenue.*

Figure 20-8. With help by a supportive person on the receiving end, a clear message can be obtained even from a nervous and hesitant sender.

Jones*: "Five twelve VRRROOOOMMM-MM..."*
Smith*: "There was a loud noise. What was the street address again, sir?"*
Jones*: "Five twelve Maple Street."*
Smith*: "Maple Street or Maple Avenue?"*
Jones*: "Street. Maple Street."*
Smith*: "What is the name of the nearest main street?"*
Jones*: "Twelfth Street. It's right off Twelfth."*
Smith*: "May I have your name, please?"*
Jones*: "Jones. Harold Jones."*
Smith*: "What is the number of the phone you are calling from, Mr. Jones?"*
Jones*: "555-6837. Please hurry."*
Smith*: "We're on our way, Mr. Jones. Thank you for calling."*

Educating citizens

You can help ensure effective communication by taking advantage of opportunities to explain to citizens how to properly report a fire or other emergency. Such opportunities present themselves when you speak at meetings (on such occasions as Fire Prevention Week), or just in the course of normal conversation.

Start out by telling the citizen that, if he or she is reasonably sure that there is a fire or other emergency, it should be reported immediately. If a large cloud of smoke should turn out to be just a trash fire, chances are good that *Dispatch* is already aware of it. Reassure the citizen that, even if the fire he or she reports turns out to be nothing more than a cloud of dust from construction work, no one is going to be angry. The fire department would rather respond to a few trash fires or investigate a cloud of dust than to have an actual fire go unreported, allowing it to get

out of hand. Actually, this happens much oftener than it should, because people fear they will be blamed for "turning in a false alarm." Assure people that there is a great difference between mistakenly reporting a fire and maliciously making a false report. Tell them that they should call Dispatch or the fire department without hesitation if they see something we should investigate.

To report a fire or other emergency, the person calling should follow these steps:
1. Call the fire emergency number. In many areas, citizens can report any type of emergency simply by dialing 911.
2. State the nature of the emergency, such as:
"Smoke coming from an upper story."
"A person lying on the sidewalk."
"A woman screaming."
"A heavy smell of smoke."
"An alarm is sounding."
3. State the location of the emergency situation. To save time and avoid mistakes, give the name of a cross street or other landmark.
4. Give your name and the number of the telephone you are calling from. Dispatch may have to call back for further information.

Alarms

At one time, many city street corners displayed a red fire alarm box. It was mounted on a pole or fixed to a wall. On the front of the box were the words, "IN CASE OF FIRE, BREAK GLASS AND PULL LEVER". When you broke the glass and pulled the lever, a signal was sent to a tickertape machine in fire headquarters. A stylus would punch a pattern of holes in a paper tape, such as this:

• • • • • • • •

which is read as "1241" (the number of the box). By consulting a chart on the wall, firefighters could establish that Box 1241 was at the corner of Fourth and Arch Streets. And away they went.

Sometimes, the box would also activate bells, sirens, whistles, or other alerting devices at the fire station or headquarters. Again, the pattern identified the box location (and thus, in general, the location of the fire). These boxes are no longer found on city streets (although they are still common in schools, hospitals, and factories). See **Figure 20-9.** Improvements in communications have made the alarm box obsolete. Also, changes in society made the street corner boxes more a liability than an asset: too many people apparently enjoyed breaking the glass and pulling the lever to see fire engines run. In some areas, over 90-percent of the alarms sent from street corners

Figure 20-9. Although alarm boxes are no longer found on street corners, they are still commonly used inside hospitals, schools, and some manufacturing plants. They may be connected directly to the fire department, a central dispatching agency, or a private security firm. (Institutional Communications Associates)

were false alarms. Although the boxes are gone, many departments still refer to the initial fire response as a "box alarm." The box itself has disappeared, but the tradition lingers.

Transmitting Alarms

Today, dispatch agencies usually receive alarms over the telephone, and alert the firefighters by either a telecommunications system or by radio. *Telecommunications systems,* making use of telephone lines or a dedicated network of wires, connect the dispatch agency with all fire stations and other emergency service agencies. Such systems are most widely used in larger cities and densely populated urban areas with a large number of fire stations. Radio is also widely used for two different purposes: transmitting the alarm to stations (for departments with on-duty firefighters), and alerting individual firefighters who carry pagers or portable personal radios (usually volunteer or paid-per-call departments).

In the fire station, an alarm signal sounds. Then a voice announcement is made stating the location and nature of the fire or other emergency. Because of the possibility of a single piece of communications equipment malfunctioning, two or more units will be activated. One may be a simple radio receiver or telecommunications speaker ("squawk box"). The other might be a radio base station that is used to communicate with the field. A printer similar to a computer printer may also type out the alarm information.

Just as fire stations have more than one unit which will receive alarms, dispatching units typically have a backup system in transmitting alarms. The radio signal from dispatch is sent simultaneously to two or more transmitters. The receiving areas of the transmitters overlap. Thus, every receiver in the area served will receive the signal from at least two transmitters. If any one transmitter should become inoperative, each receiver will still get the signal from at least one back-up transmitter.

Central dispatching agencies

While some localities maintain separate fire and police dispatch systems, many areas today have set up *central dispatching agencies* to handle fire, police, ambulance, and other emergencies. See **Figure 20-10.** A dispatch agency receives alarms in a number of ways, but most often by telephone. In many localities, a citizen can dial one three-digit telephone number, *911,* for all emergencies: fire, ambulance, and police. This is rapidly becoming the universal number, and is expected to become the nationwide emergency number within a relatively short time.

Central dispatching agencies often cover a wide area, such as an entire county. On any given day, the agency's dispatchers might have to handle literally hundreds of emergencies. At times, especially during a natural disaster like a flood or a tornado, have dozens of emergencies going on at the same time. Under these circumstances, you might sometimes get incomplete (or even wrong) information. If this should happen, do not respond in an angry or sarcastic way. That will only make matters worse. The dispatchers are doing the best they can, often under very stressful circumstances.

Security companies

Security companies that install and service fire and burglar alarm systems have their own method. When they receive an alarm from an installation, they relay the information to the proper dispatching agency by means of a *telecommunicator* (a direct, leased telephone line). No dialing is necessary, since the line is always "open." The security company simply report the location and nature of the emergency to Dispatch.

Automatic alarm systems

Automatic alarm systems are tied in, either by radio or leased telephone line, to the central dispatching agency. At Dispatch, the information is fed directly into a small computer that displays or prints out the location and cause of the alarm.

Audible alarms

In some rural and suburban departments, outside sirens and horns are still used as a way to alert firefighters to report to the station, **Figure 20-11.** Unfortunately, these

Figure 20-10. A central dispatching agency receives calls for all types of emergencies, typically through a 911 telephone system, and dispatches the proper emergency equipment and personnel — police, fire, ambulance, or other specialized units.

Figure 20-11. Many departments in rural and suburban areas have audible alarm systems, such as this roof-mounted siren, to alert their firefighters. Unfortunately, the alarm also alerts the curious and the thrill-seekers.

devices also alert the general public, allowing the curious and excitement-seekers to clog the roads. Another negative aspect of loud sirens or horns is that firefighters inside the fire station cannot hear the voice information while those devices are blasting away. For this reason, the voice information is sent before the audible alarms are activated.

If you are a volunteer or paid-per-call firefighter, it is likely that nearly all alarms that you receive will come by way of radio. Most firefighters who are not members of full-time paid departments carry radio receivers or radio-activated pagers wherever they go. They are in constant contact with Dispatch. The sirens and horns used to signal alarms often are activated by radio, as well.

Only two reasons exist for the continued use of audible alarms: tradition and occupation. Traditionally, these alarms have been a part of the whole business of firefighting. We would all kind of miss it. Some occupations, such as farming and mining, create high noise levels. Firefighters in such occupations cannot hear their little radios but they can hear the sirens. Like the alarm box, however, one day the sirens and horns will likely become obsolete.

Multiple alarms

There is little standardization in the way multiple alarms are transmitted. Sometimes, a single dispatching organization may even use differing terminology for different departments within a single area. Usually, however, all alarms after the first one are identified by number: second alarm, third alarm, and so on. What response is made to a multiple alarm will differ from department to department. In a small rural community, for example, a second alarm may call for an additional 15 firefighters to report to the scene; a larger community might specify the response of additional equipment and the firefighters assigned to those units. A third alarm, in some communities, might be the call for all off-duty firefighters to report; a fourth might be a request for mutual aid from one or more nearby communities.

In rural and suburban areas, mutual aid agreements are common. An established sequence of response for different situations helps assure sufficient equipment and personnel will be available for incidents larger than any given department could handle alone. Mutual aid also provides a plan to "cover" communities which have sent their firefighters and equipment to aid in fighting a large fire elsewhere. Mutual aid plans are sometimes general, but often are tailored to call for response of specific types of equipment that might be needed: water tankers, ladder trucks, a snorkel unit. What system is used in a given area depends upon local needs and department capabilities.

Handling an Alarm Directly

Since most areas today make use of some sort of central dispatching agency, very few emergencies are reported directly to the fire department. A veteran with many years on the fire department may have taken incoming alarms, but most firefighters have not. Once in a long while, a citizen will report a fire or other emergency directly to the fire department.

Telephone alarms

When a citizen calls the department directly to report a fire, follow this procedure:
1. If you answer the telephone, handle the call yourself. Do not refer caller to Dispatch or pass the call along to an officer. Time measured in seconds will seem like *hours* to the person whose house is on fire or whose family member is having a heart attack.
2. Speaking clearly and in a calm manner, determine the nature of the emergency (fire, illness, or whatever). Find out if anybody is trapped or in danger.
3. Determine the *exact* location of the emergency. There are still places in most localities that are commonly described as "down the road a piece from a red barn and up a gravel road." If the address is not instantly recognizable, get reference

streets or landmarks. *Write down the address and directions for getting there.*

4. If you feel that you can do so without upsetting the caller, ask for her or his name and the number of the telephone from which the call is being made. Write these down.

5. As soon as you know the nature and location of the emergency, *alert the other firefighters* so they can start moving.

6. Let the caller know that you are taking immediate action. Say something like, "All right, Mr. Jones, we are on the way."

7. As the unit responds, use the radio in the apparatus to notify Dispatch:
"Fire Headquarters to Dispatch. Urgent. *Repeat.* Urgent. Headquarters companies are responding to a house fire at (address). Alert other units."

In-person ("bicycle") alarms

From time to time, someone will physically walk into the firehouse to report a fire or other emergency. Such alarms are sometimes referred to as "bicycle alarms" because, at one time, it was common for people to ride up on bicycles to report emergencies. Handle this alarm in the same way you handle a telephone alarm.

Radio Communication

Radio communication is most efficient and effective when all persons using the radio system follow the same set of procedures. A typical complete procedure for fire department radio transmissions is shown in an Appendix to this text. You will be required to know and use the procedures followed in your department. Although procedures vary somewhat in detail from one department to another, all includes these basic elements of radio voice operations:

1. Since mobile radios in nearly all emergency apparatus, **Figure 20-12**, are powered by the unit's ignition system, the

Figure 20-12. Mobile radios like this one are powered by the vehicle's ignition system. This unit also electronically generates the vehicle's siren or warning horn. (Federal Signal Corp.)

ignition must be "on" to operate the radio. Some units may also require manually switching on the radio set.

2. Adjust the squelch control, **Figure 20-13**, which cuts out the noises normally heard

Figure 20-13. The squelch control is the knob at far right on this hand-held radio. It suppresses unwanted background noise for clearer reception. (Repco, Inc.)

with no signal present. When the knob is turned fully left or right (depending on the unit), you will hear a loud rushing sound. Turn the knob slowly in the opposite direction to cut out this noise. **CAUTION:** Turn just far enough to eliminate the noise; turning the knob further will limit the effective range of the radio reception.

3. Adjust the volume control to the degree of loudness you prefer, just as you would an ordinary broadcast receiver. Keep in mind the effect of outside noises, such as engine noise, on your ability to receive and understand all transmissions, and adjust volume accordingly. Adjusting this control does not affect transmission levels.

4. If you notice you are not hearing messages on your radio, something may be wrong. Check the on-off switch, the volume control, the frequency selector switch, the squelch control, and the microphone button. If you see that the red light indicating you are in the transmit mode is lit continuously, turn the entire radio off immediately. Notify an officer of the problem.

5. Before you transmit, listen briefly to make sure no one else is on the air. If no one else is transmitting, press the transmit button on the microphone (some units have a separate toggle switch on the radio itself that is set to "Transmit" or to "Receive") and start speaking.

6. Identify yourself and the station or unit you are calling at the start of your transmission, such as, "Snorkel one to Dispatch". Release the button when you have finished speaking and wait for a reply.

Improving Radio Communication

The following are items to keep in mind for improving your radio communication skills:

- Think of what you want to say before you press the microphone button. Keep messages brief and to the point.

- Hold the microphone close to your mouth and at a slight angle, **Figure 20-14.** Do not shout or yell into the microphone. This will cause an extremely distorted signal.

- Best results are obtained by speaking in a normal voice. Maintain a constant voice volume which does not trail off at the end.

- When requested to repeat your message, talk slowly and in a normal tone of voice.

Figure 20-14. Proper microphone technique will make radio communications easier to understand. Hold the microphone at a slight angle and speak into it with a normal tone of voice. Speaking directly into the microphone, or shouting into it, will cause distortion that makes messages hard to understand. (Globe Mfg. Co.)

- Do not blow into the microphone. This can damage the microphone mechanism.

- Use proper titles or unit designations. Avoid over-familiarity. Use proper English instead of jargon and slang.

- Some localities use the ten code. Others use standard words and phrases. Become thoroughly familiar with the system used in your area.

- If a call can wait until you are near a telephone, do not use radio. This is especially true of sensitive information, as described in the next section.

- When you finish transmitting, replace the microphone on the mike clip. Do not lay the microphone in your lap, on the seat, or on the dashboard.

Handling sensitive information

Some people seem to be irresistibly attracted to other people's misfortune and misery. They will drive twenty miles in a blinding blizzard to see a house where an explosion has occurred or where someone has been killed in a fire. This cannot be prevented. It's their right. But, at the same time, you don't have to help them. *Sensitive information* is material that should not be transmitted over the radio, if at all possible. If you need special assistance, call for it by telephone (referred to as a *landline* in some areas) if you can find one. Use a pay phone, if you must: any of your officers will be glad to reimburse you for money well-spent. It will save them more than the cost in aspirin. Instances where you should use this kind of discretion include:

- Dead on arrival (*DOA*) victims

- Accidents with severe injuries

- Drug overdose (*OD*) incidents

- Suspected arson situations

- Suicides, murders, and other violent deaths.

If it is not practical to use the telephone, then try to switch to a radio channel that is less heavily monitored than the normal communications channel. This will, at least, keep some of the curious out of your way.

Telephone Comunication

Many departments have an ongoing campaign to get citizens to call the fire department before they get into trouble. However, people are afraid to call the police or fire departments, sometimes even to report a fire or a serious crime. They feel threatened in some undefined way by talking to what they consider "official" people.

When a citizen calls in, all he or she hears is a voice. If what the citizen hears is something that sounds like a cross between a wounded elephant and a foghorn shouting, "Fire Department, Firefighter Smith speakin'," the response is most likely to be a hang-up.

We have to turn this thing around. The telephone can be one of the best fire prevention devices available, if people will only use it. It can make the firefighter's job easier and safer if we use the telephone to prevent trouble. But it will take some effort on our part to make sure that citizens who call find it a nonthreatening, even pleasant, experience.

Handling Telephone Calls

When the phone rings, you don't know who is calling or why. So the only thing to do is answer in a warm, friendly way. Your job is helping other people, and you must *sound* that way. Speak in a normal conversational tone, identifying the department and yourself. "Springfield Fire Department. Firefighter Smith speaking." or "Fire Department, Smith speaking. May I help you?" are both good examples of answering techniques. If you really sound as if you want to help, the caller will usually respond favorably.

If the call is to be handled by another person, tell the caller, "(Name) will be with you in just a minute. I'll place you on hold." It is best to put an incoming call on "hold" if you will not be handling it yourself. This will prevent possible embarrassment of private conversations in the firehouse being picked up by an open telephone line.

If the call is to be handled by someone who is not available at the moment, make every effort to take a message. A caller might say he or she will call back. But it was hard enough to call the first time, so a second call may never be made. Try to get the name and phone number of the caller. If the person says, "Oh, it's not important, I don't want to bother him," reply with "It's no bother. That's why we are here." If you do get a name and number, *write it down,* along with any additional information concerning the nature of the call. See **Figure 20-15.** Thank the caller and assure him or her that the call will be returned as soon as possible.

When you are talking with members of the public on the telephone, always use a friendly, conversational approach. The callers will tell others their reaction — good, bad, or indifferent — to their conversation with "the fire department." Always try to make a good impression.

Personal Calls

Many departments have direct outside lines that may be used for making personal calls. Firefighters are often away from home for long stretches of time and an occasional call helps out. But be considerate. Your comrades have the same rights and needs that you do, so don't tie up the only available line for a long period of time.

On incoming personal calls for someone who is not available, try to get the name and number of the caller. But if the person on the telephone doesn't want to provide that information, don't press for it.

Written Communication

If you ask ten people what they hate most about their jobs, at least seven of them will give you a one-word answer: *paperwork.* However, modern society runs on paperwork (an example: the paperwork required to build an aircraft carrier is said to weigh more than the ship itself). Even though nearly everyone hates it, it's there and it has to be done.

Almost every alarm to which you respond generates the potential for an insurance claim, a workman's compensation claim, or some kind of civil or criminal proceeding. Any of these actions will require information from you in the form of a report, a deposition, or actual courtroom testimony. As a rule, however, these actions don't happen the next day when everything about the fire or other incident is fresh in your mind. Your information may not be required for weeks, months, even a *year* or more. In the meantime, you will have been to other fires, other auto accidents, other emergency calls. You will have forgotten many of the details of any particular incident. *That's* why the paperwork is necessary.

Figure 20-15. Telephone messages should be written down, whenever possible. At minimum, they should include name and telephone number.

Clearly written reports, log entries, or other documents will be used to provide the information needed. In court cases where you will testify, by deposition or in person, they will be useful for refreshing your memory.

Communicating Effectively

As noted at the beginning of this chapter, the word "communication" refers to the process by which meanings are exchanged between individuals. Not just words, but the meanings of those words as they are used in a message. Without an exchange of meanings, there is no communication. What if you saw this sign posted on a door?

GADRI KLUGBNT AQPMIS!

This looks like communication, but isn't. The sign might mean "Danger, Keep Out!" or "Free Money Samples Here!" or "No Shirt, No Shoes, No Service!" You have no way of knowing, because no meaning has been exchanged.

When you talk to somebody, you probably watch that person's face. Imagine saying something and watching as his or her face displays an expression that says, "I don't understand that." So you explain, "Well, what I mean is..." The look is still there, so you say, "Let me put it this way..." and try again. Finally, a look of understanding comes over the other person's face. You have finally communicated!

But when somebody reads what you have written, chances are that you won't be there to see the quizzical look. You can't say, "What I meant by that is..." When you write a report, you must make sure the reader knows what you mean. You must write so that you leave no questions in your reader's mind.

Identify your audience

Before you start to write, the first question to ask yourself is: *Who is my reader?* Other questions that you should ask include: Why am I communicating with this person? How interested is this person in what I have to say? How much does this person know about firefighting? Does he or she understand the technical jargon firefighters use? When you have answered these questions accurately, you can start to think about what you are going to write.

A good way to concentrate on what you are writing is to imagine you are walking down the street and somebody on the other side shouts to you, "What are you writing about?" You shout back, "Charlie got hurt when the porch roof collapsed." What you have just done is given a *summary* of your report — picked out the most important item and stated it as briefly as possible. All you have to do is state it in a bit more formal terms, and you have the start of your report: "Firefighter Charles J. Johnson was slightly injured when..." Then, go on and provide the details that explain what happened, when it happened (date and time, if known), how it happened, and why it happened.

Another example: "What are you writing about?" "That lousy hose we have to work with." In your report, you'd put it more like this: "On January 6, 19__, at a fire on Magnolia Street, a hose burst putting a line out of service for a minute and a half until a hose jacket could be put in place. On April 3, ..." By using the summary approach, you'll be following the common-sense writing approach of "Know what you are going to say before you try to say it."

Focus on the "doer"

Look at these two sentences:

Johnny hit Billy.

Billy was hit by Johnny.

Your grade-school English courses taught you that *Johnny* is the subject of the first sentence, while *Billy* is the subject of the second. But, somehow, this doesn't seem to make sense. Johnny did the hitting in both sentences. Billy got hit in both sentences. So "subject" doesn't tell us very much.

It is better to look at a sentence in terms of the *doer of the action* and the *action done*. Johnny did the hitting and Billy got hit. But the second sentence takes more words to say it, and you have to turn the sentence around before you know *who* did *what*. Let's apply that lesson to a fire service example. In your report, don't write, "It was requested that the hydrants be inspected by Deputy Chief Wilson." Did Chief Wilson make the request, or did someone request that he do the inspection? Here's a better way to state it, one that makes the meaning more clear: "Deputy Chief Wilson requested that the hydrants be inspected." But there's still something missing. *Who* is going to inspect the hydrants? Smith, of course. So, your sentence should read, "Deputy Chief Wilson requested that Smith inspect the hydrants." Even better is this shorter, more direct sentence: "Deputy Chief Wilson told Smith to inspect the hydrants." Every sentence in your report should have the doer of the action and the action done (almost always in that order).

Provide specific, concrete information

When you write, think in terms of providing *specific* information that will answer the reader's questions. Take a close look at this sentence: "Billy was hit." What's missing? The sentence isn't complete because it doesn't tell us who or what hit Billy. Was it a truck? Was it Johnny? Maybe a custard pie? Try this one: "It was decided to inspect the fire hydrants." Who decided that the hydrants were to be inspected? When are the hydrants to be inspected? Who is supposed to do the inspecting? The sentence doesn't tell us. Newspaper reporters are taught a formula (called "5 Ws and an H") for putting all the important facts in the first sentence or two of the stories they write. In those one or two sentences, they will try to answer the questions, *Who?*, *What?*, *When?*, *Where?*, *Why?*, and *How?*

"Smoke was coming from one of the windows." This sounds like it says something, but it really doesn't provide the specific information needed. How much smoke? Who saw the smoke? What color was the smoke? Which window was it coming from? Compare this more specific sen-

tence: "Firefighter Snyder reported that thick, heavy, black smoke was pouring from the right front window on the second floor when the first engine company arrived." The revised sentence answers 4 of 5 Ws:

WHO?   Firefighter Snyder...
WHAT?   thick, black smoke...
WHERE?   the right front window on
          the second floor...
WHEN?   when the first engine
          company arrived.

The questions Why? and How? could be answered in the next sentence, or later in the report when dealing with the fire's cause and other details.

In the sentence, "Smoke was coming from one of the windows," the word "smoke" is abstract, because it can mean any kind of smoke. Window can mean any window in the building. By using concrete terms that tell how much smoke, what color, and which window, we make the sentence mean something. If a term can have more than one meaning, it is **abstract.** *Concrete* terms have only one meaning. The revised sentence is concrete. We know what happened. Always use concrete terms.

Cut unnecessary words

"We arrived on the fire scene. At the time when we got there, we observed three persons of a suspicious-looking nature lurking around in the general vicinity of the fire." The only thing wrong with this sentence is that it says what it has to say in too many words. Cut out all of the unnecessary words and make a few other minor changes, so the sentence reads: "Arriving on the fire scene, we saw three suspicious-looking persons." This says the same thing as the first version but it says it with 10 words, rather than 30 words. Don't burden your reader with unnecessary words. "We were proceeding in a westerly direction" is a wordy way of saying "We were driving west." Use as few words as possible to say what you have to say, without losing meaning.

Facts vs inferences

You are driving down the highway and notice a car ahead of you weaving noticeably. It suddenly veers to the right and stops on the shoulder. You assume the driver is drunk or ill, and pull off the road yourself to check. It turns out the car has a faulty steering mechanism.

Somebody sees smoke coming out of a house window and reports a fire. When firefighters arrive, they find that workmen are tearing out a wall; what the caller thought was smoke was actually a cloud of dust.

Assuming the driver was ill or drunk and that a cloud of dust was smoke from a burning building are both inferences. An *inference* is a conclusion based on fact. But an inference is not fact and is not necessarily correct. Sometimes, as in the two examples just stated, an inference is little more than a guess. The fact that the car was weaving led to an incorrect inference: that the cause of the weaving was an impaired driver. The fact that a cloud of *something* was coming out the window led to the incorrect inference that the material was smoke and that the house was on fire.

In your reports, never confuse inferences with facts. The rapid spread of a fire is a fact. The finding of a gasoline can near the back door is a fact. That the fire was set is not yet a fact: it's an inference based on the two preceding facts. Additional facts that turn up, such as an eyewitness report of someone running from the building just before the fire broke out or an investigator's discovery of a triggering device, could change the inference to a fact: the fire *was* set. If you *must* include an inference in a report, show it for what it is. Label it clearly with introductory statements like: "We inferred that...," "The facts suggest that...," "Based on these observations, we assumed..."

SUMMARY

In any kind of an emergency, the process of communication is a difficult one. As a firefighter, your responsibility is to obtain the facts accurately and completely, no matter how confused or terrified the other person might be.

When educating citizens on how to report an emergency, state what number should be called (in many localities, 911). Inform them that the caller should state what he sees or hears, and give the most precise location possible. The caller should state his or her name and the telephone number that the call is being made from. The Dispatcher might have to call back for more information.

Since nearly all emergency communications involve the use of radio, certain procedures have been set up governing the use of this equipment. The purpose of these procedures is not to make your job more difficult but to avoid confusion and ensure clear communication. Become thoroughly familiar with the radio procedures for your department. Whenever possible, use standard words and phrases or the ten code (depending upon which is used in your area. Don't crowd the air with needless messages; if you can handle it by telephone, do so. If your message is of a confidential or sensitive nature, use a telephone, if at all possible.

When dealing with Dispatch, remember that they might have many emergencies going on at the same time. Do not overload them with unnecessary questions, problems, or comments. Dispatching can get very hectic, at times. Always follow established communications procedures.

If your duties include handling telephone calls, remember that you are a professional. Many people are nervous about

Continued

calling any kind of government or emergency organization, even when they are simply seeking information. You should project a friendly, courteous, and helpful image with your voice and words. If the matter must be handled by someone else, tell the caller you will get him or her. If the person called isn't available, take a message in writing and be sure the other person gets it. When making outgoing calls of a personal nature on fire department lines, keep conversations as brief as possible. Remember your fellow firefighters might also need to make similar calls.

When writing reports, remember that they might be used months or even years later. For that reason, you must make them as complete and as clear as possible. Remember that the reader will not be able to ask you what you meant. You have to tell it right the first time. Keep your sentences short and in this form: who did it... and what did they do? Use specific, concrete terms, and avoid wordiness: don't use three words where one will do. State what you saw or heard, not what you think happened. Be careful to avoid confusing inferences with facts.

REVIEW QUESTIONS

1. Why is a megaphone represented on the emblems of many fire departments?
2. For an idea to be communicated between two people, the sender must _____ and the receiver must _____ it.
3. When referring to communications, what does the term "noise" mean? How can you, as the intended receiver of a message, prevent noise?
4. When instructing citizens on how to report an emergency, what three vital pieces of information should you tell them to provide?
5. Why are street corner alarm boxes no longer widely used in cities? Where are alarm boxes still found?
6. What are the two different purposes for which radio is used when an alarm is received?
7. What forms of communication, other than radio, are used to send out alarms?
8. What is the purpose of a central dispatching agency? What types of calls does it handle?
9. The three-digit number used to report emergencies in many communities is _____.
10. The use of sirens or other audible alarms to alert firefighters in many rural and suburban areas has one major drawback. What is it?
11. If a citizen should call to your fire department directly to report an emergency, to what person should you refer the caller?
12. What is a "bicycle" alarm?
13. What function does a squelch control perform? Briefly describe how it is used.
14. How should you hold a microphone when making a radio transmission?
15. Give three examples of "sensitive" information you should try to avoid transmitting by radio.

16. Describe how you should answer the telephone as a representative of the fire department. What tone of voice should you use?

17. Why should you place a caller on "hold" while they wait for the person to whom they wish to speak?

18. If you receive a telephone call at your fire station and the call is for someone who isn't there at the time, what should you do?

19. How would a clearly written report help you if you were called to testify in a court case a year after a fire or accident occurred?

20. What are the "5 Ws and an H"? How can they help you write a good report?

Today's fire communication methods are far different from those in use when this photo of the Williamsport (Pennsylvania) Fire Chief was taken in the early 1900s. Instead of radio, he had to rely on a megaphone and sheer lung power to communicate on the fireground; messengers and a telephone — if one was available — kept him in touch with headquarters. (Harold Anthony/Archive Photo)

NFPA 1001 Job Performance Requirements

The material on this page consists of those portions of the NFPA 1001 Job Performance Requirements relevant to the material presented in this chapter. Items preceded by the numeral 3 (3-x.x) are Fire Fighter I requirements; those with the numeral 4 (4-x.x) are Fire Fighter II requirements.

3-3.13 Conserve property as a member of a team, given salvage tools and equipment and an assignment, so that the building and its contents are protected from further damage.

(a) Prerequisite Knowledge: The purpose of property conservation and its value to the public, methods used to protect property, types of and uses for salvage covers, operations at properties protected with automatic sprinklers, how to stop the flow of water from an automatic sprinkler head, identification of the main control valve on an automatic sprinkler system, and forcible entry issues related to salvage.

(b) Prerequisite Skills: The ability to cluster furniture; deploy covering materials; roll and fold salvage covers for reuse; construct water chutes and catch-alls; remove water; cover building openings, including doors, windows, floor openings, and roof openings; separate, remove, and relocate charred material to a safe location while protect-

ing the area of origin for cause determination; stop the flow of water from a sprinkler with sprinkler wedges or stoppers; and operate a main control valve on an automatic sprinkler system.

(4-5.1)

(a) Prerequisite Knowledge: The sources of water supply for fire protection; the fundamentals of fire suppression and detection systems; common symbols used in diagramming construction features, utilities, hazards, and fire protection systems; departmental requirements for a preincident survey and form completion; and the importance of accurate diagrams.

(b) Prerequisite Skills: The ability to identify the components of fire suppression and detection systems; sketch the site, buildings, and special features; detect hazards and special considerations to include in the preincident sketch; and complete all related departmental forms.

Reprinted with permission from NFPA 1001, *Fire Fighter Professional Qualifications,* Copyright ©1997, National Fire Protection Association, Quincy, MA 02269. This reprinted material is not the complete and official position of the National Fire Protection Association on the referenced subject, which is represented only by the standard in its entirety.

Automatic Sprinkler Systems

OBJECTIVES

When you have completed this chapter, you will be able to:

- Distinguish between wet-pipe and dry-pipe sprinkler systems and describe situations in which each type might be installed.
- Identify the parts of an automatic sprinkler head.
- Describe how an automatic sprinkler head opens and releases water.
- Discuss how to identify a fire department sprinkler connection and a water flow alarm.
- List and describe the component parts of a sprinkler system.
- Describe how to temporarily stop the flow of water from a sprinkler head.

IMPORTANT TERMS

branch lines
cap
check valve
cross mains
deflector
dry-pipe sprinkler
  system

fire department
  connection
frame
glass bulb head
heat-responsive
  element
link-lever head

orifice
pendant sprinklers
solder pellet head
sprinkler flow alarm
sprinkler head
sprinkler riser
upright sprinklers

water flow detector
water main
water motor gong
wet-pipe sprinkler
  system

Of all firefighting devices and methods, automatic sprinklers are probably one of the most important available. Automatic sprinklers have been shown to be up to 98% effective in suppressing and extinguishing fires. They quickly and effectively control a fire, dramatically reducing the potential for release of heat and toxic gases. Losses from fires that occur in structures protected by sprinklers are one-fifth the loss experienced in non-sprinklered buildings. In a fire that is controlled by a sprinkler system, water damage is far less extensive than a fire extinguished by conventional hose line methods.

From the firefighter's point of view, these systems greatly reduce the risk of injury and loss of life by decreasing the possibility of large conflagrations. Related benefits are the potential saving of billions of gallons of water and significant reduction of fire insurance costs. Also, the "response time" of a properly maintained sprinkler system is virtually immediate — it will begin to operate within seconds after a fire starts. See **Figure 21-1.**

Figure 21-1. The "response time" of an automatic sprinkler system is virtually immediate. When the temperature at a sprinkler head reaches a preset limit, indicating the presence of fire, the head opens to spray water over a defined area.

There are two basic types of sprinkler systems in use, known as dry-pipe systems and wet-pipe systems. The more common of the two types is the *wet-pipe sprinkler system,* which is normally used in any building where the temperature remains above the freezing point of water, 32°F (0°C). In this system, water fills the pipes and begins to flow immediately when a sprinkler head is activated by the heat of a fire. *Dry-pipe sprinkler systems* are typically used in unheated spaces, where water might freeze. The pipes contain air under pressure, rather than water. When a sprinkler head opens, air pressure inside the system drops abruptly. This opens a valve, allowing water to flow into the piping system.

Fire protection engineers and insurance companies understand the purpose and functioning of sprinkler systems. Insurance organizations have strongly promoted the installation of automatic sprinkler systems to protect the buildings that they insure. According to the National Fire Protection Association, properly installed and maintained sprinkler systems are very effective. The NFPA found that most fires in such buildings were either controlled or extinguished by a small number of sprinkler heads. Historically, there has never been a large loss of life recorded in a building where the sprinkler system has been properly maintained. The value of this important tool should be obvious. As a firefighter, it is vital that you understand the automatic sprinkler system and how it performs to protect life and property.

The Sprinkler Head

The *active* component of an automatic sprinkler system — the part that goes into action when a fire occurs — is the *sprinkler head.* Spaced in a regular pattern to cover every square foot of floor area in the protected space, **Figure 21-2**, sprinkler heads are responsive to heat. When the heat-responsive element of any sprinkler head reaches a preset temperature, the flow of water is initiated.

Although there are a number of types of sprinkler heads, and some variations within each type, all have five basic elements:

- A *frame* with a threaded connection that screws into the water supply pipe.
- A *heat-responsive element* that melts or breaks when a preset temperature is reached. This releases pressure on the cap over the orifice, so that water can flow.
- An *orifice* (hole), that extends through the threaded portion of the frame to allow water to flow from the supply pipe when pressure on the cap is released.
- A *cap* that is held in place over the orifice by the heat-sensitive element. When the element melts or breaks, water pressure pushes the cap off the orifice.

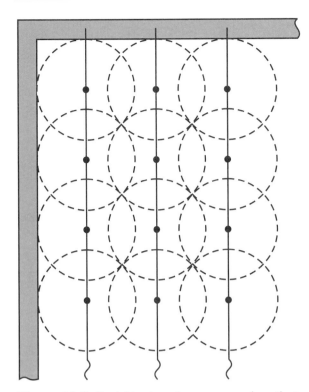

Figure 21-2. Sprinkler heads are spaced so that their spray patterns overlap, providing coverage to every square foot of protected space. Since individual heads are activated by heat, only those in the immediate vicinity of a fire will operate. This minimizes water damage to building and contents.

- A *deflector* that causes the jet of water from the orifice to break up into a spray pattern and cover a specified area.

Types of Sprinkler Heads

One of the most common sprinkler head types has a heat-responsive element that consists of a system of fusible links and levers. This sprinkler head is commonly referred to as the *link-lever head* or fusible-link type head. This sprinkler head has more components than used in other heads. As shown in **Figure 21-3**, the frame surrounds two levers that are held in place by a fusible link (the heat-responsive element). The levers, in turn, hold the cap in place over the orifice. The operating temperature at which the sprinkler head will activate is determined

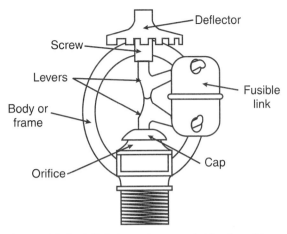

Figure 21-3. A link-lever type sprinkler head is the most common, and has more components than other types of sprinkler heads. So long as the link holds the levers in tension, the cap will keep the orifice closed, preventing water flow.

by the melting point of the solder used to hold the two link plates together. When the link plates are released, they allow the lever arms to fly apart. The cap can then be forced off the orifice by water pressure. **Figure 21-4** shows the operation of a fusible link head.

Another common sprinkler head is the *solder pellet head,* which uses a single formed piece of fusible material instead of a link and levers. As shown in **Figure 21-5**, the solder pellet holds the cap in place over the orifice. When exposed to a predetermined temperature, the pellet melts, allowing the sprinkler head to operate.

A type of sprinkler head that does not use a fusible link is the *glass bulb head,* **Figure 21-6**. In this sprinkler head, the cap over the orifice is held in place by a glass bulb that is partly filled with liquid. When the temperature rises to the preset level, the liquid inside the bulb expands. This breaks the glass bulb, releasing the cap and allowing the water to flow.

Replacing Sprinkler Heads

Sprinkler heads are initially chosen for the structure by the fire protection engineer, based upon the system environment and the

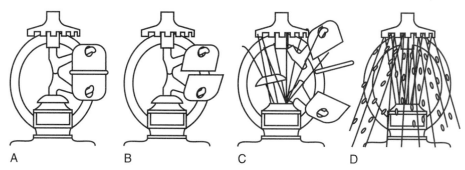

Figure 21-4. Operation of a link-lever sprinkler head. A—Solder holds the link plates together keeping tension on the levers. B—When the solder melts the link plates are no longer joined and tension on the levers is released. C—The levers, no longer under tension, fly apart and allow water pressure to act on the cap covering the orifice. D—The cap is pushed off the orifice by water pressure. The stream of water exiting the orifice strikes the deflector and is broken up into a spray.

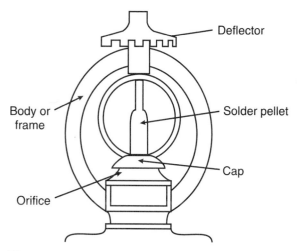

Figure 21-5. Components of the solder pellet sprinkler head. When the formed solder pellet melts, tension on the cap is released, allowing water pressure to push it off the orifice.

Figure 21-6. The glass bulb sprinkler head uses a liquid-filled glass bulb as the heat-responsive element. Heat expands the liquid, breaking the bulb and opening the orifice.

conditions under which individual heads will operate. Every sprinkler head is color-coded by the manufacturer to show the temperature rating at which it will open. The standard color coding of sprinkler heads is shown in **Figure 21-7**.

Whenever you must replace a sprinkler head that has opened, always be sure to use a replacement head with a matching temperature rating. Look at the color coding on the activated sprinkler head and replace it with one that has the same color coding. The National Fire Protection Association

Standard for the Installation of Sprinkler Systems requires that spare sprinkler heads be kept on site to replace any that have been activated. The best place to look for replacement heads would be a box mounted near the sprinkler controls, **Figure 21-8**. *Never shut down a sprinkler system to replace heads (or for any other reason) without an order from a chief officer.* While your sector may be controlled, other areas of the fire ground may need the continued operation of the system.

Figure 21-7. Color coding for replacement sprinkler heads.

Color Codes/Temperature Ratings			
Hazard	Expected Max. Ceiling Temperature	Temperature Rating Of Head In Degrees Fahrenheit	Color Code
Ordinary	100°F	135°F-165°F	No color (typically brass or chrome)
Intermediate	150°F	175°F-212°F	White
High	225°F	250°F-286°F	Blue
Extra High	300°F	325°F-360°F	Red
Very Extra High	375°F	400°F-450°F	Green
Ultra High	475°F	500°F-575°F	Orange

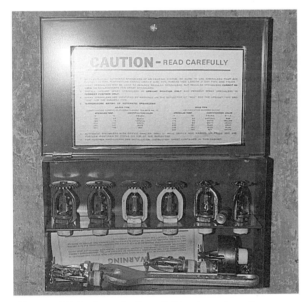

Figure 21-8. A typical sprinkler head replacement box mounted near the sprinkler riser and control valve. The NFPA standard for sprinkler systems requires spare heads to be kept on hand. (Warren Lutton)

Sprinkler System Piping

Every sprinkler system is made up of component parts that form its basic piping. This basic piping includes the water main from the source of supply, the sprinkler riser, the cross mains, and the branch lines. A fire department connection is also part of the basic system. These components are described in the following sections:

Water Main

The *water main* is the pipe extending from the water source to the point where it enters an individual building, **Figure 21-9.** The water main system for a particular area usually will include pipes of several sizes. Large *distributor* mains usually run beneath major streets and are connected directly to the water source. Smaller *branch* mains are connected to the distributor mains to serve residential neighborhoods, commercial districts, or industrial areas. Sizes and types of mains are determined by the flow requirements: a single industrial plant that uses large quantities of water may be served by a bigger main than an entire residential neighborhood.

Water supply

The most common form of water supply for an automatic sprinkler system is the public water system that feeds the community's mains. When available, a reliable public water system is preferred as the primary source of water supply for automatic

Figure 21-9. The water main is piping of various sizes that extends from the water source to the building containing the sprinkler system. It is connected to the sprinkler riser.

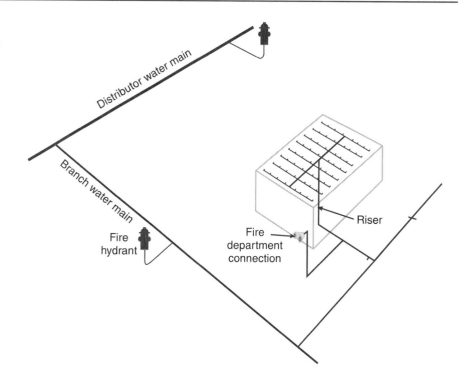

sprinklers, since the quantity of water is generally unlimited. The system must be capable of delivering efficient pressure and volume; unfortunately, public water systems are often hampered by low water pressure.

When a public water supply is not available or is inadequate, one or more types of private water supply must be used to assure sufficient volume for the sprinkler system. Private water soures can include elevated tanks, gravity tanks, and static water supplies. See **Figure 21-10.** In most cases, when the private water supply relies upon the use of an elevated tank, it is using a limited source of water. To supplement such a limited supply, fire pumps can draft from private water supplies or natural sources (rivers, lakes, ponds) to supply an adequate water flow to the sprinkler system.

Fire Department Connection

Because a large number of sprinkler heads may have to operate in an extensive fire, there may not be enough pressure at the individual heads for the system to be effective. To overcome this problem, automatic

sprinkler systems have a *fire department connection,* usually mounted on an outside wall of the building. See **Figure 21-11.** When a fire occurs in a sprinklered structure, the fire department supports the automatic sprinkler system by providing additional pressure and water volume. This is accomplished by connecting a pumper between a source of water (usually a hydrant) and the fire department connection.

Fire department connections should be properly marked and easily accessible. Each connection is equipped with a *check valve,* which ensures that the flow of water will always be in the direction of the system. See **Figure 21-12.** Also included on a fire department connection is an approved drain, **Figure 21-13,** to allow the fire department connection piping to be drained off after use of the system.

When a building has a single sprinkler system riser, the fire department connection should be attached to the sprinkler system side of the controlling gate valve for a wet type of sprinkler system. This arrangement will allow the fire department to provide a source of water in the event that the controlling gate

Figure 21-10. A water tower that has a limited capacity for serving a sprinkler system. Many industrial plants have such a private water source in addition to the public supply.

Figure 21-11. The fire department connection is usually found on the building's outside wall near the point where the water main connects to the sprinkler system riser.

valve has been closed. In buildings that have multiple sprinkler systems, each system should have its own fire department connection. In large industrial installations where many different sprinkler systems are connected to common water mains, one fire department connection can be used on the supply side of each riser. During a fire, the fire department can then pump water from a source of supply into the sprinkler system through its hoses and the fire department connection.

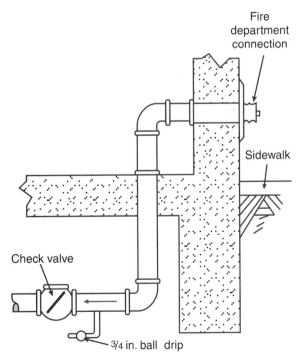

Figure 21-12. A check valve between the fire department connection and the sprinkler system ensures that water can flow in only one direction — into the system.

Figure 21-13. A drain must be provided in the fire department connection piping to allow water to be drained off after the system is used. (Warren Lutton)

One of the first priorities of a fire department responding to a sprinkler-equipped building is to support the sprinkler system with additional water. Assuming that the search and rescue operations are already under way, the first pumper on the scene will usually connect to the system's fire department connection and maintain adequate water supply and adequate water pressure. You should not wait for orders to make the hookup, but do not start pumping into the sprinkler system until told to do so.

This hookup can be accomplished even when the sprinkler system is in operation because of the check valve that is installed on the fire department connection. Making this fire department connection is not essentially different from connecting to a fire hydrant. Sprinkler connections have 2 1/2 inch female inlets, but larger or smaller hose may be used, with the proper adapters. You must practice the same precautions and follow the same basic procedures used when connecting to a hydrant. Follow this procedure:

1. Remove the caps, using a spanner wrench. (Some connections have breakaway caps that must be removed using spanners or a hydrant wrench.)
2. Check the siamese swivels to be sure that they rotate freely. Often, they will be painted shut or have grit in them, preventing free rotation. Tapping lightly with a spanner wrench will help to free them.
3. Check for presence of a gasket, **Figure 21-14.** Gaskets will sometimes be missing or

Figure 21-14. Always check the fire department connection for presence of a gasket. If gasket is missing or damaged, replace it.

Gasket

badly damaged and unusable. Always carry a few spare 2 $\frac{1}{2}$ in. gaskets on the apparatus to be prepared for such situations.

4. Connect a hose to the left side of the connection first. This will help prevent cracking your knuckles against a butt when you connect the second hose line.

Sprinkler Riser

The first component of an automatic sprinkler system *inside* the building is the *sprinkler riser,* **Figure 21-15.** This pipe

Figure 21-15. The sprinkler riser is equipped with control valves for turning the water on and off and for draining the system when necessary for repairs. Note chain on the main shutoff valve wheel to prevent inadvertent shutting off of the system. (Warren Lutton)

connects the water main to the network of pipes that makes up the sprinkler system itself. The pipe is called a "riser" because it rises up vertically from ground level or below to the ceiling of the protected space.

The riser will usually be equipped with control valves, a check valve, and a water flow detector. The control valves are used to shut off the water supply to the sprinkler system when maintenance work must be done or a sprinkler head replaced after a fire. A check valve, as noted earlier, allows water flow in only one direction — toward the sprinkler heads.

A *water flow detector,* **Figure 21-16,** is a simple device consisting of a paddle or small water wheel inside the riser. Any flow of water (indicating that a sprinkler head has opened) will move the paddle or wheel and close a switch, activating a *sprinkler flow alarm.* The alarm bell or similar sounding device is usually located on an outside wall of the building, where it can be heard by passersby or arriving firefighters. Typically, a sign is located near the alarm enclosure that reads, "SPRINKLER FIRE ALARM. If alarm sounds, call fire or police department." Many modern sprinkler systems can also send an alarm automatically

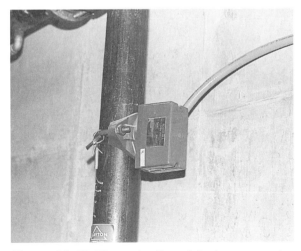

Figure 21-16. The water flow detector, on most modern sprinkler systems, will activate a flow alarm that both sends a signal to the fire department or a dispatching service and sounds an audible alarm outside the building.

to the fire department or an emergency dispatch center in case of water flow.

One of the simplest alarm devices is purely mechanical in nature. The *water motor gong* is connected by piping to a valve that opens whenever water is flowing in the sprinkler system. A small stream of water flows through the pipe and turns a water wheel, which in turn rotates a drive shaft. A striker on the drive shaft repeatedly strikes the gong.

Cross Mains and Branch Lines

Cross mains are the transmission mains or "arterials" that carry the water from the sprinkler riser to the branch lines. See **Figure 21-17.** Usually, the only connections to cross mains are the branch lines; sprinkler heads are not connected directly to them.

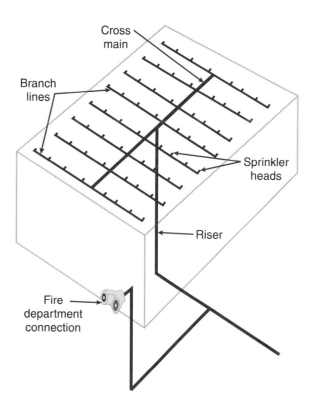

Figure 21-17. Cross mains carry water to the branch lines, upon which the sprinkler heads are mounted. This is a simple system; actual piping may be much more complex.

The *branch lines* are the pipes that transmit water from the cross mains to the sprinkler heads. Branch lines may include various sizes piping, depending upon the distance they extend from the cross mains and the number of sprinkler heads that are mounted on them. Sprinkler heads may be installed atop the branch line piping (*upright sprinklers*) or hung below it (*pendant sprinklers*). Both types of sprinkler heads have deflectors that spread or diffuse the stream of water to cover a wider area for better control of fire. In the upright position, the sprinkler head has a deflector that will diffuse the water downward. On a pendant head, the deflector diffuses the water outward and downward. Upright heads are usually found in dry-pipe sprinkler systems so that water cannot collect in the heads and freeze, making the system inoperable. A wet-pipe system may use either upright or pendant heads.

Each sprinkler head has the three initials SSU or SSP printed on it. These initials stand for *Standard Sprinkler Upright* or *Standard Sprinkler Pendant.* They are a reminder that, when replacing a sprinkler head, you must replace it with the right type — pendant with pendant; upright with upright.

Stopping Sprinkler Heads Temporarily

In most cases, fires are contained or extinguished by no more than four or five sprinkler heads. Since a single sprinkler head may be discharging 15 gpm (gallons per minute) or more, it is a good idea to discontinue the flow from activated sprinkler heads once the fire has been extinguished. This will minimize water damage and conserve water for use elsewhere. See **Figure 21-18.**

To temporarily stop the flow of water from an individual sprinkler head, without shutting down the entire system, use a sprinkler shutoff. The shutoff is inserted into the frame so the flow of water is blocked at the sprinkler orifice. Sprinkler head wrenches are

Figure 21-18. Once the fire is extinguished in your area, the sprinkler heads should be shut off temporarily to minimize water damage. It will also conserve the water supply for use in other areas of the building. (Warren Lutton)

available with a rubber pad that can be placed against the sprinkler orifice to cut off the flow of water, **Figure 21-19.** Once pressure has been placed upon the sprinkler opening by this rubber pad, simply pull back

on the ring to force the sprinkler wrench into the open position.

An alternative method, if a sprinkler head wrench is not available, is to cut a wooden wedge to fit inside the frame opening. Drive that wedge into the sprinkler frame, blocking the orifice.

No matter how you stop the flow, it eventually will be necessary to shut off the main control valve to replace the open heads of the sprinkler system. Once the system is shut off, the firefighter who shut the valve off *must* remain at the valve until the sprinkler system is restored to service. This is necessary so that, if the fire flares up again, the firefighter can immediately return the sprinkler system to service by turning the valve back on.

Figure 21-19. A sprinkler head wrench with rubber pad can be used to temporarily shut off flow of an individual sprinkler head. Several other devices are available for this purpose.

SUMMARY

Sprinklers are an extremely important tool to the fire service. Sprinklers begin to apply water as soon as the temperature becomes hot enough to activate a temperature-rated sprinkler head. Since they apply water directly to the area of the fire, sprinklers tend to conserve water and lessen the water damage to the fire building. Sprinkler systems may be of either the wet-pipe or dry-pipe type, and may be supplied by either a public water system or a private water system. Regardless of the water source, the first pumper on the scene should hook up to the fire department connection and supplement the pressure and volume to the sprinkler system.

The most common style of sprinkler head is the link-lever, or fusible link, sprinkler head. Other sprinkler heads use either a solder pellet or a breakable glass bulb in place of the link and levers. All sprinkler heads are color coded to indicate the temperature at which they will operate. When replacing a sprinkler head that has opened, use one with the same color code.

Sprinkler heads can be installed in either upright or pendant positions. Upright heads, installed above the sprinkler

Continued

piping, are typically used in dry-pipe sprinkler systems so that water cannot collect in the head and freeze making the system inoperable. A wet type system may contain either upright or pendant (below-the-pipe) heads.

When a sprinkler head activates, the flow of water may activate either a water motor gong or a water flow alarm. These audible alarms alert people in the vicinity that there is a fire in the building. Some sprinkler alarms also automatically notify the fire department or some other dispatching agency.

Once the fire is out, a sprinkler head shutoff or a simple wedge may be used to temporarily stop the discharge of water from the sprinkler head. When it becomes necessary to shut down the entire sprinkler system, the firefighter assigned the duty of shutting off the main system control valve must remain with that valve until ordered to turn it on again. By remaining at the valve, the firefighter can, in the event of a flareup, immediately reactivate the sprinkler system.

REVIEW QUESTIONS

1. Describe the importance of automatic sprinkler systems as a firefighting tool.
2. What are the two basic types of sprinkler systems? Which type would be used in an unheated warehouse in a cold climate? Why?
3. True or false? A large loss of life has never occurred from a fire in a building with a properly maintained sprinkler system.
4. Name the parts of a typical sprinkler head and describe their functions.
5. What is the most common type of sprinkler head?
6. What is the essential difference between the glass bulb sprinkler head and the types that use fusible material?
7. Why are sprinkler heads color coded?
8. Name the piping components, in order, between the water source and the sprinkler head.
9. What is the most common problem of public water systems, when serving as a supply source for a sprinkler system?
10. Name several sources for private water supply to a sprinkler system.
11. Assuming that search and rescue are already underway, what should be done immediately by the first pumper to arrive at a fire in a sprinkler-system-equipped building?
12. What feature of a fire department connection allows a pumper to connect to it even while the sprinkler system is actively operating?
13. Describe the procedure for making a hookup to the fire department connection.
14. Why is the sprinkler riser called by that name?
15. What is the purpose of the control valves on the sprinkler riser?
16. How does the water flow detector operate?
17. What is a water motor gong? Describe its operation.
18. Besides sounding an audible signal outside the building, what do the sprinkler flow alarms of most modern systems also do?
19. Why are upright sprinkler heads used in dry-pipe systems?
20. If you are directed to turn off the main control valve of a sprinkler system, what should you do after carrying out that order?

Devastating fires like this one that occurred in an Eastern U.S. city in the early decades of the century have decreased in number, but have not been entirely eliminated, by the greatly increased use of automatic sprinkler systems in commercial structures. (Harold Anthony/Archive Photo)

NFPA 1001 Job Performance Requirements

The material on this page consists of those portions of the NFPA 1001 Job Performance Requirements relevant to the material presented in this chapter. Items preceded by the numeral 3 (3-x.x) are Fire Fighter I requirements; those with the numeral 4 (4-x.x) are Fire Fighter II requirements.

3-1.1 For certification at Level I, the fire fighter shall meet the job performance requirements defined in Sections 3-2 through 3-6 of this standard and the requirements defined in Chapter 2, Competencies for the First Responder at the Awareness Level, of NFPA 472, *Standard for Professional Competence of Responders to Hazardous Materials Incidents.*

Reprinted with permission from NFPA 1001, *Fire Fighter Professional Qualifications*, Copyright ©1997, National Fire Protection Association, Quincy, MA 02269. This reprinted material is not the complete and official position of the National Fire Protection Association on the referenced subject, which is represented only by the standard in its entirety.

Hazardous Materials (Awareness Level)

OBJECTIVES

When you have completed this chapter, you will be able to:

♦ Discuss the basic Acts and Standards relating to hazardous materials.

♦ Describe the Department of Transportation Hazard Classes and Divisions and the potential outcomes of incidents involving materials from each Class.

♦ Use the various methods of determining whether a hazardous material is involved in an incident.

♦ Demonstrate proper use of the DOT Emergency Response Guidebook in identifying a hazardous material and proper response.

♦ Show understanding of the Awareness level responder's role in dealing with a HazMat incident.

IMPORTANT TERMS

Awareness Level	Response Act	HazMat	placards
chemical identification	(HAZWOPER)	Initial Isolation Zone	Protective Action Zone
DOT	Federal Superfund	initial response phase	shelter-in-place
Emergency Response	Amendments and	labels	Structural Firefighter's
Guidebook (ERG)	Reauthorization Act	Material Safety Data	Protective Clothing
evacuation	of 1986 (SARA)	Sheet (MSDS)	(SFPC)
exposure	Hazard Classes	National Fire Protection	transportation-related
Federal Hazardous	hazardous material	Association (NFPA)	incident
Waste Operations	occupancies	NFPA 472	UN/NA numbers
and Emergency	hazardous materials	NFPA 704	

Hazardous materials are manufactured, transported, stored, and processed in ever-expanding varieties and amounts. Most of the time, this is done safely and without incident. There are times, however, when hazardous materials escape containment. They then can pose a threat to people, to the environment, and to property. The danger can be immediate or long-term. When hazardous material is accidentally released, the fire department is nearly always the agency to respond first.

How often have you heard that firefighters rush in when others rush out? Although that may appeal to the ego, it also can lead to tragedy. With hazardous materials, charging in can be deadly. Over the years, firefighters have entered hazardous materials danger zones to attempt a rescue, quickly extinguish a fire, or stop a leak. Unfortunately, these firefighters were all too often blown to pieces, incinerated, poisoned, or asphyxiated. By rushing in, the responders became the victims.

Hazardous materials have changed the way firefighters conduct operations. You must learn the dangers of hazardous chemical events. Rules and standards have been developed to provide guidance and even legal regulation for both chemical users and emergency responders. But accidents involving dangerous chemicals will still happen and firefighters will be called. As a firefighter, you must be dedicated to HazMat competency. You owe that to yourself, your family, your department, and your community.

Every year, thousands of hazardous materials incidents occur. Most do not make the front page of the newspaper or lead off the evening television newscast. But any of these incidents *could* pose a serious threat to responders, the public, the environment, or property.

What Are Hazardous Materials?

What are *hazardous materials* or *HazMats?* There are many definitions, but a useful generalization is, *substances which, when released from containment, pose an unreasonable risk to life, health, the environment, or property.*

You will see similar terms like "hazardous chemicals," "hazardous substances," "extremely hazardous substances," "hazardous wastes," "toxic substances," and a number of others. These terms have different meanings, particularly for the government agencies that regulate them. But for the typical firefighter, they all can be equated with *hazardous materials.*

For decades, firefighters have been responding to "chemical" emergencies. As the number and variety of chemicals increased, so did the potential for damage when they escaped from containment. Any time that a chemical substance is spilled, the potential exists for physical damage to property and the environment, as well as danger to people and other living things. The term "HazMat" become popular in the fire service in the late 1960s and early 1970s. Through the 1970s and into the 1980s, we became more aware of HazMat incidents and their potential results to communities and responders.

Three events in the middle 1980s had a major impact on how firefighters (and other emergency service personnel) respond to HazMats today. In 1984, a methyl isocyanate release in Bhopal, India, killed thousands and injured tens of thousands. In the same year, the *National Fire Protection Association (NFPA)* was asked to develop standards for those who responded to HazMat calls. In 1986, there was another methyl isocyanate incident, this time in the United States. Fortunately, the outcome of this spill, at Institute, West Virginia, was not disastrous like the one in Bhopal. The Bhopal and Institute incidents contributed to the passage of the *Federal Superfund Amendments and Reauthorization Act of 1986 (SARA)* and the *Federal Hazardous Waste Operations and Emergency Response Act (HAZWOPER).* HazMat responder standards created by the National Fire Protection Association provided a basis for portions of HAZWOPER. This legislation became effective in 1990.

Levels of Competence for Responders

HAZWOPER and *NFPA 472, Standard for Professional Competence of Responders to Hazardous Materials Incidents,* set the minimum competencies expected of responders. Under HAZWOPER, emergency service providers responding to HazMat accidents must be competent to perform certain tasks. Initially, NFPA 472 established these five levels of competence:

- First Responder Awareness
- First Responder Operations
- Hazardous Materials Technician
- Hazardous Materials Specialist
- On-Scene Incident Commander

The first four levels built upon the previous ones. See **Figure 22-1.** The current NFPA 472 standard combines the Specialist and Technician levels and creates a new Off-Site Specialist Employee designation. The Incident Command level is based on the Awareness and Operations levels; it does not require Technician or Specialist competence. Technicians and Specialists are considered "offensive" competencies, while the others are "defensive." Responders should never attempt to perform beyond their level of training and competency.

Firefighters and others who are certified for the various levels must receive annual

Training Levels				
	Requires Employer Certification of Competence			
1st Responder Awareness	**1st Responder Operations**	**H. M. Technician**	**H. M. Specialist**	**On Scene Command**
No hours specified	Awareness Level plus 8 hrs. training or sufficient experience to show competency in areas below	24 hrs. training in Ops Level plus competency in areas below	24 hrs. training in Technician Level plus competency in areas below	24 hrs. training in Ops Level plus competency in areas below
Understand H.M. & risks				
Potential outcome of H.M. emergencies	Basic hazard & risk assessment techniques	Basic hazard & risk assessment techniques	In-depth hazard & risk assessment techniques	
Recognize outcome of H.M. emergencies				
Recognize presence of H.M.	Select/use proper personal protective equipment (PPE)	Select/use proper specialized chemical PPE	Select/use proper specialized chemical PPE	Hazards/risks in working in chemical PPE
Ability to identify H.M.	Understand basic H.M. terms	Understand basic chemical & toxicological terms/ behavior	Understand chemical, radiological, toxicological terms/ behavior	
Understand role of Awareness Level				
Understand site security	Basic control within capabilities of resources & PPE	Advanced control within capabilities of resources & PPE	Specialized control within capabilities of resources & PPE	
Understand DOT ERG	Implement basic decon	Understand/implement decon	Determine/implement decon	Understand importance of decon
Realize need for more resources	Understand relevant SOPs	Implement employer's emergency response plan (ERP)	Implement local emergency response plan (ERP)	Implement employer's ERP
Notify communication center				Implement local ERP
	Understand termination procedures	Understand termination procedures		
			Know of State ERP	Know of State ERP
	Function within Incident Command System (ICS)		Develop site safety/ control place	Implement ICS
				Know of Regional Response Team
	Field survey instruments/ equipment		Advanced survey instruments/ equipment	

Figure 22-1. The NFPA 472 Standard, as originally set up, established five levels of competence with the responsibilities shown. All levels above Awareness require certification by the employer.

refresher training to maintain competence, or must annually demonstrate competence. The department or employer is required to keep a record of training or demonstrations of competence (including a description of the methods used).

Awareness level

First Responder Awareness, according to HAZWOPER, is for those who are likely to witness or discover a hazardous substance release. Further, NFPA 472 expects *Awareness Level* responders to recognize the presence of hazardous materials and be able to protect themselves. The Awareness Level responder notifies proper authorities of the release and takes no further action regarding the release. Securing the area is an appropriate activity at the Awareness Level, so long as it is safely done.

First Responder Awareness requires sufficient training or experience to show these competencies:

- An understanding of what hazardous materials are and their associated risks in an incident.

- An understanding of the potential outcomes of a hazardous material emergency.

- The ability to recognize the presence of hazardous materials in an emergency.

- An understanding by the First Responder Awareness Level person of his or her role in the department or employer's response plan (including site security and control and the DOT Emergency Response Guidebook).

- The ability to realize the need for additional resources and how to make appropriate notification to the communications center.

Hazardous Material Classifications

The many thousands of hazardous materials and the risks they pose are easier to understand if they are logically categorized. This has been done by the U.S. Department of Transportation (*DOT*). The DOT has developed a system of *Hazard Classes* and Divisions which is the basis for transportation labeling and placarding.

Class 1: *Explosives.* These are substances or articles designed to function by an extremely rapid release of heat and gas or by a chemical reaction within itself (even if not designed to explode). Within this class, there are six divisions. Divisions 1.1 and 1.2 correspond essentially to the former Class A Explosives designation. Some examples of materials in this class are TNT and detonating fuses (UN 0107). Division 1.3 equates to the former Class B Explosives (such as flash powder), and Division 1.4, to the former Class C Explosives (such as common fireworks). Division 1.5 contains the Blasting Agents, such as Type E blasting explosives (UN 0332). Materials in Division 1.6 are insensitive and do not have mass explosion potential.

Class 2: *Gases.* Most simply defined, a gas is the formless fluid state of a substance that conforms to the shape of its container and fills the entire volume of that container. Gases are grouped into three divisions: *Flammable Gases,* such as propane, (Division 2.1); *Nonflammable, Nonpoisonous Compressed Gases,* such as nitrogen, (Division 2.2), and *Poisonous Gases,* such as chlorine, (Division 2.3). Gases can be compressed, liquefied, or cryogenic. Responders should understand that some nonflammable gases, such as anhydrous ammonia, actually can burn but do not meet the formal definition of a Flammable Gas.

Class 3: *Liquids.* Flammable Liquids have flash points not higher than 141°F (61°C). Some definitions use a flash point under 100°F (38°C). Under current DOT regulations, Combustible Liquids are those not meeting the definition of any other hazard class except Class 9 and with a flash point between 100°F and 200°F (38°C and 93°C). DOT permits shippers to reclassify materials with flash points between 100°F and 141°F (38°C and 61°C) as Combustible Liquids. Note that packages of 110 gallons or less of Combustible Liquids are not regulated by DOT, so those packages need not be labeled. The responder should examine several reference sources to determine the flash point of a particular material.

Class 4: *Flammable solid, spontaneously combustible, and dangerous when wet materials.* These materials are generally solids that can ignite. Division 4.1 is Flammable Solids (such as wetted explosives, self-reactive materials, or combustible solids like highway safety flares). Spontaneously Combustible Materials (Division 4.2) are solids or liquids that can heat or ignite when they are exposed to air. The metallic element hafnium, in dry powder form, is an example. Substances in Division 4.3, Dangerous When Wet Materials can ignite when exposed to water. Another metallic element, lithium, is an example of this type of substance.

Class 5: *Oxidizers and organic peroxides.* Oxidizers (Division 5.1) such as ammonium nitrate fertilizer (UN 2072) enhance combustion but may not themselves burn. Organic Peroxides (Division 5.2) are oxidizers which carry their own fuel. This makes some of them especially hazardous.

Class 6: *Poisonous materials.* These materials (Division 6.1) are solids or liquids, such as carbofuran, that are known or presumed to be toxic or an irritant to humans. Poisonous *gases* are classified separately, as part of Class 2. Infectious Substances (Division 6.2) are microorganisms or toxins that can cause disease. Hepatitis is an example.

Class 7: *Radioactive materials.* These substances, such as thorium ore, spontaneously emit ionizing radiation with a specific activity greater than 0.002 microcuries per gram.

Class 8: *Corrosive materials.* These liquid or solid materials, which might be acids (nitric acid is an example) or bases (such as sodium hydroxide), cause visible destruction or irreversible deterioration to living tissue at the point of contact. The term is also used for a liquid that has a high corrosion rate on steel.

Class 9: *Miscellaneous hazardous materials.* This class includes hazardous substances that are not included in any other Hazard Class, but that pose a threat during transportation.

ORM-D Materials. These are Other Regulated Materials that pose limited transportation hazards — normally, materials are in small quantities or consumer packages. Dry ice is in this class.

There are some materials whose transportation by any means is *forbidden,* because of the serious hazards they represent.

The release of hazardous materials can injure and kill living things, cause genetic damage, destroy or contaminate property, or pollute air and water. Effects can be immediate, delayed, or both. Mitigation and clean-up costs can bankrupt businesses.

Potential Outcomes in HazMat Incidents

It is imperative for you to know what might happen when you respond to an incident where hazardous materials are involved. Potential outcomes are described below, organized by DOT Hazard Classes.

- *Class 1, Explosives:* Detonation with shock wave, sound wave, flying debris, fire, and heat. Deflagration occurs with very rapid burning, fire, and heat.

- *Class 2, Gases:* Container rupture, flying debris, fire, heat, asphyxiation, poisoning, frostbite, release of oxidizers.

- *Class 3, Liquids:* Container rupture, flying debris, fire, heat, toxic products, environmental contamination.

- *Class 4, Flammable solids, etc.:* Intense combustion, high heat, toxic/corrosive products.

- *Class 5, Oxidizers and organic peroxides:* Combustion enhancement even of products normally difficult to ignite, intense combustion, sensitivity to heat, shock, friction, light, contamination.

- *Class 6, Poisons:* Poisoning, disease, fire, environmental contamination.
- *Class 7, Radioactives:* Biological burns, radiation sickness, genetic damage.
- *Class 8, Corrosives:* Chemical burns, environmental contamination, toxic products, combustion.
- *Class 9, Miscellaneous hazardous materials:* Can affect passengers and crew or the transporting vehicle itself.

Identifying Hazardous Materials

HazMat emergencies occur both at fixed sites and during transportation. There are several methods that can be used to determine, with varying degrees of accuracy, that an event involves hazardous materials. *Do not* make yourself a victim trying to identify the hazardous material. Methods used to identify whether hazardous materials are involved include:

- Occupancy.
- Container shape.
- Placards/labels.
- Markings/colors.
- Shipping papers.
- Senses.

If possible, use several methods to verify the presence of a hazardous material.

Correct **chemical identification** is essential. Develop the habit, when using telephones and department radios, of initially spelling chemical names. Spell carefully and clearly. Many hazardous materials have lengthy names which are difficult to pronounce. (try saying *tert-butyl peroxy-2-ethylhexanoate, with 2, 2-DI (tert-butylperoxy) butane* clearly.) Even though materials might have spellings or pronunciations that are similar, there is no guarantee that the hazards they present are similar hazards. As you use the methods described in the following sections to identify the hazardous material, always spell and respell the names.

Occupancy

Based on knowledge acquired before the incident, are hazardous materials probably at the site? Is it a known HazMat site? Is it a SARA Title III Planning Facility and/or Tier Two Report filer? Have there been previous HazMat releases there? Sites such as water or sewage treatment plants, chemical companies, agricultural supply centers, fuel terminals, paint stores, farms, or repair garages are obvious *hazardous material occupancies.* See **Figure 22-2.** To be safe, assume that any occupancy can have hazardous materials on site and be involved in the incident.

Figure 22-2. Occupancy is a clue to the probability of hazardous materials on site. Assume that a chemical plant such as this one, like most manufacturing facilities, will have hazardous materials stored. Tank trucks and trailers on site are also likely to be carrying hazardous cargoes. (Fruehauf)

Container Shape

At a fixed site, look for storage tanks, processing and pressure vessels, piping/tubing/hoses, vats, towers, or diked areas. Tank cars or trucks, cylinders, drums, casks, carboys, and bags may be visible on the site. If it is a *transportation-related incident,* look for tank cars or trucks, tube trailers, casks on flat trailers or railcars, cylinders, ton containers, or barrels. Remember that rail box cars and van-type trailers may also carry hazardous materials. See **Figure 22-3.**

Placards and Labels

Placards are warning signs, based on the DOT Hazard Classes, that are used on rail and highway carriers. They are displayed on all four sides of the truck or rail car. As shown in **Figure 22-4**, they are standardized square, diamond-on-point signs 10 3/4-in. (27.3 cm) on a side. You must be familiar with the colors, symbols, and hazard class numbers used with placards, since each offers general identification information. A four-digit *UN/NA number* may be placed on the placard or on a nearby 6 1/4 in. by 15 3/4 in. (15.9 cm by 40 cm) orange panel. The UN/NA number more definitively identifies the product. If the placard/panel has a four-digit number, refer to

Figure 22-4. Identification placards must be displayed on trucks and rail cars carrying materials that fall into one of the DOT Hazard Classes. The 4-digit UN/NA number for the material may be on the placard or a separate adjoining panel. This placard identifies the material (1830) as sulfuric acid. The drawings at the top of the placard and the numeral 8 at the bottom denote that the material is a corrosive. (Photo courtesy of Lab Safety Supply, Inc., Janesville, WI)

the blue section of the DOT Emergency Response Guidebook.

Any quantity of a hazardous material that is listed in **Figure 22-5** must be placarded. Hazardous materials listed in **Figure 22-6** must be placarded only if the quantity exceeds 1000 pounds (453.6 kg).

A

B

Figure 22-3. Transportation-related HazMat incidents can take place on roadways, waterways, or other locations. A—Tanker trucks often carry materials that are designated as hazardous. B—Although barges for oil and other liquid cargoes are easily identified as having hazardous contents, even dry cargo barges like these may carry materials that are dangerous.

Materials That MUST Be Placarded	
Hazard Division/Class	Placard
Division 1.1	EXPLOSIVES 1.1
Division 1.2	EXPLOSIVES 1.2
Division 1.3	EXPLOSIVES 1.3
Division 2.3	POISON GAS
Division 4.3	DANGEROUS WHEN WET
Division 6.1 PG I, Inhalation Hazard	POISON
Class 7 Yellow III label	RADIOACTIVE

Figure 22-5. A placard *must* be displayed any time that a material in a Class or Division on this list is transported.

Materials Placarded Only in Large Quantities	
Hazard Division/Class	Placard
Division 1.4	EXPLOSIVES 1.4
Division 1.5	BLASTING AGENTS or EXPLOSIVES 1.5
Division 1.6	EXPLOSIVES 1.6
Division 2.1	FLAMMABLE GAS
Division 2.2	NONFLAMMABLE GAS or OXYGEN if appropriate
Class 3	FLAMMABLE
Combustible Liquid	COMBUSTIBLE
Division 4.1	FLAMMABLE SOLID
Division 4.2	SPONTANEOUSLY COMBUSTIBLE
Division 5.1	OXIDIZER
Division 5.2	ORGANIC PEROXIDE
Division 6.1 PG I/II, not PG I, Inhalation Hazard	POISON
Division 6.1 PG III	HARMFUL-STOW AWAY FROM FOODSTUFFS
Division 6.2	No placard
Class 8	CORROSIVE
Class 9	9 on placard
ORM-D	No placard

Figure 22-6. Vehicles must display the appropriate placard if more than 1000 pounds of material in any of these Classes or Divisions is in its cargo.

The **DANGEROUS** placard may be used for mixed loads with a total hazardous materials weight in excess of 1000 pounds (unless the load contains materials that must be placarded without regard to quantity, such as Explosives 1.1 or Poison Gas).

A **GASOLINE** placard may be used in place of a **FLAMMABLE LIQUID** placard for highway shipments of gasoline.

A **COMBUSTIBLE** placard is used for bulk transportation, but is not required for nonbulk shipments.

A **FUEL OIL** placard may be used in place of **COMBUSTIBLE** for motor vehicle combustible fuel.

The **HARMFUL — STOW AWAY FROM FOODSTUFFS** placard may be used for Division 6.1, PG III poisons, instead of a **POISON** placard.

A **RESIDUE** placard is posted on empty rail tank cars for the hazardous material which was last in the car.

The **DANGER FUMIGATED** or **TREATED** placard is required on rail cars, trucks, and freight containers which have been fumigated with a Division 6.1 or 6.2 Poison/ Poison Gas.

Do not be too trusting with placards. They can be forgotten, deliberately not used, incorrect for the load, dirty or faded, torn off, or not visible as a result of an accident. Remember that hazard class placards only indicate the most *significant* hazard of the product that is placarded. As noted previously, many dangerous chemicals have multiple hazards. Also, do not mistake other signage, particularly on trucks, for HazMat information. Truck/trailer numbers and advertising or safety slogans in placard holders can be confusing.

Diamond-shaped *labels* are 4-in. (10 cm) on a side. They are affixed to nonbulk packages of hazardous materials. Like placards, labels are based on the hazard classes.

Placard/label regulations are complex, and have numerous exceptions. You must understand them but not place total reliance in them.

Markings and Colors

In transportation incidents, name references to fuels, chemicals, energy products, agricultural supplies, cleaning agents, automotive supplies, or pesticides suggest that hazardous materials may be present. For several dozen materials, including anhydrous ammonia and chlorine, DOT requires that shipping names be stenciled on railcars. Railcars owned by chemical companies can often be identified by the initials on the car. Among those commonly seen are DUPX (DuPont), DOWX (Dow), RAHX (Rohm and Haas), and DODX (Department of Defense). Trucking company names, tractor and trailer numbers, and vehicle registrations can be helpful, as well. Pipelines are often marked at points where they cross under roads.

NFPA 704 signing system

At a fixed site, the Standard System for the Identification of the Fire Hazards of Materials (*NFPA 704*) combines colors with numbers and symbols to provide nonspecific information. This signing system is not required by law, but *is* often used for fixed sites.

As shown in **Figure 22-7**, each of the four quadrants of the diamond-on-point sign offers guidance: **blue** pertains to *health* hazards, **red** to *fire* hazards, **yellow** to *reactivity* hazards, and **white** to *special information*. The numerals 0 through 4, used in the blue, red, and yellow quadrants, address the relative risk posed to the responder. Substances rated as 0 are the least hazardous; those rated 4, the most hazardous. You should be particularly cautious when the numerals 4, 3, or 2 appear.

The Special Information (white) quadrant is used to indicate the presence of oxidizers (**OX**) or the hazard of a possible reaction with water ($\mathbb{W}$). Some users put other information in this quadrant, such as *Radioactive* or *Corrosive*.

Individual sites may use other signs, decals, labels, warning markings or color codes for hazardous material areas.

Some labels on nonbulk packages convey the same type of information as NFPA 704, but use a different format and are chemical-specific. Occasionally, one gallon (3.8 liter) glass bottles have caps that correspond to the color of the highest threat under the NFPA 704 system. When dark bottle glass is used, it may suggest a sensitivity to light.

Shipping Papers

These documents provide information about the specific hazardous materials in transit. They identify the hazardous material, its hazard class, its 4-digit UN/NA number and weight. A source for emergency information is also provided. Frequently that source is CHEMTREC (the nationwide Chemical Transportation Emergency Center of the Chemical Manufacturer's Association).

Highway

Bills of lading or freight bills are the driver's responsibility. They must be within his or her reach at all times. If the driver leaves the vehicle, the papers are often on the seat or in the driver-side door pouch.

Railroad

The "consist" or waybill is the conductor's responsibility. Other similar documents are acceptable substitutes on some railroads. The conductor and/or engineer will have the documents.

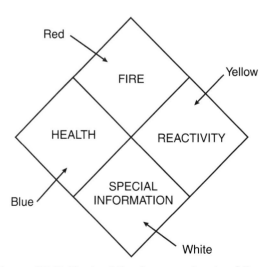

Figure 22-7. Each of the four quadrants of the NFPA 704 standard sign displays a different hazard. Numerals 0-4 in each quadrant (except white) rate the seriousness of the hazard.

Air

The airbill is the pilot's responsibility and will be in the cockpit. This information may also be attached to packages. Many hazardous materials may not be transported by air.

Water

The captain is responsible for the "dangerous cargo manifest." It's found on the bridge. Barges have a special holder for the manifest.

Material Safety Data Sheet

The ***Material Safety Data Sheet (MSDS)*** is a document, produced by the chemical manufacturer, which provides information specific to the hazards presented by the material. See **Figure 22-8.** Under various Federal and State worker safety laws, work sites are required to have an MSDS on file for each hazardous chemical used. Some MSDSs are now being carried when materials are transported. Even though it was not developed primarily for use by First Responders, the MSDS provides such important details as the brand, common, chemical, and synonym names of the material, its hazardous ingredients, and the name, address, and telephone number of its manufacturer. The MSDS also describes:

- Physical/chemical hazards (including fire, explosion and reactivity data).
- Health/medical hazards.
- Spill/disposal procedures.
- Special protection information.
- Special precautions/comments.

Mistakes occur in MSDSs and they do become outdated. Whenever possible, use other references to complement MSDS data.

When responding to an incident at a fixed site, be sure to confer with company personnel and use facility emergency plans, such as SARA Title III plans (if applicable).

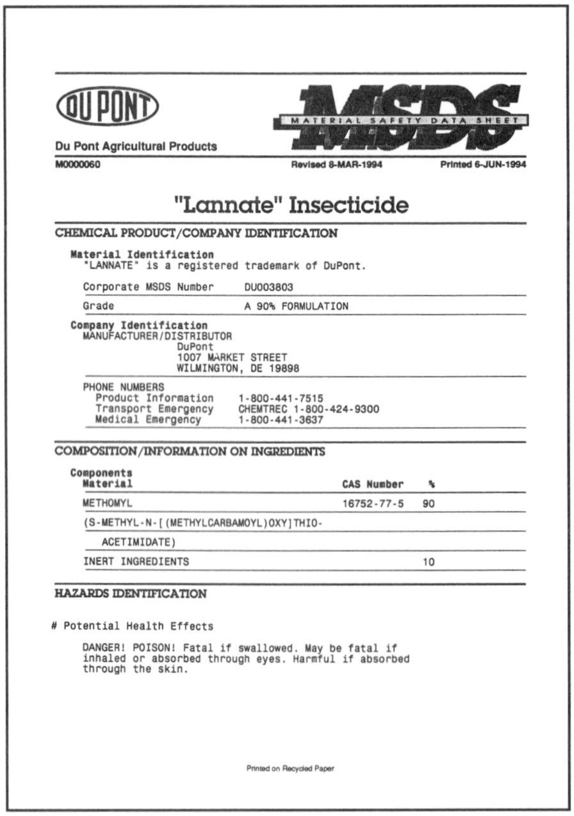
Du Pont Agricultural Products
MSDS
MATERIAL SAFETY DATA SHEET
M0000060 Revised 8-MAR-1994 Printed 6-JUN-1994

"Lannate" Insecticide

CHEMICAL PRODUCT/COMPANY IDENTIFICATION

Material Identification
"LANNATE" is a registered trademark of DuPont.

Corporate MSDS Number DU003803
Grade A 90% FORMULATION

Company Identification
MANUFACTURER/DISTRIBUTOR
DuPont
1007 MARKET STREET
WILMINGTON, DE 19898

PHONE NUMBERS
Product Information 1-800-441-7515
Transport Emergency CHEMTREC 1-800-424-9300
Medical Emergency 1-800-441-3637

COMPOSITION/INFORMATION ON INGREDIENTS

Components

Material	CAS Number	%
METHOMYL	16752-77-5	90
(S-METHYL-N-[(METHYLCARBAMOYL)OXY]THIO-		
ACETIMIDATE)		
INERT INGREDIENTS		10

HAZARDS IDENTIFICATION

Potential Health Effects

DANGER! POISON! Fatal if swallowed. May be fatal if inhaled or absorbed through eyes. Harmful if absorbed through the skin.

Printed on Recycled Paper

Figure 22-8. The Material Safety Data Sheet contains a wealth of information on a chemical's hazards and how to deal with them. This is the first page of a nine-page document.

Senses

Because of the danger involved in dealing with possibly toxic unknown materials, your senses must be used with *extreme caution;* preferably in conjunction with the other means already mentioned. *Always approach a site cautiously, from uphill and upwind.*

Sight

Use binoculars. Are vapors, clouds, fumes, or mists visible? Are liquids or powders/granules spilled? Is smoke thick or strangely colored? Are flames abnormally hued? Are there dead birds, fish, or other animals in the vicinity? Are waterways discolored? Are containers visibly damaged?

Hearing

Listen for explosions, mechanical stressing, hissing from release of pressurized material.

Smell

As a general rule, if you can smell it, you're too close. *Never inhale a material that is potentially hazardous*. Inhalation is a primary route of human *exposure*. Not all hazardous materials have detectable odors. Some have odor threshold concentrations that are greater than safe inhalation levels. Others can quickly desensitize the sense of smell, making the material indistinguishable.

Taste

Like smell, if you can *taste* the material, you're too close to the spill. *Never taste a material that is potentially hazardous*. Ingestion is a primary route of human exposure.

Touch

Do not touch a material that is potentially hazardous, unless you are wearing protective clothing. Even if protected, minimize any contact with the product. Absorption and direct dermal contact are the primary routes of human exposure.

The DOT Emergency Response Guidebook

An important goal of the United States Department of Transportation (DOT) is to place a copy of its *Emergency Response Guidebook (ERG)* in every emergency service vehicle nationwide. See **Figure 22-9.** The Guidebook lists approximately 2800 of the most commonly transported hazardous materials.

DOT states that the book is "primarily a guide to aid first responders in (1) quickly identifying the specific or generic classification of the material(s) involved...and (2) protecting themselves and the general public during this initial response phase... " The *initial response phase* is the period (immediately after arrival at the incident scene) during which the presence of a hazardous material is confirmed and if possible identified, protective actions are initiated and the area secured, and the assistance of qualified personnel is requested. Essentially, these are the actions required at the First Responder Awareness Level.

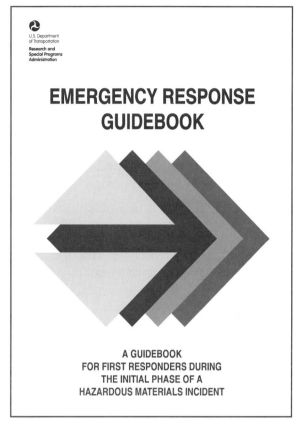

U.S. Department of Transportation
Research and Special Programs Administration

EMERGENCY RESPONSE GUIDEBOOK

A GUIDEBOOK
FOR FIRST RESPONDERS DURING
THE INITIAL PHASE OF A
HAZARDOUS MATERIALS INCIDENT

Figure 22-9. The Emergency Response Guidebook published by the U.S. Department of Transportation is a basic tool for all HazMat responders.

The ERG has five major components:

- A Table of Placards, showing 28 DOT and 3 Canadian placards, with a guide number for each.

- A Yellow-bordered Chemical Index, with the 4-digit UN/NA ID numbers listed in numerical order. A guide number is shown for each substance.

- A Blue-bordered Chemical Index, with substances sequenced alphabetically by chemical name. The corresponding UN/NA ID number is listed for each substance, along with a guide number for each.

- Orange-bordered Guides explaining potential hazards and emergency actions.

- A Green-bordered Table of Initial Isolation and Protective Action Distances for materials that have poisonous effects when inhaled.

How to Use the ERG

You must know how to effectively use the ERG and understand its limitations. For example, the ERG may be of limited value in incidents at fixed facilities.

As a First Responder, your most urgent task will be to determine that a hazardous material is or might be involved. With safety always your foremost consideration, use any or all of these methods to identify the product involved: read placards, stenciled names, or 4-digit UN/NA numbers; examine shipping papers, or speak with the driver/crew or the facility personnel. The specificity of information obtained will determine how you will use the ERG.

When no chemical name or UN/NA number is known:

If you find that there are only hazard class or **DANGEROUS** placards associated with the material (or if you only *suspect* that there is hazardous material present), use the Table of Placards section of the ERG. See **Figure 22-10.** After finding the matching placard, turn to the indicated Guide. Only very generic guidance can be provided since the specific hazardous material involved has not been determined.

When the UN/NA number is known:

If a 4-digit UN/NA number is located, use the Yellow-bordered Chemical Index section to find the chemical and its proper Guide. See **Figure 22-11.** Note that frequently several chemicals have the same UN/NA number. They all will have the same Guide number.

If the chemical line is highlighted in yellow, refer to the Green-bordered Table of Initial Isolation and Protective Action Distances by using the UN/NA number.

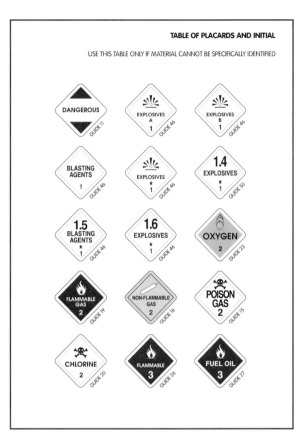

Figure 22-10. This section of the ERG is used to find the appropriate Guide for placards showing only the hazard class or a DANGEROUS message.

When the chemical name is known:

If the chemical name can be identified, use the Blue-bordered Chemical Index (alphabetical listing) section to find the Guide number, **Figure 22-12.** Not all hazardous materials in transport will be found in the ERG; sometimes they may be included, but are listed under a synonym. If the chemical's line in the listing is highlighted in blue, refer to the Green-bordered Table of Initial Isolation and Protective Action Distances. Use the UN/NA number to identify the proper procedure to follow.

Note that, in the Blue-bordered alphabetical section, some chemical names are repeated. Closer examination indicates the same names may have different UN/NA numbers and sometimes different Guide references. Be cautious and thorough.

ID No.	Guide No.	Name of Material	ID No.	Guide No.	Name of Material
——	46	AMMONIUM NITRATE - FUEL OIL MIXTURES	1012	22	BUTYLENE
——	46	BLASTING AGENT, n.o.s.	1013	21	CARBON DIOXIDE
——	46	EXPLOSIVE A	1014	14	CARBON DIOXIDE and OXYGEN MIXTURES
——	46	EXPLOSIVE B	1015	12	CARBON DIOXIDE and NITROUS OXIDE MIXTURES
——	50	EXPLOSIVE C	1016	18	CARBON MONOXIDE
——	46	EXPLOSIVES, division 1.1, 1.2, 1.3, 1.5 or 1.6	1017	20	CHLORINE
——	50	EXPLOSIVE division 1.4	1018	12	CHLORODIFLUOROMETHANE
0004	46	AMMONIUM PICRATE, dry or wetted with less than 10% water	1020	12	CHLOROPENTAFLUORO-ETHANE
0222	46	AMMONIUM NITRATE with more than 0.2% combustible material	1021	12	CHLOROTETRAFLUORO-ETHANE
0223	46	AMMONIUM NITRATE FERTILIZER, which is more liable to explode than ammonium nitrate with 0.2% combustible material	1022	12	CHLOROTRIFLUOROMETHANE
			1022	12	TRIFLUOROCHLOROMETHANE
			1023	18	COAL GAS
0331	46	AMMONIUM NITRATE - FUEL OIL MIXTURE (containing only prilled ammonium nitrate and fuel oil)	1026	18	CYANOGEN
			1026	18	CYANOGEN, liquefied
			1026	18	CYANOGEN GAS
0402	46	AMMONIUM PERCHLORATE	1027	22	CYCLOPROPANE
1001	17	ACETYLENE	1027	22	CYCLOPROPANE, liquefied
1001	17	ACETYLENE, dissolved	1028	12	DICHLORODIFLUORO-METHANE
1002	12	AIR, compressed	1029	12	DICHLOROFLUOROMETHANE
1003	23	AIR, refrigerated liquid (cryogenic liquid)	1029	12	DICHLOROMONOFLUORO-METHANE
1005	15	AMMONIA	1030	22	1,1-DIFLUOROETHANE
1005	15	AMMONIA, ANHYDROUS, liquefied	1030	22	DIFLUOROETHANE
1005	15	AMMONIA SOLUTIONS with more than 50% ammonia	1032	19	DIMETHYLAMINE, anhydrous
1005	15	ANHYDROUS AMMONIA	1033	22	DIMETHYL ETHER
1006	12	ARGON, compressed	1035	22	ETHANE, compressed
1008	15	BORON TRIFLUORIDE	1036	68	ETHYLAMINE
1009	12	BROMOTRIFLUOROMETHANE	1036	68	MONOETHYLAMINE
1010	17	BUTADIENES, inhibited	1037	27	ETHYL CHLORIDE
1011	22	BUTANE or BUTANE MIXTURES	1038	22	ETHYLENE, refrigerated liquid (cryogenic liquid)

Figure 22-11. The Yellow-bordered Chemical Index section of the ERG lists materials by their 4-digit UN/NA numbers.

Name of Material	Guide No.	ID No.	Name of Material	Guide No.	ID No.
SODA LIME	60	1907	SODIUM DICHLORO-S-TRIAZINETRIONE	45	2465
SODIUM	40	1428	SODIUM DICHROMATE	35	1479
SODIUM ALUMINATE, solid	60	2812	SODIUM DINITRO-ortho-CRESOLATE, wetted with not less than 15% water	36	1348
SODIUM ALUMINATE SOLUTION	60	1819	SODIUM DITHIONITE	37	1384
SODIUM ALUMINUM HYDRIDE	40	2835	SODIUM FLUORIDE, solid	54	1690
SODIUM AMMONIUM VANADATE	53	2863	SODIUM FLUORIDE SOLUTION	54	1690
SODIUM ARSANILATE	53	2473	SODIUM FLUOROACETATE	53	2629
SODIUM ARSENATE	53	1685	SODIUM FLUOROSILICATE	53	2674
SODIUM ARSENITE, aqueous solutions	54	1686	SODIUM HYDRATE	60	1824
SODIUM ARSENITE, solid	53	2027	SODIUM HYDRIDE	40	1427
SODIUM AZIDE	56	1687	SODIUM HYDROGEN FLUORIDE	60	2439
SODIUM BIFLUORIDE, solid	60	2439	SODIUM HYDROGEN SULFATE, solid	60	1821
SODIUM BIFLUORIDE SOLUTION	60	2439	SODIUM HYDROGEN SULFATE SOLUTION	60	2837
SODIUM BISULFATE, solid	60	1821	SODIUM HYDROGEN-DIFLUORIDE	60	2439
SODIUM BISULFATE SOLUTION	60	2837	SODIUM HYDROSULFIDE, solid with less than 25% water of crystallization	34	2318
SODIUM BISULFITE SOLUTION	60	2693	SODIUM HYDROSULFIDE, solid with not less than 25% water of crystallization	59	2923
SODIUM BOROHYDRIDE	32	1426	SODIUM HYDROSULFIDE, with not less than 25% water of crystallization	59	2949
SODIUM BROMATE	42	1494	SODIUM HYDROSULFIDE SOLUTION	59	2922
SODIUM CACODYLATE	53	1688	SODIUM HYDROSULFIDE SOLUTION	59	2949
SODIUM CHLORATE	35	1495	SODIUM HYDROSULFITE	37	1384
SODIUM CHLORATE, aqueous solution	31	2428	SODIUM HYDROXIDE, dry, solid	60	1823
SODIUM CHLORITE	43	1496	SODIUM HYDROXIDE SOLUTION	60	1824
SODIUM CHLORITE SOLUTION with more than 5% available chlorine	60	1908	SODIUM HYPOCHLORITE SOLUTION	60	1791
SODIUM CHLOROACETATE	53	2659	SODIUM METAL	40	1428
SODIUM CUPROCYANIDE, solid	53	2316	SODIUM METHYLATE, dry	40	1431
SODIUM CUPROCYANIDE SOLUTION	54	2317			
SODIUM CYANIDE	55	1689			
SODIUM 2-DIAZO-1-NAPH-THOL-4-SULFONATE	72	3040			
SODIUM 2-DIAZO-1-NAPH-THOL-5-SULFONATE	72	3041			
SODIUM DICHLORO-ISOCYANURATE	45	2465			

Figure 22-12. The Blue-bordered Chemical Index section of the ERG lists materials alphabetically by chemical name.

Using the ERG Guide Pages

The Orange-bordered Guides provide basic guidance for the responder, **Figure 22-13.** The ERG cautions that the guides are "not applicable when materials of different classes and divisions are involved..." It is extremely difficult to estimate what will occur when different hazardous chemicals are involved in a single event. This type of analysis is beyond the capabilities of Awareness-Level First Responders, however.

You should read the entire text of the indicated Guide before taking action. Each Guide consists of a Potential Hazards section and an Emergency Action section. Under Potential Hazards are "Health Hazards" and "Fire or Explosion" headings. Whichever heading is printed first represents the greater threat. Recommendations under Emergency Action include personal protective clothing and methods of dealing with fire, spills, and first aid. Note that the Isolation or Evacuation distances given in this section are for *fire* situations.

Isolation and protective action table

If the chemical name and the UN/NA number are highlighted in the index sections, the material poses a poisonous inhalation threat. Highlighting directs you to the ERG section entitled Table of Initial Isolation and Protective Action Distances. See **Figure 22-14.** This table specifies distances for population protection when the hazardous materials produce poisonous gases, vapors, or fumes. Population protection can be evacuation or in-place sheltering. Distances in the table are based on the potentially affected area during

ERG 93 **GUIDE 19**

POTENTIAL HAZARDS

FIRE OR EXPLOSION

Extremely flammable; may be ignited by heat, sparks or flames.
Vapors may travel to a source of ignition and flash back.
Container may explode in heat of fire.
Vapor explosion hazard indoors, outdoors or in sewers.

HEALTH HAZARDS

May be poisonous if inhaled.
Vapor **extremely irritating;** contact causes burns to skin and eyes.
Contact with liquid may cause frostbite.
Fire may produce irritating or poisonous gases.
Runoff from fire control or dilution water may cause pollution.

EMERGENCY ACTION

Keep unnecessary people away; isolate hazard area and deny entry.
Stay upwind; keep out of low areas.
Positive pressure self-contained breathing apparatus (SCBA) and structural firefighters' protective clothing may provide limited protection.
Isolate the leak or spill area immediately for at least 150 feet in all directions.
Isolate for 1/2 mile in all directions if tank, rail car or tank truck is involved in fire.
CALL Emergency Response Telephone Number on Shipping Paper first. If Shipping Paper not available or no answer,
CALL CHEMTREC AT 1-800-424-9300.
If water pollution occurs, notify the appropriate authorities.

FIRE

Let tank, tank car or tank truck burn unless leak can be stopped; with smaller tanks or cylinders, extinguish/isolate from other flammables.
Small Fires: Dry chemical or CO2.
Large Fires: Water spray, fog or regular foam.
Move container from fire area if you can do it without risk.
Apply cooling water to sides of containers that are exposed to flames until well after fire is out. Stay away from ends of tanks.
For massive fire in cargo area, use unmanned hose holder or monitor nozzles; if this is impossible, withdraw from area and let fire burn.
Withdraw immediately in case of rising sound from venting safety device or any discoloration of tank due to fire.

SPILL OR LEAK

Shut off ignition sources; no flares, smoking or flames in hazard area.
Stop leak if you can do it without risk.
Use water spray to reduce vapors; isolate area until gas has dispersed.

FIRST AID

Move victim to fresh air and call emergency medical care; if not breathing, give artificial respiration; if breathing is difficult, give oxygen.
In case of contact with material, immediately flush skin or eyes with running water for at least 15 minutes.
Remove and isolate contaminated clothing and shoes at the site.
Keep victim quiet and maintain normal body temperature.

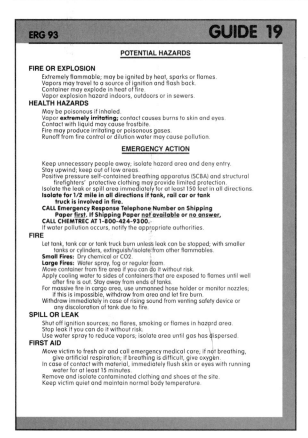

Figure 22-13. Each Guide section in the ERG has a Potential Hazards description and recommendations for Emergency Action.

TABLE OF INITIAL ISOLATION AND PROTECTIVE ACTION DISTANCES

		SMALL SPILLS (From a small package or small leak from a large package)			LARGE SPILLS (From a large package or from many small packages)		
		First ISOLATE in all Directions	Then, PROTECT persons DOWNWIND		First ISOLATE in all Directions	Then, PROTECT persons DOWNWIND	
ID #	NAME OF MATERIAL	(Feet)	DAY (Miles)	NIGHT (Miles)	(Feet)	DAY (Miles)	NIGHT (Miles)
1510	TETRANITROMETHANE	500	0.1	0.1	500	0.1	0.9
1541	ACETONE CYANOHYDRIN, stabilized	500	0.1	0.1	500	0.1	0.5
1545	ALLYL ISOTHIOCYANATE, inhibited	500	0.1	0.1	500	0.1	0.2
1545	ALLYL ISOTHIOCYANATE, stabilized	500	0.1	0.1	500	0.1	0.2
1556	METHYLDICHLOROARSINE	500	0.2	1.9	1000	1.0	3.2
1560	ARSENIC CHLORIDE	1500	2.9	5.1	1500	3.5	5.8
1560	ARSENIC TRICHLORIDE	1500	2.9	5.1	1500	3.5	5.8
1569	BROMOACETONE	500	0.1	1.4	1000	1.4	3.5
1580	CHLOROPICRIN	500	0.5	2.6	500	0.8	2.9
1581	CHLOROPICRIN and METHYL BROMIDE MIXTURES	500	0.5	2.6	500	0.8	2.9
1581	METHYL BROMIDE and CHLOROPICRIN MIXTURES	500	0.5	2.6	500	0.8	2.9
1582	CHLOROPICRIN and METHYL CHLORIDE MIXTURES	500	0.5	2.6	500	0.8	2.9
1582	METHYL CHLORIDE and CHLOROPICRIN MIXTURES	500	0.5	2.6	500	0.8	2.9
1583	CHLOROPICRIN MIXTURES, n.o.s. (When "Inhalation Hazard" is on a package or shipping paper.)	500	0.5	2.6	500	0.8	2.9
1589	CYANOGEN CHLORIDE, inhibited	500	0.5	2.4	500	0.9	3.1
1595	DIMETHYL SULFATE	500	0.1	0.2	500	0.1	0.4
1595	METHYL SULFATE	500	0.1	0.2	500	0.1	0.4
1605	1,2-DIBROMOETHANE	500	0.1	0.2	500	0.1	0.2
1605	ETHYLENE DIBROMIDE	500	0.1	0.2	500	0.1	0.2
1612	HEXAETHYL TETRAPHOSPHATE and COMPRESSED GAS MIXTURES	500	0.6	2.6	1500	3.2	5.5

Figure 22-14. When a material is (or may emit) a serious inhalation threat, this table provides isolation and protective action distances for population protection.

the initial 30 minutes of a nonfire release. Table distances may be modified due to:

- Fire.
- Leaks from multiple large containers.
- Topographic considerations.
- Wind speed.
- Snow cover.
- Temperature inversions.
- Heavy overcast.
- Building height/density.

The ***Initial Isolation Zone*** is a 360° circle around the point of the release. There is a high likelihood that anyone without appropriate protection within this zone will be exposed to life-threatening concentrations of the hazardous material. No unauthorized parties should be inside the Isolation Zone.

The ***Protective Action Zone*** is beyond the Initial Isolation Zone and extends 30° on either side of the predominant wind direction. See **Figure 22-15.** The crosswind and downwind protection distances are equal. Within the Protective Action Zone, anyone without proper protection is at risk of becoming incapacitated and/or seriously exposed.

To use the Isolation and Protective Action Distance Table, you must know the material's UN/NA number, whether the spill is small or large, and whether it is day or night. *Small spills* are those from a single small package, a drum (up to 55 gallons), or a small cylinder. A small leak from a larger container is also classified as a small spill. *Large spills* are from large containers or multiple small packages. *Day* is from sunrise to sunset. *Night* is from sunset to sunrise.

Using the appropriate row and column from the table, first determine the Isolation

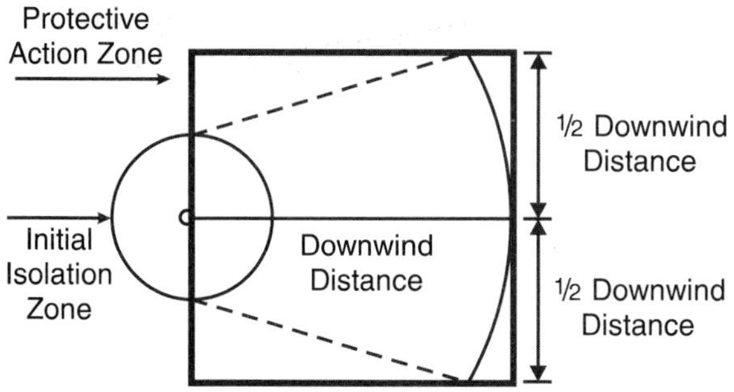

Figure 22-15. Relationship of the Protective Action Zone to the Initial Isolation Zone

Distance. Anyone within the specified distance from the spill should immediately move away from the source in an upwind or crosswind direction. Next, using the appropriate row and column, determine the Protective Action Distance. The "downwind distance will also be the width of the zone. Population protection — evacuation or in-place sheltering — should begin with those closest to the initial isolation zone, then expand outward.

Population protection

Evacuation and shelter-in-place are the population protection options. A number of factors enter into which method should be selected or if a combination of the two should be used. There are risks associated with either approach. The Awareness Level First Responder is not expected to understand the variables, but should know what some of them are.

Evacuation encompasses the removal of all civilians from a threatened area to a safe one. Some considerations: methods to be used for warning to move and why, what to take, where to go, how to get there, security, traffic and access control, making provision for special needs people and those without personal transportation, what to do with pets/livestock. Will people be exposed to dangerous levels of the hazardous material if they evacuate? Legal authority to "order" an evacuation may not be legal authority to "compel" an evacuation. Is an evacuation really necessary for this chemical? Is the

HazMat explosive or flammable? Will there be a long-term toxic cloud?

Shelter-in-place keeps people inside buildings where actions are taken to reduce outside air infiltration. Heating/air conditioning/ventilation/exhaust systems are turned off. Doors and windows are closed and taped. Occupants are instructed to stay in interior rooms with doors closed, keeping away from glass windows or doors, listening to radio for instructions, and not using the telephone except when necessary. Is the HazMat explosive or flammable? Will there be a long-term toxic hazardous cloud? Are buildings suitable for in-place sheltering or will air infiltration be difficult to seal? Can people be evacuated later if necessary?

A complete understanding of the Emergency Response Guidebook is a requisite for First Responder Awareness competency. You can achieve that understanding only by studying the actual Guidebook.

Be mindful of the importance of eliminating ignition sources, even if the HazMat is not classified as a flammable substance. Open flames and smoking materials are obvious sources, but also consider friction, static electricity, hot surfaces, mechanical sparking and chemical reactions.

Understanding Your Role

Employers formulate emergency response plans and operating procedures. Awareness Level employees need to understand their roles in such plans. The plan should be sufficient to enable the Awareness Level First Responder to perform the appropriate roles, but not put the responder at risk beyond those roles. As an Awareness Level First Responder, you must realize that you may be unable to attempt the rescue of victims or safely warn people in a hazard zone, because you lack appropriate training and protective clothing. You may be confronted with contaminated victims who need help. Decontamination is not within the competencies of the Awareness Level. Contaminated victims should be isolated in the safest possible area for handling by appropriately trained and equipped personnel. The responder must not become a victim.

Awareness Level Clothing

Awareness Level Responders are not expected to wear Chemical Protective Clothing. The ERG cautions "safe use of this type of protective clothing requires specific skills developed through training and experience. It is generally not available to, or used by, first responders."

The street clothes and work uniforms typically worn by firefighters provide little or no protection from exposure to hazardous materials.

Structural Firefighter's Protective Clothing (SFPC), **Figure 22-16**, is not intended to provide chemical protection in most HazMat incidents. Some Guides in the ERG state "structural firefighters' protective clothing will provide limited protection." It is important to understand what is meant by this. In certain circumstances, a responder wearing SFPC and a positive-pressure SCBA

may be able to perform an expedient ("quick in-and-out") operation. Be aware, however, that this type of operation can place the responder at risk of exposure, injury, or death. The Incident Commander makes the decision to perform this operation only if an overriding benefit can be gained.

The positive-pressure self-contained breathing apparatus (SCBA) goes hand-in-hand with responder personal protection. Positive-pressure SCBA provides a constant flow of air into the facepiece. Each ERG Guide refers to positive-pressure SCBA.

Notification

Awareness Level responders have too few qualifications to control a HazMat event. When it's apparent that hazardous materials may be involved, you should secure the area by whatever means are readily available, then notify competent response personnel. Notification should be accomplished by the appropriate means: telephoning 911 or other emergency number, radioing the emergency communications center, or contacting facility administrators. If the name of the product is known from placards, labels, or shipping papers, carefully

Figure 22-16. Normal firefighting turnout gear, even with an SCBA, provides only very limited protection in HazMat situations.

spell the name when making notification. Ask the notified party to spell it back. Accuracy of spelling is absolutely essential.

After you have made the initial notification, the dispatcher frequently will call one or more of the following organizations for assistance in a hazardous materials emergency:

- CHEMTREC® (Chemical Transportation Emergency Center)
  1-800-424-9300 (24 hours)
  202-483-7616 (calls originating outside continental U.S.)
  (emergencies only)

- NRC (National Response Center)
  1-800-424-8802 (24 hours)
  267-2675 in District of Columbia

- Military Shipments by or to Department of Defense (DOD) (for incidents involving explosives/ammunition)
  U.S. Army Operations Center
  703-697-0218/0219 (call collect; emergencies only)

- Defense Logistics Agency
  (for incidents involving hazardous material except explosives/ammunition; emergencies only) 800-851-8061

New Technology

The use of satellite technology for locating and identifying HazMat incidents on the highways is currently being tested in pilot projects. Under this system, a tiny electronic device called a transponder is installed on the truck and programmed with information about the type and quantity of hazardous materials being carried. If the truck is involved in a collision or goes off the road, the impact will activate the transponder. A radio signal from the transponder would be received by an orbiting satellite and relayed to the nearest 911 emergency center. The signal transmitted by the transponder would give the 911 operator the precise location of the truck and complete information on its dangerous cargo. This new technology would allow the appropriate response to be made more rapidly than by present methods.

SUMMARY

First Responder Awareness training taught you how to realize that a HazMat event may occur or is occurring. You learned about the various classes of dangerous chemicals and their hazards. A number of methods were described to help you recognize that hazardous materials may be involved. The DOT Emergency Response Guidebook was explained at length. This book must be understood by everyone who climbs into an emergency vehicle.

As an Awareness Level First Responder, you can do nothing to mitigate a spill. You understand that more resources and qualified responders are necessary and start the HazMat response process. You also initiate the vital population protection process as soon as you determine that hazardous materials may be involved.

Awareness training is merely an introduction to dangerous chemicals. It is not sufficient to enable you to respond to known or suspected HazMat emergencies. Awareness is the foundation from which you will train to the next level, Operations.

REVIEW QUESTIONS

1. What governs the actions of HazMat emergency responders?
2. For whom is HazMat First Responder Awareness training intended?
3. Are placards required for 950 pounds of flammable solids which are not water reactive? Why?
4. What is the purpose of the DOT Emergency Response Guidebook?
5. What does a **DANGEROUS** placard on a truck mean?
6. What is the most important requirement for location of shipping documents when hazardous material is being transported by truck?
7. Why is it important to always verify HazMat information?
8. Why is sense of smell not a good HazMat detector?
9. In the DOT Emergency Resource Guide, what is the significance of chemicals whose names are highlighted in the numerical or alphabetical lists?
10. Is the following statement true or false? Why? "Awareness Level Responders must report to the Incident Commander or Safety Officer before wearing chemical protective clothing."
11. What is the effect of a corrosive material on living tissue?
12. What do the colors in the NFPA 704 System mean?
13. Is the following statement correct? "The NFPA 704 signing system is required by federal law for all above ground storage tanks holding more than 3000 gallons."
14. Does structural firefighters' turnout gear offer sufficient chemical protection for entering a hazardous substance zone?
15. Why can anhydrous ammonia burn, if it is classified as a Nonflammable Gas?
16. Which of the pairs of trucks below *must be* placarded under DOT regulations? Explain your choice.
    A. Truck 1 with 600 pounds of Explosives 1.2, Truck 2 with 900 pounds of Corrosives.
    B. Truck 1 with 1100 pounds of Flammable Liquids, Truck 2 with 900 pounds of Flammable Solids Division 4.1.
    C. Truck 1 with 1500 pounds of Organic Peroxide: Truck 2 with 250 pounds of Radioactive Yellow III.
17. On a train, which crew member is responsible for producing the hazardous materials "consist" when it is needed?
18. True or False? DOT regulations forbid any shipment by air of hazardous materials.
19. Does a DOT placard indicate only the greatest hazard of the material, or all of its potential hazards?
20. Why does the DOT Emergency Response Guide distinguish between fire and nonfire situations involving the same hazardous chemical?

Although they would be considered totally inadequate for today's hazardous materials situations, the "oxygen breathing apparatus" worn by these firefighters were a major step forward in 1949. It still would be decades, however, before firefighters began wearing self-contained breathing apparatus as a part of their normal turnout gear. (Harold Anthony/Archive Photo)

NFPA 1001 Job Performance Requirements

The material on this page consists of those portions of the NFPA 1001 Job Performance Requirements relevant to the material presented in this chapter. Items preceded by the numeral 3 (3-x.x) are Fire Fighter I requirements; those with the numeral 4 (4-x.x) are Fire Fighter II requirements.

4-1.1 For certification at Level II, the Fire Fighter I shall meet the job performance requirements defined in Sections 4-2 through 4-5 of this standard and the requirements defined in Chapter 3, Competencies for the First Responder at the Operational Level, of NFPA 472, *Standard for Professional Competence of Responders to Hazardous Materials Incidents.*

Reprinted with permission from NFPA 1001, *Fire Fighter Professional Qualifications,* Copyright ©1997, National Fire Protection Association, Quincy, MA 02269. This reprinted material is not the complete and official position of the National Fire Protection Association on the referenced subject, which is represented only by the standard in its entirety.

Hazardous Materials Operations Level

OBJECTIVES

When you have completed this chapter, you will be able to:

- Demonstrate proper use and knowledge of the terminology related to HazMat incidents and their handling.

- Show understanding of the Operations Level responder's role in dealing with a HazMat incident.

- Describe the four levels of Personal Protective Equipment established by the EPA.

- Identify the types of highway tank trucks, rail cars, and stationary tanks that are likely to contain hazardous materials.

- Describe the control zone system used to deal with HazMat incidents.

- Demonstrate understanding of the decontamination procedures used for responders who enter and leave the Hot Zone.

- Discuss the Incident Termination Procedures followed after a HazMat incident.

IMPORTANT TERMS

NOTE: See the Terminology section of this chapter for additional important terms.

Action Plan
bulk containers
Chemical Protective Clothing (CPC)
CHEMTREC®
Cold Zone
confinement

containment
contamination
critique
cryogenic tanks
damming
debriefing
decontamination
Department Operating Procedures (DOPs)
diking
filter dams

Hot Zone
IDLH (Immediately Dangerous to Life and Health)
Incident Command System (ICS)
Incident Commander
inorganic mineral sorbents
intermodal portable tanks

nonbulk containers
organic natural sorbents
overflow dams
Personal Protective Equipment (PPE)
post-incident analysis
retention basin
underflow dams
Warm Zone

This chapter will prepare you to respond to a known or a suspected hazardous materials incident. At the HazMat First Responder Operations Level, you are a part of the initial response to releases or potential releases of hazardous materials. Your purpose is to protect nearby persons, the environment and/or property from the release. You'll mitigate the release from a safe distance, keep it from spreading, and prevent exposures. Your actions will be "defensive" in nature, without actually trying to stop the release. Operations

Level personnel are not expected to use chemical protective clothing or specialized equipment. Do not permit yourself contact with the hazardous chemical. As firefighters, you'll wear structural firefighting protective garments. Your work is to be done from safe locations. Most fire department personnel are trained in this category.

Over the years, many firefighters have been exposed to dangerous chemicals. Some have died in explosions and fires; others have developed chronic disabilities that cut short their lives and careers. The number of hazardous chemicals continues to grow, and their uses become more widespread. Hazardous materials and their potential for accidents are found in every community in the country, in settings ranging from commerce to transportation to municipal government to residences.

Organizations such as the National Fire Protection Association (NFPA), the U.S. Occupational Safety and Health Administration (OSHA), and the U.S. Environmental Protection Agency (EPA), have created standards and regulations aimed at reducing the number of firefighter hazardous materials casualties. Two of these are of particular importance:

- NFPA 472, *Standard for Professional Competence of Responders to Hazardous Materials Incidents.*
- *Federal Hazardous Waste Operations and Emergency Response Act (HAZWOPER).*

These documents establish competency criteria for those who respond to hazardous materials emergencies. A portion of those criteria are for Operations Level responders.

Operations Level Qualifications

According to Federal law, *Operations Level* responders must meet the following qualifications and demonstrate the appropriate competencies, with certification by the employer.

The responder must have completed Awareness Level training plus at least eight hours of training or sufficient experience to objectively show competency in the areas listed below:

1. Knowledge of basic hazard and risk assessment techniques.
2. Ability to select and use of proper personal protective equipment provided to the first responder operational level.
3. Knowledge of basic HazMat terms.
4. Familiarity with basic control, containment and/or confinement operations within the capabilities of resources and personal protective equipment available with their unit.
5. Ability to implement basic decontamination procedures.
6. Knowledge of relevant standard operating and termination procedures.

As an Operations Responder, you'll continue and improve from the Awareness objectives such as product identification and scene security. Always *assess* the situation before performing other tasks. Successful assessment relies in part in the basic skills learned in First Responder Awareness training. To more accurately assess the threat, you must be familiar with fundamental *HazMat terminology.*

HazMat Terminology

HazMat terminology is used in the processes of identification, assessment, safety, and defensive control. You are probably already familiar with many of the definitions, but if you don't know what a term means, *find out.*

Absorb: The process in which a liquid penetrates a solid substance. (Compare to Adsorb, below)

Acute: Occurring in the short term.

Adsorb: The process in which a gas or liquid collects on the surface of another material. (Compare to Absorb, above)

Ambient: Term used to describe usual or surrounding conditions. Often associated with air temperature and pressure.

Anhydrous: Literally, without water.

Aqueous: Containing water or water-based (such as "aqueous film-forming foam").

Boiling point: The temperature at which vapor pressure of a liquid equals the surrounding air pressure. The liquid begins to change state to a gas.

Carcinogen: A cancer-causing substance.

Caution: Label term used to describe the lowest level of pesticide hazard.

Celsius: Term used for temperature units (degrees Celsius) in the metric system. Water freezes at 0°C (32°F) and boils at 100°C (212°F). The Celsius scale is also sometimes referred to as "Centigrade."

CHEMTREC®: The Chemical Transportation Emergency Center of the Chemical Manufacturers Association. Provides emergency HazMat information around-the-clock at 800-424-9300.

Chronic: Describes something occurring in the longer term, such as a *chronic illness.*

Cold Zone: In a HazMat incident, the uncontaminated area where command, staging and support occur. Also known as the Support Zone.

Combustible liquids: According to DOT, combustible liquids do not meet the definition of any other hazard class except Class 9, and have a flash point of between 100°F and 200°F (38°C and 93°C). OSHA uses a flash point range of from 100°F to 200°F. See **Figure 23-1.**

Confinement: Keeping a HazMat release within a given area.

Containment: Keeping a material within its container.

Corrosive: A chemical that shows visible destruction of or irreversible alterations in living tissue by chemical action at the site of contact, or a liquid that has a severe corrosion rate on steel. The pH scale of 1 to 14 can be used to measure corrosivity. The neutral point is 7 — acid materials have a pH lower than 7, while bases (alkalis or caustics) have a pH higher than 7.

Cryogenic: A term refering to extremely low temperatures, especially in relation to

Figure 23-1. A large truck stop like this one presents a number of hazards in the combustible and flammable liquids categories. Other types of hazards may be present in the form of cargoes aboard trucks themselves.

refrigerated gases. Cryogenic materials have boiling points of -150°F (-101°C) or lower.

Danger: The label term used to describe the greatest level of pesticide hazard. May be accompanied by the word "poison." Do not confuse this term with the DANGEROUS placard.

Decomposition: A process whereby a material breaks down into simpler parts, many of which may be hazardous.

Decontaminate: To remove hazardous material from people and equipment.

EPA: Common abbreviation for the U.S. Environmental Protection Agency.

ERG: Abbreviation for the *Emergency Response Guidebook* issued by the U.S. Department of Transportation.

Explosive: Any material that produces sudden release of pressure, gas, and heat when subjected to abrupt shock, pressure, or high temperature.

Exposure routes: Ways in which a human body can be invaded by a toxic or dangerous material. They include inhalation, absorption, ingestion, and direct contact.

Fahrenheit: Term used for temperature units (degrees Fahrenheit) in the US Conventional system of measurement. Water freezes at 32°F (0°C) and boils at 212°F (100°C).

Fire point: The lowest temperature at which a liquid produces sufficient vapor to flash near its surface and continue to burn. (Compare to Flash point, below.)

Flammable: Term used for any solid, liquid, vapor, or gas that will ignite easily and burn rapidly.

Flammable gas: A gas that, at ambient temperature and pressure, forms a flammable mixture with air at a concentration of 13% or less by volume; or a gas that, at ambient temperature and pressure, forms a range (12 percentage points or more) of flammable mixtures with air by volume without regard to the lower limit.

Flammable limits or range: The minimum and maximum concentrations in air (as a percentage) between which ignition of a flammable gas or vapor can occur. Concentrations below the lower limit are too lean to burn. Concentrations above the upper limit are too lean to burn.

Flammable liquid: A burnable liquid with a flash point below 141°F (61°C).

Flammable solid: A readily ignitable solid that will continue to burn, such as magnesium or phosphorus.

Flashback: A fire condition occurring when a trail of flammable material ignites at a point distant from its source and then follows the trail back to the source.

Flash point: The lowest temperature at which a burnable liquid gives off sufficient vapor to form an ignitable mixture with air. Burning does not continue. (Compare to Fire point, above.)

Freezing point: The temperature at which a liquid changes state to a solid.

Gas: A formless fluid occupying the space of its container. It can change to a liquid or solid state as its temperature is lowered and/or pressure increased.

HAZWOPER: The Federal Hazardous Waste Operations and Emergency Response Act.

Hot Zone: In a HazMat incident, the area where contamination is known or suspected.

Also known as the *Exclusion* or *Contamination Zone.*

Hygroscopic: Term that describes a substance which readily absorbs moisture from the air.

IDLH: "Immediately Dangerous to Life and Health," the maximum concentration of a material from which one could escape within 30 minutes and not suffer irreversible health effects.

Ignition temperature: The lowest temperature at which a combustible material will ignite in air and continue to burn without an outside heat source.

Incompatible: Term used to describe materials that could react dangerously with one another.

Inhibitor: Any material that retards a chemical reaction.

LC^{50}: Abbreviation for *lethal concentration,* the concentration in air of a material that is expected to kill 50% of the test animal group after a single inhalation exposure.

LD^{50}: A lethal dose of a material which is expected to kill 50% of the test animal group after a single *noninhalation* exposure.

Melting point: The temperature at which a solid changes state to become a liquid.

Miscible: Term that is used to describe the ability of a material to mix with water or other defined material.

Mutagen: An agent that causes gene mutation.

NIOSH: Abbreviation for the National Institute for Occupational Safety and Health.

Odor threshold: The lowest concentration in air of a material that can be detected by the sense of smell.

OSHA: Abbreviation for the U.S. Occupational Safety and Health Administration.

Oxidizer: Any material that readily yields oxygen or takes electrons away from other materials, resulting in enhanced combustion of the other material.

Packing Group (PG): A hazard packaging method. The classification PG I represents the greatest danger, followed by PG II, and PG III.

Polymerization: A chemical reaction in which small molecules combine to form larger ones. Uncontrolled polymerization can result in explosions, container ruptures, generation of heat, or fire. See *Inhibitor*.

ppb: Abbreviation for parts per billion (10,000,000 ppb = 1% concentration).

ppm: Abbreviation for parts per million (10,000 ppm = 1% concentration).

psi: Abbreviation for the pressure measurement, pounds per square inch.

psia: Abbreviation for pounds per square inch absolute (pressure measurement that *includes* the normal atmospheric pressure of 14.7 psi).

psig: Abbreviation for pounds per square inch gauge (pressure reading that *excludes* atmospheric pressure. Gauges are designed to read 0 psi at normal atmospheric pressure).

Pyrophoric: Term used to describe materials which can ignite spontaneously in air below 130°F (54°C).

Radiation (ionizing): Atoms which emit particles or rays that can produce ions (charged atoms) in whatever the rays or particles touch.

Reactivity: The ability of material to chemically change by itself or with other materials. Can result in heat, explosion, or generation of dangerous substances.

Reportable quantity: An amount of hazardous material released that requires reporting to governmental agencies.

Residue: The product remaining in a container after all reasonable effort has been made to unload it. In some cases, the amount can be quite hazardous.

Solubility: The ability of a material to dissolve, generally in water. Solubility is a factor in selecting a foam to use.

Sorbent: A material used to absorb or adsorb spilled liquids. Both organic and inorganic sorbents are available.

Specific gravity: The weight of a given volume of material, compared to the weight of an equal volume of water. The specific gravity (SG) of water is 1. SG>1 means material is heavier than water and, if not soluble, will sink in water. SG<1 means material is lighter than water and, if not soluble, will float on water. Water weighs approximately 8.33 lbs. per gallon.

Sublimation: The process by which a material changes directly from a solid state to a gas, bypassing the liquid state. For example, dry ice changes directly from solid carbon dioxide to carbon dioxide gas.

Teratogen: A material that can cause a defect in a human or animal embryo.

TLV-C: Abbreviation for "Threshold Limit Value Ceiling," the exposure concentration that should not be exceeded.

Vapor: The gaseous state of a normally liquid material.

Vapor density: The weight of a given volume of a vapor or gas, compared to the weight of an equal volume of air. Air's vapor density is 1. A vapor with a density >1 will sink in air. Vapor density <1 means a vapor will rise in air.

Vapor pressure: Pressure exerted by a vapor above a liquid inside a closed container. High vapor pressure indicates the tendency of the liquid to convert to vapor. Low boiling points mean high vapor pressures. (Remember that *vapors*, not liquids, actually burn.)

Volatility: A liquid's tendency to become a vapor.

Warm Zone: In a HazMat incident, the area between the Hot and Cold Zones. Decontamination is done in the Warm Zone. The personnel and equipment backing up the Hot Zone team stays in the Warm Zone, as well. Also known as *Contamination Reduction Zone*.

Warning: The label term used to describe the middle level of pesticide hazard.

The Assessment Process

Hazard and risk assessment begin with a *cautious approach* to the scene. Reidentify the hazardous materials involved. Correct determination of the material is critical for accurate assessment and subsequent defensive operations.

What Is the Material?

Use the methods you learned in Awareness Level training to determine the name of the material. Seek to confirm the identity of the product from the highest level of sources available: the manufacturer, shipper, or user. Always look for signs that the material may not be what "authoritative" sources say it is. If the material is *supposed to be* a clear, colorless, free-flowing liquid, but is actually a thick, dark-colored, slow-moving liquid, it is likely *not* the same product. Report any unexpected signs or activities to your officers.

Product identification is critical, but is often a complicated process. Many hazardous materials have similar spellings and pronunciations. Get in the habit of slowly spelling the chemical's name in the early identification stage. This will reduce the likelihood of identification errors among the responders, communications center, and other agencies.

Be sure **CHEMTREC**® is called (emergencies only) at 800-424-9300. It's a source of immediate, quality assistance. CHEMTREC contacts the manufacturer or shipper for expert advice. Provide CHEMTREC with as much of the following information as available:

- Your name and telephone number.
- Location and nature of the incident.
- Name of the material involved.
- Shipper or manufacturer.
- Container type.
- Rail car or truck number.
- Name of carrier.
- Name of consignee.
- Local conditions, such as weather, topography, and population density.

Reference sources

Most responders initially use the DOT *Emergency Response Guidebook*. Once the material is specifically identified, use multiple references as needed to gather and confirm information. Do this even if there is an MSDS present, since the MSDS can have mistakes. Listed below are some sources for use in emergencies.

- *Emergency Handling of Hazardous Materials in Surface Transportation*, Association of American Railroads, Bureau of Explosives.
- *Fire Protection Guide to Hazardous Materials*, National Fire Protection Association.
- *NIOSH Pocket Guide to Chemical Hazards*, National Institute for Occupational Safety and Health.
- *Farm Chemical Handbook*, Meister Publishing, Willoughby, Ohio.
- *Chemical Data Notebook, Fire Engineering Books.*
- *U.S. Coast Guard CHRIS Manual*, (Chemical Hazard Response Information System), U.S. Government Printing Office.
- *Emergency Action Guides*, Association of American Railroads, Bureau of Explosives, Washington, DC.
- *Emergency Care for Hazardous Material Exposure*, C.V. Mosby Co.

Complete familiarity with any reference is essential for obtaining the most benefit from that source. The HazMat incident ground is not the time and place to be using a reference for the first time. Become familiar with your reference sources during training sessions.

How is the material harmful?

Will it poison, burn, irradiate, asphyxiate, explode, mutate genes, or do other damaging things? Placards, labels, hazard classes, hazard ID systems, MSDSs, and reference materials give you some of that information.

What Personal Protective Equipment Is Needed?

How effective is your protective clothing for the chemical involved in the incident? Understand the limitations of structural firefighting protective garments, as stated in the DOT Emergency Response Guide. What will your *Personal Protective Equipment (PPE)* permit you to do safely? Can you perform a rapid rescue? Close a valve or place a bucket under the leak? Perform a process shutdown? Turn a leaking drum? Build a dike? Cover catch basins? Or, will your PPE permit you to operate only well away from the spill?

Your PPE may be all that prevents you from becoming exposed; from becoming a victim instead of a responder. You must be fully aware of the limitations of your PPE. There are wide variations in the capabilities of PPE for responders. Remember that First Responder Operations is limited to *defensive* techniques that do not require special chemical protective clothing.

The Emergency Response Guidebook section on Protective Clothing explains the basic differences in clothing types associated with HazMat responders.

- Street clothing and typical work uniforms offer virtually no protection from hazardous materials.

- A full structural fighting protective garment ensemble, used with positive-pressure SCBA, provides "limited protection" in some cases. *"Limited protection"* is defined as a rapid entry, rapid withdrawal operation. Even so, you may be placed in serious jeopardy of exposure injury or death during such activities.

- *Chemical Protective Clothing (CPC)* is generally not available or to be used by First Responders. The level of expertise associated with the selection and use of the CPC is beyond your First Responder training. CPC offers limited-term protection against exposure to a certain chemical or group of chemicals. No single garment is suitable for use in all hazardous environments. CPC is not heat- or flame-resistant unless specifically certified by the manufacturer.

The positive-pressure SCBA is the norm in today's fire service.

You must be thoroughly familiar with this type of breathing apparatus. SCBA wearers must be adequately trained, medically fit, and psychologically prepared. OSHA/EPA HAZ-WOPER regulations require a HazMat responder to wear a positive-pressure SCBA until the Incident Commander determines that a lower level of respiratory protection is satisfactory.

Air-purifying respirators (APRs) and supplied-air respirators (SARs) may be used at some incidents. First Responders must understand the uses, techniques, and limitations of these before donning. Remember that APRs may not be used in *IDLH (Immediately Dangerous to Life and Health)* or in atmospheres that are oxygen-deficient (under 19.5%). The hazardous material must be known and must exhibit adequate exposure warning characteristics such as odor. Remember that your air supply must always allow enough air time for decontamination processing.

EPA has defined four levels of personal protection. See **Figure 23-2.** They are:

- **Level A:** The highest category of respiratory and skin protection. Fully-encapsulating chemical protective clothing designed and manufactured to prevent direct body contact with the chemical and NIOSH-approved SCBA or SAR with escape bottle required.

- **Level B:** The highest level of respiratory protection, but a lower level of skin protection. NIOSH-approved SCBA or SAR with escape bottle required and nonencapsulating chemical protective clothing are standard. This is the minimum acceptable level when the hazardous material has not been identified.

- **Level C:** A lower level of respiratory and skin protection. NIOSH-approved APR and chemical resistant clothing are acceptable.

- **Level D:** The lowest level of protection, providing no special respiratory or

EPA Levels of Protection

Level A

Recommended Equipment	Optional Equipment	Used When	
• Pressure-demand full-facepiece SCBA or demand supplied-air respirator with escape device • Fully encapsulating vapor-tight chemical resistant suit • Chemical resistant boots • Two-way radio communications	• Coveralls (Nomex) • Long cotton underwear • Hard hat • Disposable gloves and boot covers • Cooling unit	• The highest level of protection for skin, eyes, and respiratory system is required • Substances with a high skin absorption hazard are likely to be encountered • High levels of dangerous or unknown vapors or gases may be present	

Level B

Recommended Equipment	Optional Equipment	Used When	
• Pressure-demand full-facepiece SCBA or positive pressure airline respirator with escape mask • Chemical resistant suit • Inner and outer chemical • Chemical resistant boots with steel toe and shank • Two-way radio communications	• Coveralls • Long cotton underwear • Chemical resistant disposable boot covers • Hard hat	• The highest level of respiratory protection but a lesser level of skin protection is required • Atmosphere conditions exceed the criteria for air-purifying respirators, but it is unlikely that high levels of atmospheric contaminants or a splash hazard will be encountered	

Level C

Recommended Equipment	Optional Equipment	Used When	
• Full-face air-purifying respirator (MSHA/NIOSH) approved • Chemical resistant suit • Inner and outer chemical resistant gloves • Chemical resistant boots with steel toe and shank • Two-way radio communications	• Coveralls • Long cotton underwear • Chemical resistant disposable boot covers • Hard hat	• All criteria for air-purifying respirators are met • Measured air concentrations of identified substances will be reduced by use of an APR and stay within the service unit • Condition will not warrant use of self-contained breathing apparatus or exposure of unprotected areas to contaminants	

Figure 23-2. Recommended and optional equipment at each of the four levels identified by the Environmental Protection Agency. (U.S. Public Health Service)

EPA Levels of Protection (Cont)		
Level D Does not provide chemical protection!		
Recommended Equipment	**Optional Equipment**	**Used When**
• Coveralls • Safety boots/shoes • Safety glasses or chemical splash goggles • Hard hat	• Gloves • Escape masks • Face shield	• The atmosphere contains no known hazard • Work function precludes splashes, immersion, or potential for unexpected inhalation of or contact with any chemicals

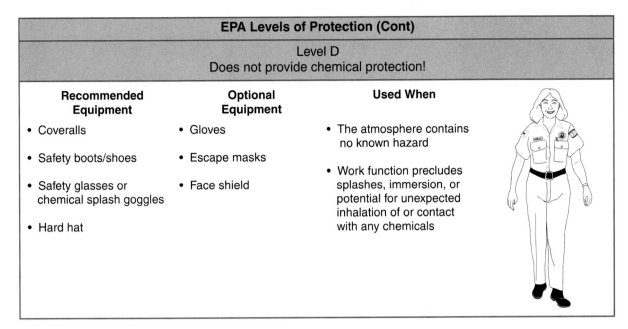

Figure 23-2. (continued)

skin protection. Since firefighting turnout gear is not chemical-resistant, it would fall into this category.

Responders must be trained in the correct use of PPE and fully understand its limitations. Never wear PPE for which you have not been adequately trained and for which you are mentally unprepared.

What Are the Decontamination Requirements?

At Operations Level, you are not to become contaminated. Never touch hazardous products and stay away from areas of airborne contamination. However, the potential for exposure *does* exist. Also, there may be contaminated victims needing treatment. That's why you must learn about basic *decontamination* (usually referred to as simply "decon").

Decon is the removal or reduction of the hazardous material from people and equipment. It should be set up before anyone operates in a potential contamination situation. Decon is required to reduce the hazard to personnel and prevent secondary contamination of people, equipment, and the environment

away from the incident. Responders and civilians who contact or might have contacted the material must be decontaminated.

What Are the Material's Physical and Chemical Properties?

Is it a liquid, solid, or gas? What are its color, odor, flash, and boiling points? Will it sink or float on water? Will it dissolve in water? Is alcohol-resistant foam needed? Is it heavier or lighter than air? What is the flammable range? Will it react with water or air? Is it incompatible with organic sorbents? (Check the *Terminology* section of this chapter if you're not sure of the definitions.)

Is There a Release?

Are there visible liquids, solids, or gases? Can you hear hissing or rushing sounds of escaping product? Are reactions occurring near the incident? Do waterways appear off-color? Are there dead animals, fish, or plants? Do you see smoke and fire colors and/or intensities which are not normal? Can you observe mechanical damage or stress to containers?

Are There Injuries?

Victims may be contaminated. Rescue may be too dangerous without proper chemical protective clothing. The rescuer must not become a casualty. Decon will be needed.

What Are Wind/Weather Conditions?

Observe wind direction; keep it at your back. Variable wind direction is a concern. Wind speed is a factor in product spread. Is the ambient temperature greater than the flash point or boiling point of the chemical? Rain or other precipitation on water reactives can be dangerous. Rain causes runoff dilemmas. Is the sun shining brightly or is it overcast?

What Type and Size Container Is Involved?

Is your 50-gallon spill from a 55-gallon drum, a 34,000 gallon rail car, or a million-gallon storage tank? How much more might be released? Is the container under stress?

In transportation, containers are classified as bulk and nonbulk. *Bulk containers* are rail cars, tanker trucks and vans, intermodal containers, large boxes/bins, and ton containers. *Nonbulk containers* are bottles, bags, pails, drums, cylinders, and smaller boxes. Fixed facilities can have any of the transportation containers on site, in addition to stationary tanks, vats, reactor vessels, bins, and piles.

Don't underestimate the potential of an incident involving a nonbulk container. Consider what is in the package involved, and how spilling of its contents can affect other packages at the incident.

As a responder, you should be familiar with some design characteristics of bulk containers. These characteristics can be indicators of the type of product carried.

Trucks

Highway trucks, **Figure 23-3**, carry both hazardous and nonhazardous materials. There are several types of these cargo vessels:

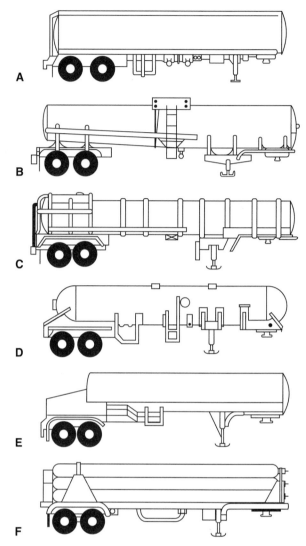

Figure 23-3. Cargo tank trucks. A—Nonpressure tanker for flammable or combustible liquids. B—Low-pressure, used for general chemical transport. C—Medium-pressure tanker for corrosives. D—High-pressure unit for liquefied petroleum gas and similar cargoes. E—Cryogenic liquid tanker. F—Tube trailer for compressed gases.

- Nonpressure/flammable-combustible liquids.
- Low-pressure/general chemical.
- Medium-pressure/corrosives.
- High-pressure.
- Specialized (cryogenic, tube trailer, covered pneumatic hopper trailer).

Nonpressure tanks can be compartmentalized and carry up to 9200 gallons (34 822 liters) of liquid cargo. The tank ends are oval in shape. They are designed for flammable and combustible liquids and have numerous safety and tank protection features. Safety relief valves operate at <3 psig (<20.6 kPa) and there are emergency shutoff controls. There also may be fusible caps and links. Tanks can collapse if product is free-flowing with the access hatch closed, thus creating a vacuum.

Low-pressure tanks are for transportation of general chemicals, including weak acids. They carry up to 7000 g (26 495 l). Tanks are often insulated. Safety relief valves normally operate near the 35 psig (241.3 kPa) working pressure of the tank. There are emergency shutoff controls and fusible links and caps. Tanks can collapse if a vacuum is drawn.

Medium-pressure/corrosives tanks can hold up to 6300 g (23 845 l). They carry strong corrosives and some materials that are poison inhalation hazards. Often loading/unloading fittings are on the top rear portion of the tank, and are fitted with turnover protection. Internal pressure can be as high as 100 psig (689.5 kPa). Tanks are usually round in cross-section, and can have external ring stiffeners. They may be insulated.

High-pressure tanks hold up to 11,500 g (43 528 l) at pressures between 100 psig and 500 psig (689.5 kPa and 3447.5 kPa). They transport anhydrous ammonia, chlorine, liquefied petroleum gas, and other highly volatile products. Tanks are round but have ellipsoidal ends and have bolted hatches on those ends. The tanks can be insulated or uninsulated. They have relief and excess flow valves.

Cryogenic tanks carry extremely cold cargoes such as liquid argon, helium, nitrogen, and hydrogen. Capacity ranges from 5000 g to 14,000 g (28 925 l to 52 990 l) at pressures ranging from 25 psig to 500 psig (172.3 kPa to 3447.5 kPa). They consist of a tank within a tank, separated by insulation in a vacuum space. Look for a box-like compartment at the end of the trailer or on the side in front of the trailer wheels.

Tube trailers permanently hold from two to twenty cylinders containing nonliquefied compressed gas. Cylinder service pressures range from 3000 psig to 5000 psig (20 685 kPa to 34 475 kPa). Oxygen, helium, nitrogen, and hydrogen are some products transported. All cylinders on such a trailer carry the same material.

Covered pneumatic hopper trailers haul solids such as ammonium nitrate fertilizer or dry caustic soda. Capacity is to 1500 cu.ft. (42.4 cu/m).

Intermodal tanks

Intermodal portable tanks are bulk units that can be carried on ships, trucks, or trains. They transport liquids, solids, and gases. They consist of a single compartment container within a lifting frame that is also used for securing the unit. See **Figure 23-4.** Tanks approved for hazardous materials have capacities from 4500 g to 6000 g (17 032.5 l to 22 710 l) and pressure ranges from 14.5 psig to 500 psig (99.9 kPa and 3447.5 kPa).

Rail cars

Railcars transport massive quantities of liquid, gaseous, and solid hazardous and nonhazardous materials. You'll find most hazardous substances in tank cars, **Figure 23-5,**

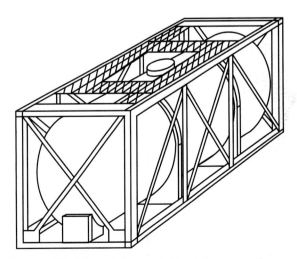

Figure 23-4. The intermodal tank is secured within a lifting frame. It may be loaded on railcars, ships, or trucks.

Figure 23-5. Rail tanker cars. A—Nonpressure tanker for general liquid cargoes and some gases. B—Older-type nonpressure tank car with expansion dome. C—Pressurized tank car used for flammable and nonflammable liquids. D—Cryogenic tank car for liquefied gases.

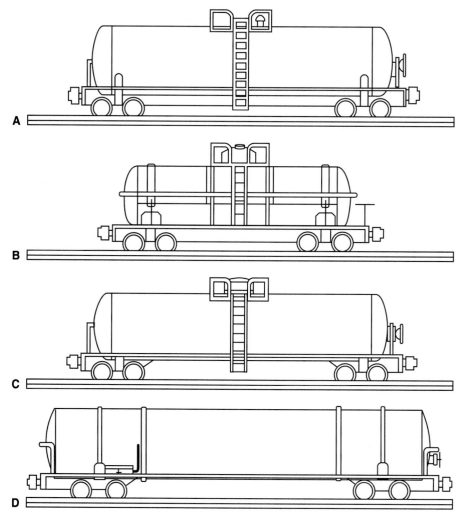

A

B

C

D

but some are transported in covered hoppers or box cars. Some tank cars always carry the same commodity and are permanently lettered to indicate their contents.

Tank cars may be insulated or noninsulated, and may or may not have thermal protection. Capacities range from 4000 g to 45,000 g (15 140 l to 170 325 l), although cars built after 1970 do not exceed 34,500 g (130 582 l).

Nonpressure tank cars are for general service use. Newer cars have visible topside fittings, while older cars have expansion domes on top. The cars may have bottom outlets and inlets. Cars may be compartmentalized to carry different products, and internal pressures may reach 100 psig (689.5 kPa). Hazardous commodities that may be carried in nonpressure tank cars include flammable and combustible liquids, Division 6.1 poisons, corrosives, oxidizers, solids, and some gases.

Pressure tank cars typically transport flammable, nonflammable, or poison gases in a liquefied state. Loading/unloading fittings are on top in a protective housing. There are neither bottom fittings nor multiple compartments. Pressures range from 100 psig to 600 psig (689.5 kPa to 4137 kPa).

Cryogenic tank cars carry extremely cold cargoes, such as liquid argon, helium, nitrogen, or hydrogen. They are constructed as a tank within a tank, separated by insulation in a vacuum space. Pressures are below 25 psig (172.3 kPa). All fittings are enclosed in cabinets on both sides of the car near the wheels or at one end above the coupler.

High-pressure tube cars have 25 to 30 cylinders mounted horizontally in an open-sided frame. All fittings are in an enclosure at the end of the car. Cylinder pressures can be up to 5000 psig (34 475 kPa). Typically, hydrogen, helium, or oxygen is transported in such cars. Such cars do not carry mixed cargo — the same material is in all cylinders.

Covered hopper cars transport such solids as adipic acid, dry caustic soda, ammonium nitrate fertilizer, or polyvinyl chloride pellets. Some cars are pneumatically unloaded by applying 15 psig (103.4 kPa) or more of air pressure.

Boxed tank cars consist of a tank within a box car. Fittings are not external to the box car.

Stationary tanks

Stationary storage tanks may be above ground, below ground, or inside a building. They can store huge quantities of liquids or gases. See **Figure 23-6.**

Atmospheric or nonpressure tanks are normally subjected to internal pressures of up to 0.5 psig (3.4 kPa). Low-pressure tanks have pressures between 0.5 psig and 15 psig (3.4 kPa and 103.4 kPa). Tanks that have pressures >15 psig (>103.4 kPa) are designated as "pressure tanks," **Figure 23-7.**

Container failure and a sudden, significant release of contents can result from stresses either on the container itself or on the contents. Stress can result from mechanical, chemical, and/or thermal causes. Always be on the lookout for signs of container stress and conditions that could affect the chemical contents. It has been determined that, when product is released, various dispersion patterns are possible: stream, cloud, plume, pool, cone, hemisphere, and irregular. The pattern will depend on type and size of breach, form of product when released (liquid, solid, or gas), ambient temperature, internal container pressure, and other factors.

Pipelines

Hazardous materials also are transported by being pumped through pipelines. Markers

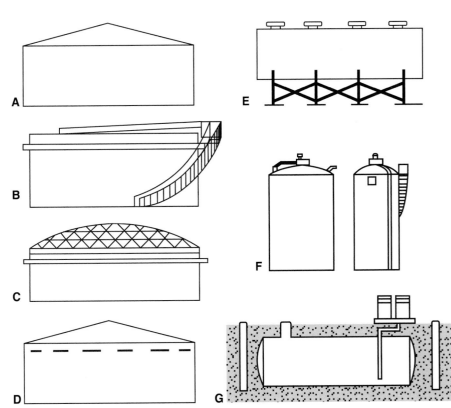

Figure 23-6. Stationary nonpressure tanks. A—Cone-roof tank. Roof-to-shell seams are designed to fail in case of fire or explosion. B—Open floating-roof tank. C—Open floating-roof tank with light geodesic dome covering. D—Internal floating-roof tank with fixed cover. E—Horizontal cylindrical tank on supports. F—Vertical dome-roof tanks. G—Underground storage tanks typically used for petroleum products.

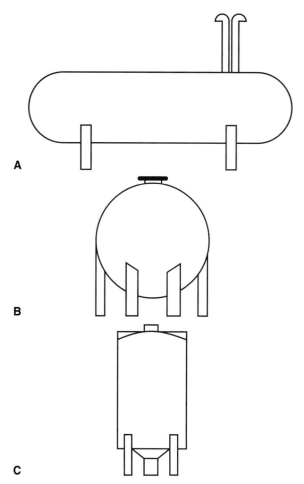

Figure 23-7. Pressure tanks. A—Horizontal high-pressure tank. B—Spherical high-pressure tank for LP gases. C—Cryogenic tank for liquid oxygen and similar products.

Consider Topography

What is the slope of the land? Will hills, valleys, or mountains channel, block, or divert the hazardous material? What is the danger of contaminating surface water or the groundwater supply?

What Is the Hazardous Material Likely to Do?

Based on your assessment of the chemical, container, weather, topography, and other conditions, what would you expect the chemical to do? Will it run downhill into a stream that flows into a town? Will vapors travel into a farming valley? Will the rate of release slow down, allowing more time for qualified responders to act?

Is Intervention Necessary?

Is the threat to the community such that Operations Level actions should be undertaken? Or should there be no Operations Level activities because the hazard is beyond your capability? Will Operations Level intervention have a positive influence? Is there really a need to act? Do you have the necessary resources? What is the likely outcome if nothing is done beyond securing the area? Do the benefits outweigh the risks?

on the pipeline must indicate who owns it, what it carries, and what telephone number to call for an emergency.

What Are the Exposures?

Are site employees safe? Are residential, commercial, institutional, or industrial occupancies in danger? Are special needs people endangered? Should there be an evacuation or in-place sheltering? Are other hazardous chemicals threatened? Are critical facilities — hospitals, power stations, water or sewage treatment plants, fire or police stations — exposed? Are waterways, drinking water supplies, or environmentally sensitive areas threatened?

Action Plan

The objective of your *Action Plan* is protection of people, the environment, and property. Actions should reduce or at least stabilize the threat; nothing you do should make the threat more severe.

Planning Bases

What are the goals you wish to achieve? Based on the Incident Assessment and the resources you have available, how many ways can you accomplish your goals? Develop your Action Plan around the way which offers the most positive outcome at an acceptable level of risk.

Federal law requires that an on-scene **Incident Commander** be in charge of a HazMat emergency and that an incident management system be utilized. Your department's standard operating procedures should explain your **Incident Command System (ICS).** The Incident Commander should be familiar with the responsibilities and legalities of the position. A safety officer must also be appointed. Locate the Incident Command Post in the Cold Zone.

Control zones

Based on the incident assessment, three zones must be established. They are designated as the **Hot Zone, Warm Zone,** and **Cold Zone.** See **Figure 23-8.** As an Operations Level First Responder, you do not belong in the Hot Zone. Event circumstances may or may not require you to operate in the Warm Zone. A major factor will be the level of personal protective clothing needed in the Warm Zone. Your functions are to be performed only at a safe distance, where you will not become contaminated.

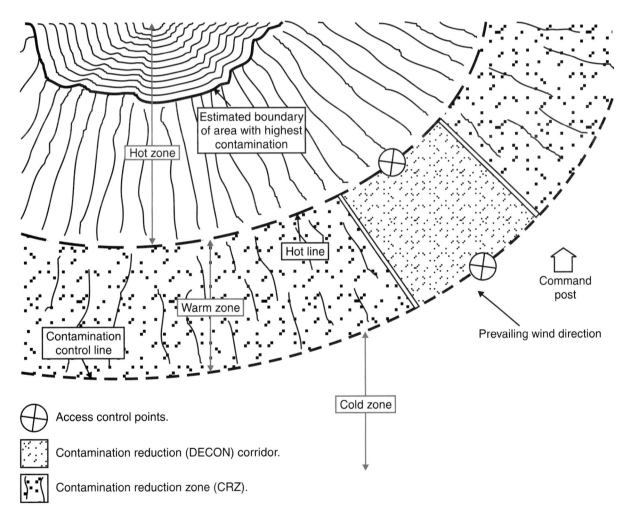

Note: Area dimensions not to scale. Distances between points may vary.

Figure 23-8. The Hot Zone, Warm Zone, and Cold Zone form concentric circles around the point of the spill. The corridor used for decontamination, as well as limiting entry, extends through the Warm Zone from the Hot Zone to the Cold Zone.

Decontamination

Facilities for decontamination must be established before exposing any responders to potential *contamination.* At the First Responder Operations level, you don't expect to become contaminated, but even defensive tasks can lead to contact with the hazardous material. In addition, contaminated victims may present themselves to you. Preparation for decontamination, under an assigned *Decon Officer,* must be made early in the incident, before contamination can occur to response personnel. If your department is not trained to perform decontamination tasks, then your plans should identify who can fulfill this need.

Avoid any form of contact with the hazardous material. Don't inhale it, walk or kneel in it, or let it get on your clothing. Never eat or drink in any hazardous areas.

Conduct decon in a corridor through the Warm Zone that starts at the Hot Zone boundary and finishes at the point where the Cold Zone begins. (Refer to **Figure 23-8.**) Decon should be carried out on level terrain, upwind and a safe distance from the spill site.

Personal protective equipment (PPE) for those doing decon is often the same as for those working in the Hot Zone. At other times, it is one level below that used in the Hot Zone. If the contaminant is unknown, decon personnel should be wearing EPA Level B as a minimum. Level C may be considered if the contaminant is known and concentrations can be determined or if there is little likelihood of contamination. These levels of recommended PPE suggest that personnel at the First Responder Operations Level probably are *not* going to be sufficiently qualified to conduct many decon operations. Decon workers may be exposed to contamination and will themselves have to be decontaminated. The Incident Commander and Safety Officer must be very aware of these considerations.

The decontamination process

As noted earlier, decontamination is the process of removing or reducing the hazardous material from personnel and equipment.

Decon methods must be compatible with the contaminant involved. For example, don't use water to decon a water reactive material. There are numerous decon methods, each with advantages and disadvantages.

The decon area must be clearly identified and protected by laying down plastic and diking around the area. Stay away from waterways and drainage systems. Provide receptacles for equipment and contaminated clothing. Have hoses, wading pools, stepladders, brushes, pails, soap, appropriate gloves/boots, duct tape, and spare SCBA bottles ready.

The most common decon procedure is rinsing and cleaning with warm water and mild soap. See **Figure 23-9.** Rinse contaminated persons from head to toe, then brush with soap/water solution, and rinse well again. See **Figure 23-10.** Use low pressures from small hose lines or hand-pump sprayers. *Dry decon* entails carefully brushing or wiping solids from the contaminated person.

Protective clothing should be turned inside-out as it is removed. This helps keep any contaminant inside the garment. Leave respiratory protection in place until decontamination has eliminated any respiratory threat.

The EPA and other organizations have developed multiple staged decon processes. Your department should adopt, in its operating procedures, appropriate methods of decon for the types of HazMat activities you are likely to encounter.

Emergency decon for medical victims

Unless the chemical is water-reactive, begin flushing with water as soon as responders can don personal protective equipment. Remove victim's clothing as necessary. Don't worry about runoff. Gross decon will normally remove the bulk of the contaminant. Even so, consider the victim to be still contaminated. Properly protected medical responders can begin lifesaving procedures simultaneously with gross decon.

Wrap the victim in plastic (use a body bag, if it is all that's available) and remove him or her to a medical facility in a properly

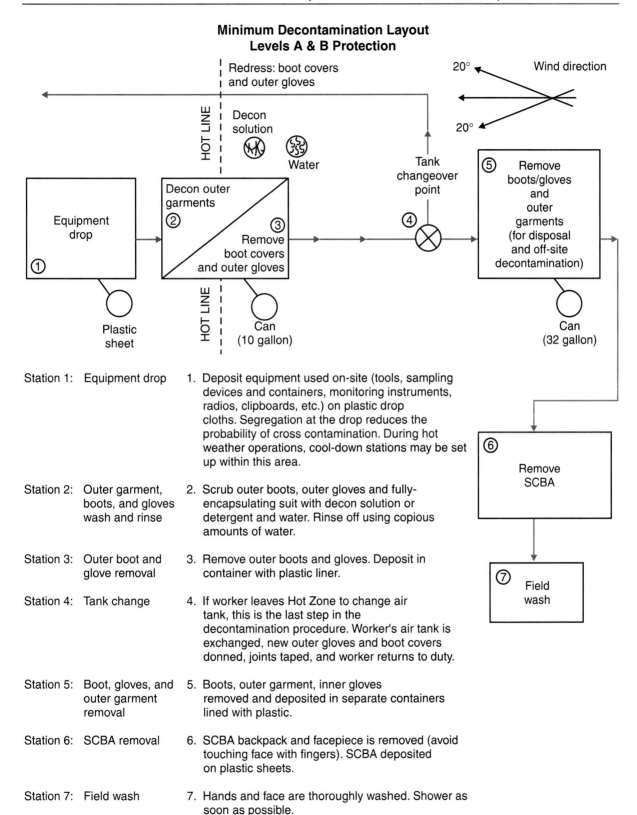

Minimum Decontamination Layout
Levels A & B Protection

Redress: boot covers and outer gloves

Wind direction

Decon solution

Water

Tank changeover point

HOT LINE

Equipment drop ①

Plastic sheet

Decon outer garments ②

Remove boot covers and outer gloves ③

Can (10 gallon)

④

⑤ Remove boots/gloves and outer garments (for disposal and off-site decontamination)

Can (32 gallon)

⑥ Remove SCBA

⑦ Field wash

Station 1: Equipment drop — 1. Deposit equipment used on-site (tools, sampling devices and containers, monitoring instruments, radios, clipboards, etc.) on plastic drop cloths. Segregation at the drop reduces the probability of cross contamination. During hot weather operations, cool-down stations may be set up within this area.

Station 2: Outer garment, boots, and gloves wash and rinse — 2. Scrub outer boots, outer gloves and fully-encapsulating suit with decon solution or detergent and water. Rinse off using copious amounts of water.

Station 3: Outer boot and glove removal — 3. Remove outer boots and gloves. Deposit in container with plastic liner.

Station 4: Tank change — 4. If worker leaves Hot Zone to change air tank, this is the last step in the decontamination procedure. Worker's air tank is exchanged, new outer gloves and boot covers donned, joints taped, and worker returns to duty.

Station 5: Boot, gloves, and outer garment removal — 5. Boots, outer garment, inner gloves removed and deposited in separate containers lined with plastic.

Station 6: SCBA removal — 6. SCBA backpack and facepiece is removed (avoid touching face with fingers). SCBA deposited on plastic sheets.

Station 7: Field wash — 7. Hands and face are thoroughly washed. Shower as soon as possible.

Figure 23-9. The layout and procedure recommended for decontamination of responders wearing Level A or Level B personal protective equipment. Level C layout and procedures are similar.

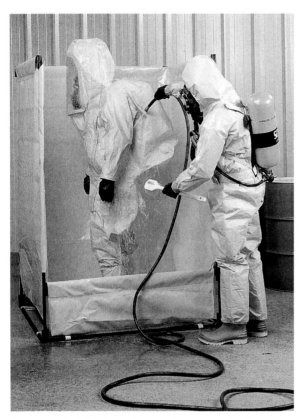

Figure 23-10. Decontamination of protective clothing is done by brushing with a soap and water solution, then rinsing thoroughly with water. Since the rinse water becomes contaminated, it must be captured and later disposed of properly. (Photo courtesy of Lab Safety Supply, Inc., Janesville, WI)

protected transport unit. Medical and transport personnel must be appropriately protected (including respiratory) while handling and moving the victim.

Transport the victim to a medical facility that has been notified that the patient is contaminated, and is willing to accept him or her. Such facilities should be identified in plans drafted *before* any incident takes place. Note that many air medical units will *not* transport contaminated victims.

Population Protection

Early responders may have to make some quick decisions to protect the population. There are sophisticated chemical monitoring devices and computer programs, but these are not normally available to Operations Level personnel. You may have to determine the size of the area that needs to be protected, and how to do so. Your quickest source of advice may be the Emergency Response Guide and other reference materials.

As noted in Chapter 22, civilians may be evacuated or sheltered in place, depending upon circumstances. Those making population-protection decisions must be aware of the many factors influencing each course of action. *Evacuation* entails moving people from the hazard zone to shelters in safe areas. It takes time to warn and instruct people (when such time may not be available), requires resources from many agencies, and can be dangerous. *Shelter-in-place* is a strategy that calls for people in the hazard zone to stay indoors, while taking steps to reduce the amount of air infiltrating from the exterior. This involves closing and taping doors, windows, vents, and other outside air intakes. Air conditioning and heating systems must be turned off. People who are sheltered in place should listen to the radio for instructions.

When ordering population protection, consider how it will impact such occupancies as hospitals, nursing homes, schools, prisons, high-density housing developments, and commercial and industrial facilities and other occupancies. Anticipate the logistical needs for evacuating the elderly, infirm, and very young. Will there be a disruption of such essential services as water, sewage treatment, or electricity?

Defensive Operations

Do not exceed your level of training, competency, and personal protective equipment. Do not place yourself in a position to become contaminated. While remaining mindful of these concerns, you may still be able to perform various actions.

Confinement keeps the released product in a limited area. See **Figure 23-11.** Most Operations Level activities will be limited to

Figure 23-11. Various methods of confinement can be used, depending upon the situation. Here, absorbent sock materials have been used to confine liquid from a leaking drum. A layer of foam was spread over the ground to control vapors from the escaped liquid. (Photo courtesy of Lab Safety Supply, Inc., Janesville, WI)

confinement. In contrast to confinement, *containment* keeps the product in its container. Few Operations Level activities will be containment.

Consider how the spill will spread on the surface, above the surface, and down through the soil or water. Cover any openings into storm and sanitary sewer systems. Plastic sheets or tarps, held down by dirt or other heavy objects, can be placed over the openings. Commercially manufactured protectors are available also.

Retention basins

One method of confinement is to retain liquid in a container or a *retention basin.* Be certain that the container and leaking material

are compatible. Use caution before digging retention basins (pits), since this can worsen soil and groundwater contamination. Line retention basins with compatible materials whenever possible.

You can control vapors by placing a layer of foam over a liquid. The type of foam used must be correct for the material. See Chapter 8.

Sorbent materials

Spreading sorbent materials onto and around a liquid may prevent its spread. Check for compatibility of the sorbent material with the spilled material. Note that, after use, sorbents are hazardous wastes. *Organic natural sorbents* such as straw, hay, pine needles, or sawdust may react with corrosives and oxidizers. They tend to become quite heavy and are less absorbent than mineral materials. *Inorganic mineral sorbents* like vermiculite, clay, perlite, and porous silicates often are more effective. Be very cautious of material typically used as cat litter, because of chemical materials in the material that could cause a reaction.

A method of confinement that also is used is to place tarps or sheeting over a spilled solid or liquid. Check the covering material for compatibility and cleanliness.

To disperse or direct a gas or vapor, use water fog or fans. This might reduce flammables below explosive range. Water runoff may pose a contamination threat, however, and must be controlled. Before use, determine reactivity of material with water. Note that fog may be less effective on materials that are not water-soluble.

Confinement can also be accomplished by *diking,* which channels a liquid to a desired location or away from a sensitive location. Dikes can be constructed from dirt, filled plastic bags, tubular-style absorbent socks, or water-filled fire hose.

Damming

Confinement by *damming* is not always practical, since fast-flowing streams and large bodies of water are very difficult to dam.

There are various types of dams. You must know the hazardous material's specific gravity and solubility before deciding which method is practical. Dams must be reinforced as water action deteriorates them. Use heavy, solid materials like rocks and logs for the base. Tie it into the banks if possible. Build up with rocks, stones, branches, and dirt. Use plastic to line the upstream face of the dam. Customize it for the need at hand.

You should build your dam downstream far enough that you won't be working in contaminated water. You may have to construct several "holdback" dams to buy time to build one or more customized ones.

There are three basic types of customized dams. They are the filter dam, the overflow dam, and the underflow dam.

Filter dams screen out undissolved material which floats on the surface (specific gravity <1). Wire mesh is attached to posts driven into the streambed. Lay straw or similar material on the surface upstream at the dam. The straw collects the floating hazardous material. Use pads to absorb the material.

Overflow dams are for hazardous materials that don't dissolve but do sink (specific gravity >1). Piping or tubing through the barrier is angled so the upstream end is higher than the downstream end. This enables surface flow to pass down dam but retains the heavier hazardous material.

Underflow dams are for hazardous materials which do not dissolve and which float on/near the surface (specific gravity <1). Piping/tubing through the barrier is angled so the upstream end is *lower* than the downstream end. Don't have the downstream ends of the pipes higher than the dam top, or water will flow over the dam rather than through the piping. Also, the piping must be angled properly to prevent the surface contaminants from flowing out if the impoundment level drops. This dam permits lower depths of relatively uncontaminated water to flow downstream while the hazardous material near the surface is retained.

The wisest action plan may be one of *no action* beyond securing the scene, and observing conditions while awaiting the arrival of more specifically trained personnel. The incident may be minor due to the nature of the material, quantity released, remote location, or other conditions. Responders may simply control access to the site, watch for deterioration, and await cleanup regulators and contractors. Or, the event may be clearly beyond the capabilities of any First Responder defensive actions. Personnel would secure a suitable safe area and wait for higher levels of responders to attempt control.

Plan Reevaluation

The action plan must be continuously reevaluated for effectiveness and changing conditions. There are very few certainties with HazMat events. Always be observant. Report any unexpected or unusual occurrences. Are your actions stabilizing the situation or are events worsening? Are unanticipated conditions developing?

Provide status reports as required in your standard operating procedures. Know your department's methods for incident ground warning to evacuate or immediately take shelter.

Should You Attempt Rescue?

You know that at the Operations Level, you are to perform "defensively" from a safe location and not get contaminated. You are not trained in wearing Chemical Protective Clothing. You probably don't understand how to quickly interpret information in the reference books. So, what do you do when faced with a HazMat rescue? Do you try or not try? When you weigh the decision, remember these points:

- There is no gain if the rescuer needs to be rescued and becomes another victim.

- Chemical hazards are often invisible.
- Some things are just not possible.
- The ERG's definition of "limited protection."

If you decide to try, wear your SCBA and the highest level of personal protective equipment available. Enter the Hot Zone from uphill and upwind. Be very careful about causing ignition. Be especially cautious of oxidizers and fuels. Get in, then get out to decontamination as quickly as possible.

Incident Termination Procedures

Debriefing, post-incident analysis, and critique are the major components of incident termination. The objective is to offer personal safety information, followed by the lessons learned or reinforced by the operation.

Debriefing

The process of *debriefing* should begin as soon as the emergency is over; preferably before emergency personnel leave the scene. A Debriefing Officer should explain or discuss the following:

- The hazardous material involved and signs/symptoms of exposure. If applicable, the officer should provide information to responders for their exposure records.
- Equipment damage. Identify unsafe conditions requiring immediate attention or isolation. Talk about the need to decon or clean equipment upon returning to the station.
- Assign information-gathering duties to appropriate individuals for follow-up analysis and critique.
- Identify a post-incident point of contact, should responders have questions or concerns.

- Briefly describe activities performed in each sector. Discuss any major problems or concerns.
- Reinforce positive points of the event.
- Thank everyone.

Keep the debriefing under an hour, and stage it away from distractions.

Post-incident Analysis

Reconstruction of the event to determine what occurred and who did what is called *post-incident analysis.* Generally, you won't be involved very deeply in this activity. You may be asked about specific actions you performed or events you observed.

Critique

This review of the event centers around what went *right* and what *did not;* what was learned or reinforced. Although *critique* formats vary, their common purpose is to improve responder safety and effectiveness. *A critique is not a time to place blame.* Critiques encourage:

- Self-correction within the system.
- Cooperation through teamwork.
- Preplanning.
- Sharing of information.
- Desire to improve skills and capabilities.

Written comments or suggestions from a critique should be forwarded to higher levels in the department for evaluation and possible implementation.

Department Operating Procedures

Department Operating Procedures (DOPs) are designed to provide operational guidance to personnel. They should be developed in a thought-provoking environment.

The language must be clear, concise, and have the same meaning to all who read them.

You need to understand your department's policies pertaining to HazMat response. Operating Procedures tell you what you may or may not do at your level of training. They tell you what to look for. They explain specific procedures or processes. Be sure to have a thorough understanding of your DOPs before responding to HazMat calls.

SUMMARY

First Responders at the Operations level protect people, the environment, and property from the effects of a hazardous materials release. They perform in a "defensive" manner without actually trying to stop the spill. Taking offensive actions requires a higher level of training and competency.

Operations responders are not to come in contact with the hazardous material. They are not expected to wear chemical protective clothing or to use specialized equipment. Qualification in the use of the SCBA is imperative, however. An understanding of HazMat terminology, and of hazard and risk evaluation, is essential. Since Operations level personnel are at some risk of exposure or may find contaminated victims, they need training in basic decontamination procedures.

Many defensive practices center around confining the released product. Construction of dikes or dams and the protection of sewer inlets are important procedures. Foam application can reduce dangerous vapors.

Responders must be versed in the department's Incident Command System, Operating Procedures, and incident termination procedures.

REVIEW QUESTIONS

1. HazMat incident assessment is made by:
   A. First Responder Awareness personnel only.
   B. Incident Commander only.
   C. Safety Officer only.
   D. Everyone involved.

2. Name three HazMat exposure routes that can affect humans.

3. Specific gravity of 1.5 means that the product:
   A. Is heavier than air.
   B. Floats on water.
   C. Sinks in water.
   D. 1.5 % of the product will dissolve in water.

4. True or False? A vapor density of less than 1 means that the gas is lighter than air.

5. Does structural firefighters' turnout gear offer a satisfactory degree of protection against most types of hazardous materials?

6. Plugging a leak in a gasoline tank truck would most likely be done by:
   A. A Technician Level responder.
   B. An Operations Level responder.
   C. An Awareness Level responder.
   D. Any of the above.

7. What is the *minimum* EPA Level of Personal Protection that should be used for an incident involving an unknown hazardous material?

8. Why is absorbent compatibility with the spilled material important?

9. Under what circumstances would a filter dam be most effective for a hazardous material waterway spill?

10. An overflow dam should not be used if the spilled material:
    A. Has a specific gravity of 0.85.
    B. Sinks in water.
    C. Has a specific gravity of 1.3.
    D. Is classed as a mutagen.

11. True or False? Decon should not be set up until the Hot Zone entry team has confirmed the identity of the hazardous material.

12. Discuss the correctness of the statement, "All rail tank cars are insulated as a precaution against fire."

13. Air Purifying Respirators might be used if:
    A. No SCBA is available.
    B. The hazardous material is unidentified.
    C. The hazardous material has a distinctive odor.
    D. The oxygen level is 17.5% or less.
    E. In none of the above situations.

14. Name the two types of population protection that are used in HazMat incidents.

15. Which factors should be considered in any Action Plan?
    A. Responder risks.
    B. Benefits.
    C. Threat to the community.
    D. All of the above.

16. Describe the location where decontamination is done in a HazMat situation, and how it relates to the Hot Zone and Cold Zone.

17. Which of the following statements about debriefing is correct?
    A. It is important only for Technician Level responders.
    B. It identifies the hazardous material and signs or symptoms of exposure.
    C. It occurs several days after the event.
    D. It is useful for determining who is at fault.

18. At what personal protection level (on the EPA scale) would the combination of fire department turnout gear and SCBA be classified?

19. A vapor density of 1.9 means that:
    A. The vapor will sink in air.
    B. The vapor will rise in air.
    C. The vapors will dissolve readily in water.
    D. None of the above.

20. What are some physical signs that a hazardous material may be escaping?

APPENDIX 1:
Ladder Testing

The following ladder test procedure has been adapted from the factory spot check test used by Duo-Safety Ladder Corporation, and is used with permission.

The ladder test procedure should be performed annually. Between annual tests, it should be used any time that you suspect a ladder has been damaged or subjected to excessive heat. Establish a permanent record card for each ladder you have in service. Faithfully record test dates and results.

To prevent possible injury to personnel while testing, use sandbags as weights. Use the required number of 50-pound sandbags for the load test and the roof hook test. Use one 30-pound sand bag for the rung torque test.

Avoid shock loads—do not throw the sandbags on the ladders. Instead, place them in position gently and carefully. *Note*: These tests are not suitable for folding ladders or pompier ladders.

Load Test

As shown in **Figure A-1,** place the ladder on test bars (sawhorses or similar supports) located under the end rungs. If ladder being tested is an extension ladder, extend it fully before placing it on the test bars. Lay a piece of 3/4" plywood on top of the rails to support the sandbags used for this test.

Next, preload the ladder, **Figure A-1A.** Carefully place seven 50-pound sandbags on the ladder as shown. Place three bags to one side of the centerpoint of the ladder and three side of the centerpoint of the ladder and three

to the other side. Lay the seventh bag on top of the others, at the ladder's centerpoint. Allow the sandbags to remain in place for one minute to "set" the ladder, then remove them. Do not move the ladder.

As shown on **Figure A-1B**, you should next measure the distance from the bottom of the ladder rail at the centerpoint to the floor. Record this distance on the ladder's permanent record card.

Load ladder with sandbags again, as shown in **Figure A-1C.** This time, use ten 50-pound sandbags for a total load of 500 pounds. Allow the load to remain in position for five minutes, then remove the sandbags. Wait for five more minutes, then repeat the ladder rail-to-floor measurement. Record this second measurement on the permanent record card.

For ladders 25 feet or less in length, the difference in the two measurements should not exceed one-half inch. For ladders more than 25 feet in length, the difference in measurements should not exceed one inch. Any ladder that deflects more than these amounts is potentially hazardous and should be removed from service.

Rung Torque Test

To conduct this test, it will be necessary to construct a test arm, as shown in **Figure A-2.** The test arm should be constructed from standard 2" x 4" lumber and a locking clamp (De-Sta-Co #52670 or equivalent). Hooks able to safely support a 50-pound load should be installed at each end of the test bar.

This test is performed on either three or five randomly chosen rungs, depending on ladder length. For a ladder 20 feet or under, choose three rungs; for a longer ladder, choose five.

Mount ladder vertically in any convenient position that will allow use of the test arm. Using a fine felt pen, draw a line about an inch long across the top of each rung to be tested. Continue the line up the inside of the beam for about one inch, as shown in

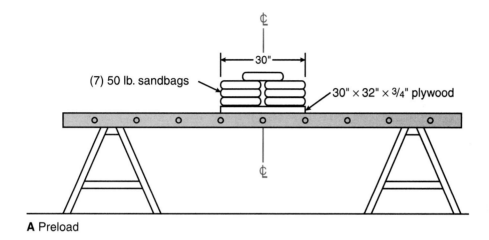

A Preload

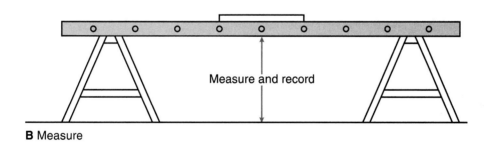

B Measure

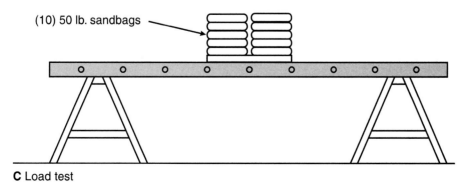

C Load test

Figure A-1. Ladder load test procedure.

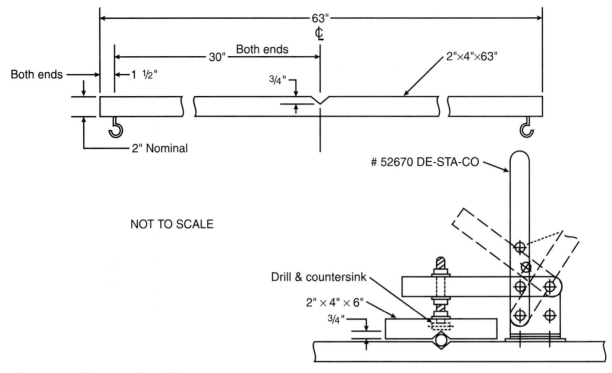

Figure A-2. Construction of the rung torque test arm.

Figure A-3A. Repeat at the opposite end of that rung. Attach the test arm to the center of the rung to be tested, clamping it tight enough that it will not move on the rung, but not so tight as to deform the rung.

Hang a 30-pound sandbag from the hook on one end of the test arms shown in **Figure A-3B.** Let it hang for one minute, then inspect the lines to determine if there has been any movement of the rung in relation to the beams. Move the weight to other end of test arm and repeat the test. Repeat one more time at each end of test arm. No movement of the rung with respect to the beam is permitted. If any one rung fails the test, all rungs on that ladder should be tested

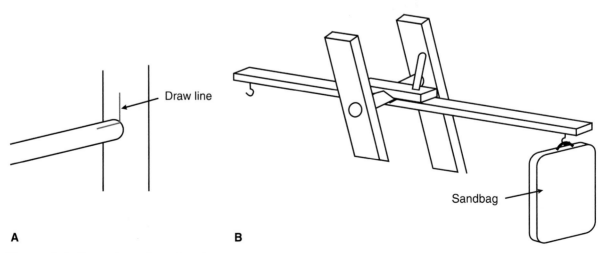

A   B

Figure A-3. Procedures for using the rung torque test arm.

for tightness. Any loose rungs must be repaired or replaced. If 25% of the rungs on a ladder show looseness, it is a good indication that the ladder has suffered considerable stress. The manufacturer should be contacted to determine if the ladder should be repaired or replaced.

Roof Hook Test

This test should be performed on all roof ladders in addition to the Load Test and the Rung Torque Test. *Caution:* Because of the great weight (in excess of 1000 pounds) involved in this test, adequate safety precautions must be taken. The surface from which the ladder is hung from must be able to withstand the total weight with a good safety margin. Further, the ladder must be secured so that if one or both hooks should fail, the ladder will not fall or whip and injure testers or observers.

Hang the ladder so that the weight is borne entirely by the points of the hooks, as shown in **Figure A-4**. Working from the top down, hang 50-pound sandbags alternately on the left and right ends of the ladder rungs. Hang a total of 20 sandbags (10 on each side of the ladder). The ladder and roof hooks must not disengage point contact and should remain fully functional after the test.

The NFPA ladder specification offers a more complete test procedure. You should procure a copy and become thoroughly familiar with this procedure. However, more complete testing should be performed by factory or professional testing personnel. Any ladder passing this test procedure will have a minimum load capacity of 500 pounds with a 4:1 safety factor at the time of testing.

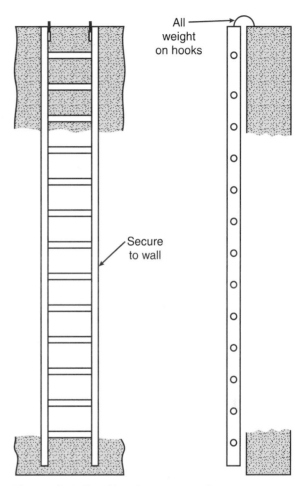

Figure A-4. Roof hook test procedure.

APPENDIX 2:
Radio Procedure

The following sample radio procedure is a composite of those used in several localities. No two dispatching organizations work in exactly the same way, nor are the terms used in dispatching identical in all areas. However, the basics are the same all over. Make yourself familiar with these procedures and then adapt them to the practices of your own department.

24-Hour Time

Most fire communications systems use the 24-hour time system to promote accuracy and help avoid misunderstandings. The 24-hour time and 12-hour time systems are compared below:

24-hour time	12-hour time
2400	Midnight (in spoken form, *"twenty-four hundred"*)
0001	One minute after midnight (*"zero zero zero one"*)
0015	Quarter past midnight (*"zero zero one five"*)
0100	1 a.m. (*"zero one hundred"*)
0130	One thirty a.m. (*"zero one three zero"*)
0200	2 a.m.
0300	3 a.m.
0400	4 a.m.
0500	5 a.m.
0600	6 a.m.
0700	7 a.m.
0800	8 a.m.
0900	9 a.m.
1000	10 a.m. (*"ten hundred"*)
1100	11 a.m.
1200	Noon (*"twelve hundred"*)
1201	One minute after noon (*"twelve zero one"*)
1215	Quarter past noon (*"twelve fifteen"*)
1300 (add 100 to 1200)	1 p.m. (*"thirteen hundred"*)
1400	2 p.m.
1500	3 p.m.
1545 (add 0045 to 1500)	3:45 p.m. (*"fifteen forty-five"*)
1600	4 p.m.
1700	5 p.m.
1800	6 p.m.
1900	7 p.m.
2000 (add 800 to 1200)	8 p.m. (*"twenty hundred"*)
2100	9 p.m.
2200	10 p.m.
2300	11 p.m.

Standard Words and Phrases

The terminology listed below is used to convey in condensed form certain frequently used orders, instructions, requests, and abbreviations. While the actual phrases may vary from locality to locality, the following are widely used:

Procedure Words	Meaning
Acknowledge	Let me know that you have received and understood the message.
Advise	Give this message to/or provide me with the necessary information.
Affirmative	What you have just said is correct.
Available	Apparatus is in service and able to respond.
Be advised	This is to advise you that (give information).
Correction	An error has been transmitted. The correct information is_____.
E.T.A.	Estimated time of arrival.
Message received	I understand your last message.
O.K.	Your message has been received and understood, and will be complied with.
On the scene	Responding apparatus has reached the location of the incident.
Out-of-service	Apparatus is not available to respond.
Proceed	Acknowledgement and direction to state your message.
Repeat	Say your last message again.
Responding	Places a unit on the air when it is running on an emergency call.
Stand-by	Listen but do not transmit until directed to do so.
Test count	For test purposes, a 5 count will be made twice (1 to 5, then 5 to 1) followed by words *"Test complete"* and the time.
Verify	Verify entire message and correct if necessary

"Ten Codes" for Police and Fire Emergencies

Code	Message
10-0	Caution
10-1	Unable to copy, change location
10-2	Signal is good
10-3	Stop transmitting
10-4	Acknowledgment
10-5	Relay
10-6	Busy, stand by unless urgent
10-7	Out of service
10-8	In service
10-9	Repeat
10-10	Fight in progress
10-12	Stand by
10-13	Weather and road conditions
10-15	Civil disturbance
10-16	Domestic trouble
10-18	Complete assignment quickly
10-19	Return to _____.
10-20	Give your location
10-21	Call by telephone
10-22	Disregard
10-23	Arrived at scene
10-24	Assignment completed
10-25	Report in person to _____.
10-30	Illegal use of radio
10-32	Man with a gun
10-34	Riot
10-36	Correct time
10-41	Beginning tour of duty
10-42	Ending tour of duty
10-43	Information
10-46	Assist motorist
10-50	Vehicle accident
10-52	Ambulance needed
10-53	Road blocked
10-55	Intoxicated driver
10-56	Intoxicated pedestrian
10-62	Reply to message

10-63	Prepare to make written copy
10-64	Message for local delivery
10-65	New message assignment
10-66	Message cancellation
10-67	Clear to read net message
10-68	Dispatch information
10-69	Message received
10-70	Fire alarm
10-71	Advise nature of fire (size, type, and contents of building)
10-72	Report progress of fire
10-73	Smoke report
10-74	Negative
10-75	In contact with _____.
10-76	En route
10-77	ETA (estimated time of arrival)
10-78	Need assistance
10-79	Notify coroner
10-85	Delayed, due to _____.
10-88	Advise phone number to contact_____.
10-91	Unnecessary use of radio
10-96	Mentally ill subject

Phonetic alphabet

A = ALPHA	N = NOVEMBER
B = BRAVO	O = OSCAR
C = CHARLIE	P = PAPA
D = DELTA	Q = QUEBEC
E = ECHO	R = ROMEO
F = FOXTROT	S = SIERRA
G = GOLF	T = TANGO
H = HOTEL	U = UNIFORM
I = INDIA	V = VICTOR
J = JULIETTE	W = WHISKEY
K = KILO	X = X-RAY
L = LIMA	Y = YANKEE
M = MIKE	Z = ZULU

Communication with Mobile Units

- All apparatus must acknowledge that they are responding.
- First unit on the scene will be acknowledged by Dispatch with unit number, on-the-scene report, if any, and the time.
- After first unit reports on the scene, Dispatch often will not acknowledge any additional units or apparatus reporting on the scene or responding.
- Placing units on the air: the term *"responding"* is used by units when enroute to an emergency call. One unit may place several units on the air.

Single-Unit Alarm Response (Field Unit)

1. Personnel on apparatus will acknowledge receipt of alarm from Dispatch by saying *"(unit number) responding"* when leaving the station.
2. When arriving at the fire or incident, report *"(unit number) on the scene."*
3. Provide a situation report within five minutes of arrival on the scene. This can also be done immediately upon arrival, if the situation is of an obvious nature.
4. When the assignment is completed, notify Dispatch or other control center of your availability status. *"(unit number) available,"* or *"(unit number) not available."*
5. If you return to quarters with a *"not available"* status, notify Dispatch by telephone when you have become *"available."* Usually, Dispatch will notify other stations over the air.
6. When requesting assistance on an incident from a Duty Officer or the police, use maximum discretion in reporting your needs. This will assist in controlling unauthorized persons who may be monitoring radio transmissions.

Multiple-Unit Alarm Response (Field Units)

1. Personnel on any apparatus will acknowledge receipt of alarm from Dispatch by saying *"(unit number) responding"* when leaving the station. If more than one piece of apparatus is responding from the same station, one

unit can acknowledge for the others. Be careful to avoid trying to transmit over another unit's transmission.

2. All units will report when they arrive at the fire or incident location, using the form, *"(unit number) on the scene."*

3. The first unit on the scene will transmit a first-in report, such as *"Nothing showing"* or *"Fire showing on second floor."* Dispatch will relay the first-in report to other responding apparatus. They should acknowledge the report by stating *"(unit number) OK"* or *"(unit number), 10-4."*

4. Any other transmission that may originate from the fire scene to apparatus not yet on the scene will be relayed by Dispatch, if there is not an immediate acknowledgement by that apparatus.

5. Upon completion of the assignment, notify Dispatch that your unit is *"available"* or *"not available."*

Ambulance Procedures (Field Unit)

1. Ambulance personnel will acknowledge receipt of call from Dispatch by saying *"(unit number) responding."*

2. Upon arrival at scene, report *"(unit number) on the scene."*

3. When departing from the scene, report *"(unit number) en route to (name of hospital)."*

4. When arriving at the hospital, report *"(unit number) at the hospital."*

5. After delivering patient to the hospital, notify Dispatch that *"(unit number) is available."*

6. When requesting assistance on a call, use maximum discretion in reporting your needs. This will help avoid attracting the attention of curious persons who monitor emergency service radio frequencies.

In-Service/Out-of-Service Announcements

1. In-service/out-of-service announcements are usually made by Dispatch as they are received.

2. Announcements typically are made to identify the status of any of the following:
   - Engine companies and other units
   - Hydrants
   - Streets
   - Sprinkler systems
   - Private fire alarm systems
   - Bridges

Recall Procedure

The purpose of this procedure is to cancel response by additional apparatus when they are not needed.

1. When the first arriving unit or officer determines that full response is not warranted or that continued emergency response by other apparatus is not necessary, the officer should radio Dispatch immediately. He or she should advise Dispatch of the situation, identify the unit or units needed at the scene, and request a recall of all other apparatus responding.

2. **Example:** *"Chief 2 to Dispatch, this is only a trash fire at the rear of the structure, Engine 2 will handle the situation. Recall the other apparatus."*

3. Dispatch will than transmit the recall request, noting the exception of the unit or units that will handle the incident.

4. **Example:** (Tone Signal) *"Attention all units responding to 2222 Almart Street, except Engine 2. Recall on the order of Chief 2."*

5. Recalled units should acknowledge by merely giving the unit number and "OK". It is not necessary for the unit to signify it is "available," or "returning to quarters" — that is the intent of the recall procedure.

6. **Example:** *"Ladder 11, OK"..... "Engine 6, OK"..... "Snorkel 3, OK"..... "Rescue 4, OK"*

7. If a unit does not acknowledge the recall message, Dispatch must contact the unit with a message such as, *"Dispatch to Engine 8. Recall in Progress. Acknowledge."*

Fireground Communications

Fire Scene Operations

Message may be classified as either urgent or routine. Urgent messages have a priority classification to clear radio traffic. Routine messages (those of normal importance) have a lower priority. For example, when a unit has an urgent message for Dispatch, especially when radio traffic is heavy, the unit should use this form: *"(unit number) to Dispatch: Urgent...Repeat...Urgent."* An urgent message will be given priority over all other messages. For this reason, its use must be restricted to emergencies where life-threatening or critical situations require immediate additional assistance.

Under certain conditions, radio and telephone traffic at Dispatch becomes heavy enough to prevent immediate answers to radio calls. When this occurs, Dispatch will advise, *"All units stand by."* This means that Dispatch is temporarily unable to answer and units should not transmit until further notice.

All fire and ambulance personnel should be aware of the need to conserve the use of radio frequencies. They should make a conscious and positive effort to eliminate unnecessary use of radio.

Fire Command Communications

1. If more than one piece of equipment is responding to a fire, a command post should be set up by the officer in charge at the scene. All communications between the fire scene and Dispatch will then be routed through this command post.
2. The officer in charge, as soon as possible after assessing the situation, must make a fireground report to the chief officer. In this report, the officer will advise the nature and severity of the situation, what units will be held on the fireground, and an estimate of how long those units will be held. During all fires and emergencies, the officer-in-charge must periodically advise Dispatch about the current situation. It is important that Dispatch be kept continuously informed of progress.
3. When several units on the fireground are available for reassignment, the officer in charge should transmit this information to Dispatch. The transmission should list all the units in a group.
4. Whenever a unit leaves the fireground in such condition that it cannot be used immediately for another alarm (i.e., with insufficient gas, water, hose, or equipment), it should be reported as "not available." Each unit leaving the fireground and reporting as "not available" should be reported as "available" as soon as it is actually ready for assignment (refueled, water tank filled, hose repacked, or equipment restored). Radio is normally used to report such units as available for duty.

Notification of Other Agencies

Outside agencies such as the police department, utility companies, or state agencies may require notification under certain situations. Fire/rescue personnel must make the determination of which agency to contact and when to contact them. Dispatch should be advised to make the proper notifications. Whenever representatives of another agency arrive on the scene Dispatch should be notified of their arrival.

Police assistance

Ambulance and fire personnel should always be alert for possible foul play or other problems that may require the presence of police for investigation or security.

Utility companies

When the service of utility companies is needed (for gas or power shutoff, for example), advise Dispatch of the situation. (An order to "lay lines" for a water supply to fight the fire often constitutes an automatic call to the electric power company.) The officer in charge should notify Dispatch when utility company personnel have arrived on the scene.

Accident involving fire/rescue apparatus

Any fire or rescue vehicle involved in a traffic accident must immediately notify Dispatch and advise whether they require any assistance.

The State Fire Marshal

This official may be notified of any fire or emergency at which the officer in charge desires assistance. *Note*: If the police request that the Fire Marshal be notified, the information is not to be transmitted over the fire frequency. Call the police department on a landline (telephone) to advise that the Fire Marshal has been notified.

Testing of Equipment

The dispatching center will provide tests of individual unit alerting equipment whenever requested, if no Dispatch operations are in progress at that time. A typical test and response sequence might be:

Dispatch	Unit Response
Headquarters	*Headquarters, OK*
Company No. 2	*Company No. 2, OK*
Company No. 3	*Company No. 3, OK*
One (5 second) Beep Tone	
Rescue 1	*Rescue 1, OK*
Rescue 1-1	*Rescue 1-1, OK*
Snorkel 1	*Snorkel 1, OK*
Ladder 1	*Ladder 1, OK*
Engine 1	*Engine 1, OK*
Engine 1-1	*Engine 1-1, OK*
(and so on)	

Representative Fire and Rescue Alarms

Alarms can be classified into single-unit response and multiple-unit response alarms, depending upon the number of units normally dispatched. The classification of alarms shown below is typical, and may differ from the practice in your community.

Single-Unit Response Alarms

- Vehicle fire
- Brush fire
- Trash or debris fire
- Shed fire
- Tree fire
- Chimney fire
- Smoke investigation (outside central business district)
- Odor investigation
- Washdown
- Furnace malfunction (no fire involved)

Multiple-Unit Response Alarms

- Residential fire (kitchen, bedroom, cellar, attic, porch)
- Automatic alarms (waterflow, etc.)
- Business establishment (all)
- Apartment buildings
- Hospitals
- Schools
- Churches
- Printing plants
- Gas stations and auto repair garages
- Smoke investigation (within central business district)
- Manufacturing plants
- Warehouses

Types of Alarms

The specific types and combinations of units responding to each level of alarm, as well as the number of levels of alarm, will vary from community to community. The examples that follow are typical.

Single unit alarm

Usually, an alarm to which one engine company responds. (Called a "still alarm" in some communities.)

Multiple unit alarm

An alarm to which a certain combination of units (varying by community) will respond. A typical response might be two engine companies, one ladder company, one snorkel, one rescue unit, and the Deputy Chief on duty. The Fire Chief may respond.

Second alarm

In some communities, this is primarily a call for more personnel. The chief officer will contact Dispatch to designate how many firefighters are to be to called and where they are to respond. In larger departments, a second alarm will bring in a set combination of additional equipment and personnel.

Third alarm

In smaller communities, this is usually a general alarm or "all hands" alarm that results in the calling in of all available firefighters. In larger communities, it is similar to a second alarm, resulting in the assignment of additional equipment and personnel. Large city departments often have as many as five levels of alarms.

Special assignment

A procedure used whenever a particular piece of apparatus is required at a fire or other incident. The unit is designated after the phrase "Special Assignment." For example, *"Special Assignment, Snorkel 1"* or *"Special Assignment, Tankers 3 and 4."*

Mutual Aid

An alarm in which equipment and personnel from neighboring communities is called in a preplanned sequence. Usually not declared until after an "all hands" general alarm by the local Fire Department indicates additional help is needed. Mutual aid plans are designed to spread resources on a regional basis so that extra equipment and personnel can be brought to bear in one community while maintaining adequate protection in adjoining communities. The decision to call for Mutual Aid is usually made by the Fire Chief or a Deputy Chief.

Sample Dispatch: Single-Unit Response

Note: The term "still alarm," as used here, indicates a single-unit response.

DISPATCH, 1st Announcement:
　　　　　　(Alert tone) *"Engine 2, still alarm"* (Address) (Details)
DISPATCH, 2nd Announcement:
　　　　　　"Still alarm" (Address) (Details) (Time)
UNIT, Acknowledgement:
　　　　　　"Engine 2, responding" (Address) (Details) (Time)

Sample Dispatch: Multiple-Unit Response

Note: The term "district alarm," as used here, indicates a multiple-unit response.

DISPATCH, 1st Announcement:
　　　　　　(Alert tone) *"District alarm"* (Address) (Details)
DISPATCH, 2nd Announcement:
　　　　　　"District alarm" (Address) (Details) (Time)
FIRST UNIT, Acknowledgment:
　　　　　　"Engine 1, responding" (Address) (Details) (Time)
OTHER UNITS, Acknowledgment:
　　　　　　"Rescue 1, responding"
　　　　　　"Ladder 2, responding"
　　　　　　"Deputy Chief, responding"

Sample Dispatch: Routine Ambulance Call

DISPATCH, 1st Announcement:
　　　　　　(Alert tone) *"Rescue 1, ambulance call, routine"* (Address) (Details)
DISPATCH, 2nd Announcement:
　　　　　　"Ambulance call, routine" (Address) (Details) (Time)
UNIT, Acknowledgement:
　　　　　　"Rescue 1, responding" (Address) (Details) (Time)

Sample Dispatch: Emergency Ambulance Call

DISPATCH, 1st Announcement:
> (Alert tone) *"Rescue 1, ambulance call, emergency"*
> (Address) (Details)

DISPATCH, 2nd Announcement:
> *"Ambulance call, emergency"*
> (Address) (Details) (Time)

UNIT, Acknowledgement:
> *"Rescue 1, responding"*
> (Address) (Details) (Time)

The police will be notified to respond on an "Ambulance call, emergency" dispatch if the nature of the call is one of the following:

* Overdose
* Carbon monoxide
* Possible suicide attempt
* Foul play
* Domestic problems
* Public disturbance

Sample Dispatch: Ambulance and Engine (Vehicle Accident)

Note: This dispatch is performed only when engine is requested by a Fire Department officer or Police officer, usually in cases of fuel spillage, an overturned vehicle, or trapped vehicle occupants.

DISPATCH, 1st Announcement:
> (Alert tone) *"Rescue 1, Engine 2, still alarm"*
> (Address) (Details)
> *"Reported vehicle accident"*

DISPATCH, 2nd Announcement:
> *"Rescue 1, Engine 2, still alarm"* (Address) (Details)
> *"Reported vehicle accident"*
> (Time)

FIRST UNIT, Acknowledgement:
> *"Rescue 1, responding"*
> (Address) (Details) (Time)

SECOND UNIT, Acknowledgement:
> *"Engine 2, responding"*

Failure to Respond

If for any reason a unit fails to come on the air and acknowledge within one minute, the dispatcher will transmit a second alarm signal and verbal dispatch. If the unit again fails to respond within one minute, the dispatcher will immediately dispatch a backup or adjacent unit to the incident or fire.

After ensuring that the second unit is responding, the dispatcher will call the first unit by station telephone. If there is no answer, the headquarters officer will be contacted by telephone.

Additional Alarm Procedure

If the situation warrants additional personnel or equipment, the officer in charge will notify Dispatch of exactly what is needed. When the officer requests off-duty personnel, he or she will designate how many firefighters are to be called and where they are to be sent.

If mutual aid assistance is needed, the officer in charge will designate what companies should be called, the types of equipment needed, and where mutual aid units should be assigned.

Calling Off-Duty Personnel

After the officer in charge relays to Dispatch how many firefighters to call and where they are to report, Dispatch will:

1. Acknowledge officer's request.
2. Sound the reed (alert) tone.
3. Transmit the message: *"(name) Fire Department requesting (number of) firefighters to report to (location) at (time)."*
4. Repeat step 3.
5. An off-duty personnel call often requires notification of the community's public safety director and the mayor.

APPENDIX 3:
Advantages and Disadvantages of Foam Generating Systems

System	Advantages	Disadvantages
Conventional Nozzle	• Can use existing equipment • More efficient use of common equipment	• Normal waterflow • Limited to foam solution applications only • Generally creates only froth
Low-Expansion Aspirating Nozzle	• Makes foam • Requires minimal equipment • Simple to operate • Simplest and initially the cheapest generating device	• Needs a high ratio of concentrate to water • Needs a high working pressure to develop foam • Needs high waterflows • Incomplete conversion of water to foam • Limited foam variability • Limited discharge distance • Same hydraulics as water • Less viable foam
Medium-Expansion Aspirating Nozzle	• Creates excellent ground firebreak • Easy to operate	• High waterflow • Requires more concentrate • Poor discharge distance • Obscures ground footing
CAFS (Compressed Air Foam System)	• Requires less water • Greater discharge distance • Complete conversion of water to foam • Requires less concentrate • Rope effect • Can produce all foam types • Light hose weight • Reduced head pressure • Stored energy in hose • Most stable foam	• More mechanical components • Slug flow • High initial cost • More complex operation • Deceiving energy stored in hose is a safety factor

(Foam Task Group, Fire Equipment Working Team, National Wildfire Coordinating Group)

APPENDIX 4:
Advantages and Limitations of Proportioning Devices

	Proportioning Device*						
	1	2	3	4	5	6	7
ADVANTAGES							
Maintain desired mix ratio despite changes in waterflow and pressure					X	X	X
Unlimited hose length	X	X		X	X	X	X
Unlimited number of hose lines	X	X		X	X	X	X
Easily adjusted mix ratios		X		X	X	X	X
No moving parts	X	X	X	X	X		
No loss in waterflow or pressure	X	X					X
Requires no equipment investment	X						
DISADVANTAGES							
Tank and pump corrosion	X	X		X			
Plumbing corrosion	X	X	X	X	X	X	X
Pump priming	X	X		X			
Pump cavitation	X	X		X			
Water tank refill	X	X		X			
Inconsistent dispersion of concentrate	X						
Foam solution degradation	X						
Excessive foam concentrate use	X	X		X			
Clean water supply contamination	X	X		X			
Removes lubricants	X	X	X	X	X	X	X
Cleaning required after every use	X	X	X	X	X	X	X
Specific waterflow requirements			X				
Specific pressure requirements			X				
Vertically mounted attitude only			X				
Limited nozzle elevation			X				
Dependent on pump vacuum	X						
Concentrate viscosity sensitive	X	X	X	X			
Concentrate resupply interrupts concentrate input				X			
Requires auxiliary power					X	X	

*Key to Proportioning Devices
1. Batch mixing
2. Suction-side regulator
3. In-line proportioning system (eductor)
4. Around-the-pump proportioning system
5. Balanced pressure bladder tank proportioning system
6. Balanced pressure pump proportioning system
7. Direct injection proportioning system

Continued

	Proportioning Device*						
	1	2	3	4	5	6	7
ACCURATE WATERFLOW RANGE							
Any flow, single mix ratio	X						
Single flow, single mix ratio		X	X	X			
Any flow, any mix ratio (between 0.1% and 1.0% for Class A Foam)					X	X	X
INITIAL EQUIPMENT INVESTMENT							
$0–$500	X	X	X	X			
$500–$1000							
$1000–$2000					X		
$2000–$4000						X	
$4000–$6000							X

(Foam Task Group, Fire Equipment Working Team, National Wildfire Coordinating Group)

*Key to Proportioning Devices
1. Batch mixing
2. Suction-side regulator
3. In-line proportioning system (eductor)
4. Around-the-pump proportioning system

5. Balanced pressure bladder tank proportioning system
6. Balanced pressure pump proportioning system
7. Direct injection proportioning system

When used with aspirating devices, such as the two blower fans shown here, a high-expansion foam can quickly fill a three-dimensional space such as this warehouse. (Ansul Fire Protection)

Glossary of Technical Terms

A

"A" ladder: A collapsible ladder, resembling a tall stepladder in appearance. Also called an "A-frame" ladder.

Abrasion-resistance: Quality of a surface that is not easily worn by contact with rough materials.

Absorb: The process in which a liquid penetrates a solid substance. (Compare to Adsorb, below)

Abstract: Situation in which a term can have more than one meaning. Compare to "concrete."

Accordion fold: A method of folding a salvage cover that allows use of ballooning or of the one-person or two-person throws. A cover folded this way is easy to carry.

Accordion load: Hose load that is more versatile than the horseshoe load. It lends itself to shoulder and underarm carries.

Action plan: In a HazMat situation, a plan to protect people, the environment, and property. Actions should reduce or at least stabilize the threat.

Acute: Occurring in the short term.

Adsorb: The process in which a gas or liquid collects on the surface of another material. (Compare to Absorb, above)

Aggravating: Making worse — usually used in referring to injuries.

Air bag: See Pneumatic lifting bag.

Ambient: Term used to describe usual or surrounding conditions. Often associated with air temperature and pressure.

Ambulatory: Term used to describe an injured person who is in good enough shape to walk.

Ammonia (NH₃): A colorless gas with an overpowering odor. In high concentrations, it can attack the skin and the mucous membranes in the nose, throat, and lungs.

Anaphylactic shock: A type of shock resulting from the inability of the human body to tolerate a particular substance, such as bee venom. In some cases, it becomes fatal.

Anchor bolts: Bolts embedded in the top surface of a foundation to fasten the building sill in place.

Anhydrous: Literally, without water.

Appliances: Anything that can be applied to a completed hose line, but that does not become a part of the line itself.

Aqueous: Containing water or water-based (such as "aqueous film-forming foam").

Aqueous film: A thin film of water.

Aqueous film-forming foam (AFFF): Concentrates that produce a high quality foam with very little energy input. They produce foams which have low viscosity and are very fast-spreading. Foams expanded from AFFF concentrates can be used on Class B fires and mixed Class A and Class B fires.

Arched roof: A roof type formed with either trusses or short rafter sections that are beveled and bolted together at an angle to form the arch.

Arson: The term for a deliberately set fire, as well as the act of setting such a fire.

Arterial bleeding: A type of bleeding in which the blood is bright red in appearance and usually "spurts" from the wound due to the pumping action of the heart.

Arterial water mains: Large diameter pipes designed to move large quantities of water to various parts of the community for further distribution.

Artery: One of the major vessels that carries blood from the heart to other parts of the body.

Asphyxia: Suffocation due to lack of oxygen. Some poisonous gases cause asphyxia by blocking the oxygen transfer from the blood to tissue.

Aspirating nozzle: A type of nozzle with an expansion chamber that mixes fine jets of solution with air to create foam.

Assessment: The process of identifying the scope and severity of a patient's illness or injury so that proper treatment can be administered.

Awareness level: The lowest of the levels of HazMat response. Awareness level responders are able to recognize the presence of hazardous materials, protect themselves, and notify proper authorities.

Axe: A basic firefighting tool that is made in different patterns. The most common patterns are the pick point and the flathead.

B

Backdraft explosion: A violent burning that results when oxygen is suddenly introduced to a confined space where a fire is in the fourth (smoldering) phase.

Bale hook: A steel hook with a wooden cross-handle. It is sometimes called a "cargo hook" or "longshoreman's hook."

Baled materials: Loose materials (such as cotton, cloth, paper, or hay) that have been gathered and fastened together in a large object called a bale.

Balloon framing: Construction type, used in older homes, the studs in both exterior walls and bearing walls extend the entire height of the building, from the foundation to the rafters.

Balloon throw: Method used by two firefighters to trap air under the salvage cover to float it over the material being covered.

Bangor ladders: Longer ladders equipped with staypoles. They are often more than 40 feet in length when fully extended.

Bar and cable cutter: A device used to cut bolts and cable up to $1/2$ in. in diameter. Also called a bolt cutter.

Barcoding: A system of light and dark bars readable by a scanner, and widely used in industry and business. Used in a personnel accountability system, the bar code on the firefighter's identification card, bracelet, or tag makes it possible to log time-in, time-out information and record the location to which the individual is assigned.

Battering ram: A heavy steel tool, typically 4 feet in length, with a notched end used to break through brick or stone walls and partitions, and a rounded end for softer material, such as plaster or cinder block.

Beam carry: Method of carrying a ladder with the rungs perpendicular to the ground.

Beam raise: A ladder raised with its rungs perpendicular to the ground.

Beams: The side rails of a ladder.

Bearing wall: A wall that supports part of the weight of the building.

Becket bend: See Sheet bend.

Bight: A bend or reversing of direction of the rope. The sides of the bight are parallel.

Biodegradable: Term for material that soil bacteria will break down into harmless components.

BLEVE: Boiling liquid expanding vapor explosion. A dangerous and powerful explosion that can occur in liquified gas containers and transport vehicles.

Boiling point: The temperature at which vapor pressure of a liquid equals the surrounding air pressure. The liquid begins to change state to a gas.

Booster hose: A rubber-covered hose, either 3/4 in. or 1 in. in diameter, mounted on a reel for rapid access.

Bowline on a bight: A knot formed in the same way as a conventional bowline, but is made with a double strand of rope. The bight formed by doubling the rope is used as the working end.

Branch lines: In a sprinkler system, the pipes that transmit water from the cross mains to the sprinkler heads.

Branch water mains: Pipes of smaller size than the arterial water mains that make up the secondary level of the distribution grid.

Brick veneer: A single layer of brick applied to the walls of a building.

Bridging: The term applied to cross pieces that go from the bottom on one joist to the top of the joist beside it, forming an "X." Bridging keeps the joists vertical and spreads the load from joist to joist.

British thermal unit (Btu): The measuring unit for heat. The amount of heat is needed to raise the temperature of one pound of water one degree Fahrenheit.

Bulk containers: In transportation, the types of containers that carry large quantities of material, such as railcars or tanker trucks.

Bunker gear: See Structural Firefighting Protective Garment.

Burn: A type of injury that can permanently damage the skin. There are four ways in which the skin can be damaged by a burn: heat, chemical, electrical, or radiation.

Burnback: The rekindling of a fire.

Burst strength: The limit of internal pressure that a hose is designed to withstand.

Butts: Hose couplings. Also, discharge ports of the fire hydrant.

C

C.O.P.E.: Acronym standing for the four items to be observed when conducting a fire inspection. They are *construction, occupancy, protection,* and *exposures*.

Capillaries: Tiny blood vessels near the surface of the skin.

Capillary bleeding: A type of bleeding that results from scrapes and abrasions. Loss of blood from capillary bleeding is usually much less than from arterial or venous bleeding.

Carbon dioxide (CO$_2$): A colorless, odorless gas making up about 1% of normal air volume. Higher concentrations cause you to breathe faster and more deeply, and could result in a reaction called hyperventilation.

Carbon monoxide (CO): A colorless, odorless, tasteless gas, created by the incomplete combustion of burning materials, that is poisonous in almost any concentration. Also, at the proper concentrations, carbon monoxide can be flammable and explosive.

Carcinogen: A cancer-causing substance.

Cardiogenic shock: A condition that is caused by the inability of the heart itself to pump adequate blood to vital organs of the body.

Cardiopulmonary resuscitation (CPR): A resuscitation technique, prescribed by the American Heart Association, that involves using external chest massage and artificial respiration.

Cargo hook: See Bale hook.

Carnivores: Creatures that are meat eaters.

Carries: Transportation methods that can be used by one or several rescuers to remove an injured person from an area of immediate hazard.

Catchall: A temporary container, formed with a salvage cover and used for removing water and debris.

Caution: Label term used to describe the lowest level of pesticide hazard.

Cave-in: A collapsed excavation.

Cellar nozzle: A nozzle with a rotating head that produces a fog which projects up, down, and sideways. It is used by cutting a small hole in a floor, lowering the nozzle a few feet into the cellar, and turning it on.

Celsius: Term used for temperature units (degrees Celsius) in the metric system. Water freezes at 0°C (32°F) and boils at 100°C (212°F). The Celsius scale is also sometimes referred to as "Centigrade".

Central dispatching agencies: Those that handle fire, police, ambulance, and other emergencies. A dispatch agency receives alarms in a number of ways, but most often by telephone. Central dispatching agencies often cover a wide area, such as an entire county.

Cervical collar: A rigid, padded device used to surround and immobilize the neck of a victim with possible damage to neck vertebrae.

Chain reaction: Process in which the heat produced by the combustion reaction of a few atoms, in turn, heats other nearby atoms to the point of combustion. They then heat others, and so on, until all of the hydrogen or oxygen atoms (or both) are used up.

Chain saw: A gasoline-powered saw used to quickly open a roof or the side of building.

Chair litter carry: A fast, easy, excellent carry to use if a chair is available. The rescuer behind the chair tilts it backward and lifts, while the rescuer in front rises and lifts. The chair and victim then can be easily transported to safety.

Char: A deep burn that occurs when wood is exposed to excessive heat.

Check valve: Valve placed in a water system to ensure that the flow of water will always be in the desired direction.

Chemical chain reaction: Reaction that takes place during the burning process, causing new products to form.

Chemical identification: Properly conveying to those concerned the correct chemical name of the substance involved. Many hazardous materials have lengthy names which are difficult to pronounce.

Chemical Protective Clothing (CPC): Specialized clothing that offers limited-term protection against exposure to a certain chemical or group of chemicals. CPC is not heat- or flame-resistant.

CHEMTREC®: The Chemical Transportation Emergency Center of the Chemical Manufacturers Association. A service that can be called around-the-clock for assistance in cases of chemical spills or fires. CHEMTREC contacts the manufacturer or shipper of the chemical for expert advice.

Chimney hitch: A slipknot that slips only when you want it to slip. The chimney hitch is used in situations where you must loosen and retighten a line frequently, tie around very large objects, or descend a steep roof (with a good strong chimney to tie onto).

Chlorine (Cl): A greenish-yellow gas with a very noxious odor. It has a very irritating effect on the throat and lungs.

Chronic: Describes something occurring in the longer term, such as a *chronic illness*.

Chute: A trough used to channel water during salvage operations.

Class A foams: Foams made from hydrocarbon-based surfactants and detergents. They do not have the strong film-forming properties of a Class B foam.

Class B foams: Foams formulated to extinguish fires involving flammable liquids and gases, grease, and melted plastics.

Claw bar: A steel bar used to break locks or perform heavy prying tasks.

Closet hook: A pike pole head with a short shaft and "D" handle, used in confined spaces such as halls, closets, and crawlspaces.

Clove hitch: A knot that is two half-hitches, with one the reverse of the other.

Codes: Municipal laws regulating the construction and use of buildings (such as the building code, plumbing code, or fire code).

Cold Zone: In a HazMat incident, the uncontaminated area where command, staging, and support occur. Also known as the Support Zone.

Collapsed building: One that has had to bear a load too heavy for its construction.

Combination construction: Situation in which different types of construction have been used in a building, typically as a result of building additions made after the original construction.

Combination load: A load that uses a baffle board. On one side of the board is 2 1/2 in. hose used for a supply line to the pump. On the other side are two 1 1/2 in. preconnected lines for attack use.

Combustible liquids: According to DOT, combustible liquids do not meet the definition of any other hazard class except Class 9, and have a flash point of between 100°F and 200°F (38°C and 93°C). OSHA uses a flash point range of from 100°F to 200°F (93°C).

Combustion: The chemical process in which oxygen and a fuel combine.

Comminuted fracture: One characterized by the bone being broken in more than two pieces.

Common hazards: Term that refers to the *frequency* with which particular hazards occur, not to their severity. Typical common hazards are poor housekeeping practices, faulty electrical systems, faulty heating systems, and unsafe materials storage.

Communication: A process in which two persons must hear and understand each others' messages.

Compound: A distinct substance formed by the union of two or more ingredients in definite proportions.

Compound fracture: An injury in which a bone is fractured and protrudes through the skin. Also called an open fracture.

Concrete: In the communication process, a term that has only one meaning. Compare to "abstract."

Condensation: Return of a gas to a liquid state as a result of cooling.

Conduction: The transferring of heat by direct contact from one material to another.

Confinement: Action taken to keep the released hazardous product in a limited area.

Conflagration hazards: Conditions in which a large number of buildings may be lost due to their proximity to other buildings and the type of material used in their construction.

Constant gallonage nozzle: A nozzle that, at any given pressure, will produce the same flow in gallons per minute (gpm) whether the setting is for a solid stream or one of the fog patterns.

Constant pressure/variable gallonage nozzle: A nozzle built to maintain a constant pressure of about 100 psi. The operator uses a throttle valve to achieve the flow (gallonage) desired.

Construction: The method and materials used to build a building. The type of construction determines the ability of a fire to burn or spread within a structure.

Containment: Action taken to keep the hazardous product in its container.

Contamination: Contact with chemicals or other hazardous materials.

Convection: The transferring of heat by moving masses of matter.

Corrosive: A chemical that causes visible destruction of or irreversible alterations in living tissue by chemical action at the site of contact, or a liquid that has a severe corrosion rate on steel. The pH scale of 1 to 14 can be used to measure corrosivity. The neutral point is 7 — acid materials have a pH lower than 7, while bases (alkalis or caustics) have a pH higher than 7.

Critical burn: Any second-degree burn that involves more than 30 percent of the body area, or any third-degree burn that covers more than 10 percent of the body area. Third-degree burns involving the face, hands, feet, or genitals — regardless of extent — should be classified as critical.

Critique: A review of an event centering around what went *right* and what *did not;* what was learned or reinforced.

Cross mains: The transmission mains that carry water from the sprinkler riser to the branch lines.

Cross-fold finish: A finish that will provide more hose than the donut finish.

Crowbar: A steel bar, longer and heavier than a claw bar, used to force doors, lift and move heavy objects, or break through plaster.

Cryogenic: A term that refers to extremely low temperatures, especially in relation to refrigerated gases. Cryogenic materials have boiling points of -150°F (-101°C) or lower.

Cryogenic tanks: Containers or vehicles that carry extremely cold cargoes such as liquid argon, helium, nitrogen, and hydrogen.

D

"D" distance: The distance of the butt of a ladder from the building.

Damming: A method of confining spills that is not always practical, since fast-flowing streams and large bodies of water are very difficult to dam.

Danger: The label term used to describe the greatest level of pesticide hazard. May be accompanied by the word "poison." Do not confuse this term with the DANGEROUS placard.

Debriefing: The process of interviewing emergency personnel as soon as the emergency is over.

Decibels (dB): Unit used to measure sounds in the workplace or other environments. Decibel measurements are usually given in dBA, indicating measurement on a scale covering the range of normal human hearing.

Deck gun: See Monitor.

Decode: To translate a message back into a mental image.

Decomposition: A process whereby a material breaks down into simpler parts, many of which may be hazardous.

Decontaminating: The process of washing or otherwise cleaning up tools, clothing, and equipment that have been exposed to poisonous or otherwise hazardous materials.

Defensive driving: The practice of anticipating problems and hazards, and allowing sufficient space around the vehicle to react safely.

Deflected stream: A solid stream that is bounced off a wall, ceiling, or other surface so that it breaks into drops.

Degree: Term used to describe how deeply skin is damaged by a burn.

Deluge set: A portable master stream device.

Demand-type breathing equipment: A type of breathing apparatus in which airflow only takes place upon inhalation.

Density: The weight per unit volume, or "thickness" of the foam.

Department Operating Procedures (DOPs): Written guidelines designed to provide operational guidance to personnel.

Dermis: The deeper layer of skin, located below the epidermis. That contains the sweat glands, oil glands, hair follicles, nerve endings, and blood vessels.

Diking: A method of confinement which channels a liquid to a desired location or away from a sensitive location. Dikes can be constructed from dirt, filled plastic bags, tubular-style absorbent socks, or water-filled fire hose.

Dispatch: Term for the central communications or dispatching office where alarms are received and emergency units ordered out.

Distribution system: A network of mains (pipes) installed to provide water to homes, businesses, and industrial plants.

Divided load: Two accordion loads in one hose bed, separated by a baffle board.

Donut finish: An excellent method for taking a hydrant, somewhat easier to use than the cross-fold finish.

Donut roll: Method of rolling hose that keeps both butts to the outside for easier access. It is done by folding the hose back on itself approximately halfway along its length.

DOT: Abbreviation for the U.S. Department of Transportation. Sometimes used to describe the corresponding agency at the state level.

Drags: Methods used to rescue an injured person from an area of immediate hazard when lifting and carrying the victim is not possible.

Drain time: The time required for foam to break down from bubbles to a water solution.

Dry chemical: A type of extinguisher containing a mixture of chemical powders that can be used effectively on various types of fires. The finely ground powders require some form of expulsion force (usually, a compressed gas) to discharge them from the extinguisher.

Dry foam: A foam that is mostly air. It consists of medium to small bubbles, and resembles whipped cream or beaten egg whites.

Dry powder: A specialized type of extinguisher specifically intended for use on fires involving combustible metals, such as magnesium or sodium. Dry powders are not effective on ordinary combustibles, burning liquids, or electrical fires.

Dry-barrel fire hydrant: One that does not have water in the barrel under normal circumstances. A valve used to control water flow is located near the base of the hydrant.

Dry-pipe sprinkler systems: These systems are typically used in unheated spaces, where water might freeze. The pipes contain air under pressure, rather than water. When a sprinkler head opens, air pressure inside the system drops abruptly. This opens a valve, allowing water to flow into the piping system.

Duck bill lock breaker: Tool with a bronze head and rubber-covered steel handle. It is inserted into a padlock shackle, then struck with flathead axe to break the shackle.

Duration: How long a sound lasts. The longer the duration of a loud noise, the more potentially damaging it is to hearing.

E

Eductor: An in-line proportioner that uses venturi action to pull foam concentrate into the water stream on the pressure side of the pump.

Effective length: The distance from the base of the ladder to the point where it rests against a portion of the building.

Elasticity: The amount (usually expressed as a percentage) that a sample of rope can be stretched and still return to its original length.

Electric-powered circular saw: A saw typically used to open walls or floors. Sometimes referred to as a rescue saw.

Element: A simple substance that cannot be broken down into anything simpler by ordinary chemical means.

Elevation loss: See Head loss.

Elongation: The amount of *permanent* stretch a rope reaches at its breaking point.

Emergency Response Guidebook (ERG): A Federal document that lists approximately 2800 of the most commonly transported hazardous materials.

Encode: To put a message or idea in a form that can be transmitted from one person to another.

Encumbrance: The difficulty in moving around and working that is a result of weight and bulk in protective clothing.

Enforcement: The process of inspecting structures for fire code violations and any followup necessary (including legal action) to ensure that any violations have been corrected.

EPA: Common abbreviation for the U.S. Environmental Protection Agency. Also used to describe the corresponding agency at the state level.

Epidermis: The outermost "wear layer" of the skin. The epidermis is watertight and is usually resistant to germs.

ERG: Abbreviation for the *Emergency Response Guidebook* issued by the U.S. Department of Transportation.

Escape plan: A prefire plan that should include at least two ways out of each room and out of the dwelling in the event of a fire. All members of the household should be familiar with it through practice.

Evacuation: The removal of all civilians from a threatened area to a safe place.

Evaporation: Changing of a liquid to a gaseous form.

Expansion: The increase in volume of the foam solution that results from the introduction of air.

Expansion ratio: The relationship of water and concentrate solution to the amount of firefighting foam produced. With a 10:1 expansion ratio, each gallon of the water-concentrate solution would result in 10 gallons of foam.

Explosive: Any material that produces sudden release of pressure, gas, and heat when subjected to abrupt shock, pressure, or high temperature.

Explosive limits: See Flammable limits or range.

Exposure: In hazardous material terms, having contact with a dangerous substance.

Exposure hazards: Hazards created by the location or proximity of one structure to another.

Exposure routes: Ways in which a human body can be invaded by a toxic or dangerous material. They include inhalation, absorption, ingestion, and direct contact.

Exposures: Term used to describe endangered areas in the fire structure or in adjacent structures.

Extinguishing agents: Materials that are used to attack one or more sides of the fire tetrahedron and put out a fire.

F

Fahrenheit: Terms used for temperature units (degrees Fahrenheit) in the conventional system of measurement. Water freezes at 32°F (0°C) and boils at 212°F (100°C).

Federal Emergency Management Agency (FEMA): Supervising agency for the National Emergency Training Center and its programs.

Federal Hazardous Waste Operations and Emergency Response Act (HAZWOPER): Regulations setting (among other items) the minimum competencies expected of HazMat responders.

Federal Superfund Amendments and Reauthorization Act of 1986 (SARA): A major piece of hazardous material legislation.

Feedback: A condition in which some of the output of a process is fed back into the input.

Filter dams: Dams made of wire mesh that screen out hazardous material which floats on the water's surface.

Fire: A chemical process that produces heat and light through combining oxygen with another substance, called a fuel.

Fire department connection: A large threaded inlet pipe, usually mounted on an outside wall of the building. It allows the fire department to support the automatic sprinkler system by providing additional pressure and water volume.

Fire hazard: A condition that could encourage a fire to start or could increase the severity of the fire once it has begun.

Fire loading: The quantity of combustibles a building contains.

Fire mark: The symbol of a specific insurance company. It was placed on the front of the insured building to make it readily visible to the volunteer fire brigade hired by the insurance company.

Fire point: The lowest temperature at which a liquid produces sufficient vapor to flash near its surface and continue to burn. (Compare to "Flash point.")

Fire prevention: Activities aimed at saving lives and protecting property through preventing fires from happening. Education, inspection, and enforcement programs are major aspects of fire prevention.

Fire prevention through education: An important part of every fire department's program to reduce the number of fires (and resulting injuries and fatalities).

Fire Prevention Week: Nationally, the second week in October, commemorating the anniversary of the Great Chicago Fire of 1871. It provides a focus for public fire safety education activities.

Fire pump: A mechanical device that increases pressure, and thus, the distance that water can be moved from the source to the fire.

Fire safety program: An organized educational program for children, carried out in cooperation with a community's school system. Each part of the program should be designed for the appropriate age group.

Fire stop: A wooden block between the studs that prevents the space from acting as a chimney that would conduct heat and smoke to the floors above.

Fire stream: Term that refers to the size, shape, and compactness that water takes as it leaves the nozzle and reaches its objective.

Fire tetrahedron: The traditional fire triangle, with a fourth side added. This fourth side is referred to as the *chemical chain reaction*.

Fire triangle: The representation of fire as consisting of three components (fuel, oxygen, heat), all of which must be present for combustion.

Fire-resistive construction: The term used to describe a building which is built completely of noncombustible material.

Firebreaks: Solid "blocks" between the studs in building partitions, designed to prevent fire rising rapidly and weakening overhead structural members.

Firefighting foam agents: Used primarily to combat flammable liquid fires, firefighting foams act as an extinguishing agent by creating a blanket to exclude the oxygen from the fire. Under special circumstances, foam may be used on fires involving ordinary combustible materials.

Fireground commander: The officer in overall charge at the fire scene or other emergency incident.

Fireman's carry: A traditional carry in which the victim is draped over the rescuer's shoulder, allowing the rescuer to walk to a place of safety.

Fireman's drag: Rescue method in which the victim's hands are tied together loosely and placed around the rescuer's neck. The rescuer can then crawl to safety with the victim.

First-degree burns: Those that affect only the outermost areas of the epidermis. They are characterized by a reddening of the skin area, and often by swelling.

Fitting: Anything that attaches to a hose, such as an adapter to connect different sizes and styles of threads.

Flammable: Term used for any solid, liquid, vapor, or gas that will ignite easily and burn rapidly.

Flammable gas: A gas that, at ambient temperature and pressure, forms a flammable mixture with air at a concentration of 13% or less by volume; or a gas that, at ambient temperature and pressure, forms a range (12 percentage points or more) of flammable mixtures with air by volume without regard to the lower limit.

Flammable limits or range: The minimum and maximum concentrations in air (as a percentage) between which ignition of a flammable gas or vapor can occur. Concentrations below the lower limit are too lean to burn. Concentrations above the upper limit are too lean to burn.

Flammable liquid: In the DOT hazardous materials classification, a burnable liquid with a flash point below 141°F (61°C). Other classification systems use 100°F (38°C).

Flammable solid: A readily ignitable solid that will continue to burn, such as magnesium or phosphorus.

Flash point: The lowest temperature at which a burnable liquid gives off sufficient vapor to form an ignitable mixture with air. Burning does not continue. (Compare to "Fire point.")

Flashback: A fire condition occurring when a trail of flammable material ignites at a point distant from its source and then follows the trail back to the source.

Flashover: A dangerous condition in which a room's contents reach ignition temperature and burst into flame simultaneously.

Flat carry: Method of carrying a ladder with the rungs parallel to the ground.

Flat raise: A ladder raised with its rungs parallel to the ground.

Flat roof: A roof type with construction similar to that of a floor. The structural material may be metal, wood, or concrete. Flat roofs are found on larger commercial, industrial, and multiple-dwelling structures.

Flexibility: A characteristic of hose that is easily folded so that the maximum amount can be placed on a truck.

Floor joists: The major supports beneath the floor of a wood-framed structure.

Flow pressure: The forward velocity or force at a discharge opening.

Flow testing: The process of checking the quantity of water available from a hydrant or hose in a given period of time. Hydrants should be flow-tested annually.

Fluid foam: A foam with a consistency somewhat like watery shaving cream. Fluid foam flows easily, and has a medium to fast drain time.

Fly: The section of ladder that is extended when an extension ladder is in position on the building.

Foam solution: A milky-looking fluid with few visible bubbles. It is almost entirely water, and can be projected as a stream from a distance to reach the burning material.

Fog nozzle: A versatile nozzle that will produce a solid stream and a range of fog patterns from narrow to extra-wide.

Fog-only nozzle: This nozzle is intended mostly for fighting electrical fires. It cannot be accidentally switched to straight stream, which could cause electrocution.

Folding ladder: A very narrow ladder that folds in half vertically (beam-to-beam). This ladder can be worked into some very tight places.

Food chain: The sequence of plants and animals from simple microscopic plants at the bottom to omnivores at the top. Each level feeds on the level below it.

Forced ventilation: Release of smoke or gases from a confined area, using water fog or mechanical forced-air ventilation.

Forcible entry: The act of using tools or other physical means to "break into" a building.

Fore-and-aft carry: A carry requiring two rescuers. One supports victim's upper torso, the other lifts at the knees.

Foundation wall: A supporting perimeter wall that allows for a cellar or a crawl space beneath the first floor of a structure.

Four-second stopping zone: In defensive driving, the minimum distance required to come to a full stop for a fixed object (such as a fallen tree) or a moving object crossing your path.

Framing anchors: Sheet metal angle plates that are nailed to a girder or joist header to fasten the joists.

Freezing point: The temperature at which a liquid changes state to a solid.

Friction: A force that occurs any time that two material surfaces rub against each other and kinetic energy is converted to heat energy.

Fuel: A material that can burn when combined with heat and oxygen.

Full-time paid fire department: A professional, usually tax-supported organization dedicated to fire prevention and fire suppression activities. The first such department in the United States was established in the city of Cincinnati, Ohio, in 1853.

G

Gas: A formless fluid occupying the space of its container. It can change to a liquid or solid state as its temperature is lowered and/or pressure increased. It is the state of matter in which atoms are farthest apart and move most freely.

Gasoline-powered circular saw: A saw similar in size and operation to the electric version, but more powerful and more portable.

Gate valve: A device used to shut off one line independently of others from the same source.

Girder: A heavy wood or metal beam used to support floor joists midway between foundation walls.

Glass bulb head: A sprinkler head in which the cap over the orifice is held in place by a glass bulb partly filled with liquid. When the temperature rises, the liquid expands and breaks the bulb, allowing the water to flow.

"Good Samaritan" law: A law passed in many states to protect medical personnel, firefighters, and others in similar roles from frivolous lawsuits when they perform their duties in good faith.

Gravity flow: Movement that takes place when the water supply is located in an elevation higher than the place in which it is going to be used.

Greenstick fracture: An injury characterized by an incomplete breaking of the bone.

Grommets: Metal-reinforced holes in a salvage cover.

Grouping: An efficient salvage practice that permits one salvage cover to be used to protect the contents of an entire room.

H

Habitable: Term describing a residential structure that is able to be occupied.

Hacksaw: A small, manually operated saw designed for cutting bolts and other metal objects.

Half-hitch: The simplest and most versatile knot used in the fire service. It consists of a simple loop that may be formed on an object or formed in the hands and then applied.

Halligan tool: A versatile device that can be used as a crowbar, pick, or sledgehammer.

Halogenated extinguishing agents: Chemical compounds created by the use of the elements bromine, chlorine, fluorine, or iodine.

Hard suction hose: A rigid, rubber-covered hose used to draft water from a pond or stream.

Hazard classes: A system developed done by the U.S. Department of Transportation as the basis for transportation labeling and placarding of hazardous materials.

Hazardous material occupancies: Sites where hazardous materials are likely to be encountered, such as water or sewage treatment plants, chemical companies, agricultural supply centers, fuel terminals, paint stores, farms, or repair garages.

Hazardous materials: Substances which, when released from containment, pose an unreasonable risk to life, health, the environment, or property.

Hazardous vapor mitigating foam: Special foams are made for use on specific chemicals or groups of chemicals, such as strong acids or alkalis.

HazMat: Commonly used abbreviation for "hazardous materials."

HAZWOPER: The Federal Hazardous Waste Operations and Emergency Response Act.

Head loss: The pressure loss resulting from the weight of the column of water above the pump.

Heat: A form of energy. Intensity of this energy is measured in degrees of temperature.

Heat detector: A hand-held electronic device that looks like a conventional flashlight. It will find heat sources behind walls, in dense smoke, and in other hiding places.

Heat indicators: Dots that change color when exposed to a temperature that could cause weakening of an aluminum ladder.

Heavy timber construction: A type of construction in which the columns, beams, and girders are large wood timbers. Wood columns must be at least eight inches in any dimension.

Hemoglobin: The blood component that combines with oxygen molecules in the lungs and carries the oxygen to other body organs.

Hemorrhagic shock: A condition caused by the loss of blood, whether inside or outside the body.

Herbivores: Creatures that are plant eaters, which are in turn the food sources for meat-eating creatures (carnivores).

High-pressure fog nozzles: Usually called "guns," they operate in a pressure range of 300-1000 psi, and are always attached to high-pressure booster lines.

High-expansion foams: Those with expansion ratios above 200:1.

Horizontal packstrap carry: Rescue method similar to the vertical packstrap carry, but performed on hands and knees.

Horizontal position: Describes moving a victim to safety in a horizontal orientation (either carried or dragged).

Horseshoe load: A load that has the advantage of eliminating about half the sharp bends that other loads have. It is not suited for shoulder or underarm hose carries.

Hose: A flexible pipe, often made from rubber, that is used to convey fluids from a hydrant to a point some distance away.

Hose adapters: Fittings used to connect two threads that normally wouldn't go together, either because of thread size or thread type.

Hose bridges: Devices used whenever hose must be laid across a street or other areas where vehicles might drive over it and cause damage.

Hose cap: A closed, threaded fitting used to block off a line or as a thread protector.

Hose clamp: A tool used any time that an emergency shutoff of a working line is needed (such as replacement of a burst line).

Hose jacket: A device that can be used to temporarily seal a burst hose.

Hose line: All of the hose, fittings, and nozzles used to bring the water from the point of origin to the point of application.

Hose pipe: A nozzle with no shutoff or control, made to fit either 1 1/2 in. or 2 1/2 in. hose. This nozzle is not much used by fire departments.

Hose roller: A device to protect a hose against chafing and cutting when it is pulled over a sharp edge.

Hose strap: Originally intended for securing a charged line to a ladder, it also can be employed to secure a ladder to a building, to serve as a carrying strap or a safety belt, or many other uses.

Hot Zone: In a HazMat incident, the area where contamination is known or suspected. Also known as the Exclusion or Contamination Zone.

HVAC: Acronym for a building's heating, ventilation, and air conditioning system.

Hydraulic shearing and prying rescue kit: A gasoline or electrically powered tool that may be used to pry open steel doors, cut auto centerposts, jack up a vehicle, or pull steering wheels or other vehicle parts to extricate accident victims.

Hydraulic ventilation: A method of smoke removal accomplished by placing the nozzle on full fog and pointing it out an open window. The venturi effect of the fog stream will draw hot gases and smoke from the room.

Hydraulics: The branch of science that deals with the effects of liquids in motion.

Hydrocarbons: Compounds of hydrogen and carbon that make up a large family of organic chemical compounds.

Hydrogen cyanide (HCN): An extremely poisonous gas formed when rubber, plastics, wool, silk, or rayon are burned.

Hydrogen sulfide (H_2S): A gas produced by the burning of rubber, certain plastics, wool, silk, and some synthetic materials. When inhaled, hydrogen sulfide is a very deadly poison.

Hydrologic cycle: The natural water cycle, consisting of continuous movement of water between the earth and the atmosphere.

Hydrology: The science concerned with the distribution of water on earth.

Hydroplaning: Loss of traction due to tires skidding on a film of water.

Hygroscopic: Term that describes a substance which readily absorbs moisture from the air.

Hyperventilation: A respiratory problem caused by overexertion and heavy breathing. When you breathe greater-than-normal amounts of air, the level of oxygen in your bloodstream rises. It can cause dizziness, impaired vision, anxiety (fear), and numbness or tingling in the extremities.

I

IDLH: "Immediately Dangerous to Life and Health," the maximum concentration of a material from which one could escape within 30 minutes and not suffer irreversible health effects.

Ignition temperature: The lowest temperature at which a combustible material will ignite in air and continue to burn without an outside heat source.

Impacted fracture: An injury characterized by many fine incomplete fracture lines at the point of injury. This type of break results from the ends of the bones being forced together.

Impeller pump: A pump with a rotating element (the impeller) that picks up water at the inlet and impels (throws) it toward the outlet.

Improvise: Solve a problem with whatever equipment, material, and/or personnel that might be available.

In-line pumping: A system in which the water flow from the hydrant to the attack lines is through the truck's pump, for better control of pressure in the attack lines.

Incident Command System (ICS): A system for management of personnel and equipment, usable for many kinds of incidents, from structure fires to HazMat emergencies. All emergency service providers operating at an incident must follow the same rules.

Incident Commander: Under the Incident Command System, the person who is ultimately responsible for all decisions at an emergency scene.

Incipient phase: The beginning stage of burning, with oxygen at normal level (21% of the air). The flame burns brightly and combustion is nearly complete.

Incline drag: Method used for easing a victim down a stairway in a lying position.

Incompatible: Term used to describe materials that could react dangerously with one another.

Inference: A conclusion based on fact.

Inhibitor: Any material that retards a chemical reaction.

Initial Isolation Zone: A 360° circle around the point of a hazardous materials release.

Initial response phase: The period (immediately after arrival at the incident scene) during which the presence of a hazardous material is confirmed and if possible identified, protective actions are initiated and the area secured, and the assistance of qualified personnel is requested.

Inorganic mineral sorbents: Materials such as vermiculite, clay, perlite, and porous silicates often used to absorb spills.

Inspections: Physical examinations of property done to assure that fire prevention codes are being properly met.

Insulated wire cutter: Tool used to cut all charged electrical wires 110 volt or above. It must be used with an approved insulated glove.

Insurance companies: Companies that sell individuals, businesses, and organizations policies to protect them against losses such as those caused by a fire. In exchange for monthly or annual payments, the company will pay for the loss. Fire insurance companies were first established after the Great London Fire of 1666.

Insurers: Another name for insurance companies.

Intake manifold: A three-way hydrant wye normally attached to a vehicle and used to bring three intake lines into a 6 in. pump intake.

Intensity: The volume or loudness of a sound.

Intermodal portable tanks: Bulk units that can be carried on ships, trucks, or trains to transport liquids, solids, and gases. They consist of a single compartment container within a lifting frame that is also used for securing the unit.

K

Kelly tool: A strong, lightweight, highly versatile tool that has many prying and pounding uses.

Kernmantle: Type of construction method for nylon ropes. The kern (or core) is composed of braided or twisted nylon strands. The mantle (sheath) is braided nylon.

Kickback: The force exerted in the opposite direction by the pressure and flow of a hose stream.

Kinetic energy: The energy of motion.

Kits: Groupings of salvage equipment assembled for specific applications, such as roof repair.

L

Labels: Diamond-shaped 4-in. labels affixed to nonbulk packages of hazardous materials. Like placards, labels are based on the hazard classes.

LC^{50}: Abbreviation for *lethal concentration,* the concentration in air of a material that is expected to kill 50% of the test animal group after a single inhalation exposure.

LD^{50}: A lethal dose of a material which is expected to kill 50% of the test animal group after a single *noninhalation* exposure.

Leverage: Term used to describe multiplied force.

Life belt (life safety harness): A seldom-used rescue device that requires thorough training to use safely.

Life net: A seldom-used device consisting of a fabric stretched over a circular frame that is supported by rescuers to cushion the fall of victims who leap from upper stories of a building.

Line functions: Duties that are directly related to the delivery of emergency services to the citizens, such as fire suppression and emergency medical services. Firefighter and paramedic training also fall under line function heading.

Link-lever head: A sprinkler head with a heat-responsive element that consists of a system of fusible links and levers.

Liquefied petroleum gas (LPG): Propane or a combination of flammable gases stored in a liquid state under pressure in tanks of various sizes. LPG is often used for heating or cooking fuel.

Liquid: State of matter in which atoms show less movement than a gas, but more than a solid.

Lofted: Projected into the air (used to describe a method of applying foam, so the blanket of material can settle down on top of the burning fuel).

Loop: A shape formed when one of the sides of a bight in a rope is crossed over the other.

Low-expansion foams: Those with expansion ratios lower than 20:1.

LPG: Common acronym for liquefied petroleum gas, also called "bottled gas."

M

Master stream: A fire stream that is too large to hold and control by hand. Any stream with a waterflow of 350 gpm or higher is considered a master stream, but many master streams have flow rates of 500 to 1000 gpm.

Material Safety Data Sheet (MSDS): A document, produced by the chemical manufacturer, which provides information specific to the hazards presented by a given material.

Medical history: Information on existing conditions, prior illnesses, or other factors that might influence emergency treatment.

Medium-expansion foams: Those with expansion ratios ranging from 20:1 to 200:1.

Melting point: The temperature at which a solid changes state to become a liquid.

Metabolic shock: A condition that results from prolonged periods of fluid loss due to vomiting, diarrhea, or urination.

Methane: A common hydrocarbon produced by the decay of plant matter.

Methane series: A family of related hydrocarbons (also called the "paraffin series").

Minor burns: Usually, first-degree burns that cover less than 20 percent of the body surface, or second-degree burns that cover less than 15 percent.

Miscible: Term used to describe the ability of a material to mix with water or other defined material.

Moderate burns:. First-degree burns that cover more than 50 percent of the body surface, or second-degree burns that cover 15 percent or more. A moderate burn requires prompt medical attention.

Molecule: The smallest unit of a substance that still retains the characteristics of that substance.

Momentum: Kinetic energy, the energy of a body in motion.

Monitor: A master stream nozzle that is permanently mounted on the apparatus body. Also known as a deck gun.

Motorization: The process of changing fire departments from horse-drawn apparatus to equipment powered by gasoline engines. Motorization allowed faster response and a better deployment of equipment, as well as more powerful pumps with more reliable sources of power.

Mutagen: An agent that causes gene mutation.

N

911 system: A telephone system for emergency calls that uses special computer equipment and programs to help dispatchers identify the location from which the call is being made. The system allows a citizen to dial the same three-digit telephone number (911) for all emergencies (fire, ambulance, and police).

National Emergency Training Center: A federal agency, with facilities located in Emmitsburg, Maryland. It provides a number of valuable services, such the National Fire Academy, the Emergency Management Institute, the Learning Resource Center, the Emergency Management Information Center, the Emergency Education Network, and the publications program of the United States Fire Administration.

National Fire Protection Association (NFPA): Organization that develops, maintains, and publishes standards related to firefighting.

Natural ventilation: The use of all openings found or made in the fire building.

Negative pressure ventilation: A method in which a fan is positioned in a doorway or window opening. The airstream is directed outward, causing a lowering of air pressure inside the building and pulling the smoke out of the structure.

Negligence: Failure to act responsibly, with the result of causing an injury or loss to another person.

Neurogenic shock: A condition in which the central nervous system is unable to convey messages to various parts of the body. The most common cause of neurogenic shock is an injury to the spine.

Neutral position: When a fracture has occurred, the "neutral position" for the injured area is the one that causes the patient the least pain, and thus can best be tolerated.

NFPA 472: The "Standard for Professional Competence of Responders to Hazardous Materials Incidents."

NFPA 704: The "Standard System for the Identification of the Fire Hazards of Materials." The system, often used for fixed sites, combines colors with numbers and symbols to provide nonspecific information.

NIOSH: Abbreviation for the National Institute for Occupational Safety and Health.

Noise: In communications science, anything that interferes with the purity of the message.

Nonadecane: A waxy methane solid.

Nonane: One of the components of kerosene. A liquid whose molecule has 9 carbon atoms and 20 hydrogen atoms.

Nonaspirating nozzle: A straight bore nozzle or a fog nozzle without an expansion chamber. Neither type produces a stable foam.

Nonbulk containers: In transportation, containers holding relatively small quantities of material, such as bottles, bags, boxes, pails, or drums.

Noncombustible construction: A construction type with bearing walls that have a minimum fire resistance rating of two hours.

Normal operating pressure: The pressure found on the distribution system while normal consumption demands are being met.

Nozzle: A short tube with a taper or constriction that is used to direct a flow of fluid.

Nozzle reaction: See Kickback.

O

Oblique fracture: A break that is characterized by a break line angling through the bone. It differs from the spiral break since the break line is diagonally across the bone, rather than spiraling around it.

Occupancy: Classifications made for the purpose of fire inspection according to the type of hazard that they present.

Occupational Safety and Health Act: The federal workplace safety program.

Occupational Safety and Health Administration: The federal agency is responsible for inspecting for safety and health hazards, investigating workplace accidents, and requiring corrective action.

Odor threshold: The lowest concentration in air of a material that can be detected by the sense of smell.

Omnivores: Creatures at the top of the food chain which eat both plants and animals.

One-person crutch assist: Method usable by a single rescuer to support and move an ambulatory victim who is not severely injured.

One-person fold: A method of preparing a salvage cover so that one firefighter can put the cover into use. The fold is preferred over the one-person roll by some departments.

One-person roll: A method of preparing a salvage cover so that one firefighter can put the cover into use.

One-person throw: A means of covering a pile of furniture in a residence or grouped stock in a store by one firefighter using a properly folded or rolled salvage cover.

Open-burning phase: The second phase that fire enters when burning in a confined space. Oxygen in the room is reduced below the normal level, down to 16 to 19 percent, so combustion is less complete.

Ordinary joist construction: A type of building that has bearing walls with a minimum fire resistance rating of two hours and nonbearing walls of noncombustible construction.

Organic natural sorbents: Straw, hay, pine needles, or sawdust used to soak up spilled materials. They may react with corrosives and oxidizers, however, and are less absorbent than mineral materials.

Organization chart: A graphic representation of the fire department, showing the lines of responsibility for both staff and line functions.

OSHA: Letters that stand for both the Occupational Safety and Health Administration and the act of Congress that created it.

Overflow dams: Dams used to trap hazardous materials that don't dissolve but do sink. Piping or tubing through the barrier is angled so the upstream end is higher than the downstream end. This enables surface flow to pass the dam but retains the heavier hazardous material.

Overhaul: The process of conducting a thorough search for and then extinguishing any hidden fire or smoldering material in the structure or its contents. Overhaul also means leaving the building in as safe, secure, and serviceable condition as possible.

Oxidizer: Any material that readily yields oxygen or takes electrons away from other materials, resulting in enhanced combustion of the other material.

Oxyacetylene cutting outfit: A portable unit consisting of tanks, hoses, and torch used to cut steel bars or other obstructions.

Oxygen: A gas that makes up approximately 21% of the volume of our atmosphere, or normal breathing air. To sustain a free-burning fire, air must contain 15% to 16% oxygen.

Oxygen depletion: The displacing of oxygen with the byproducts of combustion as a fire continues to burn in a confined space. When the oxygen content of the air drops below 6%, death will occur in four to six minutes.

Oxygen rebreathing apparatus: A closed-circuit system that includes a small cylinder of pure oxygen. As the firefighter breathes, exhaled air passes through a filter which removes the carbon dioxide. A small amount of pure oxygen is then added to the cleaned air.

Oxygen-generating equipment: Apparatus that is similar to that used for oxygen rebreathing, but chemically generates oxygen rather than supplying it from a cylinder.

P

Packaging: Term for preparation of an injured victim for safe movement.

Packing group (PG): A hazard packaging method. The classification PG I represents the greatest danger, followed by PG II and PG III.

Paramedics: Ambulance personnel specially trained as emergency medical technicians. They can perform various procedures at the direction of a physician.

PASS: See Personal alert safety system.

Pendant sprinklers: Sprinkler heads hung below the branch line piping.

Permanent set: The difference between the base measurement and the load measurement in a ladder load test.

Permeability: Ability of the soil to absorb moisture.

Personal alert safety system (PASS): An electronic device worn by a firefighter that will emit a loud signal if the firefighter becomes unconscious or immobilized and fails to move for a specified period of time (typically 30 seconds).

Personal hazards: Those that arise from an individual's disregard of common-sense fire safety rules, such as smoking in a clearly designated nonsmoking area.

Personal protective equipment (PPE): The clothing and associated items (such as an SCBA) worn by a firefighter to protect against various hazards.

Personnel accountability systems (PAS): A system designed to identify the location of each firefighter at a fire scene or incident.

Piercing nozzle: A fog nozzle with an end made of sharpened tool steel, hard stainless steel, or carbide, so that it can be pushed or driven into or through a wall, ceiling, or floor.

Pike pole: A tool consisting of a steel head with spike and hook, mounted on a long wood or fiberglass handle. It is typically used to pull down ceilings.

Pitched roof: One that is higher in the center that it is at the edges, or higher at one side than the other.

Pitot tube: A device with a movable blade and a pressure gauge, used to read flow pressure from a nozzle or hydrant.

Placards: Warning signs, based on the DOT Hazard Classes, that are used on rail and highway carriers. They are displayed on all four sides of the truck or railcar.

Platform construction: A type of building framing in which a deck or platform is built at each floor level.

Pneumatic chisel: An air-powered tool used for both rescue and forcible entry tasks.

Pneumatic lifting bag: An inflatable container of heavy , air-tight fabric used in collapsed building rescue work. When deflated, these bags can be slipped into spaces only an inch or two high, then inflated to lift up to several tons.

Polar solvents: A class of flammable liquids (alcohols, ketones, esters, and aldehydes) that are water-soluble and quickly break down most foams. Special foaming concentrates are made to fight fires involving polar solvents.

Polymer: A substance with large molecules formed through the repeated linking of smaller molecules.

Polymerization: A chemical reaction in which small molecules combine to form larger ones. Uncontrolled polymerization can result in explosions, container ruptures, generation of heat, or fire. See Inhibitor.

Pompier ladder: An unusual ladder with a top hook and rungs passing through the single center beam. Pompier ladders are very light, and can be used in a lot of tight places.

Portable electric generator: A gasoline-driven source of power for lights, smoke ejectors, saws, and other tools when no other source is available.

Positive pressure: Term applied when air is at a pressure slightly higher than the atmosphere outside the mask of breathing apparatus.

Positive pressure ventilation: A method in which a fan is placed outside the building to blow a stream of air directly into a door or window opening. This creates a pressure inside the building that is higher than the outside atmospheric pressure, forcing smoke and heated gases out of the structure.

Positive-pressure-type breathing equipment: The most commonly used type today, in which a small amount of air is allowed to leak past the regulator at all times. The positive pressure within the mask keeps contaminants from leaking into the mask.

Post-incident analysis: In HazMat incidents, reconstruction of the event to determine what occurred and who did what.

ppb: Abbreviation for parts per billion (10,000,000 ppb = 1% concentration).

ppm: Abbreviation for parts per million (10,000 ppm = 1% concentration).

Practical training sessions: Training sessions in which firefighters take part in exercises or "hands-on evolutions."

Precipitation: Water in the form of rain or snow.

Pre-fire plan: A document that is developed in anticipation of a fire in a given building. It includes information regarding the building's construction, occupancy, exposures, and the available public and private protection.

Primary survey: The initial phase of patient assessment, involving checking of the patient's airway, breathing, and circulation.

Products of combustion: The result of burning a fuel; typically water, carbon dioxide, carbon monoxide, soot, and heat.

Protection: Term used to describe the public and private means of preventing or combating a fire in a given structure. Public protection is, basically, the fire protection capabilities of the community. Private protection capabilities include such items as automatic fire detection systems and automatic sprinkler systems.

Protective Action Zone: An area beyond the Initial Isolation Zone in a hazardous materials situation. The Protective Action Zone extends 30° on either side of the predominant wind direction. The crosswind and downwind protection distances are equal.

Protective equipment: Helmets, breathing apparatus, turnout coats, boots, lifelines, and other items supplied to protect the firefighter.

Protein foaming agents: Concentrates made from natural proteins found in animal byproducts. The protein provides strength and elasticity to the bubbles in the foam developed from the concentrate.

psi: Abbreviation for pounds per square inch, a unit used to measure pressure.

psia: Abbreviation for pounds per square inch absolute (pressure measurement that *includes* the normal atmospheric pressure of 14.7 psi).

psig: Abbreviation for pounds per square inch gauge (pressure reading that *excludes* atmospheric pressure. Gauges are designed to read 0 psi at normal atmospheric pressure).

Psychogenic shock: The immediate reaction of the nervous system to a temporary reduction of the blood supply to the vital organs. Often referred to as fainting.

Public relations value: The positive results of a program or action in terms of building community support for the fire department.

Public service announcements (PSAs): Messages over radio and television that serve the public interest. An example would be fire safety tips.

Pumping stations: Facilities at the source of supply that use pumps to increase the pressure and discharge the water into the distribution system.

Pyrophoric: Term that describes materials which can ignite spontaneously in air below 130°F (54°C).

Q

Quadrants: The four sections into which the fireground or incident area is divided in personnel accountability systems.

R

Radiation: The transfer of heat through the air from a heat source, such as the sun. Radiated heat travels in straight lines in all directions from the source.

Radiation (ionizing): Atoms which emit particles or rays that can produce ions (charged atoms) in whatever the rays or particles touch.

Radiation hazards: Those involving radioactive materials. Any incident involving radioactive materials must be handled with the most extreme caution.

Radioactive materials: Materials that emit harmful atomic particles (radiation). Proper shielding is important during storage and transportation, and special decontamination procedures must be used if you become exposed to radioactivity.

Reactivity: The ability of material to chemically change by itself or with other materials. Can result in heat, explosion, or generation of dangerous substances.

Reciprocating saw: A small portable saw with a blade that moves in an up-and-down direction. Sometimes called a saber saw.

Rehabilitation area: A place where a firefighter can be sent for rest and evaluation of his or her ability to continue operating effectively.

Re-ignition: Term used to describe the sudden, unexpected flaring up again of a fire.

Reportable quantity: An amount of hazardous material released that requires reporting to governmental agencies.

Rescue knot: A combination of two knots: the bowline on a bight and the slippery hitch.

Residual pressure: That part of the pressure in a distribution system that is not used to overcome friction loss while forcing water through pipe, fittings, or adaptors.

Residue: The product remaining in a container after all reasonable effort has been made to unload it. In some cases, the amount can be quite hazardous.

Respiratory process: The act of breathing.

Respiratory shock: Usually referred to as "respiratory failure," it results from the inability of the patient to breathe adequate amounts of oxygen.

Retention basin: A lined pit or other container used to temporarily retain a hazardous liquid spill or leak.

Reverse lay: A hose lay from the fire to the hydrant.

Right-hand and left-hand search: A means of using the sense of touch to find a way out of a smoke-filled structure.

Rope hose tool: A length of rope about six feet long, with its ends joined to form a circle. A strong metal hook is attached.

Round turn: A continuation of the loop, in which the pieces of the rope are again parallel. It can be described as a bight with a loop in it.

Rule of nines: A general guide to determining the amount of body surface that has been burned. The body is divided into areas, with a percentage of the body surface area assigned to each.

Rungs: The "steps" or climbing portion of a ladder, made from a tough hardwood. Rungs may be glued or bolted (or both) to the beams.

Running bowline: A bowline with the standing part passed through it to form a loop that is easily tightened or loosened.

Runoff: Excess that occurs when the amount of water returning to the earth exceeds the ability of the ground to absorb it.

S

Safety line: A rope tied around victim's chest just under the armpits, to act as a support and "fail safe" while lowering the victim down a ladder.

Safety ropes: Ropes that are used for rescue or other activities upon which human life might depend.

Salvage: The practice of protecting building and contents from unnecessary damage.

Salvageable: Term used for materials that are not destroyed or heavily damaged in a fire.

Scanning: In defensive driving, the correct and continual use of the eyes to sweep the entire intended path of travel.

SCBA: See Self-contained breathing apparatus.

Screw jack: A powerful manual jack that can be used to raise a vehicle or force an overhead door.

Seat carry: A means of moving a victim in which two rescuers use their arms to form a "chair" for the victim.

Secondary survey: The physical examination of a patient before taking action to treat the illness or injury.

Second-degree burns: Those that involve deeper damage to the skin than first-degree burns. They are usually characterized by a considerable amount of pain, a deep reddening, and the presence of blisters.

Self-contained breathing apparatus (SCBA): A device consisting of an air supply and mask, designed to provide respiratory protection from smoke and gases.

Sensitive information: Material that should not be transmitted over the radio, if at all possible.

Septic shock: A condition resulting from the presence of extreme amount of poisons or bacteria within the cardiovascular system.

Service drop: The point where the power lines enter a building.

Sheepshank: A knot that is used to shorten or tighten a rope tied between two objects.

Sheet bend: A knot used principally to tie together two ropes of different diameters. It is not likely to slip once it has been set.

Shelter-in-place: A method of dealing with hazardous materials incidents that keeps people inside buildings where actions are taken to reduce outside air infiltration. It may be used where evacuation is not possible.

Shock: A general term for a condition in which the body's cardiovascular system breaks down and fails to provide sufficient blood circulation to the body.

Shutoff: The handle on a straight-bore playpipe, used to open and close it.

Siamese: A fitting that has a male thread at one end and two female threads at the other, used for combining two supply lines into one working line.

Sill: In a wood-framed structure, the first piece of wood attached to the top of the foundation.

Simple fracture: A broken bone injury where the skin has *not* been broken. Also called a closed fracture.

Single roll: Method of rolling hose with the male butt inside to protect the thread.

Skid finish: The best finish for advancing hose to the fire. It is adaptable for the shoulder carry, the underarm carry, or any of the other common hose advancement methods.

Sledgehammer: A heavy, long-handled hammer used to break out wall tile or concrete, freeing iron bars set in masonry, or similar tasks.

Smoke detector: A device that sounds a loud alarm when smoke is detected. Considered to be one of the most important lifesaving inventions of the twentieth century.

Smoke ejector: In the negative pressure ventilation method, a fan that is positioned in a doorway or window opening with the air-stream directed outward.

Smolder: Term used to describe a fire that burns without visible flame, in materials like a mattress or a pile of debris.

Smoldering phase: The third phase of burning, in which oxygen content in the fire area is reduced to approximately 15 percent. The flames are barely visible, and smoke is dense. The increasingly incomplete combustion produces larger amounts of carbon monoxide and other flammable and toxic gases.

Social services: Special services provided by public or private agencies to persons with special needs, such as fire victims who require temporary housing.

Soil pipe: The large drainpipe to which a toilet is connected.

Solder pellet head: A common sprinkler head that uses a single formed piece of fusible material (pellet). When the pellet melts, the sprinkler head operates.

Sole plate: Bottommost element of a wood-framed wall, installed by nailing through the subfloor to the joists.

Solid: State of matter in which atoms are closest together and show little movement.

Solid stream: A fire stream that has the force and penetrating power that neither the fog nor the deflected stream can provide.

Solubility: The ability of a material to dissolve, generally in water. Solubility is a factor in selecting a foam to use.

Sorbent: A material that is used to absorb or adsorb spilled liquids. Both organic and inorganic sorbents are available.

Space margin: The hazard-free space in front, in back, and on both sides of your vehicle. This margin gives you time to see, to evaluate, and to react to any hazard.

Special hazards: Those hazards particular to an occupancy or process, such as spray painting, storage of flammable liquids, welding, grain dusts, and the use of processing chemicals.

Specific gravity: The weight of a given volume of material, compared to the weight of an equal volume of water. The specific gravity (SG) of water is 1. SG>1 means material is heavier than water and, if not soluble, will sink in water. SG<1 means material is lighter than water and, if not soluble, will float on water. Water weighs approximately 8.33 lbs. per gallon.

Specific heat: The ratio of the amount of heat needed to raise the temperature of a given mass of a substance by one degree Fahrenheit, compared to the amount of heat needed to raise the temperature of the same mass of water by one degree Fahrenheit.

Spiral fracture: One that is characterized by a twisting type of break line.

Sprinkler flow alarm: An alarm bell or similar device on an outside wall of the building, where it can be heard by passersby or arriving firefighters.

Sprinkler head: The active component of an automatic sprinkler system. Sprinkler heads are responsive to heat. When they reach a preset temperature, the flow of water is initiated.

Sprinkler riser: The pipe that connects the water main to the network of pipes that makes up the sprinkler system itself.

Square knot: A knot that has only one use on the fireground: tying together two ropes of the same diameter.

Staff functions: Those that can be classified as nonfirefighting duties, such as department administration, budget preparation, or personnel management.

Standing part: The section of rope that will be used for work, such as pulling or hoisting.

State Fire Marshal: In most states, the Fire Marshal is responsible for fire prevention and control, fire data collection, organization of statewide training programs, fire cause and origin investigation, arson investigation, and the protection of state-owned property.

Static: A term implies that there is no motion (something is at rest).

Static pressure: Stored potential energy that is available to force water through pipe, hose, fittings, or adaptors.

Statutory requirements: The provisions of both local and state laws governing a particular activity, such as fire inspections.

Steam fire engine: Fire apparatus that substituted a more powerful steam-powered pump for a pump operated by human musclepower. First used in the 1850s.

Stop, Drop, and Roll: A burn prevention technique taught to students by many fire departments. Students are taught that, if their clothing catches fire, they should *stop*, *drop* to the floor or ground, then *roll* back and forth to extinguish the fire.

Straight lay: A hose lay in which hose is laid from the hydrant to the fire.

Straight-bore playpipe: A simple hose nozzle with a handle to open and close it, available in several tip sizes.

Straight-to-reverse lay: Hose lay in which one truck will start a straight lay from the hydrant and proceed as close to the fire as possible. Another truck will start a reverse lay from the fire toward the hydrant. Where the lays meet, a double female is used to connect the two lines.

Strainer: A fitting attached to the end of a hard suction hose when drafting from a pond or stream to keep rocks and other debris out of the pump.

Strip ventilation: See Trench ventilation.

Structural Firefighting Protective Garment: Protective clothing composed of three parts: an outer shell, a vapor barrier, and a thermal liner. The garments ("turnout gear") normally worn by firefighters while fighting a fire.

Subflooring: Rough boards or plywood laid on top of the floor joists. Finish flooring will be applied over this layer.

Sublimation: The process by which a material changes directly from a solid state to a gas, bypassing the liquid state. For example, dry ice changes directly from solid carbon dioxide to carbon dioxide gas.

Suction hose: Available in various lengths, in hard and soft types, with diameters ranging from 2 1/2 in. to 6 in.

Sulfur dioxide (SO_2): A colorless gas with an irritating odor, considered to be very poisonous.

Summary: A brief statement, covering the most important item or items in a report.

Supply water mains: The distribution grid arranged to serve the needs of individual customers, and also provide the water supply for all fire hydrants.

Suppressants: Water or other extinguishing agents used on fires.

Surfactant: An agent that reduces the surface tension of the water, causing it to spread more rapidly and penetrate more deeply.

T

Taking a hydrant: The process of connecting a line to a hydrant.

Target hazards: Any hazards that could potentially lead to large life loss or large property loss from fire. Examples include nursing homes, hospitals, lumberyards, and chemical plants.

Teasers: See Tormenters.

Telecommunications systems: The telephone lines or dedicated network of wires that connect the dispatch agency with all fire stations and other emergency service agencies.

Telecommunicator: A direct, leased telephone line connecting a security company with a dispatching agency.

Tensile strength: The breaking point of the rope when one end is anchored and a pull is exerted on the other end. Tensile strength is often expressed as the number of pounds of pull it takes to break a sample.

Teratogen: A material that can cause a defect in a human or animal embryo.

Test fire: A standard used in assigning ratings to fire extinguishers. The number 2 preceding the letter designation indicates that this extinguisher could be expected to extinguish fire twice as large as a normal test fire.

Theory sessions: Classroom training sessions in which firefighters study topics that they will later apply on hands-on practical sessions.

Third-degree burns: These are the most serious burns in which both the dermis and epidermis have been damaged. Skin often will appear to be dry, white, or pale; however, it may also be brown or even heavily charred. There is a loss of pain sensation, since the nerve endings in the dermis have been burned away.

Tie rods: Long bolts that go through every fourth rung of some wood ladders, from beam to beam, for greater strength.

Tin snips: Cutting tool used to open sheet metal roofing, cut flashing, or cut steel window casements.

Tip: The orifice of a nozzle, where water exits.

TLV-C: Abbreviation for "Threshold Limit Value Ceiling," the exposure concentration that should not be exceeded.

Tormenters: Poles attached to the sides of an extension ladder to aid in raising and steadying it. Most ladders of this type are 40 feet or more in length.

Tourniquet: Material that is tightly wrapped around a limb to stop bleeding. Tourniquets are not recommended, because the pressure applied can cause damage to nerves and blood vessels. Use of a tourniquet should be considered a last resort.

Trachea: The relatively large tube which extends from the mouth down into the chest cavity.

Transmit: To move a message through time and/or space.

Transportation hazards: A group of hazards associated with the movement of materials.

Transportation-related incident: In hazardous materials situations, an incident involving tank cars or trucks, tube trailers, casks on flat trailers or railcars, cylinders, ton containers, or barrels. Rail box cars and van-type trailers also may carry hazardous materials.

Trench ventilation: A method in which an opening is made through the roof completely across the building's width. Smoke and heated air will vent out of the trench, preventing spread of the fire to areas beyond.

Truss construction: A method used to support the roof of commercial or residential buildings. Failure of a truss can lead to partial or complete roof collapse.

Trusses: Connecting pieces between two rails of smaller cross-section that form the beam of a truss ladder. They also serve as rung support blocks.

Turnout: See Structural Firefighting Protective Garment.

Twelve-second travel path: The distance your vehicle will travel in twelve seconds, giving you time to identify, evaluate, and decide what to do about any potential hazard.

Two-person crutch assist: A rescue method similar to the one-person version, except that one rescuer is on each side of the victim.

Two-person fold: A method of preparing a salvage cover that should be used only if two firefighters will be available to spread the cover.

Two-person throw: A throw similar to the balloon throw, except that the salvage cover is only partially unfolded before being spread.

Two-second following zone: When driving an emergency vehicle, the amount of space to keep between your vehicle and the vehicles in front and behind. It refers to the distance your vehicle will travel in two seconds at the current rate of speed.

U

UN/NA number: A four-digit identifying number that may be placed on a placard or on a nearby orange panel. The UN/NA number definitively identifies the product.

Underflow dams: Dams used to retain hazardous materials which do not dissolve and which float on/near the surface. Piping/tubing through the barrier is angled so the upstream end is lower than the downstream end.

Universal spanner wrench: A steel or aluminum tool used for tasks such as connecting hose or shutting off a gas cock.

Unresponsive: Term for a patient that is not reacting to sound or physical stimuli.

Upright sprinklers: Sprinkler heads installed atop the branch line piping.

Utility bar: A heavy, multipurpose steel bar with a hammer head at one end and a claw at the other. It can be used as a wrecking bar, crowbar, hatchet, hammer, or sheet metal ripper.

Utility ropes: Those used for hauling equipment, securing ladders, or any of the other assorted tying and pulling activities on the fireground or in the station.

V

Vapor: The gaseous state of a normally liquid material.

Vapor density: The weight of a given volume of a vapor or gas, compared to the weight of an equal volume of air. Air's vapor density is 1. A vapor with a density >1 will sink in air. Vapor density <1 means a vapor will rise in air.

Vapor Pressure: Pressure exerted by a vapor above a liquid inside a closed container. A high vapor pressure indicates the tendency of the liquid to convert to vapor. A low boiling point means high vapor pressures.

(Remember that *vapors,* not liquids, actually burn.)

Vaporize: Term used to describe a change of state of a material from solid or liquid to a gas.

Variable gallonage nozzle: A type of fog nozzle that permits the operator to determine the amount of flow.

Vein: One of the blood vessels that carries blood from the system back to the patient's heart.

Venous bleeding: A type of bleeding in which the blood is a darker red color than arterial blood and does not spurt from the vessel.

Ventilation: The planned release of smoke and gases from a confined area.

Venting devices: Mechanisms that will help to vent the products of combustion in the event of a fire. Some are designed for automatic operation; others are manual.

Vertical packstrap carry: A method of moving a victim by looping a length of cloth under the victim's arms and over the rescuer's shoulders. The victim is then lifted and supported on the rescuer's back. The carry is performed while standing.

Vertical position: Describes moving a victim to safety in an upright orientation (either walking or being carried).

Vigil: A group of watchmen in ancient Rome who stood guard at night to protect the city from fire. When they detected a fire in a specific district, they alerted the citizens.

Vital signs: A patient's pulse count, respiratory rate, and blood pressure.

Voids: Vertical or horizontal openings in the structure through which fire can move rapidly.

Volatility: A liquid's tendency to become a vapor.

Volunteer fire brigades: First formed in early 18th century in the major cities of the United States, these fire brigades were hired by individual insurance companies to protect the properties that the company insured.

W

Wall studs: Vertical supports of wood or metal that form building walls in frame construction.

Warm Zone: In a HazMat incident, the area between the Hot and Cold Zones. Decontamination is done in the Warm Zone. The personnel and equipment backing up the Hot Zone team stays in the Warm Zone, as well. Also known as Contamination Reduction Zone.

Warning: The label term used to describe the middle level of pesticide hazard.

Water curtain: A specialized nozzle that produces a broad, fan-shaped stream of water used to absorb radiated heat and prevent the spread of fire to an adjacent structure.

Water flow detector: A simple device consisting of a paddle or small waterwheel inside a sprinkler riser. Any flow of water (indicating that a sprinkler head has opened) will move the paddle or wheel and close a switch, activating an alarm.

Water hammer: A sharp clanking sound like a hammer striking a steel pipe, caused by the flow of water through a hose being suddenly cut off by a sudden closing of nozzle.

Water main: The pipe extending from the water source to the point where it enters an individual building.

Water motor gong: A simple alarm device that sounds whenever water is flowing in the sprinkler system. A waterwheel rotates a drive shaft, making a striker on the drive shaft repeatedly hit the gong.

Water table: Depth at which water is found in the earth.

Water thief: Hydrant device with one gated outlet the same size as the inlet and two or more smaller gated outlets. It provides the option of using one large line or two or more smaller ones.

Water vapor: Water that has changed to a gaseous state. It is lighter than air.

Wear surface: The exposed part of the roof that protects the building from weather.

Wet foam: A firefighting foam that exhibits many more visible bubbles than foam solution, but still consists of far more water than air. It has the ability to penetrate deep-seated fires.

Wet water: A term used to describe water to which a wetting agent has been added to improve its extinguishing ability. Wetting agents decrease the surface tension of water, helping it to better penetrate below the surface of burning materials.

Wet-barrel fire hydrant: One that has water in the barrel at all times. It is not recommended for areas that are subject to freezing temperatures.

Wet-pipe sprinkler system: The method normally used in a building where the temperature will remain above the freezing point of water. Water fills the pipes and begins to flow immediately when a sprinkler head is activated by the heat of a fire.

Wildlands: Land that is not used for cultivation or urban structures.

Wood-frame structure: A building that has nearly all its weight supported by the wooden wall studs.

Working end: The portion of the rope used to make bights, loops, and round turns as a knot is formed.

Working equipment: This equipment includes axes, hoses, nozzles, wrenches, and many other items used to perform the job of firefighting.

Working hose: The common fabric-covered hose used for firefighting, available in fifty-foot lengths, with diameters from 1 1/2 in. to 3 in.

Working strength: In practice, the elastic limits of the rope.

Wye: A fitting with a female thread on one end and two male threads on the other, used to divide one supply line into two working lines.

Vehicle fires can be dangerous and destructive when they occur in the open, but are even more so when they take place inside a structure. This car fire destroyed the vehicle, the garage it was housed in, and an adjacent residence.

Index